# **Contents**

# Acknowledgements

**Editorial Director**
Hilary McGlynn

**Managing Editor**
Roger Tritton

**Project Editors**
Catherine Thompson
Fran Alexander

**Design**
Matt Braund
Brand Design
WHSmith Ltd

**Technical Lead**
Tracey Auden

**Database Management**
Claire Lishman

**Production**
John Normansell
Stacey Penny

# Preface

The *WHSmith Pocket Encyclopedia* is a compact guide to world events, history, arts, science, medicine, and information technology for home, school, and library use. The aim throughout has been to provide up-to-date, readable entries, using clear and nontechnical language. As well as text entries and illustrations there are clearly presented tables and carefully selected Web links. The Appendix provides additional tabular material for quick reference.

# Guide to the Encyclopedia

### Arrangement of entries

Entries are ordered alphabetically, as if there were no spaces between words. Thus, entries for words beginning 'East' follow the order:

East Anglia
Easter
Easter Island

However, we have avoided a purely mechanical alphabetization in cases where a different order corresponds more with human logic. For example, sovereigns with the same name are grouped according to country before number. Words beginning 'Mc' and 'Mac' are all treated as if they begin 'Mac'; 'St' is treated as if spelt out in full.

### Foreign names

Names of foreign sovereigns and places are usually shown in their English form, except where the foreign name is more familiar, for example Cinque Ports and not Five Ports, but Florence and not Firenze.

### Titles

Entries for people with titles are under the name by which they are best known, for example the entry for Anthony Eden is under E for Eden and not under A for Lord Avon.

### Cross references

These are indicated by the → symbol. Cross referencing is selective; a cross reference is shown when another entry contains material directly relevant to the subject matter of an entry, and to where the reader may not otherwise think of looking.

## Units

SI (metric) units are used throughout with the imperial conversion given after the metric measurement.

## Chinese names

Pinyin, the preferred system for transcribing Chinese names, is generally used: thus, there is an entry at Mao Zedong and not Mao Tsetung.

**aardvark** (Afrikaans 'earth pig') nocturnal mammal *Orycteropus afer*, the only species in the order Tubulidentata, found in central and southern Africa. A timid, defenceless animal about the size of a pig, it has a long head, a piglike snout, large ears, sparse body hair, a thick tail, and short legs.

**Aberdeen City** city and unitary authority in northeast Scotland. The unitary authority was created in 1996 from the district of the same name that was part of Grampian region from 1975; before that it was part of Aberdeenshire. The city of Aberdeen, as well as being the administrative headquarters of the Aberdeen City unitary authority, is the administrative headquarters of Aberdeenshire unitary authority; **area:** 185 sq km/71 sq mi; **physical:** low-lying coastal area on the banks of the rivers Dee and Don; it has 3 km/2 mi of sandy beaches; **features:** St Andrew's Episcopal Cathedral (consecrated in 1816), King's College (from 1500) and Marischal College (founded in 1593, and housed in one of the world's largest granite buildings constructed in 1836), which together form Aberdeen University, Brig O'Balgownie (1314–18), Municipal Buildings (1867), St Machar Cathedral (from 1370). Aberdeen's granite buildings have given it the name of 'Silver City', although the last granite quarry, in Rubislaw, closed in 1971; **agriculture:** white and salmon fishing; **industries:** oil and gas service industries, paper manufacturing, textiles, engineering, food processing, chemicals, fish processing; **population:** (1996) 219,100; **famous people:** poet John Barbour, archdeacon of Aberdeen; Scottish historian Hector Boece (*c.* 1465–1536), principal of King's College; theologian George Campbell; the poet Lord Byron received his early education at the grammar school here.

**aberration of starlight** apparent displacement of a star from its true position, due to the combined effects of the speed of light and the speed of the Earth in orbit around the Sun (about 30 km per second/18.5 mi per second). *See illustration on page 2.*

**Abidjan** port and former capital (until 1983) of the Republic of Côte d'Ivoire; population (1995 est) 2,722,000. There is an airport and communication by rail, as well as by sea, and the city has become increasingly important for its industries which include metallurgy, farm machinery, car and electrical

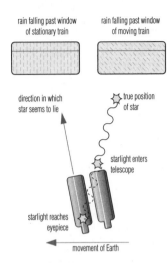

**aberration of starlight** The aberration of starlight is an optical illusion caused by the motion of the Earth. Rain falling appears vertical when seen from the window of a stationary train; when seen from the window of a moving train, the rain appears to follow a sloping path. In the same way, light from a star 'falling' down a telescope seems to follow a sloping path because the Earth is moving. This causes an apparent displacement, or aberration, in the position of the star.

assembly. Products include coffee, palm oil, cocoa, and timber (mahogany). There are tourist markets trading in handicrafts and traditional medicines. Around 10% of adults carry the AIDS virus (1996).

**aborigine** (Latin *ab origine* 'from the beginning') any indigenous inhabitant of a region or country. The word often refers to the original peoples of areas colonized by Europeans, and especially to →Australian Aborigines.

**Abruzzi** mountainous region of southern central Italy, comprising the provinces of L'Aquila, Chieti, Pescara, and Teramo; area 10,800 sq km/4,169 sq mi; population (1992) 1,255,500. L'Aquila, the capital, and Pescara are the principal towns. Gran Sasso d'Italia, 2,914 m/9,564 ft, is the highest point of the →Apennines.

**abstract art** nonrepresentational art. Ornamental art without figurative representation occurs in most cultures. The modern abstract movement in sculpture and painting emerged in Europe and North America between 1910 and 1920. Two approaches produce different abstract styles: images that have been 'abstracted' from nature to the point where they no longer reflect a conventional reality, and nonobjective, or 'pure', art forms, without any reference to reality.

**Abu Dhabi** sheikhdom in southwest Asia, on the Gulf, capital of the United Arab Emirates; area 67,350 sq km/26,000 sq mi; population (1995) 928,400. Formerly under British protection, it has been ruled since 1971 by Sheikh Sultan Zayed bin al-Nahayan, who is also president of the Supreme Council of Rulers of the United Arab Emirates.

**abyssal zone** dark ocean region 2,000–6,000 m/6,500–19,500 ft deep;

temperature 4°C/39°F. Three-quarters of the area of the deep-ocean floor lies in the abyssal zone, which is too far from the surface for photosynthesis to take place. Some fish and crustaceans living there are blind or have their own light sources. The region above is the bathyal zone; the region below, the hadal zone.

**Abyssinia** former name of →Ethiopia.

**AC** in physics, abbreviation for →alternating current.

**acacia** any of a large group of shrubs and trees that includes the thorn trees of the African savanna and the gum arabic tree (*Acacia senegal*) of North Africa, and several North American species of the southwestern USA and Mexico. The hardy tree commonly known as acacia is the false acacia (*Robinia pseudacacia*, of the subfamily Papilionoideae). True acacias are found in warm regions of the world, particularly Australia. (Genus *Acacia*, family Leguminosae.)

**Academy Award** annual honour awarded since 1927 by the American Academy of Motion Picture Arts and Sciences in a number of categories that reflect the diversity and collaborative nature of film-making. The Academy Award is one of the highest accolades in the film industry, and a virtual guarantor of increased financial returns. The trophy itself is a gold-plated statuette which since 1931 has been popularly nicknamed an 'Oscar'. The most prestigious awards are for Best Picture, Best Director, Best Actor, and Best Actress.

**Acapulco** (or Acapulco de Juarez) port and holiday resort in southern Mexico; population (1990) 593,200. There is deep-sea fishing, and tropical products are exported. Acapulco was founded 1550 and was Mexico's major Pacific coast port until about 1815.

**acceleration** rate of change of the velocity of a moving body. It is usually measured in metres per second per second (m s$^{-2}$) or feet per second per second (ft s$^{-2}$). Because velocity is a vector quantity (possessing both magnitude and direction) a body travelling at constant speed may be said to be accelerating if its direction of motion changes. According to Newton's second law of motion, a body will accelerate only if it is acted upon by an unbalanced, or resultant, →force.

Acceleration due to gravity is the acceleration of a body falling freely under the influence of the Earth's gravitational field; it varies slightly at different latitudes and altitudes. The value adopted internationally for gravitational acceleration is 9.806 m s$^{-2}$/32.174 ft s$^{-2}$.

**accelerator** in physics, a device to bring charged particles (such as protons and electrons) up to high speeds and energies, at which they can be of use in industry, medicine, and pure physics. At low energies, accelerated particles can be used to produce the image on a television screen and generate X-rays (by means of a →cathode-ray tube), destroy tumour cells, or kill bacteria. When high-energy particles collide with other particles, the fragments formed reveal the nature of the fundamental forces. *See illustration on page 4.*

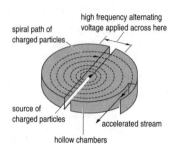

**accelerator** The cyclotron, an early accelerator, consisted of two D-shaped hollow chambers enclosed in a vacuum. An alternating voltage was applied across the gap between the hollows. Charged particles spiralled outward from the centre, picking up energy and accelerating each time they passed through the gap.

## Achebe, Chinua (Albert Chinualumogo)

(1930– ) Nigerian novelist. His themes include the social and political impact of European colonialism on African people, and the problems of newly independent African nations. Among his works are the seminal *Things Fall Apart* (1958), one of the first African novels to achieve a global reputation, and *Anthills of the Savannah* (1987).

**Achilles** Greek hero of Homer's *Iliad*. He was the son of Peleus, King of the Myrmidons in Thessaly, and of the sea nymph Thetis, who rendered him invulnerable, except for the heel by which she held him, by dipping him in the River Styx. Achilles killed Hector at the climax of the *Iliad*, and according to subsequent Greek legends was himself killed by Paris, who shot a poisoned arrow into Achilles' heel.

**acid** in chemistry, compound that releases hydrogen ions ($H^+$ or protons) in the presence of an ionizing solvent (usually water). Acids react with →bases to form salts, and they act as solvents. Strong acids are corrosive; dilute acids have a sour or sharp taste, although in some organic acids this may be partially masked by other flavour characteristics. The strength of an acid is measured by its hydrogen-ion concentration, indicated by the →pH value. All acids have a pH below 7.0.

**acid rain** acidic precipitation thought to be caused principally by the release into the atmosphere of sulphur dioxide ($SO_2$) and oxides of nitrogen, which dissolve in pure rainwater making it acidic. Sulphur dioxide is formed by the burning of fossil fuels, such as coal, that contain high quantities of sulphur; nitrogen

---

**WEB SITE** > > > > > > > >
### Acid Rain
http://qlink.queensu.ca/%7E4lrm/table.htm

Canadian site explaining acid rain and its consequences for the aquatic environment, trees and soils, and human beings. It includes an account of an acid rain attack in New England, USA, where the rain was as acidic as vinegar.

---

oxides are contributed from various industrial activities and from vehicle exhaust fumes.

**acoustics** in general, the experimental and theoretical science of sound and its transmission; in particular, that branch of the science that has to do with the phenomena of sound in a particular space such as a room or theatre. In architecture, the sound-reflecting character of an internal space.

**acquired immune deficiency syndrome** full name for the disease →AIDS.

**Actium, Battle of** naval battle in which Octavian defeated the combined fleets of →Mark Antony and →Cleopatra on 2 September 31 BC to become the undisputed ruler of the Roman world (as the emperor →Augustus). The site of the battle is at Akri, a promontory in western Greece.

**act of Congress** in the USA, a bill or resolution passed by both houses of Congress, the Senate and the House of Representatives, which becomes law with the signature of the president. If vetoed by the president, it may still become law if it returns to Congress again and is passed by a majority of two-thirds in each house.

**act of Parliament** in Britain, a change in the law originating in Parliament and called a statute. Before an act receives the royal assent and becomes law it is a bill. The US equivalent is an →act of Congress.

**acupuncture** in alternative medicine, a system of inserting long, thin metal needles into the body at predetermined points to relieve pain, as an anaesthetic in surgery, and to assist healing. The needles are rotated manually or electrically. The method, developed in ancient China and increasingly popular in the West, is thought to work by stimulating the brain's own painkillers, the →endorphins.

**Adams, Gerry** (1948– ) born Gerard Adams, Northern Irish politician, president of →Sinn Fein (the political wing of the Irish Republican Army, IRA) from 1978. Adams was elected member of Parliament for Belfast West in 1983 but declined to take up his Westminster seat, as he refused to take an oath of allegiance to the British queen. He lost his seat in 1992 but regained it in 1997, still refusing to sit in the Westminster Parliament. He has been a key figure in Irish peace negotiations. He was the main architect of the IRA ceasefire in 1994 and in 1997 he entered into multiparty talks with the British government which, on Good Friday, 10 April 1998, resulted in an agreement accepted by all parties and subsequently endorsed in referenda held simultaneously in Northern Ireland and in the Irish Republic.

**Addis Ababa** (or Adis Abeba; Amharic 'new flower') capital of Ethiopia; population (1992) 2,213,000. The city is at an altitude of 2,500 m/8,200 ft. It was founded in 1887 by Menelik II, chief of Shoa, who ascended the throne of Ethiopia in 1889. His former residence, Menelik Palace, is now occupied by the government. Industries include light engineering, food processing, brewing, livestock processing, chemicals, cement, textiles, footwear, clothing, and handicrafts.

**Adelaide** capital and chief port of →South Australia; population (1996) 978,100. Adelaide is situated on the River Torrens, 11 km/7 mi from the Gulf of St Vincent. Industries include oil refining, shipbuilding, electronics, and the manufacture of electrical goods and cars. Grain, wool, fruit, and wine are exported from Port Adelaide, 11 km/7 mi northwest of the city. Adelaide was founded in 1836 and named after the queen of William IV. The city's fine buildings include Parliament House, Government House, the Anglican cathedral of St Peter, and the Roman Catholic Cathedral of St Francis Xavier (built 1856–1926).

**adenoids** masses of lymphoid tissue, similar to →tonsils, located in the upper part of the throat, behind the nose. They are part of a child's natural defences against the entry of germs but usually shrink and disappear by the age of ten.

**adobe** in architecture, a building method employing sun-dried earth bricks; also the individual bricks. The use of earth bricks and the construction of walls by enclosing earth within moulds (*pisé de terre*) are the two principal methods of raw-earth building. The techniques are commonly found in Spain, Latin America, and the southwestern USA.

**Adonis** (Semitic *Adon*, 'the Lord') in Greek mythology, a beautiful youth loved by the goddess →Aphrodite. He was killed while boar-hunting but was allowed to return from the underworld for a period every year to rejoin her. The anemone sprang from his blood.

**adrenal gland** (or suprarenal gland) triangular gland situated on top of the →kidney. The adrenals are soft and yellow, and consist of two parts: the cortex and medulla. The **cortex** (outer part) secretes various steroid hormones and other hormones that control salt and water metabolism and regulate the use of carbohydrates, proteins, and fats. The **medulla** (inner part) secretes the hormones adrenaline and noradrenaline which, during times of stress, cause the heart to beat faster and harder, increase blood flow to the heart and muscle cells, and dilate airways in the lungs, thereby delivering more oxygen to cells throughout the body and in general preparing the body for 'fight or flight'.

**adrenaline** (or epinephrine) hormone secreted by the medulla of the →adrenal glands. Adrenaline is synthesized from a closely related substance, noradrenaline, and the two hormones are released into the bloodstream in situations of fear or stress.

**Adrian IV** (*c.* 1100–1159) Nicholas Breakspear, pope 1154–59, the only English pope. He secured the execution of Arnold of Brescia and crowned Frederick I Barbarossa as German emperor. When he died, Adrian IV was at the height of a quarrel with

Barbarossa over papal supremacy. He allegedly issued the controversial bull giving Ireland to Henry II of England in 1154. He was attacked for false representation, and the bull was subsequently refuted.

**Aegean Islands** region of Greece comprising the Dodecanese islands, the Cyclades islands, Lesvos, Samos, and Chios; area 9,122 sq km/3,523 sq mi; population (1991) 460,800.

**aerial** (or antenna) in radio and television broadcasting, a conducting device that radiates or receives electromagnetic waves. The design of an aerial depends principally on the wavelength of the signal. Long waves (hundreds of metres in wavelength) may employ long wire aerials; short waves (several centimetres in wavelength) may employ rods and dipoles; microwaves may also use dipoles – often with reflectors arranged like a toast rack – or highly directional parabolic dish aerials. Because microwaves travel in straight lines, requiring line-of-sight communication, microwave aerials are usually located at the tops of tall masts or towers.

**aerobic** in biology, term used to describe those organisms that require oxygen (usually dissolved in water) for the efficient release of energy contained in food molecules, such as glucose. They include almost all organisms (plants as well as animals) with the exception of certain bacteria, yeasts, and internal parasites.

**aerobics** (Greek 'air' and 'life') exercises to improve the performance of the heart and lungs, involving strenuous application of movement to raise the heart rate to 120 beats per minute or more for sessions of 5–20 minutes' duration, 3–5 times per week.

**aerodynamics** branch of fluid physics that studies the forces exerted by air or other gases in motion. Examples include the airflow around bodies moving at speed through the atmosphere (such as land vehicles, bullets, rockets, and aircraft), the behaviour of gas in engines and furnaces, air conditioning of buildings, the deposition of snow, the operation of air-cushion vehicles (hovercraft), wind loads on buildings and bridges, bird and insect flight, musical wind instruments, and meteorology. For maximum efficiency, the aim is usually to design the shape of an object to produce a streamlined flow, with a minimum of turbulence in the moving air. The behaviour of aerosols or the pollution of the atmosphere by foreign particles are other aspects of aerodynamics.

**aeroplane** (US airplane) powered heavier-than-air craft supported in flight by fixed wings. Aeroplanes are propelled by the thrust of a jet engine, a rocket engine, or airscrew (propeller), as well as combinations of these. They must be designed aerodynamically, since streamlining ensures maximum flight efficiency. The Wright brothers flew the first powered plane (a biplane) in Kitty Hawk, North Carolina, USA, in 1903. For the history of aircraft and aviation, see →flight.

**aerosol** particles of liquid or solid suspended in a gas. Fog is a common natural example. Aerosol cans contain a substance such as scent or cleaner packed under pressure with a device for releasing it as a fine spray. Most aerosols used chlorofluorocarbons (CFCs) as propellants until these were found to cause destruction of the →ozone layer in the stratosphere.

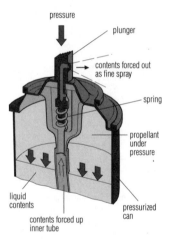

**aerosol** The aerosol can produces a fine spray of liquid particles, called an aerosol. When the top button is pressed, a valve is opened, allowing the pressurized propellant in the can to force out a spray of the liquid contents. As the liquid sprays from the can, the small amount of propellant dissolved in the liquid vaporizes, producing a fine spray of small droplets.

**Aeschylus** (c. 525–c. 456 BC) Athenian dramatist. He developed Greek tragedy by introducing the second actor, thus enabling true dialogue and dramatic action to occur independently of the chorus. Ranked with →Euripides and →Sophocles as one of the three great tragedians, Aeschylus composed some 90 plays between 500 and 456 BC, of which seven complete tragedies survive in his name: *Persians* (472 BC), *Seven Against Thebes* (467), *Suppliants* (463), the *Oresteia* trilogy (*Agamemnon*, *Libation-Bearers*, and *Eumenides*) (458), and *Prometheus Bound* (the last, although attributed to him, is of uncertain date and authorship).

**Aesop** by tradition, a writer of Greek fables. According to the historian Herodotus, he lived in the mid-6th century BC and was a slave. The fables that are ascribed to him were collected at a later date and are anecdotal stories using animal characters to illustrate moral or satirical points.

> **WEB SITE** > > > > > > > >
> **Aesop's Fables**
> http://www.pacificnet.net/~johnr/aesop/
> Full text of 398 of the most popular of Aesop's fables. Several have pictures to illustrate the story and some also have sound effects.

**aesthetics** branch of philosophy that deals with the nature of beauty, especially in art. Aesthetics emerged as a distinct branch of enquiry in the mid-18th century.

**affirmative action** government policy of positive discrimination by the use of legal measures and moral persuasion that favours women and members of minority ethnic groups in such areas as employment and education. It is designed to counter the effects of long-term discrimination against these groups, and in Europe, Sweden, Belgium, the Netherlands, and Italy actively promote affirmative action through legal and financial incentives.

**Afghanistan** Republic of; **national name:** *Islamic Emirate of Afghanistan*; **area:** 652,090 sq km/251,771 sq mi; **capital:** Kabul; **major towns/cities:** Kandahar, Herat, Mazar-i-Sharif, Jalalabad; **physical features:** mountainous in centre and northeast (Hindu Kush mountain range; Khyber and Salang passes, Wakhan salient, and Panjshir Valley), plains in north and southwest, Amu Darya (Oxus) River, Helmand River, Lake Saberi; **head of state and government:** Muhammad Rabbani from 1996; **political system:** transitional; **currency:** afghání; **GNP per capita (PPP):** (US$) 819 (1992); **exports:** fruit and nuts, carpets, wool, karakul skins, cotton, natural gas. Principal market Kyrgyzstan 37.3% (1995); **population:** 21,923,000 (1999 est); **language:** Pushtu, Dari (Persian), Uzbek, Turkoman, Kirgiz; **religion:** Muslim (85% Sunni, 15% Shiite); **life expectancy:** 45 (men); 46 (women) (1995–2000).

**Afghan Wars** three wars waged between Britain and Afghanistan to counter the threat to British India from expanding Russian influence in Afghanistan. **First Afghan War** 1838–42, when the British garrison at Kabul was wiped out. **Second Afghan War** 1878–80, when General Roberts captured Kabul and relieved Kandahar. **Third Afghan War** 1919, when peace followed the dispatch by the UK of the first aeroplane ever seen in Kabul.

**Africa** second largest of the five continents. Africa is connected with Asia by the isthmus of Suez, and separated from Europe by the Mediterranean Sea. The name Africa was first given by the Romans to their African provinces with the city of Carthage, and it has since been extended to the whole continent. **area:** 30,097,000 sq km/11,620,451 sq mi (three times the area of Europe); **largest cities:** (population over 2 million; population given in millions) Abidjan (2.9), Addis Ababa (2.6), Alexandria (3.7), Algiers (3.8), Cairo (9.9), Casablanca (3.2), Johannesburg (2.2), Khartoum (2.3), Kinshasa (4.4), Lagos (10.9), Luanda (2.2), Maputo (2.4); **features:** Great Rift Valley, containing most of the great lakes of East Africa (except Lake Victoria); Atlas Mountains in the northwest; Drakensberg mountain range in the southeast; Sahara Desert (world's largest desert) in the north; Namib, Kalahari, and Great Karoo deserts in the south; Nile, Congo-Zaire, Niger, Zambezi, Limpopo, Volta, and Orange rivers; **physical:** dominated by a uniform central plateau comprising a southern tableland with a mean altitude of 1,070 m/3,000 ft that falls northwards to a lower elevated plain with a mean altitude of 400 m/1,300 ft. Although there are no great alpine regions or extensive coastal plains, Africa has a mean altitude of 610 m/ 2,000 ft, two times greater than Europe. The highest points are Mount Kilimanjaro 5,900 m/19,364 ft, and Mount Kenya 5,200 m/17,058 ft; the lowest point is Lac Assal in Djibouti −144 m/−471 ft. Compared with other continents, Africa has few broad estuaries or inlets and therefore has proportionally the shortest coastline (24,000 km/15,000 mi). The geographical extremities of the continental mainland are Cape Hafun in the east, Cape Almadies in the west, Ras Ben Sekka in the north, and Cape Agulhas in the south. The Sahel is a narrow belt of savanna and scrub forest which covers 700 million hectares/1.7 billion acres of west and central Africa; 75% of the continent lies within the tropics.

**African National Congress** (ANC) South African political party, founded in 1912 as a multiracial nationalist organization with the aim of extending the franchise to the whole population and ending all racial discrimination. Its president from 1997 is Thabo Mbeki.

The ANC was banned by the government from 1960 to January 1990. Talks between the ANC and the South African government began in December 1991 and culminated in the adoption of a nonracial constitution in 1993 and the ANC's agreement to participate in a power-sharing administration, as a prelude to full majority rule. In the country's first universal suffrage elections in April 1994, the ANC won a sweeping victory, capturing 62% of the vote, and Nelson →Mandela was elected president. The ANC also won a majority in South Africa's first democratic local government elections in November 1995, when it won 66.3% of the vote.

The ANC won 66% of the vote in the country's second non-racial election in June 1999, but fell just short of a two-thirds majority in parliament and entered into a coalition agreement with a minority party.

**afterimage** persistence of an image on the retina of the eye after the object producing it has been removed. This leads to persistence of vision, a necessary phenomenon for the illusion of continuous movement in films and television. The term is also used for the persistence of sensations other than vision.

**agate** cryptocrystalline (with crystals too small to be seen with an optical microscope) silica, $SiO_2$, composed of cloudy and banded chalcedony, sometimes mixed with →opal, that forms in rock cavities.

**Agincourt, Battle of** battle fought on 25 October 1415 at Agincourt during the Hundred Years' War, between Henry V of England and a much larger force of French under a divided command. Henry decimated the French and enabled the English conquest of Normandy. Some 6,000 French died and hundreds, including the richest nobles, were taken prisoner. Henry gained France and the French princess Catherine of Valois as his wife. The village of Agincourt (modern Azincourt) is south of Calais, in northern France.

**Agra** city in Uttar Pradesh, northern India, on the River Jumna (or Yamuna), 160 km/100 mi southeast of Delhi; population (1991) 892,000. It is a centre for commerce, tourism, and industry. There are many small-scale engineering plants, and carpets, leather goods, gold and silver embroidery, and engraved marble are produced. The capital of the Mogul empire from 1566–69 and 1601–1658, it is the site of the →Taj Mahal, built during the latter period. Other notable buildings include the Moti Masjid (Pearl Mosque), and the Jama Masjid (Great Mosque), and the Red Fort, with red sandstone walls over 20 m/65 ft high and 2.5 km/1.5 mi long. It has a university (1927).

**Agricola, Gnaeus Julius** (AD 40–93) Roman general and politician. Born at Forum Julii (Fréjus) in Provence, he became consul in AD 77, and then governor of Britain 78–85. He extended Roman rule to the Firth of Forth in Scotland and in 84 won the Battle of Mons Graupius. His fleet sailed round the north of Scotland and proved Britain an island.

**agricultural revolution** sweeping changes that took place in British agriculture over the period 1750–1850. The changes were a response to the increased demand for food from a rapidly expanding population. Major events included the enclosure of open fields; the development of improved breeds of livestock; the introduction of four-course crop rotation; and the use of new crops such as turnips as animal fodder. Recent research has shown that these changes were only part of a much larger, ongoing process of development: many were in fact underway before 1750, and other breakthroughs, such as farm mechanization, did not occur until after 1859.

**agriculture** (Latin *ager* 'field', *colere* 'to cultivate') the practice of farming, including the cultivation of the soil (for raising crops) and the raising of domesticated animals. The units for managing agricultural production vary from smallholdings and individually owned farms to corporate-run farms and collective farms run by entire communities.

**Crops** are for human or animal food, or commodities such as cotton and sisal. For successful production, the land must be prepared (ploughed, cultivated, harrowed, and rolled). Seed must be planted and the growing plants nurtured. This may involve fertilizers, →irrigation, pest control by chemicals, and monitoring of acidity or nutrients. When the crop has grown, it must be harvested and, depending on the crop, processed in a variety of ways before it is stored or sold.

Greenhouses allow cultivation of plants that would otherwise find the climate too harsh. Hydroponics allows commercial cultivation of crops using nutrient-enriched solutions instead of soil. Special methods, such as terracing, may be adopted to allow cultivation in hostile terrain and to retain topsoil in mountainous areas with heavy rainfall.

**Animals** are raised for wool, milk, leather, dung (as fuel), or meat. They may be semidomesticated, such as reindeer, or fully domesticated but nomadic (where naturally growing or cultivated food supplies are sparse), or kept in one location. Animal farming involves accommodation (buildings, fencing, or pasture), feeding, breeding, gathering the produce (eggs, milk, or wool), slaughtering, and further processing such as tanning.

**Ahmadabad** (or Ahmedabad) city in Gujarat, India, situated on the Sabarmati River, 430 km/260 mi north of Mumbai; population (1991) 3,298,000. The former state capital and Gujarat's largest city, it is a major industrial centre specializing in cotton manufacturing. It has many sacred buildings of the Hindu, Muslim, and Jain faiths, as well as buildings designed by 20th-century architects, such as Le Corbusier, reflecting commercial success.

**Ahura Mazda** (or Ormuzd) in Zoroastrianism, the spirit of supreme good. As god of life and light he will finally prevail over his enemy, Ahriman.

**AI** abbreviation for →artificial intelligence.

**AIDS** (acronym for acquired immune deficiency syndrome) gravest of the sexually transmitted diseases, or STDs. It is caused by the human immunodeficiency virus (HIV), now known to be a →retrovirus, an organism first identified in 1983. HIV is transmitted in body fluids, mainly blood and genital secretions.

**air** the mixture of gases making up the Earth's →atmosphere.

**aircraft** any aeronautical vehicle capable of flying through the air. It may be lighter than air (supported by buoyancy) or heavier than air (supported by the dynamic action of air on its surfaces). →Balloons and airships are lighter-than-air craft. Heavier-than-air craft include the →aeroplane, glider, autogiro, and helicopter.

**Alabama** state in southern USA. It is nicknamed Heart of Dixie or the Camellia State. Alabama was admitted to the Union in 1819 as the 22nd US state. Historically it was a plantation state associated with slavery and, in the 20th century, the civil-rights movement. It is bordered to the east by Georgia, with the Chattahoochee River forming the lower half of the boundary, to the north by Tennessee, and to the west by Mississippi, with the Tennessee River forming a small part of the boundary in the northwest. To the south is the Florida panhandle and a 100-km/60-mi long stretch of coast on the Gulf of Mexico, bisected by Mobile Bay; **population:** (1996 est) 4,273,100; **area:** 134,700 sq km/51,994 sq mi; **capital:** Montgomery; **towns and cities:** Birmingham, Mobile, Huntsville, Tuscaloosa; **industries and products:** cotton (still important though no longer prime crop), soybeans, peanuts, wood products, marble, coal, oil, natural gas, livestock, poultry, fishing, iron, steel, aluminium, chemicals, textiles, paper, power generation, aerospace industry.

**Alaska** largest state of the USA, located on the northwest extremity of North

America, and separated from the lower 48 states by British Columbia. It is nicknamed Last Frontier. Alaska was admitted to the Union in 1959 as the 49th US state. Historically and commercially the state has been associated with mineral exploitation. It is bordered to the east by the Yukon Territory, Canada, and to the southeast, along its panhandle, by the Yukon Territory and British Columbia, Canada. Northern Alaska lies on the Beaufort Sea, part of the Arctic Ocean. To the northwest is the Chukchi Sea, narrowing to c. 80 km/50 mi at the Bering Strait, which separates the Alaskan Seward Peninsula from Russian East Asia. The Bering Sea is bounded to the south by Alaska's long →Aleutian Island chain, extending in an east–west arc across the North Pacific Ocean from the Alaska Peninsula. To the peninsula's east is the Gulf of Alaska; **population:** (1996 est) 607,000; including 15% American Indians, Aleuts, and Inuit; **total area:** 1,530,700 sq km/591,004 sq mi; **land area:** 1,478,457 sq km/570,833 sq mi; **capital:** Juneau; **towns and cities:** Anchorage, Fairbanks, Fort Yukon, Holy Cross, Nome, College, Sitka; **industries and products:** oil, natural gas, coal, copper, iron, gold, tin, fur, salmon fisheries and canneries, lumber; tourism is a large and growing industry (tourists outnumber residents each year).

**Albania** Republic of; **national name:** *Republika e Shqipërisë*; **area:** 28,748 sq km/11,099 sq mi; **capital:** Tiranë (Tirana); **major towns/cities:** Durrës, Shkodër, Elbasan, Vlorë, Korçë; **major ports:** Durrës; **physical features:** mainly mountainous, with rivers flowing east–west, and a narrow coastal plain; **head of state:** Rexhep Mejdani from 1998; **head of government:** Ilir Meta from 1999; **political system:** emergent democracy; **currency:** lek; **GNP per capita (PPP):** (US$) 3,200 (1998 est); **exports:** chromium and chrome products, processed foodstuffs, textiles and footwear, base metals, machinery and equipment, bitumen, tobacco. Principal market Italy 49.1% (1997); **population:** 3,113,000 (1999 est); **language:** Albanian, Greek; **religion:** Muslim, Orthodox, Roman Catholic; **life expectancy:** 70 (men); 76 (women) (1995–2000).

**albatross** large seabird, genus *Diomedea*, with long narrow wings adapted for gliding and a wingspan of up to 3 m/10 ft, mainly found in the southern hemisphere. It belongs to the family Diomedeidae, order Procellariiformes, the same group as petrels and shearwaters. The external nostrils of birds in this order are more or less tubular, and the bills are hooked.

**Albert, Prince Consort** (1819–1861) husband of British Queen →Victoria from 1840. A patron of the arts, science, and industry, Albert was the second son of the Duke of Saxe Coburg-Gotha and first cousin to Queen Victoria, whose chief adviser he became. He planned the Great Exhibition of 1851, the profits from which were used to buy the sites in London of all the South Kensington museums and colleges and the Royal Albert Hall, built in 1871. He died of typhoid. The Queen never fully recovered from his premature death, and remained in mourning for him for the rest of her life.

**albumin** any of a group of sulphur-containing →proteins. The best known is in the form of egg white (albumen); others occur in milk, and as a major component of serum. Many vegetables and fluids also contain albumins. They are soluble in water and dilute salt solutions, and are coagulated by heat.

**alchemy** (Arabic *al-Kimya*) supposed technique of transmuting base metals, such as lead and mercury, into silver and gold by the philosopher's stone, a hypothetical substance, that was also attributed the power to give eternal life.

**alcohol** any member of a group of organic chemical compounds characterized by the presence of one or more aliphatic OH (hydroxyl) groups in the molecule, and which form →esters with acids. The main uses of alcohols are as solvents for gums, resins, lacquers, and varnishes; in the making of dyes; for essential oils in perfumery; and for medical substances in pharmacy. The alcohol produced naturally in the fermentation process and consumed as part of alcoholic beverages is called →ethanol.

**aldehyde** any of a group of organic chemical compounds prepared by oxidation of primary alcohols, so that the OH (hydroxyl) group loses its hydrogen to give an oxygen joined by a double

| Alkane | Alcohol | Aldehyde | Ketone | Carboxylic acid | Alkene |
|--------|---------|----------|--------|-----------------|--------|
| $CH_4$ methane | $CH_3OH$ methanol | HCHO methanal | — | $HCO_2H$ methanoic acid | — |
| $CH_3CH_3$ ethane | $CH_3CH_2OH$ ethanol | $CH_3CHO$ ethanal | — | $CH_3CO_2H$ ethanoic acid | $CH_2CH_2$ ethene |
| $CH_3CH_2CH_3$ propane | $CH_3CH_2CH_2OH$ propanol | $CH_3CH_2CHO$ propanal | $CH_3COCH_3$ propanone | $CH_3CH_2CO_2H$ propanoic acid | $CH_2CHCH_3$ propene |
| methane | methanol | methanal | propanone | methanoic acid | ethene |

**alcohol** The systematic naming of simple straight-chain organic molecules.

bond to a carbon atom (the aldehyde group, with the formula CHO).

**Aleutian Islands** volcanic island chain in the North Pacific, stretching 1,900 km/1,200 mi southwest of Alaska, of which it forms part, towards Kamchatka; population (1990) 12,000. There are 14 large and more than 100 small islands running along the Aleutian Trench; the largest island is Unimak (with an area of 3,500 sq km/1,360 sq mi), which contains two active volcanoes. The islands are mountainous, barren, and treeless; they are ice-free all year but are often foggy, with only about 25 days of sunshine recorded annually. The only industries are fishing, seal hunting, and sheep farming; the main exports are fish and furs. Unalaska is the chief island for trade as it has a good harbour.

**Alexander (III) the Great** (356–323 BC) king of Macedon 336–323 BC and conqueror of the Persian Empire. As commander of the powerful Macedonian army he conquered Greece in 336, defeated the Persian king Darius III in Asia Minor in 333, then moved on to Egypt where he founded Alexandria. He defeated the Persians again in Assyria in 331, then advanced further east, invading India in 327. He conquered the Punjab before mutinous troops forced his retreat.

**Alexandria** (or Al Iskandariya) city, chief port, and second-largest city of Egypt, situated between the Mediterranean and Lake Maryut; population (1992) 3,380,000. It is linked by canal with the Nile. There is oil refining, gas processing, and trade in cotton and grain. Founded in 331 BC by Alexander the Great, Alexandria was the capital of Egypt for over 1,000 years.

**Alfred the Great** (c. 849–c. 901) Anglo-Saxon king 871–899 who defended England against Danish invasion and founded the first English navy. He succeeded his brother Aethelred to the throne of Wessex in 871, and a new legal code came into force during his reign. He encouraged the translation of scholarly works from Latin (some he translated himself), and promoted the development of the Anglo-Saxon Chronicle.

**algae** (singular alga) highly varied group of plants, ranging from single-celled forms to large and complex seaweeds. They live in both fresh and salt water, and in damp soil. Algae do not have true roots, stems, or leaves.

**Algeria** Democratic and Popular Republic of; **national name:** al-Jumhuriya al-Jazairiya ad-Dimuqratiya ash-Shabiya; **area:** 2,381,741 sq km/919,590 sq mi; **capital:** Algiers (al-Jaza'ir); **major towns/cities:** Oran, Annaba, Blida, Sétif, Constantine (Qacentina); **major ports:** Oran (Ouahran), Annaba (Bône); **physical features:** coastal plains backed by mountains in north, Sahara desert in south; Atlas mountains, Barbary Coast, Chott Melrhir depression, Hoggar mountains; **head of state:** Abdel Aziz Bouteflika from 1999; **head of government:** Ismail Hamdani from 1998;

**political system:** military rule; **currency:** Algerian dinar; **GNP per capita (PPP):** (US$) 4,380 (1998 est); **exports:** crude oil, gas, vegetables, tobacco, hides, dates. Principal market Italy 19.8% (1997); **population:** 30,774,000 (1999 est); **language:** Arabic (official); Berber, French; **religion:** Sunni Muslim (state religion); **life expectancy:** 68 (men); 70 (women) (1995–2000).

**Algiers** (Arabic *al-Jazair*; French *Alger*) capital of Algeria, situated on the narrow coastal plain between the Atlas Mountains and the Mediterranean; population (1995) 2,168,000. It distributes grain, iron, phosphates, wines, and oil from central Algeria. The main industries are oil refining, petrochemicals, and metal working. The city is a popular winter resort.

**algorithm** procedure or series of steps that can be used to solve a problem.

In computer science, it describes the logical sequence of operations to be performed by a program. A →flow chart is a visual representation of an algorithm.

**Ali** (*c.* 598–661) 4th caliph of Islam. He was born in Mecca, the son of Abu Talib, and was the cousin and close friend and supporter of the prophet Muhammad, who gave him his daughter Fatima in marriage. He was one of the first to believe in Islam. On Muhammad's death 632, Ali had a claim to succeed him, but this was not conceded until 656, following the murder of the third caliph, Uthman. After a brief and stormy reign, Ali was assassinated. Controversy has raged around Ali's name between the Sunni Muslims and the Shiites, the former denying his right to the caliphate and the latter supporting it.

**Ali, Muhammad** (1942– ) adopted name of Cassius Marcellus Clay, Jr, US boxer. Olympic light-heavyweight champion in 1960, he went on to become world professional heavyweight champion in 1964, and was the only man to regain the title twice. He was known for his fast footwork and extrovert nature. In December 1999, he was voted the British Broadcasting Corporation (BBC) 'Sports Personality of the Century', and the US magazine *Sports Illustrated* and the US newspaper *USA Today* both named him 'Sportsman of the Century'.

**alimentary canal** in animals, the tube through which food passes; it extends from the mouth to the anus. It is a complex organ, adapted for digestion. In human adults, it is about 9 m/30 ft long, consisting of the mouth cavity, pharynx, oesophagus, stomach, and the small and large intestines.

**aliphatic compound** any organic chemical compound in which the carbon atoms are joined in straight chains, as in hexane ($C_6H_{14}$), or in branched chains, as in 2-methylpentane ($CH_3CH(CH_3)CH_2CH_2CH_3$).

**alkali** in chemistry, a →base that is soluble in water. Alkalis neutralize acids and are soapy to the touch. The strength of an alkali is measured by its hydrogen-ion concentration, indicated by the →pH value. They may be divided into strong and weak alkalis: a strong alkali (for example, potassium hydroxide, KOH) ionizes completely when disssolved in water, whereas a weak alkali (for example, ammonium hydroxide, $NH_4OH$) exists in a partially ionized state in solution. All alkalis have a pH above 7.0.

The hydroxides of metals are alkalis. Those of sodium and potassium are chemically powerful; both were historically derived from the ashes of plants.

**alkane** member of a group of →hydrocarbons having the general formula $C_nH_{2n+2}$, commonly known as **paraffins**. As they contain only single →covalent bonds, alkanes are said to be saturated. Lighter alkanes, such as methane, ethane, propane, and butane, are colourless gases; heavier ones are liquids or solids. In nature they are found in natural gas and petroleum.

**Allah** (Arabic *al-Ilah* 'the God') Islamic name for God.

**allele** one of two or more alternative forms of a →gene at a given position (locus) on a chromosome, caused by a difference in the →DNA. Blue and brown eyes in humans are determined by different alleles of the gene for eye colour.

**Allen, Woody** (1935– ) adopted name of Allen Stewart Konigsberg, US film writer, director, and actor. Allen's filmography includes such critically acclaimed works as *Annie Hall* (1977), which won an Academy Award in 1977 for Best Picture, *Manhattan* (1979), *Hannah and Her Sisters* (1986), *Radio Days* (1987), *Crimes and Misdemeanours* (1989), *Bullets Over Broadway* (1994), and *Deconstructing Harry* (1997). In 1998 he wrote and directed *Celebrity*.

**allergy** special sensitivity of the body that makes it react with an exaggerated response of the natural immune defence mechanism to the introduction of an otherwise harmless foreign substance (allergen).

**Allies, the** in World War I, the 23 countries allied against the Central Powers (Germany, Austro-Hungary, Turkey, and Bulgaria), including France, Italy, Russia, the UK, Australia and other Commonwealth nations, and, in the latter part of the war, the USA. In World War II they were the 49 countries allied against the Axis Powers (Germany, Italy, and Japan), including France, the UK, Australia and other Commonwealth nations, the USA, and the former Soviet Union.

**alligator** (Spanish *el lagarto* 'the lizard') reptile of the genus *Alligator*, related to the crocodile. There are only two living species: *A. mississipiensis*, the Mississippi alligator of the southern states of the USA, and *A. sinensis* from the swamps of the lower Chang Jiang River in China. The former grows to about 4 m/12 ft, but the latter only to 1.5 m/5 ft. Alligators lay their eggs in waterside nests of mud and vegetation and are good mothers. They swim well with lashing movements of the tail and feed on fish and mammals but seldom attack people.

**allotropy** property whereby an element can exist in two or more forms (allotropes), each possessing different physical properties but the same state of matter (gas, liquid, or solid). The allotropes of carbon are diamond, fullerene, and graphite. Sulphur has several allotropes (flowers of sulphur, plastic, rhombic, and monoclinic). These solids have different crystal structures, as do the white and grey forms of tin and the black, red, and white forms of phosphorus.

**alloy** metal blended with some other metallic or nonmetallic substance to give it special qualities, such as resistance to corrosion, greater hardness, or tensile strength. Useful alloys include bronze, brass, cupronickel, duralumin, German silver, gunmetal, pewter, solder, steel, and stainless steel.

**alluvial deposit** layer of broken rocky matter, or sediment, formed from material that has been carried in suspension by a river or stream and dropped as the velocity of the current decreases. River plains and deltas are made entirely of alluvial deposits, but smaller pockets can be found in the beds of upland torrents.

**Alps** the highest and most extensive mountain range in Europe. The Alps run in an arc from the Mediterranean coast of France in the west through northern Italy, Switzerland, southern Germany, and Austria to the outskirts of Vienna and the River Danube in the east – a total distance of some 960 km/597 mi. Alpine ranges also extend down the Adriatic coast into Slovenia and Croatia. The Alps form a natural frontier between several countries in south-central Europe. The highest peak, at 4,808 m/15,774 ft, is Mont Blanc, on the Franco-Italian border. The Alps are the source of many of Europe's major rivers – or their tributaries – including the Rhine, the Rhône, the Po, and the Danube.

**Alsace** region of France; area 8,300 sq km/3,204 sq mi; population (1990) 1,624,400. It consists of the *départements* of Bas-Rhin and Haut-Rhin; its administrative centre is →Strasbourg. Alsace has much rich agricultural land, and is noted for its white wines.

**alternating current** (AC) electric current that flows for an interval of time in one direction and then in the opposite direction, that is, a current that flows in alternately reversed directions through or around a circuit. Electric energy is usually generated as alternating current in a power station, and alternating currents may be used for both power and lighting.

**alternative medicine** see →medicine, alternative.

**alternator** electricity generator that produces an alternating current.

**aluminium** lightweight, silver-white, ductile and malleable, metallic element, symbol Al, atomic number 13, relative atomic mass 26.9815, melting point 658°C/1,216°F. It is the third most abundant element (and the most abundant metal) in the Earth's crust, of

## COMMON ALLOYS

| Name | Approximate composition | Uses |
|------|------------------------|------|
| brass | 35–10% zinc, 65–90% copper | decorative metalwork, plumbing fittings, industrial tubing |
| bronze – common | 2% zinc, 6% tin, 92% copper | machinery, decorative work |
| bronze – aluminium | 10% aluminium, 90% copper | machinery castings |
| bronze – coinage | 1% zinc, 4% tin, 95% copper | coins |
| cast iron | 2–4% carbon, 96–98% iron | decorative metalwork, engine blocks, industrial machinery |
| dentist's amalgam | 30% copper, 70% mercury | dental fillings |
| duralumin | 0.5 % magnesium, 0.5% manganese, 5% copper, 94% aluminium | framework of aircraft |
| gold – coinage | 10% copper, 90% gold | coins |
| gold – dental | 14–28% silver, 14–28% copper, 58% gold | dental fillings |
| lead battery plate | 6% antimony, 94% lead | car batteries |
| manganin | 1.5% nickel, 16% manganese, 82.5% copper | resistance wire |
| nichrome | 20% chromium, 80% nickel | heating elements |
| pewter | 20% lead, 80% tin | utensils |
| silver – coinage | 10% copper, 90% silver | coins |
| solder | 50% tin, 50% lead | joining iron surfaces |
| steel – stainless | 8–20% nickel, 10–20% chromium, 60–80% iron | kitchen utensils |
| steel – armour | 1–4% nickel, 0.5–2% chromium, 95–98% iron | armour plating |
| steel – tool | 2–4% chromium, 6–7% molybdenum, 90–95% iron | tools |

which it makes up about 8.1% by mass. It is non-magnetic, an excellent conductor of electricity, and oxidizes easily, the layer of oxide on its surface making it highly resistant to tarnish.

**Alzheimer's disease** common manifestation of →dementia, thought to afflict one in 20 people over 65. After heart disease, cancer, and strokes it is the most common cause of death in the Western world. Attacking the brain's 'grey matter', it is a disease of mental processes rather than physical function, characterized by memory loss and progressive intellectual impairment. It was first described by Alois Alzheimer 1906. It affects up to 4 million people in the USA and around 600,000 in Britain.

**amalgam** any alloy of mercury with other metals. Most metals will form amalgams, except iron and platinum. Amalgam is used in dentistry for filling teeth, and usually contains copper, silver, and zinc as the main alloying ingredients. This amalgam is pliable when first mixed and then sets hard, but the mercury leaches out and may cause a type of heavy-metal poisoning.

**Amazon** (Portuguese and Spanish *Rio Amazonas*; Indian *Amossona* 'destroyer of boats'), river in South America, the second longest in the world; length 6,516 km/4,050 mi. The Amazon ranks as the largest river in the world in terms of the volume of water it discharges (between 34 million and 121 million l/7.5 million and 27 million gall), its number of tributaries (over 500), and the total basin area that it drains (7 million sq km/2.7 million sq mi – almost half the landmass of South America). It has 48,280 km/30,000 mi of navigable waterways. The river empties into the Atlantic Ocean on the Equator, through an estuary 80 km/50 mi wide. Over 5 million sq km/2 million sq mi of the Amazon basin is virgin rainforest, containing 30% of all known plant and animal species. This is the wettest region on Earth, with an average annual rainfall of 2.54 m/8.3 ft.

**Amazon** in Greek mythology, a member of a group of female warriors living near the Black Sea, who cut off their right breasts to use the bow more easily. Their queen Penthesilea was killed by →Achilles at the siege of Troy. The term Amazon has come to mean a large, strong woman.

**amber** fossilized resin from coniferous trees of the Middle →Tertiary period. It is often washed ashore on the Baltic coast with plant and animal specimens preserved in it; many extinct species have been found preserved in this way. It ranges in colour from red to yellow, and is used to make jewellery.

**American Civil War** 1861–65; see →Civil War, American.

**American Independence, War of** alternative name of the American Revolution, the revolt 1775–83 of the British North American colonies that resulted in the establishment of the United States of America.

**American Indian** (or Native American) member of one of the aboriginal peoples of the Americas; the Arctic peoples (Inuit and Aleut) are often included, especially by the Bureau of Indian Affairs (BIA) of the US Department of the Interior, responsible for overseeing policy on US American Indian life, their reservations, education, and social welfare. The first American Indians arrived during the last ice age, approximately 20,000–30,000 years ago, passing from northeastern Siberia into Alaska over a land-bridge across the Bering Strait. The earliest reliably dated archaeological sites in North America are about 13,000–14,000 years old. In South America they are generally dated at about 12,000–13,000 years old, but discoveries made in 1989 suggest an even earlier date, perhaps 35,000–40,000 years ago. There are about 1.9 million (1995) American Indians in the USA and Canada.

**amethyst** variety of →quartz, $SiO_2$, coloured violet by the presence of small quantities of impurities such as manganese or iron; used as a semiprecious stone. Amethysts are found chiefly in the Ural Mountains, India, the USA, Uruguay, and Brazil.

**Amin (Dada), Idi** (1925– ) Ugandan politician, president 1971–79. He led the coup that deposed Milton Obote in 1971, expelled the Asian community in 1972, and exercised a reign of terror over his people during which an estimated 300,000 people were killed. After he invaded Tanzania in 1978, the Tanzanian army combined with dissident Ugandans to counter-attack. Despite assistance from Libya, Amin's forces collapsed and he fled in 1979. He now lives in Saudi Arabia.

**amino acid** water-soluble organic →molecule, mainly composed of carbon, oxygen, hydrogen, and nitrogen, containing both a basic amino group ($NH_2$) and an acidic carboxyl (COOH) group. They are small molecules able to pass through membranes. When two or more amino acids are joined together, they are known as →peptides; →proteins are made up of peptide chains folded or twisted in characteristic shapes. *See illustration on page 22.*

**Amis, Kingsley William** (1922–1995) English novelist and poet. He was associated early on with the Angry Young Men group of writers. His sharply ironic works include the best-selling *Lucky Jim* (1954; his first novel), a comic portrayal of life at a provincial university. His later novels include the satiric comedy *The Old Devils* (1986), for which he won the Booker Prize.

**Amman** capital and chief industrial centre of Jordan, 80 km/50 mi northeast of Jerusalem; population (1994 est) 1,300,000. It is a major communications centre, linking historic trade routes across the Middle East.

**ammonia** $NH_3$ colourless pungent-smelling gas, lighter than air and very soluble in water. It is made on an industrial scale by the Haber (or Haber–Bosch) process, and used mainly to produce nitrogenous fertilizers, nitric acid, and some explosives.

**ammonite** extinct marine →cephalopod mollusc of the order Ammonoidea,

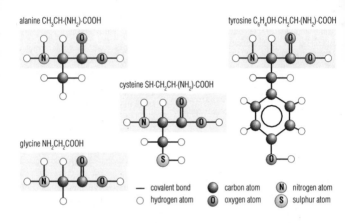

alanine CH$_3$CH·(NH$_2$)·COOH

tyrosine C$_6$H$_4$OH·CH$_2$CH·(NH$_2$)·COOH

cysteine SH·CH$_2$CH·(NH$_2$)·COOH

glycine NH$_2$CH$_2$COOH

— covalent bond
○ hydrogen atom
● carbon atom
(O) oxygen atom
(N) nitrogen atom
(S) sulphur atom

**amino acid** Amino acids are natural organic compounds that make up proteins and can thus be considered the basic molecules of life. There are 20 different common amino acids. They consist mainly of carbon, oxygen, hydrogen, and nitrogen. Each amino acid has a common core structure (consisting of two carbon atoms, two oxygen atoms, a nitrogen atom, and four hydrogen atoms) to which is attached a variable group, known as the R group. In glycine, the R group is a single hydrogen atom; in alanine, the R group consists of a carbon and three hydrogen atoms.

related to the modern nautilus. The shell was curled in a plane spiral and made up of numerous gas-filled chambers, the outermost containing the body of the animal. Many species flourished between 200 million and 65 million years ago, ranging in size from that of a small coin to 2 m/6 ft across.

**amnesia** loss or impairment of memory. As a clinical condition it may be caused by disease or injury to the brain, by some drugs, or by shock; in some cases it may be a symptom of an emotional disorder.

**amniocentesis** sampling the amniotic fluid surrounding a fetus in the womb for diagnostic purposes. It is used to detect Down's syndrome and other genetic abnormalities. The procedure carries a 1 in 200 risk of miscarriage.

**amoeba** (plural amoebae) one of the simplest living animals, consisting of a single cell and belonging to the →protozoa group. The body consists of colourless protoplasm. Its activities are

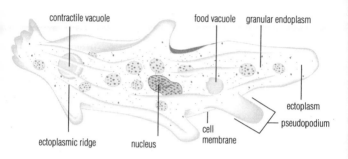

**amoeba** The amoebae are among the simplest living organisms, consisting of a single cell. Within the cell, there is a nucleus, which controls cell activity, and many other microscopic bodies and vacuoles (fluid-filled spaces surrounded by a membrane) with specialized functions. Amoebae eat by flowing around food particles, engulfing the particle, a process called phagocytosis.

controlled by the nucleus, and it feeds by flowing round and engulfing organic debris. It reproduces by binary fission. Some species of amoeba are harmful parasites.

**ampere** SI unit (symbol A) of electrical current. Electrical current is measured in a similar way to water current, in terms of an amount per unit time; one ampere represents a flow of about $6.28 \times 10^{18}$ →electrons per second, or a rate of flow of charge of one coulomb per second.

**amphetamine** (or speed) powerful synthetic stimulant. Benzedrine was the earliest amphetamine marketed, used as a 'pep pill' in World War II to help soldiers overcome fatigue, and until the 1970s amphetamines were prescribed by doctors as an appetite suppressant for weight loss; as an antidepressant, to induce euphoria; and as a stimulant, to increase alertness.

Indications for its use today are very restricted because of severe side effects, including addiction. It is a sulphate or phosphate form of $C_9H_{13}N$.

**amphibian** (Greek 'double life') member of the vertebrate class Amphibia, which generally spend their larval (tadpole) stage in fresh water, transferring to land at maturity (after →metamorphosis) and generally returning to water to breed. Like fish and reptiles, they continue to grow throughout life, and cannot maintain a temperature greatly differing from that of their environment. The class contains 4,553 known species, 4,000 of which are frogs and toads, 390 salamanders, and 163 caecilians (wormlike in appearance).

**amplifier** electronic device that magnifies the strength of a signal, such as a radio signal. The ratio of output signal strength to input signal strength is called the **gain** of the amplifier. As well as achieving high gain, an amplifier should be free from distortion and able to operate over a range of frequencies. Practical amplifiers are usually complex circuits, although simple amplifiers can be built from single transistors or valves.

**Amritsar** industrial city in the Punjab, India; population (1991) 709,000. It is the holy city of →Sikhism, with the Guru Nanak University (named after the first Sikh guru), and the Golden Temple, surrounded by the sacred pool Amrita Saras. The Jallianwala Bagh area of the city was the scene of the Amritsar Massacre in 1919, when the British Gen Dyer ordered troops to fire on a crowd agitating for self-government; 379 were killed and 1,200 wounded. In 1984, armed Sikh demonstrators were evicted from the Golden Temple by the Indian army, in Operation Bluestar, led by Gen Dayal. Over 300 were killed. Later in 1984, Indian prime minister Indira Gandhi was assassinated in reprisal by Sikh extremists wanting an independent Sikh state in Punjab. The whole of Punjab was put under presidential control in 1987 following riots. Rajiv Gandhi ordered further attacks on the Golden Temple in 1988.

**Amundsen, Roald Engelbrecht Gravning** (1872–1928) Norwegian explorer who in 1903–06 became the first person to navigate the Northwest Passage. Beaten to the North Pole by US explorer Robert Peary 1910, he reached the South Pole ahead of Captain Scott 1911.

**anabolic steroid** any →hormone of the steroid group that stimulates tissue growth. Its use in medicine is limited to the treatment of some anaemias and breast cancers; it may help to break up blood clots. Side effects include aggressive behaviour, masculinization in women, and, in children, reduced height.

**anaemia** condition caused by a shortage of haemoglobin, the oxygen-carrying component of red blood cells. The main symptoms are fatigue, pallor, breathlessness, palpitations, and poor resistance to infection. Treatment depends on the cause.

**anaesthetic** drug that produces loss of sensation or consciousness; the resulting state is **anaesthesia**, in which the patient is insensitive to stimuli. Anaesthesia may also happen as a result of nerve disorder.

**analgesic** agent for relieving pain. Opiates alter the perception or appreciation of pain and are effective in controlling 'deep' visceral (internal) pain. Non opiates, such as →aspirin, →paracetamol, and NSAIDs (nonsteroidal anti-inflammatory drugs), relieve musculoskeletal pain and reduce inflammation in soft tissues.

**analogue** (of a quantity or device) changing continuously; by contrast a digital quantity or device varies in series of distinct steps. For example, an analogue clock measures time by means of a continuous movement of hands around a dial, whereas a digital clock measures time with a numerical display that changes in a series of discrete steps.

**anarchism** (Greek *anarkhos*, 'without ruler') political belief that society should have no government, laws, police, or other authority, but should be a free association of all its members. It does not mean 'without order'; most theories of anarchism imply an order of a very strict and symmetrical kind, but they maintain that such order can be achieved by cooperation. Anarchism must not be confused with nihilism (a purely negative and destructive activity directed against society); anarchism is essentially a pacifist movement.

**Anatolia** (Turkish *Anadolu*) Asian part of Turkey, consisting of a mountainous peninsula with the Black Sea to the north, the Aegean Sea to the west, and the Mediterranean Sea to the south.

**ANC** abbreviation for →African National Congress, a South African political party and former nationalist organization.

**Anchorage** port and largest city in Alaska, USA, at the head of Cook Inlet; population (1994 est) 253,600. It is an important centre of administration, communication, and commerce for much of central and western Alaska.

Local industries include oil and gas extraction, tourism, and fish canning.

**Andalusia** (Spanish *Andalucía*) autonomous community of southern Spain, including the provinces of Almería, Cádiz, Córdoba, Granada, Huelva, Jaén, Málaga, and Seville; area 87,300 sq km/33,698 sq mi; population (1991) 6,940,500. The Guadalquivir River flows through Andalusia, which is bounded on the north by the Sierra Morena mountain range. The region is fertile, and produces oranges and wine (especially sherry); horses are bred here also, and copper is mined at Rio Tinto. Seville, an inland port, is the administrative capital and the largest industrial centre; Málaga, Cádiz, and Algeciras are the chief ports and also important industrial centres. The **Costa del Sol** on the south coast has many tourist resorts, including Marbella and Torremolinos; the Sierra Nevada mountain range in the southeast is a winter ski destination.

**Andersen, Hans Christian** (1805–1875) Danish writer of fairy tales. Examples include 'The Ugly Duckling', 'The Snow Queen', 'The Little Mermaid', and 'The Emperor's New Clothes'. Their inventiveness, sensitivity, and strong sense of wonder have given these stories perennial and universal appeal; they have been translated into many languages. He also wrote adult novels and travel books.

**Andes** great mountain system or **cordillera** that forms the western fringe of South America, extending through some 67° of latitude and the republics of Colombia, Venezuela, Ecuador, Peru, Bolivia, Chile, and Argentina. It is the longest mountain range in the world, 8,000 km/5,000 mi, and its peaks exceed 3,600 m/12,000 ft in height for half that length.

**Andhra Pradesh** state in east central India; **area:** 275,100 sq km/106,216 sq mi; **capital:** Hyderabad; **towns and cities:** Secunderabad, Visakhapatnam, Vijayawada, Kakinda, Guntur, Nellore; **physical:** coastal plains with extensive river valleys (Krishna and Godavari) reaching into the Eastern Ghats; smaller rivers Pennar and Cheyyar; Deccan plateau inland; **industries:** mica, coal, iron ore, oil refining, shipbuilding, fertilizers; **agriculture:** rice, millet, sugar cane, tobacco, groundnuts, sorghum, cotton; **population:** (1994 est) 71,800,000; **language:** Telugu, Urdu, Tamil; **history:** formed in 1953 from the Telugu-speaking areas of Madras, and enlarged on a similar linguistic basis in 1956 with parts of the former Hyderabad state.

**Andorra** Principality of; **national name:** *Principat d'Andorra;* **area:** 468 sq km/181 sq mi; **capital:** Andorra-la-Vella; **major towns/cities:** Les Escaldes, Escaldes-Engordany (suburb of capital); **physical features:** mountainous, with narrow valleys; the eastern Pyrenees, Valira River; **heads of state:** Joan Marti i Alanis (bishop of Urgel, Spain) and Jacques Chirac (president of France); **head of government:** Marc Forne from 1994; **political system:** co-principality; **currency:** French franc and Spanish peseta; **GNP per capita (PPP):** (US$) 16,630 (1995 est); **exports:** cigars and cigarettes, furniture, electricity. Principal market Spain 47.5% (1997); **population:** 66,000 (1999 est); **language:** Catalan (official); Spanish, French; **religion:** Roman Catholic; **life expectancy:** 70 (men); 73 (women) (1994 est).

**aneurysm** weakening in the wall of an artery, causing it to balloon outwards with the risk of rupture and serious, often fatal, blood loss. If detected in time, some accessible aneurysms can be repaired by bypass surgery, but such major surgery carries a high risk for patients in poor health.

**Angelico, Fra** (*c.* 1400–1455) Guido di Pietro, Italian painter. He was a monk, active in Florence, and painted religious scenes. His series of frescoes at the monastery of San Marco, Florence, was begun after 1436. He also produced several altarpieces in a style characterized by a delicacy of line and colour.

**angina** (or angina pectoris) severe pain in the chest due to impaired blood supply to the heart muscle because a coronary artery is narrowed. Faintness and difficulty in breathing accompany the pain. Treatment is by drugs or bypass surgery.

**angiosperm** flowering plant in which the seeds are enclosed within an ovary, which ripens into a fruit. Angiosperms are divided into monocotyledons (single seed leaf in the embryo) and dicotyledons (two seed leaves in the embryo). They include the majority of flowers, herbs, grasses, and trees except conifers.

**angle** in mathematics, the amount of turn or rotation; it may be defined by a pair of rays (half-lines) that share a common endpoint but do not lie on the same line. Angles are measured in →degrees (°) or radians (rads) – a complete turn or circle being 360° or 2π rads.

Angles are classified generally by their degree measures: acute angles are less than 90°; right angles are exactly 90° (a quarter turn); obtuse angles are greater than 90° but less than 180°(a straight line); reflex angles are greater

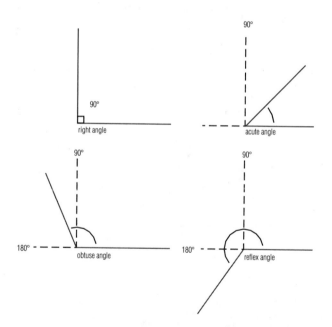

**angle** The four types of angle, as classified by their degree measures. No angle is classified as having a measure of 180°, as by definition such an 'angle' is actually a straight line.

than 180° but less than 360°. Angles that add up to 180° are called supplementary angles.

**Anglo-Saxon** one of several groups of Germanic invaders (including Angles, Saxons, and Jutes) that conquered much of Britain between the 5th and 7th centuries. Initially they established conquest kingdoms, commonly referred to as the **Heptarchy**; these were united in the early 9th century under the overlordship of Wessex. The Norman invasion in 1066 brought Anglo-Saxon rule to an end.

**Angola** People's Republic of; **national name:** *República Popular de Angola*; **area:** 1,246,700 sq km/481,350 sq mi; **capital:** Luanda (and chief port); **major towns/cities:** Lobito, Benguela, Huambo, Lubango, Malange, Namibe (formerly Moçâmedes); **major ports:** Huambo, Lubango, Malange; **physical features:** narrow coastal plain rises to vast interior plateau with rainforest in northwest; desert in south; Cuanza, Cuito, Cubango, and Cunene rivers; **head of state:** José Eduardo dos Santos from 1979; **head of government:** Fernando Franca van Dunem from 1996; **political system:** emergent democracy; **currency:** kwanza; **GNP per capita (PPP):** (US\$) 840 (1998 est); **exports:** petroleum and petroleum products, diamonds, gas. Principal market USA 65% (1997); **population:** 12,478,000 (1999 est); **language:** Portuguese (official); Bantu dialects; **religion:** Roman Catholic 68%, Protestant 20%, animist 12%; **life**

**expectancy:** 45 (men); 48 (women) (1995–2000).

**Anguilla** island in the eastern Caribbean; **area:** 160 sq km/62 sq mi; **capital:** The Valley; **features:** white coral-sand beaches; 80% of its coral reef has been lost through tourism (pollution and souvenir sales); **exports:** lobster, salt; **currency:** Eastern Caribbean dollar; **population:** (1992) 8,960; **language:** English, Creole; **government:** from 1982, governor, executive council, and legislative house of assembly; **history:** a British colony from 1650, Anguilla was long associated with St Christopher–Nevis but revolted against alleged domination by the larger island and seceded in 1967. A small British force restored order in 1969, and Anguilla retained a special position at its own request; since 1980 it has been a separate dependency of the UK.

**animal** (or metazoan; Latin *anima* 'breath', 'life') member of the →kingdom Animalia, one of the major categories of living things, the science of which is **zoology**. Animals are all →heterotrophs (they obtain their energy from organic substances produced by other organisms); they have eukaryotic cells (the genetic material is contained within a distinct nucleus) bounded by a thin cell membrane rather than the thick cell wall of plants. Most animals are capable of moving around for at least part of their life cycle.

**animism** in anthropology, the belief that everything, whether animate or inanimate, possesses a soul or spirit. It is a fundamental system of belief in certain religions, particularly those of some pre-industrial societies. Linked with this is the worship of natural objects such as stones and trees, thought to harbour spirits (naturism); fetishism; and ancestor worship.

**anion** ion carrying a negative charge. During electrolysis, anions in the electrolyte move towards the anode (positive electrode).

**Ankara** (formerly Angora) capital of Turkey; population (1990) 2,559,500. Industries include cement, textiles, and leather products. It replaced Istanbul (then in Allied occupation) as capital 1923.

**Anne** (1665–1714) queen of Great Britain and Ireland 1702–14. She was the second daughter of James, Duke of York, who became James II, and his first wife, Anne Hyde, daughter of Edward Hyde, Earl of Clarendon. She succeeded William III in 1702. Events of her reign include the War of the Spanish Succession, Marlborough's victories at Blenheim, Ramillies, Oudenarde, and Malplaquet, and the union of the English and Scottish parliaments in 1707.

**annelid** any segmented worm of the phylum Annelida. Annelids include earthworms, leeches, and marine worms such as lugworms.

**annual plant** plant that completes its life cycle within one year, during which time it germinates, grows to maturity, bears flowers, seeds, and then dies.

**annelid** Annelids are worms with segmented bodies. The ragworm, lugworm, and peacock worm shown here are all marine species. Ragworms commonly live in mucous-lined burrows on muddy shores or under stones, and lugworms occupy U-shaped burrows. The peacock worm, however, builds a smooth, round tube from fine particles of mud.

**anode** in chemistry, the positive electrode of an electrolytic →cell, towards which negative particles (anions), usually in solution, are attracted. See →electrolysis.

**anorexia** lack of desire to eat, or refusal to eat, especially the pathological condition of **anorexia nervosa**, most often found in adolescent girls and young women. Compulsive eating, or →bulimia, distortions of body image, and depression often accompany anorexia.

**ant** insect belonging to the family Formicidae, and to the same order (Hymenoptera) as bees and wasps. Ants are characterized by a conspicuous waist and elbowed antennae. About 10,000 different species are known; all are social in habit, and all construct nests of various kinds. Ants are found in all parts of the world, except the polar regions. It is estimated that there are about 10 million billion ants.

**Antananarivo** (formerly Tananarive) capital and administrative centre of Madagascar, on the interior plateau, with a rail link to Tamatave; population (1993) 1,052,800. Industries include food processing, leather goods, clothing, wood pulp and paper manufacturing, and brewing.

**Antarctica** continent surrounding the South Pole, arbitrarily defined as the region lying south of the Antarctic Circle. Occupying 10% of the world's surface, it is almost 1.5 times the size of the USA. Antarctica contains 90% of the world's ice, representing nearly three-quarters of its fresh water. It is thought that if all Antarctica's ice suddenly melted, the world sea level would rise by 60 m/197 ft; **area:** 13,000,000 sq km/5,019,300 sq mi; ice shelves which fill the surrounding seas add a further 1,300,000 sq km/501,930 sq mi to this figure; **features:** Mount Erebus on Ross Island is the world's southernmost active volcano; the Ross Ice Shelf is formed by several glaciers coalescing in the Ross Sea; **physical:** Antarctica can be divided into two regions, separated by the Transantarctic Mountains, which extend for 3,500 km/2,175 mi and whose peaks, many of them exceeding 3,000 m/9,850 ft in height, protrude through the ice. The larger region, known as Greater or east Antarctica, is comprised of ancient rocks lying mostly at sea level, which are approximately 3,800 million years old. In contrast, Lesser or west Antarctica is 150–200 million years old and has mountain ranges buried under the ice. These include the Antarctic Peninsular and the Ellsworth Mountains, in which the highest peak in Antarctica, the Vinson Massif, is located; height 5,140 m/16,863 ft. The few peaks that are visible above the ice are known as nunataks. Two vast seas, the Ross Sea and the Weddell Sea, cut into the continent. Between them lies the mountainous Antarctic Peninsula, which was originally connected to South America before continental drift.

**antelope** any of numerous kinds of even-toed, hoofed mammals belonging to the cow family, Bovidae. Most antelopes are lightly built and good runners. They are grazers or browsers, and chew the cud. They range in size from the dik-diks and duikers, only 30 cm/1 ft high, to the eland, which can be 1.8 m/6 ft at the shoulder.

**antenna** in zoology, an appendage ('feeler') on the head. Insects, centipedes, and millipedes each have one pair of antennae but there are two pairs in crustaceans, such as shrimps. In insects, the antennae are involved with the senses of smell and touch; they are frequently complex structures with large surface areas that increase the ability to detect scents.

**Anthony, St** (c. 251–356) or Anthony of Thebes, Egyptian founder of Christian monasticism. At the age of 20, he renounced all his possessions and began a hermetic life of study and prayer, later seeking further solitude in a cave in the desert.

**anthracite** (from Greek *anthrax*, 'coal') hard, dense, shiny variety of →coal, containing over 90% carbon and a low percentage of ash and impurities, which causes it to burn without flame, smoke, or smell. Because of its purity, anthracite gives off relatively little sulphur dioxide when burnt.

**anthrax** disease of livestock, occasionally transmitted to humans, usually via infected hides and fleeces. It may develop as black skin pustules or severe pneumonia. Treatment is with antibiotics. Vaccination is effective.

**anthropology** (Greek *anthropos* 'man', *logos* 'discourse') the study of humankind. It investigates the cultural, social, and physical diversity of the human species, both past and present. It is divided into two broad categories: biological or physical anthropology, which attempts to explain human biological variation from an evolutionary perspective; and the larger field of social or cultural anthropology, which attem pts to explain the variety of human cultures. This differs from sociology in that anthropologists are concerned with cultures and societies other than their own.

**antibiotic** drug that kills or inhibits the growth of bacteria and fungi. It is derived from living organisms such as fungi or bacteria, which distinguishes it from synthetic antimicrobials.

**antibody** protein molecule produced in the blood by →lymphocytes in response to the presence of foreign or invading substances (→antigens); such substances include the proteins carried on the surface of infecting microorganisms. Antibody production is only one aspect of →immunity in vertebrates.

**antigen** any substance that causes the production of →antibodies by the body's immune system. Common antigens include the proteins carried on the surface of bacteria, viruses, and pollen grains. The proteins of incompatible blood groups or tissues also act as antigens, which has to be taken into account in medical procedures such as blood transfusions and organ transplants.

**Antigua and Barbuda** State of; **area:** Antigua 280 sq km/108 sq mi, Barbuda 161 sq km/62 sq mi, plus Redonda 1 sq km/0.4 sq mi (440 sq km/169 sq mi altogether); **capital** (and chief port): St John's (on Antigua); **major towns/cities:** Codrington (on Barbuda); **physical features:** lowlying tropical islands of limestone and coral with some higher volcanic outcrops; no rivers and low rainfall result in frequent droughts and deforestation. Antigua is the largest of the Leeward Islands; Redonda is an uninhabited island of volcanic rock rising to 305 m/1,000 ft; **head of state:** Elizabeth II from 1981, represented by governor general James B Carlisle from 1993; **head of government:** Lester Bird from 1994; **political system:** liberal democracy; **currency:** Eastern Caribbean dollar; **GNP per capita (PPP):** (US$) 9,440 (1998); **exports:** petroleum products, food, manufactures, machinery and transport equipment. Principal market USA (mainly re-exports); **population:** 69,000 (1999 est); **language:** English; **religion:** Christian (mostly Anglican); **life expectancy:** 72 (men); 76 (women) (1998 est).

**antihistamine** any substance that counteracts the effects of histamine. Antihistamines may occur naturally or they may be synthesized.

**Antilles** group of West Indian islands, divided N–S into the **Greater Antilles** (Cuba, Jamaica, Haiti–Dominican Republic, Puerto Rico) and **Lesser Antilles**, subdivided into the Leeward Islands (Virgin Islands, St Christopher–Nevis, Antigua and Barbuda, Anguilla, Montserrat, and Guadeloupe) and the Windward Islands (Dominica, Martinique, St Lucia, St Vincent and the Grenadines, Barbados, and Grenada).

**antimatter** in physics, a form of matter in which most of the attributes (such as electrical charge, magnetic moment, and spin) of →elementary particles are reversed. Such particles (→antiparticles) can be created in particle accelerators, such as those at CERN in Geneva, Switzerland, and at Fermilab in the USA. In 1996 physicists at CERN created the first atoms of antimatter: nine atoms of antihydrogen survived for 40 nanoseconds.

**Antioch** ancient capital of the Greek kingdom of Syria, founded 300 BC by Seleucus I in memory of his father Antiochus, and famed for its splendour and luxury. Under the Romans it was an early centre of Christianity. St Paul set off on his missionary journeys from here. It was captured by the Arabs 637. After a five-month siege 1098 Antioch was taken by the crusaders, who held it until 1268. The site is now occupied by the Turkish town of Antakya.

**antiparticle** in nuclear physics, a particle corresponding in mass and properties to a given →elementary particle but with the opposite electrical charge, magnetic properties, or coupling to other fundamental forces. For example, an electron carries a negative charge whereas its antiparticle, the positron, carries a positive one. When a particle and its antiparticle collide, they destroy each other, in the process called 'annihilation', their total energy being converted to lighter particles and/or photons. A substance consisting entirely of antiparticles is known as →antimatter.

**antipope** rival claimant to the elected pope for the leadership of the Roman Catholic Church, for instance in the Great Schism 1378–1417 when there were rival popes in Rome and Avignon.

**Antrim** county of Northern Ireland; **area:** 2,830 sq km/1,092 sq mi; **towns and cities:** →Belfast (county town), Larne (port), Antrim, Ballymena, Lisburn, Carrickfergus; **physical:** peat bogs; Antrim borders Lough Neagh, and is separated from Scotland by the North Channel, which is only 21 km/13 mi wide at Torr Head, the narrowest point; the main rivers are the Bann and the Lagan; **features:** Giant's Causeway, a World Heritage Site, consisting of natural polygonal, mainly hexagonal basalt columns on the north coast; Antrim Mountains (highest point Trostan 554 m/1,817 ft) and the Glen of Antrim; Kebble National Nature Reserve on Rathlin Island, off the coast near Ballycastle; **industries:** traditional linen production was largely replaced by the manufacture of artificial fibres, in turn now mostly closed down, whiskey, agriculture (the Bann Valley is particularly fertile); **agriculture:** potatoes, oats, livestock.

**Antwerp** (Flemish *Antwerpen*, French *Anvers*) port in Belgium on the River Schelde, capital of the province of Antwerp, 43 km/27 mi north of Brussels; population (1997) 453,000. One of the world's busiest ports, it has shipbuilding, oil refining, petrochemical, textile, and diamond cutting industries. The home of the artist Rubens is preserved, and several of his works are in the Gothic cathedral.

**apartheid** (Afrikaans 'apartness') racial-segregation policy of the government of South Africa from 1948 to 1994. Under the apartheid system, nonwhites – classified as Bantu (black), coloured (mixed), or Indian – did not share full rights of citizenship with the white minority. For example, black people could not vote in parliamentary elections, and until 1990 many public facilities and institutions were restricted to the use of one race only. The establishment of →Black

National States was another manifestation of apartheid. In 1991, after years of internal dissent and violence and the imposition of international trade sanctions by the United Nations (UN) and other organizations, President F W de Klerk repealed the key elements of apartheid legislation and by 1994 apartheid had ceased to exist.

The term apartheid has also been loosely applied to similar movements and other forms of racial separation, for example social or educational, in other parts of the world.

**ape** primate of the family Pongidae, closely related to humans, including gibbon, orang-utan, chimpanzee, and gorilla.

**Apennines** chain of mountains stretching the length of the Italian peninsula. An older and more weathered continuation of the Maritime Alps, from Genoa the Apennines swing across the peninsula to Ancona on the east coast, and then back to the west coast and into the 'toe' of Italy. The system is continued over the Strait of Messina along the north Sicilian coast, then across the Mediterranean Sea in a series of islands to the Atlas Mountains of North Africa. The highest peak is Monte Corno in Gran Sasso d'Italia at 2,914 m/9,560 ft.

**aphid** any of the family of small insects, Aphididae, in the order Hemiptera, suborder Homoptera, that live by sucking sap from plants. There are many species, often adapted to particular plants; some are agricultural pests.

**Aphrodite** in Greek mythology, the goddess of love (Roman Venus, Phoenician Astarte, Babylonian Ishtar). She is said to be either a daughter of →Zeus (in Homer) or sprung from the foam of the sea (in Hesiod). She was the unfaithful wife of Hephaestus, the god of fire, and the mother of Eros.

**Apocrypha** (Greek *apokryptein* 'to hide away') appendix to the Old Testament of the Bible, 14 books not included in the final Hebrew canon but recognized by Roman Catholics. There are also disputed New Testament texts known as Apocrypha.

**Apollo** in Greek and Roman mythology, the god of sun, music, poetry, prophecy, agriculture, and pastoral life, and leader of the Muses. He was the twin child (with Artemis) of Zeus and Leto. Ancient statues show Apollo as the embodiment of the Greek ideal of male beauty. His chief cult centres were his supposed birthplace on the island of Delos, in the Cyclades, and Delphi.

**Apollo project** US space project to land a person on the Moon, achieved 20 July 1969, when Neil →Armstrong was the first to set foot there. He was accompanied on the Moon's surface by 'Buzz' Aldrin; Michael Collins remained in the orbiting command module.

**Appalachian Mountains** mountain system in eastern North America, stretching about 2,400 km/1,500 mi from Alabama to Québec. The chain, composed of ancient eroded rocks and rounded peaks, includes the Allegheny, Catskill, and Blue Ridge Mountains. Its width in some parts reaches 500 km/311 mi. Mount Mitchell, in the Blue Ridge Mountains, is the highest peak at 2,045 m/6,712 ft. The eastern edge has a fall line to the coastal plain where Philadelphia, Baltimore, and Washington stand. The Appalachians are heavily forested and have deposits of coal and other minerals.

**appendicitis** inflammation of the appendix, a small, blind extension of the bowel in the lower right abdomen. In an acute attack, the pus-filled appendix may burst, causing a potentially lethal spread of infection. Treatment is by removal (appendicectomy).

**Aqaba, Gulf of** gulf extending northwards from the Red Sea for 160 km/100 mi to the Negev; its coastline is uninhabited except at its head, where the frontiers of Israel, Egypt, Jordan, and Saudi Arabia converge. The two ports of Elat (Israeli Elath) and Aqaba, Jordan's only port, are situated here. A border crossing near the two ports was opened 1994, for non-Israelis and non-Jordanians, to encourage the eastern Mediterranean tourist industry.

**aqualung** (or scuba) underwater breathing apparatus worn by divers, developed in the early 1940s by French diver Jacques Cousteau. Compressed-air cylinders strapped to the diver's back are regulated by a valve system and by a mouth tube to provide air to the diver at the same pressure as that of the surrounding water (which increases with the depth).

**aqueduct** any artificial channel or conduit for water, originally applied to water supply tunnels, but later used to refer to elevated structures of stone, wood, or ironcarrying navigable canals across valleys. One of the first great aqueducts was built in 691 BC, carrying water for 80 km/50 mi to Ninevah, capital of the ancient Assyrian Empire. Many Roman aqueducts are still standing, for example the one carried by the Pont du Gard at Nîmes in southern France, built about 8 BC (48 m/160 ft high).

**aquifer** a body of rock through which appreciable amounts of water can flow. The rock of an aquifer must be porous and permeable (full of interconnected holes) so that it can conduct water. Aquifers are an important source of fresh water, for example, for drinking and irrigation, in many arid areas of the world, and are exploited by the use of artesian wells.

**Aquinas, St Thomas** (1225–1274) Italian philosopher and theologian, the greatest figure of the school of scholasticism. He was a Dominican monk, known as the 'Angelic Doctor'. In 1879 his works were recognized as the basis of Catholic theology. His *Summa contra Gentiles/Against the Errors of the Infidels* (1259–64) argues that reason and faith are compatible. He assimilated the philosophy of Aristotle into Christian doctrine. He was canonized 1323.

**Arabia** Arabian Peninsula (Arabic *Jazirat al-Arab*, the 'peninsula of the Arabs'), peninsula between the Gulf and the Red Sea, in southwest Asia; area 2,600,000 sq km/1,000,000 sq mi. The length from north to south is about 2,400 km/1,490 mi and the greatest width about 1,600 km/994 mi. The peninsula contains the world's richest gas reserves and half the world's oil reserves. It comprises the states of Bahrain, Kuwait, Oman, Qatar, Saudi Arabia, the United Arab Emirates, and Yemen.

**arachnid** (or arachnoid) type of arthropod of the class Arachnida, including spiders, scorpions, ticks, and mites. They differ from insects in possessing only two main body regions, the cephalothorax and the abdomen, and in having eight legs.

**Arafat, Yassir** (1929– ) born Muhammad Abed Ar'ouf Arafat, Palestinian nationalist politician, cofounder of al-Fatah in 1957, president of the Palestinian Authority, and leader of the →Palestine Liberation Organization (PLO) from 1969. He was influential in the Middle East peace talks and in 1993 reached a historic peace accord of mutual recognition with Israel, under which the Gaza Strip and Jericho were transferred to PLO control. He returned to the former occupied territories in 1994 as head of an embryonic Palestinian state, and in 1994 Arafat was awarded the Nobel Prize for Peace jointly with Israeli prime minister Yitzhak Rabin and Israeli foreign minister Shimon Peres.

In November 1995 Rabin, was assassinated by an Israeli extremist and the peace process appeared to be threatened. The hard-line Likud leader

Binjamin Netanyahu was elected prime minister in 1996. Despite this, Arafat continued his efforts for a lasting peace. He was elected president of the self-governing Palestinian National Council in 1996.

In May 1999 Labour candidate Ehud Barak was elected as Israel's prime minister, and Arafat announced that an independent Palestine state would be declared by the end of the year. Later that month Arafat met with King Abdullah of Jordan prior to the reopening of peace talks with Israel.

**Aragón** autonomous community and former kingdom of northeast Spain, including the provinces of Huesca, Teruel, and Zaragoza; area 47,700 sq km/18,412 sq mi; population (1991) 1,188,800. Products include cereals, rice, olive oil, almonds, figs, grapes, and olives; merino wool is a major export. The principal river of Aragón is the Ebro, which receives numerous tributaries both from the mountains of the south and from the Pyrenees in the north. Aragón was an independent kingdom from 1035 to 1479. The capital of modern Aragón is Zaragoza.

**Aral Sea** (Russian *Aralskoye More*) inland sea divided between Kazakhstan and Uzbekistan, the world's fourth-largest lake; former area 62,000 sq km/24,000 sq mi, but decreasing. Water from its tributaries, the Amu Darya and Syr Darya, has been diverted for irrigation and city use, and the sea is disappearing, with long-term consequences for the climate.

**Ararat, Mount** double-peaked mountain in Turkey near the Iranian border; Great Ararat, at 5,137 m/16,854 ft, is the highest mountain in Turkey. It was the reputed resting place of Noah's Ark after the Flood.

**arc** in geometry, a section of a curved line or circle. A circle has three types of arc: a **semicircle**, which is exactly half of the circle; **minor arcs**, which are less than the semicircle; and **major arcs**, which are greater than the semicircle.

**Archaean** (or Archaeozoic) widely used term for the earliest era of geological time; the first part of the Precambrian eon, spanning the interval from the formation of Earth to about 2,500 million years ago.

**archaeology** (Greek *archaia* 'ancient things', *logos* 'study') study of prehistory and history, based on the examination of physical remains. Principal activities include preliminary field (or site) surveys, excavation (where necessary), and the classification, dating, and interpretation of finds.

**archaeopteryx** (Greek *archaios* 'ancient', *pterux* 'wing') extinct primitive bird, known from fossilized remains, about 160 million years old, found in limestone deposits in Bavaria, Germany. It is popularly known as 'the first bird', although some earlier bird ancestors are now known. It was about the size of a crow and had feathers and wings, with three clawlike digits at the end of each wing, but in many respects its skeleton is reptilian (teeth and a long, bony tail) and very like some small meat-eating dinosaurs of the time.

**Archimedes** (*c.* 287–212 BC) Greek mathematician who made major discoveries in geometry, hydrostatics, and mechanics, and established the sciences of statics and hydrostatics. He also formulated a law of fluid displacement (Archimedes' Principle), and is credited with the invention of the Archimedes screw, a cylindrical device for raising water. His method of finding mathematical proof to substantiate experiment and observation became the method of modern science in the High Renaissance.

**architecture** art of designing structures. The term covers the design of the visual appearance of structures; their internal arrangements of space; selection of external and internal building materials; design or selection of natural and artificial lighting systems, as well as mechanical, electrical, and plumbing systems; and design or selection of decorations and furnishings. Architectural style may emerge from evolution of techniques and styles particular to a culture in a given time period with or without identifiable individuals as architects, or may be attributed to specific individuals or groups of architects working together on a project.

**Arctic Ocean** ocean surrounding the North Pole; area 14,000,000 sq km/5,405,400 sq mi. Because of the Siberian and North American rivers flowing into it, it has comparatively low salinity and freezes readily.

**Ardennes** hilly, wooded plateau in northeast France, southeast Belgium, and northern Luxembourg, cut through by the River Meuse. The area gives its name to the region of Champagne-Ardenne and the *département* of the Ardennes in France. The highest hills are about 590 m/1,936 ft. Cattle and sheep are raised and the area is rich in timber and minerals. There was heavy fighting here in both world wars, notably in the Battle of the Bulge (1944–1945, also known as the Ardennes offensive). In World War I it was the route of the main German advance in 1914.

**Argentina** Republic of; **national name:** *República Argentina*; **area:** 2,780,092 sq km/1,073,393 sq mi; **capital:** Buenos Aires; **major towns/cities:** Rosario, Córdoba, San Miguel de Tucumán, Mendoza, Santa Fé, La Plata; **major ports:** La Plata and Bahía Blanca; **physical features:** mountains in west, forest and savanna in north, pampas (treeless plains) in east-central area, Patagonian plateau in south; rivers Colorado, Salado, Paraná, Uruguay, Río de La Plata estuary; Andes mountains, with Aconcagua the highest peak in western hemisphere; Iguaçu Falls; **territories:** claims Falkland Islands (*Islas Malvinas*), South Georgia, the South Sandwich Islands, and part of Antarctica; **head of state and government:** Fernando de la Rua from 1999; **political system:** democratic federal republic; **currency:** peso = 10,000 australs (which it replaced in 1992); **GNP per capita (PPP):** (US$) 10,200 (1998);

**exports:** meat and meat products, prepared animal fodder, cereals, petroleum and petroleum products, soybeans, vegetable oils and fats. Principal market Brazil 30.4% (1997); **population:** 36,577,000 (1999 est); **language:** Spanish 95% (official); Italian 3%; **religion:** Roman Catholic (state-supported); **life expectancy:** 70 (men); 77 (women) (1995–2000).

**argon** (Greek *argos* 'idle') colourless, odourless, nonmetallic, gaseous element, symbol Ar, atomic number 18, relative atomic mass 39.948. It is grouped with the →inert gases, since it was long believed not to react with other substances, but observations now indicate that it can be made to combine with boron fluoride to form compounds. It constitutes almost 1% of the Earth's atmosphere, and was discovered in 1894 by British chemists John Rayleigh and William Ramsay after all oxygen and nitrogen had been removed chemically from a sample of air. It is used in electric discharge tubes and argon lasers.

**Argonauts** in Greek mythology, the band of heroes who accompanied →Jason when he set sail in the *Argo* to find the Golden Fleece.

**Aristarchus of Samos** (c. 320–c. 250 BC) Greek astronomer. The first to argue that the Earth moves around the Sun, he was ridiculed for his beliefs. He was also the first astronomer to estimate (quite inaccurately) the sizes of the Sun and Moon and their distances from the Earth.

**Aristophanes** (c. 445–c. 380 BC) Greek comedy dramatist. Of his 11 extant plays (of a total of over 40), the early comedies are remarkable for the violent satire with which he ridiculed the democratic war leaders. He also satirized contemporary issues such as the new learning of Socrates in *The Clouds* (423 BC) and the obsession with war, with the sex-strike of women in *Lysistrata* (411 BC). The chorus plays a prominent role, frequently giving the play its title, as in *The Wasps* (422 BC), *The Birds* (414 BC), and *The Frogs* (405 BC).

**Aristotle** (384–322 BC) Greek philosopher who advocated reason and moderation. He maintained that sense experience is our only source of knowledge, and that by reasoning we can discover the essences of things, that is, their distinguishing qualities. In his works on ethics and politics, he suggested that human happiness consists in living in conformity with nature. He derived his political theory from the recognition that mutual aid is natural to humankind, and refused to set up any one constitution as universally ideal. Of Aristotle's works, around 22 treatises survive, dealing with logic, metaphysics, physics, astronomy, meteorology, biology, psychology, ethics, politics, and literary criticism.

**arithmetic** branch of mathematics concerned with the study of numbers and their properties. The fundamental operations of arithmetic are addition, subtraction, multiplication, and division. Raising to powers (for example, squaring or cubing a number), the extraction of roots (for example, square roots), percentages, fractions, and ratios are developed from these operations.

**Arizona** state in southwestern USA. It is nicknamed Grand Canyon State. Arizona was admitted to the Union in 1912 as the 48th US state. The state is renowned for its natural wonders, including Monument Valley and the Grand Canyon, and is strongly associated with such indigenous peoples as the Navajo and Hopi; **population:** (1996 est) 4,428,100; including 5.6% American Indians (Navajo, Hopi, Apache), who by treaty own 25% of the state; **area:** 294,100 sq km/113,500 sq mi; **capital:** Phoenix; **towns and cities:** Tucson, Scottsdale, Tempe, Mesa, Glendale, Flagstaff; **industries and products:** cotton under irrigation, livestock ranching, copper (more than half of US annual output), silver, uranium mining, molybdenum, electronics, aircraft.

**Arkwright, Richard** (1732–1792) English inventor and manufacturing pioneer who in 1768 developed a machine for spinning cotton (he called it a 'water frame'). In 1771 he set up a water-powered spinning factory and in 1790 he installed steam power in a Nottingham factory. Knighted 1786.

**Armada** fleet sent by Philip II of Spain against England in 1588. See →Spanish Armada.

**armadillo** mammal of the family Dasypodidae, with an armour of bony plates along its back or, in some species, almost covering the entire body. Around 20 species live between Texas and Patagonia and range in size from the fairy armadillo, or pichiciego, *Chlamyphorus truncatus*, at 13 cm/5 in, to the giant armadillo *Priodontes giganteus*, 1.5 m/4.5 ft long. Armadillos feed on insects, snakes, fruit, and carrion. Some can roll into an armoured ball if attacked; others defend themselves with their claws or rely on rapid burrowing for protection.

**Armageddon** in the New Testament (Revelation 16:16), the site of the final battle between the nations that will end the world; it has been identified with Megiddo in Israel.

**Armagh** Irish *Ard Mhacha* ('the height of Mhacha' (a legendary queen), county of Northern Ireland, **area:** 1,250 sq km/ 483 sq mi; **towns and cities:** Armagh (county town), Lurgan and Portadown (merged to form Craigavon), Keady; **physical:** smallest county of Northern Ireland; flat in the north, with many bogs and mounds formed from glacial deposits; low hills in the south, the highest of which is Slieve Gullion (577 m/1,893 ft); principal rivers are the Bann, the Blackwater and its tributary, the Callan; **features:** Blackwater River Park; the 17th-century manor Ardress House; Camagh Forest; Oxford Island Nature Reserve; Gosford Forest Park; **agriculture:** good farmland (apart from the marshy areas by Lough Neagh) with apple orchards; potatoes; flax; emphasis on livestock rearing in the south; fruit-growing and market gardening in the north; **industries:** linen manufacture (Portadown and Lurgan were the principal centres of the linen industry); milling; light engineering; concrete; potato crisps; **population:** (1981) 119,000.

**Armenia** Republic of; **national name:** *Haikakan Hanrapetoutioun*; **area:** 29,800 sq km/11,505 sq mi; **capital:** Yerevan; **major towns/cities:** Gyumri (formerly Leninakan), Vanadzor (formerly Kirovakan); **physical features:** mainly mountainous (including Mount Ararat), wooded; **head of state:** Robert Kocharian from 1998; **head of government:** Amen Sarkisian from 1999; **political system:** authoritarian nationalist; **currency:** dram (replaced Russian rouble in 1993); **GNP per capita (PPP):** (US$) 2,180 (1998 est); **exports:** machinery and metalworking products, chemical and petroleum products. Principal market CIS 36.3% (1998); **population:** 3,525,000 (1999 est); **language:** Armenian; **religion:** Armenian Christian; **Life expectancy:** 67 (men); 74 (women) (1995–2000).

**armistice** cessation of hostilities while awaiting a peace settlement. **The Armistice** refers specifically to the end of World War I between Germany and the Allies on 11 November 1918. On 22 June 1940, following the German invasion of France, French representatives signed an armistice with Germany in the same railway carriage at Compiègne as in 1918. No armistice was signed with either Germany or Japan in 1945; both nations surrendered and there was no provision for the suspension of fighting. The Korean armistice, signed at Panmunjom on 27 July 1953, terminated the Korean War 1950–53.

**Armstrong, Louis** (1901–1971) nicknamed Satchmo, US jazz cornet and trumpet player and singer. His Chicago recordings in the 1920s with the Hot Five and Hot Seven brought him recognition for his warm and pure trumpet tone, his skill at improvisation, and his quirky, gravelly voice. From the 1930s he also appeared in films.

**Armstrong, Neil Alden** (1930– ) US astronaut. In 1969, he became the first person to set foot on the Moon, and said, 'That's one small step for a man, one giant leap for mankind.' The Moon landing was part of the →Apollo project.

**WEB SITE** > > > > > > > >
**Armstrong, Neil**

http://www.3d-interact.com/ SpaceMuseum/armstrong.html

Biography of the first man on the moon from the Neil A Armstrong Museum. It traces Armstrong's childhood interest in flying, his first flying lessons aged 15, his military service, his epic mission, and his post-NASA career as academic, farmer, and businessman.

**Arnold, Matthew** (1822–1888) English poet and critic. His poem 'Dover Beach' (1867) was widely regarded as one of the most eloquent expressions of the spiritual anxieties of Victorian England. In his highly influential critical essays collected in *Culture and Anarchy* (1869), he attacked the smugness and philistin-ism of the Victorian middle classes, and argued for a new culture based on the pursuit of artistic and intellectual val-ues. He was he son of Thomas Arnold, headmaster of Rugby school.

**aromatic compound** organic chemical compound in which some of the bond-ing electrons are delocalized (shared among several atoms within the mole-cule and not localized in the vicinity of the atoms involved in bonding). The commonest aromatic compounds have ring structures, the atoms comprising the ring being either all carbon or con-taining one or more different atoms (usually nitrogen, sulphur, or oxygen). Typical examples are benzene ($C_6H_6$) and pyridine ($C_6H_5N$).

**arsenic** brittle, greyish-white, semi-metallic element (a metalloid), symbol As, atomic number 33, relative atomic mass 74.92. It occurs in many ores and occasionally in its elemental state, and is widely distributed, being present in minute quantities in the soil, the sea, and the human body. In larger quanti-ties, it is poisonous. The chief source of arsenic compounds is as a by-product from metallurgical processes. It is used in making semiconductors, alloys, and solders.

**art deco** style in the decorative arts which influenced design and architec-ture. It emerged in Europe in the 1920s and continued through the 1930s, becoming particularly popular in the USA and France. A self-consciously modern style, originally called 'Jazz Modern', it is characterized by angular, geometrical patterns and bright colours, and by the use of materials such as enamel, chrome, glass, and plastic. The

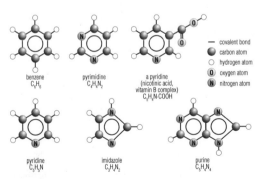

benzene
$C_6H_6$

pyrimidine
$C_4H_4N_2$

a pyridine
(nicotinic acid,
vitamin B complex)
$C_5H_4N \cdot COOH$

— covalent bond
⬤ carbon atom
◯ hydrogen atom
Ⓞ oxygen atom
Ⓝ nitrogen atom

pyridine
$C_5H_5N$

imidazole
$C_3H_4N_2$

purine
$C_5H_4N_4$

**aromatic compound** Compounds whose molecules contain the benzene ring, or variations of it, are called aromatic. The term was originally used to distinguish sweet-smelling compounds from others.

graphic artist Erté was a fashionable exponent.

**arteriosclerosis** hardening of the arteries, with thickening and loss of elasticity. It is associated with smoking, ageing, and a diet high in saturated fats.

**artery** vessel that carries blood from the heart to the rest of the body. It is built to withstand considerable pressure, having thick walls which contain smooth muscle fibres. During contraction of the heart muscle, arteries expand in diameter to allow for the sudden increase in pressure that occurs; the resulting pulse or pressure wave can be felt at the wrist. Not all arteries carry oxygenated (oxygen-rich) blood; the pulmonary arteries convey deoxygenated (oxygen-poor) blood from the heart to the lungs.

**arthritis** inflammation of the joints, with pain, swelling, and restricted motion. Many conditions may cause arthritis, including gout, infection, and trauma to the joint. There are three main forms of arthritis: rheumatoid arthritis; osteoarthritis; and septic arthritis.

**arthropod** member of the phylum Arthropoda; an invertebrate animal with jointed legs and a segmented body with a horny or chitinous casing (exoskeleton), which is shed periodically and replaced as the animal grows. Included are arachnids such as spiders and mites, as well as crustaceans, millipedes, centipedes, and insects.

**Arthur** (lived 6th century) semi-legendary Romano-British warleader who led British resistance against the Saxons, Picts, and Scots in the first half of the 6th century. He was probably a warlord rather than a king. He operated throughout Britain, commanding a small force of mobile warriors, reminiscent of the late Roman *comitatenses* (line units). Arthur is credited with a great victory over the Saxons at Mount Badon, possibly in Dorset.

**artificial intelligence** (AI) branch of science concerned with creating computer programs that can perform actions comparable with those of an intelligent human. Current AI research covers such areas as planning (for robot behaviour), language understanding, pattern recognition, and knowledge representation.

**artificial respiration** emergency procedure to restart breathing once it has stopped; in cases of electric shock or apparent drowning, for example, the first choice is the expired-air method, the **kiss of life** by mouth-to-mouth breathing until natural breathing is restored.

**artificial selection** in biology, selective breeding of individuals that exhibit the particular characteristics that a plant or animal breeder wishes to develop. In plants, desirable features might include resistance to disease, high yield (in crop plants), or attractive appearance. In animal breeding, selection has led to the development of particular breeds of cattle for improved meat production (such as the Aberdeen Angus) or milk production (such as Jerseys).

**art nouveau** in the visual arts, interior design, and architecture, a decorative style flourishing from 1890 to 1910 and characterized by organic, sinuous patterns and ornamentations based on plant forms. In England, it appears in the illustrations of Aubrey Beardsley; in Scotland, in the interior and exterior designs of Charles Rennie Mackintosh; in France, in the glass of René Lalique and the posters of Alphonse Mucha; and in the USA, in the lamps and metalwork of Louis Comfort Tiffany. It was known as **Jugendstil** in Germany and **Stile Liberty** in Italy, after a fashionable London department store.

**Arunachal Pradesh** state of India, in the Himalayas on the borders of Tibet and Myanmar; **area:** 83,700 sq km/ 32,316 sq mi; **capital:** Itanagar; **towns:** Bomdila; Ziro; **physical:** stretches from the foothills of the Himalayas to their peaks; largely forested, ranging from Alpine to sub-tropical conditions: Parasuram Kund, a lake visited by pilgrims; Brahmaputra (or Siang) River flows north–south in a deeply cut valley; **features:** Tawang Monastery; Namdapha National Park; **industries:** timber, coal mining; **agriculture:** rice, coffee, spices, fruit, rubber; **population:** (1994 est) 965,000; over 80 ethnic groups; **language:** 50 different dialects; **history:** formerly part of the state of Assam, it became a state of India in 1987.

**asbestos** any of several related minerals of fibrous structure that offer great heat resistance because of their nonflammability and poor conductivity. Commercial asbestos is generally either made from serpentine ('white' asbestos) or from sodium iron silicate ('blue' asbestos). The fibres are woven together or bound by an inert material. Over time the fibres can work loose and, because they are small enough to float freely in the air or be inhaled, asbestos usage is now strictly controlled; exposure to its dust can cause cancer.

**ASCII** (acronym for American standard code for information interchange) in computing, coding system in which numbers are assigned to letters, digits, and punctuation symbols. Although computers work in code based on the →binary number system, ASCII numbers are usually quoted as decimal or hexadecimal numbers. For example, the decimal number 45 (binary 0101101) represents a hyphen, and 65 (binary 1000001) a capital A. The first 32 codes are used for control functions, such as carriage return and backspace.

**ascorbic acid** $C_6H_8O_6$ (or vitamin C) relatively simple organic acid found in citrus fruits and vegetables. It is soluble in water and destroyed by prolonged boiling, so soaking or overcooking of vegetables reduces their vitamin C content. Lack of ascorbic acid results in scurvy.

**asexual reproduction** in biology, reproduction that does not involve the manufacture and fusion of sex cells, nor the necessity for two parents. The process carries a clear advantage in that

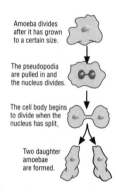

Amoeba divides after it has grown to a certain size.

The pseudopodia are pulled in and the nucleus divides.

The cell body begins to divide when the nucleus has split.

Two daughter amoebae are formed.

**asexual reproduction** Asexual reproduction is the simplest form of reproduction, occurring in many simple plants and animals. Binary fission, shown here occurring in an amoeba, is one of a number of asexual reproduction processes

there is no need to search for a mate nor to develop complex pollinating mechanisms; every asexual organism can reproduce on its own. Asexual reproduction can therefore lead to a rapid population build-up.

**Asia** largest of the continents, occupying one-third of the total land surface of the world. The origin of the name is unknown, though it seems probable that it was at first used with a restricted local application, gradually extended to the whole continent; **area:** 44,000,000 sq km/17,000,000 sq mi; **largest cities:** (population over 5 million) Bangkok, Beijing, Bombay, Calcutta, Delhi, Dhaka, Hong Kong, Hyderabad, Istanbul, Jakarta, Karachi, Lahore, Madras, Manila, Osaka, Seoul, Shanghai, Shenyang, Tehran, Tianjin, Tokyo; **features:** Mount Everest, at 8,872 m/29,118 ft is the world's highest mountain; the Dead Sea at −394 m/ −1,293 ft is the world's lowest point below sea level; rivers (over 3,200 km/ 2,000 mi) include Chang Jiang (Yangtze), Huang He (Yellow River), Ob-Irtysh, Amur, Lena, Mekong, Yenisey; lakes (over 18,000 sq km/7,000 sq mi) include the Caspian Sea (the largest lake in the world), the Aral Sea, Lake Baikal (largest freshwater lake in Eurasia), Balkhash; deserts include the Gobi, Takla Makan, Syrian Desert, Arabian Desert, Negev; **physical:** lying in the eastern hemisphere, Asia extends from the Arctic Circle to just over 10° south of the Equator. The Asian mainland, which forms the greater part of the Eurasian continent, lies entirely in the northern hemisphere and stretches from Cape Chelyubinsk at its northern extremity to Cape Piai at the southern tip of the Malay Peninsula. From Dezhneva Cape in the east, the mainland extends west over more than 165° longitude to Cape Baba in Turkey.

**Asmara** (or Asmera) capital of Eritrea, 64 km/40 mi southwest of Massawa on the Red Sea and 2,300 m/7,546 ft above sea level; population (1991) 367,300. Products include beer, clothes, and textiles. The University of Asmara is here, together with a naval school, a cathedral and many modern buildings. The population is half Christian and half Muslim.

**aspirin** acetylsalicylic acid, a popular

pain-relieving drug (→analgesic) developed in the late 19th century as a household remedy for aches and pains. It relieves pain and reduces inflammation and fever. It is derived from the white willow tree *Salix alba*, and is the world's most widely used drug.

**Assam** state of northeast India; **area:** 78,400 sq km/30,262 sq mi; **capital:** Dispur (a suburb of Guwahati); **towns and cities:** Guwahati, Dibrugarh, Silchar; **industries:** half of India's oil produced here; coal, petrochemicals, paper, cement; **agriculture:** half of India's tea is grown here; rice, jute, sugar, cotton; **population:** (1994 est) 24,200,000, including 12 million Assamese (Hindus), 5 million Bengalis (chiefly Muslim immigrants from Bangladesh), Nepalis, and 2 million indigenous people (Christian and traditional religions); **language:** Assamese.

**assassin bug** member of a family of blood-sucking bugs that contains about 4,000 species. Assassin bugs are mainly predators, feeding on other insects, but some species feed on birds and mammals, including humans. They are found, mainly in tropical regions, although some have established themselves in Europe and North America. (Family Reduviidae, suborder Heteroptera, order Hemiptera.)

**Assyria** empire in the Middle East *c.* 2500–612 BC, in northern Mesopotamia (now Iraq); early capital Ashur, later Nineveh. It was initially subject to Sumer and intermittently to Babylon. The Assyrians adopted largely the Sumerian religion and structure of society. At its greatest extent the empire included Egypt and stretched from the eastern Mediterranean coast to the head of the Persian Gulf.

**Astaire, Fred** (1899–1987) adopted name of Frederick Austerlitz, US dancer, actor, singer, and choreographer. The greatest popular dancer of his time, he starred in numerous films, including *Top Hat* (1935), *Easter Parade* (1948), and *Funny Face* (1957), many containing inventive sequences which he designed and choreographed himself. He made ten classic films with the most popular of his dancing partners, Ginger Rogers.

**asteroid** (or minor planet) any of many thousands of small bodies, composed of rock and iron, that orbit the Sun. Most lie in a belt between the orbits of Mars and Jupiter, and are thought to be fragments left over from the formation of the →Solar System. About 100,000 may exist, but their total mass is only a few hundredths the mass of the Moon.

**asthma** chronic condition characterized by difficulty in breathing due to spasm of the bronchi (air passages) in the lungs. Attacks may be provoked by allergy, infection, and stress. The incidence of asthma may be increasing as a result of air pollution and occupational hazard. Treatment is with bronchodilators to relax the bronchial muscles and thereby ease the breathing, and in severe cases by inhaled steroids that reduce inflammation of the bronchi.

**astronomy** science of the celestial bodies: the Sun, the Moon, and the planets; the stars and galaxies; and all other objects in the universe. It is concerned with their positions, motions, distances, and physical conditions and with their origins and evolution. Astronomy thus divides into fields such as astrophysics, celestial mechanics, and →cosmology. See also →radio astronomy.

**astrophysics** study of the physical nature of stars, galaxies, and the universe. It began with the development of spectroscopy in the 19th century, which allowed astronomers to analyse the composition of stars from their light. Astrophysicists view the universe as a vast natural laboratory in which they can study matter under conditions of temperature, pressure, and density that are unattainable on Earth.

**Asunción** capital and chief port of Paraguay, situated on the east bank of the Paraguay River, near its confluence with the River Pilcomayo; population (1992) 502,400 (metropolitan area 637,700); there are textile, footwear, and food processing industries. The climate is subtropical, and cattle are raised in the surrounding area, and maize, cotton, sugar, fruit, and tobacco are grown.

**asylum, political** in international law, refuge granted in another country to a person who, for political reasons, cannot return to his or her own country without putting himself or herself in danger. A person seeking asylum is a type of refugee.

**Atatürk, Mustafa Kemal** (1881–1938) (Turkish 'Father of the Turks'), name assumed in 1934 by Mustafa Kemal Pasha, Turkish politician and general, first president of Turkey from 1923. After World War I he established a provisional rebel government and in 1921–22 the Turkish armies under his leadership expelled the Greeks who were occupying Turkey. He was the founder of the modern republic, which he ruled as a virtual dictator, with a policy of consistent and radical westernization.

**Athens** (Greek *Athinai*) capital city of Greece and of ancient Attica; population (1991) 784,100, metropolitan area (1991) 3,096,800. Situated 8 km/5 mi northeast of its port of Piraeus on the Gulf of Aegina, it is built around the rocky hills of the Acropolis 169 m/555 ft and the Areopagus 112 m/368 ft, and is overlooked from the northeast by the hill of Lycabettus, 277 m/909 ft high. It lies in the south of the central plain of Attica, watered by the mountain streams of Cephissus and Ilissus. It has less green space than any other European capital (4%) and severe air and noise pollution.

**atherosclerosis** thickening and hardening of the walls of the arteries, associated with atheroma.

**athletics** competitive track and field events consisting of running, throwing, and jumping disciplines. **Running events** range from sprint races (100 metres) and hurdles to cross-country running and the →marathon (26 miles 385 yards). **Jumping events** are the high jump, long jump, triple jump, and pole vault. **Throwing events** are javelin, discus, shot put, and hammer throw.

**Atlantic, Battle of the** during World War II, continuous battle fought in the Atlantic Ocean by the sea and air forces of the Allies and Germany, to control the supply routes to the UK. The Allies destroyed nearly 800 U-boats during the war and at least 2,200 convoys of 75,000 merchant ships crossed the Atlantic, protected by US naval forces.

**Atlantic Ocean** ocean lying between Europe and Africa to the east and the Americas to the west; area of basin 81,500,000 sq km/31,500,000 sq mi; including the Arctic Ocean and Antarctic seas, 106,200,000 sq km/41,000,000 sq mi. It is generally divided by the equator into the North Atlantic and South Atlantic. It was probably named after the legendary island continent of Atlantis. The average depth is 3 km/2 mi; greatest depth is at the Milwaukee Depth in the Puerto Rico Trench 8,648 m/28,374 ft. The Mid-Atlantic Ridge, of which the Azores, Ascension, St Helena, and Tristan da Cunha form part, divides it from north to south. Lava welling up from this central area annually increases the distance between South America and Africa. The North Atlantic is the saltiest of the main oceans and has the largest tidal range.

**Atlas** in Greek mythology, one of the Titans who revolted against the gods; as punishment, he was compelled to support the heavens on his head and shoulders. Growing weary, he asked Perseus to turn him into stone by showing him the Medusa's head, and was transformed into Mount Atlas.

**Atlas Mountains** mountain system of northwest Africa, stretching 2,400 km/1,500 mi from the Atlantic coast of Morocco to the Gulf of Gabes, Tunisia, and lying between the Mediterranean on the north and the Sahara on the south. The highest peak is Mount Toubkal 4,165 m/13,665 ft.

**atmosphere** mixture of gases surrounding a planet. Planetary atmospheres are prevented from escaping by the pull of gravity. On Earth, atmospheric pressure decreases with altitude. In its lowest layer, the atmosphere consists of nitrogen (78%) and oxygen (21%), both in molecular form (two atoms bonded together) and 1% argon. Small quantities of other gases are important to the chemistry and physics of the Earth's atmosphere, including

---

**WEB SITE** > > > > > > > >

**Atlantic Ocean**

http://www.wusl.edu/services/govdocs/wofont96/24.htm

Geographical and political details of the second-largest ocean. A downloadable map is also available from this CIA-run Web site. As with all of the sites from the World Factbook, there is a lot of information here, on such things as ports, economy, conflicts, natural resources, and the environment.

---

## ATMOSPHERE: COMPOSITION

| Gas | Symbol | Volume (%) | Role |
|---|---|---|---|
| nitrogen | $N_2$ | 78.08 | cycled through human activities and through the action of micro-organisms on animal and plant waste |
| oxygen | $O_2$ | 20.94 | cycled mainly through the respiration of animals and plants and through the action of photosynthesis |
| carbon dioxide | $CO_2$ | 0.03 | cycled through respiration and photosynthesis in exchange reactions with oxygen. It is also a product of burning fossil fuels |
| argon | Ar | 0.93 | chemically inert and with only a few industrial uses |
| neon | Ne | 0.0018 | as argon |
| helium | He | 0.0005 | as argon |
| krypton | Kr | trace | as argon |
| xenon | Xe | trace | as argon |
| ozone | $O_3$ | 0.00006 | a product of oxygen molecules split into single atoms by the Sun's radiation and unaltered oxygen molecules |
| hydrogen | $H_2$ | 0.00005 | unimportant |

water and carbon dioxide. The atmosphere plays a major part in the various cycles of nature (the water cycle, the →carbon cycle, and the nitrogen cycle). It is the principal industrial source of nitrogen, oxygen, and argon, which are obtained by fractional distillation of liquid air.

**atom** (Greek *atomos* 'undivided') smallest unit of matter that can take part in a chemical reaction, and which cannot be broken down chemically into anything simpler. An atom is made up of protons and neutrons in a central nucleus surrounded by electrons (see →atomic structure). The atoms of the various elements differ in atomic number, relative atomic mass, and chemical behaviour.

**atomic bomb** (or atom bomb) bomb deriving its explosive force from nuclear fission (see →nuclear energy) as a result of a neutron chain reaction, developed in the 1940s in the USA into a usable weapon.

**atomic mass unit** (or dalton unit; symbol amu or u) unit of mass that is used to measure the relative mass of atoms and molecules. It is equal to one-twelfth of the mass of a carbon-12 atom, which is equivalent to the mass of a proton or $1.66 \times 10^{-27}$ kg. The

sodium 2.8.1          sulphur 2.8.6

**atomic structure** The arrangement of electrons in a sodium atom and a sulphur atom. The number of electrons in a neutral atom gives that atom its atomic number: sodium has an atomic number of 11 and sulphur has an atomic number of 16.

→relative atomic mass of an atom has no units; thus oxygen-16 has an atomic mass of 16 daltons but a relative atomic mass of 16.

**atomic number** (or proton number) number (symbol $Z$) of protons in the nucleus of an atom. It is equal to the positive charge on the nucleus.

In a neutral atom, it is also equal to the number of electrons surrounding the nucleus. The chemical elements are arranged in the →periodic table of the elements according to their atomic number.

**atomic structure** internal structure of an →atom.

**nucleus:** The core of the atom, a dense body only one ten-thousandth the diameter of the atom itself. The simplest nucleus, that of hydrogen, comprises a single stable positively charged particle, the **proton**. Nuclei of other elements contain more protons and additional particles, called **neutrons**, of about the same mass as the proton but with no electrical charge. Each element has its own characteristic nucleus with a unique number of protons, the atomic number. The number of neutrons may vary. Where atoms of a single element have different numbers of neutrons, they are called →isotopes. Although some isotopes tend to be unstable and exhibit →radioactivity, they all have identical chemical properties.

**electrons:** The nucleus is surrounded by a number of moving **electrons**, each of which has a negative charge equal to the positive charge on a proton, but which weighs only 1/1,839 times as much. In a neutral atom, the nucleus is surrounded by the same number of electrons as it contains protons. According to →quantum theory, the position of an electron is uncertain; it may be found at any point. However, it is more likely to be found in some places than others. The region of space in which an electron is most likely to be found is called an orbital. The chemical properties of an element are determined by the ease with which its atoms can gain or lose electrons from its outer orbitals.

**atonement** in Christian theology, the doctrine that Jesus suffered on the cross to bring about reconciliation and forgiveness between God and humanity.

**Atonement, Day of** Jewish holy day (**Yom Kippur**) held on the tenth day of Tishri (Sept–Oct), the first month of the Jewish year. It is a day of fasting, penitence, and cleansing from sin, ending the Ten Days of Penitence that follow **Rosh Hashanah**, the Jewish New Year.

**ATP** (abbreviation for adenosine triphosphate) nucleotide molecule found in all cells. It can yield large amounts of energy, and is used to drive the thousands of biological processes needed to sustain life, growth, movement, and reproduction. Green plants use light energy to manufacture ATP as part of the process of →photosynthesis. In animals, ATP is formed by the breakdown of glucose molecules, usually obtained from the carbohydrate component of a diet, in a series of reactions termed →respiration. It is the driving force behind muscle contraction and the synthesis of complex molecules needed by individual cells.

**Attica** (Greek *Attiki*) region of Greece comprising Athens and the district around it; area 3,381 sq km/1,305 sq mi; population (1991) 3,522,800. It is renowned for its language, art, and philosophical thought in classical times. It is a prefecture of modern Greece with Athens as its capital.

**Attlee, Clement Richard** (1883–1967) 1st Earl Attlee British Labour politician. In the coalition government during World War II he was Lord Privy Seal 1940–42, dominions secretary 1942–43, and Lord President of the Council 1943–45, as well as deputy prime minister from 1942. As prime minister 1945–51 he introduced a sweeping programme of nationalization and a whole new system of social services.

**Attorney General** in the UK, principal law officer of the crown and head of the English Bar; the post is one of great political importance. In the USA, it is the chief law officer of the government and head of the Department of Justice.

**Auckland** largest city of North Island, New Zealand, in the north of the island, in an area of impressive volcanic scenery; population (1996) 997,900. It fills the isthmus that separates its two harbours (Waitemata and Manukau), and its suburbs spread north across the

Harbour Bridge. It is the country's chief port and leading industrial centre, having iron and steel plants, engineering, car assembly, textiles, food processing, sugar refining, and brewing. Auckland was officially founded as New Zealand's capital in 1840, remaining so until 1865.

**Auden, W(ystan) H(ugh)** (1907–1973) English-born US poet. He wrote some of his most original poetry, such as *Look, Strangere* (1936), in the 1930s when he led the influential left-wing literary group that included Louis MacNeice, Stephen Spender, and C Day-Lewis. He became a US citizen in 1946.

**Augustine of Hippo, St** (Aurelius Augustinus) (354–430) one of the early Christian leaders and writers known as the Fathers of the Church. He was converted to Christianity by Ambrose in Milan and became bishop of Hippo (modern Annaba, Algeria) 396. Among Augustine's many writings are his *Confessions*, a spiritual autobiography, and *De Civitate Dei/The City of God*, vindicating the Christian church and divine providence in 22 books.

**Augustus** (63 BC–AD 14) title of Octavian (born Gaius Octavius), first Roman emperor 31 BC–AD 14. He joined forces with →Mark Antony and Lepidus in the Second Triumvirate. Following Mark Antony's liaison with the Egyptian queen →Cleopatra, Augustus defeated her troops at Actium 31 BC. As emperor he reformed the government of the empire, the army, and Rome's public services, and was a patron of the arts.

The period of his rule is known as the Augustan Age.

**aurora** coloured light in the night sky near the Earth's magnetic poles, called **aurora borealis** ('northern lights') in the northern hemisphere and **aurora australis** in the southern hemisphere. Although aurorae are usually restricted to the polar skies, fluctuations in the solar wind occasionally cause them to be visible at lower latitudes. An aurora is usually in the form of a luminous arch with its apex towards the magnetic pole followed by arcs, bands, rays, curtains, and coronas, usually green but often showing shades of blue and red, and sometimes yellow or white. Aurorae are caused at heights of over 100 km/60 mi by a fast stream of charged particles from solar flares and low-density 'holes' in the Sun's corona.

These are guided by the Earth's magnetic field towards the north and south magnetic poles, where they enter the upper atmosphere and bombard the gases in the atmosphere, causing them to emit visible light.

**Auschwitz** (Polish Oświęcim) town near Kraków in Poland, the site of a notorious concentration camp used by the Nazis in World War II to exterminate Jews and other political and social minorities, as part of the 'final solution'. Each of the four gas chambers could hold 6,000 people.

**Austen, Jane** (1775–1817) English novelist. She described her raw material as 'three or four families in a Country Village'. *Sense and Sensibility* was published in 1811, *Pride and Prejudice* in 1813, *Mansfield Park* in 1814, *Emma* in 1816, and *Northanger Abbey* and *Persuasion* together in 1818, all anonymously. She observed speech and manners with wit and precision, and her penetrating observation of human behaviour results in insights that transcend period. Many of her works have been successfully adapted for film and television.

---

**WEB SITE** > > > > > > > >

**Jane Austen: *Emma***

http://www.bibliomania.com/Fiction/Austen/Emma/index.html

E-text of Jane Austen's novel *Emma*.

---

**Austerlitz, Battle of** battle on 2 December 1805, in which the French forces of Emperor Napoleon Bonaparte defeated those of Alexander I of Russia and Francis II of Austria at a small town in the Czech Republic (formerly in Austria), 19 km/12 mi east of Brno. The battle was one of Napoleon's greatest victories, resulting in the end of the coalition against France – the Austrians signed the Treaty of Pressburg and the Russians retired to their own territory.

**Australia** Commonwealth of; **area:** 7,682,300 sq km/2,966,136 sq mi; **capital:** Canberra; **major towns/cities:** Adelaide, Alice Springs, Brisbane, Darwin, Melbourne, Perth, Sydney, Hobart, Geelong, Newcastle, Townsville, Wollongong; **physical features:** Ayers Rock; Arnhem Land; Gulf of Carpentaria; Cape York Peninsula; Great Australian Bight; Great Sandy Desert; Gibson Desert; Great Victoria Desert; Simpson Desert; the Great Barrier Reef; Great Dividing Range and Australian Alps in the east (Mount Kosciusko, 2,229 m/7,136 ft, Australia's highest peak). The fertile southeast region is watered by the Darling, Lachlan, Murrumbridgee, and Murray rivers. Lake Eyre basin and Nullarbor Plain in the south; **territories:** Norfolk Island, Christmas Island, Cocos (Keeling) Islands, Ashmore and Cartier Islands, Coral Sea Islands, Heard Island and McDonald Islands, Australian Antarctic Territory; **head of state:** Elizabeth II from 1952, represented by governor general Sir William Deane from 1996; **head of government:** John Howard from 1996; **political system:** federal constitutional monarchy; **currency:** Australian dollar; **GNP per capita (PPP):** (US\$) 20,130 (1998); **exports:** major world producer of raw materials iron ore, aluminium, coal, nickel, zinc, lead, gold, tin, tungsten, uranium, crude oil; wool, meat, cereals, fruit, sugar, wine. Principal markets Japan 19.6% (1998); **population:** 18,705,000 (1999 est); **language:** English, Aboriginal languages; **religion:** Anglican 26%, other Protestant 17%, Roman Catholic 26%; **life expectancy:** 76 (men); 81 (women) (1995–2000).

**Australian Aborigine** member of any of the 500 groups of indigenous inhabitants of the continent of Australia, who migrated to this region from South Asia about 40,000 years ago. Traditionally hunters and gatherers, they are found throughout the continent and their languages probably belong to more than one linguistic family. They are dark-skinned, with fair hair in childhood and heavy dark beards and body hair in adult males. There are about 228,000 Aborigines in Australia, making up about 1.5% of the population of 16 million.

**Austria** Republic of; **national name:** *Republik Österreich*; **area:** 83,500 sq km/ 32,239 sq mi; **capital:** Vienna; **major towns/cities:** Graz, Linz, Salzburg, Innsbruck, Klagenfurt; **physical features:** landlocked mountainous state, with Alps in west and south (Austrian Alps, including Grossglockner and Brenner and Semmering passes, Lechtaler and Allgauer Alps north of River Inn, Carnic Alps on Italian border) and low relief in east where most of the population is concentrated; River Danube; **head of state:** Thomas Klestil from 1992; **head of government:** Wolfgang Schüssel from 2000; **political system:** democratic federal republic; **currency:** schilling; **GNP per capita (PPP):** (US$) 22,740 (1998); **exports:** dairy products, food products, wood and paper products, machinery and transport equipment, metal and metal products, chemical products. Principal market for exports Germany 35.1% (1997); **population:** 8,177,000 (1999 est); **language:** German; **religion:** Roman Catholic 78%, Protestant 5%; **life expectancy:** 74 (men); 80 (women) (1995–2000).

**Austro-Hungarian Empire** Dual Monarchy established by the Habsburg Franz Joseph in 1867 between his empire of Austria and his kingdom of Hungary (including territory that became Czechoslovakia as well as parts of Poland, the Ukraine, Romania, Yugoslavia, and Italy).

It collapsed in the autumn of 1918 with the end of World War I. Only two king-emperors ruled: Franz Joseph and Charles.

**autism, infantile** rare disorder, generally present from birth, characterized by a withdrawn state and a failure to develop normally in language or social behaviour. Although the autistic child may, rarely, show signs of high intelligence (in music or with numbers, for example), many have impaired intellect. The cause is unknown, but is thought to involve a number of factors, possibly including an inherent abnormality of the child's brain. Special education may bring about some improvement.

**autoimmunity** in medicine, condition where the body's immune responses are mobilized not against 'foreign' matter, such as invading germs, but against the body itself. Diseases considered to be of autoimmune origin include myasthenia gravis, rheumatoid arthritis, and →lupus erythematous.

**autonomic nervous system** in mammals, the part of the nervous system that controls those functions not controlled voluntarily, including the heart rate, activity of the intestines, and the production of sweat.

There are two divisions of the autonomic nervous system. The **sympathetic** system responds to stress, when it speeds the heart rate, increases blood pressure, and generally prepares the body for action. The **parasympathetic** system is more important when the body is at rest, since it slows the heart rate, decreases blood pressure, and stimulates the digestive system.

**autotroph** any living organism that synthesizes organic substances from inorganic molecules by using light or chemical energy. Autotrophs are the **primary producers** in all food chains since the materials they synthesize and store are the energy sources of all other organisms. All green plants and many planktonic organisms are autotrophs, using sunlight to convert carbon dioxide and water into sugars by →photosynthesis.

**Auvergne** ancient province of central France and modern region comprising the *départements* of Allier, Cantal, Haute-Loire, and Puy-de-Dôme; administrative centre Clermont-Ferrand; area 26,000 sq km/10,036 sq mi; population (1990) 1,321,200. It is a mountainous area, composed chiefly of volcanic rocks in several masses. Products include cattle, sheep, tyres, and metal goods.

**auxin** plant →hormone that promotes stem and root growth in plants. Auxins influence many aspects of plant growth and development, including cell enlargement, inhibition of development of axillary buds, →tropisms, and the initiation of roots. **Synthetic auxins** are used in rooting powders for cuttings, and in some weedkillers, where high auxin concentrations cause such rapid growth that the plants die. They are also used to prevent premature fruitdrop in orchards. The most common naturally occurring auxin is known as indoleacetic acid, or IAA. It is produced in the shoot apex and transported to other parts of the plant.

**avant-garde** (French 'forward guard') in the arts, those artists or works that are in the forefront of new developments in their media. The term was introduced (as was 'reactionary') after the French Revolution, when it was used to describe any socialist political movement.

**Avebury** Europe's largest stone circle (diameter 412 m/1,350 ft), in Wiltshire, England. This megalithic henge monument is thought to be part of a ritual complex, and contains 650 massive blocks of stone arranged in circles and avenues. It was probably constructed around 3,500 years ago, and is linked with nearby Silbury Hill.

**Avignon** city in Provence, France, administrative centre of Vaucluse *département*, on the River Rhône, 80 km/ 50 mi northwest of Marseille; population (1990) 89,400, conurbation 180,000. Tourism, food processing, and wine are important. An important Gallic and Roman city, it has a 12th-century bridge (only half of which still stands), a 13th-century cathedral, 14th-century walls, and the Palais des Papes, the enormous fortress-palace of the popes, one of the most magnificent Gothic buildings of the 14th century.

**Avogadro's hypothesis** in chemistry, the law stating that equal volumes of all gases, when at the same temperature and pressure, have the same numbers of molecules. It was first propounded by Amedeo Avogadro.

**Avon** (Upper Avon or Warwickshire Avon; Celtic *afon* 'river') river in southern England; length 154 km/96 mi. It rises in the Northamptonshire uplands near Naseby and flows southwest through Warwick, Stratford-upon-Avon, and Evesham, before joining the River Severn near Tewkesbury, Gloucestershire.

**axis** (plural axes) in geometry, one of the reference lines by which a point on a graph may be located. The horizontal axis is usually referred to as the *x*-axis, and the vertical axis as the *y*-axis. The term is also used to refer to the imaginary line about which an object may be said to be symmetrical (**axis of symmetry**) – for example, the diagonal of a square – or the line about which an object may revolve (**axis of rotation**).

**Ayckbourn, Alan** (1939– ) English playwright and artistic director of the Stephen Joseph Theatre, Scarborough, North Yorkshire, from 1970. His plays include *Relatively Speaking* (1967), *Absurd Person Singular* (1972), *Intimate Exchanges* (1982), *A Woman in Mind* (1986), and *Haunting Julia* (1994).

**Ayers Rock** (Aboriginal *Uluru*) vast ovate mass of pinkish rock in Northern Territory, Australia; 335 m/1,110 ft high and 9 km/6 mi around. For the Aboriginals, whose paintings decorate its caves, it has magical significance.

**Azerbaijan** Republic of; **national name:** *Azarbaijchan Respublikasy*; **area:** 86,600 sq km/33,436 sq mi; **capital:** Baku; **major towns/cities:** Gyandzha (formerly Kirovabad), Sumgait, Nakhichevan, Stepanakert; **physical features:** Caspian Sea with rich oil reserves; the country ranges from semidesert to the Caucasus Mountains; **head of state:** Geidar Aliyev from 1993; **head of government:** Artur Rasizade from 1996; **political system:** authoritarian nationalist; **currency:** manat (left rouble zone in 1993); **GNP per capita (PPP):** (US$) 1,820 (1998); **exports:** refined petroleum products, machinery, food products, textiles. Principal market Turkey 22.4% (1998); **population:** 7,697,000 (1999 est); **language:** Azeri; **religion:** Shiite Muslim 62%, Sunni Muslim 26%, Orthodox Christian 12%; **life expectancy:** 66 (men); 74 (women) (1995–2000).

**Aztec** member of an American Indian people who migrated south into the valley of Mexico in the AD 1100s, and in 1325 began reclaiming lake marshland to build their capital, Tenochtitlán, on the site now occupied by Mexico City. Under their emperor Montezuma I, who reigned from 1440, the Aztecs created an empire in central Mexico.

After the Spanish conquistador Hernán Cortés landed in 1519, →Montezuma II, who reigned from 1502, was killed and Tenochtitlañ was destroyed. Nahuatl is the Aztec language; it belongs to the Uto-Aztecan family of languages, and is still spoken by some Mexicans.

# Bb

**Babbage, Charles** (1792–1871) English mathematician who devised a precursor of the computer. He designed an analytical engine, a general-purpose mechanical computing device for performing different calculations according to a program input on punched cards (an idea borrowed from the Jacquard loom). This device was never built, but it embodied many of the principles on which digital computers are based.

**Babylon** capital of ancient Babylonia, on the bank of the lower Euphrates River. The site is now in Iraq, 88 km/55 mi south of Baghdad and 8 km/5 mi north of Hilla, which is built chiefly of bricks from the ruins of Babylon. The Hanging Gardens of Babylon, one of the →Seven Wonders of the World, were probably erected on a vaulted stone base, the only stone construction in the mud-brick city. They formed a series of terraces, irrigated by a hydraulic system.

**Bach, Johann Sebastian** (1685–1750) German composer. A master of counterpoint, his music epitomizes the baroque polyphonic style. His orchestral music includes the six *Brandenburg Concertos* (1721), other concertos for keyboard instrument and violin, four orchestral suites, sonatas for various instruments, three partitas and three sonatas for violin solo, and six unaccompanied cello suites. Bach's keyboard music, for clavier and organ, his fugues, and his choral music are of equal importance. He also wrote chamber music and songs.

**Bacon, Francis** (1909–1992) Irish painter. Self-taught, he practised abstract art, then developed a stark Expressionist style characterized by distorted, blurred figures enclosed in loosely defined space. He aimed to 'bring the figurative thing more up onto the nervous system more violently and more poignantly'. One of his best-known works is *Study after Velázquez's Portrait of Pope Innocent X* (1953; Museum of Modern Art, New York).

**Bacon, Francis,** 1st Baron Verulam and Viscount St Albans (1561–1626) English philosopher, politician, and writer, a founder of modern scientific research. His works include *Essays* (1597, revised and augmented 1612 and 1625), characterized by pith and brevity; *The Advancement of Learning* (1605), a seminal work discussing scientific method; *Novum Organum* (1620), in which he redefined the task of natural science, seeing it as a means of empirical discovery and a method of increasing human power over nature; and *The New Atlantis* (1626), describing a utopian state in which scientific knowledge is systematically sought and exploited. He was briefly Lord Chancellor in 1618 but lost his post through corruption.

**Bacon, Roger** (c. 1214–1294) English philosopher and scientist. He was interested in alchemy, the biological and physical sciences, and magic. Many discoveries have been credited to him, including the magnifying lens. He foresaw the extensive use of gunpowder and mechanical cars, boats, and planes. Bacon was known as *Doctor Mirabilis* (Wonderful Teacher).

**bacteria** (singular bacterium) microscopic single-celled organisms lacking a nucleus. Bacteria are widespread, present in soil, air, and water, and as parasites on and in other living things. Some parasitic bacteria cause disease by producing toxins, but others are harmless and may even benefit their hosts. Bacteria usually reproduce by binary

---

**WEB SITE** > > > > > > > >
**Bacteria in Sickness and in Health**
http://microbios1.mds.qmw.ac.uk/under ground/bactsick/bactsick.html
Guide to the bacteria that form the healthy flora of the human body. The site looks at various parts of the body, such as the gut, mouth, nose, and throat, and the bacteria that they normally contain, and explains how to tell when a bacteria is acting as a pathogen.

---

fission (dividing into two equal parts), and this may occur approximately every 20 minutes. Only 4,000 species of bacteria are known (in 1998); bacteriologists believe that around 3 million species may actually exist.

**badminton** racket game similar to lawn →tennis but played on a smaller court and with a shuttlecock (a half sphere of cork or plastic with a feather or nylon skirt) instead of a ball. The object of the game is to prevent the opponent from being able to return the shuttlecock.

**Baghdad** historic city and capital of Iraq, on the River Tigris; population (1995 est) 5,385,000. Industries include oil refining, distilling, tanning, tobacco processing, and the manufacture of textiles and cement. Founded in 762, it became Iraq's capital in 1921. During the Gulf War of 1991, the UN coalition forces bombed it in repeated air raids.

**Baha'i Faith** religion founded in the 19th century from a Muslim splinter group, Babism, by the Persian Baha'u'llah. His message in essence was that all great religious leaders are manifestations of the unknowable God and all scriptures are sacred. There is no priesthood: all Baha'is are expected to teach, and to work towards world unification. There are about 6 million Baha'is worldwide.

**Bahamas** Commonwealth of the; **area:** 13,864 sq km/5,352 sq mi; **capital:** Nassau (on New Providence Island); **major towns/cities:** Freeport (on Grand Bahama); **physical features:**

comprises 700 tropical coral islands and about 1,000 cays; the Exumas are a narrow spine of 365 islands; only 30 of the desert islands are inhabited; Blue Holes of Andros, the world's longest and deepest submarine caves; **principal islands:** Andros, Grand Bahama, Abaco, Eleuthera, New Providence, Berry Islands, Bimini Islands, Great Inagua, Acklins Island, Exuma Islands, Mayguana, Crooked Island, Long Island, Cat Islands, Rum Cay, Watling (San Salvador) Island, Inagua Islands; **head of state:** Elizabeth II from 1973, represented by governor general Orville Turnquest from 1995; **head of government:** Hubert Ingraham from 1992; **political system:** constitutional monarchy; **currency:** Bahamian dollar; **GNP per capita (PPP):** (US$) 10,460 (1998); **exports:** foodstuffs (fish), oil products and transhipments, chemicals, rum, salt. Principal market USA 24.5% (1997); **population:** 301,000 (1999 est); **language:** English and some Creole; **religion:** Christian 94% (Roman Catholic 26%, Anglican 21%, other Protestant 48%); **life expectancy:** 71 (men); 77 (women) (1995–2000).

**Bahrain** State of; **national name:** *Dawlat al Bahrayn*; **area:** 688 sq km/266 sq mi; **capital:** Al Manamah on the largest island (also called Bahrain); **major towns/cities:** Muharraq, Jiddhafs, Isa Town, Hidd, Rifa'a, Sitra; **major ports:** Mina Sulman; **physical features:** archipelago of 35 islands in Arabian Gulf, composed largely of sand-covered limestone; generally poor and infertile soil; flat and hot; causeway

linking Bahrain to mainland Saudi Arabia; **head of state:** Sheikh Hamad bin Isa al-Khalifa from 1999; **head of government:** Sheikh Khalifa bin Salman al-Khalifa from 1970; **political system:** absolute emirate; **currency:** Bahraini dinar; **GNP per capita (PPP):** (US$) 13,700 (1998 est); **exports:** petroleum and petroleum products, aluminium, chemicals (1996). Principal market India 14% (1997); **population:** 607,000 (1999 est); **language:** Arabic (official); Farsi, English, Urdu; **religion:** 85% Muslim (Shiite 60%, Sunni 40%), Christian; Islam is the state religion; **life expectancy:** 71 (men); 75 (women) (1995–2000).

**Baird, John Logie** (1888–1946) Scottish electrical engineer who pioneered television. In 1925 he gave the first public demonstration of television, transmitting an image of a recognizable human face. The following year, he gave the world's first demonstration of true television before an audience of about 50 scientists at the Royal Institution, London. By 1928 Baird had succeeded in demonstrating colour television.

**Baku** capital city of the republic of Azerbaijan, located on the Apsheron Peninsula on the western shore of the Caspian Sea. Baku is an important industrial city and port. It has been a major centre of oil extraction and refining since the 1870s; the oilfields here are linked by pipelines with the Georgian Black Sea port of Batumi, while petroleum exports to Russia are shipped across the Caspian to Astrakhan. Heavy engineering enterprises in the city produce equipment for the oil industry and ships; light industries include leather tanning and food processing. Baku has a hot climate and is subject to strong northwest winds.

**Balaclava, Battle of** a Russian attack on 25 October 1854, during the Crimean War, on British positions, near a town in Ukraine, 10 km/6 mi southeast of Sevastopol. It was the scene of the ill-timed **Charge of the Light Brigade** of British cavalry against the Russian entrenched artillery. Of the 673 soldiers who took part, there were 272 casualties. Balaclava helmets were knitted hoods worn here by soldiers in the bitter weather.

**balance of nature** in ecology, the idea that there is an inherent equilibrium in most ecosystems, with plants and animals interacting so as to produce a stable, continuing system of life on Earth. The activities of human beings can, and frequently do, disrupt the balance of nature.

**Baldwin, James Arthur** (1924–1987) US writer and civil-rights activist. He portrayed with vivid intensity the suffering and despair of African-Americans in contemporary society. After his first novel, *Go Tell It on the Mountain* (1953), set in Harlem, and *Giovanni's Room* (1956), about a homosexual relationship in Paris, his writing became more politically indignant with *Another Country* (1962) and *The Fire Next Time* (1963), a collection of essays.

**Baldwin, Stanley** (1867–1947) 1st

Earl Baldwin of Bewdley British Conservative politician, prime minister 1923–24, 1924–29, and 1935–37. He weathered the general strike of 1926, secured complete adult suffrage in 1928, and handled the abdication crisis of Edward VIII in 1936, but failed to prepare Britain for World War II.

**Balearic Islands** (Spanish *Baleares*) group of Mediterranean islands forming an autonomous region of Spain; including →Mallorca, Menorca, Ibiza, Cabrera, and Formentera; **area:** 5,014 sq km/1,936 sq mi; **capital:** Palma de Mallorca; **industries:** figs, olives, oranges, wine, brandy, coal, iron, slate; tourism is crucial; **population:** (1991) 709,100; **history:** held successively by Greeks and Carthaginians, the islands became a Roman colony from 123 BC, and an independent Moorish kingdom from 1009 until 1232; they were incorporated into the Christian Spanish kingdom of Aragón in 1349.

**Balfour Declaration** letter, dated 2 November 1917, from British foreign secretary A J Balfour to Lord Rothschild (chair, British Zionist Federation) stating: 'HM government view with favour the establishment in Palestine of a national home for the Jewish people.' It helped form the basis for the foundation of Israel in 1948.

**Bali** island of Indonesia, east of Java, one of the Sunda Islands; area 5,800 sq km/2,240 sq mi; population (1990) 2,777,800. The capital is Denpasar. The island features volcanic mountains. Industries include gold and silver work, woodcarving, weaving, copra, salt, coffee, and tourism, with 1 million tourists a year (1990); arts include Balinese dancing, music, and drama. Bali's Hindu culture goes back to the 7th century; the Dutch gained control of the island by 1908.

**Balkans** (Turkish 'mountains') peninsula of southeastern Europe, stretching into Slovenia between the Adriatic and Aegean seas, comprising Albania, Bosnia-Herzegovina, Bulgaria, Croatia, Greece, Romania, the part of Turkey in Europe, and Yugoslavia. It is joined to the rest of Europe by an isthmus 1,200 km/750 mi wide between Rijeka on the west and the mouth of the Danube on the Black Sea to the east.

**Balkan Wars** two wars 1912–13 and 1913 (preceding World War I) which resulted in the expulsion by the Balkan states of Ottoman Turkey from Europe, except for a small area around Istanbul.

**ballet** (Italian *balletto* 'a little dance') theatrical representation in dance form in which music also plays a major part in telling a story or conveying a mood. Some such form of entertainment existed in ancient Greece, but Western ballet as we know it today first appeared in Renaissance Italy, where it was a court entertainment. From there it was brought by Catherine de' Medici to France in the form of a spectacle combining singing, dancing, and declamation. During the 18th century there were major developments in technique and ballet gradually became divorced from opera, emerging as an art form in its own right.

In the 20th century Russian ballet had a vital influence on the classical tradition in the West, and ballet developed further in the USA through the work of George Balanchine and the American Ballet Theater, and in the UK through the influence of Marie Rambert.

Modern dance is a separate development.

**ballistics** study of the motion and impact of projectiles such as bullets, bombs, and missiles. For projectiles from a gun, relevant exterior factors include temperature, barometric pressure, and wind strength; and for nuclear missiles these extend to such factors as the speed at which the Earth turns.

**balloon** lighter-than-air craft that consists of a gasbag filled with gas lighter than the surrounding air and an attached basket, or gondola, for carrying passengers and/or instruments. In 1783, the first successful human ascent was in Paris, in a hot-air balloon designed by the →Montgolfier brothers Joseph Michel and Jacques Etienne. In 1785, a hydrogen-filled balloon designed by French physicist Jacques Charles travelled across the English Channel.

**ballot** (Italian *ballotta*, diminutive of *balla*, 'a ball') the process of voting in an election. In political elections in democracies ballots are usually secret: voters indicate their choice of candidate on a voting slip that is placed in a sealed ballot box. **Ballot rigging** is a term used to describe elections that are fraudulent because of interference with the voting process or the counting of votes.

**Baltic Sea** shallow sea, extending northeast from the narrow Skagerrak and Kattegat, between Sweden and Denmark, to the Gulf of Bothnia between Sweden and Finland. Its coastline is 8,000 km/5,000 mi long; the sea is 1,500 km/930 mi long and 650 km/404 mi wide, and its area, including the gulfs of Riga, Finland, and Bothnia, is 422,300 sq km/163,000 sq mi. Its average depth is 65 m/213 ft, but it is 460 m/1,500 ft at its deepest.

Its shoreline is shared by Denmark, Germany, Poland, the Baltic States, Russia, Finland, and Sweden.

**Baltic States** collective name for the states of Estonia, Latvia, and Lithuania. They were formed as independent states after World War I out of former territories of the Russian Empire. The government of the USSR recognized their independence in peace treaties signed in 1920, but in 1939 forced them to allow occupation of important military bases by Soviet troops. In the following year, the Baltic states were absorbed into the Soviet Union as constituent republics. They regained their independence in September 1991 after the collapse of the Soviet Union.

**Balzac, Honoré de** (1799–1850) French writer. He was one of the major novelists of the 19th century. His first success was *Les Chouans/The Chouans*, inspired by Walter Scott. This was the beginning of the long series of novels *La Comédie humaine/The Human Comedy* which includes *Eugénie Grandet* (1833), *Le Père Goriot* (1834), and *Cousine Bette* (1846). He also wrote the Rabelaisian *Contes drolatiques/Ribald Tales* (1833).

**Bamako** capital and port of Mali on the River Niger; population (1992) 746,000. It produces pharmaceuticals, chemicals, textiles, food products, beer, tobacco, and metal products. The Grand Mosque, Malian Museum, and BCEAO Tower are situated here.

**Banda, Hastings Kamuzu** (1905–1997) Malawi politician, physician, and president (1966–94). He led his country's independence movement and was prime minister of Nyasaland (the former name of Malawi) from 1964. He became Malawi's first president in 1966 and was named president for life in 1971; his rule was authoritarian. Having bowed to opposition pressure and opened the way for a pluralist system, Banda stood in the first free presidential elections for 30 years in 1994, but was defeated by Bakili Muluzi.

**Bangalore** capital of Karnataka state, southern India, lying 950 m/3,000 ft above sea-level; population (1991) 4,087,000. Industries include electronics, aircraft and machine-tools construction, and coffee. Bangalore University and the University of Agriculture Sciences were founded in 1964, and the National Aeronautical Institute in 1960.

**Bangkok** (Thai *Krung Thep* 'City of Angels') capital and port of Thailand, on the River Chao Phraya; population (1993) 5,572,700. Products include paper, ceramics, cement, textiles, aircraft, and silk. It is the headquarters of the Southeast Asia Treaty Organization (SEATO).

**Bangladesh** People's Republic of (formerly **East Pakistan**); **national name:** *Gana Prajatantri Bangladesh*; **area:** 144,000 sq km/55,598 sq mi; **capital:** Dhaka (formerly Dacca); **major towns/cities:** Rajshahi, Khulna, Chittagong, Comilla, Barisal, Sylhet; **major ports:** Chittagong, Khulna; **physical features:** flat delta of rivers Ganges (Padma) and Brahmaputra (Jamuna), the largest estuarine delta in the world; annual rainfall of 2,540 mm/100 in; some 75% of the land is less than 3 m/10 ft above sea level; hilly in extreme southeast and northeast; **head of state:** Abdur Rahman Biswas from 1991; **head of government:** Sheikh Hasina Wazed from 1996; **political system:** emergent democracy; **currency:** taka; **GNP per capita (PPP):** (US$) 1,100 (1998); **exports:** raw jute and jute goods, tea, clothing, leather and leather products, shrimps and frogs' legs. Principal market USA 33.3% (1997); **population:** 126,948,000 (1999 est); **language:** Bengali (official); English; **religion:** Sunni Muslim 85%, Hindu 12%; Islam is the state religion; **life expectancy:** 58 (men); 58 (women) (1995–2000).

**Bannister, Roger Gilbert** (1929– ) English track and field athlete. He was the first person to run a mile in under four minutes. He achieved this feat at Oxford, England, on 6 May 1954, in a time of 3 min 59.4 sec.

**Bannockburn, Battle of** battle fought on 24 June 1314 at Bannockburn, Scotland, between Robert (I) the Bruce, King of Scotland, and Edward II of England. The defeat of the English led to the independence of Scotland.

**baobab** tree with rootlike branches, hence the nickname 'upside-down tree', and a disproportionately thick girth, up to 9 m/30 ft in diameter. The pulp of its fruit is edible and is known as monkey bread. (Genus *Adansonia*, family Bombacaceae.)

**Baptist** member of any of several Protestant and evangelical Christian sects that practise baptism by immersion only upon profession of faith. Baptists seek their authority in the Bible. They originated among English Dissenters who took refuge in the Netherlands in the early 17th century, and spread by emigration and, later, missionary activity. Of the world total of approximately 31 million, some 26.5 million are in the USA and 265,000 in the UK.

**Barbados** **area:** 430 sq km/166 sq mi; **capital:** Bridgetown; **major towns/cities:** Speightstown, Holetown, Oistins; **physical features:** most easterly island of the West Indies; surrounded by coral reefs; subject to hurricanes in June to November; highest point Mount Hillaby 340 m/1,115 ft; **head of state:** Elizabeth II from 1966, represented by Governor General Sir Clifford Straughn Husbands from 1996; **head of government:** Owen Arthur from 1994; **political system:** constitutional monarchy;

**currency:** Barbados dollar; **GNP per capita (PPP):** (US$) 12,260 (1998); **exports:** sugar, molasses, syrup-rum, chemicals, electrical components. Principal market USA 17.7% (1997); **population:** 269,000 (1999 est); **language:** English and Bajan (Barbadian English dialect); **religion:** 33% Anglican, 13% Pentecostalist, 6% Methodist, 4% Roman Catholic; **life expectancy:** 74 (men); 79 (women) (1995–2000).

**barbiturate** hypnosedative drug, commonly known as a 'sleeping pill', consisting of any salt or ester of barbituric acid $C_4H_4O_3N_2$. It works by depressing brain activity. Most barbiturates, being highly addictive, are no longer prescribed and are listed as controlled substances.

**Barcelona** port and capital of Barcelona province and of the autonomous community of Cataluña, northeast Spain; population (1994) 1,631,000. Industries include textiles, engineering, and chemicals. As the chief centre of Catalan nationalism, Barcelona was prominent in the overthrow of the monarchy in 1931 and was the last city of the republic to surrender to Franco in 1939. The city hosted the Summer Olympics in 1992.

**Barebones Parliament** English assembly called by Oliver →Cromwell to replace the 'Rump Parliament' in July 1653. Although its members attempted to pass sensible legislation (civil marriage; registration of births, deaths, and marriages; custody of lunatics), their attempts to abolish tithes, patronage, and the court of chancery, and to codify the law, led to the resignation of the moderates and its dissolution in December 1653.

**baritone** male voice pitched between bass and tenor, of approximate range G2–F4. As a prefix to the name of an instrument, for example baritone saxophone, it indicates that the instrument sounds in approximately the same range.

**bar mitzvah** (Hebrew 'son of the commandment') in Judaism, initiation of a boy, which takes place at the age of 13, into the adult Jewish community; less common is the **bat mitzvah** or **bat** for girls aged 12. The child reads a passage from the Torah in the synagogue on the Sabbath and is subsequently regarded as a full member of the congregation.

**barnacle** marine crustacean of the subclass Cirripedia. The larval form is free-swimming, but when mature, it fixes itself by the head to rock or floating wood. The animal then remains attached, enclosed in a shell through which the cirri (modified legs) protrude to sweep food into the mouth. Barnacles include the stalked **goose barnacle** *Lepas anatifera* found on ships' bottoms, and the **acorn barnacles**, such as *Balanus balanoides*, common on rocks.

**Barnardo, Thomas John** (1845–1905) British philanthropist. He was known as Dr Barnardo, although he was not medically qualified. He opened the first of a series of homes for destitute children 1867 in Stepney, East London.

**barometer** instrument that measures atmospheric pressure as an indication of weather. Most often used are the mercury barometer and the aneroid barometer.

**baroque** in the visual arts, architecture, and music, a style flourishing in Europe 1600–1750, broadly characterized as expressive, flamboyant, and dynamic. Playing a central role in the crusading work of the Catholic Counter-Reformation, the baroque used elaborate effects to appeal directly to the emotions. In some of its most characteristic works – such as Giovanni Bernini's Cornaro Chapel (Sta Maria della Vittoria, Rome), containing his sculpture *Ecstasy of St Theresa* (1645–52) – painting, sculpture, decoration, and architecture were designed to create a single, dramatic effect. Many masterpieces of the baroque emerged in churches and palaces in Rome, but the style soon spread throughout Europe, changing in character as it did so. The term baroque has also by extension been used to describe the music and literature of the period, but it has a much less clear meaning in these fields, and is more a convenient label than a stylistic description.

**barrow** (Old English *beorgh* 'hill or mound') burial mound, usually composed of earth but sometimes of stones. Examples are found in many parts of the world. The two main types are **long**, dating from the Neolithic period (New Stone Age), and **round**, dating from the Mesolithic period (early Bronze Age). Barrows made entirely of stones are known as cairns.

**Bartók, Béla** (1881–1945) Hungarian composer. His works combine folk elements with mathematical concepts of

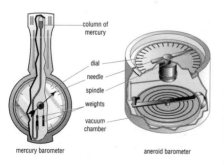

mercury barometer                    aneroid barometer

**barometer** The mercury barometer (left) and the aneroid barometer (right). In the mercury barometer, the weight of the column of mercury is balanced by the pressure of the atmosphere on the lower end. A change in height of the column indicates a change in atmospheric pressure. In the aneroid barometer, any change of atmospheric pressure causes the metal box which contains the vacuum to be squeezed or to expand slightly. The movements of the box sides are transferred to a pointer and scale via a chain of levers.

Labels (mercury barometer): column of mercury; dial; needle; spindle; weights; vacuum chamber tonal and rhythmic proportion. His large output includes six string quartets, a *Divertimento* for string orchestra (1939), concertos for piano, violin, and viola, the *Concerto for Orchestra* (1943–44), a one-act opera *Duke Bluebeard's Castle* (1911), and graded teaching pieces for piano.

**Bartolommeo, Fra** (c. 1472–1517) also called Baccio della Porta, Italian religious painter of the High Renaissance, active in Florence. He introduced Venetian artists to the Florentine High Renaissance style during a visit to Venice in 1508, and took back with him to Florence a Venetian sense of colour. His style is one of classic simplicity and order, as in *The Mystical Marriage of St Catherine* (1511, Louvre, Paris).

**base** in chemistry, a substance that accepts protons. Bases can contain negative ions such as the hydroxide ion ($OH^-$), which is the strongest base, or be molecules such as ammonia ($NH_3$). Ammonia is a weak base, as only some of its molecules accept protons.

$$OH^- + H^+_{(aq)} \rightarrow H_2O_{(l)}$$

$$NH_3 + H_2O \rightarrow NH_4^+ + OH^-$$

Bases that dissolve in water are called alkalis.

**base** in mathematics, the number of different single-digit symbols used in a particular number system. In our usual (decimal) counting system of numbers (with symbols 0, 1, 2, 3, 4, 5, 6, 7, 8, 9) the base is 10. In the →binary number system, which has only the symbols 1 and 0, the base is two. A base is also a number that, when raised to a particular power (that is, when multiplied by itself a particular number of times as in $10^2 = 10 \times 10 = 100$), has a →logarithm equal to the power. For example, the logarithm of 100 to the base ten is 2.

In geometry, the term is used to denote the line or area on which a polygon or solid stands.

**baseball** national summer game of the USA, derived in the 19th century from the English game of rounders. Baseball is a bat-and-ball game played between two teams, each of nine players, on a pitch ('field') marked out in the form of a diamond, with a base at each corner. The ball is struck with a cylindrical bat, and the players try to score ('make a run') by circuiting the bases. A 'home run' is a circuit on one hit.

**Basel** (*or* Basle, French *Bâle*) commercial and industrial city, capital of Basel canton, Switzerland, situated on the Rhine at the point where the French, German, and Swiss borders meet; population (1994) 179,600. Manufactured goods include dyes, textiles, vitamins, agrochemicals, dietary products, and genetic products. Basel was a strong military station under the Romans. In 1501 it joined the Swiss confederation and later developed as a centre for the Reformation.

**base pair** in biochemistry, the linkage of two base (purine or pyrimidine) molecules in →DNA. They are found in nucleotides, and form the basis of the genetic code.

**Bashō** (1644–1694) pen-name of Matsuo Munefusa, Japanese poet. He was a master of the **haiku**, a 17-syllable poetic form with lines of 5, 7, and 5 syllables, which he infused with subtle allusiveness.

**basic–oxygen process** most widely used method of steelmaking, involving the blasting of oxygen at supersonic speed into molten pig iron.

**basilica** Roman public building; a large roofed hall flanked by columns, generally with an aisle on each side, used for judicial or other public business. The earliest known basilica, at Pompeii, dates from the 2nd century BC. This architectural form was adopted by the early Christians for their churches.

**basketball** ball game between two teams of five players on an indoor enclosed court. The object is, via a series of passing moves, to throw the large inflated ball through a circular hoop and net positioned at each end of the court, 3.05 m/10 ft above the ground. The first world championship for men was held in 1950, and 1953 for women. They are now held every four years.

**Basque Country** (Basque *Euskal Herria*) homeland of the Basque people in the western Pyrenees, divided by the Franco-Spanish border. The Spanish Basque Country (Spanish *País Vasco*) is an autonomous region (created in 1979) of central northern Spain, comprising the provinces of Vizcaya, Alava, and Guipúzcoa (Basque *Bizkaia*, *Araba*,

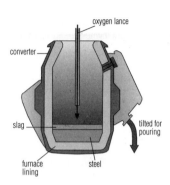

**basic–oxygen process** The basic–oxygen process is the primary method used to produce steel. Oxygen is blown at high pressure through molten pig iron and scrap steel in a converter lined with basic refractory materials. The impurities, principally carbon, quickly burn out, producing steel.

and *Gipuzkoa*); area 7,300 sq km/2,818 sq mi; population (1991) 2,104,000. The French Basque Country (French *Pays Basque*) is the area occupied by Basques in the *département* of Pyrénées-Atlantiques. It is estimated that there are about 170,000 Basques in France.

**bassoon** double-reed woodwind instrument in C, the bass of the oboe family. It doubles back on itself in a tube about 2.5 m/7.5 ft long and has a rich and deep tone. The bassoon concert repertoire extends from the early baroque via Vivaldi, Mozart, and Dukas to Stockhausen.

**Bastille** castle of St Antoine, built about 1370 as part of the fortifications of Paris. It was made a state prison by Cardinal →Richelieu and was stormed by the mob that set the French Revolution in motion 14 July 1789. Only seven prisoners were found in the castle when it was stormed; the governor and most of the garrison were killed, and the Bastille was razed.

**bat** any mammal of the order Chiroptera, related to the Insectivora (hedgehogs and shrews), but differing from them in being able to fly. Bats are the only true flying mammals. Their forelimbs are developed as wings capable of rapid and sustained flight. There are two main groups of bats: **megabats**, which eat fruit, and **microbats**, which mainly eat insects. Although by no means blind, many microbats rely largely on echolocation for navigation and finding prey, sending out pulses of high-pitched sound and listening for the echo. Bats are nocturnal, and those native to temperate countries hibernate in winter. There are about 977 species forming the order Chiroptera, making this the second-largest mammalian order; bats make up nearly one-quarter of the world's mammals.

**Bath** historic city and administrative headquarters of Bath and North East Somerset unitary authority, southwest England, 171 km/106 mi west of London; population (1991) 78,700. Industries include printing, plastics, engineering, and tourism. Bath was the site of the Roman town of **Aquae Sulis**, and in the 18th century flourished as a fashionable spa, with the only naturally occurring hot mineral springs in Britain. Although the baths were closed to the public in 1977, a Millennium Spa Project is intended to bring back public bathing to Bath's hot springs.

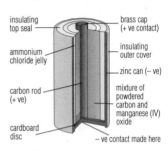

**battery** The common dry cell relies on chemical changes occurring between the electrodes – the central carbon rod and the outer zinc casing – and the ammonium chloride electrolyte to produce electricity. The mixture of carbon and manganese is used to increase the life of the cell.

**battery** any energy-storage device allowing release of electricity on demand. It is made up of one or more electrical →cells. Primary-cell batteries are disposable; secondary-cell batteries, or accumulators, are rechargeable. Primary-cell batteries are an extremely uneconomical form of energy, since they produce only 2% of the power used in their manufacture. It is dangerous to try to recharge a primary-cell battery.

**Baudelaire, Charles Pierre** (1821–1867) French poet. His immensely influential work combined rhythmical and musical perfection with a morbid romanticism and eroticism, finding beauty in decadence and evil. His first and best-known book of verse was *Les Fleurs du mal/Flowers of Evil* (1857). He was one of the main figures in the development of Symbolism.

**bauxite** principal ore of →aluminium, consisting of a mixture of hydrated aluminium oxides and hydroxides, generally contaminated with compounds of iron, which give it a red colour. It is formed by the chemical weathering of rocks in tropical climates. Chief producers of bauxite are Australia, Guinea, Jamaica, Russia, Kazakhstan, Suriname, and Brazil.

**Bavaria** (German *Bayern*) administrative region (German *Land*) in southeast Germany; bordered on the west by Hesse and Baden Württemberg, on the north by Thuringia and Saxony, on the northeast by the Czech Republic, and on the south and southeast by Austria; **area:** 70,600 sq km/27,252 sq mi; **capital:** →Munich; **towns and cities:** Nuremberg, Augsburg, Würzburg, Regensburg, Passau, Fürth, Ingolstadt; **physical:** largest of the German *Länder*; forms the Danube and Main basins; around one-third of the state is woodland, the principal forests being the Frankenwald in the north and the Bavarian Forest, or Bohemian Forest (Böhmerwald), in the northeast; Bavarian Alps in the south; **features:** festivals at Bayreuth (Wagner), Oberammergau (Passion Play), Ansbach (Bach), Augsburg (Mozart), Munich (opera), Nuremberg (organ), Würzburg (Mozart); the Oktoberfest, an internationally known beer festival, is held annually in Munich; ski resorts in the Bavarian Alps attract many visitors; the state includes 11 universities; **industries:** electronics, electrical engineering, optics, automobile assembly (BMW cars are manufactured at the Bayerische Motoren Werke), aerospace, brewing, chemicals, plastics, oil refining, textiles, glass, toys; **agriculture:** wheat, rye, barley, oats, potatoes, and sugar beet; livestock farming; forestry; **population:** (1995) 12,100,000; **famous people:** Lucas Cranach, Richard Strauss, Bertolt Brecht, Hermann Goering, Heinrich Himmler, Franz Josef Strauss; **religion:** 70% Roman Catholic, 26% Protestant; **history:** settled by Germanic tribes in the 5th century; part of the Holy Roman Empire; ruled for most of its history by the Wittelsbach dynasty; bastion of Roman Catholicism; became a kingdom under Napoleon Bonaparte; last king of Bavaria, Ludwig III, abdicated in 1918; birthplace of national socialist movement.

**bean** seed of a large number of leguminous plants. Beans are rich in nitrogen compounds and proteins and are grown both for human consumption and as food for cattle and horses. Varieties of bean are grown throughout Europe, the USA, South America, China, Japan, Southeast Asia, and Australia.

**bear** large mammal with a heavily built body, short powerful limbs, and a very short tail. Bears breed once a year, producing one to four cubs. In northern regions they hibernate, and the young are born in the winter den. They are found mainly in North America and northern Asia. The skin of the polar bear is black to conserve 80–90% of the solar energy trapped and channelled down the hollow hairs of its fur.

**Bear, Great and Little** common names (and translations of the Latin) for the constellations →Ursa Major and →Ursa Minor respectively.

**bearing** device used in a machine to allow free movement between two parts, typically the rotation of a shaft in a housing. **Ball bearings** consist of two rings, one fixed to a housing, one to the rotating shaft. Between them is a set, or race, of steel balls. They are widely used to support shafts, as in the spindle in the hub of a bicycle wheel.

**Beat Generation** (or Beat movement) US social and literary movement of the 1950s and early 1960s. Members of the Beat Generation, called **beatniks**, responded to the conformist materialism of the period by adopting lifestyles derived from Henry David Thoreau's social disobedience and Walt Whitman's poetry of the open road. The most influential writers were Jack →Kerouac (who is credited with coining the term), Allen →Ginsberg, and William Burroughs.

**Beatles, the** English pop group 1960–70. The members, all born in Liverpool, were John →Lennon (1940–1980, rhythm guitar, vocals), Paul McCartney (1942– , bass, vocals), George Harrison (1943– , lead guitar, vocals), and Ringo Starr (formerly Richard Starkey, 1940– , drums). Using songs written largely by Lennon and McCartney, the Beatles dominated rock music and pop culture in the 1960s.

**Beaufort scale** system of recording wind velocity (speed), devised by Francis Beaufort in 1806. It is a numerical scale ranging from 0 to 17, calm being indicated by 0 and a hurricane by 12; 13–17 indicate degrees of hurricane force.

**Becket, St Thomas à** (1118–1170) English priest and politician. He was chancellor to Henry II 1155–62, when he was appointed archbishop of Canterbury. The interests of the church

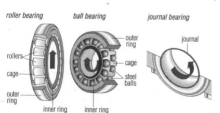

*roller bearing*    *ball bearing*    *journal bearing*

rollers — cage — outer ring — inner ring — outer ring — cage — steel balls — inner ring — journal

**bearing** Three types of bearing. The roller and the ball bearing are similar, differing only in the shape of the parts that roll when the middle shaft turns. The simpler journal bearing consists of a sleeve, or journal, lining the surface of the rotating shaft. The bearing is lubricated to reduce friction and wear.

## THE BEAUFORT SCALE

The Beaufort scale is a system of recording wind velocity (speed) devised in 1806 by Francis Beaufort (1774–1857). It is a numerical scale ranging from 0 to 12, calm being indicated by 0 and a hurricane by 12. The scale received international recognition in 1874. Measurements are made at 10 m/33 ft above ground level.

| Force | Description | Features | Air Speed | |
|-------|-------------|----------|-----------|-----|
| | | | kph | mph |
| 0 | calm | smoke rises vertically; water smooth | 0–2 | 0–1 |
| 1 | light air | smoke shows wind direction; water ruffled | 2–5 | 1–3 |
| 2 | light breeze | leaves rustle; wind felt on face | 6–11 | 4–7 |
| 3 | gentle breeze | loose paper blows around | 12–19 | 8–12 |
| 4 | moderate breeze | branches sway | 20–29 | 13–18 |
| 5 | fresh breeze | small trees sway, leaves blown off | 30–39 | 19–24 |
| 6 | strong breeze | whistling in telephone wires; sea spray from waves | 40–50 | 25–31 |
| 7 | near gale | large trees sway | 51–61 | 32–38 |
| 8 | gale | twigs break from trees | 62–74 | 39–46 |
| 9 | strong gale | branches break from trees | 75–87 | 47–54 |
| 10 | storm | trees uprooted; weak buildings collapse | 88–101 | 55–63 |
| 11 | violent storm | widespread damage | 102–117 | 64–73 |
| 12 | hurricane | widespread structural damage | above 118 | above 74 |

soon conflicted with those of the crown and Becket was assassinated; he was canonized in 1172.

**Beckett, Samuel Barclay** (1906–1989) Irish dramatist, novelist, and poet, who wrote in both French and English. His play *En attendant Godot* – first performed in Paris 1952, and then in his own translation as *Waiting for Godot* in London in 1955 and New York in 1956 – and his later drama, such as *Fin de partie/Endgame* (1957–58) and *Happy Days* (1961), won him international acclaim. He was awarded the Nobel Prize for Literature in 1969.

**Bede** (c. 673–735) English theologian and historian, known as **the Venerable Bede**. Active in Durham and Northumbria, he wrote many scientific, theological, and historical works. His *Historia Ecclesiastica Gentis Anglorum* (*Ecclesiastical History of the English People*) of 731 is a primary source for early English history, and was translated into the vernacular by King Alfred.

**bee** four-winged insect of the superfamily Apoidea in the order Hymenoptera, usually with a sting. There are over 12,000 species, of which fewer than 1 in 20 are social in habit. The **hive bee** or **honeybee** *Apis mellifera* establishes perennial colonies of about 80,000, the majority being infertile females (workers), with a few larger fertile males (drones), and a single very large fertile female (the queen). Worker bees live for no more than a few weeks, while a drone may live a few months, and a queen several years. Queen honeybees lay two kinds of eggs: fertilized, female eggs, which have two sets of chromosomes and develop into workers or queens, and unfertilized, male eggs, which have only one set of chromosomes and develop into drones.

**Beethoven, Ludwig van** (1770–1827) German composer and pianist. His mastery of musical expression in every genre made him the dominant influence on 19th-century music. Beethoven's repertoire includes concert overtures; the opera *Fidelio* (1805, revised 1806

and 1814); 5 piano concertos and 2 for violin (one unfinished); 32 piano sonatas, including the *Moonlight* (1801) and *Appassionata* (1804–05); 17 string quartets; the Mass in D (*Missa solemnis*) (1819–22); and 9 symphonies, as well as many youthful works. He usually played his own piano pieces and conducted his orchestral works until he was hampered by deafness in 1801; nevertheless he continued to compose.

**beetle** common name for insects in the order Coleoptera (Greek 'sheath-winged') with leathery forewings folding down in a protective sheath over the membranous hindwings, which are those used for flight. They pass through a complete metamorphosis. They include some of the largest and smallest of all insects: the largest is the **Hercules beetle** *Dynastes hercules* of the South American rainforests, 15 cm/6 in long; the smallest is only 0.05 cm/0.02 in long. Comprising more than 50% of the animal kingdom, beetles number some 370,000 named species, with many not yet described.

---

### WEB SITE > > > > > > > >

**Beetles**

http://www.ent.iastate.edu/imagegal/coleoptera/

Colour photographs of numerous beetle species from Iowa State University's Entomology Image Gallery.

---

**Begin, Menachem** (1913–1992) Israeli politician. He was leader of the extremist Irgun Zvai Leumi organization in

Palestine from 1942 and prime minister of Israel 1977–83, as head of the right-wing Likud party. Following strong encouragement from US president Jimmy Carter, he entered into negotiations with President Anwar Sadat of Egypt, which resulted in the Camp David Agreements. In 1978 he and Sadat were jointly awarded the Nobel Peace Prize. In 1981 Begin won a new term of office but his health was failing. The death of his wife in 1982 was a grave blow, resulting in his retirement in September 1983. For the rest of his life he was a virtual recluse.

**behaviour therapy** in psychology, the application of behavioural principles, derived from learning theories, to the treatment of clinical conditions such as phobias, obsessions, and sexual and interpersonal problems.

**Beijing** (or Peking, 'northern capital') capital of China; parts of the northeast municipal boundary coincide with sections of the Great Wall of China; population (1994) 7,084,000. The municipality of Beijing has an area of 17,800 sq km/6,871 sq mi and a population (1996) of 12,590,000. Industries include engineering and the production of steel, vehicles, textiles, and petrochemicals.

**Beirut** (or Beyrouth) capital and port of Lebanon, 90 km/60 mi northwest of Damascus, situated on a promontory into the eastern Mediterranean with the Lebanon Mountains behind it; population (1993) 1,200,000. It was devastated by civil war in the 1970s and 1980s. The city dates back to at least 1400 BC.

**Belarus** Republic of; **national name:** *Respublika Belarus*; **area:** 207,600 sq km/80,154 sq mi; **capital:** Minsk (Mensk); **major towns/cities:** Gomel, Vitebsk, Mogilev, Bobruisk, Hrodna, Brest; **physical features:** more than 25% forested; rivers Dvina, Dnieper and its tributaries, including the Pripet and Beresina; the Pripet Marshes in the east; mild and damp climate; **head of state:** Alexandr Lukashenko from 1994; **head of government:** Syargey Ling from 1996; **political system:** emergent democracy; **currency:** rouble and zaichik; **GNP per capita (PPP):** (US$) 4,100 (1998 est); **exports:** machinery, chemicals and petrochemicals, iron and steel, light industrial goods. Principal market Russia 65.5% (1998); **population:** 10,275,000 (1999 est); **language:** Belorussian (official); Russian, Polish; **religion:** Russian Orthodox, Roman Catholic; Baptist, Muslim, and Jewish minorities; **life expectancy:** 62 (men); 74 (women) (1995–2000).

**Belfast** (Irish *Beal Feirste* 'the mouth of the Farset') city and industrial port in County Antrim and County Down, Northern Ireland, at the mouth of the River Lagan on Belfast Lough; county town of County →Antrim, and capital of Northern Ireland since 1920; **population:** (1994 est) 290,000 (Protestants form the majority in east Belfast, Catholics in the west); **industries:** aircraft components, engineering, electronics, fertilizers, food processing, textiles; linen and shipbuilding have declined in importance since the 19th century, although some attempt is being made to revive these industries; **features:** City Hall (1906); Stormont (the former parliament buildings and from 1998 the seat of the Northern Ireland Assembly); Waterfront Hall, opened in 1997; the Linen Hall Library (1788); Belfast Castle (built 1870; former home of the Donegall family); Queen's University (1849, 1909).

**Belgium** Kingdom of; **national name:** French *Royaume de Belgique*, Flemish *Koninkrijk België*; **area:** 30,510 sq km/11,779 sq mi; **capital:** Brussels; **major towns/cities:** Antwerp, Ghent, Liège, Charleroi, Bruges, Mons, Namur, Leuven; **major ports:** Antwerp, Ostend, Zeebrugge; **physical features:** fertile coastal plain in north-west, central rolling hills rise eastwards, hills and forest in southeast; Ardennes Forest; rivers Schelde and Meuse; **head of state:** King Albert II from 1993; **head of government:** Guy Verhofstadt from 1999; **political system:** federal constitutional monarchy; **currency:** Belgian franc; **GNP per capita (PPP):** (US$) 23,480 (1998); **exports:** food, livestock and livestock products, gem diamonds, iron and steel manufacturers, machinery and transport equipment, chemicals and related products. Principal market Germany 19% (1998); **population:** 10,152,000 (1999 est); **language:** in the north (Flanders) Flemish (a Dutch dialect, known as *Vlaams*) 55%; in the south (Wallonia) Walloon (a French dialect) 32%; bilingual 11%; German

(eastern border) 0.6%. Dutch is official in the north, French in the south; Brussels is officially bilingual; **religion:** Roman Catholic 75%, various Protestant denominations; **life expectancy:** 74 (men); 81 (women) (1995–2000).

**Belize** (formerly **British Honduras**); **area:** 22,963 sq km/8,866 sq mi; **capital:** Belmopan; **major towns/cities:** Belize City, Dangriga, Orange Walk, Corozal; **major ports:** Belize City, Dangriga, Punta Gorda; **physical features:** tropical swampy coastal plain, Maya Mountains in south; over 90% forested; **head of state:** Elizabeth II from 1981, represented by governor general Dr Norbert Colville Young from 1993; **head of government:** Said Musa from 1998; **political system:** constitutional monarchy; **currency:** Belize dollar; **GNP per capita (PPP):** (US$) 3,940 (1998); **exports:** sugar, clothes, citrus products, forestry and fish products, bananas. Principal market UK 45.5% (1997); **population:** 235,000 (1999 est); **language:** English (official), Spanish (widely spoken), Creole dialects; **religion:** Roman Catholic 60%, Protestant 35%; **life expectancy:** 73 (men); 76 (women) (1995– 2000).

**Bell, Alexander Graham** (1847–1922) Scottish-born US scientist and inventor. He was the first person ever to transmit speech from one point to another by electrical means. This invention – the telephone – was made in 1876. Later Bell experimented with a type of phonograph and, in aeronautics, invented the tricycle undercarriage.

**Bellini, Vincenzo** (1801–1835) Italian composer of operas. He collaborated with the tenor Giovanni Battista Rubini (1794–1854) to develop a new simplicity of melodic expression in romantic evocations of classic themes, as in *La sonnambula/The Sleepwalker* and *Norma* (both 1831). In *I puritani/The Puritans* (1835), his last work, he discovered a new boldness and vigour of orchestral effect.

**Benares** alternative transliteration of →Varanasi, a holy Hindu city in Uttar Pradesh, India.

**Benedict, St** (*c.* 480–*c.* 547) founder of Christian monasticism in the West and of the Benedictine order. He founded the monastery of Monte Cassino and others in Italy. His feast day is 11 July.

**Bengal, Bay of** part of the Indian Ocean lying between the east coast of India and the west coast of Myanmar (Burma) and the Malay Peninsula.

**Ben-Gurion, David** (1886–1973) adopted name of David Gruen, Israeli statesman and socialist politician. He was one of the founders of the state of Israel, the country's first prime minister 1948–53, and again 1955–63. He retired from politics in 1970, but remained a lasting symbol of the Israeli state.

**Benin** former African kingdom 1200–1897, now a province of Nigeria. It reached the height of its power in the 14th–17th centuries when it ruled the area between the Niger Delta and Lagos. The province trades in timber and rubber.

**Benin** People's Republic of (formerly known as **Dahomey** 1904–75); **national name:** *République Populaire du Bénin*; **area:** 112,622 sq km/43,483 sq mi; **capital:** Porto-Novo (official), Cotonou (de facto); **major towns/cities:** Abomey, Natitingou, Parakou, Kandi, Ouidah, Djougou, Bohicou; **major ports:** Cotonou; **physical features:** flat to undulating terrain; hot and humid in south; semiarid in north; coastal lagoons with fishing villages on stilts; Niger River in northeast; **head of state:** Mathieu Kerekou from 1996; **head of government:** vacant from 1998; **political system:** socialist pluralist republic; **currency:** franc CFA; **GNP per capita (PPP):** (US$) 1,250 (1998); **exports:** cotton, crude petroleum, palm oil and other palm products. Principal market Brazil 18.2% (1997); **population:** 5,937,000 (1999 est); **language:** French (official); Fon 47% and Yoruba 9% in south; six major tribal languages in north; **religion:** animist 60%, Muslim, Roman Catholic; **life expectancy:** 52 (men); 55 (women) (1995–2000).

**Bennett, Alan** (1934– ) English dramatist and screenwriter. His works (often set in his native north of England) treat such subjects as class, senility, illness, and death with macabre comedy. They include the series of monologues for television *Talking Heads* (1988) and *Talking Heads 2* (1998), and the play *The Madness of George III* (1991), made into the critically acclaimed film *The Madness of King George* (1995) (Academy Award for best adapted screenplay).

**Bennett, (Enoch) Arnold** (1867–1931) English novelist, playwright, and journalist. His major works are set in the industrial 'five towns' of the Potteries in Staffordshire (now Stoke-on-Trent) and are concerned with the manner in which the environment dictates the pattern of his characters' lives. They include *Anna of the Five Towns* (1902), *The Old Wives' Tale* (1908), and the trilogy *Clayhanger*, *Hilda Lessways*, and *These Twain* (1910–15).

**Ben Nevis** highest mountain in the British Isles (1,344 m/4,409 ft), 7 km/4 mi southeast of Fort William, Scotland.

**Benz, Karl Friedrich** (1844–1929) German automobile engineer. He produced the world's first petrol-driven motor vehicle. He built his first model engine 1878 and the petrol-driven car 1885.

**benzene** $C_6H_6$ clear liquid hydrocarbon of characteristic odour, occurring in coal tar. It is used as a solvent and in the synthesis of many chemicals.

**Beowulf** Old English poem of 3,182 lines, thought to have been composed in the first half of the 8th century. It is the only complete surviving example of Germanic folk epic and exists in a single manuscript copied in England about 1000 and now housed in the Cottonian collection of the British Museum, London.

**Bergman, (Ernst) Ingmar** (1918– ) Swedish stage and film director. He is regarded by many as a unique auteur and one of the masters of modern cinema. His work deals with complex moral, psychological, and metaphysical problems. Bergman gained an international reputation with *Det sjunde inseglet/The Seventh Seal* and *Smultronstället/Wild Strawberries*, both 1957. He has also directed *Junfrukällan/The Virgin Spring* (1959), *Tystnaden/The Silence* (1963), *Persona* (1966), *Viskningar och rop/Cries and Whispers* (1972), and *Fanny och Alexander/Fanny and Alexander* (1982).

**Bergman, Ingrid** (1915–1982) Swedish-born actor. Having moved to the USA 1939 to appear in David O Selznick's remake of the Swedish film *Intermezzo* (1936) in which she had first come to prominence, she went on to

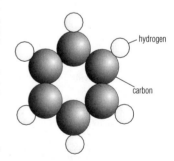

**benzene** The molecule of benzene consists of six carbon atoms arranged in a ring, with six hydrogen atoms attached. The benzene ring structure is found in many naturally occurring organic compounds.

appear in such Hollywood classics as *Casablanca* (1942), *For Whom the Bell Tolls* (1943), *Gaslight* (1944) (for which she won an Academy Award), and *Notorious* (1946).

**Berlin** industrial city and capital of the Federal Republic of Germany, lying on the River Spree; population (1995) 3,470,200. Products include machine tools, engineering goods (including cars), electrical goods, paper, food and drink, and printed works. After the division of Germany in 1949, East Berlin became the capital of East Germany and Bonn was made the provisional capital of West Germany. The Berlin Wall divided the city from 1961 until it was dismantled in 1989. Following the reunification of Germany on 3 October 1990, East and West Berlin were once more reunited as the 16th *Land* (state) of the Federal Republic.

**Berlin, Irving** (1888–1989) adopted name of Israel Baline, Russian-born US songwriter. His songs include hits such as 'Alexander's Ragtime Band' (1911), 'Always' (1925), 'God Bless America' (1917, published 1939), and 'White Christmas' (1942), and the musicals *Top Hat* (1935), *Annie Get Your Gun* (1946), and *Call Me Madam* (1950). He also provided songs for films like *Blue Skies* (1946) and *Easter Parade* (1948). His 'White Christmas' has been the most performed Christmas song in history, with more than 500 versions recorded.

**Berlioz, (Louis) Hector** (1803–1869) French Romantic composer. He is noted as the founder of modern orchestration. Much of his music was inspired by drama and literature and has a theatrical quality. He wrote symphonic works, such as *Symphonie fantastique* (1830–31) and *Roméo et Juliette* (1839); dramatic cantatas including *La Damnation de Faust* (1846) and *L'Enfance du Christ* (1850–54); sacred music; and three operas: *Benvenuto Cellini* (1838), *Les Troyens* (1856–58), and *Béatrice et Bénédict* (1860–62).

**Bermuda** British colony in the Northwest Atlantic Ocean; **area:** 54 sq km/21 sq mi; **capital:** and chief port Hamilton; **features:** consists of about 150 small islands, of which 20 are inhabited, linked by bridges and causeways; **industries:** Easter lilies, pharmaceuticals; tourism, banking, and insurance are important; **currency:** Bermuda dollar; **population:** (1994) 60,500; **language:** English; **religion:** Christian; **government:** under the constitution of 1968, Bermuda is a fully self-governing British colony, with a governor (Lord Waddington from 1992), senate, and elected House of Assembly (premier from 1997 Pamela Gordon, United Bermuda Party); **history:** the islands were named after Juan de Bermudez, who visited them in 1515, and were settled by British colonists in 1609. It is Britain's oldest colony, officially taken by the crown in 1684. Indian and African slaves were transported from 1616 and soon outnumbered the white settlers. Racial violence in 1977 led to intervention, at the request of the government, by British troops. A 1995 referendum rejected independence.

**Bernoulli's principle** law stating that the pressure of a fluid varies inversely with speed, an increase in speed producing a decrease in pressure (such as a drop in hydraulic pressure as the fluid speeds up flowing through a constriction in a pipe) and vice versa. The principle also explains the pressure differences on each surface of an aerofoil, which gives lift to the wing of an aircraft. The principle was named after Swiss mathematician and physicist Daniel Bernoulli.

**Bernstein, Leonard** (1918–1990) US composer, conductor, and pianist. He is one of the most energetic and versatile 20th-century US musicians. His works, which established a vogue for realistic, contemporary themes, include symphonies such as *The Age of Anxiety* (1949), ballets such as *Fancy Free* (1944), and scores for musicals, including *Wonderful Town* (1953), *West Side Story* (1957), and *Mass* (1971) in memory of President J F Kennedy.

**Bessemer process** the first cheap method of making steel, invented by Henry Bessemer in England 1856. It has since been superseded by more efficient steel-making processes, such as the →basic–oxygen process. In the Bessemer process compressed air is blown into the bottom of a converter, a furnace shaped like a cement mixer, containing molten pig iron. The excess carbon in the iron burns out, other impurities form a slag, and the furnace is emptied by tilting.

**beta particle** electron ejected with great velocity from a radioactive atom that is undergoing spontaneous disintegration. Beta particles do not exist in the nucleus but are created on disintegration, beta decay, when a neutron converts to a proton to emit an electron.

**Bethlehem** (Arabic *Beit-Lahm*) city on the west bank of the River Jordan, 8 km/5 mi south of Jerusalem; population (1997 est) 135,000. It was occupied by Israel in 1967 and came under control of the Palestinian Authority in December 1995. In the Bible it is mentioned as the birthplace of King David and Jesus, and in 326 AD the Church of the Nativity was built over the grotto said to be the birthplace of Jesus.

**Betjeman, John** (1906–1984) English poet and essayist. He was the originator of a peculiarly English light verse, nostalgic, and delighting in Victorian and Edwardian architecture. He also wrote prose works on architecture and social history which reflect his interest in the Gothic Revival. His *Collected Poems* appeared in 1958 and a verse autobiography, *Summoned by Bells*, in 1960.

**Bevan, Aneurin (Nye)** (1897–1960) British Labour politician. Son of a Welsh miner, and himself a miner at 13, he was member of Parliament for Ebbw Vale 1929–60. As minister of health 1945–51, he inaugurated the National Health Service (NHS).

***Bhagavad-Gītā*** (Hindi 'the Song of the Blessed') religious and philosophical Sanskrit poem, dating from around 300 BC, forming an episode in the sixth book of the *Mahābhārata*, one of the two great Hindu epics. It is the supreme religious work of Hinduism.

**Bhopal** industrial city and capital of Madhya Pradesh, central India, 525 km/326 mi southwest of Allahabad; population (1991) 1,064,000. Textiles, chemicals, electrical goods, and jewellery are manufactured. Nearby Bhimbetka Caves, discovered in 1973, have the world's largest collection of prehistoric paintings, about 10,000 years old. In 1984 some 2,600 people died from an escape of the poisonous gas methyl isocyanate from a factory owned by US company Union Carbide; another 300,000 suffer from long-term health problems.

**Bhutan** Kingdom of; **national name:** *Druk-yul;* **area:** 46,500 sq km/17,953 sq mi; **capital:** Thimphu (Thimbu); **major towns/cities:** Paro, Punakha, Mongar, P'sholing, W'phodrang, Bumthang; **physical features:** occupies southern slopes of the Himalayas; Gangkar Punsum (7,529 m/24,700 ft) is one of the world's highest unclimbed peaks; cut by valleys formed by tributaries of the Brahmaputra; thick forests in south; **head of state:** Jigme Singye Wangchuk from 1972; **head of government:** Lyonpo Jigme Thimley from 1998; **political system:** absolute monarchy to 1998, when the king conceded political powers to the National Assembly; **currency:** ngultrum; also Indian currency;

**GNP per capita (PPP):** (US$) 1,180 (1997 est); **exports:** cardamon, cement, timber, fruit, electricity (to India), precious stones, spices. Principal market India 90.7% (1997); **population:** 2,064,000 (1999 est); **language:** Dzongkha (official, a Tibetan dialect), Sharchop, Bumthap, Nepali, and English; **religion:** 70% Mahayana Buddhist (state religion), 25% Hindu; **life expectancy:** 60 (men); 62 (women) (1995–2000).

**Bhutto, Benazir** (1953–  ) Pakistani politician. She was leader of the Pakistan People's Party (PPP) from 1984, a position she held in exile until 1986. Bhutto became prime minister of Pakistan from 1988–90, when the opposition manoeuvred her from office and charged her with corruption. She again rose to the office of prime minister (1993–96), only to be removed for a second time under suspicion of corruption, an offence for which she was charged late in 1998.

**Biafra, Republic of** African state proclaimed 1967 when fears that Nigerian central government was increasingly in the hands of the rival Hausa tribe led the predominantly Ibo Eastern Region of Nigeria to secede under Lt-Col Odumegwu Ojukwu. On the proclamation of Biafra, civil war ensued with the rest of the federation. In a bitterly fought campaign federal forces confined the Biafrans to a shrinking area of the interior by 1968, and by 1970 Biafra ceased to exist. Around 1 million Biafrans died in the famine caused by the civil war.

**Bible** (Greek *ta biblia* 'the books') the sacred book of the Jewish and Christian religions. The Hebrew Bible, recognized by both Jews and Christians, is called the **Old Testament** by Christians. The **New Testament** comprises books recognized by the Christian church from the 4th century as canonical. The Roman Catholic Bible also includes the →**Apocrypha**.

**Big Bang** in astronomy, the hypothetical 'explosive' event that marked the origin of the universe as we know it. At the time of the Big Bang, the entire universe was squeezed into a hot, superdense state. The Big Bang explosion threw this compact material outwards, producing the expanding universe (see →red shift). The cause of the Big Bang is unknown; observations of the current rate of expansion of the universe suggest that it took place about 10–20 billion years ago. The Big Bang theory began modern →cosmology.

**Bihar** (or Behar state) of northeast India; **area:** 173,900 sq km/67,125 sq mi; **capital:** Patna; **physical:** River Ganges runs west–east in the north, through intensely cultivated alluvial plains, prone to drought and floods; Rajmahal Hills, Chota Nagpur plateau in the south, much of which is forested; **industries:** copper, iron, coal; 40% of India's mineral production; **agriculture:** rice, jute, sugar cane, cereals, oilseed, tobacco, potatoes; **language:** Hindi, Bihari; **population:** (1994 est) 93,080,000, 75% living in northern plains; **famous people:** Chandragupta Maurya, Asoka; **history:** the ancient kingdom of Magadha roughly corresponded to central and south Bihar. Many Bihari people were massacred as a result of their protest at the establishment of Bangladesh in 1971. Elections were postponed and direct rule imposed after public disturbances in 1995.

**bile** brownish alkaline fluid produced by the liver. Bile is stored in the gall bladder and is intermittently released into the duodenum (small intestine) to aid digestion. Bile consists of bile salts, bile pigments, cholesterol, and lecithin. Bile salts assist in the breakdown and absorption of fats; bile pigments are the breakdown products of old red blood cells that are passed into the gut to be eliminated with the faeces.

**billiards** indoor game played, normally by two players, with tapered poles (cues) and composition balls (one red, two white) on a rectangular table covered with a green, feltlike cloth (baize). The table has six pockets, one at each corner and in each of the long sides at the middle. Scoring strokes are made by potting the red ball, potting the opponent's ball, or potting another ball off one of these two. The cannon (when the cue ball hits the two other balls on the table) is another scoring stroke. In 1998 billiards received recognition from the International Olympic Committee as an Olympic sport, along with snooker, pool, and carom (or French) billiards.

**Bill of Rights** in the USA, the first ten amendments to the US Constitution, incorporated 1791:

1 guarantees freedom of worship, of speech, of the press, of assembly, and to petition the government;

2 grants the right to keep and bear arms;

3 prohibits billeting of soldiers in private homes in peacetime;

4 forbids unreasonable search and seizure;

5 guarantees none be 'deprived of life, liberty or property without due process of law' or compelled in any criminal case to be a witness against himself or herself;

6 grants the right to speedy trial, to call witnesses, and to have defence counsel;

7 grants the right to trial by jury of one's peers;

8 prevents the infliction of excessive bail or fines, or 'cruel and unusual punishment';

9 provide a safeguard to the states and

10 people for all rights not specifically delegated to the central government.

**Bill of Rights** in Britain, an act of Parliament of 1689 which established Parliament as the primary governing body of the country. It made provisions limiting royal prerogative with respect to legislation, executive power, money levies, courts, and the army, and stipulated Parliament's consent to many government functions.

**binary number system** system of numbers to →base two, using combinations of the digits 1 and 0. Codes based on binary numbers are used to represent instructions and data in all modern digital computers, the values of the binary digits (contracted to 'bits') being stored or transmitted as, for example, open/closed switches, magnetized/unmagnetized disks and tapes, and high/low voltages in circuits.

**binary star** pair of stars moving in orbit around their common centre of mass. Observations show that most stars are binary, or even multiple – for example, the nearest star system to the Sun, Rigil Kent.

**biochemistry** science concerned with the chemistry of living organisms: the structure and reactions of proteins (such as enzymes), nucleic acids, carbohydrates, and lipids.

**biodiversity** contraction of **biological diversity** measure of the variety of the Earth's animal, plant, and microbial species; of genetic differences within species; and of the ecosystems that support those species. Its maintenance is important for ecological stability and as a resource for research into, for example, new drugs and crops. In the 20th century, the destruction of habitats is believed to have resulted in the most

**binary number code**

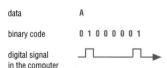

| data | A |
| binary code | 0 1 0 0 0 0 0 1 |
| digital signal in the computer | |

**binary number system** The capital letter A represented in binary form.

severe and rapid loss of biodiversity in the history of the planet.

**biological control** control of pests such as insects and fungi through biological means, rather than the use of chemicals. This can include breeding resistant crop strains; inducing sterility in the pest; infecting the pest species with disease organisms; or introducing the pest's natural predator. Biological control tends to be naturally self-regulating, but as ecosystems are so complex, it is difficult to predict all the consequences of introducing a biological controlling agent.

**biology** (Greek *bios* 'life', *logos* 'discourse') science of life. Biology includes all the life sciences – for example, anatomy and physiology (the study of the structure of living things), cytology (the study of cells), zoology (the study of animals) and botany (the study of plants), ecology (the study of habitats and the interaction of living species), animal behaviour, embryology, and taxonomy, and plant breeding. Increasingly in the 20th century biologists have concentrated on molecular structures: biochemistry, biophysics, and genetics (the study of inheritance and variation).

**biosphere** the narrow zone that supports life on our planet. It is limited to the waters of the Earth, a fraction of its crust, and the lower regions of the atmosphere. The biosphere is made up of all the Earth's ecosystems. It is affected by external forces such as the Sun's rays, which provide energy, the gravitational effects of the Sun and Moon, and cosmic radiations.

**biotechnology** industrial use of living organisms to manufacture food, drugs, or other products. The brewing and baking industries have long relied on the yeast micro-organism for fermentation purposes, while the dairy industry employs a range of bacteria and fungi to convert milk into cheeses and yoghurts. →Enzymes, whether extracted from cells or produced artificially, are central to most biotechnological applications.

**bird** backboned animal of the class Aves, the biggest group of land vertebrates, characterized by warm blood, feathers, wings, breathing through lungs, and egg-laying by the female. Birds are bipedal; feet are usually adapted for perching and never have more than four toes. Hearing and eyesight are well developed, but the sense of smell is usually poor. No existing species of bird possesses teeth.

Most birds fly, but some groups (such as ostriches) are flightless, and others include flightless members. Many communicate by sounds (nearly half of all known species are songbirds) or by visual displays, in connection with which many species are brightly coloured, usually the males. Birds have highly developed patterns of instinctive behaviour. There are nearly 8,500 species of birds.

**Birmingham** industrial city and administrative headquarters of West Midlands metropolitan county, central England, second-largest city in the UK, 177 km/ 110 mi northwest of London; population (1994 est) 1,220,000, metropolitan area 2,632,000. It is a major manufacturing, engineering, commercial, and service centre. The city's concert halls, theatres, and three universities also make it an important cultural and educational centre. Its chief products are motor vehicles, vehicle components and accessories, machine tools, aerospace control systems, electrical equipment, plastics, chemicals, food, chocolate (Cadbury), jewellery, tyres, glass, cars, and guns.

**birth** act of producing live young from within the body of female animals. Both viviparous and ovoviviparous animals give birth to young. In viviparous animals, embryos obtain nourishment from the mother via a →placenta or other means.

In ovoviviparous animals, fertilized eggs develop and hatch in the oviduct of the mother and gain little or no nourishment from maternal tissues. See also →pregnancy.

**Biscay, Bay of** bay of the Atlantic Ocean between northern Spain and western France, known for rough seas and high tides. It is traditionally a rich fishing area.

**Bismarck, Otto Eduard Leopold von** (1815–1898) German politician, prime minister of Prussia 1862–90 and chancellor of the German Empire 1871–90. He pursued an aggressively expansionist policy, waging wars against Denmark 1863–64, Austria 1866, and France

1870–71, which brought about the unification of Germany. He became Prince 1871.

**Bissau** capital and chief port of Guinea-Bissau, on an island at the mouth of the Geba River; population (1992) 145,000. Originally a Portuguese fortified slave-trading centre (1687), Bissau became a free port in 1869. Industries include agricultural processing, fishing, textiles, and crafts. There are refrigeration units at the port, and there is an international airport and a university. Bissau replaced Bolama as the capital in 1941.

**bit** (contraction of binary digit) in computing, a single binary digit, either 0 or 1. A bit is the smallest unit of data stored in a computer; all other data must be coded into a pattern of individual bits. A →byte represents sufficient computer memory to store a single character of data, and usually contains eight bits. For example, in the →ASCII code system used by most microcomputers the capital letter A would be stored in a single byte of memory as the bit pattern 01000001.

**bitumen** impure mixture of hydrocarbons, including such deposits as petroleum, asphalt, and natural gas, although sometimes the term is restricted to a soft kind of pitch resembling asphalt.

**Bizet, Georges (Alexandre César Léopold)** (1838–1875) French composer of operas. Among his works are *Les Pêcheurs de perles*/*The Pearl Fishers* (1863) and *La Jolie Fille de Perth*/*The Fair Maid of Perth* (1866). He also wrote the concert overture *Patrie* and incidental music to Alphonse Daudet's play *L'Arlésienne* (1872), which has remained a standard work in the form of two suites for orchestra. His operatic masterpiece *Carmen* was produced a few months before his death in 1875. His Symphony in C, written when he was 17, is now frequently performed.

**Black Death** great epidemic of bubonic →plague that ravaged Europe in the mid-14th century, killing between one-third and half of the population (about 75 million people). The cause of the plague was the bacterium *Yersinia pestis*, transmitted by fleas borne by migrating Asian black rats. The name Black Death was first used in England in the early 19th century.

---

**WEB SITE** > > > > > > > >

**Black Death**

http//history.idbsu.edu/westciv/plague

Part of a larger site on the history of western civilization maintained by Boise State University, this page provides an introduction to the Black Death. Information is organized into 22 brief articles, each concerning a specific aspect of the plague. There is also a list of references for further study.

---

**Black Forest** (German *Schwarzwald*) mountainous region of coniferous forest in Baden-Württemberg, western Germany; length 160 km/100 mi, greatest breadth 57 km/35 mi. Bounded to the west and south by the Rhine, which separates it from the Vosges, it rises to 1,493 m/4,898 ft in the Feldberg. It extends to the Swiss border in the south and to the Neckar valley in the north. Parts of the forest have recently been affected by →acid rain. The region is a popular tourist destination and lumbering is an important industry.

**black hole** object in space whose gravity is so great that nothing can escape from it, not even light. Thought to form when massive stars shrink at the end of their lives, a black hole sucks in more matter, including other stars, from the space around it. Matter that falls into a black hole is squeezed to infinite density at the centre of the hole. Black holes can be detected because gas falling towards them becomes so hot that it emits X-rays.

**Black National State** area in the Republic of South Africa set aside 1971–94 for development towards self-government by black Africans, in accordance with →apartheid. Before 1980 these areas were known as **black homelands** or **bantustans**. Making up less than 14% of the country, they tended to be situated in arid areas (though some had mineral wealth), often in scattered blocks. Those that achieved nominal independence were Transkei in 1976, Bophuthatswana in 1977, Venda in 1979, and Ciskei in 1981. They were not recognized outside South Africa because of their racial basis.

**Black Sea** (Russian *Chernoye More*) inland sea in southeast Europe, linked with the seas of Azov and Marmara, and via the Dardanelles strait with the

Mediterranean; area 423,000 sq km/ 163,320 sq mi; maximum depth 2,245 m/7,365 ft, decreasing in the Sea of Azov to only 13.5 m/44 ft. It is bounded by Ukraine, Russia, Georgia, Turkey, Bulgaria, and Romania, and the rivers Danube, Volga, Bug, Dniester and Dnieper flow into it, keeping salinity levels low. Uranium deposits beneath it are among the world's largest. About 90% of the water is polluted, mainly by agricultural fertilizers.

**bladder** hollow elastic-walled organ which stores the urine produced in the kidneys. It is present in the →urinary systems of some fishes, most amphibians, some reptiles, and all mammals. Urine enters the bladder through two ureters, one leading from each kidney, and leaves it through the urethra.

**Blair, Tony (Anthony Charles Lynton)** (1953– ) British politician, born in Edinburgh, Scotland, leader of the Labour Party from 1994, prime minister from 1997. A centrist in the manner of his predecessor John Smith, he became Labour's youngest leader by a large majority in the first fully democratic elections to the post in July 1994. In 1995 he won approval of a new Labour Party charter, intended to distance the party from its traditional socialist base and promote 'social market' values. He and his party secured a landslide victory in the 1997 general election with a 179-seat majority.

**Blake, William** (1757–1827) English poet, artist, engraver, and visionary, and one of the most important figures of

English →Romanticism. His lyrics, often written with a childlike simplicity, as in *Songs of Innocence* (1789) and *Songs of Experience* (1794), express a unique spiritual vision. In his 'prophetic books', including *The Marriage of Heaven and Hell* (1790), he created a vast personal mythology. He illustrated his own works with hand-coloured engravings.

**blast furnace** smelting furnace used to extract metals from their ores, chiefly pig iron from iron ore. The temperature is raised by the injection of an air blast.

**Blériot, Louis** (1872–1936) French aviator. In a 24-horsepower monoplane of his own construction, he made the first flight across the English Channel 25 July 1909.

**Blitzkrieg** (German 'lightning war') swift military campaign, as used by Germany at the beginning of World War II 1939–41. It was characterized by rapid movement by mechanized forces, supported by tactical air forces acting as 'flying artillery' and is best exemplified by the campaigns in Poland 1939 and France 1940.

**Blixen, Karen (Christentze), Baroness Blixen** (1885–1962) born Dinesen Danish writer. She wrote mainly in English and is best known for her short stories, Gothic fantasies published in such collections as *Seven Gothic Tales* (1934) and *Winter's Tales* (1942) under the pen-name **Isak Dinesen**. Her autobiography *Out of Africa* (1937; filmed 1985) is based on her experience of running a coffee plantation in Kenya.

**blood** fluid circulating in the arteries, veins, and capillaries of vertebrate animals; the term also refers to the corresponding fluid in those invertebrates that possess a closed →circulatory system. Blood carries nutrients and oxygen to each body cell and removes waste products, such as carbon dioxide. It is also important in the immune response and, in many animals, in the distribution of heat throughout the body.

**blood clotting** complex series of events (known as the blood clotting cascade) that prevents excessive bleeding after injury. The result is the formation of a meshwork of protein fibres (fibrin) and trapped blood cells over the cut blood vessels.

**blood group** any of the types into which blood is classified according to the presence or otherwise of certain →antigens on the surface of its red cells. Red blood cells of one individual may carry molecules on their surface that act as antigens in another individual whose red blood cells lack these molecules. The two main antigens are designated A and B. These give rise to four blood groups: having A only (A), having B only (B), having both (AB), and having neither (O). Each of these groups may or may not contain the →rhesus factor. Correct typing of blood groups is vital in transfusion, since incompatible types of donor and recipient blood will result in coagulation, with possible death of the recipient.

**blood pressure** pressure, or tension, of the blood against the inner walls of blood vessels, especially the arteries, due to the muscular pumping activity of the heart. Abnormally high blood pressure (→hypertension) may be associated with various conditions or arise with no obvious cause; abnormally low blood pressure (hypotension) occurs in shock and after excessive fluid or blood loss from any cause.

**Bloomsbury Group** intellectual circle of writers and artists based in Bloomsbury, London, which flourished in the 1920s. It centred on the house of publisher Leonard Woolf and his wife, novelist Virginia →Woolf. Typically modernist, their innovative artistic contributions represented an important section of the English avant-garde.

**blowfly** any fly of the genus *Calliphora*, also known as bluebottle, or of the related genus *Lucilia*, when it is greenbottle. It lays its eggs in dead flesh, on which the maggots feed.

**blue-green algae** (or cyanobacteria) single-celled, primitive organisms that resemble bacteria in their internal cell organization, sometimes joined together in colonies or filaments. Blue-green algae are among the oldest known living organisms and, with bacteria, belong to the kingdom Monera; remains have been found in rocks up to 3.5 billion years old. They are widely distributed in aquatic habitats, on the damp surfaces of rocks and trees, and in the soil.

**Blue Nile** (Arabic *Al Bahr al-Azraq*) river rising at a spring site upstream of Lake Tana in Ethiopia, 2,150 m/7,054 ft above sea level. Flowing west then north for 1,460 km/907 mi, it eventually meets the White Nile at Khartoum. A length of 800 km/500 mi is navigable at high water. Some 80% of Sudan's electricity is provided by hydroelectric schemes at Roseires and Sennar, and these dams provide irrigation water for over 10,000 sq km/3,860 sq mi of the Gezira Plain.

**blues** African-American music that originated in the work songs and Negro spirituals of the rural American South in the late 19th century. It is characterized by a 12-bar, or occasionally 16-bar, construction and melancholy lyrics which relate tales of woe or unhappy love. The guitar has been the dominant instrument; harmonica and piano are also common. Blues guitar and vocal styles have played a vital part in the development of jazz, rock, and pop music in general.

**Blyton, Enid Mary** (1897–1968) English writer of children's books. Her books, though criticized for their predictability and lack of characterization, and more recently for social, racial, and sexual stereotyping, satisfy the reader's need for security. Her best-selling series were, the *Famous Five*, the *Secret Seven*, and *Noddy*.

**Boadicea** alternative (Latin) spelling of British queen →Boudicca.

**Boccaccio, Giovanni** (1313–1375) Italian writer and poet. He is chiefly known for the collection of tales called the *Decameron* (1348–53). Equally at home with tragic and comic narrative, he laid the foundations for the humanism of the Renaissance and raised vernacular literature to the status enjoyed by the ancient classics.

**Boer War** the second of the →South African Wars 1899–1902, waged between Dutch settlers in South Africa and the British.

**Boethius, Anicius Manlius Severinus** (AD 480–524) Roman philosopher. He wrote treatises on music and mathematics and *De Consolatione Philosophiae/The Consolation of Philosophy*, a dialogue in prose. It was translated into European languages during the Middle Ages.

**Bogart, Humphrey (DeForest)** (1899–1957) US film actor. He became an international cult figure through roles as a tough, romantic loner in such films as *High Sierra* (1941), *The Maltese Falcon* (1941), *Casablanca* (1942), *To Have and Have Not* (1944), *The Big Sleep* (1946), and *In a Lonely Place* (1950). He won an Academy Award for his role in *The African Queen* (1952).

**Bogotá** (originally Santa Fé de Bogotá) capital of Colombia, and of Cundinamarca department, situated at 2,640 m/8,660 ft above sea level, on the edge of the Eastern Cordillera plateau of the Andes; population (1994) 5,132,000. Main industries include textiles, chemicals, food processing, and tobacco. Bogotá is Colombia's largest city, and the financial, commercial, and cultural centre of the country. It has several universities and museums.

**Bohr, Niels Henrik David** (1885–1962) Danish physicist whose theoretical work established the structure of the atom and the validity of →quantum theory by showing that the nuclei of atoms are surrounded by shells of electrons, each assigned particular sets of quantum numbers according to their orbits. For this work he was awarded the Nobel Prize for Physics in 1922. He explained the structure and behaviour of the nucleus, as well as the process of nuclear fission. Bohr also proposed the doctrine of **complementarity**, the theory that a fundamental particle is neither a wave nor a particle, because these are complementary modes of description.

**boiling point** for any given liquid, the temperature at which the application of heat raises the temperature of the liquid no further, but converts it into vapour.

**Boleyn, Anne** (c. 1507–1536) Queen of England 1533–36 as the second wife of Henry VIII. She gave birth to the future Queen Elizabeth I in 1533, but was unable to produce a male heir to the throne, and was executed on a false charge.

**Bolívar, Simón** (1783–1830) South American nationalist, leader of revolutionary armies, known as **the Liberator**. He fought the Spanish colonial forces in several uprisings and eventually liberated Colombia in 1819, his native Venezuela in 1821, Ecuador in 1822, Peru in 1824, and Bolivia (a new state named after him, formerly Upper Peru) in 1825.

**Bolivia** Republic of; **national name:** *República de Bolivia*; **area:** 1,098,581 sq km/424,162 sq mi; **capital:** La Paz (seat of government), Sucre (legal capital and seat of judiciary); **major towns/cities:** Santa Cruz, Cochabamba, Oruro, El Alto, Potosí; **physical features:** high plateau (Altiplano) between mountain ridges (cordilleras); forest and lowlands (llano) in east; Andes; lakes Titicaca (the world's highest navigable lake, 3,800 m/12,500 ft) and Poopó; **head of state and government:** Hugo Banzer Suarez from 1997; **political system:** emergent democracy; **currency:** boliviano; **GNP per capita (PPP):** (US$) 2,820 (1998); **exports:** metallic minerals, natural gas, jewellery, soybeans, wood. Principal market UK 16.1% (1998). Illegal trade in coca and its derivatives (mainly cocaine) was worth approximately $600 million in 1990 – almost equal to annual earnings from official exports.; **population:** 8,142,000 (1999 est); **language:** Spanish (official); Aymara, Quechua; **religion:** Roman Catholic 95% (state-recognized); **life expectancy:** 60 (men); 63 (women) (1995–2000).

**Bolshevik** (from Russian *bolshinstvo* 'a majority') member of the majority of the Russian Social Democratic Party who split from the Mensheviks 1903. The Bolsheviks, under →Lenin, advocated the destruction of capitalist political and economic institutions, and the setting-up of a socialist state with power in the hands of the workers. The Bolsheviks set the →Russian Revolution 1917 in motion. They changed their name to the Russian Communist Party in 1918.

**Bonaparte** Corsican family of Italian origin that gave rise to the Napoleonic dynasty: Napoleon I, Napoleon II, and Napoleon III. Others were the brothers and sister of Napoleon I: **Joseph** (1768–1844) whom Napoleon made king of Naples 1806 and Spain 1808; **Lucien** (1775–1840) whose handling of the Council of Five Hundred on 10 November 1799 ensured Napoleon's future; **Louis** (1778–1846) the father of Napoleon III, who was made king of Holland 1806–10; also called (from 1810) comte de Saint Leu; **Caroline** (1782–1839) who married Joachim Murat 1800; full name Maria Annunciata Caroline; **Jerome** (1784–1860) made king of Westphalia 1807.

**bone** hard connective tissue comprising the →skeleton of most vertebrate animals. Bone is composed of a network of collagen fibres impregnated with mineral salts (largely calcium phosphate and calcium carbonate), a combination that gives it great density and strength, comparable in some cases with that of reinforced concrete. Enclosed within this solid matrix are bone cells, blood vessels, and nerves. The interior of the long bones of the limbs consists of a spongy matrix filled with a soft marrow that produces blood cells.

**section through a long bone (the femur)**

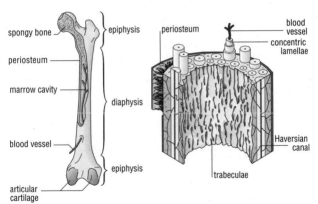

**bone** Bone is a network of fibrous material impregnated with mineral salts and as strong as reinforced concrete. The upper end of the thighbone or femur is made up of spongy bone, which has a fine lacework structure designed to transmit the weight of the body. The shaft of the femur consists of hard compact bone designed to resist bending. Fine channels carrying blood vessels, nerves, and lymphatics interweave even the densest bone.

**Boole, George** (1815–1864) English mathematician. His work *The Mathematical Analysis of Logic* (1847) established the basis of modern mathematical logic, and his **Boolean algebra** can be used in designing computers.

**boot** (or bootstrap) in computing, the process of starting up a computer. Most computers have a small, built-in boot program that starts automatically when the computer is switched on – its only task is to load a slightly larger program, usually from a hard disk, which in turn loads the main operating system.

**Bordeaux** administrative centre of the *département* of Gironde and of the Aquitaine region, southwest France, situated on the River Garonne, 100 km/62 mi from the Atlantic; population (1990) 213,300, conurbation 685,000. Bordeaux is accessible to seagoing ships and is a major port; it is a centre for the wine trade, oil refining, chemicals, and the aircraft and aeronautics industries. Other industries include shipbuilding, sugar refining, and the manufacture of electrical goods, motor vehicles, and processed foods. Bordeaux was under the English crown for three centuries until 1453. In 1870, 1914, and 1940 the French government was moved here because of German invasions.

**Borgia, Cesare** (c. 1475–1507) Italian general, illegitimate son of Pope Alexander VI. Made a cardinal at 17 by his father, he resigned to become captain-general of the papacy, campaigning successfully against the city republics of Italy. Ruthless and treacherous in war, he was an able ruler (a model for Machiavelli's *The Prince*), but his power crumbled on the death of his father. He was a patron of artists, including Leonardo da Vinci.

**Borgia, Lucrezia** (1480–1519) Duchess of Ferrara from 1501. She was the illegitimate daughter of Pope Alexander VI and sister of Cesare →Borgia. She was married at 12 and again at 13 to further her father's ambitions, both marriages being annulled by him. At 18 she was married again, but her husband was murdered in 1500 on the order of her brother, with whom (as well as with her father) she was said to have committed incest. Her final marriage was to the Alfonso d'Este, the heir to the duchy of Ferrara. She made the court a centre of culture and was a patron of authors and artists such as Ariosto and Titian.

**Borneo** third-largest island in the world, one of the Sunda Islands in the West Pacific; area 754,000 sq km/290,000 sq mi. It comprises the Malaysian territories of →Sabah and →Sarawak; Brunei; and, occupying by far the largest part, the Indonesian territory of **Kalimantan**. It is mountainous and densely forested. A forest fire in early 1998 destroyed 30,000 sq km/11,583 sq mi of forest.

**Bosch, Hieronymus** (c. 1460–1516) Jerome van Aken, early Dutch painter. His fantastic visions, often filled with bizarre and cruel images, depict a sinful world in which people are tormented by demons and weird creatures, as in *Hell*, a panel from the triptych *The Garden of Earthly Delights* (about 1505–10, Prado, Madrid). In their richness, complexity, and sheer strangeness, his pictures fore-shadow surrealism.

**Bosnia-Herzegovina** Republic of; **national name:** *Republika Bosna i Hercegovina*; **area:** 51,129 sq km/ 19,740 sq mi; **capital:** Sarajevo; **major towns/cities:** Banja Luka, Mostar, Prijedor, Tuzla, Zenica; **physical features:** barren, mountainous country, part of the Dinaric Alps; limestone gorges; 20 km/12 mi of coastline with no harbour; **heads of state:** Rotating chairman of the collective presidency, Ante Jelavic from 1999; **heads of government:** Co-prime ministers Haris Silajdzic (from 1997) and Svetozar Mihajlovic (from 1998); **political system:** emergent democracy; **currency:** dinar; **GNP per capita (PPP):** (US$) 450 (1996 est); **exports:** coal, domestic appliances (industrial production and mining remain low). Principal market Croatia 34.3% (1997); **population:** 3,838,000 (1999 est); **language:** Serbian variant of Serbo-Croatian; **religion:** Sunni Muslim, Serbian Orthodox, Roman Catholic; **life expectancy:** 71 (men); 76 (women) (1995–2000).

**Boston** industrial port and commercial centre, capital of Massachusetts, USA, on Massachusetts Bay; population (1992) 551,700; metropolitan area (1992) 5,439,000. Its economy is dom-inated by financial and health services and government. It is also a publishing and academic centre. The subway system (begun 1897) was the first in the USA. Boston's baseball team, the Red Sox, is based at Fenway Park. Boston was founded by Puritans in 1630 and has played an important role in American history.

**Boston Tea Party** protest 1773 by colonists in Massachusetts, USA, against the tea tax imposed on them by the British government before the American Revolution.

**Boswell, James** (1740–1795) Scottish biographer and diarist. He was a mem-ber of Samuel →Johnson's Literary Club and the two men travelled to Scotland together in 1773, as recorded in Boswell's *Journal of a Tour to the Hebrides* (1785). His *Life of Samuel Johnson* was published in 1791. Boswell's ability to record Johnson's pithy conversation ver-batim makes this a classic of English biography.

**Bosworth, Battle of** battle fought on 22 August 1485, during the English Wars of the Roses (see →Roses, Wars of the). Richard III, the Yorkist king, was defeated and killed by Henry Tudor, who became Henry VII. The battlefield is near the village of Market Bosworth, 19 km/12 mi west of Leicester, England.

**botany** (Greek *botane* 'herb') the study of living and fossil →plants, including form, function, interaction with the environment, and classification.

**Botany Bay** inlet on the east coast of New South Wales, Australia, 8 km/5 mi south of Sydney. It is the outlet of the River Georges. The English explorer

Captain James →Cook landed here in 1770. In 1787 the bay was chosen as the site for a British penal colony, but proved unsuitable, and the colony was located at Port Jackson.

**botfly** any fly of the family Oestridae. The larvae are parasites that feed on the skin (warblefly of cattle) or in the nasal cavity (nostrilflies of sheep and deer). The horse botfly belongs to another family, the Gasterophilidae. It has a parasitic larva that feeds in the horse's stomach.

**Botswana** Republic of; **area:** 582,000 sq km/224,710 sq mi; **capital:** Gaborone; **major towns/cities:** Mahalapye, Serowe, Tutume, Bobonong Francistown, Selebi-Phikwe, Lobatse, Molepolol, Kange; **physical features:** Kalahari Desert in southwest (70–80% of national territory is desert), plains (Makgadikgadi salt pans) in east, fertile lands and Okavango Delta in north; **head of state and government:** Festus Mogae from 1998; **political system:** democracy; **currency:** franc CFA; **GNP per capita (PPP):** (US$) 8,310 (1998); **exports:** diamonds, copper and nickel, beef. Principal market EU 79.7% (1997); **population:** 1,597,000 (1999 est); **language:** English (official), Setswana (national); **religion:** Christian 50%, animist, Baha'i, Muslim, Hindu; **life expectancy:** 46 (men); 48 (women) (1995–2000).

**Botticelli, Sandro, born Alessandro Filipepi** (1445–1510) Florentine painter. He depicted religious and mythological subjects. He was patronized by the ruling →Medici family and was deeply influenced by their Neo-Platonic circle. It was for the Medicis that he painted *Primavera* (1478) and *The Birth of Venus* (about 1482–84). From the 1490s he was influenced by the religious fanatic →Savonarola, and developed a harshly expressive and emotional style, as seen in his *Mystic Nativity* (1500).

**Boudicca** (died AD 61) Queen of the Iceni (native Britons), often referred to by the Latin form of her name, **Boadicea**. Her husband, King Prasutagus, had been a tributary of the Romans, but on his death AD 60 the territory of the Iceni was violently annexed. Boudicca was scourged and her daughters raped. Boudicca raised the whole of southeastern England in revolt, and before the main Roman armies could return from campaigning in Wales she burned Londinium (London), Verulamium (St Albans), and Camulodunum (Colchester). Later the Romans under governor Suetonius Paulinus defeated the British between London and Chester; they were virtually annihilated and Boudicca poisoned herself.

**bovine spongiform encephalopathy** (BSE or mad cow disease) disease of cattle, related to →scrapie in sheep, which attacks the nervous system, causing aggression, lack of coordination, and collapse. First identified in 1985, it is almost entirely confined to the UK. By 1996 it had claimed 158,000 British cattle.

**boxing** fighting with gloved fists, almost entirely a male sport. The sport dates from the 18th century, when fights were fought with bare knuckles and untimed rounds. Each round ended with a knockdown. Fighting with gloves became the accepted form in the latter part of the 19th century after the formulation of the Queensberry Rules in 1867.

**Boyle's law** law stating that the volume of a given mass of gas at a constant temperature is inversely proportional to its pressure. For example, if the pressure of a gas doubles, its volume will be reduced by a half, and vice versa. The law was discovered in 1662 by Irish physicist and chemist Robert Boyle.

**Boyne, Battle of the** battle fought on 1 July 1690 in eastern Ireland, in which the exiled king James II was defeated by William III and fled to France. It was the decisive battle of the War of English Succession, confirming a Protestant monarch. It took its name from the River Boyne which rises in County Kildare and flows 110 km/69 mi northeast to the Irish Sea.

**Brahe, Tycho** (1546–1601) Danish astronomer. His accurate observations of the planets enabled German astronomer and mathematician Johannes →Kepler to prove that planets orbit the Sun in ellipses. Brahe's discovery and report of the 1572 supernova brought him recognition, and his observations of the comet of 1577 proved that it moved in an orbit among the planets, thus disproving Aristotle's view that comets were in the Earth's atmosphere.

**Brahma** in Hinduism, the creator of the cosmos, who forms with Vishnu and Siva the Trimurti, or three aspects of the absolute spirit.

**Brahms, Johannes** (1833–1897) German composer, pianist, and conductor. He is considered one of the greatest composers of symphonic music and of songs. His works include four symphonies, lieder (songs), concertos for piano and for violin, chamber music, sonatas, and the choral *Ein Deutsches Requiem/A German Requiem* (1868). He performed and conducted his own works.

**brain** in higher animals, a mass of interconnected →nerve cells forming the anterior part of the →central nervous system, whose activities it coordinates and controls. In →vertebrates, the brain is contained by the skull. At the base of the brainstem, the **medulla oblongata** contains centres for the control of respiration, heartbeat rate and strength, and blood pressure. Overlying this is the **cerebellum**; which is concerned with coordinating complex muscular processes such as maintaining posture and moving limbs.

The cerebral hemispheres (**cerebrum**) are paired outgrowths of the front end of the forebrain, in early vertebrates mainly concerned with the senses, but in higher vertebrates greatly developed and involved in the integration of all sensory input and motor

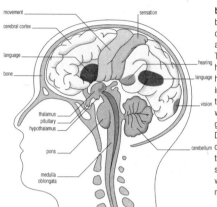

**brain** The structure of the human brain. At the back of the skull lies the cerebellum, which coordinates reflex actions that control muscular activity. The medulla controls respiration, heartbeat, and blood pressure. The hypothalamus is concerned with instinctive drives and emotions. The thalamus relays signals to and from various parts of the brain. The pituitary gland controls the body's hormones. Distinct areas of the large convoluted cerebral hemispheres that fill most of the skull are linked to sensations, such as hearing and sight, and voluntary activities, such as movement.

output, and in thought, emotions, memory, and behaviour.

**brake** device used to slow down or stop the movement of a moving body or vehicle. The mechanically applied calliper brake used on bicycles uses a scissor action to press hard rubber blocks against the wheel rim. The main braking system of a car works hydraulically: when the driver depresses the brake pedal, liquid pressure forces pistons to apply brakes on each wheel.

**Branagh, Kenneth Charles** (1960– ) Northern Irish stage and film actor, director, and producer. He co-founded the Renaissance Theatre Company in 1987. His first film as both actor and director was *Henry V* (1989); he

returned to Shakespeare with lavish film versions of *Much Ado About Nothing* (1993) and *Hamlet* (1996).

**Braque, Georges** (1882–1963) French painter. With Picasso, he played a decisive role in the development of cubism 1907–1910. It was during this period that he began to experiment with collage and invented the technique of gluing paper, wood, and other materials to canvas.

**brass** metal →alloy of copper and zinc with not more than 5% or 6% of other metals. The zinc content ranges from 20% to 45%, and the colour of brass varies accordingly from coppery to whitish yellow. Brasses are characterized by the ease with which they may be shaped and machined; they are strong and ductile, resist many forms of corrosion, and are used for electrical fittings, ammunition cases, screws, household fittings, and ornaments.

**brass instrument** any of a class of musical instruments made of brass or other metal, including trumpets, bugles, trombones, and horns. The function of a reed is served by the lips, shaped and tensed by the mouthpiece, acting as a valve releasing periodic pulses of pressurized air into the tube. Orchestral brass instruments are derived from signalling instruments that in their natural or valveless form produce a directionally focused range of ones from the harmonic series by overblowing to as high as the 16th harmonic. They are powerful and efficient generators, and produce tones of great depth and resonance.

**Brazil** Federative Republic of; **national name:** *República Federativa do Brasil*; **area:** 8,511,965 sq km/3,286,469 sq mi; **capital:** Brasília; **major towns/cities:** São Paulo, Belo Horizonte, Nova Iguaçu, Rio de Janeiro, Belém, Recife, Pôrto Alegre, Salvador, Curitiba, Manaus, Fortaleza; **major ports:** Rio de Janeiro, Belém, Recife, Pôrto Alegre, Salvador; **physical features:** the densely forested Amazon basin covers the northern half of the country with a network of rivers; south is fertile; enormous energy resources, both hydroelectric (Itaipú Reservoir on the Paraná, and Tucuruí on the Tocantins) and nuclear (uranium ores); mostly tropical climate; **head of state and government:** Fernando Henrique Cardoso from 1995; **political system:** democratic federal republic; **currency:** real; **GNP per capita (PPP):** (US$) 6,160 (1998); **exports:** steel products, transport equipment, coffee, iron ore and concentrates, aluminium, iron, tin, soybeans, orange juice (85% of world's concentrates), tobacco, leather footwear, sugar, beef, textiles. Principal market USA 17.8% (1998); **population:** 167,988,000 (1998 est); **language:** Portuguese (official); 120 Indian languages; **religion:** Roman Catholic 89%; Indian faiths; **life expectancy:** 63 (men); 71 (women) (1995–2000).

**Brazzaville** river port and capital of the Republic of the Congo (Congo-Brazzaville), on the west bank of the Congo River, opposite Kinshasa; population (1995 est) 937,600. Industries include foundries, railway repairs, shipbuilding, beverages, textiles, food processing, shoes, soap, furniture, and bricks. There is a cathedral built in 1892 and the Pasteur Institute founded in 1908. The city stands on Malebo Pool (Stanley Pool).

**breathing** in terrestrial animals, the muscular movements whereby air is taken into the lungs and then expelled, a form of gas exchange. Breathing is sometimes referred to as external respiration, for true respiration is a cellular (internal) process.

**Brecht, Bertolt (Eugen Berthold Friedrich)** (1898–1956) German dramatist and poet. He was one of the most influential figures in 20th-century theatre. A committed Marxist, he sought to develop an 'epic theatre' which aimed to destroy the 'suspension of disbelief' usual in the theatre and so encourage audiences to develop an active and critical attitude to a play's subject. He adapted John Gay's *The Beggar's Opera* as *Die Dreigroschenoper/ The Threepenny Opera* (1928), set to music by Kurt Weill. Later plays include *Mutter Courage und ihre Kinder/Mother Courage and her Children* (1941), set during the Thirty Years' War, and *Der kaukasische Kreidekreis/The Caucasian Chalk Circle* (1945).

**Bremen** industrial port and capital of the *Land* (state) of Bremen, Germany, on the River Weser 69 km/43 mi from the open sea; population (1995) 549,000. Industries include iron, steel, oil refining, the manufacture of chemicals, aircraft, and cars, ship repairing, marine engineering, and electronics. The Bremer Vulkan Shipyards closed in 1996. Nearby Bremerhaven serves as an outport.

**Brest** naval base and industrial port in the *département* of Finistère, situated on two hills separated by the River Penfeld at **Rade de Brest** (Brest Roads), a great bay whose only entrance is a narrow channel, at the western extremity of Brittany in northwest France; population (1990) 201,500. The town has a naval academy, several schools of nautical science, a university and an oceanographic research centre. Industries include electronics, shipbuilding, and the manufacture of chemicals and paper. Occupied as a U-boat base by the Germans 1940–44, part of the old city was destroyed by Allied bombing and the retreating Germans.

**Breton, André** (1896–1966) French writer and poet. He was among the leaders of the →Dada art movement and was also a founder of surrealism, publishing *Le Manifeste de surréalisme/ Surrealist Manifesto* (1924).

**brewing** making of beer, ale, or other alcoholic beverage, from malt and barley by steeping (mashing), boiling, and fermenting. Mashing the barley releases its sugars. Yeast is then added, which contains the enzymes needed to convert the sugars into ethanol (alcohol) and carbon dioxide. Hops are added to give a bitter taste.

**Brezhnev, Leonid Ilyich** (1906–1982) Soviet leader, president 1977–82. Domestically he was conservative; abroad the USSR was established as a military and political superpower during the Brezhnev era, extending its influence in Africa and Asia.

**bridge** structure that provides a continuous path or road over water, valleys, ravines, or above other roads. The basic designs and composites of these are based on the way they bear the weight of the structure and its load. **Beam**, or **girder**, bridges are supported at each end by the ground with the weight thrusting downwards. **Cantilever** bridges are a complex form of girder in which only one end is supported. **Arch** bridges thrust outwards and downwards at their ends. **Suspension** bridges use cables under tension to pull inwards against anchorages on either side of the span, so that the roadway hangs from the main cables by the network of vertical cables. The **cable-stayed** bridge relies on diagonal cables connected directly between the bridge deck and supporting towers at each end. Some bridges are too low to allow traffic to pass beneath easily, so they are designed with movable parts, like swing and draw bridges.

**Bridgetown** port and capital of Barbados; population (1990) 6,700. Sugar is exported through the nearby deep-water port. Bridgetown was founded 1628.

**Brighton** seaside resort in Brighton and Hove unitary authority, on the south coast of England; population (1994 est) 155,000. The town was part of the county of East Sussex until 1997. It is an education and service centre with two universities, language schools, and tourist and conference business facilities.

**Bristol** industrial port and unitary authority in southwest England, at the junction of the rivers Avon and Frome; it was part of the former county of Avon to 1996; **area:** 109 sq km/42 sq mi; **features:** new city centre, with British engineer and inventor Isambard Kingdom →Brunel's Temple Meads railway station as its focus; there is a 12th-century cathedral and 13th–14th-century St Mary Redcliffe church; National Lifeboat Museum; Clifton Suspension Bridge (completed in 1864), designed by Brunel; Wildscreen World, the world's first electronic zoo;

**industries:** engineering, microelectronics, tobacco, printing, metal refining, banking, insurance, sugar refining, and the manufacture of aircraft engines, chemicals, paper, soap, Bristol 'blue' glass, and chocolate; **population:** (1996) 374,300, urban area (1991) 516,500; **famous people:** Thomas Chatterton, W G Grace, Cary Grant.

**Britain, ancient** period in the British Isles (excluding Ireland) extending through prehistory to the Roman occupation (1st century AD). Settled agricultural life evolved in Britain during the 3rd millennium BC. A peak was reached in Neolithic society in southern England early in the 2nd millennium BC, with the construction of the great stone circles of Avebury and Stonehenge. It was succeeded in central southern Britain by the Early Bronze Age Wessex culture, with strong trade links across Europe. The Iron Age culture of the Celts was predominant in the last few centuries BC, and the Belgae (of mixed Germanic and Celtic stock) were partially Romanized in the century between the first Roman invasion of Britain under Julius Caesar (54 BC) and the Roman conquest (AD 43). For later history, see →Roman Britain.

**Britain, Battle of** World War II air battle between German and British air forces over Britain 10 July–31 October 1940.

**British Columbia** most westerly, and only Pacific, province of Canada. It is bordered on the east by Alberta, with the Continental Divide in the Rocky Mountains forming its southeastern boundary. To the south, it has a frontier along the 49th Parallel with the US states of Montana, Idaho, and Washington. To the north, along the 60th Parallel, lie the Northwest Territories and Yukon Territory. British Columbia borders in the northwest on the panhandle of Alaska for about half its length (the other half forming the frontier with Yukon Territory); **area:** 947,800 sq km/365,851 sq mi; **capital:** Victoria; **towns and cities:** Vancouver, Prince George, Kamloops, Kelowna, Surrey, Richmond, Nanaimo; **population:** (1996) 3,724,500; **physical:** Rocky Mountains, Coast Mountains, and Coast Range; deeply indented coastline; rivers include the Fraser and Columbia; over 80 major lakes; **industries:** lumbering and manufacture of finished wood products; fishing; mining (coal, copper, iron, lead); extraction of oil and natural gas; hydroelectric power generation; fruit and vegetable growing.

**British Isles** group of islands off the northwest coast of Europe, consisting of Great Britain (England, Wales, and Scotland), Ireland, the Channel Islands, the Orkney and Shetland islands, the Isle of Man, and many other islands that are included in various counties, such as the Isle of Wight, Scilly Isles, Lundy Island, and the Inner and Outer Hebrides. The islands are divided from Europe by the North Sea, Strait of Dover, and the English Channel, and face the Atlantic to the west.

**Brittany** (French *Bretagne*; Breton *Breiz*) modern region of northwest France and former province, on the Breton peninsula between the Bay of Biscay and the English Channel; area 27,200 sq km/10,499 sq mi; population (1990) 2,795,600. A farming region, it includes the *départements* of Côtes-d'Armor, Finistère, Ille-et-Vilaine, and Morbihan. The administrative centre is Rennes.

**Britten, (Edward) Benjamin, Baron Britten** (1913–1976) English composer. He often wrote for the individual voice; for example, the role in the opera *Peter Grimes* (1945), based on verses by George Crabbe, was written for his life companion, the tenor Peter Pears. Among his many works are the *Young Person's Guide to the Orchestra* (1946); the chamber opera *The Rape of Lucretia* (1946); *A Midsummer Night's Dream* (Shakespeare; 1960); and *Death in Venice* (after Thomas Mann; 1973).

---

**WEB SITE** > > > > > > > >

**Britten, Benjamin**

http//www.geocities.com/Vienna/Strasse/1523/britten.htm

Comprehensive source of information on the British composer. In addition to a biography, there is a huge bibliography of books, articles, and dissertations about Britten, a complete discography, and a listing of recordings of Britten as conductor, pianist, and violist.

---

**Brodsky, Joseph Alexandrovich** (1940–1996) Russian poet. He emigrated to the USA in 1972. His work, often dealing with themes of exile, is admired for its wit and economy of language. Many of his poems, written in Russian, have been translated into English (*A Part of Speech* 1980). He was awarded the Nobel Prize for Literature 1987 and became US poet laureate 1991.

**bromine** (Greek *bromos* 'stench') dark, reddish-brown, nonmetallic element, a volatile liquid at room temperature, symbol Br, atomic number 35, relative atomic mass 79.904. It is a member of the →halogen group, has an unpleasant odour, and is very irritating to mucous membranes. Its salts are bromides.

**Brontë** three English novelists, daughters of a Yorkshire parson. **Charlotte** (1816–1855), notably with *Jane Eyre* (1847) and *Villette* (1853), reshaped autobiographical material into vivid narrative. **Emily** (1818–1848) in *Wuthering Heights* (1847) expressed the intensity and nature mysticism which also pervades her poetry (*Poems*, 1846).

---

**WEB SITE** > > > > > > > >
**Brontë Sisters**

http//www2.sbbs.se/hp/cfalk/
bronteng.htm

Extensive collection of information on each of the Brontë sisters, including online novels and poems, literary criticism and interpretation, biographies, bibliographies, and mailing lists.

---

Anne (1820–1849) produced *Agnes Grey* (1847) and *The Tenant of Wildfell Hall* (1848).

**bronze** alloy of copper and tin, yellow or brown in colour. It is harder than pure copper, more suitable for casting, and also resists →corrosion. Bronze may contain as much as 25% tin, together with small amounts of other metals, mainly lead.

**Bronze Age** stage of prehistory and early history when copper and bronze (an alloy of tin and copper) became the first metals worked extensively and used for tools and weapons. One of the classifications of the Danish archaeologist Christian Thomsen's Three Age System, it developed out of the Stone Age and generally preceded the Iron Age. It first began in the Far East and may be dated 5000–1200 BC in the Middle East and about 2000–500 BC in Europe.

**Brooke, Rupert Chawner** (1887–1915) English poet. He stands as a symbol of the World War I 'lost generation'. His five war sonnets, including 'The Soldier', were published posthumously. Other notable poems are 'Grantchester' (1912) and 'The Great Lover', written in 1914.

**brown dwarf** in astronomy, an object less massive than a star, but heavier than a planet. Brown dwarfs do not have enough mass to ignite nuclear reactions at their centres, but shine by heat released during their contraction from a gas cloud. Some astronomers believe that vast numbers of brown dwarfs exist throughout the Galaxy.

**Browning, Robert** (1812–1889) English poet. His work includes *Pippa Passes* (1841) (written in dramatic form) and the poems 'The Pied Piper of Hamelin' (1842), 'My Last Duchess' (1842), 'Home Thoughts from Abroad' (1845), and 'Rabbi Ben Ezra' (1864). He was married to Elizabeth Barrett Browning.

**Brueghel** (or Bruegel) family of Flemish painters. **Pieter Brueghel the Elder** (*c.* 1525–1569) was one of the greatest artists of his time. His pictures of peasant life helped to establish genre painting, and he also popularized works illustrating proverbs, such as *The Blind Leading the Blind* (1568, Museo di Capodimonte, Naples). A contemporary taste for the macabre can be seen in *The Triumph of Death* (1562, Prado, Madrid), which clearly shows the influence of Hieronymus Bosch. One of his best-known works is *Hunters in the Snow* (1565, Kunsthistorisches Museum, Vienna).

**Brundtland, Gro Harlem** (1939– ) Norwegian Labour politician, head of the World Health Organization (WHO) from 1998. Environment minister 1974–76, she briefly took over as prime minister in 1981, a post to which she was re-elected in 1986, 1990, and again held 1993–96, when she resigned. Leader of the Norwegian Labour Party from 1981, she resigned the post in 1992 but continued as prime minister. Retaining her seat count in the 1993 general election, she led a minority Labour government committed to European Union membership, but failed to secure backing for the membership application in a 1994 national referendum.

**Brunei** State of; **national name:** *Negara Brunei Darussalam*; **area:** 5,765 sq km/2,225 sq mi; **capital:** Bandar Seri Begawan; **major towns/cities:** Seria, Kuala Belait, Bangar; **physical features:** flat coastal plain with hilly lowland in west and mountains in east (Mount Pagon 1,850 m/6,070 ft); 75% of the area is forested; the Limbang valley splits Brunei in two, and its cession to Sarawak in 1890 is disputed by Brunei; tropical climate; Temburong, Tutong, and Belait rivers; **head of state and government:** HM Musa Hassanal Bolkiah Mu'izzaddin Waddaulah, Sultan of Brunei, from 1967; **political system:** absolute monarchy; **currency:** Brunei dollar (ringgit); **GNP per capita (PPP):** (US$) 25,500 (1998 est); **exports:** crude petroleum, natural gas and refined products. Principal market Japan 50.9% (1998); **population:** 321,000 (1999 est); **language:** Malay (official), Chinese (Hokkien), English; **religion:** Muslim 66%, Buddhist 14%, Christian 10%; **life expectancy:** 73 (men); 78 (women) (1995–2000).

**Brunel, Isambard Kingdom** (1806–1859) English engineer and inventor. In 1833 he became engineer to the Great Western Railway, which adopted the 2.1-m/7-ft gauge on his advice. He built the Clifton Suspension Bridge over the River Avon at Bristol and the Saltash Bridge over the River Tamar near Plymouth. His shipbuilding designs include the *Great Western* (1837), the first steamship to cross the Atlantic regularly; the *Great Britain* (1843), the first large iron ship to have a screw propeller; and the *Great Eastern* (1858), which laid the first transatlantic telegraph cable.

**Brunelleschi, Filippo** (1377–1446) Italian Renaissance architect. The first and one of the greatest of the Renaissance architects, he pioneered the scientific use of perspective. He was responsible for the construction of the dome of Florence Cathedral (completed 1436), a feat deemed impossible by many of his contemporaries.

**Brussels** (Flemish *Brussel*; French *Bruxelles*) city and capital of Belgium and the province of Brabant, situated almost in the centre of the country in the Senne river valley; city population (1997) 133,800; metropolitan/capital region population (1997) 950,600. Industries include lace, textiles, machinery, and chemicals. It is the headquarters of the European Union (EU) and, since 1967, of the international secretariat of →NATO. It contains the Belgian royal seat, the chief courts, the chamber of commerce, and is the centre of the principal banks of the country. Founded on an island in the River Senne *c.* 580, Brussels became a city in 1312, and was declared capital of the Spanish Netherlands in 1530 and of Belgium in 1830.

**Brutus, Marcus Junius** (*c.* 85–42 BC) Roman senator and general who conspired with →Cassius to assassinate Julius →Caesar in order to restore the purity of the Republic. He and Cassius were defeated by the united forces of →Mark Antony and Octavian at Philippi 42 BC, and Brutus committed suicide.

**bubonic plague** epidemic disease of the Middle Ages; see →plague and →Black Death.

**Bucharest** (Romanian *Bucureşti*) capital and largest city of Romania; population (1993) 2,343,800. The conurbation of Bucharest district has an area of 1,520 sq km/587 sq mi. It was originally a citadel built by Vlad the Impaler to stop the advance of the Ottoman invasion in the 14th century. Bucharest became the capital of the princes of Wallachia 1698 and of Romania 1861. Savage fighting took place in the city during Romania's 1989 revolution.

**buckminsterfullerene** form of carbon, made up of molecules (buckyballs) consisting of 60 carbon atoms arranged in 12 pentagons and 20 hexagons to form a perfect sphere. It was named after the US architect and engineer Richard Buckminster Fuller because of its structural similarity to the geodesic dome that he designed. See →fullerene.

**bud** undeveloped shoot usually enclosed by protective scales; inside is a very short stem and numerous undeveloped leaves, or flower parts, or both. Terminal buds are found at the tips of shoots, while axillary buds develop in the axils of the leaves, often remaining dormant unless the terminal bud is removed or damaged. Adventitious buds may be produced anywhere on the plant, their formation sometimes stimulated by an injury, such as that caused by pruning.

**Budapest** capital of Hungary, industrial city (chemicals, textiles) on the River Danube; population (1993 est) 2,009,000. Buda, on the right bank of the Danube, became the Hungarian capital 1867 and was joined with Pest, on the left bank, 1872.

**Buddha** (*c.* 563–483 BC) 'enlightened one', title of Prince **Gautama Siddhārtha** religious leader, founder of →Buddhism, born at Lumbini in Nepal. At the age of 29 he left his wife and son and a life of luxury, to resolve the problems of existence. After six years of austerity he realized that asceticism, like overindulgence, was futile, and chose the middle way of meditation. He became enlightened under a bo, or bodhi, tree near Buddh Gaya in Bihar, India. He began teaching at Varanasi, and founded the Sangha, or order of monks. He spent the rest of his life travelling around northern India, and died at Kusinagara in Uttar Pradesh.

**Buddhism** one of the great world religions, which originated in India in the 5th century BC. It derives from the teaching of the →Buddha, who is regarded as one of a series of such enlightened beings. The chief doctrine is that all phenomena share three characteristics: they are impermanent, unsatisfactory, and lack a permanent essence (such as a soul). All beings, including gods, are subject to these characteristics, but can achieve freedom through enlightenment. The main

forms of Buddhism are **Theravāda** (or Hīnayāna) in Southeast Asia and **Mahāyāna** in North and East Asia; **Lamaism** in Tibet and **Zen** in Japan are among the many Mahāyāna forms of Buddhism. There are over 300 million Buddhists worldwide (1994).

**Buenos Aires** industrial city, chief port, and capital of Argentina, situated in the 'Capital Federal' – a separate federal district, on the south bank of the Río de la Plata, at its estuary; population (1992 est) 11,662,050. Industries include motor vehicles, engineering, oil, chemicals, textiles, paper, and food processing. Main exports are grain, beef, and wool, which are produced in the surrounding pampas. The administrative Federal District of Buenos Aires has an area of 200 sq km/77 sq mi, with a population of (1991) 2,960,976. Buenos Aires is the financial and cultural centre of Argentina, and has many museums and libraries. It is a major railway terminus, and has an international airport 35 km/22 mi southwest of the city centre.

**bug** in computing, an error in a program. It can be an error in the logical structure of a program or a syntax error, such as a spelling mistake. Some bugs cause a program to fail immediately; others remain dormant, causing problems only when a particular combination of events occurs. The process of finding and removing errors from a program is called **debugging**.

**bug** in entomology, an insect belonging to the order Hemiptera. All these have two pairs of wings with forewings partly thickened.

They also have piercing mouthparts adapted for sucking the juices of plants or animals, the 'beak' being tucked under the body when not in use.

**Bujumbura** formerly (until 1962) Usumbura, capital of Burundi, located at the northeastern end of Lake Tanganyika; population (1996 est) 300,000. Bujumbura is the main banking and financial centre of Burundi; industries include food processing and paint manufacture. It was founded in 1899 by German colonists, and a university was established in 1960.

**Bulgaria** Republic of; **national name:** *Republika Bulgaria*; **area:** 110,912 sq km/42,823 sq mi; **capital:** Sofia; **major towns/cities:** Plovdiv, Varna, Ruse, Burgas, Stara Zagora; **major ports:** Black Sea ports Burgas and Varna; **physical features:** lowland plains in north and southeast separated by mountains (Balkan and Rhodope) that cover three-quarters of the country; River Danube in north; **head of state:** Petar Stoyanov from 1997; **head of government:** Ivan Kostov from 1997; **political system:** emergent democracy; **currency:** lev; **GNP per capita (PPP):** (US$) 3,920 (1998 est); **exports:** base metals, chemical and rubber products, processed food, beverages, tobacco, chemicals, textiles, footwear. Principal market Italy 12.7% (1998); **population:** 8,280,000 (1999 est); **language:** Bulgarian, Turkish; **religion:** Eastern Orthodox Christian, Muslim, Roman Catholic,

Protestant; **life expectancy:** 68 (men); 75 (women) (1995–2000).

**bulimia** (Greek 'ox hunger') eating disorder in which large amounts of food are consumed in a short time ('binge'), usually followed by depression and self-criticism. The term is often used for **bulimia nervosa**, an emotional disorder in which eating is followed by deliberate vomiting and purging. This may be a chronic stage in →anorexia nervosa.

**Bunker Hill, Battle of** the first significant engagement in the American Revolution, 17 June 1775, near a small hill in Charlestown (now part of Boston), Massachusetts; the battle actually took place on Breed's Hill, but is named after Bunker Hill as this was the more significant of the two. Although the colonists were defeated, they were able to retreat to Boston in good order.

**Buñuel, Luis** (1900–1983) Spanish-born film director. He is widely considered one of the giants of European art cinema, responsible for such enduring classics as *Belle de Jour* (1966), and *Le Charme discret de la bourgeoisie/The Discreet Charm of the Bourgeoisie* (1972).

**Bunyan, John** (1628–1688) English writer, author of *The Pilgrim's Progress* (first part 1678, second part 1684), one of the best-known religious allegories in English. A Baptist, he was imprisoned in Bedford 1660–72 for unlicensed preaching and wrote *Grace Abounding* in 1666, which describes his early spiritual life. He started to write *The Pilgrim's Progress* during a second jail sentence

(1676–77). Written in straightforward language with fervour and imagination, it achieved immediate popularity and was highly influential.

**Burgess, Anthony** (1917–1993) penname of John Anthony Burgess Wilson, English novelist, critic, and composer. His work includes *A Clockwork Orange* (1962) (made into a film by Stanley Kubrick in 1971) and the panoramic *Earthly Powers* (1980).

**Burgundy** (French *Bourgogne*) modern region and former duchy of east-central France that includes the *départements* of Ain, Côte-d'Or, Nièvre, Saône-et-Loire, and Yonne; area 31,600 sq km/12,198 sq mi; population (1990) 1,609,700. Its administrative centre is Dijon.

**Burke, Edmund** (1729–1797) British Whig politician and political theorist, born in Dublin, Ireland. During a parliamentary career spanning more than 30 years, he was famous for opposing the government's attempts to coerce the American colonists, for example in *Thoughts on the Present Discontents* (1770), and for supporting the emancipation of Ireland. However, he was a vehement opponent of the French Revolution, which he denounced in *Reflections on the Revolution in France* (1790), and attacked the suggestion of peace with France in *Letters on a Regicide Peace* (1795–97).

**Burkina Faso** The People's Democratic Republic of (formerly Upper Volta); **national name:** *République Démocratique Populaire de Burkina Faso*; **area:** 274,122 sq km/105,838 sq mi; **capital:** Ouagadougou; **major towns/ cities:** Bobo-Dioulasso, Koudougou; **physical features:** landlocked plateau with hills in west and southeast; headwaters of the River Volta; semiarid in north, forest and farmland in south; linked by rail to Abidjan in Côte d'Ivoire, Burkina Faso's only outlet to the sea; **head of state:** Blaise Compaoré from 1987; **head of government:** Kadre Desire Ouedraogo from 1996; **political system:** emergent democracy; **currency:** franc CFA; **GNP per capita (PPP):** (US$) 1,020 (1998 est); **exports:** cotton, gold, livestock and livestock products. Principal market Côte d'Ivoire 12.7% (1997); **population:** 11,616,000 (1999 est); **language:** French (official); about 50 Sudanic languages spoken by 90% of population; **religion:** animist 53%, Sunni Muslim 36%, Roman Catholic 11%; **life expectancy:** 44 (men); 45 (women) (1995–2000).

**Burma** former name (to 1989) of →Myanmar.

**Burne-Jones, Edward Coley** (1833–1898) English painter. In 1856 he was apprenticed to the Pre-Raphaelite painter and poet Dante Gabriel →Rossetti, who remained a dominant influence. His paintings include *King Cophetua and the Beggar Maid* (1880–84; Tate Gallery, London). He collaborated with William →Morris in designing stained-glass windows, tapestries, and book decorations for the Kelmscott Press. His work influenced both →Symbolism and →art nouveau. He was created a baronet in 1894.

**Burns, Robert** (1759–1796) Scottish poet. He used a form of Scots dialect at a time when it was not considered suitably 'elevated' for literature. Burns's first volume, *Poems, Chiefly in the Scottish Dialect*, appeared in 1786. In addition to his poetry (such as 'To a Mouse'), Burns wrote or adapted many songs, including 'Auld Lang Syne'. **Burns Night** is celebrated on 25 January, his birthday.

**Burundi** Republic of; **national name:** *Republika y'Uburundi*; **area:** 27,834 sq km/10,746 sq mi; **capital:** Bujumbura; **major towns/cities:** Kitega, Bururi, Ngozi, Muhinga, Muramuya; **physical features:** landlocked grassy highland straddling watershed of Nile and Congo; Lake Tanganyika, Great Rift Valley; **head of state:** Pierre Buyoya from 1996; **head of government:** Pascal-Firmin Ndimira from 1996; **political system:** authoritarian nationalist; **currency:** Burundi franc; **GNP per capita (PPP):** (US$) 620 (1998 est); **exports:** coffee, tea, glass products, hides and skins. Principal market UK 29.1% (1997); **population:** 6,565,000 (1999 est); **language:** Kirundi (a Bantu language) and French (both official), Kiswahili; **religion:** Roman Catholic 62%, Pentecostalist 5%, Anglican 1%, Muslim 1%, animist; **life expectancy:** 41 (men); 44 (women) (1995–2000).

**Butler, Samuel** (1835–1902) English writer. He made his name in 1872 with a satiric attack on contemporary utopianism, *Erewhon* (an anagram of *nowhere*). He is now remembered for his unfinished, semi-autobiographical discursive novel, *The Way of All Flesh*, a study of Victorian conventions, the causes and effects of the clash between generations, and religious hypocrisy (written and frequently revised 1873–84 and posthumously published in 1903).

**butterfly** insect belonging, like moths, to the order Lepidoptera, in which the wings are covered with tiny scales, often brightly coloured. There are some 15,000 species of butterfly, many of which are under threat throughout the world because of the destruction of habitat.

---

**WEB SITE** > > > > > > >
**Butterfly Web Site**
http/mgfx.com/butterfly/
Useful link page to the world of butterflies, with graphics, articles, and discoveries, as well as information on related topics.

---

**byte** sufficient computer memory to store a single character of data. The character is stored in the byte of memory as a pattern of →bits (binary digits), using a code such as →ASCII. A byte usually contains eight bits – for example, the capital letter F can be stored as the bit pattern 01000110.

**Byzantine Empire** the Eastern Roman Empire 395–1453, with its capital at Constantinople (formerly Byzantium, modern Istanbul). It was the direct continuation of the Roman Empire in the East, and inherited many of its traditions and institutions.

**Byzantium** (modern Istanbul) ancient Greek city on the Bosporus, between the Black Sea and the Sea of Marmara. Byzantium was founded as a colony of the Greek city of Megara on the important strategic site at the entrance to the Black Sea in about 660 BC. In AD 330 the capital of the Roman Empire was transferred there by Constantine the Great, who renamed it Constantinople and it became the capital of the →Byzantine Empire to which it gave its name.

# Cc

**cabinet** ('a small room, implying secrecy') in politics, the group of ministers holding a country's highest executive offices who decide government policy. In Britain the cabinet system originated under the Stuarts. Under William III it became customary for the king to select his ministers from the party with a parliamentary majority. The US cabinet, unlike the British, does not initiate legislation, and its members, appointed by the president, must not be members of Congress. The term was used in the USA from 1793.

**cable television** distribution of broadcast signals through cable relay systems. Narrow-band systems were originally used to deliver services to areas with poor regular reception; systems with wider bands, using coaxial and fibreoptic cable, are increasingly used for distribution and development of home-based interactive services, typically telephones.

**cactus** (plural cacti) strictly, any plant of the family Cactaceae, although the word is commonly used to describe many different succulent and prickly plants. True cacti have a woody axis (central core) surrounded by a large fleshy stem, which takes various forms and is usually covered with spines (actually reduced leaves). They are all specially adapted to growing in dry areas.

**Cádiz** Spanish city and naval base, capital and seaport of the province of Cádiz, sited on a peninsula on the south side of Cádiz Bay, an inlet of the Atlantic Ocean, 103 km/64 mi south of Seville; population (1991) 153,600. After the discovery of the Americas in 1492, Cádiz became one of Europe's most vital trade ports. The English adventurer Francis →Drake burned a Spanish fleet here in 1587 to prevent the sailing of the →Armada.

**Caesar, Gaius Julius** (100–44 BC) Roman general and dictator, considered Rome's most successful military commander. He formed with Pompey the Great and Marcus Licinius Crassus (the Elder) the First Triumvirate in 60 BC. He conquered Gaul in 58–50 and invaded Britain in 55–54. By leading his army across the river Rubicon into Italy in 49, an act of treason, he provoked a civil war which ended in 45 with the defeat of Pompey and his supporters. He was voted dictator for life, but was assassinated by conspirators on 15 March 44 BC. Caesar was a skilled historian whose *Commentarii*, recounting his campaigns, has had a major impact on the way military history is written.

**Caesarean section** surgical operation to deliver a baby by way of an incision in the mother's abdominal and uterine walls. It may be recommended for almost any obstetric complication implying a threat to mother or baby.

**caesium** (Latin *caesius* 'bluish-grey') soft, silvery-white, ductile metallic element, symbol Cs, atomic number 55, relative atomic mass 132.905. It is one of the alkali metals, and is the most electropositive of all the elements. In air it ignites spontaneously, and it reacts vigorously with water. It is used in the manufacture of photocells.

**caffeine** alkaloid organic substance found in tea, coffee, and kola nuts; it stimulates the heart and central nervous system. When isolated, it is a bitter crystalline compound, $C_8H_{10}N_4O_2$. Too much caffeine (more than six average cups of tea or coffee a day) can be detrimental to health.

**Cairo** (Arabic *El Qahira* 'the victorious') capital of Egypt, and the largest city in Africa and in the Middle East, situated on the east bank of the River Nile 13 km/ 8 mi above the apex of the delta and 160 km/100 mi from the Mediterranean; population (1995 est) 6,955,000. Industries include the manufacture of textiles, cement, vegetable oils, tourism and steel. At Helwan, 24 km/15 mi to the south, an industrial centre is powered by electricity from the Aswan High Dam.

**calcium** (Latin *calcis* 'lime') soft, silvery-white metallic element, symbol Ca, atomic number 20, relative atomic mass 40.08. It is one of the alkaline-earth metals. It is the fifth most abundant element (the third most abundant metal) in the Earth's crust. It is found mainly as its carbonate $CaCO_3$, which occurs in a fairly pure condition as chalk and limestone. Calcium is an essential component of bones, teeth, shells, milk, and leaves, and it forms 1.5% of the human body by mass.

**calculus** (Latin 'pebble') branch of mathematics which uses the concept of a derivative to analyse the way in which the values of a function vary. Calculus is probably the most widely used part of mathematics. Many real-life problems are analysed by expressing one quantity as a function of another – position of a moving object as a function of time, temperature of an object as a function of distance from a heat source, force on an object as a function of distance from the source of the force, and so on – and calculus is concerned with such functions.

**Calcutta** city in India, on the River Hooghly, the westernmost mouth of the River Ganges, some 130 km/80 mi north of the Bay of Bengal; population (1994) 11,500,000. The capital of West Bengal, it is chiefly a commercial and industrial centre, its industries including engineering, shipbuilding, jute, and other textiles. It was the seat of government of British India 1773–1912.

**California** western state of the USA. It is nicknamed the Golden State, originally because of its gold mines, and more recently because of its orange groves and sunshine. California was admitted to the Union in 1850 as the 31st US state. It is bordered to the south by the Mexican state of Baja California, to the east by Arizona and Nevada, to the north by Oregon, and to the west by the Pacific Ocean; **population:** (1996 est) 31,878,000, the most populous state of the USA; **area:** 411,100 sq km/158,685 sq mi; **capital:** Sacramento; **towns and cities:** Los Angeles, San Diego, San Francisco, San Jose, Fresno; **industries and products:** leading agricultural state with fruit (peaches, citrus, grapes in the valley of the San Joaquin and Sacramento rivers); beef cattle; timber; fish; oil; natural gas; aerospace technology; electronics (Silicon Valley); financial sector; food processing; films and television programmes; tourism; leisure industry; great reserves of energy (geothermal) in the hot water that lies beneath much of the state.

**Caligula** (AD 12–41) Gaius Julius Caesar Germanicus, Roman emperor AD 37–41, son of Germanicus and Agrippina the Elder, and successor to Tiberius. Caligula was a cruel tyrant and was assassinated by an officer of his guard. He appears to have been mentally unstable.

**Callas, Maria** (1923–1977) adopted name of Maria Kalogeropoulos, US lyric soprano. She was born in New York of Greek parents. With a voice of fine range and a gift for dramatic expression, she excelled in operas including *Aïda*, *Tosca*, and *Medea*.

**calorie** c.g.s. unit of heat, now replaced by the joule (one calorie is approximately 4.2 joules). It is the heat required to raise the temperature of one gram of water by 1°C. In dietetics, the Calorie or kilocalorie is equal to 1,000 calories.

**Calvin, John** (1509–1564) also known as Cauvin or Chauvin, French-born Swiss Protestant church reformer and theologian. He was a leader of the Reformation in Geneva and set up a strict religious community there. His theological system is known as Calvinism, and his church government as →Presbyterianism.

**Calvinism** Christian doctrine as interpreted by John →Calvin and adopted in Scotland, parts of Switzerland, and the Netherlands; by the →Puritans in England and New England, USA; and by the subsequent Congregational and Presbyterian churches in the USA. Its central doctrine is predestination, under which certain souls (the elect) are predestined by God through the sacrifice of Jesus to salvation, and the rest to damnation. Although Calvinism is rarely accepted today in its strictest interpretation, the 20th century has seen a neo-Calvinist revival through the work of Karl Barth.

**calyx** collective term for the sepals of a flower, forming the outermost whorl of the perianth. It surrounds the other flower parts and protects them while in bud. In some flowers, for example, the campions *Silene*, the sepals are fused along their sides, forming a tubular calyx.

**Cambodia** State of (Khmer Republic

1970–76, Democratic Kampuchea 1976–79, People's Republic of Kampuchea 1979–89); **national name:** *Roat Kampuchea*; **area:** 181,035 sq km/69,897 sq mi; **capital:** Phnom Penh; **major towns/cities:** Battambang, Kompong Cham; **major ports:** Kompong Cham; **physical features:** mostly flat, forested plains with mountains in southwest and north; Mekong River runs north–south; Lake Tonle Sap; **head of state:** King Norodom Sihanouk from 1991; **head of government:** Hun Sen from 1998; **political system:** limited constitutional monarchy; **currency:** Cambodian riel; **GNP per capita (PPP):** (US$) 1,240 (1998); **Exports:** timber, rubber, fishery products, garments. Principal market Vietnam 18% (1997); **population:** 10,946,000 (1999 est); **language:** Khmer (official), French; **religion:** Theravāda Buddhist 95%, Muslim, Roman Catholic; **life expectancy:** 52 (men); 55 (women) (1995–2000).

**Cambrian** period of geological time 570–510 million years ago; the first period of the Palaeozoic era. All invertebrate animal life appeared, and marine algae were widespread. The **Cambrian Explosion** 530–520 million years ago saw the first appearance in the fossil record of all modern animal phyla; the earliest fossils with hard shells, such as trilobites, date from this period.

**Cambridge** city and administrative headquarters of Cambridgeshire, eastern England, on the River Cam, 80 km/50 mi north of London; population (1994 est) 117,000. It is the seat of Cambridge University (founded in the 13th century). Industries include the manufacture of computers and electronic products, scientific instruments, and paper, printing, publishing, financial services, and insurance.

**camera** apparatus used in →photography, consisting of a lens system set in a light-proof box inside of which a sensitized film or plate can be placed. The lens collects rays of light reflected from the subject and brings them together as a sharp image on the film. The opening or hole at the front of the camera, through which light enters, is called an aperture. The aperture size controls the amount of light that can enter. A shutter controls the amount of time light has to affect the film. There are small-, medium-, and large-format cameras; the format refers to the size of recorded image and the dimensions of the image obtained.

**camera obscura** darkened box with a tiny hole for projecting the inverted image of the scene outside on to a screen inside. For its development as a device for producing photographs, see →photography.

**Cameroon** Republic of; **national name:** *République du Cameroun*; **area:** 475,440 sq km/183,567 sq mi; **capital:** Yaoundé; **major towns/cities:** Garoua, Douala, Nkongsamba, Maroua, Bamenda, Bafoussam; **major ports:** Douala; **physical features:** desert in far north in the Lake Chad basin, mountains in west, dry savanna plateau in the intermediate area, and dense tropical rainforest in south; Mount Cameroon 4,070 m/13,358 ft, an active volcano on the coast, west of the Adamawa Mountains; **head of state:** Paul

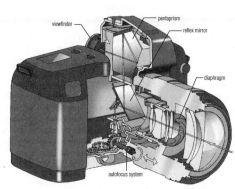

**camera** The single-lens reflex (SLR) camera in which an image can be seen through the lens before a picture is taken. The reflex mirror directs light entering the lens to the viewfinder. The SLR allows different lenses, such as close-up or zoom, to be used because the photographer can see exactly what is being focused on.

viewfinder
pentaprism
reflex mirror
diaphragm
autofocus system

Biya from 1982; **head of government:** Simon Achidi Achu from 1992; **political system:** emergent democracy; **currency:** franc CFA; **GNP per capita (PPP):** (US$) 1,810 (1998); **exports:** crude petroleum and petroleum products, timber and timber products, coffee, aluminium, cotton, bananas. Principal market Italy 25.4% (1997); **population:** 14,710,000 (1999 est); **language:** French and English in pidgin variations (official); there has been some discontent with the emphasis on French – there are 163 indigenous peoples with their own African languages (Sudanic languages in north, Bantu languages elsewhere); **religion:** Roman Catholic 35%, animist 25%, Muslim 22%, Protestant 18%; **life expectancy:** 53 (men); 56 (women) (1995–2000).

**camouflage** colours or structures that allow an animal to blend with its surroundings to avoid detection by other animals. Camouflage can take the form of matching the background colour, of countershading (darker on top, lighter below, to counteract natural shadows), or of irregular patterns that break up the outline of the animal's body. More elaborate camouflage involves closely resembling a feature of the natural environment, as with the stick insect; this is closely akin to mimicry. Camouflage is also important as a military technique, disguising either equipment, troops, or a position in order to conceal them from an enemy.

**Camus, Albert** (1913–1960) Algerian-born French writer. His works, such as the novels *L'Etranger*/*The Outsider* (1942) and *La Peste*/*The Plague* (1948), owe much to →existentialism in their emphasis on the absurdity and arbitrariness of life. Nobel Prize for Literature 1957.

**Canada** area: 9,970,610 sq km/ 3,849,652 sq mi; **capital:** Ottawa; **major towns/cities:** Toronto, Montréal, Vancouver, Edmonton, Calgary, Winnipeg, Québec, Hamilton, Saskatoon, Halifax, Regina, Windsor, Oshawa, London, Kitchener; **physical features:** mountains in west, with low-lying plains in interior and rolling hills in east; St Lawrence Seaway, Mackenzie River; Great Lakes; Arctic Archipelago; Rocky Mountains; Great Plains or Prairies; Canadian Shield; Niagara Falls; climate varies from temperate in south to arctic in north; 45% of country forested; **head of state:** Elizabeth II from 1952, represented by governor general Roméo A LeBlanc from 1995; **head of government:** Jean Chrétien from 1993; **political system:** federal constitutional monarchy; Progressive Conservative Party (PCP), free enterprise, right of centre; **currency:** Canadian dollar; **GNP per capita (PPP):** (US$) 24,050 (1998); **exports:** motor vehicles and parts, lumber, wood pulp, paper and newsprint, crude petroleum, natural gas, aluminium and alloys, petroleum and coal products. Principal market USA 83.7% (1998); **population:** 30,857,000 (1999 est); **language:** English, French (both official; 60% English mother tongue, 24% French mother tongue); there are also American Indian languages and the Inuit Inuktitut; **religion:** Roman Catholic, various Protestant denominations; **life expectancy:** 76 (men); 82 (women) (1995–2000).

**canal** artificial waterway constructed for drainage, irrigation, or navigation. **Irrigation canals** carry water for irrigation from rivers, reservoirs, or wells, and are designed to maintain an even flow of water over the whole length. **Navigation and ship canals** are constructed at one level between →locks, and frequently link with rivers or sea inlets to form a waterway system. The Suez Canal in 1869 and the Panama Canal in 1914 eliminated long trips around continents and dramatically shortened shipping routes.

**Canary Islands** (Spanish *Islas Canarias*) group of volcanic islands and autonomous Spanish community 100 km/ 60 mi off the northwest coast of Africa, comprising the provinces of Las Palmas and Santa Cruz de Tenerife; area 7,300 sq km/2,818 sq mi; population (1991) 1,456,500. Products include bananas and tomatoes, both grown for export. Tourism is the major industry.

The Northern Hemisphere Astronomical Observatory (1981) is on the island of La Palma. Observation conditions are exceptionally good here because there is little moisture, no artificial-light pollution, and little natural airglow.

The aboriginal inhabitants of the Canary Islands were called Guanches, and the Organization of African Unity (OAU) supports the creation of an independent state, the Guanch Republic, and the revival of the Guanch language.

**Canberra** capital of Australia and seat of the federal government, situated in the Australian Capital Territory in southeast Australia; population (1996) 299,243. Canberra is enclosed within the state of New South Wales, 289 km/180 mi southwest of Sydney and 655 km/407 mi northeast of Melbourne, on the River Molonglo, a tributary of the Murrumbidgee. It succeeded Melbourne as capital of Australia in 1927. It is an administrative, cultural, and tourist centre. The new Parliament House (1988) is located here, as well as government offices, foreign embassies, and many buildings of national importance.

**cancer** group of diseases characterized by abnormal proliferation of cells. Cancer (malignant) cells are usually degenerate, capable only of reproducing themselves (tumour formation). Malignant cells tend to spread from their site of origin by travelling through the bloodstream or lymphatic system. Cancer kills about 6 million people a year worldwide.

**cannabis** dried leaves and female flowers (marijuana) and resin (hashish) of certain varieties of hemp, which are smoked or swallowed to produce a range of effects, including feelings of happiness and altered perception. (*Cannabis sativa*, family Cannabaceae.)

**Canterbury** (Old English *Cantwarabyrig* 'fortress of the men of Kent') historic cathedral city in Kent, southeast England, on the River Stour, 100 km/62 mi southeast of London; population (1991) 36,500. The city is the metropolis of the Anglican Communion and seat of the archbishop of Canterbury. It is a popular tourist destination. Paper, paper products, and electrical goods are manufactured.

**cantilever** beam or structure that is fixed at one end only, though it may be supported at some point along its length; for example, a diving board. The cantilever principle, widely used in construction engineering, eliminates the need for a second main support at the free end of the beam, allowing for more elegant structures and reducing the amount of materials required. Many large-span bridges have been built on the cantilever principle.

**Canute** (*c.* 995–1035) also known as Cnut, the Great king of England from 1016, Denmark from 1018, and Norway from 1028. Having invaded England in 1013 with his father, Sweyn, king of Denmark, he was acclaimed king on Sweyn's death in 1014 by his →Viking army. Canute defeated Edmund (II) Ironside at Assandun, Essex, in 1016, and became king of all England on Edmund's death. He succeeded his brother Harold as king of Denmark in 1018, compelled King Malcolm to pay homage by invading Scotland in about 1027, and conquered Norway in 1028. He was succeeded by his illegitimate son Harold I.

**Cape Town** (Afrikaans *Kaapstad*) port and oldest city (founded 1652) in South Africa, situated at the northern end of the Cape Peninsula, on Table Bay;

population (1991) 854, 616 (urban area); (1991) 2,350,200 (peninsula). Industries include horticulture and trade in wool, wine, fruit, grain, and oil. Tourism is important. It is the legislative capital of the Republic of South Africa and capital of Western Cape province.

**Cape Verde** Republic of; **national name:** *República de Cabo Verde*; **area:** 4,033 sq km/1,557 sq mi; **capital:** Praia; **major towns/cities:** Mindelo; **major ports:** Mindelo; **physical features:** archipelago of ten volcanic islands 565 km/350 mi west of Senegal; the windward (Barlavento) group includes Santo Antão, São Vicente, Santa Luzia, São Nicolau, Sal, and Boa Vista; the leeward (Sotovento) group comprises Maio, São Tiago, Fogo, and Brava; all but Santa Luzia are inhabited; **head of state:** Mascarenhas Monteiro from 1991; **head of government:** Carlos Viega from 1991; **political system:** emergent democracy; **currency:** Cape Verde escudo; **GNP per capita (PPP):** (US$) 2,950 (1998); **exports:** fish, shellfish and fish products, salt, bananas. Principal market Portugal 45% (1997); **population:** 418,000 (1999 est); **language:** Portuguese (official), Creole; **religion:** Roman Catholic 93%, Protestant (Nazarene Church); **life expectancy:** 66 (men); 71 (women) (1995–2000).

**capitalism** economic system in which the principal means of production, distribution, and exchange are in private (individual or corporate) hands and competitively operated for profit. A **mixed economy** combines the private enterprise of capitalism and a degree of state monopoly, as in nationalized industries and welfare services.

**capital punishment** punishment by death. Capital punishment is retained in 92 countries and territories (1990), including the USA (38 states), China, and Islamic countries. It was abolished in the UK in 1965 for all crimes except treason and piracy, and in 1998 it was entirely abolished in the UK. Methods of execution include electrocution, lethal gas, hanging, shooting, lethal injection, garrotting, and decapitation.

**capybara** world's largest rodent *Hydrochoerus hydrochaeris*, up to 1.3 m/ 4 ft long and 50 kg/110 lb in weight. It is found in South America, and belongs to the guinea-pig family. The capybara inhabits marshes and dense vegetation around water. It has thin, yellowish hair, swims well, and can rest underwater with just eyes, ears, and nose above the surface.

**carat** (Arabic *quirrat* 'seed') unit for measuring the mass of precious stones; it is equal to 0.2 g/0.00705 oz, and is part of the troy system of weights. It is also the unit of purity in gold (US 'karat'). Pure gold is 24-carat; 22-carat (the purest used in jewellery) is 22 parts gold and two parts alloy (to give greater strength); 18-carat is 75% gold.

**Caravaggio, Michelangelo Merisi da** (1573–1610) Italian early baroque painter. He was active in Rome 1592–1606, then in Naples, and finally in Malta. He created a forceful style, using contrasts of light and shade, dramatic foreshortening, and a meticulous attention to detail. His life was as dramatic as his art (he had to leave Rome after killing a man in a brawl).

**carbohydrate** chemical compound composed of carbon, hydrogen, and oxygen, with the basic formula $C_m(H_2O)_n$, and related compounds with the same basic structure but modified functional groups. As sugar and starch, carbohydrates are an important part of a balanced human diet, providing energy for life processes including growth and movement. Excess carbohydrate intake can be converted into fat and stored in the body.

**carbon** (Latin *carbo, carbonaris* 'coal') nonmetallic element, symbol C, atomic number 6, relative atomic mass 12.011. It occurs on its own as diamond, graphite, and as fullerenes (the allotropes), as compounds in carbonaceous rocks such as chalk and limestone, as carbon dioxide in the atmosphere, as hydrocarbons in petroleum, coal, and natural gas, and as a constituent of all organic substances.

**carbon cycle** sequence by which →carbon circulates and is recycled through the natural world. Carbon dioxide is released into the atmosphere by living things as a result of →respiration. The $CO_2$ is taken up and converted into carbohydrates during →photosynthesis by plants and by organisms such as diatoms and dinoflagellates in the oceanic →plankton; the oxygen component is released back into the atmosphere. The carbon they accumulate is later released back into circulation in various ways. The simplest occurs when an animal eats a plant and carbon is transferred from, say, a leaf cell to the animal body. Carbon is also released through the decomposition of decaying plant matter, and the burning of fossil fuels such as →coal (fossilized plants). The oceans absorb 25–40% of all carbon dioxide released into the atmosphere.

**carbohydrate** A molecule of the polysaccharide glycogen (animal starch) is formed from linked glucose ($C_6H_{12}O_6$) molecules. A typical glycogen molecule has 100–1,000 glucose units.

**carbon dioxide** $CO_2$ colourless, odourless gas, slightly soluble in water and denser than air. It is formed by the complete oxidation of carbon.

**Carboniferous** period of geological time 362.5–290 million years ago, the fifth period of the Palaeozoic era. In the USA it is divided into two periods: the Mississippian (lower) and the Pennsylvanian (upper).

Typical of the lower-Carboniferous rocks are shallow-water →limestones, while upper-Carboniferous rocks have →delta deposits with →coal (hence the name). Amphibians were abundant, and reptiles evolved during this period.

**cardinal number** in mathematics, one of the series of numbers 0, 1, 2, 3, 4, … . Cardinal numbers relate to quantity, whereas ordinal numbers (first, second, third, fourth,…) relate to order.

**Carroll, Lewis** (1832–1898) pen-name of Charles Lutwidge Dodgson, English author of the children's classics *Alice's Adventures in Wonderland* (1865) and its sequel *Through the Looking-Glass, and What Alice Found There* (1872). Among later works was the mock-heroic

---

**WEB SITE** > > > > > > > >
**Lewis Carroll Home Page**

http://www.lewiscarroll.org/carroll.html

Large site dedicated to Lewis Carroll as a writer, photographer, and mathematician. There is a large amount of information about studies of Carroll, together with information about his place in popular culture.

---

narrative poem *The Hunting of the Snark* (1876). He was a lecturer in mathematics at Oxford University from 1855–81 and also published mathematical works.

**Carthage** ancient Phoenician port in North Africa founded by colonists from Tyre in the late 9th century BC; it lay 16 km/10 mi north of Tunis, Tunisia. A leading trading centre, it was in conflict with Greece from the 6th century BC, and then with Rome, and was destroyed by Roman forces 146 BC at the end of the →Punic Wars. About 45 BC, Roman colonists settled in Carthage, and it became the wealthy capital of the province of Africa. After its capture by the Vandals AD 439 it was little more than a pirate stronghold. From 533 it formed part of the Byzantine Empire until its final destruction by Arabs 698, during their conquest in the name of Islam.

**cartilage** flexible bluish-white connective tissue made up of the protein collagen. In cartilaginous fish it forms the skeleton; in other vertebrates it forms the greater part of the embryonic skeleton, and is replaced by →bone in the course of development, except in areas of wear such as bone endings, and the discs between the backbones. It also forms structural tissue in the larynx, nose, and external ear of mammals.

**Casablanca** (Arabic *Dar el-Beida*) port, commercial, and industrial centre on the Atlantic coast of Morocco; population (1993) 2,943,000. Casablanca is one of the major ports of Africa, and the industrial centre of Morocco. It trades in fish, phosphates, and manganese. The Great Hassan II Mosque, completed in 1989, is the world's largest; it is built on a platform (40,000 sq m/430,000 sq ft) jutting out over the Atlantic, with walls 60 m/200 ft high, topped by a hydraulic sliding roof, and a minaret 175 m/574 ft high.

**cash crop** crop grown solely for sale rather than for the farmer's own use, for example, coffee, cotton, or sugar beet. Many Third World countries grow cash crops to meet their debt repayments rather than grow food for their own people. The price for these crops depends on financial interests, such as those of the multinational companies and the International Monetary Fund.

**Caspian Sea** world's largest inland sea, on the border between Europe and Asia east of the Black Sea, divided between Iran, Azerbaijan, Russia, Kazakhstan, and Turkmenistan. It extends north–south for 1,200 km/745 mi, and its average width is 300 km/186 mi; area about 400,000 sq km/155,000 sq mi, with a maximum depth of 1,000 m/3,250 ft. An underwater ridge divides it into two halves, of which the shallow northern half is almost salt-free. There are no tides, but violent storms make navigation hazardous. The chief ports are Astrakhan (Russia), Baku (Azerbaijan), and Bandar Shah (Iran). The River Volga supplies 80% of freshwater inflow; the Ural, Emba, Terek, Kura, and Atrek rivers also flow into the Caspian Sea. Prolonged drought, drainage in the north, and regulation of the

Volga and Kura rivers reduced the area from 430,000 sq km/166,000 sq mi in 1930 to 382,000 sq km/147,000 sq mi in 1957, and left the sea approximately 28 m/90 ft below sea level.

**Cassius** (c. 85 BC–42 BC) Gaius Cassius Longinus, Roman general and politician, one of Julius →Caesar's assassins. He fought with Marcus Licinius Crassus (the Elder) against the Parthians in 53 BC and distinguished himself after Carrhae by defending the province of Syria. He sided with Pompey against Julius Caesar on the outbreak of the civil war in 49, but was pardoned after the battle of Pharsalus in 48. Nevertheless, he became a leader in the conspiracy against Caesar which resulted in his murder in 44.

**caste** (Portuguese *casta* 'race') a system of stratifying a society into ranked groups defined by marriage, descent, and occupation. Most common in South Asia, caste systems are also found in other societies such as in Mali and Rwanda, and in the past, in Japan, in South Africa under apartheid, and among the Natchez.

The system in Hindu society dates from ancient times and there are over 3,000 castes, known as 'jatis', which are loosely ranked into four classes known as 'varnas': **Brahmans** (priests), **Kshatriyas** (nobles and warriors), **Vaisyas** (traders and farmers), and **Sudras** (servants); plus a fifth group, **Harijan** (untouchables).

**Castile** kingdom founded in the 10th century, occupying the central plateau of Spain. Its union with →Aragón in 1479, based on the marriage of Ferdinand and Isabella, effected the foundation of the Spanish state, which at the time was occupied and ruled by the Moors. Castile comprised the two great basins separated by the Sierra de Gredos and the Sierra de Guadarrama, known traditionally as Old and New Castile. The area now forms the regions of Castilla–León and Castilla–La Mancha.

**Castro (Ruz), Fidel** (1927–  ) Cuban communist politician, prime minister 1959–76, and president from 1976. He led two unsuccessful coups against the right-wing regime of Fulgencio Batista, and led the revolution that overthrew the dictator 1959. He raised the standard of living for most Cubans but dealt harshly with dissenters. From 1990, deprived of the support of the USSR and experiencing the long-term effects of a US trade embargo, Castro faced increasing pressure for reform; in September 1995 he moved towards greater economic flexibility by permitting foreign ownership in major areas of commerce and industry.

**cat** small, domesticated, carnivorous mammal *Felis catus*, often kept as a pet or for catching small pests such as rodents. Found in many colour variants, it may have short, long, or no hair, but the general shape and size is constant. Cats have short muzzles, strong limbs, and flexible spines which enable them to jump and climb. All walk on the pads of their toes (digitigrade) and

have retractile claws, so are able to stalk their prey silently. They have large eyes and an acute sense of hearing. The canine teeth are long and very well-developed, as are the shearing teeth in the side of the mouth.

**catalyst** substance that alters the speed of, or makes possible, a chemical or biochemical reaction but remains unchanged at the end of the reaction. →Enzymes are natural biochemical catalysts. In practice most catalysts are used to speed up reactions.

---

**WEB SITE** > > > > > > > >

**Catalysts**

http://www.puchon.co.uk/science/catalyst.html

Clear explanation of catalysts and what they do. Designed to help GCSE chemists with their revision, this page is part of a larger site of scientific revision aids. The clearly written text includes definitions of important terms such as absorption and intermediate compounds.

---

**catalytic converter** device fitted to the exhaust system of a motor vehicle in order to reduce toxic emissions from the engine. It converts harmful exhaust products to relatively harmless ones by passing the exhaust gases over a mixture of catalysts coated on a metal or ceramic honeycomb (a structure that increases the surface area and therefore the amount of active catalyst with which the exhaust gases will come into contact). **Oxidation catalysts** (small amounts of precious palladium and platinum metals) convert hydrocarbons (unburnt fuel) and carbon monoxide into carbon dioxide and water, but do not affect nitrogen oxide emissions. **Three-way catalysts** (platinum and rhodium metals) convert nitrogen oxide gases into nitrogen and oxygen.

**cataract** eye disease in which the crystalline lens or its capsule becomes cloudy, causing blindness. Fluid accumulates between the fibres of the lens and gives place to deposits of →albumin. These coalesce into rounded bodies, the lens fibres break down, and areas of the lens or the lens capsule become filled with opaque products of degeneration. The condition is estimated to have blinded more than 25 million people worldwide, and 150,000 in the UK.

**cathode** in chemistry, the negative electrode of an electrolytic →cell, towards which positive particles (cations), usually in solution, are attracted. See →electrolysis.

**cathode-ray tube** (CRT) vacuum tube in which a beam of electrons is produced and focused onto a fluorescent screen. The electrons' kinetic energy is converted into light energy as they collide with the screen. It is an essential component of television receivers, computer visual display units, and oscilloscopes.

**Catullus, Gaius Valerius** (c. 84–54 BC) Roman lyric poet. He wrote in a variety of metres and forms, from short narratives and hymns to epigrams. His love affair with the woman he called 'Lesbia' provided the inspiration for many of his poems.

**cave** roofed-over cavity in the Earth's crust usually produced by the action of underground water or by waves on a seacoast. Caves of the former type commonly occur in areas underlain by limestone, such as Kentucky and many Balkan regions, where the rocks are soluble in water. A **pothole** is a vertical hole in rock caused by water descending a crack; it is thus open to the sky.

**Caxton, William** (c. 1422–1491) English printer. He learned the art of printing in Cologne, Germany, in 1471 and set up a press in Belgium where he produced the first book printed in English, his own version of a French romance, *Recuyell of the Historyes of Troye* (1474). Returning to England in 1476, he established himself in London, where he produced the first book printed in England, *Dictes or Sayengis of the Philosophres* (1477).

**CD-ROM** (abbreviation for compact-disc read-only memory) computer storage device developed from the technology of the audio compact disc. It consists of a plastic-coated metal disk, on which binary digital information is etched in the form of microscopic pits. This can then be read optically by passing a laser beam over the disk. CD-ROMs typically hold about 650 megabytes of data, and are used in distributing large amounts of text, graphics, audio, and video, such as encyclopedias, catalogues, technical manuals, and games.

**Ceauşescu, Nicolae** (1918–1989) Romanian politician, leader of the Romanian Communist Party (RCP), in power 1965–89. He pursued a policy line independent of and critical of the USSR. He appointed family members, including his wife Elena (1919–1989), to senior state and party posts, and governed in an increasingly repressive manner, zealously implementing schemes that impoverished the nation. The Ceauşescus were overthrown in a bloody revolutionary coup in December 1989 and executed on Christmas Day that year.

**cell** in biology, the basic structural unit of life. It is the smallest unit capable of independent existence which can reproduce itself exactly. All living organisms – with the exception of →viruses – are composed of one or more cells. Single cell organisms such as bacteria, protozoa, and other micro-organisms are termed **unicellular**, while plants and animals which contain many cells are termed **multicellular** organisms. Highly complex organisms such as human beings consist of billions of cells, all of which are adapted to carry out specific functions – for instance, groups of these

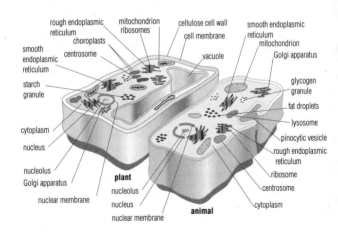

**cell structure** Typical plant and animal cell. Plant and animal cells share many structures, such as ribosomes, mitochondria, and chromosomes, but they also have notable differences: plant cells have chloroplasts, a large vacuole, and a cellulose cell wall. Animal cells do not have a rigid cell wall but have an outside cell membrane only.

specialized cells are organized into tissues and organs. Although these cells may differ widely in size, appearance, and function, their essential features are similar.

Cells divide by mitosis, or by meiosis when →gametes are being formed.

**cell, electrical** (or voltaic cell or galvanic cell) device in which chemical energy is converted into electrical energy; the popular name is →'battery', but this actually refers to a collection of cells in one unit. The reactive chemicals of a **primary cell** cannot be replenished, whereas **secondary cells** – such as storage batteries – are rechargeable: their chemical reactions can be reversed and the original condition restored by applying an electric current. It is dangerous to attempt to recharge a primary cell.

**cellular phone** (or cellphone) mobile radio telephone, one of a network connected to the telephone system by a computer-controlled communication system. Service areas are divided into small 'cells', about 5 km/3 mi across, each with a separate low-power transmitter.

**cellulose** complex →carbohydrate composed of long chains of glucose units, joined by chemical bonds called glycosidic links. It is the principal constituent of the cell wall of higher plants, and a vital ingredient in the diet of many →herbivores. Molecules of cellulose are organized into long, unbranched microfibrils that give support to the cell wall. No mammal produces the enzyme cellulase, necessary for digesting cellulose; mammals such as rabbits and cows are only able to digest grass because the bacteria present in their gut can manufacture it.

**Celsius** scale of temperature, previously called centigrade, in which the range from freezing to boiling of water is divided into 100 degrees, freezing point being 0° and boiling point 100°.

**Celt** (Greek *Keltoi*) Indo-European people that originated in Alpine Europe and spread to the Iberian peninsula and beyond. They were ironworkers and farmers. In the 1st century BC they were defeated by the Roman Empire and by Germanic tribes and confined largely to Britain, Ireland, and northern France.

**Cenozoic** (or Caenozoic) era of geological time that began 65 million years ago and continues to the present day. It is divided into the Tertiary and Quaternary periods. The Cenozoic marks the emergence of mammals as a dominant group, including humans, and the formation of the mountain chains of the Himalayas and the Alps.

**centigrade** former name for the →Celsius temperature scale.

**central nervous system** (CNS) the brain and spinal cord, as distinct from other components of the nervous system. The CNS integrates all nervous function.

**cephalopod** any predatory marine mollusc of the class Cephalopoda, with the mouth and head surrounded by tentacles. Cephalopods are the most intelligent, the fastest-moving, and the largest of all animals without backbones, and there are remarkable luminescent forms which swim or drift at great depths. They have the most highly developed nervous and sensory systems of all invertebrates, the eye in some closely paralleling that found in vertebrates. Examples include squid, octopus, and →cuttlefish. Shells are rudimentary or absent in most cephalopods.

**ceramics** objects made from clay, hardened into a permanent form by baking (firing) at very high temperatures in a kiln. Ceramics are used for building construction and decoration (bricks, tiles), for specialist industrial uses (linings for furnaces used to manufacture steel, fuel elements in nuclear reactors, and so on), and for plates and vessels used in the home. Different types of clay and different methods and temperatures of firing create a variety of results. Ceramics may be cast in a mould or hand-built out of slabs of clay, coiled, or thrown on a wheel. Technically, the main categories are earthenware, stoneware, and hard- and softpaste porcelain (see under →pottery and porcelain).

**Central African Republic** national name: *République Centrafricaine*; area: 622,436 sq km/240,322 sq mi; capital: Bangui; major towns/cities: Berbérati, Bouar, Bambari, Bossangoa, Carnot; physical features: landlocked flat plateau, with rivers flowing north and south, and hills in northeast and southwest; dry in north, rainforest in southwest; mostly wooded; Kotto and Mbali river falls; the Oubangui River rises 6 m/20 ft at Bangui during the wet season (June–November); head of state: Ange-Felix Patasse from 1993; head of government: Anicet Georges Dologuele from 1999; political system: emergent democracy; currency: franc CFA; GNP per capita (PPP): (US$) 1,290 (1998 est); exports: diamonds, coffee, timber, cotton. Principal market Belgium – Luxembourg 36.2% (1997); population: 3,594,000 (1999 est); language: French (official), Sangho (national), Arabic, Hunsa, and Swahili; religion: Protestant, Roman Catholic, Muslim, animist; life expectancy: 43 (men); 47 (women) (1995–2000).

**Cervantes, Saavedra, Miguel de** (1547–1616) Spanish novelist, dramatist, and poet. His masterpiece *Don Quixote de la Mancha* (in full *El ingenioso hidalgo Don Quixote de la Mancha*) was published in 1605. In 1613 his *Novelas ejemplares/Exemplary Novels* appeared, followed by *Viaje del Parnaso/The Voyage to Parnassus* (1614). A spurious second part of *Don Quixote* prompted Cervantes to bring out his own second part in 1615, often considered superior to the first in construction and characterization.

**Cézanne, Paul** (1839–1906) French post-Impressionist painter. He was a leading figure in the development of modern art. He broke away from the Impressionists' concern with the ever-changing effects of light to develop a style that tried to capture the structure of natural forms, whether in landscapes, still lifes, or portraits. *Joueurs de Cartes* (*Cardplayers*) (about 1890–95; Louvre, Paris) is typical of his work.

**Chad** Republic of; **national name:** *République du Tchad*; **area:** 1,284,000 sq km/495,752 sq mi; **capital:** N'djaména (formerly Fort Lamy); **major towns/cities:** Sarh, Moundou, Abéché, Bongor, Doba; **physical features:** landlocked state with mountains (Tibetsi) and part of Sahara Desert in north; moist savanna in south; rivers in south flow northwest to Lake Chad; **head of state:** Idriss Deby from 1990; **head of government:** Nassour Ouaidou Guelendouksia from 1997; **political system:** emergent democracy; **currency:** franc CFA; **GNP per capita (PPP):** (US$) 1,020 (1998 est); **exports:** cotton, live cattle, meat, hides and skins. Principal market Portugal 29.8% (1997); **population:** 7,458,000 (1999 est); **language:** French, Arabic (both official), over 100 African languages spoken; **religion:** Muslim, Christian, animist; **life expectancy:** 46 (men); 49 (women) (1995–2000).

**Chagall, Marc** (1887–1985) Belorussian-born French painter and designer. Much of his highly coloured, fantastic imagery was inspired by the village life of his boyhood and by Jewish and Russian folk traditions. He was often seen as a precursor of surrealism. *I and the Village* (1911; Museum of Modern Art, New York) is characteristic.

**chain reaction** in chemistry, a succession of reactions, usually involving →free radicals, where the products of one stage are the reactants of the next. A chain reaction is characterized by the continual generation of reactive substances.

**chain reaction** in nuclear physics, a fission reaction that is maintained because neutrons released by the splitting of some atomic nuclei themselves go on to split others, releasing even more neutrons. Such a reaction can be controlled (as in a nuclear reactor) by using moderators to absorb excess neutrons. Uncontrolled, a chain reaction produces a nuclear explosion (as in an atom bomb).

**chalk** soft, fine-grained, whitish sedimentary rock composed of calcium carbonate, $CaCO_3$, extensively quarried for use in cement, lime, and mortar, and in the manufacture of cosmetics and toothpaste. **Blackboard chalk** in fact consists of gypsum (calcium sulphate, $CaSO_4.2H_2O$).

**chamber music** music intended for performance in a small room or chamber, rather than in the concert hall, and usually written for instrumental combinations, played with one instrument to a part, as in the string quartet.

**chameleon** any of 80 or so species of lizard of the family Chameleontidae. Some species have highly developed colour-changing abilities, caused by stress and changes in the intensity of light and temperature, which alter the dispersal of pigment granules in the layers of cells beneath the outer skin.

**Chandler, Raymond Thornton** (1888–1959) US novelist. He turned the pulp detective mystery form into a successful genre of literature and created the quintessential private eye in the tough but chivalric loner, Philip Marlowe. Marlowe is the narrator of such books as *The Big Sleep* (1939; filmed 1946), *Farewell My Lovely* (1940; filmed 1944), *The Lady in the Lake* (1943; filmed 1947), and *The Long Goodbye* (1954 filmed 1975).

**chaos theory** (or chaology or complexity theory) branch of mathematics that attempts to describe irregular, unpredictable systems – that is, systems whose behaviour is difficult to predict because there are so many variable or unknown factors. Weather is an example of a chaotic system.

**Chaplin, Charlie (Charles Spencer)** (1889–1977) English film actor and director. One of cinema's most popular stars, he made his reputation as a tramp with a smudge moustache, bowler hat, and twirling cane in silent comedies, including *The Rink* (1916), *The Kid* (1921), and *The Gold Rush* (1925). His work combines buffoonery with pathos, as in *The Great Dictator* (1940) and *Limelight* (1952).

**charcoal** black, porous form of →carbon, produced by heating wood or other organic materials in the absence of air. It is used as a fuel in the smelting of metals such as copper and zinc, and by artists for making black line drawings **Activated charcoal** has been powdered and dried so that it presents a much increased surface area for adsorption; it is used for filtering and purifying liquids and gases – for example, in drinking-water filters and gas masks.

**Charlemagne, Charles I, the Great** (742–814) king of the Franks from 768 and Holy Roman Emperor from 800. By inheritance (his father was Pepin the Short) and extensive campaigns of conquest, he united most of western Europe by 804, when after 30 years of war the Saxons came under his control.

**Charles I** (1600–1649) king of Great Britain and Ireland from 1625, son of James I of England (James VI of Scotland). He accepted the petition of right in 1628 but then dissolved Parliament and ruled without a parliament 1629–40. His advisers were Strafford and Laud, who persecuted the Puritans and provoked the Scots to revolt. The →Short Parliament, summoned in 1640, refused funds, and the →Long Parliament later that year rebelled. Charles declared war on Parliament in 1642 but surrendered in 1646 and was beheaded in 1649. He was the father of Charles II.

**Charles II** (1630–1685) king of Great Britain and Ireland from 1660, when Parliament accepted the restoration of the monarchy after the collapse of Oliver Cromwell's Commonwealth; son of Charles I. His chief minister Edward Clarendon, who arranged Charles marriage in 1662 with Catherine of Braganza, was replaced in 1667 with the Cabal of advisers. His plans to restore Catholicism in Britain led to war with the Netherlands 1672–74 in support of Louis XIV of France and a break with Parliament, which he dissolved in 1681. He was succeeded by James II.

**Charles Edward Stuart** (1720–1788) (the Young Pretender or Bonnie Prince Charlie) British prince, grandson of James II and son of James, the Old Pretender. In the Jacobite rebellion of 1745 Charles won the support of the Scottish Highlanders; his army invaded England to claim the throne but was beaten back by the duke of Cumberland and routed at →Culloden on 16 April 1746. Charles fled; for five months he wandered through the Highlands with a price of £30,000 on his head before escaping to France. He visited England secretly in 1750, and may have made other visits. In later life he degenerated into a friendless drunkard. He settled in Italy in 1766.

**Charles's law** law stating that the volume of a given mass of gas at constant pressure is directly proportional to its absolute temperature (temperature in kelvin). It was discovered by French physicist Jacques Charles 1787, and independently by French chemist Joseph Gay-Lussac in 1802.

**Chartism** radical British democratic movement, mainly of the working classes, which flourished around 1838–48. It derived its name from the People's Charter, a six-point programme comprising universal male suffrage, equal electoral districts, secret ballot, annual parliaments, and abolition of the property qualification for, and payment of, members of Parliament.

**Chateaubriand, François Auguste René, Vicomte de** (1768–1848) French writer. He was a founder of Romanticism. Having lived in exile from the French Revolution 1794–1800, he wrote *Atala* (1801) (based on his encounters with North American Indians), *Le Génie du christianisme/The Genius of Christianity* (1802) – a defence of the Christian faith in terms of social, cultural, and spiritual benefits – and the autobiographical *René* (1805).

**Chaucer, Geoffrey** (c. 1340–1400) English poet. *The Canterbury Tales*, a collection of stories told by a group of pilgrims on their way to Canterbury, reveals his knowledge of human nature and his stylistic variety, from urbane and ironic to simple and bawdy. His early work shows formal French influence, as in the dream-poem *The Book of the Duchess* and his adaptation of the French allegorical poem on courtly love, *The Romaunt of the Rose*. More mature works reflect the influence of Italian realism, as in *Troilus and Criseyde*, a substantial narrative poem about the tragic betrayal of an idealized courtly love, adapted from →Boccaccio. In *The Canterbury*

*Tales* he shows his own genius for metre and characterization. Chaucer was the most influential English poet of the Middle Ages.

**Chekhov, Anton Pavlovich** (1860–1904) Russian dramatist and writer of short stories. His plays concentrate on the creation of atmosphere and delineation of internal development, rather than external action. His first play, *Ivanov* (1887), was a failure, as was *The Seagull* (1896) until revived by Stanislavsky (1898) at the Moscow Art Theatre, for which Chekhov went on to write his finest plays: *Uncle Vanya* (1897), *The Three Sisters* (1901), and *The Cherry Orchard* (1904).

**chemistry** branch of science concerned with the study of the structure and composition of the different kinds of matter, the changes which matter may undergo and the phenomena which occur in the course of these changes.

**Organic chemistry** is the branch of chemistry that deals with carbon compounds. **Inorganic chemistry** deals with the description, properties, reactions, and preparation of all the elements and their compounds, with the exception of carbon compounds. **Physical chemistry** is concerned with the quantitative explanation of chemical phenomena and reactions, and the measurement of data required for such explanations. This branch studies in particular the movement of molecules and the effects of temperature and pressure, often with regard to gases and liquids.

**chemotherapy** any medical treatment with chemicals. It usually refers to treatment of cancer with cytotoxic and other drugs. The term was coined by the German bacteriologist Paul Ehrlich for the use of synthetic chemicals against infectious diseases.

**Chernobyl** town in northern Ukraine 100 km/62 mi north of Kiev; site of a nuclear power station. On 26 April 1986, two huge explosions occurred at the plant, destroying a central reactor and breaching its 1,000-tonne roof. In the immediate vicinity of Chernobyl, 31 people died (all firemen or workers at the plant) and 135,000 were permanently evacuated. It has been estimated that there will be an additional 20–40,000 deaths from cancer in the following 60 years; 600,000 are officially classified as at risk.

**chess** board game originating as early as the 2nd century AD. Two players use 16 pieces each, on a board of 64 squares of alternating colour, to try to force the opponent into a position where the main piece (the king) is threatened and cannot move to another position without remaining threatened.

**Chicago** (Ojibway 'wild onion place') financial and industrial city in Illinois, USA, on Lake Michigan. It is the third largest US city; population (1992) 2,768,500; metropolitan area (1992) 8,410,000. Industries include iron, steel, chemicals, electrical goods, machinery, meatpacking and food processing, publishing, and fabricated metals. The once famous stockyards are now closed. Chicago grew from a village in the mid-19th century. The world's first skyscraper was built here 1885 and some of the world's tallest skyscrapers, including the Sears Tower (443 m/ 1,454 ft high), are in Chicago.

**chickenpox** (or varicella) common, usually mild disease, caused by a virus of the →herpes group and transmitted by airborne droplets. Chickenpox chiefly attacks children under the age of ten. The incubation period is two to three weeks. One attack normally gives immunity for life.

**Chile** Republic of; **national name:** *República de Chile;* **area:** 756,950 sq km/292,258 sq mi; **capital:** Santiago; **major towns/cities:** Concepción, Viña del Mar, Valparaiso, Talcahuano, San Bernardo, Puente Alto, Chillán, Rancagua, Talca, Temuco; **major ports:** Valparaíso, Antofagasta, Arica, Iquique, Punta Arenas; **physical features:** Andes mountains along eastern border, Atacama Desert in north, fertile central valley, grazing land and forest in south; **territories:** Easter Island, Juan Fernández Islands, part of Tierra del Fuego, claim to part of Antarctica; **head of state:** Ricardo Lagos from 2000; **head of government:** Dante Cordova from 1995; **political system:** emergent democracy; **currency:** Chilean peso; **GNP per capita (PPP):** (US$) 12,890 (1998); **exports:** copper, fruits, timber products, fishmeal, vegetables, manufactured foodstuffs and beverages. Principal market USA 17.7% (1998); **population:** 15,019,000 (1999 est); **language:** Spanish; **Religion:** Roman Catholic; **life expectancy:** 72 (men); 78 (women) (1995–2000).

**chilli** pod, or powder made from the pod, of a variety of capsicum (*Capsicum frutescens*), a small, hot, red pepper. It is widely used in cooking. The hot ingredient of chilli is capsaicin. It causes a burning sensation in the mouth by triggering nerve branches in the eyes, nose, tongue, and mouth.

Capsaicin does not activate the taste buds and therefore has no flavour. It is claimed that people can become physically addicted to it.

**chimpanzee** highly intelligent African ape *Pan troglodytes* that lives mainly in rainforests but sometimes in wooded savanna. Chimpanzees are covered in thin but long black body hair, except for the face, hands, and feet, which may have pink or black skin. They normally walk on all fours, supporting the front of the body on the knuckles of the fingers, but can stand or walk upright for a short distance. They can grow to 1.4 m/4.5 ft tall, and weigh up to 50 kg/110 lb. They are strong and climb well, but spend time on the ground, living in loose social groups. The bulk of the diet is fruit, with some leaves, insects, and occasional meat. Females reach sexual maturity at 8–12 years of age, males at

---

**WEB SITE** > > > > > > > >

**Chimpanzee**

http://www.seaworld.org/animal_bytes /chimpanzeeab.html

Illustrated guide to the chimpanzee including information about genus, size, life span, habitat, gestation, diet, and a series of fun facts.

17–18. Chimpanzees give birth to a single infant approximately every five years. Chimpanzees can use 'tools', fashioning twigs to extract termites from their nests. According to a 1998 estimate by the Worldwide Fund for Nature, the world population of chimpanzees stands at 200,000.

The **bonobo** or pygmy chimpanzee, *Pan paniscus* is found only in a small area of rainforest in the Democratic Republic of Congo (formerly Zaire). Bonobos are a distinct species about the same height as 'common' chimpanzees, but they are of a slighter build, with less hair, and stand upright more frequently. In 1999 there were believed to be fewer than 15,000 bonobos left and these were threatened by the civil war in the Democratic Republic of Congo.

**China** People's Republic of; **national name:** *Zhonghua Renmin Gonghe Guo;* **area:** 9,572,900 sq km/3,696,000 sq mi; **capital:** Beijing (Peking); **major towns/ cities:** Shanghai, Hong Kong, Chongqing (Chungking), Tianjin, Guangzhou (Canton), Shenyang (Mukden), Wuhan, Nanjing (Nanking), Harbin, Chengdu, Xi'an, Zibo; **major ports:** Tianjin (Tientsin), Shanghai, Hong Kong, Qingdao (Tsingtao), Guangzhou (Canton); **physical features:** two-thirds of China is mountains or desert (north and west); the lowlying east is irrigated by rivers Huang He (Yellow River), Chang Jiang (Yangtze-Kiang), Xi Jiang (Si Kiang); **head of state:** Jiang Zemin from 1993; **head of government:** Zhu Rongji from 1998; **political system:** communist republic; **currency:** yuan; **GNP per capita (PPP):** (US$) 3,220 (1998); **exports:** basic manufactures, miscellaneous manufactured articles (particularly clothing and toys), crude petroleum, machinery and transport equipment, fishery products, cereals, canned food, tea, raw silk, cotton cloth. Principal market Hong Kong 21.1% (1998); **population** 1,273,639,000 (1999 est); **language:** Chinese, including Mandarin (official) Cantonese, Wu, and other dialects **religion:** Taoist, Confucianist, and Buddhist; Muslim 20 million; Catholic 3–6 million (divided between the 'patriotic' church established in 1958 and the 'loyal' church subject to Rome) Protestant 3 million; **life expectancy** 68 (men); 72 (women) (1995–2000).

**China Sea** area of the Pacific Ocean bordered by China, Vietnam, Borneo, the Philippines, and Japan. Various groups of small islands and shoals, including the Paracels, 500 km/300 mi east of Vietnam, have been disputed by China and other powers because they lie in oil-rich areas. The chief rivers which flow into the South China Sea are the Red River and Mekong; the main ports include Canton, Hong Kong, Manila, Bangkok, Singapore, and Ho Chi Minh City.

**Chinese Revolution** series of great political upheavals in China between 1911 and 1949 which eventually led to Communist Party rule and the establishment of the People's Republic of China. In 1912 a nationalist revolt overthrew the imperial Manchu dynasty. Under the leaders Sun Zhong Shan (Sun Yat-sen) (1923–25) and Jiang Jie Shi (Chiang Kai-shek) (1925–49) the nationalists, or Guomindang, were increasing challenged by the growing communist movement. The 10,000-km/6,000-mi →Long March to the north-west, undertaken by the communists in 1934–35 to escape Guomindang harassment, resulted in the emergence of →Mao Zedong as a communist leader. During World War II the various Chinese political groups pooled military resources against the Japanese invaders, but in 1946 the conflict reignited into open civil war. In 1949 the Guomindang were defeated at Nanjing and forced to flee to Taiwan. Communist rule was established in the People's Republic of China under the leadership of Mao Zedong.

**chip** (or silicon chip) another name for an →integrated circuit, a complete electronic circuit on a slice of silicon (or other semiconductor) crystal only a few millimetres square.

**chiropractic** in alternative medicine, technique of manipulation of the spine and other parts of the body, based on the principle that physical disorders are attributable to aberrations in the functioning of the nervous system, which manipulation can correct.

**chitin** complex long-chain compound, or polymer; a nitrogenous derivative of glucose. Chitin is widely found in invertebrates. It forms the exoskeleton of insects and other arthropods. It combines with protein to form a covering that can be hard and tough, as in beetles, or soft and flexible, as in caterpillars and other insect larvae. It is insoluble in water and resistant to acids, alkalis, and many organic solvents. In crustaceans such as crabs, it is impregnated with calcium carbonate for extra strength.

**chlorine** (Greek *chloros* 'green') greenish-yellow, gaseous, nonmetallic element with a pungent odour, symbol Cl, atomic number 17, relative atomic mass 35.453. It is a member of the →halogen group and is widely distributed, in combination with the alkali metals, as chlorates or chlorides.

**chlorofluorocarbon** (CFC) a class of synthetic chemicals that are odourless, nontoxic, nonflammable, and chemically inert. The first CFC was synthesized in 1892, but no use was found for it until the 1920s. Since then their stability and apparently harmless properties have made CFCs popular as propellants in →aerosol cans, as refrigerants in refrigerators and air conditioners, as degreasing agents, and in the manufacture of foam packaging. They are partly responsible for the destruction of the →ozone layer. In June 1990 representatives of 93 nations, including the UK and the USA, agreed to phase out production of CFCs and various other ozone-depleting chemicals.

**chlorophyll** green pigment present in most plants; it is responsible for the absorption of light energy during →photosynthesis. The pigment absorbs the red and blue-violet parts of sunlight but reflects the green, thus giving plants their characteristic colour.

**cholera** disease caused by infection with various strains of the bacillus *Vibrio cholerae*, transmitted in contaminated water and characterized by violent diarrhoea and vomiting. It is prevalent in many tropical areas.

**cholesterol** white, crystalline sterol found throughout the body, especially in fats, blood, nerve tissue, and bile; it is also provided in the diet by foods such as eggs, meat, and butter. A high level of cholesterol in the blood is thought to contribute to atherosclerosis (hardening of the arteries).

**Chopin, Frédéric François** (1810–1849) Polish composer and pianist. He made his debut as a pianist at the age of eight. His compositions for piano, which include two concertos and other works with orchestra, are characterized by great volatility of mood, and rhythmic fluidity.

**chordate** animal belonging to the phylum Chordata, which includes vertebrates, sea squirts, amphioxi, and others. All these animals, at some stage of their lives, have a supporting rod of tissue (notochord or backbone) running down their bodies.

**Christ** (Greek *khristos* 'anointed one') the Messiah as prophesied in the Hebrew Bible, or Old Testament.

**Christianity** world religion derived from the teaching of Jesus, as found in the New Testament, during the first third of the 1st century. It has a present-day membership of about 1 billion, and is divided into groups or denominations that differ in some areas of belief and practice. Its main divisions are the →Roman Catholic, →Eastern Orthodox, and →Protestant churches; **beliefs:** Christians believe in one God with three aspects: God the Father, God the Son (Jesus), and God the Holy Spirit, who is the power of God working in the world. God created everything that exists and showed his love for the world by coming to Earth as Jesus, and suffering and dying in order to reconcile humanity to himself. Christians believe that three days after his death by crucifixion Jesus was raised to life by God's power, appearing many times in bodily form to his followers, and that he is now alive in the world through the Holy Spirit. Christians speak of the sufferings they may have to endure because of their faith, and the reward of everlasting life in God's presence, which is promised to those who have faith in Jesus Christ and who live according to his teaching.

**Christie, Agatha Mary Clarissa** (1890–1976) born Miller, English detective novelist. She is best known for her ingenious plots and for the creation of the characters Hercule Poirot and Miss Jane Marple. She wrote more than 70 novels, including *The Murder of Roger Ackroyd* (1926) and *The Body in the Library* (1942). Her play *The Mousetrap*, which opened in London in 1952, is the longest continuously running show in the world.

**Christopher, St** patron saint of travellers. His feast day, 25 July, was dropped from the Roman Catholic liturgical calendar 1969.

**chromatography** (Greek *chromos* 'colour') technique for separating or analysing a mixture of gases, liquids, or dissolved substances. This is brought about by means of two immiscible substances, one of which (the mobile phase) transports the sample mixture through the other (the stationary phase). The mobile phase may be a gas or a liquid; the stationary phase may be a liquid or a solid, and may be in a column, on paper, or in a thin layer on a glass or plastic support. The components of the mixture are absorbed or impeded by the stationary phase to different extents and therefore become separated. The technique is used for both qualitative and quantitive analyses in biology and chemistry.

---

**WEB SITE** > > > > > > > >

**Chromatography**

http://www.eng.rpi.edu/dept/ chem-eng/Biotech-Environ/CHROMO/ chromintro.html

Explanation of the theory and practice of chromatography. Designed for school students (and introduced by a Biotech Bunny), the contents include equipment, analysing a chromatogram, and details of the various kinds of chromatography.

---

**chromium** (Greek *chromos* 'colour') hard, brittle, grey-white, metallic element, symbol Cr, atomic number 24, relative atomic mass 51.996. It takes a high polish, has a high melting point, and is very resistant to corrosion. It is used in chromium electroplating, in the manufacture of stainless steel and other alloys, and as a catalyst. Its compounds are used for tanning leather and for alums. In human nutrition it is a vital trace element. In nature, it occurs chiefly as chrome iron ore or chromite ($FeCr_2O_4$). Kazakhstan, Zimbabwe, and Brazil are sources.

**chromosome** structure in a cell nucleus that carries the →genes. Each chromosome consists of one very long strand of DNA, coiled and folded to produce a compact body. The point on a chromosome where a particular gene occurs is known as its locus. Most higher organisms have two copies of each chromosome, together known as a **homologous pair** (they are →diploid) but some have only one (they are →haploid). There are 46 chromosomes in a normal human cell. *See illustration on page 132.*

**Churchill, Winston Leonard Spencer** (1874–1965) British Conservative politician, prime minister 1940–45 and 1951–55. In Parliament from 1900, as a Liberal until 1923, he held a number of ministerial offices, including First Lord of the Admiralty 1911–15 and chancellor of the Exchequer 1924–29. Absent from the cabinet in the 1930s, he returned in September 1939 to lead a coalition government 1940–45, negotiating with Allied leaders in World War II to achieve the unconditional surrender of Germany in 1945. He led a Conservative government 1951–55. He received the Nobel Prize for Literature in 1953.

**Church of England** established form of

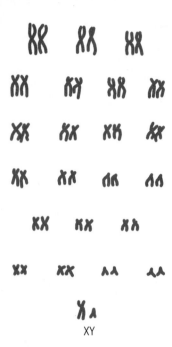

**chromosome** The 23 pairs of chromosomes of a normal human male.

Christianity in England, a member of the Anglican Communion. It was dissociated from the Roman Catholic Church in 1534 under Henry VIII; the British monarch is still the supreme head of the Church of England today. The service book is the Book of Common Prayer.

**Church of Scotland** established form of Christianity in Scotland, first recognized by the state in 1560. It is based on the Protestant doctrines of the reformer →Calvin and governed on Presbyterian lines. The church went through several periods of episcopacy (government by bishops) in the 17th century, and those who adhered to episcopacy after 1690 formed the Episcopal Church of Scotland, an autonomous church in communion with the Church of England. In 1843 there was a split in the Church of Scotland (the Disruption), in which almost a third of its ministers and members left and formed the Free Church of Scotland. By an Act of Union of 3 October 1929 the Church of Scotland was united with the United Free Church of Scotland to form the United Church of Scotland. There are 680,000 members of the Church of Scotland (1998).

**Cicero, Marcus Tullius** (106–43 BC) Roman orator, writer, and politician. His speeches and philosophical and rhetorical works are models of Latin prose, and his letters provide a picture of contemporary Roman life. As consul in 63 BC he exposed the Roman politician Catiline's conspiracy in four major orations.

**Cid, El, Rodrigo Díaz de Viva** (c. 1043–1099) Spanish soldier, nicknamed El Cid ('the lord') by the Moors. Born in Castile of a noble family, he fought against the king of Navarre and won his nickname *el Campeador* ('the Champion') by killing the Navarrese champion in single combat. Essentially a mercenary, fighting both with and against the Moors, he died while defending Valencia against them, and in subsequent romances became Spain's national hero.

**Cinque Ports** group of ports in southern England, originally five, Sandwich, Dover, Hythe, Romney, and Hastings, later including Rye, Winchelsea, and others. Probably founded in Roman times, they rose to importance after the Norman conquest and until the end of the 15th century were bound to supply the ships and men necessary against invasion. Their importance declined in the 16th and 17th centuries with the development of a standing navy.

**circle** perfectly round shape, the path of a point that moves so as to keep a constant distance from a fixed point (the centre). Each circle has a **radius** (the distance from any point on the circle to the centre), a **circumference** (the boundary of the circle, part of which is called an arc), **diameters** (straight lines crossing the circle through the centre), **chords** (lines joining two points on the circumference), **tangents** (lines that touch the circumference at one point only), **sectors** (regions inside the circle between two radii), and **segments** (regions between a chord and the circumference).

**circuit** in physics or electrical engineering, an arrangement of electrical components through which a current can flow. There are two basic circuits, series and parallel. In a series circuit, the components are connected end to end so that the current flows through all

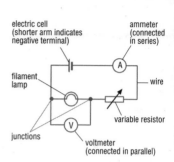

**circuit** A circuit diagram shows in graphical form how the components of an electric circuit are connected together. Each component is represented by an internationally recognized symbol, and the connecting wires are shown by straight lines. A dot indicates where wires join.

components one after the other. In a parallel circuit, components are connected side by side so that part of the current passes through each component.

**circulatory system** system of vessels in an animal's body that transports essential substances (→blood or other circulatory fluid) to and from the different parts of the body. It was first discovered and described by English physician, William →Harvey. All mammals except for the simplest kinds – such as sponges, jellyfish, sea anemones, and corals – have some type of circulatory system. Some invertebrates (animals without a backbone), such as insects, spiders, and most shellfish, have an 'open' circulatory system which consists of a simple network of tubes and hollow spaces. Other invertebrates have pumplike structures that send blood through a system of blood vessels. All vertebrates (animals with a backbone), including human beings, have a 'closed' circulatory system which principally consists of a pumping organ – the →heart – and a network of blood vessels.

**cirrhosis** any degenerative disease in an organ of the body, especially the liver, characterized by excessive development of connective tissue, causing scarring and painful swelling. Cirrhosis of the liver may be caused by an infection such as viral hepatitis, chronic obstruction of the common bile duct, chronic alcoholism or drug use, blood disorder, heart failure, or malnutrition. However, often no cause is apparent. If cirrhosis is diagnosed early, it can be arrested by treating the cause; otherwise it will progress to coma and death.

**civil engineering** branch of engineering that is concerned with the construction of roads, bridges, airports, aqueducts, waterworks, tunnels, canals, irrigation works, and harbours.

**Civil War, American** also called the War Between the States, war 1861–65 between the Southern or Confederate States of America and the Northern or Union states. The former wished to maintain certain 'states' rights', in particular the right to determine state law on the institution of slavery, and claimed the right to secede from the Union; the latter fought primarily to maintain the Union, with slave emancipation (proclaimed 1863) a secondary issue.

**Civil War, English** conflict between King Charles I and the Royalists (also called Cavaliers) on one side and the Parliamentarians (also called Roundheads) under Oliver →Cromwell on the other. Their differences centred initially on the king's unconstitutional acts, but later became a struggle over the relative powers of crown and Parliament. Hostilities began in 1642 and a series of Royalist defeats (at Marston Moor in 1644, and then at Naseby in 1645) culminated in Charles's capture in 1647, and execution in 1649. The war continued until the final defeat of Royalist forces at Worcester in 1651. Cromwell then became Protector (ruler) from 1653 until his death in 1658.

**Civil War, Spanish** war 1936–39 precipitated by a military revolt led by General Franco against the Republican government. Inferior military capability led to the gradual defeat of the Republicans by 1939, and the establishment of Franco's dictatorship.

**Clare** county on the west coast of the Republic of Ireland, in the province of Munster, situated between Galway Bay in the north and the Shannon estuary in the south; county town Ennis; area 3,190 sq km/1,231 sq mi; population (1996) 94,000. Other towns include Kilrush, Kilkee, and Shannon, an important 'new' town noted for its light industry, and electronics and aerospace industries. Dairying and cattle rearing are the principal farming activities; there are also important salmon fisheries and extensive oyster beds. Slate and black marble are quarried and worked; lead is also found. The Shannon is a source of hydroelectricity: there is a power station at Ardnacrusha, 5 km/3 mi north of Limerick.

**clarinet** any of a family of single-reed woodwind instruments of cylindrical bore. The clarinet did not establish itself in the orchestra until after the middle of the 18th century. In their concertos for clarinet, Mozart and Weber exploited the instrument's range of tone from the dark low register rising to brilliance, and its capacity for sustained dynamic control. The ability of the clarinet both to blend and to contrast with other instruments makes it popular for chamber music and as a solo instrument. It is also heard in military and concert bands and as a jazz instrument.

**class** in biological classification, a group of related orders. For example, all mammals belong to the class Mammalia and all birds to the class Aves. Among plants, all class names end in 'idae' (such as Asteridae) and among fungi in 'mycetes'; there are no equivalent conventions among animals. Related classes are grouped together in a phylum.

**classicism** term used in art, music, and literature, to characterize work that emphasizes the qualities traditionally associated with ancient Greek and Roman art, that is, reason, balance, objectivity, and restraint, as opposed to the individuality of expression typical of Romanticism. Classicism and Romanticism are often considered as opposite poles of art, but

in fact many artists show elements of both in their work. At certain times,

**Claudius I** (10 BC–AD 54) Tiberius Claudius Drusus Nero Germanicus, nephew of Tiberius, and son of Drusus Nero, made Roman emperor by the Praetorian Guard AD 41, after the murder of his nephew →Caligula. Claudius was a scholar and historian. During his reign the Roman empire was considerably extended, and in 43 he took part in the invasion of Britain.

**clay** very fine-grained →sedimentary deposit that has undergone a greater or lesser degree of consolidation. When moistened it is plastic, and it hardens on heating, which renders it impermeable. It may be white, grey, red, yellow, blue, or black, depending on its composition. Clay minerals consist largely of hydrous silicates of aluminium and magnesium together with iron, potassium, sodium, and organic substances. The crystals of clay minerals have a layered structure, capable of holding water, and are responsible for its plastic properties. According to international classification, in mechanical analysis of soil, clay has a grain size of less than 0.002 mm/ 0.00008 in.

**Cleopatra** (c. 68–30 BC) queen of Egypt 51–48 and 47–30 BC. When the Roman general Julius Caesar arrived in Egypt, he restored Cleopatra to the throne from which she had been ousted. Cleopatra and Caesar became lovers and she went with him to Rome. After Caesar's assassination 44 BC she returned to Alexandria and resumed her position as queen of Egypt. In 41 BC she was joined there by Mark Antony, one of Rome's rulers. In 31 BC Rome declared war on Egypt and scored a decisive victory in the naval Battle of Actium off the west coast of Greece. Cleopatra fled with her 60 ships to Egypt; Antony abandoned the struggle and followed her. Both he and Cleopatra committed suicide.

**Clinton, Bill (William Jefferson)** (1946– ) 42nd president of the USA from 1993, a Democrat. He served as governor of Arkansas 1979–81 and 1983–93, establishing a liberal and progressive reputation. As president, he sought to implement a **New Democrat** programme, combining social reform with economic conservatism as a means of bringing the country out of recession. He introduced legislation to reduce the federal deficit and cut crime, but the loss of both houses of Congress to the Republicans in 1994 presented a serious obstacle to further social reform. However, he successfully repositioned himself on the centre-right to become, in November 1996, the first Democrat since F D Roosevelt to be elected for a second term. Following accusations of perjury and obstruction of justice, concerning mainly his improper relationship with a White House intern, Clinton underwent an impeachment trial (the second such trial in US history) in early 1999 and was acquitted.

**clitoris** (Greek *kleitoris* 'little hill') in anatomy, part of the female reproductive system. The glans of the clitoris is visible externally. It connects to a pyramid-shaped pad of erectile tissue. Attached to this are two 'arms' that extend backwards into the body towards the anus and are approximately 9 cm/3.5 in in length. Between these arms are the clitoral bulbs, lying one on each side of the vaginal cavity.

**clone** an exact replica. In genetics, any one of a group of genetically identical cells or organisms. An identical →twin is a clone; so, too, are bacteria living in the same colony. The term 'clone' has also been adopted by computer technology to describe a (nonexistent) device that mimics an actual one to enable certain software programs to run correctly.

**cloud** water vapour condensed into minute water particles that float in masses in the atmosphere. Clouds, like fogs or mists, which occur at lower levels, are formed by the cooling of air containing water vapour, which generally condenses around tiny dust particles.

---

**WEB SITE** > > > > > > > >
### Clouds and Precipitation

http://ww2010.atmos.uiuc.edu/(GH)/guides/mtr/cld/home.rxm/

Illustrated guide to how clouds form and to the various different types. The site contains plenty of images and a glossary of key terms in addition to further explanations of the various types of precipitation.

---

**cloud chamber** apparatus for tracking ionized particles. It consists of a vessel fitted with a piston and filled with air or other gas, saturated with water vapour. When the volume of the vessel is suddenly expanded by moving the piston outwards, the vapour cools and a cloud of tiny droplets forms on any nuclei, dust, or ions present. As fast-moving ionizing particles collide with the air or gas molecules, they show as visible tracks.

**Cnut** alternative spelling of →Canute.

**coal** black or blackish mineral substance formed from the compaction of ancient plant matter in tropical swamp conditions. It is used as a fuel and in the chemical industry. Coal is classified according to the proportion of carbon it contains. The main types are →anthracite (shiny, with about 90% carbon), **bituminous coal** (shiny and dull patches, about 75% carbon), and **lignite** (woody, grading into peat, about 50% carbon). Coal burning is one of the main causes of →acid rain.

**coastal erosion** the erosion of the land by the constant battering of the sea's waves, primarily by the processes of hydraulic action, corrasion, attrition, and corrosion. Hydraulic action occurs when the force of the waves compresses air pockets in coastal rocks and cliffs. The air expands explosively, breaking the rocks apart. Rocks and pebbles flung by waves against the cliff face wear it away by the process of corrasion. Chalk and limestone coasts are often broken down by solution (also called corrosion). Attrition is the process by which the eroded rock particles themselves are worn down, becoming smaller and more rounded.

**cocaine** alkaloid $C_{17}H_{21}NO_4$ extracted from the leaves of the coca tree. It has limited medical application, mainly as a local anaesthetic agent that is readily absorbed by mucous membranes (lining tissues) of the nose and throat. It is both toxic and addictive. Its use as a stimulant is illegal. Crack is a derivative of cocaine.

**cockatoo** any of several crested parrots, especially of the genus *Cacatua*, family Psittacidae, of the order Psittaciformes. They usually have light-coloured plumage with tinges of red, yellow, or orange on the face, and an erectile crest on the head. They are native to Australia, New Guinea, and nearby islands.

**cocoa and chocolate** (Aztec *xocolatl*) food products made from the cacao (or cocoa) bean, fruit of a tropical tree *Theobroma cacao*, now cultivated mainly in Africa. Chocolate as a drink was introduced to Europe from the New World by the Spanish in the 16th century; eating-chocolate was first produced in the late 18th century. Cocoa and chocolate are widely used in confectionery and drinks.

**Cocos Islands** (or Keeling Islands) group of 27 small coral islands in the Indian Ocean, about 2,700 km/1,678 mi northwest of Perth, Australia; area 14 sq km/5.5 sq mi; population (1996) 655. An Australian external territory since 1955, the islanders voted to become part of Australia in 1984, and in 1992 they became subject to the laws of Western Australia. The main product is copra (dried kernels of coconut, used to make coconut oil), and the islands are a site for ecotourism.

**codeine** opium derivative that provides →analgesia in mild to moderate pain. It also suppresses the cough centre of the brain. It is an alkaloid, derived from morphine but less toxic and addictive.

**coelenterate** any freshwater or marine organism of the phylum Coelenterata, having a body wall composed of two layers of cells. They also possess stinging cells. Examples are jellyfish, hydra, and coral.

**coffee** drink made from the roasted and ground beanlike seeds found inside the red berries of any of several species of shrubs, originally native to Ethiopia and now cultivated throughout the tropics. It contains a stimulant, →caffeine. (Genus *Coffea*, family Rubiaceae.)

**Cold War** ideological, political, and economic tensions 1945–89 between the USSR and Eastern Europe on the one hand and the USA and Western Europe on the other. The Cold War was fuelled by propaganda, undercover activity by intelligence agencies, and economic sanctions; and was intensified by signs of conflict anywhere in the world. Arms-reduction agreements between the USA and USSR in the late 1980s, and a reduction of Soviet influence in Eastern Europe, led to a reassessment of positions, and the 'war' was officially ended in December 1989. The term 'Cold War' was first used by Bernard Baruch, advisor to US President Truman, in a speech made in April 1947. He spoke about Truman's intent for the USA to 'support free peoples who are resisting attempted subjugation by armed minorities or by outside pressures'.

**Coleridge, Samuel Taylor** (1772–1834) English poet, critic, and philosopher. A friend of the poets Robert Southey and William →Wordsworth, he collaborated with the latter on the highly influential collection *Lyrical Ballads* (1798), which expressed their theory of poetic sensation and spearheaded the English Romantic Movement. His poems include 'The Rime of the Ancient Mariner', 'Christabel', and 'Kubla Khan' (all written 1797–98); his critical works include Biographia Literaria (1817).

**Colette, Sidonie-Gabrielle** (1873–1954) French writer. Her best novels reveal an exquisite sensitivity, largely centred on the joys and sorrows of love, and include *Chéri* (1920), *La Fin de Chéri/The End of Chéri* (1926), and *Gigi* (1944).

**collagen** protein that is the main constituent of connective tissue. Collagen is present in skin, cartilage, tendons, and ligaments. Bones are made up of collagen, with the mineral calcium phosphate providing increased rigidity.

**Collins, (William) Wilkie** (1824–1889) English author of mystery and suspense novels. He wrote *The Woman in White* (1860) (with its fat villain Count Fosco), often called the first English detective novel, and *The Moonstone* (1868) (with

Sergeant Cuff, one of the first detectives in English literature).

**Cologne** (German *Köln*) industrial and commercial port in North Rhine-Westphalia, Germany, on the left bank of the Rhine, 35 km/22 mi southeast of Düsseldorf; population (1995) 964,200. Cologne is an important transhipment centre, and a major industrial centre for the manufacture of cars (Ford), machinery, electrical goods, chemicals, clothing, and food; other industries include environmental and chemical engineering, and waste management.

**Colombia** Republic of; **national name:** *República de Colombia*; **area:** 1,141,748 sq km/440,828 sq mi; **capital:** Bogotá; **major towns/cities:** Medellín, Cali, Barranquilla, Cartagena, Bucaramanga, Buenaventura; **major ports:** Barranquilla, Cartagena, Buenaventura; **physical features:** the Andes mountains run north–south; flat coastland in west and plains (llanos) in east; Magdalena River runs north to Caribbean Sea; includes islands of Providencia, San Andrés, and Mapelo; almost half the country is forested; **head of state and government:** Andres Pastrana from 1998; **political system:** democracy; **currency:** Colombian peso; **GNP per capita (PPP):** (US$) 7,500 (1998); **exports:** coffee, petroleum and petroleum products, coal, gold, bananas, cut flowers, cotton, chemicals, textiles, paper. Principal market USA 36% (1998). Illegal trade in cocaine in 1995; it was estimated that approximately 3.5 billion (equivalent to about 4% of GDP) was entering Colombia as the proceeds of drug-trafficking; **population:** 41,564,000 (1999 est); **language:** Spanish; **religion:** Roman Catholic; **life expectancy:** 67 (men); 74 (women) (1995–2000).

**Colorado** state of the western central USA. It is nicknamed the Centennial State. Colorado was admitted to the Union in 1876 as the 38th US state. Its expansion from World War II onwards has been closely associated with the US's military-industrial surge, with the state serving as the home of numerous military facilities and weapons plants; **population:** (1996 est) 3,823,000; **area:** 269,700 sq km/104,104 sq mi; **capital:** Denver; **towns and cities:** Colorado Springs, Aurora, Lakewood, Fort Collins, Greeley, Pueblo, Boulder, Arvada; **industries and products:** cereals, meat and dairy products, oil, coal, molybdenum, uranium, iron, steel, scientific instruments, machinery.

**colour** quality or wavelength of light emitted or reflected from an object. Visible white light consists of electromagnetic radiation of various wavelengths, and if a beam is refracted through a prism, it can be spread out into a spectrum, in which the various colours correspond to different wavelengths. From long to short wavelengths (from about 700 to 400 nanometres) the colours are red, orange, yellow, green, blue, indigo, and violet.

**colour blindness** hereditary defect of vision that reduces the ability to discriminate certain colours, usually red and green. The condition is sex-linked, affecting men more than women.

**Columba, St** (521–597) (Latin form of **Colum-cille**, 'Colum of the cell') Irish Christian abbot, missionary to Scotland. He was born in County Donegal of royal descent, and founded monasteries and churches in Ireland. In 563 he sailed with 12 companions to Iona, and built a monastery there that was to play a leading part in the conversion of Britain. Feast day 9 June.

**Columbus, Christopher** (1451–1506) (Spanish Cristóbal Colón) Italian navigator and explorer who made four voyages to the New World: 1492 to San Salvador Island, Cuba, and Haiti; 1493–96 to Guadaloupe, Montserrat, Antigua, Puerto Rico, and Jamaica; 1498 to Trinidad and the mainland of South America; 1502–04 to Honduras and Nicaragua.

Believing that Asia could be reached by sailing westwards, he eventually won the support of King Ferdinand and Queen Isabella of Spain and set off on his first voyage from Palos on 3 August 1492 with three small ships, the *Niña*, the *Pinta*, and his flagship the *Santa Maria*. Land was sighted on 12 October, probably Watling Island (now San Salvador Island), and within a few weeks he reached Cuba and Haiti, returning to Spain in March 1493.

**combustion** burning, defined in chemical terms as the rapid combination of a substance with oxygen, accompanied by the evolution of heat and usually light. A slow-burning candle flame and the explosion of a mixture of petrol vapour and air are extreme examples of combustion. Combustion is an exothermic reaction (exothermic reaction) as heat energy is given out.

**comedy** drama that aims to make its audience laugh, usually with a happy or amusing ending, as opposed to →tragedy. The comic tradition has undergone many changes since its Greek roots; the earliest comedy developed in ancient Greece, in the topical and fantastic satires of Aristophanes. Great comic dramatists include William Shakespeare, Molière, Carlo Goldoni, Pierre de Marivaux, George Bernard Shaw, and Oscar Wilde. Genres of comedy include pantomime, satire, farce, black comedy, and commedia dell'arte.

**comet** small, icy body orbiting the Sun, usually on a highly elliptical path. A comet consists of a central nucleus a few kilometres across, and has been likened to a dirty snowball because it consists mostly of ice mixed with dust. As a comet approaches the Sun its nucleus heats up, releasing gas and dust which form a tenuous coma, up to 100,000 km/60,000 mi wide, around the nucleus. Gas and dust stream away from the coma to form one or more tails, which may extend for millions of kilometres. US astronomers concluded in 1996 that there are two distinct types of comet: one rich in methanol and one low in methanol. Evidence for this comes in part from observations of the spectrum of Comet Hyakutake.

**commensalism** in biology, a relationship between two →species whereby one (the commensal) benefits from the association, whereas the other neither benefits nor suffers. For example, certain

## SOME MAJOR COMETS

A comet is a small, icy body orbiting the Sun, usually on a highly elliptical path. Comets consist of a central nucleus a few kilometres across, and are often likened to dirty snowballs because they consist mostly of ice mixed with dust. (− = not applicable.)

| Name | First recorded sighting | Orbital period (yrs) | Interesting facts |
|---|---|---|---|
| Halley's comet | 240 BC | 76 | parent of Eta Aquarid and Orionid meteor showers |
| Comet Tempel-Tuttle | AD 1366 | 33 | parent of Leonid meteors |
| Biela's comet | 1772 | 6.6 | broke in half in 1846; not seen since 1852 |
| Encke's comet | 1786 | 3.3 | parent of Taurid meteors |
| Comet Swift-Tuttle | 1862 | 130 | parent of Perseid meteors; reappeared 1992 |
| Comet Ikeya-Seki | 1965 | 880 | so-called 'Sun-grazing' comet, passed 500,000 km/300,000 mi above surface of the Sun on 21 October 1965 |
| Comet Kohoutek | 1973 | − | observed from space by *Skylab* astronauts |
| Comet West | 1975 | 500,000 | nucleus broke into four parts |
| Comet Bowell | 1980 | − | ejected from Solar System after close encounter with Jupiter |
| Comet IRAS-Araki-Alcock | 1983 | − | passed only 4.5 million km/2.8 million mi from the Earth on 11 May 1983 |
| Comet Austin | 1989 | − | passed 32 million km/20 million mi from the Earth in 1990 |
| Comet Shoemaker-Levy 9 | 1993 | − | made up of 21 fragments; crashed into Jupiter in July 1994 |
| Comet Hale-Bopp | 1995 | 1,000 | spitting out of gas and debris produced a coma, a surrounding hazy cloud of gas and dust, of greater volume than the Sun; the bright coma is due to an outgassing of carbon monoxide; clearly visible with the naked eye in March 1997 |
| Comet Hyakutake | 1996 | − | passed 15 million km/9.3 million mi from the Earth in 1996 |

species of millipede and silverfish inhabit the nests of army ants and live by scavenging on the refuse of their hosts, but without affecting the ants.

**common law** that part of the English law not embodied in legislation. It consists of rules of law based on common custom and usage and on judicial decisions. English common law became the basis of law in the USA and many other English-speaking countries.

**Commonwealth Games** multisport gathering of competitors from British Commonwealth countries, held every four years. The first meeting (known as the British Empire Games) was in Hamilton, Canada, in August 1930. It has been held in Britain on four occasions: London in 1934; Cardiff in 1958; Edinburgh in 1970 and 1986. Manchester will host the 2002 games.

**Commonwealth, the (British)** voluntary association of 54 sovereign countries and their dependencies, the majority of which once formed part of the British Empire and are now independent sovereign states. They are all regarded as 'full members of the Commonwealth'; the newest member being Mozambique, which was admitted in November 1995. Additionally, there are some 20 territories that are not completely sovereign and remain dependencies of the UK or one of the other fully sovereign members, and are regarded as 'Commonwealth countries'. Heads of government meet every two years, apart from those of Nauru and Tuvalu; however, Nauru and Tuvalu

have the right to participate in all functional activities. The Commonwealth, which was founded in 1931, has no charter or constitution, and is founded more on tradition and sentiment than on political or economic factors. However, it can make political statements by withdrawing membership; an example is Nigeria's suspension in 1995 because of human-rights abuses.

**communication** in biology, the signalling of information by one organism to another, usually with the intention of altering the recipient's behaviour. Signals used in communication may be **visual** (such as the human smile or the display of colourful plumage in birds), **auditory** (for example, the whines or barks of a dog), **olfactory** (such as the odours released by the scent glands of a deer), **electrical** (as in the pulses emitted by electric fish), or **tactile** (for example, the nuzzling of male and female elephants).

**communism** (French *commun* 'common, general') revolutionary socialism based on the theories of the political philosophers Karl →Marx and Friedrich →Engels, emphasizing common ownership of the means of production and a planned economy. The principle held is that each should work according to his or her capacity and receive according to his or her needs. Politically, it seeks the overthrow of capitalism through a proletarian revolution. The first communist state was the USSR after the revolution of 1917. Revolutionary socialist parties and groups united to form communist parties in other countries during the interwar years. After World War II, communism was enforced in those countries that came under Soviet occupation.

China emerged after 1961 as a rival to the USSR in world communist leadership, and other countries attempted to adapt communism to their own needs. The late 1980s saw a movement for more individual freedoms in many communist countries, culminating in the abolition or overthrow of communist rule in Eastern European countries and Mongolia, and further state repression in China. The failed hard-line coup in the USSR against President Gorbachev in 1991 resulted in the abandonment of communism there.

Communism as the ideology of a nation state survives in only a few countries, notably China, Cuba, North Korea, Laos, and Vietnam, where market forces are being encouraged in the economic sphere.

**Comoros** Federal Islamic Republic of; **national name:** *Jumhuriyat al-Qumur al-Itthādīyah al-Islāmīyah* or *République Fédérale Islamique des Comoros;* **area:** 1,862 sq km/718 sq mi; **capital:** Moroni; **major towns/cities:** Mutsamudu, Domoni, Fomboni, Dzaoudzi; **physical features:** comprises the volcanic islands of Njazídja, Nzwani, and Mwali (formerly Grande Comore, Anjouan, Moheli); at northern end of Mozambique Channel in Indian Ocean between Madagascar and coast of Africa; **head of state and government:** Azali Hassounani from 1999; **political system:** transitional; **currency:** Comorian franc; **GNP per capita (PPP):** (US$) 1,480 (1998);

**exports:** vanilla, cloves, ylang-ylang, essences, copra, coffee. Principal market France 42.9% (1997); **population:** 676,000 (1999 est); **language:** Arabic (official), Comorian (Swahili and Arabic dialect), Makua, French; **religion:** Muslim; Islam is the state religion; **life expectancy:** 57 (men); 60 (women) (1995–2000).

**compass** any instrument for finding direction. The most commonly used is a magnetic compass, consisting of a thin piece of magnetic material with the north-seeking pole indicated, free to rotate on a pivot and mounted on a compass card on which the points of the compass are marked. When the compass is properly adjusted and used, the north-seeking pole will point to the magnetic north, from which true north can be found from tables of magnetic corrections. *See illustration on page 144.*

**complementary medicine** in medicine, systems of care based on methods of treatment or theories of disease that differ from those taught in most western medical schools. See →medicine, alternative.

**computer** programmable electronic device that processes data and performs calculations and other symbol-manipulation tasks. There are three types: the **digital computer**, which manipulates information coded as binary numbers (see →binary number system); the **analogue computer**, which works with continuously varying quantities; and the **hybrid computer**, which has characteristics of both analogue and digital computers.

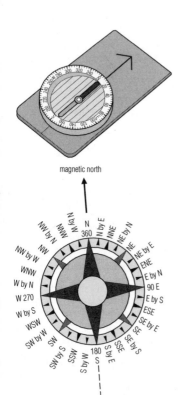

magnetic north

**compass** As early as 2500 BC, the Chinese were using pieces of magnetic rock, magnetite, as simple compasses. By the 12th century, European navigators were using compasses consisting of a needle-shaped magnet floating in a bowl of water.

**computer graphics** use of computers to display and manipulate information in pictorial form. Input may be achieved by scanning an image, by drawing with a mouse or stylus on a graphics tablet, or by drawing directly on the screen with a light pen.

**computerized axial tomography** medical technique, usually known as CAT scan, for noninvasive investigation of disease or injury.

**concave** of a surface, curving inwards, or away from the eye. For example, a bowl appears concave when viewed from above. In geometry, a concave polygon is one that has an interior angle greater than 180°. Concave is the opposite of convex.

**concerto** composition, usually in three movements, for solo instrument (or instruments) and orchestra. It developed during the 18th century from the **concerto grosso** form for string orchestra, in which a group of solo instruments (concerto) is contrasted with a full orchestra (ripieno).

**concrete** building material composed of cement, stone, sand, and water. It has been used since Egyptian and Roman times. Since the late 19th century, it has been increasingly employed as an economical alternative to materials such as brick and wood, and has been combined with steel to increase its tension capacity.

**cone** in botany, the reproductive structure of the conifers and cycads; also known as a strobilus. It consists of a central axis surrounded by numerous, overlapping, scalelike, modified leaves (sporophylls) that bear the reproductive organs. Usually there are separate male and female cones, the former bearing pollen sacs containing pollen grains, and the larger female cones bearing the ovules that contain the ova or egg cells. The pollen is carried from male to female cones by the wind (anemophily). The seeds develop within the female cone and are released as the scales open in dry atmospheric conditions, which favour seed dispersal.

**cone** in geometry, a solid or surface consisting of the set of all straight lines passing through a fixed point (the vertex) and the points of a circle or ellipse whose plane does not contain the vertex.

**Confucius** (551–479 BC) Latinized form of Kong Zi or K'ung Fu Tzu, 'Kong the master' Chinese sage whose name is given to the ethical system of Confucianism. He placed emphasis on moral order and observance of the established patriarchal family and social relationships of authority, obedience, and mutual respect. His emphasis on tradition and ethics attracted a growing number of pupils during his lifetime. *The Analects of Confucius*, a compilation of his teachings, was published after his death.

**Congo, Democratic Republic of** formerly **Zaire**; **national name:** *République Démocratique du Congo*; **area:** 2,344,900 sq km/905,366 sq mi; **capital:** Kinshasa; **major towns/cities:** Lubumbashi, Kananga, Mbuji-Mayi, Kisangani, Bukavu, Kikwit, Matadi; **major ports:** Matadi, Kalemie; **physical features:** Congo River basin has tropical rainforest (second-largest remaining in world) and savanna; mountains in east and west; lakes Tanganyika, Albert, Edward; Ruwenzori Range; Victoria Falls; **head of state and government:** Laurent Kabila from 1997; **political system:** transitional; Progress (UPDS), left of centre; Congolese National Movement–Lumumba (MNC), left of centre; **currency:** congolese franc; **GNP per capita (PPP):** (US$) 750 (1998 est); **exports:** mineral products (mainly copper, cobalt, industrial diamonds, and petroleum), agricultural products (chiefly coffee). Principal market Belgium – Luxembourg 42.7% (1997); **population:** 50,336,000 (1999 est); **language:** French (official); Swahili, Lingala, Kikongo, and Tshiluba are recognized as national languages; over 200 other languages; **religion:** Roman Catholic, Protestant, Kimbanguist; also half a million Muslims; **life expectancy:** 50 (men); 52 (women) (1995–2000).

**Congo, Republic of** **national name:** *République du Congo*; **area:** 342,000 sq km/132,046 sq mi; **capital:** Brazzaville; **major towns/cities:** Pool, Pointe-Noire, Nkayi, Loubomo, Bouenza, Cuvette, Niari, Plateaux; **major ports:** Pointe-Noire; **physical features:** narrow coastal plain rises to central plateau, then falls into northern basin; Congo River on the border with the Democratic Republic of Congo; half the country is rainforest; **head of state:** Denis Sassou-Nguessou from 1997; **head of government:**

Charles David Ganao from 1996; **political system:** emergent democracy; **currency:** franc CFA; **GNP per capita (PPP):** (US$) 1,430 (1998); **exports:** petroleum and petroleum products, saw logs and veneer logs, veneer sheets. Principal market USA 36.9% (1997); **population:** 2,864,000 (1999 est); **language:** French (official); Kongo languages; local patois Monokutuba and Lingala; **religion:** animist, Christian, Muslim; **life expectancy:** 48 (men); 51 (women) (1995–2000).

**Congo River** second-longest river in Africa, rising near the Zambia–Democratic Republic of Congo border (and known as the **Lualaba River** in the upper reaches) and flowing 4,500 km/ 2,800 mi to the Atlantic Ocean, running in a great curve that crosses the equator twice, and discharging a volume of water second only to the River Amazon. The chief tributaries are the Ubangi, Sangha, and Kasai.

**Congress** national legislature of the USA, consisting of the House of Representatives (435 members, apportioned to the states of the Union on the basis of population, and elected for two-year terms) and the Senate (100 senators, two for each state, elected for six years, one-third elected every two years). Both representatives and senators are elected by direct popular vote. Congress meets in Washington DC, in the Capitol Building. An →act of Congress is a bill passed by both houses.

**conic section** curve obtained when a conical surface is intersected by a plane. If the intersecting plane cuts both extensions of the cone, it yields a hyperbola; if it is parallel to the side of the cone, it produces a parabola. Other intersecting planes produce →circles or ellipses.

**conifer** any of a large number of cone-bearing trees or shrubs. They are often pyramid-shaped, with leaves that are either scaled or needle-shaped; most are evergreen. Conifers include pines, spruces, firs, yews, junipers, monkey puzzles, and larches. (Order Coniferales.)

**Connacht** (or Connaught) historic province of the Republic of Ireland, comprising the counties of Galway, Leitrim, Mayo, Roscommon, and Sligo; area 17,130 sq km/6,612 sq mi; population (1996) 433,200. The chief towns are Galway, Roscommon, Castlebar, Sligo, and Carrick-on-Shannon. Mainly lowland, it is agricultural and stock-raising country, with poor land in the west.

**Connecticut** state in New England, USA. It is nicknamed Constitution State or the Nutmeg State. Connecticut ratified the US Constitution in 1788, becoming the 5th state in the Union; **population:** (1996 est) 3,274,000; **area:** 13,000 sq km/5,018 sq mi; **capital:** Hartford; **towns and cities:** Bridgeport, New Haven, Waterbury, Stamford; **industries and products:** dairy, poultry, and market-garden products; tobacco, watches, clocks, silverware, helicopters, jet engines, nuclear submarines, hardware and locks, electrical and electronic equipment, guns and ammunition, optical instruments. Hartford is the centre of the nation's insurance industry.

**Conrad, Joseph** (1857–1924) pen-name of Teodor Józef Konrad Nałęcz Korzeniowski, British novelist, born in Ukraine of Polish parents. His greatest works include the novels *Lord Jim* (1900), *Nostromo* (1904), *The Secret Agent* (1907), and *Under Western Eyes* (1911); the short story 'Heart of Darkness' (1902); and the short novel *The Shadow Line* (1917).

**conservation** action taken to protect and preserve the natural world, usually from pollution, overexploitation, and other harmful features of human activity. The late 1980s saw a great increase in public concern for the environment, with membership of conservation groups, such as Friends of the Earth, Greenpeace, and the US Sierra Club, rising sharply. Globally the most important issues include the depletion of atmospheric ozone by the action of →chlorofluorocarbons (CFCs), the build-up of carbon dioxide in the atmosphere (thought to contribute to an intensification of the →greenhouse effect), and →deforestation.

**Conservative Party** UK political party, one of the two historic British parties; the name replaced **Tory** in general use from 1830 onwards. Traditionally the party of landed interests, it broadened its political base under Benjamin Disraeli's leadership in the 19th century. The present Conservative Party's free-market capitalism is supported by the world of finance and the management of industry. In recent history, the Conservative Party was in power under Margaret Thatcher (1979–90) and John Major (1990–97). After the party's defeat in the 1997 general election, John Major resigned and was succeeded by William Hague. The party's Central Office is located in Smith Square, London, and the current party chairman is Cecil Parkinson.

**Constable, John** (1776–1837) English artist; one of the greatest landscape painters of the 19th century. He painted scenes of his native Suffolk, including *The Haywain* (1821; National Gallery, London), as well as castles, cathedrals, landscapes, and coastal scenes in other parts of Britain. Constable inherited the Dutch tradition of sombre realism, in particular the style of Jacob Ruisdael. He aimed to capture the momentary changes of the weather as well as to create monumental images of British scenery, as in *The White Horse* (1819; Frick Collection, New York) and *Salisbury Cathedral from the Bishop's Grounds* (1827; Victoria and Albert Museum, London).

**constellation** one of the 88 areas into which the sky is divided for the purposes of identifying and naming celestial objects. The first constellations were simple, arbitrary patterns of stars in which early civilizations visualized gods, sacred beasts, and heroes. *See Web site on page 148.*

**continental drift** in geology, the theory that, about 250–200 million years ago, the Earth consisted of a single large continent (Pangaea), which subsequently broke apart to form the continents known today. The theory was proposed 1912 by German meteorologist Alfred Wegener, but such vast continental movements could not be satisfactorily explained until the study of →plate tectonics in the 1960s.

**contraceptive** any drug, device, or technique that prevents pregnancy. The contraceptive pill (the →Pill) contains female hormones that interfere with egg production or the first stage of pregnancy. The 'morning-after' pill can be taken up to 72 hours after unprotected intercourse. Barrier contraceptives include condoms (sheaths) and diaphragms, also called caps or Dutch caps; they prevent the sperm entering the cervix (neck of the womb).

→Intrauterine devices, also known as IUDs or coils, cause a slight inflammation of the lining of the womb; this prevents the fertilized egg from becoming implanted.

**Cook, James** (1728–1779) English naval explorer. After surveying the St Lawrence River in North America in 1759, he made three voyages: 1768–71 to Tahiti, New Zealand, and Australia; 1772–75 to the South Pacific; and 1776–79 to the South and North Pacific, attempting to find the Northwest Passage and charting the Siberian coast. He was largely responsible for Britain's initial interest in acquiring colonies in Australasia. He was killed in Hawaii early in 1779 in a scuffle with islanders.

**coordinate** in geometry, a number that defines the position of a point relative to a point or axis (reference line). Cartesian coordinates define a point by its perpendicular distances from two or more axes drawn through a fixed point mutually at right angles to each other. Polar coordinates define a point in a plane by its distance from a fixed point and direction from a fixed line.

**coordinate geometry** (or analytical geometry) system of geometry in which points, lines, shapes, and surfaces are represented by algebraic expressions. In plane (two-dimensional) coordinate geometry, the plane is usually defined by two axes at right angles to each other, the horizontal $x$-axis and the vertical $y$-axis, meeting at O, the origin. A point on the plane can be represented by a pair of Cartesian coordinates, which define its position in terms of its distance along the $x$-axis and along the $y$-axis from O. These distances are respectively the $x$ and $y$ coordinates of the point.

**Copenhagen, Battle of** naval victory on 2 April 1801 by a British fleet under Sir Hyde Parker (1739–1807) and →Nelson over the Danish fleet. Nelson put his telescope to his blind eye and refused to see Parker's signal for withdrawal.

**Copernicus, Nicolaus** (1473–1543) Latinized form of Mikołaj Kopernik, Polish astronomer who believed that the Sun, not the Earth, is at the centre of the Solar System, thus defying the Christian church doctrine of the time. For 30 years, he worked on the hypothesis that the rotation and the orbital motion of the Earth are responsible for the apparent movement of the heavenly bodies. His great work *De Revolutionibus Orbium Coelestium/On the Revolutions of the Heavenly Spheres* was the important first step to the more accurate picture of the Solar System built up by Tycho →Brahe, →Kepler, →Galileo, and later astronomers.

**Copland, Aaron** (1900–1990) US composer. His early works, such as his piano concerto (1926), were in the jazz idiom but he gradually developed a gentler style drawn from American folk music. Among his works are the ballet scores *Billy the Kid* (1938), *Rodeo* (1942), and *Appalachian Spring* (1944; based on a poem by Hart Crane). Among his orchestral works is *Inscape* (1967).

**copper** orange-pink, very malleable and ductile, metallic element, symbol Cu (from Latin *cuprum*), atomic number 29, relative atomic mass 63.546. It is used for its durability, pliability, high thermal and electrical conductivity, and resistance to corrosion.

**coral** marine invertebrate of the class Anthozoa in the phylum Cnidaria, which also includes sea anemones and jellyfish. It has a skeleton of lime (calcium carbonate) extracted from the surrounding water. Corals exist in warm seas, at moderate depths with sufficient light. Some coral is valued for decoration or jewellery, for example, Mediterranean red coral *Corallum rubrum*.

**Coral Sea** (or Solomon Sea) part of the →Pacific Ocean bounded by northeastern Australia, New Guinea, the Solomon Islands, Vanuatu, and New Caledonia; area 4,790,000 sq km/ 1,849,000 sq mi, with an average depth of 2,400 m/7,870 ft, with three deep trenches on its eastern edge. It contains numerous coral islands and reefs. The Coral Sea Islands are a territory of Australia; they comprise scattered reefs and islands over an area of about 1,000,000 sq km/386,000 sq mi. They are uninhabited except for a meteorological station on Willis Island. The →Great Barrier Reef lies along its western edge, just off the east coast of Australia.

**Corbusier,** →Le French architect; see Le Corbusier.

**Córdoba** industrial city and capital of Córdoba province, central Argentina, situated on the Primero (or Suquiá) River, 400 m/1,310 ft above sea level at the foot of the Sierra Chica, between the pampas on the east and the Andes on the west; population (1992 est) 1,179,400. Main industries include cement, glass, textiles, and motor vehicles.

**Coriolis effect** the effect of the Earth's rotation on the atmosphere and on all objects on the Earth's surface. In the northern hemisphere it causes moving objects and currents to be deflected to the right; in the southern hemisphere it causes deflection to the left. The effect is named after its discoverer, French mathematician Gaspard de Coriolis (1792–1843).

**cork** light, waterproof outer layers of the bark covering the branches and roots of almost all trees and shrubs. The cork oak (*Quercus suber*), a native of southern Europe and North Africa, is cultivated in Spain and Portugal; the exceptionally thick outer layers of its bark provide the cork that is used commercially.

**corm** short, swollen, underground plant stem, surrounded by protective scale leaves, as seen in the genus *Crocus*. It stores food, provides a means of vegetative reproduction, and acts as a perennating organ.

**Corn Laws** in Britain until 1846, laws used to regulate the export or import of cereals in order to maintain an adequate supply for consumers and a secure price for producers. For centuries the Corn Laws formed an integral part of the mercantile system in England; they were repealed because they became an unwarranted tax on food and a hindrance to British exports.

**corona** faint halo of hot (about

flower
foliage leaf
this year's developing corm
contractile root
last year's corm
preceding year's corm withering
adventitious roots

**corm** Corms, found in plants such as the gladiolus and crocus, are underground storage organs. They provide the food for growth during adverse conditions such as cold or drought.

2,000,000°C/3,600,000°F) and tenuous gas around the Sun, which boils from the surface. It is visible at solar →eclipses or through a **coronagraph**, an instrument that blocks light from the Sun's brilliant disc. Gas flows away from the corona to form the solar wind.

**coronary artery disease** (Latin *corona* 'crown', from the arteries encircling the heart) condition in which the fatty deposits of →atherosclerosis form in the coronary arteries that supply the heart muscle, narrowing them and restricting the blood flow.

**corrosion** the eating away and eventual destruction of metals and alloys by chemical attack. The rusting of ordinary iron and steel is the most common form of corrosion. Rusting takes place in moist air, when the iron combines with oxygen and water to form a brown-orange deposit of →rust (hydrated iron oxide). The rate of corrosion is increased where the atmosphere is polluted with sulphur dioxide. Salty road and air conditions accelerate the rusting of car bodies.

**Corsica** (French *Corse*) island region of France, in the Mediterranean off the west coast of Italy, north of Sardinia; it comprises the *départements* of Haute Corse and Corse du Sud; **area:** 8,700 sq km/3,358 sq mi; **capital:** Ajaccio (port); **physical:** mountainous; maquis vegetation (drought-tolerant shrubs such as cork oak and myrtle); Corsica's mountain bandits were eradicated 1931, but the tradition of the vendetta or blood feud lingers. The island is the main base of the Foreign Legion; **government:** its special status involves a 61-member regional parliament with the power to scrutinize French National Assembly bills applicable to the island and propose amendments; **products:** wine, olive oil; **population:** (1990) 250,400, including just under 50% native Corsicans. There are about 400,000 *émigrés*, mostly in Mexico and Central America, who return to retire; **language:** French (official); the majority speak Corsican, an Italian dialect; **famous people:** Napoleon.

**corticosteroid** any of several steroid hormones secreted by the cortex of the →adrenal glands; also synthetic forms with similar properties. Corticosteroids have anti-inflammatory and immunosuppressive effects and may be used to treat a number of conditions, including rheumatoid arthritis, severe allergies, asthma, some skin diseases, and some cancers. Side effects can be serious.

**cosine** in trigonometry, a function of an angle in a right-angled triangle found by dividing the length of the side adjacent to the angle by the length of the hypotenuse (the longest side). It is usually shortened to **cos**.

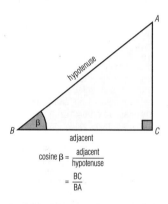

$$\text{cosine } \beta = \frac{\text{adjacent}}{\text{hypotenuse}}$$

$$= \frac{BC}{BA}$$

**cosine** The cosine of angle $\beta$ is equal to the ratio of the length of the adjacent side to the length of the hypotenuse (the longest side, opposite to the right angle).

**cosmic radiation** streams of high-energy particles from outer space, consisting of protons, alpha particles, and light nuclei, which collide with atomic nuclei in the Earth's atmosphere, and produce secondary nuclear particles (chiefly mesons, such as pions and muons) that shower the Earth.

**cosmology** branch of astronomy that deals with the structure and evolution of the universe as an ordered whole. Its method is to construct 'model universes' mathematically and compare their large-scale properties with those of the observed universe.

**Costa Rica** Republic of; **national name:** *República de Costa Rica*; **area:** 51,100 sq km/19,729 sq mi; **capital:** San José; **major towns/cities:** Alajuela, Cartago, Limón, Puntarenas; **major ports:** Limón, Puntarenas; **physical features:** high central plateau and tropical coasts; Costa Rica was once entirely forested, containing an estimated 5% of the Earth's flora and fauna; **head of state and government:** Miguel Angel Rodriguez Echeverria, from 1998; **political system:** liberal democracy; **currency:** colón; **GNP per capita (PPP):** (US$) 6,620 (1997); **exports:** bananas, coffee, sugar, cocoa, textiles, seafood, meat, tropical fruit. Principal market USA 52.5% (1998); **population:** 3,933,000 (1999 est); **language:** Spanish (official); **religion:** Roman Catholic 90%; **life expectancy:** 74 (men); 79 (women) (1995–2000).

**cot death** (or sudden infant death syndrome, SIDS) death of an apparently healthy baby, almost always during sleep. It is most common in the winter months, and strikes more boys than girls. The cause is not known but risk factors that have been identified include prematurity, respiratory infection, overheating, and sleeping position.

**Côte d'Ivoire** Republic of; **national name:** *République de la Côte d'Ivoire*; **area:** 322,463 sq km/124,502 sq mi; **capital:** Yamoussoukro; **major towns/ cities:** Abidjan, Bouaké, Daloa, Man, Korhogo; **major ports:** Abidjan, San Pedro; **physical features:** tropical rainforest (diminishing as exploited) in south; savannah and low mountains in north; coastal plain; Vridi canal, Kossou dam, Monts du Toura; **head of state:** General Robert Guei from 1999; **head of government:** Kablan Daniel Duncan from 1993; **political system:** emergent democracy; **currency:** franc CFA. **GNP per capita (PPP):** (US$) 1,730 (1998); **exports:** cocoa beans and products, petroleum products, timber, coffee, cotton, tinned tuna. Principal market Netherlands 16.6% (1997); **population:** 14,527,000 (1999 est); **language:** French (official); over 60 local languages; **religion:** animist, Muslim (mainly in north), Christian (mainly Roman Catholic in south); **life expectancy:** 46 (men); 47 (women) (1995–2000).

**cotyledon** structure in the embryo of a seed plant that may form a 'leaf' after germination and is commonly known as a seed leaf. The number of cotyledons present in an embryo is an important character in the classification of flowering plants ( →angiosperms).

**Council of Europe** body constituted in 1949 to achieve greater unity between European countries, to facilitate their economic and social progress, and to uphold the principles of parliamentary democracy and respect for human rights. It has a Committee of foreign ministers, a Consultative Assembly, a Parliamentary Assembly (with members from national parliaments), and, to fulfil one of its main functions, a **European Commission on Human Rights**, which examines complaints about human-rights abuses. If the commission is unable to achieve a friendly settlement after examining alleged violations, the case may be taken to the European Court of Human Rights for adjudication. Its headquarters are in Strasbourg, France.

**Counter-Reformation** movement initiated by the Catholic church at the Council of Trent (1545–63) to counter the spread of the →Reformation. Extending into the 17th century, its dominant forces included the rise of the Jesuits as an educating and missionary group and the deployment of the Spanish Inquisition in Europe and the Americas.

**Courbet, Gustave** (1819–1877) French artist. He was a portrait, genre, and landscape painter. He became a major exponent of →realism, depicting contemporary life with an unflattering frankness. His *Burial at Ornans* (1850; Musée d'Orsay, Paris), showing ordinary working people gathered around a village grave, shocked the public and the critics with its 'vulgarity'.

**covalent bond** chemical bond produced when two atoms share one or more pairs of electrons (usually each atom contributes an electron). The bond is often represented by a single line drawn between the two atoms. Covalently bonded substances include hydrogen ($H_2$), water ($H_2O$), and most organic substances.

**crab** any decapod (ten-legged) crustacean of the division Brachyura, with a broad, rather round, upper body shell (carapace) and a small abdomen tucked beneath the body. Crabs are related to lobsters and crayfish. Mainly marine, some crabs live in fresh water or on land. They are alert carnivores and scavengers. They have a typical sideways walk, and strong pincers on the first pair of legs, the other four pairs being used for walking. Periodically, the outer shell is cast to allow for growth. The name 'crab' is sometimes used for similar arthropods, such as the horseshoe crab, which is neither a true crab nor a crustacean.

**Crab nebula** cloud of gas 6,000 light years from Earth, in the constellation Taurus. It is the remains of a star that according to Chinese records, exploded as a →supernova observed as a brilliant point of light on 4 July 1054. At its centre is a →pulsar that flashes 30 times a second. It was named by Lord Rosse after its crablike shape.

**crane fly** (or daddy-long-legs) any fly of the family Tipulidae, with long, slender, fragile legs. They look like giant mosquitoes, but the adults are quite harmless. The larvae live in soil or water. Females have a pointed abdomen; males have a club-shaped one.

**Cranmer, Thomas** (1489–1556) English cleric, archbishop of Canterbury from 1533. A Protestant convert, he helped to shape the doctrines of the Church of England under Edward VI. He was responsible for the issue of the Prayer Books of 1549 and 1552, and supported the succession of Lady Jane Grey in 1553.

**Cretaceous** (Latin *creta* 'chalk') period of geological time approximately 144.2–65 million years ago. It is the last period of the Mesozoic era, during which angiosperm (seed-bearing) plants evolved, and dinosaurs reached a peak before their extinction at the end of the period. The north European chalk, which forms the white cliffs of Dover, was deposited during the latter half of the Cretaceous.

**Crick, Francis Harry Compton** (1916–  ) English molecular biologist. From 1949 he researched the molecular structure of →DNA, and the means whereby characteristics are transmitted from one generation to another. For this work he was awarded a Nobel prize (with Maurice Wilkins and James →Watson) in 1962.

**cricket** in zoology, an insect belonging to any of various families, especially the Gryllidae, of the order Orthoptera. Crickets are related to grasshoppers. They have somewhat flattened bodies and long antennae. The males make a chirping noise by rubbing together special areas on the forewings. The females have a long needlelike egglaying organ (ovipositor). There are around 900 species known worldwide.

**cricket** bat-and-ball game between two teams of 11 players each. It is played with a small solid ball and long flat-sided wooden bats, on a round or oval field, at the centre of which is a finely mown pitch, 20 m/22 yd long. At each end of the pitch is a wicket made up of three upright wooden sticks (stumps), surmounted by two smaller sticks (bails). The object of the game is to score more runs than the opposing team. A run is normally scored by the batsman striking the ball and exchanging ends with his or her partner until the ball is returned by a fielder, or by hitting the ball to the boundary line for an automatic four or six runs.

**Crimean War** war 1853–56 between Russia and the allied powers of England, France, Turkey, and Sardinia. The war arose from British and French mistrust of Russia's ambitions in the Balkans. It began with an allied Anglo-French expedition to the Crimea to attack the Russian Black Sea city of Sevastopol. The battles of the River Alma, Balaclava (including the charge of the Light Brigade), and Inkerman 1854 led to a siege which, owing to military mismanagement, lasted for a year until September 1855. The war was ended by the Treaty of Paris in 1856. The scandal surrounding French and British losses through disease led to the organization of proper military nursing services by Florence Nightingale.

**Croatia** Republic of; **national name:** *Republika Hrvatska*; **area:** 56,538 sq km/21,829 sq mi; **capital:** Zagreb; **major**

**towns/cities:** Osijek, Split, Dubrovnik, Rijeka, Zadar, Pula; **major ports:** chief port Rijeka (Fiume); other ports Zadar, Sibenik, Split, Dubrovnik; **physical features:** Adriatic coastline with large islands; very mountainous, with part of the Karst region and the Julian and Styrian Alps; some marshland; **head of state:** Stipe Mesic from 2000; **head of government:** Zlatko Matesa from 1995; **political system:** emergent democracy; **currency:** kuna; **GNP per capita (PPP):** (US$) 7,100 (1998 est); **exports:** machinery and transport equipment, chemicals, foodstuffs, miscellaneous manufactured items (mainly clothing). Principal market Italy 17.7% (1998); **population:** 4,477,000 (1999 est); **language:** Croatian variant of Serbo-Croatian (official); Serbian variant of Serbo-Croatian also widely spoken, particularly in border areas in east; **religion:** Roman Catholic (Croats); Orthodox Christian (Serbs); **life expectancy:** 69 (men); 77 (women) (1995–2000).

**Cromwell, Oliver** (1599–1658) English general and politician, Puritan leader of the Parliamentary side in the →Civil War. He raised cavalry forces (later called **Ironsides**) which aided the victories at Edgehill in 1642 and →Marston Moor in 1644, and organized the New Model Army, which he led (with General Fairfax) to victory at Naseby in 1645. He declared Britain a republic ('the Commonwealth') in 1649, following the execution of Charles I. As Lord Protector (ruler) from 1653, Cromwell established religious toleration and raised Britain's prestige in Europe on the basis of an alliance with France against Spain.

**Crosby, Bing (Harry Lillis)** (1904–1977) US film actor and singer. He achieved world success with his distinctive style in such songs as 'Pennies from Heaven' (1936) (featured in a film of the same name) and 'White Christmas' (1942). He won an Academy Award for his acting in *Going My Way* (1944).

**crow** any of 35 species of omnivorous birds in the genus *Corvus*, family Corvidae, order Passeriformes, which also includes choughs, jays, and magpies. Crows are usually about 45 cm/1.5 ft long, black, with a strong bill feathered at the base. The tail is long and graduated, and the wings are long and pointed, except in the jays and magpies, where they are shorter. Crows are considered to be very intelligent. The family is distributed throughout the world, though there are very few species in eastern Australia or South America. The common crows are *C. brachyrhynchos* in North America, and *C. corone* in Europe and Asia.

**crusade** (French *croisade*) European war against non-Christians and heretics, sanctioned by the pope; in particular, the Crusades, a series of wars undertaken 1096–1291 by European rulers to recover Palestine from the Muslims. Motivated by religious zeal, the desire for land, and the trading ambitions of the major Italian cities, the Crusades were varied in their aims and effects.

**crustacean** one of the class of arthropods that includes crabs, lobsters, shrimps, woodlice, and barnacles. The external skeleton is made of protein and chitin hardened with lime. Each segment bears a pair of appendages that may be modified as sensory feelers (antennae), as mouthparts, or as swimming, walking, or grasping structures.

**crystal** substance with an orderly three-dimensional arrangement of its atoms or molecules, thereby creating an external surface of clearly defined smooth faces having characteristic angles between them. Examples are table salt and quartz.

*sodium chloride*

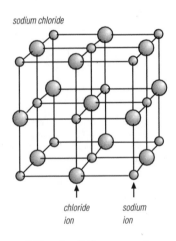

chloride     sodium
ion         ion

**crystal** The sodium chloride, or common salt, crystal is a regular cubic array of charged atoms (ions) – positive sodium atoms and negative chlorine atoms. Repetition of this structure builds up into cubic salt crystals.

**Cuba** Republic of; **national name:** *República de Cuba*; **area:** 110,860 sq km/42,803 sq mi; **capital:** Havana; **major towns/cities:** Santiago de Cuba, Camagüey, Holguín, Guantánamo, Santa Clara, Bayamo, Cienfuegos; **physical features:** comprises Cuba and smaller islands including Isle of Youth; low hills; Sierra Maestra mountains in southeast; Cuba has 3,380 km/2,100 mi of coastline, with deep bays, sandy beaches, coral islands and reefs; **head of state and government:** Fidel Castro Ruz from 1959; **political system:** communist republic; **currency:** Cuban peso; **GNP per capita (PPP):** (US$) 3,520 (1997 est); **Exports:** sugar, minerals, tobacco, citrus fruits, fish products. Principal market Russia 17.6% (1997); **population:** 11,160,000 (1999 est); **language:** Spanish; **religion:** Roman Catholic; also Episcopalians and Methodists; Life expectancy: 74 (men); 78 (women) (1995–2000).

**cubism** revolutionary style of painting created by Georges Braque and Pablo Picasso in Paris in 1907–14. It was the most radical of the developments that revolutionized art in the years of unprecedented experimentation leading up to World War I, and it changed the course of painting by introducing a new way of seeing and depicting the world. To the cubists, a painting was first and foremost a flat object that existed in its own right, rather than a kind of window through which a representation of the world is seen. Cubism also had a marked, though less fundamental, effect on sculpture, and even influenced architecture and the decorative arts.

**Culloden, Battle of** defeat in 1746 of the →Jacobite rebel army of the British prince →Charles Edward Stuart (the 'Young Pretender') by the Duke of Cumberland on a stretch of moorland in Inverness-shire, Scotland. This battle effectively ended the military challenge of the Jacobite rebellion.

**Cumbria** county of northwest England, created in 1974 from Cumberland, Westmorland, the Furness district of northwest Lancashire, and the Sedbergh district of northwest Yorkshire; **area:** 6,810 sq km/2,629 sq mi; **towns and cities:** Carlisle (administrative headquarters), Barrow, Kendal, Penrith, Whitehaven, Workington; **physical:** Scafell Pike (978 m/3,210 ft), the highest mountain in England, Helvellyn (950 m/3,118 ft); Lake Windermere, the largest lake in England (17 km/10.5 mi long, 1.6 km/1 mi wide), and other lakes (Derwentwater, Grasmere, Haweswater, Ullswater); the rivers Eden and Derwent; the M6 motorway runs north to south through the centre of the county; **features:** Lake District National Park; Grizedale Forest sculpture project; Furness peninsula; western part of Hadrian's Wall; **agriculture:** in the north and east there is dairy farming; sheep are also reared; **industries:** the traditional coal, iron, and steel industries of the coast towns have been replaced by newer industries including chemicals, plastics, marine engineering, electronics, and shipbuilding (at Barrow-in-Furness, nuclear submarines and

warships); tourism; salmon fishing; **population:** (1996) 490,600; **famous people:** Samuel Taylor Coleridge, Stan Laurel, Beatrix Potter, Thomas de Quincey, John Ruskin, Robert Southey, William Wordsworth.

**Curie, Marie** (1867–1934) born Manya Sklodowska, Polish scientist who, with husband Pierre Curie, discovered in 1898 two new radioactive elements in pitchblende ores: polonium and radium. They isolated the pure elements in 1902. Both scientists refused to take out a patent on their discovery and were jointly awarded the Nobel Prize for Physics in 1903, with Henri Becquerel. Marie Curie was also awarded the Nobel Prize for Chemistry in 1911.

**current** flow of a body of water or air, or of heat, moving in a definite direction. Ocean currents are fast-flowing currents of seawater generated by the wind or by variations in water density between two areas. They are partly responsible for transferring heat from the Equator to the poles and thereby evening out the global heat imbalance. There are three basic types of ocean current: **drift currents** are broad and slow-moving; **stream currents** are narrow and swift-moving; and **upwelling currents** bring cold, nutrient-rich water from the ocean bottom.

**cuttlefish** any of a family, Sepiidae, of squidlike cephalopods with an internal calcareous shell (cuttlebone). The common cuttle *Sepia officinalis* of the Atlantic and Mediterranean is up to 30 cm/1 ft long. It swims actively by means of the fins into which the sides of its oval, flattened body are expanded, and jerks itself backwards by shooting a jet of water from its 'siphon'.

**cyanide** CN⁻ ion derived from hydrogen cyanide (HCN), and any salt containing this ion (produced when hydrogen cyanide is neutralized by alkalis), such as potassium cyanide (KCN). The principal cyanides are potassium, sodium, calcium, mercury, gold, and copper. Certain cyanides are poisons.

**cycad** any of a group of plants belonging to the →gymnosperms, whose seeds develop in cones. Some are superficially similar to palms, others to ferns. Their large cones (up to 0.5 m/1.6 ft in length) contain fleshy seeds. There are ten genera and about 80–100 species, native to tropical and subtropical countries. Cycads were widespread during the Mesozoic era (245–65 million years ago). (Order Cycadales.)

**cylinder** in geometry, a tubular solid figure with a circular base. In everyday use, the term applies to a **right cylinder**, the curved surface of which is at right angles to the base.

**Cyprus** Greek Republic of Cyprus in south, and **Turkish Republic of Northern Cyprus** in north; national name: *Kypriakí Dimokratía* (south), and *Kıbrıs Cumhuriyeti* (north); **area:** 9,251 sq km/ 3,571 sq mi (3,335 sq km/1,287 sq mi is Turkish-occupied); **capital:** Nicosia (divided between Greek and Turkish Cypriots); **major towns/cities:** Morphou, Limassol, Larnaca, Famagusta,

$$\text{volume} = \pi r^2 h$$
$$\text{area or curved surface} = 2\pi r h$$

**cylinder** The volume and area of a cylinder are given by simple formulae relating the dimensions of the cylinder.

Paphos; **major ports:** Limassol, Larnaca, and Paphos (Greek); Kyrenia and Famagusta (Turkish); **physical features:** central plain between two east–west mountain ranges; **head of state and government:** Glafkos Clerides (Greek) from 1993, Rauf Denktaş (Turkish) from 1976; **political system:** democratic divided republic; **Currency:** Cyprus pound and Turkish lira; **GNP per capita (PPP):** (US\$) 14,090 (1997 est); **exports:** clothing, potatoes, pharmaceutical products, manufactured foods, minerals, citrus fruits, industrial products. Principal market UK 15.5% (1998); **population:** 779,000 (1999 est); **language:** Greek and Turkish (official), English; **religion:** Greek Orthodox, Sunni Muslim; **life expectancy:** 76 (men); 80 (women) (1995–2000).

**cystic fibrosis** hereditary disease involving defects of various tissues, including the sweat glands, the mucous glands of the bronchi (air passages), and the pancreas. The sufferer experiences repeated chest infections and digestive disorders and generally fails to thrive. In 1989 a gene for cystic fibrosis was identified by teams of researchers in Michigan, USA, and Toronto, Canada. This discovery enabled the development of a screening test for carriers; the disease can also be detected in the unborn child.

**cystitis** inflammation of the bladder, usually caused by bacterial infection, and resulting in frequent and painful urination. It is more common in women. Treatment is by antibiotics and copious fluids with vitamin C.

**cytoplasm** the part of the cell outside the →nucleus. Strictly speaking, this includes all the organelles (mitochondria, chloroplasts, and so on), but often cytoplasm refers to the jelly-like matter in which the organelles are embedded (correctly termed the cytosol). The cytoplasm is the site of protein synthesis.

**Czech Republic;** National name: *Česká Republika*; **area:** 78,864 sq km/30,449 sq mi; **capital:** Prague; **major towns/cities:** Brno, Ostrava, Olomouc, Liberec, Plzeň, Ustí nad Labem, Hradec Králové; **physical features:** mountainous; rivers Morava, Labe (Elbe), Vltava (Moldau); **head of state:** Václav Havel from 1993; **head of government:** Miloš Zeman from 1998; **political system:** emergent democracy; **currency:** koruna (based on Czechoslovak koruna); **GNP per capita (PPP):** (US$) 11,640 (1998 est); **exports:** basic manufactures, machinery and transport equipment, miscellaneous manufactured articles, chemicals, beer. Principal market Germany 35.6% (1998); **population:** 10,263,000 (1999 est); **Language:** Czech (official); **religion:** Roman Catholic, Hussite, Presbyterian Evangelical Church of Czech Brethren, Orthodox; **life expectancy:** 70 (men); 77 (women) (1995–2000).

# Dd

**Dada** (or Dadaism) artistic and literary movement founded in 1915 in a spirit of rebellion and disillusionment during World War I and lasting until about 1922. Although the movement had a fairly short life and was concentrated in only a few centres (New York being the only non-European one), Dada was highly influential, establishing the tendency for avant-garde art movements to question traditional artistic conventions and values. There are several accounts of how the name Dada (French for hobby horse) originated; the most often quoted is that it was chosen at random by inserting a penknife into a dictionary, symbolizing the antirational nature of the movement.

**Daguerre, Louis Jacques Mandé** (1787–1851) French pioneer of photography. Together with Joseph Niépce, he is credited with the invention of photography (though others were reaching the same point simultaneously). In 1838 he invented the daguerreotype, a single image process superseded ten years later by Fox Talbot's negative/positive process.

**Dahl, Roald** (1916–1990) British writer, of Norwegian ancestry. He is celebrated for short stories with a twist, such as *Tales of the Unexpected* (1979), and for his children's books, including *James and the Giant Peach* (1961), *Charlie and the Chocolate Factory* (1964), *The BFG* (1982), and *Matilda* (1988).

**Daimler, Gottlieb Wilhelm** (1834–1900) German engineer who pioneered the car and the internal-combustion engine together with Wilhelm Maybach. In 1885 he produced a motor bicycle and in 1889 his first four-wheeled motor vehicle. He combined the vaporization of fuel with the high-speed four-stroke petrol engine.

**Dakar** capital, chief port (with artificial harbour), and administrative centre of Senegal; population (1992) 1,729,800. It is situated at the tip of the Cape Verde peninsula, the westernmost point of Africa. It is a major industrial centre, with industries including crude-oil refining, engineering, chemicals, brewing, and tobacco and food processing. Dakar contains the Grand Mosque, National Museum, and a university (established in 1949).

**Dalai Lama** (1935– ) title of Tenzin Gyatso (Tibetan 'oceanic guru') Tibetan Buddhist monk, political ruler of Tibet from 1940 until 1959, when he went into exile in protest against Chinese annexation and oppression. He has continued to campaign for self-government, and was awarded the Nobel Peace Prize in 1989. Tibetan Buddhists believe that each Dalai Lama is a reincarnation of his predecessor and also of Avalokiteśvara (emanation of Amida Buddha). His deputy is called the Panchen Lama.

**Dalí, Salvador Felipe Jacinto** (1904–1989) Spanish painter and designer. In 1929 he joined the surrealists (see →surrealism) and became notorious for his flamboyant eccentricity. *The Persistence of Memory* (1931) (Museum of Modern Art, New York) is typical. By the late 1930s he had developed a more conventional style – this, and his apparent fascist sympathies, led to his expulsion from the surrealist movement in 1938. It was in this more traditional though still highly inventive and idiosyncratic style that he painted such celebrated religious works as *The Crucifixion* (1951) (Glasgow Art School). He also painted portraits of his wife Gala.

**Dallas** commercial city in northeastern Texas, USA, on the Trinity River; seat of Dallas County; population (1994 est) 1,023,000, metropolitan area (with Fort Worth) (1994 est) 4,362,000. The second-largest city in Texas (Houston is the largest), Dallas is the hub of a rich cotton-farming and oil-producing region, and is one of the leading cultural and manufacturing centres in the Southwest; its industries include banking, insurance, oil, aerospace, and electronics. Dallas was founded in 1841, and was incorporated as a city in 1871.

**Dalton, John** (1766–1844) English chemist who proposed the theory of atoms, which he considered to be the smallest parts of matter. He produced the first list of relative atomic masses in 'Absorption of Gases' in 1805 and put forward the law of partial pressures of gases (**Dalton's law**).

**dam** structure built to hold back water in order to prevent flooding, to provide water for irrigation and storage, and to provide hydroelectric power. The biggest dams are of the earth- and rock-fill type, also called **embankment dams**. Early dams in Britain, built before and about 1800, had a core made from puddled clay (clay which has been mixed with water to make it impermeable). Such dams are generally built on broad valley sites. Deep, narrow gorges dictate a **concrete dam**, where the strength of reinforced concrete can withstand the water pressures involved.

**Daman and Diu** Union Territory of west India; **area:** 112 sq km/43 sq mi; **capital:** Daman; **population:** (1991) 101,400. **Daman** has an area of 72 sq km/28 sq mi. The port and capital, Daman, is on the west coast, 160 km/100 mi north of Mumbai (formerly Bombay), on the estuary of the Daman Ganga River flowing in the Gulf of Khambhat. The economy is based on tourism and fishing. **Diu** is an island off the Kathiawar peninsula with an area of 40 sq km/15 sq mi. The main town is also called Diu. The economy is based on tourism, coconuts, pearl millet, and salt; **history:** Daman was seized by Portugal in 1531 and ceded to Portugal by the Shah of Gujarat in 1539; Diu was captured by the Portuguese in 1534. Both areas were annexed by India in 1961 and were part of the Union Territory of Goa, Daman, and Diu until Goa became a separate state in 1987.

**Damascus** (Arabic *Dimashq* or *ash-Sham*) capital of Syria, on the River Barada, 100 km/62 mi southeast of Beirut; population (1993) 1,497,000. It produces silk, wood products, textiles, brass, and copperware. Said to be the oldest continuously inhabited city in the world, Damascus was an ancient city even in Old Testament times.

**Danelaw** 11th-century name for the area of northern and eastern England settled by the Vikings in the 9th century. It occupied about half of England, from the River Tees to the River Thames. Within its bounds, Danish law, customs, and language prevailed, rather than West Saxon or Mercian law. Its linguistic influence is still apparent in place names in this area.

**Dante Alighieri** (1265–1321) Italian poet. His masterpiece *La divina commedia/The Divine Comedy* (1307–21) is an epic account in three parts of his journey through Hell, Purgatory, and Paradise, during which he is guided part of the way by the poet Virgil; on a metaphorical level, the journey is also one of Dante's own spiritual development. Other works include *De vulgari eloquentia/Concerning the Vulgar Tongue* (1304–06), an original Latin work on Italian, its dialects, and kindred languages; the philosophical prose treatise

*Convivio/The Banquet* (1306–08), the first major work of its kind to be written in Italian rather than Latin; *De monarchia/On World Government* (1310–13), expounding his political theories; and *Canzoniere/Lyrics.*

**Danube** (German *Donau*) second longest of European rivers, rising on the eastern slopes of the Black Forest, and flowing 2,858 km/1,776 mi across Europe to enter the Black Sea in Romania by a swampy delta.

**Dar es Salaam** (Arabic 'haven of peace') chief seaport in Tanzania, on the Indian Ocean, and capital of Tanzania until its replacement by →Dodoma in 1974; population (1996 est) 1,747,000, having grown very rapidly from 150,000 in 1964. Industries include food processing, textiles, clothing, footwear, petroleum refining, glass, printing, timber, aluminium, steel, polystyrene, machinery, and car components. Exports include copper, coffee, sisal, and cotton. As well as being the chief port and largest city, it is also the main industrial, commercial, and financial centre of Tanzania, and includes the main international airport.

**Darwin** port and capital of Northern Territory, Australia; population (1996) 70,251. Darwin is situated on the centre of Australia's north coast, in the northwest of Arnhem Land. It is a service centre for the northern part of Northern Territory, and industries include mining (uranium and copper), horticulture, fruit growing, and tourism. Darwin was destroyed in 1974 by Cyclone Tracy, and rebuilt on the same site.

**Darwin, Charles Robert** (1809–1882) English naturalist who developed the modern theory of →evolution and proposed, with Alfred Russel Wallace, the principle of →natural selection.

---

**WEB SITE** > > > > > > > >
**Darwin, Charles**

http://www.literature.org/Works/
Charles-Darwin

Complete text of Darwin's seminal work
*On the Origin of Species.*

---

**data** (singular datum) facts, figures, and symbols, especially as stored in computers. The term is often used to mean raw, unprocessed facts, as distinct from information, to which a meaning or interpretation has been applied.

**Continuous data** is data that can take any of an infinite number of values between whole numbers and so may not be measured completely accurately. This type of data contrasts with **discrete data**, in which the variable can only take one of a finite set of values. For example, the sizes of apples on a tree form continuous data, whereas the numbers of apples form discrete data.

**database** in computing, a structured collection of data, which may be manipulated to select and sort desired items of information. For example, an accounting system might be built around a database containing details of customers and suppliers. In larger computers, the database makes data available to the various programs that need it, without the need for those programs to be aware of how the data are stored. The term is also sometimes used for simple record-keeping systems, such as mailing lists, in which there are facilities for searching, sorting, and producing records.

**David, Jacques-Louis** (1748–1825) French painter. One of the greatest of the neoclassicists, he sought to give his art a direct political significance. He was an active supporter of the republic during the French Revolution, and was imprisoned 1794–95. In his *Death of Marat* (1793; Musées Royaux, Brussels), he turned political murder into classical tragedy. Later he devoted himself to the newly created empire in grandiose paintings such as *The Coronation of Napoleon* (1805–07; Louvre, Paris).

**David, St** (or Dewi; lived 5th–6th century) Patron saint of Wales, Christian abbot and bishop. According to legend he was the son of a prince of Dyfed and uncle of King Arthur. He was responsible for the adoption of the leek as the national emblem of Wales, but his own emblem is a dove. Feast day 1 March.

**da Vinci** Italian painter, sculptor, architect, engineer, and scientist; see →Leonardo da Vinci.

**Davy, Humphry** (1778–1829) English chemist. He discovered, by electrolysis, the metallic elements sodium and potassium in 1807, and calcium, boron, magnesium, strontium, and barium in 1808. In addition, he established that chlorine is an element and proposed that hydrogen is present in all acids. He invented the safety lamp for use in mines where methane was present, enabling miners to work in previously unsafe conditions. Knighted 1812, baronet 1818.

**Day-Lewis, C(ecil)** (1904–1972) Irish poet. With W H Auden and Stephen Spender, he was one of the influential left-wing poets of the 1930s. His later poetry moved from political concerns to a more traditional personal lyricism. He also wrote detective novels under the pseudonym **Nicholas Blake**. He was British poet laureate from 1968 to 1972.

**D-day** 6 June 1944, the day of the Allied invasion of Normandy under the command of General Eisenhower to commence Operation Overlord, the liberation of Western Europe from German occupation. The Anglo-US invasion fleet landed on the Normandy beaches on the stretch of coast between the Orne River and St Marcouf. Artificial harbours known as 'Mulberries' were constructed and towed across the Channel so that equipment and armaments could be unloaded on to the beaches. After overcoming fierce resistance the allies broke through the German defences; Paris was liberated on 25 August, and Brussels on 2 September. D-day is also military jargon for any day on which a crucial operation is planned. D+1 indicates the day after the start of the operation.

**DDT** (abbreviation for **dichloro-diphenyl-trichloroethane**) ($ClC_6H_5)_2$ $CHC(HCl_2)$ insecticide discovered in 1939 by Swiss chemist Paul Müller. It is useful in the control of insects that spread malaria, but resistant strains develop. DDT is highly toxic and persists in the environment and in living tissue. Despite this and its subsequent danger to wildlife, it has evaded a worldwide ban because it remains one of the most effective ways of controlling malaria. China and India were the biggest DDT users in 1999.

**Dead Sea** large lake, partly in Israel and partly in Jordan, lying 394 m/1,293 ft below sea level; it is the lowest surface point on earth; area 1,020 sq km/394 sq mi. The chief river entering it is the Jordan; it has no outlet and the water is very salty (340 grams of salt per litre of water). The sea is not, however, completely dead. *Dunaliella parva*, a single-celled green alga, and a group of halophilic (salt-loving) Archaea are found here. In 1998, three species of fungi were discovered to be living in the Dead Sea. One of the species was new to science and cannot survive without salt.

**Dead Sea Scrolls** collection of ancient scrolls (rolls of writing) and fragments of scrolls found 1947–56 in caves on the western side of the Jordan, at Qumran. They include copies of Old Testament books a thousand years older than those previously known to be extant. The documents date mainly from about 150 BC–AD 68, when the monastic community that owned them, the Essenes, was destroyed by the Romans because of its support for a revolt against their rule.

**Debussy, (Achille-)Claude** (1862–1918) French composer. He broke with German Romanticism and introduced new qualities of melody and harmony based on the whole-tone scale, evoking oriental music. His work includes *Prélude à l'après-midi d'un faune/Prelude to the Afternoon of a Faun* (1894), illustrating a poem by Stéphane Mallarmé, and the opera *Pelléas et Mélisande* (1902).

**decibel** unit (symbol dB) of measure used originally to compare sound intensities and subsequently electrical or electronic power outputs; now also used to compare voltages. An increase of 10 dB is equivalent to a 10-fold increase in intensity or power, and a 20-fold increase in voltage. The decibel scale is used for audibility measurements, as one decibel, representing an increase of about 25%, is about the smallest change the human ear can detect. A whisper has an intensity of 20 dB; 140 dB (a jet aircraft taking off nearby) is the threshold of pain.

**deciduous** of trees and shrubs, that shed their leaves at the end of the growing season or during a dry season to reduce →transpiration (the loss of water by evaporation).

**decimal number system** (or denary number system) most commonly used number system, to the base ten. Decimal numbers do not necessarily contain a decimal point; 563, 5.63, and −563 are all decimal numbers. Other systems are mainly used in computing and include the →binary number system, octal number system, and hexadecimal number system.

**Declaration of Independence** historic US document stating the theory of government on which the USA was founded, based on the right 'to life, liberty, and the pursuit of happiness'. The statement was issued by the Continental Congress 4 July 1776, renouncing all allegiance to the British crown and ending the connection with Britain.

**Defoe, Daniel** (1660–1731) English writer. His *Robinson Crusoe* (1719), though purporting to be a factual account of shipwreck and solitary survival, was influential in the development of the novel. A prolific journalist and pamphleteer, he was imprisoned in 1703 for the ironic *The Shortest Way with Dissenters* (1702).

**deforestation** destruction of forest for timber, fuel, charcoal burning, and clearing for agriculture and extractive industries, such as mining, without planting new trees to replace those lost (reafforestation) or working on a cycle that allows the natural forest to regenerate. Deforestation causes fertile soil to be blown away or washed into rivers, leading to soil erosion, drought, flooding, and loss of wildlife. It may also increase the carbon dioxide content of the atmosphere and intensify the →greenhouse effect, because there are fewer trees absorbing carbon dioxide from the air for photosynthesis.

**Degas, (Hilaire Germain) Edgar** (1834–1917) French Impressionist (see →Impressionism) painter and sculptor. He devoted himself to lively, informal studies (often using pastels) of ballet, horse racing, and young women working. From the 1890s he turned increasingly to sculpture, modelling figures in wax in a fluent, naturalistic style.

**de Gaulle, Charles André Joseph Marie** (1890–1970) French general and first president of the Fifth Republic 1958–69. He organized the Free French troops fighting the Nazis 1940–44, was head of the provisional French government 1944–46, and leader of his own Gaullist party. In 1958 the national assembly asked him to form a government during France's economic recovery and to solve the crisis in Algeria. He became president at the end of 1958, having changed the constitution to provide for a presidential system, and served until 1969.

**degree** in mathematics, a unit (symbol °) of measurement of an angle or arc. A circle or complete rotation is divided into 360°. A degree may be subdivided into 60 minutes (symbol ′), and each minute may be subdivided in turn into 60 seconds (symbol ″). **Temperature** is also measured in degrees, which are divided on a decimal scale. See also →Celsius, and →Fahrenheit.

**Delaware** state in northeastern USA. It is nicknamed the First State or the Diamond State. Delaware ratified the US Constitution in 1787, becoming the first state in the Union, hence its nickname. It is one of the most industrialized states in the USA. It is bordered to the north by Pennsylvania, to the west and south by Maryland, with which it shares the upper part of the Delmarva Peninsula, and to the east by the Atlantic Ocean; **population:** (1996 est) 725,000; **area:** 5,300 sq km/2,046 sq mi; **capital:** Dover; **towns and cities:** Wilmington, Newark; **industries and products:** dairy, poultry, and market-garden produce; fishing; chemicals, motor vehicles, and textiles.

**Delhi** (also Old Delhi) city of India, and administrative capital of the Union Territory of Delhi (state); population (1991) 8,375,000. It borders on →New Delhi, capital of India, to the south. Manufactured goods include electronic goods, chemicals, and precision instruments, as well as traditional handicrafts such as hand-woven textiles and jewellery. An international airport is 13 km/ 8 mi away at Palam. The University of Delhi (1922) has over 20,000 students.

**Delors, Jacques Lucien Jean** (1925– ) French socialist politician, economy and finance minister (1981– 84) under François Mitterrand's presidency, and president of the European Commission (1985–94), when he oversaw significant budgetary reform, the introduction of the Single European Market, and the negotiation and ratification of the 1992 Maastricht Treaty on European Union.

**Delphi** city of ancient Greece, situated in a rocky valley north of the gulf of Corinth, on the southern slopes of Mount Parnassus, site of a famous →oracle in the temple of Apollo. The site was supposed to be the centre of the Earth and was marked by a conical stone, the *omphalos*. Towards the end of the 6th century BC the Athenian family of the Alcmaeonidae helped to rebuild the temple. The oracle was interpreted by priests from the inspired utterances of the Pythian priestess until it was closed down by the Roman emperor Theodosius I AD 390.

**delta** tract of land at a river's mouth, composed of silt deposited as the water slows on entering the sea. Familiar examples of large deltas are those of the Mississippi, Ganges and Brahmaputra, Rhône, Po, Danube, and Nile; the shape of the Nile delta is like the Greek letter *delta* δ, and thus gave rise to the name.

**dementia** mental deterioration as a result of physical changes in the brain. It may be due to degenerative change, circulatory disease, infection, injury, or chronic poisoning. **Senile dementia**, a progressive loss of mental faculties such as memory and orientation, is typically a disease process of old age, and can be accompanied by →depression.

**democracy** (Greek *demos* 'the community', *kratos* 'sovereign power') government by the people, usually through elected representatives. In the modern world, democracy has developed from the American and French revolutions.

**Democratic Party** one of the two main political parties of the USA. It tends to be the party of the working person, as opposed to the Republicans, the party of big business, but the divisions between the two are not clear cut. Its stronghold since the Civil War has traditionally been industrial urban centres and the Southern states, but conservative Southern Democrats were largely supportive of Republican positions in the 1980s and helped elect President Reagan. Bill Clinton became the first Democrat president for 13 years 1993. The party lost control of both chambers of Congress to the Republicans November 1994, and increasing numbers of Southern Democrat politicians later defected. However, in November 1996 Clinton became the first Democrat president since F D Roosevelt to be elected for a second term, winning 31 states, chiefly in the northeast and west.

**Demosthenes** (*c.* 384–322 BC) Athenian politician, famed for his oratory. From 351 BC he led the party that advocated resistance to the growing power of Philip of Macedon, and in his *Philippics*, a series of speeches, incited the Athenians to war. This policy resulted in the defeat of Chaeronea 338, and the establishment of Macedonian supremacy. After the death of Alexander he organized a revolt; when it failed, he took poison to avoid capture by the Macedonians.

**Deng Xiaoping** (1904–1997) (or Teng Hsiao-ping) Chinese political leader. A member of the Chinese Communist Party (CCP) from the 1920s, he took part in the →Long March (1934–36). He was in the Politburo from 1955 until ousted in the Cultural Revolution (1966–69). Reinstated in the 1970s, he gradually took power and introduced a radical economic modernization programme. He retired from the Politburo in 1987 and from his last official position (as chair of the State Military Commission) in March 1990. He was last seen in public in February 1994. He appointed President Jiang Zemin to succeed him on his death in 1997.

**Denmark** Kingdom of; **national name:** *Kongeriget Danmark*; **area:** 43,075 sq km/ 16,631 sq mi; **capital:** Copenhagen; **major towns/cities:** Århus, Odense, Ålborg, Esbjerg, Randers; **major ports:** Århus, Odense, Ålborg, Esbjerg; **physical features:** comprises the Jutland peninsula and about 500 islands (100 inhabited) including Bornholm in the Baltic Sea; the land is flat and cultivated; sand dunes and lagoons on the west coast and long inlets on the east; the main island is Sjælland (Zealand), where most of Copenhagen is located (the rest is on the island of Amager); **territories:** the dependencies of Faroe Islands and Greenland; **head of state:** Queen Margrethe II from 1972; **head of government:** Poul Nyrup Rasmussen from 1993; **political system:** liberal democracy; **currency:** Danish krone; **GNP per capita (PPP):** (US$) 23,830 (1998); **exports:** pig meat and pork products, other food products, fish, industrial machinery, chemicals, transport equipment. Principal market Germany 21.4% (1998); **population:** 5,283,000 (1999 est); **language:** Danish (official); there is a German-speaking minority; **religion:** Lutheran 97%; **life expectancy:** 73 (men); 78 (women) (1995–2000).

**density** measure of the compactness of a substance; it is equal to its mass per unit volume and is measured in kg per cubic metre/lb per cubic foot. Density is a scalar quantity. The average density $D$ of a mass $m$ occupying a volume $V$ is given by the formula:

$$D = m/V$$

Relative density is the ratio of the density of a substance to that of water at 4°C/32.2°F.

**dentition** type and number of teeth in a species. Different kinds of teeth have different functions; a grass-eating animal will have large molars for grinding its food, whereas a meat-eater will need powerful canines for catching and killing its prey. The teeth that are less useful to an animal's lifestyle may be reduced in size or missing altogether. An animal's dentition is represented diagramatically by a dental formula.

**deoxyribonucleic acid** full name of →DNA.

**depression** in medicine, an emotional state characterized by sadness, unhappy thoughts, apathy, and dejection. Sadness is a normal response to major losses such as bereavement or unemployment. After childbirth, postnatal depression is common. Clinical depression, which is prolonged or unduly severe, often requires treatment, such as antidepressant medication, cognitive therapy, or in very rare cases, electroconvulsive therapy (ECT), in which an electrical current is passed through the brain.

**depression** (or cyclone or low) in meteorology, a region of low atmospheric pressure. In mid latitudes a depression forms as warm, moist air from the tropics mixes with cold, dry polar air, producing warm and cold boundaries ( →fronts) and unstable weather – low cloud and drizzle, showers, or fierce storms. The warm air, being less dense, rises above the cold air to produce the area of low pressure on the ground. Air spirals in towards the centre of the depression in an anticlockwise direction in the northern hemisphere, clockwise in the southern hemisphere, generating winds up to gale force. Depressions tend to travel eastwards and can remain active for several days.

**Derbyshire** county of north central England (since April 1997 Derby City has been a separate unitary authority); **area:** 2,550 sq km/984 sq mi; **towns and cities:** Matlock (administrative headquarters), Buxton, Chesterfield, Glossop, Ilkeston, Long Eaton; **physical:** Peak District National Park (including Kinder Scout 636 m/2,088 ft); rivers Dane, Derwent, Dove, Goyt, Rother, Trent, Wye; Dove Dale; **features:** Chatsworth House, Bakewell (seat of the Duke of Devonshire); Haddon Hall; Hardwick Hall; Kedleston Hall (designed by Robert Adam); well-dressing at Tissington, Wirksworth, Eyam, and other villages; Castleton Caverns; **agriculture:** cereals, root crops, and dairy farming (in the south); sheep farming (in the northern hills); **industries:** heavy engineering; manufacturing (cotton, hosiery, lace, porcelain, textiles); mineral and metal working (barytes, gypsum, lead, zinc); quarrying (marble, sandstone, pipeclay); motor cars; limestone quarrying; **population:** (1996) 962,000; **famous people:** Thomas Cook, Marquess Curzon of Kedleston, Samuel Richardson.

**Descartes, René** (1596–1650) French philosopher and mathematician. He believed that commonly accepted knowledge was doubtful because of the subjective nature of the senses, and attempted to rebuild human knowledge using as his foundation the dictum *cogito ergo sum* ('I think, therefore I am'). He also believed that the entire material universe could be explained in terms of mathematical physics, and founded coordinate geometry as a way of defining and manipulating geometrical shapes by means of algebraic expressions. Cartesian coordinates, the means by which points are represented in this system, are named after him. Descartes also established the science of optics, and helped to shape contemporary theories of astronomy and animal behaviour.

**desert** arid area with sparse vegetation (or, in rare cases, almost no vegetation). Soils are poor, and many deserts include areas of shifting sands. Deserts can be either hot or cold. Almost 33% of the Earth's land surface is desert, and this proportion is increasing.

**desktop publishing** (DTP) use of microcomputers for small-scale typesetting and page makeup. DTP systems are capable of producing camera-ready pages (pages ready for photographing and printing), made up of text and graphics, with text set in different typefaces and sizes. The page can be previewed on the screen before final printing on a laser printer.

**detergent** surface-active cleansing agent. The common detergents are made from →fats (hydrocarbons) and sulphuric acid, and their long-chain molecules have a type of structure similar to that of soap molecules: a salt group at one end attached to a long hydrocarbon 'tail'. They have the advantage over soap in that they do not produce scum by forming insoluble salts with the calcium and magnesium ions present in hard water.

**Detroit** industrial city and port in southeastern Michigan, USA, 788 km/489 mi west of New York and 395 km/245 mi east of Chicago, situated on the Detroit River opposite the city of Windsor in Ontario, Canada; seat of Wayne County; area 370 sq km/143 sq mi (excluding neighbouring cities), metropolitan area 10,093 sq km/3,897 sq mi; population (1998) 970,196, metropolitan area 5,246,000. Detroit is the headquarters of Ford, Chrysler, and General Motors, hence its nickname, Motown (from 'motor town'). Other manufactured products include steel, machine tools, chemicals, and pharmaceuticals. It is the seventh-largest city in the USA.

**de Valera, Éamon** (1882–1975) Irish nationalist politician, president/Taoiseach (prime minister) of the Irish Free State/Eire/Republic of Ireland 1932–48, 1951–54, and 1957–59, and president 1959–73. Repeatedly imprisoned, de Valera participated in the →Easter Rising of 1916 and was leader of the nationalist →Sinn Féin party 1917–26, when he formed the republican →Fianna Fáil party. He opposed the Anglo-Irish Treaty (1921) but formulated a constitutional relationship with Britain in the 1930s that achieved greater Irish sovereignty.

**de Valois, Ninette** (1898– ) (stage name of Edris Stannus) Irish choreographer, dancer, and teacher. In setting up the Vic-Wells Ballet in 1931 (later the Royal Ballet and Royal Ballet School) she was, along with choreographer Frederick Ashton, one of the architects of British ballet. Among her works are *Job* (1931), *The Rake's Progress* (1935), *Checkmate* (1937), and *The Prospect Before Us* (1940), revived by the Birmingham Royal Ballet in honour of her 100th birthday in June 1998. She is reverentially and affectionately known as 'Madam' in the ballet world.

**Devon** (or Devonshire) county of southwest England; Plymouth and Torbay have been separate unitary authorities since April 1998; **area:** 6,720 sq km/2,594 sq mi; **towns and cities:** Exeter (administrative headquarters); resorts: Barnstaple, Bideford, Exmouth, Ilfracombe, Sidmouth, Teignmouth, Tiverton; **physical:** rivers: Dart, Exe, Plym, Tamar (94 km/58 mi); Taw, Teign, Torridge; National Parks: Dartmoor, Exmoor; **features:** Lundy bird sanctuary and marine nature reserve in the Bristol Channel; **agriculture:** sheep and dairy farming, beef cattle; cider and clotted cream; fishing; **industries:** kaolin in the south; lace (at

Honiton); Dartington glass; carpets (Axminster); quarrying (granite, limestone, sandstone); minerals (copper, iron, lead, manganese); tourism; **population:** (1996) 1,059,300; **famous people:** St Boniface, Henry de Bracton, Samuel Taylor Coleridge, John Davis, Francis Drake, Humphrey Gilbert, Richard Grenville, John Hawkins, Charles Kingsley, Thomas Newcomen, Walter Raleigh, Joshua Reynolds, Robert F Scott, Joanna Southcott.

**Devonian** period of geological time 408–360 million years ago, the fourth period of the Palaeozoic era. Many desert sandstones from North America and Europe date from this time. The first land plants flourished in the Devonian period, corals were abundant in the seas, amphibians evolved from air-breathing fish, and insects developed on land.

**Dhaka** (or Dacca) capital of Bangladesh since 1971, in Dhaka region, west of the River Meghna on the →Ganges delta; population (1991) 3,397,200. It trades in rice, oilseed, sugar, and tea; industries include jute-processing, tanning, and productions of textiles, chemicals, glass, and metal products.

**diabetes** disease *diabetes mellitus*, in which a disorder of the islets of Langerhans in the pancreas prevents the body producing the hormone →insulin, so that sugars cannot be used properly.

Treatment is by strict dietary control and oral or injected insulin, depending on the type of diabetes.

**Diaghilev, Sergei Pavlovich** (1872– 1929) Russian ballet impresario. In 1909 he founded the Ballets Russes/ Russian Ballet (headquarters in Monaco), which he directed for 20 years. Through this company he brought Russian ballet to the West, introducing and encouraging a dazzling array of dancers, choreographers, composers, and artists, such as Anna Pavlova, Vaslav Nijinsky, Bronislava Nijinksa, Mikhail Fokine, Léonide Massine, George Balanchine, Igor Stravinsky, Sergey Prokofiev, Pablo Picasso, and Henri Matisse.

**dialysis** technique for removing waste products from the blood of those suffering chronic or acute kidney failure. There are two main methods, haemodialysis and peritoneal dialysis.

**diamond** generally colourless, transparent mineral, an →allotrope of carbon. It is regarded as a precious gemstone, and is the hardest substance known (10 on the →Mohs scale). Industrial diamonds, which may be natural or synthetic, are used for cutting, grinding, and polishing.

**Diana** in Roman mythology, the goddess of chastity, hunting, and the Moon; daughter of Jupiter and twin of →Apollo. Her Greek equivalent is the goddess Artemis.

**Diana, Princess of Wales** (1961– 1997) born Diana Frances Spencer, daughter of the 8th Earl Spencer, Diana married Prince Charles in St Paul's Cathedral, London, in 1981. She had two sons, William and Harry, before her separation from Charles in 1992.

In February 1996 she agreed to a divorce, after which she became known as Diana, Princess of Wales. Her worldwide prominence for charity work contributed to a massive outpouring of public grief after her death in a car crash in Paris, France, on 31 August 1997. Her funeral proved to be the biggest British televised event in history.

**diaphragm** in mammals, a thin muscular sheet separating the thorax from the abdomen. It is attached by way of the ribs at either side and the breastbone and backbone, and a central tendon. Arching upwards against the heart and lungs, the diaphragm is important in the mechanics of breathing. It contracts at each inhalation, moving downwards to increase the volume of the chest cavity, and relaxes at exhalation.

**diarrhoea** frequent or excessive action of the bowels so that the faeces are liquid or semiliquid. It is caused by intestinal irritants (including some drugs and poisons), infection with harmful organisms (as in dysentery, salmonella, or cholera), or allergies.

**Diaspora** (Greek 'dispersion') dispersal of the Jews, initially from Palestine after the Babylonian conquest 586 BC, and then following the Roman sacking of Jerusalem AD 70 and their crushing of the Jewish revolt of 135. The term has come to refer to all the Jews living outside Israel.

**Diaz, Bartholomeu** (c. 1450–1500) Portuguese explorer, the first European to reach the Cape of Good Hope, in 1488, and to establish a route around

Africa. He drowned during an expedition with Pedro Cabral.

**Dickens, Charles John Huffam** (1812–1870) English novelist. He is enduringly popular for his memorable characters and his portrayal of the social evils of Victorian England. In 1836 he published the first number of the *Pickwick Papers*, followed by *Oliver Twist* (1837), the first of his 'reforming' novels; *Nicholas Nickleby* (1838); *The Old Curiosity Shop* (1840); *Barnaby Rudge* (1841); and *David Copperfield* (1850). Among his later books are *A Tale of Two Cities* (1859) and *Great Expectations* (1861). All his novels were written as serials.

---

**WEB SITE** > > > > > > > >
**Dickens, Charles**

http://landow.stg.brown.edu/victorian/dickens/dickensov.html

Biographical page from the Victorian Web – including a chronology of Dickens's life, features on his working methods and his affair with Ellen Ternan, and overviews of *Little Dorrit* and *Great Expectations*.

---

**Dickinson, Emily Elizabeth** (1830–1886) US poet. She wrote most of her poetry between 1850 and the late 1860s and was particularly prolific during the Civil War years. She experimented with poetic rhythms, rhymes, and forms, as well as language and syntax. Her work is characterized by a wit and boldness that seem to contrast sharply with the reclusive life she led. Very few of her many short, mystical poems were published during her lifetime, and her work became well known only in the 20th century. The first collection of her poetry, *Poems by Emily Dickinson*, was published 1890.

---

**WEB SITE** > > > > > > > >

**Emily Dickinson Page**

http://userweb.interactive.net/~krisxlee/emily/

Life and works of US poet Emily Dickinson. Resources include an illustrated biography, several hundred of her poems online, links to discussion groups and the Emily Dickinson International Society, and further links to numerous related sites.

---

**Diderot, Denis** (1713–1784) French philosopher. He is closely associated with the Enlightenment, the European intellectual movement for social and scientific progress, and was editor of the enormously influential *Encyclopédie* (1751–80).

**diesel engine** →internal-combustion engine that burns a lightweight fuel oil. The diesel engine operates by compressing air until it becomes sufficiently hot to ignite the fuel. It is a piston-in-cylinder engine, like the petrol engine, but only air (rather than an air-and-fuel mixture) is taken into the cylinder on the first piston stroke (down). The piston moves up and compresses the air until it is at a very high temperature. The fuel oil is then injected into the hot air, where it burns, driving the piston

down on its power stroke. For this reason the engine is called a compression-ignition engine.

**Dietrich, Marlene** (1901–1992) born Maria Magdalene Dietrich von Losch, German-born US actor and singer. She became a star in *Der Blaue Engel/The Blue Angel* (1930), directed by Josef von Sternberg, with whom she would collaborate throughout the 1930s. Her films include *Morocco* (1930), *Blonde Venus* 1932, *The Devil is a Woman* (1935), *Destry Rides Again* (1939), and *Touch of Evil* (1958). In the 1960s she stopped acting and began a career as a concert singer.

**diffraction** the spreading out of waves when they pass through a small gap or around a small object, resulting in some change in the direction of the waves. In order for this effect to be observed the size of the object or gap must be comparable to or smaller than the →wavelength of the waves. Diffraction occurs with all forms of progressive waves – electromagnetic, sound, and water waves – and explains such phenomena as why long-wave radio waves can bend round hills better than short-wave radio waves.

**diffusion** spontaneous and random movement of molecules or particles in a fluid (gas or liquid) from a region in which they are at a high concentration to a region of lower concentration, until a uniform concentration is achieved throughout. The difference in concentration between two such regions is called the **concentration gradient**. No mechanical mixing or stirring is involved. For instance, if a drop of ink is added to water, its molecules will diffuse until their colour becomes evenly distributed throughout. Diffusion occurs more rapidly across a higher concentration gradient and at higher temperature.

**digestive system** in the body, all the organs and tissues involved in the digestion of food. In animals, these consist of the mouth, stomach, intestines, and their associated glands. The process of digestion breaks down the food by physical and chemical means into the different elements that are needed by the body for energy and tissue building and repair. Digestion begins in the mouth and is completed in the →stomach; from there most nutrients are absorbed into the small intestine from where they pass through the intestinal wall into the bloodstream; what remains is stored and concentrated into faeces in the large intestine. Birds have two additional digestive organs – the crop and gizzard. In smaller, simpler animals such as jellyfish, the digestive system is simply a cavity (coelenteron or enteric cavity) with a 'mouth' into which food is taken; the digestible portion is dissolved and absorbed in this cavity, and the remains are ejected back through the mouth.

**digitalis** any of a group of plants belonging to the figwort family, which includes the foxgloves. The leaves of the common foxglove (*Digitalis purpurea*) are the source of the drug **digitalis** used in the treatment of heart disease. (Genus *Digitalis*, family Scrophulariaceae.)

**WEB SITE** > > > > > > > >

**Your Digestive System and How it Works**

http://www.niddk.nih.gov/health/digest/pubs/digestsyst/newdiges.htm

Health information on the digestive system, detailed enough to interest biology students. Part of a much larger site from the US National Institute of Diabetes and Digestive and Kidney Diseases, it explains what happens as food travels through the body, and discusses the hormones and nerves that regulate the digestive process.

**digital recording** technique whereby the pressure of sound waves is sampled more than 30,000 times a second and the values converted by computer into precise numerical values. These are recorded and, during playback, are reconverted to sound waves.

**dilution** process of reducing the concentration of a solution by the addition of a solvent.

**dinosaur** (Greek *deinos* 'terrible', *sauros* 'lizard') any of a group (sometimes considered as two separate orders) of extinct reptiles living between 205 million and 65 million years ago. Their closest living relations are crocodiles and birds. Many species of dinosaur evolved during the millions of years they were the dominant large land animals. Most were large (up to 27 m/90 ft), but some were as small as chickens. They disappeared 65 million years ago for reasons not fully understood, although many theories exist.

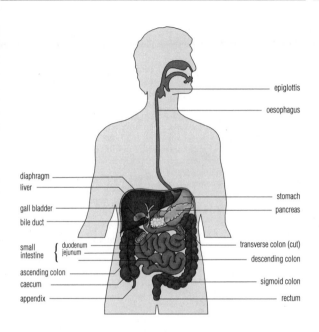

epiglottis

oesophagus

diaphragm

liver

gall bladder

bile duct

small intestine { duodenum jejunum

ascending colon

caecum

appendix

stomach

pancreas

transverse colon (cut)

descending colon

sigmoid colon

rectum

**digestive system** The human digestive system. When food is swallowed, it is moved down the oesophagus by the action of muscles (peristalsis) into the stomach. Digestion starts in the stomach as the food is mixed with enzymes and strong acid. After several hours, the food passes to the small intestine. Here more enzymes are added and digestion is completed. After all nutrients have been absorbed, the indigestible parts pass into the large intestine and thence to the rectum. The liver has many functions, such as storing minerals and vitamins and making bile, which is stored in the gall bladder until needed for the digestion of fats. The pancreas supplies enzymes. The appendix appears to have no function in human beings.

**Diocletian** (AD 245–313) Gaius Aurelius Valerius Diocletianus Roman emperor 284–305 who initiated severe persecution of Christians in 303. In 293 he appointed Maximian (c. 240–c. 310) as co-ruler and reorganized and subdivided the empire, with two joint and two subordinate emperors. This was known as the Tetrarchic system. In 305 he abdicated in favour of Galerius, living in retirement until his death.

**diode** combination of a cold anode and a heated cathode, or the semiconductor equivalent, which incorporates a *p–n* junction. Either device allows the passage of direct current in one direction only, and so is commonly used in a →rectifier to convert alternating current (AC) to direct current (DC).

**Diogenes** (*c.* 412–*c.* 323 BC) Ascetic Greek philosopher of the cynic school. He believed in freedom and self-sufficiency for the individual, and that the virtuous life was the simple life; he did not believe in social mores. His writings do not survive.

**Dionysius** two tyrants of the ancient Greek city of Syracuse in Sicily. **Dionysius the Elder** (c. 430–367 BC) seized power 405 BC. His first two wars with Carthage further extended the power of Syracuse, but in a third (383–378 BC) he was defeated. He was a patron of →Plato. He was succeeded by his son, **Dionysius the Younger**, who was driven out of Syracuse by Dion 356; he was tyrant again 353, but in 343 returned to Corinth.

**diphtheria** acute infectious disease in which a membrane forms in the throat (threatening death by asphyxia), along with the production of a powerful toxin that damages the heart and nerves. The organism responsible is a bacterium (*Corynebacterium diphtheriae*). It is treated with antitoxin and antibiotics.

**diploid** having paired →chromosomes in each cell. In sexually reproducing species, one set is derived from each parent, the →gametes, or sex cells, of each parent being →haploid (having only one set of chromosomes) due to meiosis (reduction cell division).

**Dirac, Paul Adrien Maurice** (1902–1984) British physicist who worked out a version of quantum mechanics consistent with special →relativity. The existence of antiparticles, such as the positron (positive electron), was one of its predictions. He shared the Nobel Prize for Physics in 1933 with Austrian physicist Erwin →Schrödinger.

**direct current** (DC) electric current that flows in one direction, and does not reverse its flow as →alternating current does. The electricity produced by a battery is direct current.

**discrimination** distinction made (social, economic, political, legal) between individuals or groups such that one has the power to treat the other unfavourably. **Negative discrimination**, often based on stereotype, includes anti-Semitism, apartheid, caste, racism, sexism, and slavery. **Positive discrimination**, or 'affirmative action', is sometimes practised in an attempt to counteract the effects of previous long-term discrimination.

**discus** circular disc thrown by athletes who rotate the body to gain momentum from within a circle 2.5 m/8 ft in diameter. The men's discus weighs 2 kg/4.4 lb and the women's 1 kg/2.2 lb. Discus throwing was a competition in ancient Greece at gymnastic contests, such as those of the Olympic Games. It is an event in the modern Olympics and athletics meetings.

**disk** in computing, a common medium for storing large volumes of data (an alternative is magnetic tape). A **magnetic disk** is rotated at high speed in a disk-drive unit as a read/write (playback or record) head passes over its surfaces to record or read the magnetic variations that encode the data. Recently, **optical disks**, such as →CD-ROM (compact-disc read-only memory) and WORM (write once, read many times), have been used to store computer data. Data are recorded on the disk surface as etched microscopic pits and are read by a laser-scanning device.

Optical disks have an enormous capacity – ranging from 650 megabytes for CD-ROM to 2.6 gigabytes for magneto-optical drives.

**Disney, Walt(er Elias)** (1901–1966) US film-maker and animator, a pioneer of family entertainment. He and his brother established an animation studio in Hollywood in 1923, and his first Mickey Mouse cartoons (*Plane Crazy*, which was silent, and *Steamboat Willie*, which had sound and was also in colour) appeared in 1928.

The studio later made feature-length animated films, including *Snow White and the Seven Dwarfs* (1938), *Pinocchio* (1940), and *Dumbo* (1941). Disney's cartoon figures, such as Donald Duck, also appeared in comic books worldwide. In 1955, Disney opened the first theme park, Disneyland, in California.

**Disraeli, Benjamin** (1804–1881) 1st Earl of Beaconsfield, British Conservative politician and novelist. Elected to Parliament in 1837, he was chancellor of the Exchequer under Lord Derby 1852, 1858–59, and 1866–68, and prime minister 1868 and 1874–80. His imperialist policies brought India directly under the crown, and he was personally responsible for purchasing control of the Suez Canal. The central Conservative Party organization is his creation. His popular, political novels reflect an interest in social reform and include *Coningsby* (1844) and *Sybil* (1845).

**distemper** any of several infectious diseases of animals characterized by catarrh, cough, and general weakness. Specifically, it refers to a virus disease in young dogs, also found in wild animals, which can now be prevented by vaccination. In 1988 an allied virus killed over 10,000 common seals in the Baltic and North seas.

**diuretic** any drug that increases the output of urine by the kidneys. It may be used in the treatment of high blood pressure and to relieve oedema associated with heart, lung, kidney, or liver disease, and some endocrine disorders.

**Djibouti** (or Jibuti) chief port and capital of the Republic of Djibouti, on a peninsula 240 km/149 mi southwest of Aden and 565 km/351 mi northeast of Addis Ababa; population (1995) 383,000. Industries include petroleum refining, textiles, and rail freighting. The city is an important regional bunkering and supply centre for the export trade in petroleum, and is the main export route for Ethiopian coffee.

**Djibouti** Republic of; **national name:** *Jumhouriyya Djibouti*; **area:** 23,200 sq km/8,957 sq mi; **capital:** Djibouti (and chief port); **major towns/cities:** Tadjoura, Obock, Dikhil, Ali-Sabieh; **physical features:** mountains divide an inland plateau from a coastal plain; hot and arid; **head of state:** Hassan Gouled Aptidon from 1977; **head of government:** Barkat Gourad from 1981; **political system:** emergent democracy; **currency:** Djibouti franc; **GNP per capita (PPP):** (US\$) 1,100 (1997 est); **exports:** hides, cattle, coffee (exports are largely re-exports). Principal market Somalia 41% (1997); **population:** 629,000 (1999 est); **language:** French (official), Somali, Afar, Arabic; **religion:** Sunni Muslim; **life expectancy:** 49 (men); 52 (women) (1995–2000).

**DNA** (abbreviation for deoxyribonucleic acid) complex giant molecule that contains, in chemically coded form, the information needed for a cell to make proteins. DNA is a ladderlike double-stranded nucleic acid which forms the basis of genetic inheritance in all organisms, except for a few viruses that have only →RNA. DNA is organized into →chromosomes and, in organisms other than bacteria, it is found only in the cell nucleus.

**dodo** extinct flightless bird *Raphus cucullatus*, order Columbiformes, formerly found on the island of Mauritius, but exterminated by early settlers around 1681. Although related to the pigeons, it was larger than a turkey, with a bulky body, rudimentary wings, and short curly tail-feathers. The bill was blackish in colour, forming a horny hook at the end.

**Dodoma** capital (replacing Dar es Salaam in 1974) of Tanzania; 1,132 m/3,713 ft above sea level; population (1994 est) 215,000. It is a centre of communications, linked by rail with Dar es Salaam and Kigoma on Lake Tanganyika, and by road with Kenya to the north and Zambia and Malawi to the south. There is an airport. Dodoma is a marketplace for locally grown coffee and peanuts, but has a limited industrial base, which includes the manufacture of bricks.

**dog** any carnivorous mammal of the family Canidae, including wild dogs, wolves, jackals, coyotes, and foxes. Specifically, the domestic dog *Canis familiaris*, the earliest animal descended from the wolf. Dogs were first domesticated around 14,000 years ago, and migrated with humans to all the continents. They have been selectively bred into many different varieties for working animals and pets.

**doldrums** area of low atmospheric pressure along the Equator, in the intertropical convergence zone where the northeast and southeast trade winds converge. The doldrums are characterized by calm or very light winds, during which there may be sudden squalls and stormy weather. For this reason the areas are avoided as far as possible by sailing ships.

**dolphin** any of various highly intelligent aquatic mammals of the family Delphinidae, which also includes porpoises. There are about 60 species. Most inhabit tropical and temperate oceans, but there are some freshwater forms in rivers in Asia, Africa, and South America. The name 'dolphin' is generally applied to species having a beaklike snout and slender body, whereas the name 'porpoise' is reserved for the smaller species with a blunt snout and stocky body. Dolphins use sound (echolocation) to navigate, to find prey, and for communication. The common dolphin *Delphinus delphis* is found in all temperate and tropical seas. It is up to 2.5 m/8 ft long, and is dark above and white below, with bands of grey, white, and yellow on the sides. It has up to 100 teeth in its jaws, which make the 15 cm/6 in 'beak' protrude forward from the rounded head. The corners of its mouth are permanently upturned, giving the appearance of a smile, though dolphins cannot actually smile. Dolphins feed on fish and squid.

**Domesday Book** record of the survey of England carried out in 1086 by officials of William the Conqueror in order to assess land tax and other dues, ascertain the value of the crown lands, and enable the king to estimate the power of his vassal barons. The name is derived from the belief that its judgement was as final as that of Doomsday.

**Domingo, Placido** (1941– ) Spanish lyric tenor. He specializes in Italian and French 19th-century operatic roles to which he brings a finely tuned dramatic temperament. He has established a world reputation as a sympathetic leading tenor, and has made many films including the 1988 version of Puccini's *Tosca* set in Rome, and the 1990

Zeffirelli production of Leoncavallo's *I pagliacci/The Strolling Players*. He became artistic director of the Los Angeles Opera in 2000.

**Dominica** Commonwealth of; **area:** 751 sq km/290 sq mi; **capital:** Roseau, with a deepwater port; **major towns/cities:** Portsmouth, Berekua, Marigot, Rosalie; **major ports:** Roseau, Portsmouth, Berekua, Marigot, Rosalie; **physical features:** second-largest of the Windward Islands, mountainous central ridge with tropical rainforest; **head of state:** Vernon Shaw from 1998; **head of government:** Edison James from 1995; **political system:** liberal democracy; **currency:** Eastern Caribbean dollar; pound sterling; French franc; **GNP per capita (PPP):** (US$) 3,940 (1998); **exports:** bananas, soap, coconuts, grapefruit, galvanized sheets. Principal market UK 32.8% (1997); **population:** 75,000 (1999 est); **language:** English (official), but the Dominican patois reflects earlier periods of French rule; **religion:** Roman Catholic 80%; **life expectancy:** 75 (men); 81 (women) (1998 est).

**Dominican Republic** national name: *República Dominicana*; **area:** 48,442 sq km/18,703 sq mi; **capital:** Santo Domingo; **major towns/cities:** Santiago de los Caballeros, La Romana, San Pedro de Macoris, San Francisco de Macoris, Concepcion de la Vega, San Juan; **physical features:** comprises eastern two-thirds of island of Hispaniola; central mountain range with fertile valleys; Pico Duarte 3,174 m/10,417 ft, highest point in Caribbean islands; **head of state and government:** Leonel Fernández from 1996; **political system:** democracy; **currency:** Dominican Republic peso; **GNP per capita (PPP):** (US$) 4,700 (1998); **exports:** raw sugar, molasses, coffee, cocoa, tobacco, ferro-nickel, gold, silver. Principal market USA 44.7% (1997); **population:** 8,365,000 (1999 est); **language:** Spanish (official); **religion:** Roman Catholic; **life expectancy:** 69 (men); 73 (women) (1995–2000).

**Don Juan** (Italian Don Giovanni) character of Spanish legend, Don Juan Tenorio, supposed to have lived in the 14th century and notorious for his debauchery. Tirso de Molina, Molière, Mozart, Byron, and George Bernard Shaw have featured the legend in their works.

**Donne, John** (1572–1631) English metaphysical poet. His work consists of love poems, religious poems, verse satires, and sermons. His sermons rank him with the century's greatest orators, and his fervent poems of love and hate, violent, tender, or abusive, give him a unique position among English poets. A Roman Catholic in his youth, he converted to the Church of England and finally became dean of St Paul's Cathedral, London.

**Doomsday Book** variant spelling of →Domesday Book, the English survey of 1086.

**Doppler effect** change in the observed frequency (or wavelength) of waves due to relative motion between the wave source and the observer. The Doppler effect is responsible for the perceived change in pitch of a siren as it approaches and then recedes, and for the →red shift of light from distant galaxies. It is named after the Austrian physicist Christian Doppler.

**WEB SITE** > > > > > > > >
**Doppler Effect**
http://www.lifeintheuniverse.com//doppler.html
Explanation of the Doppler effect and links to other related sites.

**Dorset** county of southwest England (since April 1997 Bournemouth and Poole have been separate unitary authorities); **area:** 2,541 sq km/981 sq mi; **towns and cities:** Dorchester (administrative headquarters), Shaftesbury, Sherborne; Lyme Regis, Weymouth, Poole (resorts); **physical:** Chesil Beach, a shingle bank along the coast 19 km/11 mi long, connecting Isle of Portland to the mainland; Dorset Downs (chalk); River Stour, and rivers Frome and Piddle (which flow into Poole Harbour); clay beds in the north and west; Canford Heath, the home of some of Britain's rarest breeding birds and reptiles (including the nightjar, Dartford warbler, sand lizard, and smooth snake); **features:** Isle of Purbeck, a peninsula where china clay and Purbeck 'marble' are quarried, and which includes Corfe Castle and the holiday resort of Swanage; Cranborne Chase; Maiden Castle (prehistoric earthwork); Tank Museum at Royal Armoured Corps Centre, Bovington, where the cottage of the soldier and writer T E Lawrence is a museum; **agriculture:** dairy farming; **industries:** Wytch Farm is the largest onshore oilfield in the UK; production at Wareham onshore oilfield started in 1991; quarrying (marble from the Isle of Purbeck, and Portland stone, which has been used for buildings all over the world); manufacturing (rope, twine, and net at Bridport); sand and gravel extraction; tourism; **population:** (1996) 681,900; **famous people:** Anthony Ashley Cooper, Thomas Hardy, Thomas Love Peacock.

**DOS** (acronym for disk operating system) computer operating system specifically designed for use with disk storage; also used as an alternative name for a particular operating system, MS-DOS.

**Dostoevsky, Fyodor Mikhailovich** (1821–1881) Russian novelist. Remarkable for their profound psychological insight, Dostoevsky's novels have been increasingly influential. In 1849 he was sentenced to four years' hard labour in Siberia, followed by army service, for printing socialist propaganda. *The House of the Dead* (1861) recalls his prison experiences, followed by his major works *Crime and Punishment* (1866), *The Idiot* (1868–69), and *The Brothers Karamazov* (1879–80).

**double bass** large, bowed four-stringed (sometimes five-stringed) musical instrument, the bass of the violin family. It is descended from the bass viol or violone. Until 1950, after which it was increasingly superseded by the electric bass, it also provided bass support (plucked) for jazz and dance bands. Performers include the Russian-born US conductor Serge Koussevitsky (1874–1951), and the jazz player and composer Charles Mingus. The double bass features in the well loved 'Elephants' solo, No. 5 of Saint-Saëns's *Carnival of the Animals* (1897).

**Dounreay** site of the world's first fast-breeder nuclear reactor (1962) on the north coast of Scotland, in the Highland unitary authority, 12 km/7 mi west of Thurso. It is now a nuclear reprocessing plant.

**Dow Jones Index** (Dow Jones Industrial 30 Share Index) scale for measuring the average share price and percentage change of 30 major US industrial companies. It has been calculated and published since 1897 by the financial news publisher Dow Jones and Co.

**Down** county of southeastern Northern Ireland; **area:** 2,470 sq km/953 sq mi; **towns and cities:** Downpatrick (county town), Bangor, Newtownards, Newry, and Banbridge; the northern part lies within the commuter belt for Belfast, and includes part of the city of Belfast, east of the River Lagan; **physical:** Mourne Mountains; Strangford sea lough; **industries:** light manufacturing, plastics, linen, high technology and computer companies, fishing, quarrying; **agriculture:** County Down has very fertile land in the north. The principal crops are barley, potatoes, and oats; there is livestock rearing and dairying; **population:** (1981) 339,200; **government:** the county returns two members to the UK Parliament.

**Down's syndrome** condition caused by a chromosomal abnormality (the presence of an extra copy of chromosome 21), which in humans produces mental retardation; a flattened face; coarse, straight hair; and a fold of skin at the inner edge of the eye (hence the former name 'mongolism'). The condition can be detected by prenatal testing.

**Doyle, Arthur Conan** (1859–1930) Scottish writer. He created the detective Sherlock Holmes and his assistant Dr Watson, who first appeared in *A Study in Scarlet* (1887) and featured in a number of subsequent stories, including *The Hound of the Baskervilles* (1902).

**dragonfly** any of numerous insects of the order Odonata, including the damselfly. They all have long narrow bodies, two pairs of almost equal-sized, glassy wings with a network of veins; short, bristlelike antennae; powerful, 'toothed' mouthparts; and very large compound eyes which may have up to 30,000 facets. They can fly at speeds of up to 64–96 kph/40–60 mph.

**Drake, Francis** (*c.* 1540–1596) English buccaneer and explorer. Having enriched himself as a pirate against Spanish interests in the Caribbean 1567–72, he was sponsored by Elizabeth I for an expedition to the Pacific, sailing round the world 1577–80 in the *Golden Hind*, robbing Spanish ships as he went. This was the

second circumnavigation of the globe (the first was by the Portuguese explorer Ferdinand Magellan). Drake also helped to defeat the →Spanish Armada in 1588 as a vice admiral in the *Revenge*.

**Dresden** capital of the *Land* (state) of Saxony, Germany, lying in a wide basin in the upper Elbe Valley; population (1995) 472,900. Products include chemicals, machinery, glassware, and musical instruments; telecommunications and high-tech industries are also important. One of the most beautiful German cities, with a rich architectural and cultural heritage, it was devastated by Allied bombing in 1945; much rebuilding has since taken place, and the city has become an important tourist destination.

**Dreyfus, Alfred** (1859–1935) French army officer, victim of miscarriage of justice, anti-Semitism, and cover-up. Employed in the War Ministry, in 1894 he was accused of betraying military secrets to Germany, court-martialled, and sent to the penal colony on Devil's Island, French Guiana. When his innocence was discovered in 1896 the military establishment tried to conceal it, and the implications of the Dreyfus affair were passionately discussed in the press until he was exonerated in 1906.

**Druidism** religion of the Celtic peoples of the pre-Christian British Isles and Gaul. The word is derived from the Greek *drus* ('oak'), a tree regarded by the Druids as sacred. One of the Druids' chief rites was the cutting of mistletoe from the oak with a golden sickle. They taught the immortality of the soul and a reincarnation doctrine, and were expert in astronomy. The Druids are thought to have offered human sacrifices.

**Dryden, John** (1631–1700) English poet and dramatist. He is noted for his satirical verse and for his use of the heroic couplet. His poetry includes the verse satire *Absalom and Achitophel* (1681), *Annus Mirabilis* (1667), and 'A Song for St Cecilia's Day' (1687). Plays include the heroic drama *The Conquest of Granada* (1672), the comedy *Marriage à la Mode* (1673), and *All for Love* (1678), a reworking of Shakespeare's *Antony and Cleopatra*.

**DTP** abbreviation for →desktop publishing.

**Dubai** one of the United Arab Emirates; population (1995) 674,100.

**Dublin** offical Irish name *Baile átha Cliath*, 'the town of the ford of the hurdles' (Gaelic *dubh linn*, 'dark pool') city and port on the east coast of Ireland, at the mouth of the River Liffey, facing the Irish Sea; capital of the Republic of Ireland, and county town of County Dublin; population (1996) 481,600; Greater Dublin, including Dún Laoghaire (1996) 953,000. Dublin is the site of one of the world's largest breweries (Guinness); other industries include textiles, pharmaceuticals, electrical goods, whiskey distilling, glass, food processing, and machine tools. Dublin is also an important cultural centre and a significant tourist centre.

**duck** any of about 50 species of short-legged waterbirds with webbed feet and flattened bills, of the family Anatidae, order Anseriformes, which also includes the larger geese and swans. Ducks were domesticated for eggs, meat, and feathers by the ancient Chinese and the ancient Maya. Most ducks live in fresh water, feeding on worms and insects as well as vegetable matter. They are generally divided into dabbling ducks and diving ducks.

**ductless gland** alternative name for an →endocrine gland.

**Dumas, Alexandre** (1802–1870) French writer, known as Dumas *père* (the father). His popular historical romances were the reworked output of a 'fiction-factory' of collaborators. They include *Les Trois Mousquetaires/The Three Musketeers* (1844) and its sequels and *Le Comte de Monte Cristo/The Count of Monte Cristo*, which appeared in 12 volumes 1845. His play *Henri III et sa cour/Henry III and his Court* (1829) established French romantic historical drama.

**Dumfries and Galloway** unitary authority in southern Scotland, formed in 1996 from the regional council of the same name (1975–96); **area:** 6,421 sq km/2,479 sq mi; **towns:** Annan, Dumfries (administrative headquarters), Kirkcudbright, Stranraer, Castle Douglas, Newton Stewart; **physical:** area characterized by an indented coastline, including Luce Bay and Wigtown Bay, backed by a low-lying coastal strip of varying width; intensively forested in the Galloways. Much of the inland area is upland: east to west this includes Eskdalemuir (Hart Fell 808 m/2,651 ft), the Lowther Hills (Green Lowther 732 m/2,402 ft) and the Galloway Hills (the Merrick 843 m/2,766 ft); **features:** Wanlockhead (the highest village in Scotland); the oldest working post office in the world at Sanquhar; Glen Trool National Park; Ruthwell Cross, Whithorn archaeological dig; **industries:** timber, chemicals, food processing; **agriculture:** beef and dairy cattle, sheep, forestry; **population:** (1996) 147,800.

**dune** mound or ridge of wind-drifted sand common on coasts and in deserts. Loose sand is blown and bounced along by the wind, up the windward side of a dune. The sand particles then fall to rest on the lee side, while more are blown up from the windward side. In this way a dune moves gradually downwind.

**Dunfermline** industrial town north of the Firth of Forth in Fife, Scotland; population (1991) 55,100. Industries include engineering, electronics, and textiles. It was the ancient capital of Scotland, with many sites of royal historical significance. Many Scottish kings, including Robert the Bruce and Malcolm Canmore, are buried in **Dunfermline Abbey**.

**Du Pré, Jacqueline Mary** (1945– 1987) English cellist. She was celebrated for her proficient technique and powerful interpretations of the classical cello repertory, particularly of Elgar. She had an international concert career while still in her teens and made many recordings.

**Durban** principal port of KwaZulu-Natal, South Africa, and main harbour of the republic; population (urban area 1996) 1,320,000. Exports include coal, chemicals, steel, granite, wood products, sugar, fruit, grain, rice, and wool; imports include heavy machinery and mining equipment. Durban is also a holiday resort.

**Dürer, Albrecht** (1471–1528) German artist. He was the leading figure of the northern Renaissance. He was born in Nürnberg and travelled widely in Europe. Highly skilled in drawing and a keen student of nature, he perfected the technique of woodcut and engraving, producing woodcut series such as the *Apocalypse* (1498) and copperplate engravings such as *The Knight, Death, and the Devil* (1513) and *Melancholia* (1514). His paintings include altarpieces and meticulously observed portraits, including many self-portraits.

**Durkheim, Emile** (1858–1917) French sociologist, one of the founders of modern sociology, who also influenced social anthropology. He worked to establish sociology as a respectable and scientific discipline, capable of diagnosing social ills and recommending possible cures.

**Dushanbe** (formerly (1929–61) Stalinabad) capital of Tajikistan, situated in the Gissar Valley 160 km/100 mi north of the Afghan frontier; population (1996) 582,000. Dushanbe is a road, rail, and air centre. Its industries include cotton and silk mills, tanneries meat-packing factories, and printing works. It is the seat of the Tajik state university.

**Düsseldorf** commercial city and capital of North Rhine-Westphalia, Germany, on the right bank of the River Rhine, 26 km/16 mi northwest of Cologne; population (1995) 571,900. It is a river port and the commercial and financial centre of the Ruhr area, with food processing, brewing, agricultural machinery, textile, and chemical industries.

**Dvořák, Antonín Leopold** (1841–1904) Czech composer. His Romantic music extends the classical tradition of Beethoven and Brahms and displays the influence of Czech folk music. He wrote nine symphonies; tone poems; operas, including *Rusalka* (1900); large-scale choral works; the *Carnival* (1891–92) and other overtures; violin and cello concertos; chamber music; piano pieces; and songs. International recognition came with two sets of *Slavonic Dances* (1878 and 1886). Works such as his *New World Symphony* (1893) reflect his interest in American folk themes, including black and American Indian music. He was director of the National Conservatory, New York, 1892–95.

**Dylan, Bob** (1941–  ) (adopted name of Robert Allen Zimmerman) US singer and songwriter. His lyrics provided catchphrases for a generation and influenced innumerable songwriters. He began in the folk-music tradition. His early songs, as on his albums *The Freewheelin' Bob Dylan* (1963) and *The Times They Are A-Changin'* (1964), were associated with the US civil-rights movement and antiwar protest. From 1965 he worked in an individualistic rock style, as on the albums *Highway 61 Revisited* (1965) and *Blonde on Blonde* (1966). His 15th album, *Time Out of Mind*, was released in 1997.

**dynamics** (or kinetics) in mechanics, the mathematical and physical study of the behaviour of bodies under the action of forces that produce changes of motion in them.

**dysentery** infection of the large intestine causing abdominal cramps and painful →diarrhoea with blood. There are two kinds of dysentery: **amoebic** (caused by a protozoan), common in the tropics, which may lead to liver damage; and **bacterial**, the kind most often seen in the temperate zones.

**dyslexia** (Greek 'bad' plus 'pertaining to words') malfunction in the brain's synthesis and interpretation of written information, popularly known as 'word blindness'.

**eagle** any of several genera of large birds of prey of the family Accipitridae, order Falconiformes, including the golden eagle *Aquila chrysaetos* of Eurasia and North America, which has a 2 m/ 6 ft wingspan. Eagles occur worldwide, usually building eyries or nests in forests or mountains, and all are fierce and powerful birds of prey. The harpy eagle is the largest eagle.

**ear** organ of hearing in animals. It responds to the vibrations that constitute sound, which are translated into nerve signals and passed to the brain. A mammal's ear consists of three parts: outer ear, middle ear, and inner ear. The **outer ear** is a funnel that collects sound, directing it down a tube to the **ear drum** (tympanic membrane), which separates the outer and **middle ears**. Sounds vibrate this membrane, the mechanical movement of which is transferred to a smaller membrane leading to the **inner ear** by three small bones, the auditory ossicles. Vibrations of the inner ear membrane move fluid contained in the snail-shaped cochlea, which vibrates hair cells that stimulate the auditory nerve connected to the brain. There are approximately 30,000 sensory hair cells (**stereocilia**). Exposure to loud noise and the process of ageing damages the stereocilia, resulting in hearing loss. Three fluid-filled canals

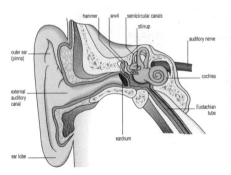

**ear** The structure of the ear. The three bones of the middle ear – hammer, anvil, and stirrup – vibrate in unison and magnify sounds about 20 times. The spiral-shaped cochlea is the organ of hearing. As sound waves pass down the spiral tube, they vibrate fine hairs lining the tube, which activate the auditory nerve connected to the brain. The semicircular canals are the organs of balance, detecting movements of the head.

of the inner ear detect changes of position; this mechanism, with other sensory inputs, is responsible for the sense of balance.

**Earth** third planet from the Sun. It is almost spherical, flattened slightly at the poles, and is composed of three concentric layers: the core, the mantle, and the crust. About 70% of the surface

(including the north and south polar icecaps) is covered with water. The Earth is surrounded by a life-supporting atmosphere and is the only planet on which life is known to exist; **mean distance from the Sun:** 149,500,000 km/ 92,860,000 mi; **equatorial diameter:** 12,756 km/7,923 mi; **circumference:** 40,070 km/24,900 mi; **rotation period:** 23 hr 56 min 4.1 sec; **year:** (complete

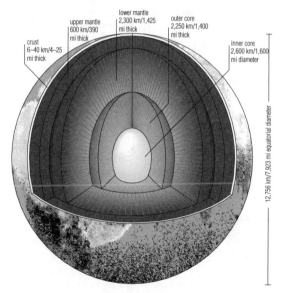

**Earth** Inside the Earth. The surface of the Earth is a thin crust about 6 km/4 mi thick under the sea and 40 km/25 mi thick under the continents. Under the crust lies the mantle about 2,900 km/1,800 mi thick and with a temperature of 1,500–3,000°C/2,700–5,400°F. The outer core is about 2,250 km/1,400 mi thick, of molten iron and nickel. The inner core is probably solid iron and nickel at about 5,000°C/9,000°F.

orbit, or sidereal period) 365 days 5 hr 48 min 46 sec. Earth's average speed around the Sun is 30 kps/18.5 mps; the plane of its orbit is inclined to its equatorial plane at an angle of 23.5°, the reason for the changing seasons; **atmosphere:** nitrogen 78.09%; oxygen 20.95%; argon 0.93%; carbon dioxide 0.03%; and less than 0.0001% neon, helium, krypton, hydrogen, xenon, ozone, radon; **surface:** land surface 150,000,000 sq km/57,500,000 sq mi (greatest height above sea level 8,872 m/29,118 ft Mount Everest); water surface 361,000,000 sq km/139,400,000 sq mi (greatest depth 11,034 m/36,201 ft →Mariana Trench in the Pacific). The interior is thought to be an inner core about 2,600 km/1,600 mi in diameter, of solid iron and nickel; an outer core about 2,250 km/1,400 mi thick, of molten iron and nickel; and a mantle of mostly solid rock about 2,900 km/1,800 mi thick, separated from the Earth's crust by the Mohorovičić discontinuity (the boundary that separates the Earth's crust and mantle). The crust and the topmost layer of the mantle form about twelve major moving plates, some of which carry the continents. The plates are in constant, slow motion, called tectonic drift. US geophysicists announced in 1996 that they had detected a difference in the spinning time of the Earth's core and the rest of the planet; the core is spinning slightly faster; **satellite:** the →Moon; **age:** 4.6 billion years. The Earth was formed with the rest of the →Solar System by consolidation of interstellar dust. Life began 3.5–4 billion years ago.

**earthquake** abrupt motion that propagates through the Earth and along its surfaces. Earthquakes are caused by the sudden release in rocks of strain accumulated over time as a result of tectonics. The study of earthquakes is called →seismology. Most earthquakes occur along →faults (fractures or breaks) and Benioff zones. Plate tectonic movements generate the major proportion: as two plates move past each other they can become jammed. When sufficient strain has accumulated, the rock breaks releasing a series of elastic waves (seismic waves) as the plates spring free. The force of earthquakes (magnitude) is measured on the →Richter scale, and their effect (intensity) on the Mercalli scale. The point at which an earthquake originates is the seismic focus or hypocentre; the point on the Earth's surface directly above this is the epicentre.

---

**WEB SITE** > > > > > > > >

**Earthquakes and Plate Tectonics**

http://wwwneic.cr.usgs.gov/neis/plate_tectonics/rift_man.html

US Geological Survey National Earthquake Information Centre site, explaining the relationship between plate tectonics and earthquakes.

---

**East Anglia** region of eastern England formerly a Saxon kingdom, including Norfolk, Suffolk, and parts of Essex and Cambridgeshire. Norwich is the principal city of East Anglia. The Sainsbury Centre for Visual Arts, opened in 1978 at the University of East Anglia, has a collection of ethnographic art and sculpture. East Anglian ports such as Harwich and Felixstowe have greatly developed as trade with the rest of Europe has increased.

**Easter** spring feast of the Christian church, commemorating the Resurrection of Jesus. It is a moveable feast, falling on the first Sunday following the full moon after the vernal equinox (21 March); that is, between 22 March and 25 April.

**Easter Island** (or Rapa Nui, Spanish *Isla de Pascua*) Chilean island in the south Pacific Ocean, part of the Polynesian group, about 3,500 km/2,200 mi west of Chile; area about 166 sq km/64 sq mi; population (1994) 2,800. It was first reached by Europeans on Easter Sunday 1722. On it stand over 800 huge carved statues (*moai*) and the remains of boat-shaped stone houses, the work of Neolithic peoples from Polynesia. The chief centre is Hanga-Roa.

**Easter Rising** (or Easter Rebellion) in Irish history, a republican insurrection against the British government that began on Easter Monday, April 1916, in Dublin. The rising was organized by the Irish Republican Brotherhood (IRB), led by Patrick Pearce, along with sections of the Irish Volunteers and James Connolly's socialist Irish Citizen Army. Although a military failure, it played a central role in shifting nationalist opinion from allegiance to the constitutional Irish Parliamentary Party (IPP) to separatist republicanism.

**East Timor** disputed territory on the island of →Timor in the Malay Archipelago, claimed by Indonesia as the province of Timor Timur; prior to 1975, it was a Portuguese colony for almost 460 years. **area:** 14,874 sq km/5,706 sq mi; **capital:** Dili; **industries:** coffee; **population:** (1990) 747,750.

**ebony** any of a group of hardwood trees belonging to the ebony family, especially some tropical persimmons native to Africa and Asia. (Genus chiefly *Diospyros*, family Ebenaceae.)

**echinoderm** marine invertebrate of the phylum Echinodermata ('spiny-skinned'), characterized by a five-radial symmetry. Echinoderms have a water-vascular system which transports substances around the body. They include starfishes (or sea stars), brittle-stars, sea lilies, sea urchins, and sea cucumbers. The skeleton is external, made of a series of limy plates. Echinoderms generally move by using tube-feet, small water-filled sacs that can be protruded or pulled back to the body.

**eclipse** passage of an astronomical body through the shadow of another. The term is usually used for solar and lunar eclipses, which may be either partial or total, but may also refer to other bodies, for example, to an eclipse of one of Jupiter's satellites by Jupiter itself. An eclipse of a star by a body in the Solar System is also called an occultation. *See illustration on page 190.*

**ecology** (Greek *oikos* 'house') study of the relationship among organisms and

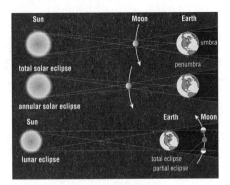

**eclipse** The two types of eclipse, lunar and solar. A lunar eclipse occurs when the Moon passes through the shadow of the Earth. A solar eclipse occurs when the Moon passes between the Sun and the Earth, blocking out the Sun's light. During a total solar eclipse, when the Moon completely covers the Sun, the Moon's shadow sweeps across the Earth's surface from west to east at a speed of 3,200kph/2,000mph.

the environments in which they live, including all living and nonliving components. The chief environmental factors governing the distribution of plants and animals are temperature, humidity, soil, light intensity, daylength, food supply, and interaction with other organisms. The term was coined by the biologist Ernst Haeckel in 1866.

---

**WEB SITE** > > > > > > > >
**Environmental Education Network**
http://envirolink.org/enviroed
Environmental information divided into sections for teachers and students, with subject subdivisions.

---

**economics** (Greek 'household management') social science devoted to studying the production, distribution, and consumption of wealth. It consists of the disciplines of **microeconomics**, the study of individual producers, consumers, or markets, and **macroeconomics**, the study

of whole economies or systems (in particular, areas such as taxation and public spending).

**ECU** (abbreviation for European Currency Unit), official monetary unit of the European Union. It is based on the values of the different currencies used in the European Monetary System (EMS).

**Ecuador** Republic of; **national name** *República del Ecuador*; **area:** 270,670 sq km/104,505 sq mi; **capital:** Quito; **major towns/cities:** Guayaquil, Cuenca, Machala, Portoviejo, Manta, Ambeto, Esmeraldas; **major ports:** Guayaquil; **physical features:** coastal plain rises sharply to Andes Mountains, which are divided into a series of cultivated valleys; flat, low-lying rainforest in the east; Galápagos Islands; Cotopaxi, the world's highest active volcano. Ecuador crossed by the equator, from which it derives its name; **head of state and government:** Jamil Mahuad Witt from 1998; **political system:** emergent democracy;

**currency:** sucre; **GNP per capita (PPP):** (US$) 4,630 (1998); **exports:** petroleum and petroleum products, bananas, shrimps (a major exporter), coffee, seafood products, cocoa beans and products, cut flowers. Principal market USA 39.2% (1998); **population:** 12,411,000 (1999 est); **language:** Spanish (official), Quechua, Jivaro, and other indigenous languages; **religion:** Roman Catholic; **life expectancy:** 67 (men); 73 (women) (1995–2000).

**Eden, (Robert) Anthony** (1897–1977) 1st Earl of Avon British Conservative politician, foreign secretary 1935–38, 1940–45, and 1951–55; prime minister 1955–57, when he resigned after the failure of the Anglo-French military intervention in the →Suez Crisis.

**Edinburgh** capital of Scotland and, as **the City of Edinburgh**, a unitary authority, located near the southern shores of the Firth of Forth; **area:** 263 sq km/122 sq mi; **physical:** Water of Leith, Salisbury Crags, Arthur's Seat; **industries:** printing, publishing, banking, insurance, chemical manufacture, electronics, distilling, brewing; **population:** (1996) 477,600.

**Edmund (II) Ironside** (c. 981–1016) king of England in 1016, the son of Ethelred II 'the Unready' (c. 968–1016). He led the resistance to Canute's invasion in 1015, and on Ethelred's death in 1016 was chosen king by the citizens of London. Meanwhile, the Witan (the king's council) elected Canute. In the struggle for the throne, Canute defeated Edmund at Ashingdon (or Assandun),

and they divided the kingdom between them. When Edmund died the same year, Canute ruled the whole kingdom.

**Edward VIII** (1894–1972) King of Great Britain and Northern Ireland January–December 1936, when he renounced the throne to marry Wallis Warfield Simpson. He was created Duke of Windsor and was governor of the Bahamas 1940–45.

**Edward the Confessor** (c. 1003–1066) King of England from 1042, the son of Ethelred II. He lived in Normandy until shortly before his accession. During his reign, power was held by Earl Godwin and his son →Harold, while the king devoted himself to religion, including the rebuilding of Westminster Abbey (consecrated in 1065), where he is buried. His childlessness led ultimately to the Norman Conquest in 1066. He was canonized in 1161.

**egg** in animals, the ovum, or female →gamete (reproductive cell). After fertilization by a sperm cell, it begins to divide to form an embryo. Eggs may be deposited by the female (oviparity) or they may develop within her body (vivipary and ovovivipary). In the oviparous reptiles and birds, the egg is protected by a shell, and well supplied with nutrients in the form of yolk. *See illustration on page 192.*

**Egypt** Arab Republic of; **national name:** *Jumhuriyat Misr al-Arabiya*; **area:** 1,001,450 sq km/386,659 sq mi; **capital:** Cairo; **major towns/cities:** El Gîza, Shubra Al Khayma, Alexandria, Port Said, El-Mahalla el-Koubra, Tauta, El-Mansoura; **major ports:** Alexandria,

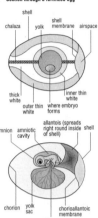

**Section through a fertilized egg**

shell
chalaza
yolk
shell membrane
airspace
thick white
outer thin white
inner thin white
where embryo forms

amnion
amniotic cavity
allantois (spreads right round inside of shell)
shell

chorion
yolk sac
chorioallantoic membrane
umbilicus

**egg** Inside a bird's egg is a complex structure of liquids and membranes designed to meet the needs of the growing embryo. The yolk, which is rich in fat, is gradually absorbed by the embryo. The white of the egg provides protein and water. The chalaza is a twisted band of protein which holds the yolk in place and acts as a shock absorber. The airspace allows gases to be exchanged through the shell. The allantois contains many blood vessels which carry gases between the embryo and the outside.

Port Said, Suez, Damietta, Shubra Al Khayma; **physical features:** mostly desert; hills in east; fertile land along Nile valley and delta; cultivated and settled area is about 35,500 sq km/13,700 sq mi; Aswan High Dam and Lake Nasser; Sinai; **head of state:** Hosni Mubarak from 1981; **head of government:** Kamal Ahmed Ganzour from 1996; **political system:** democracy; **currency:** Egyptian pound; **GNP per capita (PPP):** (US$) 3,130 (1998); **exports:** petroleum and petroleum products, textiles, clothing, food, live animals. Principal market EU 32% (1998); **population:** 67,226,000 (1999 est); **language:** Arabic (official); ancient Egyptian survives to some extent in Coptic; English; French; **religion:** Sunni Muslim 90%, Coptic Christian 7%; **life expectancy:** 65 (men); 68 (women) (1995–2000).

**Egypt, ancient** ancient civilization based around the River Nile in Egypt which emerged 5,000 years ago and reached its peak in the 16th century BC. Ancient Egypt was famed for its great power and wealth, due to the highly fertile lands of the Nile delta, which were rich sources of grain for the whole Mediterranean region. Egyptians were advanced in agriculture, engineering, and applied sciences. Many of their monuments, such as the →pyramid. and the sphinx, survive today.

**Eiffel, (Alexandre) Gustave** (1832–1923) French engineer who constructed the **Eiffel Tower** for the 1889 Paris Exhibition. The tower, made of iron, is 320 m/1,050 ft high and stands in the Champ de Mars, Paris. Sightseers may ride to the top for a view.

**Einstein, Albert** (1879–1955) German-born US physicist whose theories of →relativity revolutionized our understanding of matter, space, and time. Einstein established that light may have particle nature and deduced the **photo-electric law**, for which he was awarded the Nobel Prize for Physics in 1921. He also investigated Brownian motion, confirming the existence of atoms. His last conception of the basic laws governing the universe was outlined in his →unified field theory, made public in 1953.

**Eisenhower, Dwight David ('Ike')** (1890–1969) 34th president of the USA 1953–60, a Republican. A general in World War II, he commanded the Allied forces in Italy 1943, then the Allied invasion of Europe, and from October 1944 all the Allied armies in the West. As president he promoted business interests at home and conducted the →Cold War abroad. His vice-president was Richard Nixon.

**electric current** the flow of electrically charged particles through a conducting circuit due to the presence of a →potential difference. The current at any point in a circuit is the amount of charge flowing per second; its SI unit is the ampere (coulomb per second).

**electric field** in physics, a region in which a particle possessing electric charge experiences a force owing to the presence of another electric charge. The strength of an electric field, $E$, is measured in volts per metre (V m$^{-1}$). It is a type of electromagnetic field.

**electricity** all phenomena caused by electric charge, whether static or in motion. Electric charge is caused by an excess or deficit of electrons in the charged substance, and an electric current is the movement of charge through

**WEB SITE** > > > > > > > >
**Electricity and Magnetism**
http://www.library.thinkquest.org/12632/magnetism
Clearly presented explanation of 'electric charge', 'electromagnetism' and other aspects relating to this area of study.

a material. Substances may be electrical conductors, such as metals, that allow the passage of electricity through them readily, or insulators, such as rubber, that are extremely poor conductors. Substances with relatively poor conductivities that can be improved by the addition of heat or light are known as semiconductors.

**electrolysis** in chemistry, the production of chemical changes by passing an electric current through a solution or molten salt (the electrolyte), resulting in the migration of ions to the electrodes: positive ions (cations) to the negative electrode (cathode) and negative ions (anions) to the positive electrode (anode). *See illustration on page 194.*

**electromagnetic force** one of the four fundamental →forces of nature, the other three being the gravitational force or gravity, the weak nuclear force, and the strong nuclear force. The particle that is the carrier for the electromagnetic force is the photon.

**electromagnetic waves** oscillating electric and magnetic fields travelling together through space at a speed of nearly 300,000 km/186,000 mi per second. The (limitless) range of possible

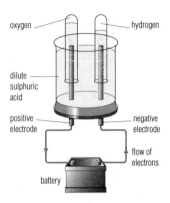

electrolysis Passing an electric current through acidified water (such as diluted sulphuric acid) breaks down the water into its constituent elements – hydrogen and oxygen.

wavelengths and →frequencies of electromagnetic waves, which can be thought of as making up the **electromagnetic spectrum**, includes radio waves, infrared radiation, visible light, ultraviolet radiation, X-rays, and gamma rays.

**electromotive force** (emf) loosely, the voltage produced by an electric battery or generator in an electrical circuit or, more precisely, the energy supplied by a source of electric power in driving a unit charge around the circuit. The unit is the →volt.

**electron** stable, negatively charged →elementary particle; it is a constituent of all atoms, and a member of the class of particles known as leptons. The electrons in each atom surround the nucleus in groupings called shells; in a neutral atom the number of electrons is equal to the number of protons in the nucleus. This electron structure is responsible for the chemical properties of the atom (see →atomic structure).

**electronics** branch of science that deals with the emission of →electrons from conductors and semiconductors, with the subsequent manipulation of these electrons, and with the construction of electronic devices. The first electronic device was the thermionic valve, or vacuum tube, in which electrons moved in a vacuum, and led to such inventions as →radio, →television, radar, and the digital →computer. Replacement of valves with the comparatively tiny and reliable →transistor from 1948 revolutionized electronic development. Modern electronic devices are based on minute →integrated circuits (silicon chips), wafer-thin crystal slices holding tens of thousands of electronic components.

**elementary particle** in physics, a subatomic particle that is not made up of smaller particles, and so can be considered one of the fundamental units of matter. There are three groups of elementary particles: quarks, leptons, and gauge bosons.

**Elgar, Edward William** (1857–1934) English composer. Although his celebrated oratorio *The Dream of Gerontius* (1900), based on the written work by the theologian John Henry Newman, was initially unpopular in Britain, its good reception in Düsseldorf, Germany, in 1902 led to a surge of interest in his earlier works, including the *Pomp and Circumstance Marches* (1901). His *Enigma Variations* (1899) brought him lasting fame.

**Eliot, George** (1819–1880) pen-name of Mary Ann (later Marian) Evans, English novelist. Her works include the pastoral *Adam Bede* (1859); *The Mill on the Floss* (1860), with its autobiographical elements; *Silas Marner* (1861), containing elements of the folk tale; and *Daniel Deronda* (1876). *Middlemarch*, published serially (1871–72), is considered her greatest novel for its confident handling of numerous characters and central social and moral issues. She developed a subtle psychological presentation of character, and her work is pervaded by a penetrating and compassionate intelligence.

**Eliot, T(homas) S(tearns)** (1888–1965) US-born poet, playwright, and critic, who lived in England from 1915. His first volume of poetry, *Prufrock and Other Observations* (1917), introduced new verse forms and rhythms; subsequent major poems were *The Waste Land* (1922), a long symbolic poem of disillusionment, and 'The Hollow Men' (1925). For children he published *Old Possum's Book of Practical Cats* (1939). Eliot's plays include *Murder in the Cathedral* (1935) and *The Cocktail Party* (1950). His critical works include *The Sacred Wood* (1920), setting out his views on poetic tradition.

**Elizabeth I** (1533–1603) Queen of England (1558–1603), the daughter of Henry VIII and Anne Boleyn. Through her Religious Settlement of 1559 she enforced the Protestant religion by law. She had →Mary Queen of Scots executed in 1587. Her conflict with Roman Catholic Spain led to the defeat of the →Spanish Armada in 1588. The Elizabethan age was expansionist in commerce and geographical exploration, and arts and literature flourished. The rulers of many European states made unsuccessful bids to marry Elizabeth, and she used these bids to strengthen her power. She was succeeded by James I.

**Ellington, Duke (Edward Kennedy)** (1899–1974) US pianist. He had an outstanding career as a composer and arranger of jazz. He wrote numerous pieces for his own jazz orchestra, accentuating the strengths of individual virtuoso instrumentalists, and became one of the leading figures in jazz over a 55-year period. Some of his most popular compositions include 'Mood Indigo', 'Sophisticated Lady', 'Solitude', and 'Black and Tan Fantasy'. He was one of the founders of bigband jazz.

**El Salvador** Republic of; **national name:** *República de El Salvador*; **area:** 21,393 sq km/8,259 sq mi; **capital:** San Salvador; **Major towns/cities:** Soyapango, Santa Ana, San Miguel, Nueva San Salvador, Mejicanos; **physical features:** narrow coastal plain, rising to mountains in north with central plateau; **head of state and government:**

Francisco Guillermo Flores Pérez from 1999; **political system:** emergent democracy; **currency:** Salvadorean colón; **GNP per capita (PPP):** (US) 2,850 (1998); **exports:** coffee, textiles and garments, sugar, shrimp, footwear, pharmaceuticals. Principal market USA 59.4 % (1998); **population:** 6,154,000 (1999 est); **language:** Spanish, Nahuatl; **religion:** Roman Catholic, Protestant; **life expectancy:** 67 (men); 73 (women) (1995–2000).

**e-mail** abbreviation for electronic mail.

**embryo** early developmental stage of an animal or a plant following fertilization of an ovum (egg cell), or activation of an ovum by parthenogenesis. In humans, the term embryo describes the fertilized egg during its first seven weeks of existence; from the eighth week onwards it is referred to as a fetus.

**Emerson, Ralph Waldo** (1803–1882) US philosopher, essayist, and poet. He settled in Concord, Massachusetts, which he made a centre of transcendentalism, and wrote *Nature* 1836, which states the movement's main principles emphasizing the value of self-reliance and the godlike nature of human souls. His two volumes of *Essays* (1841, 1844) made his reputation: 'Self-Reliance' and 'Compensation' in the earlier volume are among the best known.

**emf** in physics, abbreviation for →electromotive force.

**endocrine gland** gland that secretes hormones into the bloodstream to regulate body processes. Endocrine glands are most highly developed in vertebrates, but are also found in other animals, notably insects. In humans the main endocrine glands are the pituitary, thyroid, parathyroid, adrenal, pancreas, ovary, and testis.

**endorphin** natural substance (a polypeptide) that modifies the action of nerve cells. Endorphins are produced by the pituitary gland and hypothalamus of vertebrates. They lower the perception of pain by reducing the transmission of signals between nerve cells.

**energy** capacity for doing work. Energy can exist in many different forms. For example, potential energy (PE) is energy deriving from position; thus a stretched spring has elastic PE, and an object raised to a height above the Earth's surface, or the water in an elevated reservoir, has gravitational PE. Moving bodies possess kinetic energy (KE). Energy can be converted from one form to another, but the total quantity in a system stays the same (in accordance with the conservation of energy principle). Energy cannot be created or destroyed. For example, as an apple falls it loses gravitational PE but gains KE.

Although energy is never lost, after a number of conversions it tends to finish up as the kinetic energy of random motion of molecules (of the air, for example) at relatively low temperatures. This is 'degraded' energy that is difficult to convert back to other forms.

**energy, alternative** energy from sources

that are renewable and ecologically safe, as opposed to sources that are nonrenewable with toxic by-products, such as coal, oil, or gas (fossil fuels), and uranium (for nuclear power). The most important alternative energy source is flowing water, harnessed as →hydroelectric power. Other sources include the oceans' tides and waves, →wind power (harnessed by windmills and wind turbines), the Sun (→solar energy), and the heat trapped in the Earth's crust (→geothermal energy).

**Engels, Friedrich** (1820–1895) German social and political philosopher, a friend of, and collaborator with, Karl →Marx on *The Communist Manifesto* (1848) and other key works. His later interpretations of Marxism, and his own philosophical and historical studies such as *Origins of the Family, Private Property, and the State* (1884) (which linked patriarchy with the development of private property), developed such concepts as historical materialism. His use of positivism and Darwinian ideas gave Marxism a scientific and deterministic flavour which was to influence Soviet thinking.

**engine** device for converting stored energy into useful work or movement. Most engines use a fuel as their energy store. The fuel is burnt to produce heat energy – hence the name 'heat engine' – which is then converted into movement. Heat engines can be classified according to the fuel they use (petrol engine or →diesel engine), or according to whether the fuel is burnt inside (→internal combustion engine) or outside (→steam engine) the engine, or according to whether they produce a reciprocating or rotary motion (→turbine or Wankel engine).

**England** largest division of the United Kingdom. **area:** 130,357 sq km/50,318 sq mi; **capital:** London; **towns and cities:** Birmingham, Cambridge, Coventry, Leeds, Leicester, Manchester, Newcastle upon Tyne, Nottingham, Oxford, Sheffield, York; ports Bristol, Dover, Felixstowe, Harwich, Liverpool, Portsmouth, Southampton; **features:** variability of climate and diversity of scenery; among European countries, only the Netherlands is more densely populated; **exports:** agricultural (cereals, rape, sugar beet, potatoes); meat and meat products; electronic (software) and telecommunications equipment; scientific instruments; textiles and fashion goods; North Sea oil and gas, petrochemicals, pharmaceuticals, fertilizers; beer; china clay, pottery, porcelain, and glass; film and television programmes, and sound recordings. Tourism is important. There are worldwide banking and insurance interests; **currency:** pound sterling; **population:** (1993 est) 48,500,000; **language:** English, with more than 100 minority languages; **religion:** Christian, with the Church of England as the established church, 31,500,000; and various Protestant groups, of which the largest is the Methodist 1,400,000; Roman Catholic about 5,000,000; Muslim 900,000; Jewish 410,000; Sikh 175,000; Hindu 140,000; **government:** returns

529 members to Parliament; a mixture of 2-tier and unitary local authorities, with 34 non-metropolitan counties, 46 unitary authorities, 6 metropolitan counties (with 36 metropolitan boroughs), 32 London boroughs, and the Corporation of London.

For **government** and **history**, see →Britain, ancient; →United Kingdom.

**English Channel** stretch of water between England and France, leading in the west to the Atlantic Ocean, and in the east via the Strait of Dover to the North Sea; it is also known as **La Manche** (French 'the sleeve') from its shape. The Channel Tunnel, opened in 1994, runs between Folkestone, Kent, and Sangatte, west of Calais.

**Enlightenment** European intellectual movement that reached its high point in the 18th century. Enlightenment thinkers were believers in social progress and in the liberating possibilities of rational and scientific knowledge. They were often critical of existing society and were hostile to religion, which they saw as keeping the human mind chained down by superstition.

**entropy** in →thermodynamics, a parameter representing the state of disorder of a system at the atomic, ionic, or molecular level; the greater the disorder, the higher the entropy. Thus the fast-moving disordered molecules of water vapour have higher entropy than those of more ordered liquid water, which in turn have more entropy than the molecules in solid crystalline ice.

**enzyme** biological →catalyst produced in cells, and capable of speeding up the chemical reactions necessary for life. They are large, complex →proteins, and are highly specific, each chemical reaction requiring its own particular enzyme. The enzyme's specificity arises from its **active site**, an area with a shape corresponding to part of the molecule with which it reacts (the substrate). The enzyme and the substrate slot together forming an enzyme–substrate complex that allows the reaction to take place, after which the enzyme falls away unaltered.

**Eocene** second epoch of the Tertiary period of geological time, 56.5–35.5 million years ago. Originally considered the earliest division of the Tertiary, the name means 'early recent', referring to the early forms of mammals evolving at the time, following the extinction of the dinosaurs.

**Epicureanism** system of moral philosophy named after the Greek philosopher Epicurus. He argued that pleasure is the basis of the ethical life, and that the most satisfying form of pleasure is achieved by avoiding pain, mental or physical. This is done by limiting desire as far as possible, and by choosing pleasures of the mind over those of the body.

**epidermis** outermost layer of →cells on an organism's body. In plants and many invertebrates such as insects, it consists of a single layer of cells. In vertebrates, it consists of several layers of cells.

**epilepsy** medical disorder characterized by a tendency to develop fits, which are convulsions or abnormal feelings caused by abnormal electrical discharges in the cerebral hemispheres of the →brain. Epilepsy can be controlled with a number of anticonvulsant drugs.

**epiphyte** any plant that grows on another plant or object above the surface of the ground, and has no roots in the soil. An epiphyte does not parasitize the plant it grows on but merely uses it for support. Its nutrients are obtained from rainwater, organic debris such as leaf litter, or from the air.

**Epstein, Jacob** (1880–1959) US-born British sculptor. Initially influenced by Rodin, he turned to primitive forms after Brancusi and is chiefly known for his controversial muscular nude figures, such as *Genesis* (1931; Whitworth Art Gallery, Manchester). He was better appreciated as a portraitist; his bust of Albert Einstein (1933) demonstrating a characteristic vigorous modelling in clay. In later years he executed several monumental figures, notably the bronze *St Michael and the Devil* (1959; Coventry Cathedral) and *Social Consciousness* (1953; Fairmount Park, Philadelphia).

**Equator** (or terrestrial equator) the great circle whose plane is perpendicular to the Earth's axis (the line joining the poles). Its length is 40,092 km/24,901.8 mi, divided into 360° of longitude. The Equator encircles the broadest part of the Earth, and represents 0° latitude. It divides the Earth into two halves, called the northern and the southern hemispheres.

**Equatorial Guinea** Republic of; **national name:** *República de Guinea Ecuatorial*; **area:** 28,051 sq km/10,830 sq mi; **capital:** Malabo; **major towns/cities:** Bata, Evinayong, Ebebiyin, Mongomo; **physical features:** comprises mainland Río Muni, plus the small islands of Corisco, Elobey Grande and Elobey Chico, and Bioko (formerly Fernando Po) together with Annobón (formerly Pagalu); nearly half the land is forested; volcanic mountains on Bioko; **head of state:** Teodoro Obiang Nguema Mbasogo from 1979; **head of government:** Angel Serafin Seriche Dougan, from 1996; **political system:** emergent democracy; **currency:** franc CFA; **GNP per capita (PPP):** (US$) 4,400 (1998 est); **exports:** timber, re-exported ships and boats, textile fibres and waste, cocoa, coffee. Principal market USA 66% (1997); **population:** 442,000 (1999 est); **language:** Spanish (official); pidgin English is widely spoken, and on Annobón (whose people were formerly slaves of the Portuguese) a Portuguese patois; Fang and other African patois spoken on Río Muni; **religion:** Roman Catholic, Protestant, animist; **life expectancy:** 48 (men); 52 (women) (1995–2000).

**equestrianism** skill in horse riding, as practised under International Equestrian Federation rules. An Olympic sport, there are three main branches of equestrianism: show-jumping, dressage, and three-day eventing. Three other disciplines are under the authority of the International Equestrian Federation (FEI):

carriage driving, endurance riding, and vaulting.

**Erasmus, Desiderius** (*c.* 1469–1536) Dutch scholar and leading humanist of the Renaissance era, who taught and studied all over Europe and was a prolific writer. His pioneer translation of the Greek New Testament (with parallel Latin text, 1516) exposed the Vulgate as a second-hand document. Although opposed to dogmatism and abuse of church power, he remained impartial during Martin →Luther's conflict with the pope.

**ergonomics** study of the relationship between people and the furniture, tools, and machinery they use at work. The object is to improve work performance by removing sources of muscular stress and general fatigue: for example, by presenting data and control panels in easy-to-view form, making office furniture comfortable, and creating a generally pleasant environment.

**Eric the Red** (*c.* 950–1010) allegedly the first European to find Greenland. According to a 13th-century saga, he was the son of a Norwegian chieftain, and was banished from Iceland about 982 for murder. He then sailed westward and discovered a land that he called Greenland.

**Erie, Lake** fourth largest of the Great Lakes of North America, connected to Lake Ontario by the Niagara River and bypassed by the Welland Canal; length 388 km/241 mi; width 48–91 km/30–56 mi; area 25,720 sq km/9,930 sq mi. The most southerly of the Great Lakes, it is bounded on the north by Ontario, Canada; on the south and south-east by Ohio, Pennsylvania, and New York; and on the west by Michigan. Lake Erie is an important link in the St Lawrence Seaway.

**Eritrea** State of; **area:** 125,000 sq km/48,262 sq mi; **capital:** Asmara; **major towns/cities:** Asab, Keren, Massawa; **major ports:** Asab, Massawa; **physical features:** coastline along the Red Sea 1,000 km/620 mi; narrow coastal plain that rises to an inland plateau; Dahlak Islands; **head of state and government:** Issaias Afwerki from 1993; **political system:** emergent democracy; **currency:** Ethiopian nafka; **GNP per capita (PPP):** (US$) 950 (1998); **exports:** textiles, leather and leather products, beverages, petroleum products, basic household goods. Principal market Ethiopia 63.5% (1997); **population:** 3,720,000 (1999 est); **languages:** Afar, Amharic, Arabic, Tigre, Kunama, Tigrinya; **religion:** Sunni Muslim, Coptic Christian; **life expectancy:** 49 (men); 52 (women) (1995–2000).

**Ernst, Max** (1891–1976) German artist, a major figure in →Dada and then →surrealism. He worked in France 1922–38 and in the USA from 1941. He experimented with collage, photomontage, and surreal images, creating some of the most haunting and distinctive images of 20th-century art. His works include *The Elephant Celebes* (1921; Tate Gallery, London) and *The Temptation of St Anthony* (1945; Lehmbruck Museum, Duisburg).

**erosion** wearing away of the Earth's surface, caused by the breakdown and transportation of particles of rock or soil (by contrast, weathering does not involve transportation). Agents of erosion include the sea, rivers, glaciers, and wind. Water, consisting of sea waves and currents, rivers, and rain; ice, in the form of glaciers; and wind, hurling sand fragments against exposed rocks and moving dunes along, are the most potent forces of erosion.

People also contribute to erosion by bad farming practices and the cutting down of forests, which can lead to the formation of dust bowls.

> **WEB SITE** > > > > > > > >
>
> **Erosion and Deposition**
>
> http://www.geog.ouc.bc.ca/physgeog/contents/11g.html
>
> Description of two important geological processes, part of a much larger site on physical geography, set up by a Canadian university. The hyperlinked text explains the three stages in the process of erosion – detachment, entrainment, and transport – as well as the causes of deposition.

**escape velocity** in physics, minimum velocity with which an object must be projected for it to escape from the gravitational pull of a planetary body. In the case of the Earth, the escape velocity is 11.2 kps/6.9 mps; the Moon, 2.4 kps/1.5 mps; Mars, 5 kps/3.1 mps; and Jupiter, 59.6 kps/37 mps.

**Essex, Robert Devereux, 2nd Earl of Essex** (1566–1601) English soldier and politician. Having taken part in the Dutch fight against Spain, he became a favourite with Queen Elizabeth I in 1587, but he fell from grace because of his policies in Ireland, where he was Lieutenant from 1599, and was executed.

**ester** organic compound formed by the reaction between an alcohol and an acid, with the elimination of water. Unlike →salts, esters are covalent compounds.

**Estonia** Republic of; **national name:** *Eesti Vabariik*; **area:** 45,000 sq km/17,374 sq mi; **capital:** Tallinn; **major towns/cities:** Tartu, Narva, Kohtla-Järve, Pärnu; **physical features:** lakes and marshes in a partly forested plain; 774 km/481 mi of coastline; mild climate; Lake Peipus and Narva River forming boundary with Russian Federation; Baltic islands, the largest of which is Saaremaa; **head of state:** Lennart Meri from 1992; **head of government:** Mart Siimann from 1997; **political system:** emergent democracy; **currency:** kroon; **GNP per capita (PPP):** (US$) 6,120 (1998 est); **exports:** foodstuffs, animal products, textiles, timber products, base metals, mineral products, machinery. Principal market Finland 22.1% (1998); **population:** 1,412,000 (1999 est); **language:** Estonian (official), Russian; **religion:** Lutheran, Russian Orthodox; **life expectancy:** 63 (men); 75 (women) (1995–2000).

**ethanol** (common name ethyl alcohol $C_2H_5OH$) alcohol found in beer, wine, cider, spirits, and other alcoholic drinks. When pure, it is a colourless liquid with a pleasant odour, miscible with water or ether; it burns in air with a pale blue flame. The vapour forms an explosive mixture with air and may be used in high-compression internal combustion engines.

It is produced naturally by the fermentation of carbohydrates by yeast cells. Industrially, it can be made by absorption of ethene and subsequent reaction with water, or by the reduction of ethanal in the presence of a catalyst, and is widely used as a solvent.

**Ethelred (II) the Unready** (968–1016) king of England from 978, following the murder of his half-brother, Edward the Martyr. He was son of King Edgar. Ethelred tried to buy off the Danish raiders by paying Danegeld. In 1002 he ordered the massacre of the Danish settlers, provoking an invasion by Sweyn I of Denmark. War with Sweyn and Sweyn's son, Canute, occupied the rest of Ethelred's reign. His nickname is a corruption of the Old English 'unrede', meaning badly counselled or poorly advised.

**ether** in chemistry, any of a series of organic chemical compounds having an oxygen atom linking the carbon atoms of two hydrocarbon radical groups (general formula R-O-R'); also the common name for ethoxyethane (also called diethyl ether) $C_2H_5OC_2H_5$.

Ether is used as an anaesthetic and as an external cleansing agent before surgical operations. It is also used as a solvent, and in the extraction of oils, fats, waxes, resins, and alkaloids.

**ethics** (or moral philosophy) branch of →philosophy concerned with the systematic study of human values. It involves the study of theories of conduct and goodness, and of the meanings of moral terms.

**Ethiopia** Federal Democratic Republic of (formerly known as **Abyssinia**); **national name:** *Hebretesebawit Ityopia*; **area:** 1,096,900 sq km/423,513 sq mi; **capital:** Addis Ababa; **major towns/ cities:** Jimma, Dire Dawa, Harar, Nazret, Dessie, Gonder, Mek'ele; **physical features:** a high plateau with central mountain range divided by Rift Valley; plains in east; source of Blue Nile River; Danakil and Ogaden deserts; **head of state:** Negasso Ghidada from 1995; **head of government:** Meles Zenawi from 1995; **political system:** transition to democratic republic; **currency:** Ethiopian birr; **GNP per capita (PPP):** (US$) 500 (1998); **exports:** coffee, hides and skins, petroleum products, fruit and vegetables. Principal market Germany 22.4% (1997); **population:** 61,095,000 (1999 est); **language:** Amharic (official), Tigrinya, Orominga, Arabic; **religion:** Sunni Muslim, Christian (Ethiopian Orthodox Church, which has had its own patriarch since 1976) 40%, animist; **life expectancy:** 42 (men); 44 (women) (1995–2000)

**ethnic cleansing** the forced expulsion of one ethnic group by another to create an homogenous population, for example, of more than 2 million Muslims by Serbs in Bosnia-Herzegovina 1992–95. The term has also been used to describe the killing of Hutus and Tutsis in Rwanda and Burundi 1994, and for earlier mass exiles, as far back as the book of Exodus.

**ethology** comparative study of animal behaviour in its natural setting. Ethology is concerned with the causal mechanisms (both the stimuli that elicit behaviour and the physiological mechanisms controlling it), as well as the development of behaviour, its function, and its evolutionary history.

**Etna, Mount** volcano on the east coast of Sicily, 3,323 m/10,906 ft, the highest in Europe. About 90 eruptions have been recorded since 1800 BC, yet because of the rich soil, the cultivated zone on the lower slopes is densely populated, including the coastal town of Catania. The most recent eruption was in December 1985.

**Etruscan** member of an ancient people inhabiting Etruria, Italy (modern-day Tuscany and part of Umbria) from the 8th to 2nd centuries BC. The Etruscan dynasty of the Tarquins ruled Rome 616–509 BC. At the height of their civilization, in the 6th century BC, the Etruscans achieved great wealth and power from their maritime strength. They were driven out of Rome 509 BC and eventually dominated by the Romans.

**etymology** study of the origin and history of words within and across languages. It has two major aspects: the study of the phonetic and written forms of words, and of the semantics or meanings of those words.

**eucalyptus** any tree of a group belonging to the myrtle family, native to Australia, where they are commonly known as gumtrees. About 90% of Australian timber belongs to the eucalyptus genus, which contains about 500 species. The trees have dark hardwood timber which is used for heavy construction work such as railway and bridge building. They are mostly tall, aromatic, evergreen trees with pendant leaves and white, pink, or red flowers. (Genus *Eucalyptus*, family Myrtaceae.)

**Eucharist** chief Christian sacrament, in which bread is eaten and wine drunk in memory of the death of Jesus. Other names for it are the **Lord's Supper**, **Holy Communion**, and (among Roman Catholics, who believe that the bread and wine are transubstantiated, that is, converted to the body and blood of Christ) the **Mass**. The doctrine of transubstantiation was rejected by Protestant churches during the Reformation.

**Euclid** (*c.* 330–*c.* 260 BC) Greek mathematician who wrote the *Stoicheia/ Elements* in 13 books, nine of which deal with plane and solid geometry and four with number theory. His great achievement lay in the systematic arrangement of previous mathematical discoveries and a methodology based on axioms, definitions, and theorems.

**Euphrates** (Turkish *Firat*, Arabic *Al Furat*) river rising in east Turkey and flowing through Syria and Iraq, joining the River Tigris above Basra to form the River Shatt-al-Arab at the head of the Gulf; length 3,600 km/2,240 mi. The ancient cities of Babylon, Eridu, and Ur were situated along its course.

**Euripides** (c. 485–c. 406 BC) Athenian tragic dramatist. He is ranked with Aeschylus and Sophocles as one of the three great tragedians. His plays deal with the emotions and reactions of ordinary people and social issues rather than with deities and the grandiose themes of his contemporaries. He wrote about 90 plays, of which 18 and some long fragments survive. These include *Alcestis* (438 BC), *Medea* (431), *Andromache* about (430), *Hippolytus* (428), the satyr-drama *Cyclops* (c. 424–423), *Electra* (417), *Trojan Women* (415), *Iphigenia in Tauris* (413), *Iphigenia in Aulis* (c. 414–412), and *The Bacchae* (c. 405) (the last two were produced shortly after his death).

**European Community** (EC) former name (to 1993) of the →European Union.

**European Monetary Union** EMU the proposed European Union (EU) policy for a single currency and common economic policies. The proposal was announced by what was then a European Community (EC) committee headed by EC Commission president Jacques Delors in April 1989. In May 1998 EU leaders formalized the creation of the euro monetary zone, to take effect from 1 January 1999.

**European Parliament** the parliament of the →European Union, which meets in Strasbourg and Brussels to comment on the legislative proposals of the European Commission. Members are elected for a five-year term. The European Parliament has 626 seats, apportioned on the basis of population, of which Germany has 99; the UK, France, and Italy have 87 each; Spain 64; the Netherlands 31; Belgium, Greece, and Portugal 25 each; Sweden 22; Austria 21; Denmark and Finland 16 each; the Republic of Ireland 15; and Luxembourg 6.

**European Union** (EU) formerly (to 1993) European Community political and economic alliance consisting of the European Coal and Steel Community (1952), the European Economic Community (EEC, popularly called the Common Market, 1957), and the European Atomic Energy Community (Euratom, 1957). The original six members – Belgium, France, West Germany, Italy, Luxembourg, and the Netherlands – were joined by the UK, Denmark, and the Republic of Ireland in 1973, Greece in 1981, and Spain and Portugal in 1986. East Germany was incorporated on German reunification in 1990. Austria, Finland, and Sweden joined in 1995. In 1999 leaders of the EU agreed that another seven countries should be recognised as candidates to join the union. Bulgaria, Latvia, Lithuania, Malta, Romania, Slovakia, and Turkey joined six other countries who were also waiting to join: Cyprus, the Czech Republic, Estonia, Hungary, Poland, and Slovenia. On 1 January 2000, Portugal took over the rotating EU presidency, with aims that included expanding membership, defence policy, and a pledge to tackle unemployment.

**euthanasia** in medicine, 'mercy killing' of someone with a severe and incurable condition or illness. Euthanasia is an issue that creates much controversy on medical and ethical grounds. A patient's right to refuse life-prolonging treatment is recognized in several countries.

**evaporation** process in which a liquid turns to a vapour without its temperature reaching boiling point. A liquid left to stand in a saucer eventually evaporates because, at any time, a proportion of its molecules will be fast enough (have enough kinetic energy) to escape through the attractive intermolecular forces at the liquid surface into the atmosphere. The temperature of the liquid tends to fall because the evaporating molecules remove energy from the liquid. The rate of evaporation rises with increased temperature because as the mean kinetic energy of the liquid's molecules rises, so will the number possessing enough energy to escape.

**evening primrose** any of a group of plants that typically have pale yellow flowers which open in the evening. About 50 species are native to North America, several of which now also grow in Europe. Some are cultivated for their oil, which is rich in gamma-linoleic acid (GLA). The body converts GLA into substances which resemble hormones, and **evening primrose oil** is beneficial in relieving the symptoms of →premenstrual tension. It is also used in treating eczema and chronic fatigue syndrome. (Genus *Oenothera*, family Onagraceae.)

**evening primrose** The evening primrose belongs to a large family of flowering shrubs and plants, many of which bear four-petalled yellow flowers. The evening primrose opens its blooms at night and is pollinated by moths. Oil from the pressed seeds of one species of evening primrose is a source of gamma-linoleic acid which may be used medicinally for a variety of ailments including the reduction of high cholesterol.

**Everest, Mount** Tibetan Qomolungma ('goddess mother of the world'), Nepalese Sagarmatha ('head of the Earth') world's highest mountain above sea level, in the →Himalaya range, on the China–Nepal frontier; height 8,848 m/29,028 ft. It was first climbed by New Zealand mountaineer Edmund →Hillary and Sherpa Tenzing Norgay in 1953. More than 360 climbers have reached the summit; over 100 have died during the ascent.

**Everglades** subtropical area of swamps, marsh, and lakes in southern Florida,

USA; area 7,000 sq km/2,700 sq mi. Formed by the overflow of Lake Okeechobee after heavy rains, it is one of the wildest areas in the USA, with distinctive plant and animal life. The natural vegetation of the swamplands is sawgrass and rushes, with trees such as cypress, palm, and hardwoods where the conditions are slightly drier. Several hundred Seminole, an American Indian people, live here. A national park (established in 1947) covers the southern tip of the Everglades, making up about one-fifth of the Everglades' original area.

**evergreen** in botany, a plant such as pine, spruce, or holly, that bears its leaves all year round. Most →conifers are evergreen. Plants that shed their leaves in autumn or during a dry season are described as →deciduous.

**evolution** the slow, gradual process of change from one form to another, as in the evolution of the universe from its formation to its present state, or in the evolution of life on Earth. In biology, it is the process by which life has developed by stages from single-celled organisms into the multiplicity of animal and plant life, extinct and existing, that inhabit the Earth. The development of the concept of evolution is usually associated with the English naturalist Charles →Darwin who attributed the main role in evolutionary change to →natural selection acting on randomly occurring variations. However, these variations in species are now known to be adaptations produced by spontaneous changes or →mutations in the genetic material of organisms.

**Exchange Rate Mechanism** (ERM) voluntary system for controlling exchange rates within the European Monetary System of the European Union (EU) intended to prepare the way for a single currency. The member currencies of the ERM are fixed against each other within a narrow band of fluctuation based on a central European Currency Unit (ECU) rate, but floating against nonmember countries. If a currency deviates significantly from the central ECU rate, the European Monetary Cooperation Fund and the central banks concerned intervene to stabilize the currency.

**existentialism** branch of philosophy based on the situation of the individual in an absurd or meaningless universe where humans have free will. Existentialists argue that people are responsible for and the sole judge of their actions as they affect others. The origin of existentialism is usually traced back to the Danish philosopher →Kierkegaard; among its proponents were Martin Heidegger in Germany and Jean-Paul →Sartre in France.

**expressionism** style of painting, sculpture, and literature that expresses inner emotions; in particular, a movement in early 20th-century art in northern and central Europe. Expressionists tended to distort or exaggerate natural appearance in order to create a reflection of an inner world; the Norwegian painter Edvard Munch's *Skriket/The Scream* (1893; National Gallery, Oslo) is perhaps the most celebrated example. Expressionist writers include August Strindberg and Frank Wedekind.

**extinction** in biology, the complete disappearance of a species or higher taxon. Extinctions occur when an animal becomes unfit for survival in its natural habitat usually to be replaced by another, better-suited animal. An organism becomes ill-suited for survival because its environment is changed or because its relationship to other organisms is altered. For example, a predator's fitness for survival depends upon the availability of its prey.

**eye** the organ of vision. In the human eye, the light is focused by the combined action of the curved cornea, the internal fluids, and the lens. The insect eye is compound – made up of many separate facets – known as ommatidia, each of which collects light and directs it separately to a receptor to build up an image. Invertebrates have much simpler eyes, with no lenses. Among molluscs, cephalopods have complex eyes similar to those of vertebrates.

The mantis shrimp's eyes contain ten colour pigments with which to perceive colour; some flies and fishes have five, while the human eye has only three.

---

**WEB SITE** > > > > > > > >
**Eye**

http://retina.anatomy.upenn.edu/~lance/eye/eye.html

Thorough information on the physical structures of the eye, from the University of Pennsylvania, USA. The page is divided into sections covering the main parts of the eye, such as the retina, cornea, iris, pupil, and lens.

---

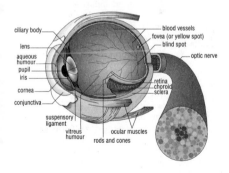

ciliary body
lens
aqueous humour
pupil
iris
cornea
conjunctiva
suspensory ligament
vitreous humour
ocular muscles
rods and cones
blood vessels
fovea (or yellow spot)
blind spot
optic nerve
retina
choroid
sclera

**eye** The human eye. The retina of the eye contains about 137 million light-sensitive cells in an area of about 650 sq mm/1 sq in. There are 130 million rod cells for black and white vision and 7 million cone cells for colour vision. The optic nerve contains about 1 million nerve fibres. The focusing muscles of the eye adjust about 100,000 times a day. To exercise the leg muscles to the same extent would need an 80 km/50 mi walk.

**Ff**

**factory farming** intensive rearing of poultry or other animals for food, usually on high-protein foodstuffs in confined quarters. Chickens for eggs and meat, and calves for veal are commonly factory farmed. Some countries restrict the use of antibiotics and growth hormones as aids to factory farming because they can persist in the flesh of the animals after they are slaughtered. The emphasis is on productive yield rather than animal welfare so that conditions for the animals are often very poor. For this reason, many people object to factory farming on moral as well as health grounds.

**FA Cup** (abbreviation for Football Association Challenge Cup), the major annual soccer knockout competition in England and Wales, open to all member clubs of the English Football Association. First held in 1871–72, it is the oldest football knockout competition.

**Fahrenheit scale** temperature scale invented in 1714 by Gabriel Fahrenheit that was commonly used in English-speaking countries until the 1970s, after which the →Celsius scale was generally adopted, in line with the rest of the world. In the Fahrenheit scale, intervals are measured in degrees (°F); °F = (°C × 9/5) + 32.

**Falkland Islands** (Argentine *Islas Malvinas*) British crown colony in the South Atlantic, 480 km/300 mi east of the Straits of Magellan; **area** 12,173 sq km/4,700 sq mi, made up of two main islands: East Falkland 6,760 sq km/2,610 sq mi, and West Falkland 5,413 sq km/2,090 sq mi; **capital** Stanley; new port facilities opened in 1984, Mount Pleasant airport in 1985; **features** in addition to the two main islands, there are about 200 small islands, all with wild scenery and rich bird life; Mount Usborne (705 m/2,312 ft); moorland; **industries** wool, alginates (used as dyes and as a food additive) from seaweed beds, fishing (especially squid); **population** (1991) 2,120.

**Falklands War** war between Argentina and Britain over disputed sovereignty of the Falkland Islands initiated when Argentina invaded and occupied the islands on 2 April 1982. On the following day, the United Nations Security Council passed a resolution calling for Argentina to withdraw. A British task force was immediately dispatched and, after a fierce conflict in which more than 1,000 Argentine and British lives were lost, 12,000 Argentine troops surrendered and the islands were returned to British rule on 14–15 June 1982.

**Fallopian tube** (or oviduct) in mammals, one of two tubes that carry eggs from the ovary to the uterus. An egg is fertilized by sperm in the Fallopian tubes, which are lined with cells whose cilia move the egg towards the uterus.

**Faraday, Michael** (1791–1867) English chemist and physicist. In 1821, he began experimenting with electromagnetism, and discovered the induction of electric currents and made the first dynamo, the first electric motor, and the first transformer. Faraday isolated benzene from gas oils and produced the basic laws of →electrolysis in 1834. He also pointed out that the energy of a magnet is in the field around it and not in the magnet itself, extending this basic conception of field theory to electrical and gravitational systems.

**fascism** political ideology that denies all rights to individuals in their relations with the state; specifically, the totalitarian nationalist movement founded in Italy 1919 by →Mussolini and followed by Hitler's Germany 1933.

Fascism was essentially a product of the economic and political crisis of the years after World War I. Units called *fasci di combattimento* (combat groups), from the Latin fasces, were originally established to oppose communism. The fascist party, the *Partitio Nazionale Fascista*, controlled Italy 1922–43. Fascism protected the existing social order by forcible suppression of the working-class movement and by providing scapegoats for popular anger, such as minority groups: Jews, foreigners, or blacks; it also prepared the citizenry for the economic and psychological mobilization of war.

**fast reactor** (or fast breeder reactor) nuclear reactor that makes use of fast neutrons to bring about fission. Unlike other reactors used by the nuclear-power industry, it has little or no moderator, to slow down neutrons. The reactor core is surrounded by a 'blanket' of uranium carbide. During operation, some of this uranium is converted into plutonium, which can be extracted and later used as fuel.

**fat** in the broadest sense, a mixture of →lipids – chiefly triglycerides (lipids containing three fatty acid molecules linked to a molecule of glycerol). More specifically, the term refers to a lipid mixture that is solid at room temperature (20°C); lipid mixtures that are liquid at room temperature are called **oils**. The higher the proportion of saturated fatty acids in a mixture, the harder the fat.

**Faulkner, William Cuthbert** (1897–1962) US novelist. His works employ difficult narrative styles in their epic mapping of a quasi-imaginary region of the American South. His third novel, *The Sound and the Fury* (1929), deals with the decline of a Southern family, told in four voices, beginning with an especially complex stream-of-consciousness narrative. He was awarded the Nobel Prize for Literature in 1949.

**fault** in geology, a fracture in the Earth either side of which rocks have moved past one another. Faults involve displacements, or offsets, ranging from the microscopic scale to hundreds of kilometres. Large offsets along a fault are the result of the accumulation of smaller movements (metres or less) over long periods of time. Large motions cause detectable →earthquakes.

**fauvism** (French *fauve*, 'wild beast') movement in modern French painting characterized by the use of very bold, vivid colours. The name is a reference to the fact that the works seemed to many people at the time to be crude and untamed. Although short-lived, lasting only about two years (1905–07), the movement was highly influential. It was the first of the artistic movements that transformed European art between the turn of the century and World War I.

**Fawkes, Guy** (1570–1606) English conspirator in the Gunpowder Plot to blow up King James I and the members of both Houses of Parliament. Fawkes, a Roman Catholic convert, was arrested in the cellar underneath the House of Lords on 4 November 1605, tortured, and executed. The event is still commemorated in Britain and elsewhere every 5 November with bonfires, fireworks, and the burning of the 'guy', an effigy.

**fax** (common name for facsimile transmission or telefax) transmission of images over a telecommunications link, usually the telephone network. When placed on a fax machine, the original image is scanned by a transmitting device and converted into coded signals, which travel via the telephone lines to the receiving fax machine, where an image is created that is a copy of the original. Photographs as well as printed text and drawings can be sent. The standard transmission takes place at 4,800 or 9,600 bits of information per second.

**federalism** system of government in which two or more separate states unite into a →federation under a common central government. A federation should be distinguished from a **confederation**, a looser union of states for mutual assistance. The USA is an example of federal government.

**federation** political entity made up from a number of smaller units or states where the central government has powers over national issues such as foreign policy and defence, while the individual states retain a high degree of regional and local autonomy. A federation should be distinguished from a **confederation**, a looser union of states for mutual assistance. Contemporary examples of federated states established since 1750 include the USA, Canada, Australia, India, the Federal Republic of Germany, Malaysia, and Micronesia.

**feldspar** a group of silicate minerals. Feldspars are the most abundant mineral type in the Earth's crust. They are the chief constituents of →igneous rock and are present in most metamorphic and sedimentary rocks. All feldspars contain silicon, aluminium, and oxygen, linked together to form a framework. Spaces within this framework structure are occupied by sodium, potassium, calcium, or occasionally barium, in various proportions. Feldspars form white, grey, or pink crystals and rank 6 on the →Mohs scale of hardness.

**Fenian movement** Irish-American republican secret society, founded in 1858 to campaign for Irish-American support for armed rebellion following the death of the Irish nationalist leader Daniel O'Connell and the breakup of Young Ireland. Its name, a reference to the ancient Irish legendary warrior band of the **Fianna**, became synonymous with underground Irish republicanism in the 19th century. The collapse of the movement began when an attempt to establish an independent Irish republic by an uprising in Ireland in 1867 failed, as did raids into Canada in 1866 and 1870, and England in 1867. In the 1880s the US-based Fenian society Clan-Na-Gael conducted assassinations and bombings through its agents in England and Ireland in an attempt to force Irish home rule.

**Fens, the** level, low-lying tracts of reclaimed marsh in eastern England, west and south of the Wash, covering an area of around 40,000 sq km/15,500 sq mi, about 115 km/70 mi north–south and 55 km/34 mi east–west. They fall within the counties of Lincolnshire, Cambridgeshire, and Norfolk. Formerly a bay of the North Sea, they are now crossed by numerous drainage canals and form some of the most fertile and productive agricultural land in Britain. The southern peat portion of the Fens is known as the Bedford Level.

**Fermanagh** county of Northern Ireland; **area** 1,680 sq km/648 sq mi; **towns** Enniskillen (county town), Lisnaskea, Irvinestown; **physical** in the centre is a broad trough of low-lying land, in which lie Upper and Lower Lough Erne; **industries** clothing, tweeds, cotton thread, food processing, light engineering, china, tourism, electronics; **agriculture** small farms, livestock, potatoes; **population** (1991) 50,000.

**Fermat, Pierre de** (1601–1665) French mathematician who, with Blaise →Pascal, founded the theory of →probability and the modern theory of numbers. Fermat also made contributions to analytical geometry. In 1657, Fermat published a series of problems as challenges to other mathematicians, in the form of theorems to be proved.

**Fermi, Enrico** (1901–1954) Italian-born US physicist who proved the existence of new radioactive elements produced by bombardment with neutrons, and discovered nuclear reactions produced by low-energy neutrons. This research won him the Nobel Prize for Physics in 1938 and was the basis for studies leading to the atomic bomb and nuclear energy. Fermi built the first nuclear reactor in 1942 at Chicago University and later took part in the Manhattan Project to construct an atom bomb. His theoretical work included the study of the weak nuclear force, one of the fundamental forces of nature, and beta decay.

**fern** any of a group of plants related to horsetails and clubmosses. Ferns are spore-bearing, not flowering, plants and most are perennial, spreading by slow-growing roots. The leaves, known as fronds, vary widely in size and shape. Some taller types, such as tree ferns, grow in the tropics. There are over 7,000 species. (Order Filicales.)

**fertilization** in →sexual reproduction, the union of two →gametes (sex cells, often called egg and sperm) to produce a zygote, which combines the genetic material contributed by each parent. In self-fertilization the male and female gametes come from the same plant; in cross-fertilization they come from different plants. Self-fertilization rarely occurs in animals; usually even hermaphrodite animals cross-fertilize each other.

**fetus** (or foetus) stage in mammalian →embryo development. The human embryo is usually termed a fetus after the eighth week of development, when the limbs and external features of the head are recognizable.

**Fianna Fáil** (Gaelic 'Soldiers of Destiny') Republic of Ireland political party, founded by the Irish nationalist Éamon →de Valera in 1926, and led since 1994 by Bertie Ahern. A broad-based party, it is conservative socially and economically, and generally right of centre. It was the governing party in the Republic of Ireland 1932–48, 1951–54, 1957–73, 1977–81, 1982, 1987–94 (from 1993 in coalition with Labour), and from 1997. Its official aims include the establishment of a united and completely independent all-Ireland republic.

**fibreglass** glass that has been formed into fine fibres, either as long continuous filaments or as a fluffy, short-fibred glass wool. Fibreglass is heat- and fire-resistant and a good electrical insulator. It has applications in the field of fibre optics and as a strengthener for plastics in GRP (glass-reinforced plastics).

**fibre optics** branch of physics dealing with the transmission of light and images through glass or plastic fibres known as →optical fibres.

**field** in physics, a region of space in which an object exerts a force on another separate object because of certain properties they both possess. For example, there is a force of attraction between any two objects that have mass when one is in the gravitational field of the other.

**Fielding, Henry** (1707–1754) English novelist. His greatest work, *The History of Tom Jones, a Foundling* (1749), which he described as 'a comic epic poem in prose', was an early landmark in the development of the English novel, realizing for the first time in English the form's potential for memorable characterization, coherent plotting, and perceptive analysis. The vigour of its comic impetus, descriptions of high and low life in town and country, and its variety of characters made it immediately popular.

**Fife** unitary authority in eastern Scotland, which was formerly a region of three districts (1975–96) and a county until 1974; **area:** 1,321 sq km/510 sq mi; **towns:** Cupar, Dunfermline, Glenrothes (administrative headquarters),

Kirkcaldy, St Andrews; **physical:** coastal area, predominantly low lying, undulating interior with dramatic escarpment at Lomond Hills; rivers Eden and Leven flow through; **features:** Rosyth naval base; Old Course, St Andrews; **industries:** electronics, petrochemicals, light engineering, oil servicing, paper; **agriculture:** potatoes, cereals, sugar beet, fishing (Pittenweem); **population:** (1996) 351,200; **history:** Tentsmuir, a coastal sand-dune area in the north, is possibly the earliest settled site in Scotland; the ancient palace of the Stuarts (16th century) was at Falkland; eight Scottish kings buried at Dunfermline.

**Fiji Islands** Republic of; **area:** 18,333 sq km/7,078 sq mi; **capital:** Suva; **major towns/cities:** Lautoka, Nadi, Ba, Labasa; **major ports:** Lautoka and Levuka; **physical features:** comprises about 844 Melanesian and Polynesian islands and islets (about 100 inhabited), the largest being Viti Levu (10,429 sq km/4,028 sq mi) and Vanua Levu (5,556 sq km/2,146 sq mi); mountainous, volcanic, with tropical rainforest and grasslands; almost all islands surrounded by coral reefs; high volcanic peaks; **head of state and government:** government overthrown in a coup 2000; **political system:** democracy; **currency:** Fiji dollar; **GNP per capita (PPP):** (US$) 3,580 (1998); **exports:** sugar, gold, fish and fish products, clothing, re-exported petroleum products, timber, ginger, molasses. Principal market Australia 33.1% (1997); **population:** 806,000 (1999 est); **language:** English (official), Fijian, Hindi; **religion:** Methodist, Hindu, Muslim, Sikh; **life expectancy:** 71 (men); 75 (women) (1995–2000).

**filtration** technique by which suspended solid particles in a fluid are removed by passing the mixture through a filter, usually porous paper, plastic, or cloth. The particles are retained by the filter to form a residue and the fluid passes through to make up the filtrate. For example, soot may be filtered from air, and suspended solids from water.

**Fine Gael** (Gaelic 'United Ireland') Republic of Ireland political party founded in 1933 by William Cosgrave and led by John Bruton from 1990. It has been socially liberal in recent years but fiscally conservative. Though it formed a coalition government with the Labour and Democratic Left parties 1994–97, it has typically been the main opposition party.

**Finland** Republic of; **national name:** *Suomen Tasavalta*; **area:** 338,145 sq km/130,557 sq mi; **capital:** Helsinki (Helsingfors); **major towns/cities:** Tampere, Turku, Espoo, Vantaa; **major ports:** Turku, Oulu; **physical features:** most of the country is forest, with low hills and about 60,000 lakes; one-third is within the Arctic Circle; archipelago in south includes Åland Islands; Helsinki is the most northerly national capital on the European continent. At the 70th parallel there is constant daylight for 73 days in summer and 51 days of uninterrupted night in winter; **head**

**of state:** Tarja Halonen from 2000; **head of government:** Paavo Lipponen from 1995; **political system:** democracy; **currency:** markka; **GNP per capita (PPP):** (US$) 20,270 (1998); **exports:** metal and engineering products, gold, paper and paper products, machinery, ships, wood and pulp, clothing and footwear, chemicals. Principal market Germany 11.8% (1998); **population:** 5,165,000 (1999 est); **language:** Finnish 93%, Swedish 6% (both official); small Saami- and Russian-speaking minorities; **religion:** Lutheran 90%, Orthodox 1%; **life expectancy:** 73 (men); 81 (women) (1995–2000).

**fish** aquatic vertebrate that uses gills to obtain oxygen from fresh or sea water.

There are three main groups: the bony fishes or Osteichthyes (goldfish, cod, tuna) the cartilaginous fishes or Chondrichthyes (sharks, rays); and the jawless fishes or Agnatha (hagfishes, lampreys).

Fishes of some form are found in virtually every body of water in the world except for the very salty water of the Dead Sea and some of the hot larval springs. Of the 30,000 fish species, approximately 2,500 are freshwater.

**Fitzgerald, Ella** (1917–1996) US jazz singer. She is recognized as one of the finest, most lyrical voices in jazz, both in solo work and with big bands. She is celebrated for her smooth interpretations of George and Ira Gershwin and Cole Porter songs.

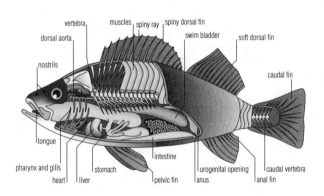

**fish** The anatomy of a fish. All fish move through water using their fins for propulsion. The bony fishes, like the specimen shown here, constitute the largest group of fishes with about 20,000 species.

**Fitzgerald, F(rancis) Scott (Key)** (1896–1940) US novelist and short-story writer. His early autobiographical novel *This Side of Paradise* (1920) made him known in the post-war society of the East Coast, and *The Great Gatsby* (1925) epitomizes the Jazz Age.

**fjord** (or fiord) narrow sea inlet enclosed by high cliffs. Fjords are found in Norway, New Zealand, and western parts of Scotland. They are formed when an overdeepened U-shaped glacial valley is drowned by a rise in sea-level. At the mouth of the fjord there is a characteristic lip causing a shallowing of the water. This is due to reduced glacial erosion and the deposition of moraine at this point.

**Flanders** region of the Low Countries that in the 8th and 9th centuries extended from Calais to the Schelde and is now covered by the Belgian provinces of Oost Vlaanderen and West Vlaanderen (East and West Flanders), the French *département* of Nord, and part of the Dutch province of Zeeland. The language is Flemish. East Flanders, capital Ghent, has an area of 3,000 sq km/1,158 sq mi and a population (1995) of 1,349,400. West Flanders, capital Bruges, has an area of 3,100 sq km/1,197 sq mi and a population (1995) of 1,121,100.

**Flaubert, Gustave** (1821–1880) French writer. One of the major novelists of the 19th century, he was the author of *Madame Bovary* (1857), *Salammbô* (1862), *L'Education sentimentale/Sentimental Education* (1869), and *La Tentation de Saint Antoine/The Temptation of St Anthony*

(1874). Flaubert also wrote the short stories *Trois Contes/ Three Tales* (1877). His dedication to art resulted in a meticulous prose style, realistic detail, and psychological depth, which is often revealed through interior monologue.

**flea** wingless insect of the order Siphonaptera, with blood-sucking mouthparts. Fleas are parasitic on warm-blooded animals. Some fleas can jump 130 times their own height.

**Fleming, Alexander** (1881–1955) Scottish bacteriologist who discovered the first antibiotic drug, →penicillin, in 1928. In 1922 he had discovered lysozyme, an antibacterial enzyme present in saliva, nasal secretions, and tears. While studying this, he found an unusual mould growing on a culture dish, which he isolated and grew into a pure culture; this led to his discovery of penicillin. It came into use in 1941. In 1945 he won the Nobel Prize for Physiology or Medicine with Howard W Florey and Ernst B Chain, whose research had brought widespread realization of the value of penicillin.

**flight** (or aviation) method of transport in which aircraft carry people and goods through the air. People first took to the air in →balloons in 1783 and began powered flight in 1852 in airships, but the history of flying, both for civilian and military use, is dominated by the →aeroplane. The earliest planes were designed for gliding; the advent of the petrol engine saw the first powered flight by the →Wright brothers in 1903 in the USA. This inspired the development of aircraft throughout Europe. Biplanes were succeeded by monoplanes in the 1930s. The first jet plane was produced in 1939, and after the end of World War II the development of jetliners brought about a continuous expansion in passenger air travel. In 1969 came the supersonic aircraft Concorde.

**flint** compact, hard, brittle mineral (a variety of chert), brown, black, or grey in colour, found as nodules in limestone or shale deposits. It consists of cryptocrystalline (grains too small to be visible even under a light microscope) silica, $SiO_2$, principally in the crystalline form of →quartz. Implements fashioned from flint were widely used in prehistory.

**Flodden, Battle of** defeat of the Scots by the English under the Earl of Surrey on 9 September 1513, on a site 5 km/ 3 mi southeast of Coldstream, in Northumberland, England. James IV of Scotland, declaring himself the active ally of France, crossed the border to England with an invading army of 30,000. The Scots were defeated, suffering heavy losses, and James himself was killed.

**floppy disk** in computing, a storage device consisting of a light, flexible disk enclosed in a cardboard or plastic jacket. The disk is placed in a disk drive, where it rotates at high speed. Data are recorded magnetically on one or both surfaces.

**Florence** (Italian *Firenze*, Roman *Florentia*) capital of →Tuscany, northern Italy, on the River Arno, 88 km/55 mi from the river's mouth; population (1992) 397,400. It has printing, engineering, and optical industries; many crafts, including leather, gold and silver work, and embroidery; and its art and architecture attract large numbers of tourists. Notable medieval and Renaissance citizens included the writers Dante and Boccaccio, and the artists Giotto, Leonardo da Vinci, and Michelangelo.

**flow chart** diagram, often used in computing, to show the possible paths that data can take through a system or program.

**flower** the reproductive unit of an angiosperm or flowering plant, typically consisting of four whorls of modified leaves: sepals, petals, →stamens, and carpels. These are borne on a central axis or receptacle. The many variations in size, colour, number, and arrangement of parts are closely related to the method of pollination. Flowers adapted for wind pollination typically have reduced or absent petals and sepals and long, feathery stigmas that hang outside the flower to trap airborne pollen. In contrast, the petals of insect-pollinated flowers are usually conspicuous and brightly coloured.

**fluoride** negative ion ($F^-$) formed when hydrogen fluoride dissolves in water; compound formed between fluorine and another element in which the fluorine is the more electronegative element.

**fluorine** pale yellow, gaseous, non-metallic element, symbol F, atomic

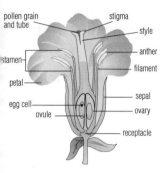

pollen grain and tube
stigma
style
anther
stamen
filament
petal
sepal
egg cell
ovary
ovule
receptacle

**flower** Cross section of a typical flower showing its basic components: sepals, petals, stamens (anthers and filaments), and carpel (ovary and stigma). Flowers vary greatly in the size, shape, colour, and arrangement of these components.

number 9, relative atomic mass 19. It is the first member of the halogen group of elements, and is pungent, poisonous, and highly reactive, uniting directly with nearly all the elements. It occurs naturally as the minerals fluorite ($CaF_2$) and cryolite ($Na_3AlF_6$). Hydrogen fluoride is used in etching glass, and the freons, which all contain fluorine, are widely used as refrigerants.

**flute** (or transverse flute) side-blown woodwind instrument of considerable antiquity. The flute is difficult to master but capable of intricate melodies and expressive tonal shading. The player blows across an end hole, the air current being split by the opposite edge, which causes pressure waves to form within the tube. The fingers are placed

over holes in the tube to create different notes. The standard soprano flute has a range of three octaves or more.

**fly** any insect of the order Diptera. A fly has a single pair of wings, antennae, and compound eyes; the hind wings have become modified into knoblike projections (halteres) used to maintain equilibrium in flight. There are over 90,000 species.

---

**WEB SITE** > > > > > > > >

**Flies and Mosquitoes**

http://www.ent.iastate.edu/Imagegal/dipteral/

Colour photographs of flies and mosquitoes from Iowa State University's Entomology Image Gallery. They include the crane fly and crane fly larva, and several dozen images of different species of mosquito and mosquito parts. Click on a link to view each insect. There is a search engine at the top of the page to look for other species of insect.

---

**fog** cloud that collects at the surface of the Earth, composed of water vapour that has condensed on particles of dust in the atmosphere. Cloud and fog are both caused by the air temperature falling below dew point. The thickness of fog depends on the number of water particles it contains. Officially, fog refers to a condition when visibility is reduced to 1 km/0.6 mi or less, and mist or haze to that giving a visibility of 1–2 km or about 1 mi.

**food chain** in ecology, a sequence

showing the feeding relationships between organisms in a particular ecosystem. Each organism depends on the next lowest member of the chain for its food. A pyramid of numbers can be used to show the reduction in food energy at each step up the food chain.

**food poisoning** any acute illness characterized by vomiting and diarrhoea and caused by eating food contaminated with harmful bacteria (for example, listeriosis), poisonous food (for example, certain mushrooms, puffer fish), or poisoned food (such as lead or arsenic introduced accidentally during processing). A frequent cause of food poisoning is →Salmonella bacteria. Salmonella comes in many forms, and strains are found in cattle, pigs, poultry, and eggs.

**football, American** contact sport similar to the English game of rugby, played between two teams of 11 players, with an inflated oval ball. Players are well padded for protection and wear protective helmets. The **Super Bowl**, first held in 1967, is now an annual meeting between the winners of the National and American Football Conferences.

**football, association** (or soccer) form of football originating in the UK, popular throughout the world. The modern game is played in the UK according to the rules laid down by the home countries' football associations. Slight amendments to the rules take effect in certain competitions and international matches as laid down by the sport's world governing body, Fédération Internationale de Football Association (FIFA, 1904). FIFA organizes the competitions for the World Cup, held every four years since 1930.

**force** any influence that tends to change the state of rest or the uniform motion in a straight line of a body. The action of an unbalanced or resultant force results in the acceleration of a body in the direction of action of the force, or it may, if the body is unable to move freely, result in its deformation. Force is a vector quantity, possessing both magnitude and direction; its SI unit is the newton.

**forces, fundamental** in physics, the four fundamental interactions believed to be at work in the physical universe. There are two long-range forces: the **gravitational force**, or **gravity**, which keeps the planets in orbit around the Sun, and acts between all particles that have mass; and the **electromagnetic force**, which stops solids from falling apart, and acts between all particles with electric charge. There are two very short-range forces which operate only inside the atomic nucleus: the **weak nuclear force**, responsible for the reactions that fuel the Sun and for the emission of →beta particles from certain nuclei; and the **strong nuclear force** which binds together the protons and neutrons in the nuclei of atoms. The relative strengths of the four forces are strong, 1; electromagnetic, $10^{-2}$; weak $10^{-6}$; gravitational, $10^{-40}$.

**Ford, Henry** (1863–1947) US automobile manufacturer. He built his first ca in 1896 and founded the Ford Motor Company in 1903. His Model T (1908–27) was the first car to be constructed solely by assembly-line methods and to be mass-marketed; 15 million of these cars were sold.

**forensic science** the use of scientific techniques to solve criminal cases. A multidisciplinary field embracing chemistry, physics, botany, zoology, and medicine, forensic science includes the identification of human bodies or traces and the establishment of time and cause of death. Ballistics (the study of projectiles, such as bullets) is another traditional forensic field.

**formula** in chemistry, a representation of a molecule, radical, or ion, in which the component chemical elements are represented by their symbols. An **empirical formula** indicates the simplest ratio of the elements in a compound, without indicating how many of them there are or how they are combined. A **molecular formula** gives the number of each type of element present in one molecule. A **structural formula** shows the relative positions of the atoms and the bonds between them. For example, for ethanoic acid, the empirical formula is $CH_2O$, the molecular formula is $C_2H_4O_2$, and the structural formula is $CH_3COOH$.

**Forster, E(dward) M(organ)** (1879–1970) English novelist, short-story writer, and critic. He was concerned with the interplay of personality and the conflict between convention and instinct. His novels include *A Room with a View* (1908), *Howards End* (1910), and *A Passage to India* (1924). Collections of stories include *The Celestial Omnibus* (1911) and *Collected Short Stories* (1948), and of essays and reviews 'Abinger Harvest' (1936). His most lasting critical work is *Aspects of the Novel* (1927).

**fossil** (Latin *fossilis* 'dug up') a cast, impression, or the actual remains of an animal or plant preserved in rock. Fossils were created during periods of rock formation, caused by the gradual accumulation of sediment over millions of years at the bottom of the sea bed or an inland lake. Fossils may include footprints, an internal cast, or external impression. A few fossils are preserved intact, as with mammoths fossilized in Siberian ice, or insects trapped in tree resin that is today amber. The study of fossils is called palaeontology. Palaeontologists are able to deduce much of the geological history of a region from fossil remains.

**WEB SITE > > > > > > > >**
**Fossil Collections of the World**

http://www.geocities.com/
CapeCanaveral/Lab/8147/index.html

Comprehensive pages of information about fossils and fossil sites around the world. This is where to find out about geological timescales, the history of fossil-collecting, famous fossil collections and collectors, and maps of sites. There are also links to numerous other related sites.

**fossil fuel** fuel, such as coal, oil, and natural gas, formed from the fossilized remains of plants that lived hundreds of millions of years ago. Fossil fuels are a nonrenewable resource and will eventually run out. Extraction of coal and oil causes considerable environmental pollution, and burning coal contributes to problems of →acid rain and the →greenhouse effect.

> **WEB SITE** > > > > > > > >
> **Fossil Fuels Page**
> http://members.xoom.com/
> coddfish14/FF.html
> Thoughtful, easy-to-understand page on fossil fuels, including information on fuel conservation. The site contains diagrams and pictures of coal-fired power plants.

**four-stroke cycle** the engine-operating cycle of most petrol and diesel →engines. The 'stroke' is an upward or downward movement of a piston in a cylinder. In a petrol engine the cycle begins with the induction of a fuel mixture as the piston goes down on its first stroke. On the second stroke (up) the piston compresses the mixture in the top of the cylinder. An electric spark then ignites the mixture, and the gases produced force the piston down on its third, power, stroke. On the fourth stroke (up) the piston expels the burned gases from the cylinder into the exhaust.

**France** French Republic; **national name:** *République Française*; **area:** (including Corsica) 543,965 sq km/210,024 sq mi; **capital:** Paris; **major towns/cities:** Lyon, Lille, Bordeaux, Toulouse, Nantes, Strasbourg, Montpellier, Saint-Etienne, Rennes, Reims, Grenoble; **major ports:** Marseille, Nice, Le Havre; **physical features:** rivers Seine, Loire, Garonne, Rhône; mountain ranges Alps, Massif Central, Pyrenees, Jura, Vosges, Cévennes; Auvergne mountain region; Mont Blanc (4,810 m/15,781 ft); Ardennes forest; Riviera; caves of Dordogne with relics of early humans; the island of Corsica; **territories:** Guadeloupe, French Guiana, Martinique, Réunion, St Pierre and Miquelon, Southern and Antarctic Territories, New Caledonia, French Polynesia, Wallis and Futuna, Mayotte; **head of state:** Jacques Chirac from 1995; **head of government:** Lionel Jospin from 1997; **political system:** liberal democracy; **currency:** franc; **GNP per capita (PPP):** (US$) 22,320 (1997); **exports:** machinery and transport equipment, food and live animals, chemicals, beverages and tobacco, textile yarn, fabrics and other basic manufactures, clothing and accessories, perfumery and cosmetics. Principal market Germany 15.9% (1998); **population:** 58,886,000 (1999 est); **language:** French (regional languages include Basque, Breton, Catalan, and Provençal); **religion:** Roman Catholic; also Muslim, Protestant, and Jewish minorities; **life expectancy:** 74 (men); 82 (women) (1995–2000).

**Francis of Assisi, St** (1182–1226) born Giovanni Bernadone Italian founder of the Roman Catholic Franciscan order of friars 1209 and, with St Clare, of the Poor Clares 1212. In 1224 he is said to have undergone a mystical experience during which he received the stigmata (five wounds of Jesus). Many stories are told of his ability to charm wild animals, and he is the patron saint of ecologists. His feast day is 4 October. Canonized 1228.

**Franco-Prussian War** 1870–71. The Prussian chancellor Otto von Bismarck put forward a German candidate for the vacant Spanish throne with the deliberate, and successful, intention of provoking the French emperor Napoleon III into declaring war. The Prussians defeated the French at Sedan, then besieged Paris. The Treaty of Frankfurt May 1871 gave Alsace, Lorraine, and a large French indemnity to Prussia. The war established Prussia, at the head of a newly established German empire, as Europe's leading power.

**Frank, Anne (Anneliese Marie)** (1929–1945) German diarist. She fled to the Netherlands with her family 1933 to escape Nazi anti-Semitism (the →Holocaust).

During the German occupation of Amsterdam, they and two other families remained in a sealed-off room, protected by Dutch sympathizers 1942–44, when betrayal resulted in their deportation and Anne's death in Belsen concentration camp. Her diary of her time in hiding was published 1947.

**Frankfurt am Main** (German 'ford of the Franks') city in Hessen, Germany, 72 km/45 mi northeast of Mannheim; population (1995) 651,200. It is a commercial and banking centre, with electrical and machine industries, and an inland port on the River Main. The International Book Fair is held here annually in the autumn. It is the site of the Bundesbank (German Central Bank), and the European Central Bank (from 1999).

**Franz Joseph** (1830–1916) or Francis Joseph, emperor of Austria-Hungary from 1848, when his uncle Ferdinand I abdicated. After the suppression of the 1848 revolution, Franz Joseph tried to establish an absolute monarchy but had to grant Austria a parliamentary constitution 1861 and Hungary equality with Austria 1867. He was defeated in the Italian War 1859 and the Prussian War 1866. In 1914 he made the assassination of his heir and nephew Franz Ferdinand the excuse for attacking Serbia, thus precipitating World War I.

**Frederick (II) the Great** (1712–1786) King of Prussia from 1740, when he succeeded his father Frederick William I. In that year he started the War of the Austrian Succession by his attack on Austria. In the peace of 1745 he secured Silesia. The struggle was renewed in the →Seven Years' War 1756–63. He acquired West Prussia in the first partition of Poland 1772 and left Prussia as Germany's foremost state. He was an efficient and just ruler in the spirit of the Enlightenment and a patron of the arts.

**free radical** in chemistry, an atom or molecule that has an unpaired electron and is therefore highly reactive. Most free radicals are very short-lived. They are by-products of normal cell chemistry and rapidly oxidize other molecules they encounter. Free radicals are thought to do considerable damage. They are neutralized by protective enzymes.

**Freetown** capital of Sierra Leone; population (1992) 505,000. It has a naval station and a harbour. Industries include cement, plastics, footwear, oil refining, food production, and tobacco processing. Platinum, chromite, rutile, diamonds, and gold are traded. Freetown was founded as a settlement for freed slaves in 1787. It was made capital of the independent Sierra Leone in 1961. The beaches of Freetown peninsula attract tourists.

**freezing** change from liquid to solid state, as when water becomes ice. For a given substance, freezing occurs at a definite temperature, known as the **freezing point**, that is invariable under similar conditions of pressure, and the temperature remains at this point until all the liquid is frozen. The amount of heat per unit mass that has to be removed to freeze a substance is a constant for any given substance, and is known as the latent heat of fusion.

**French Polynesia** French Overseas Territory in the South Pacific, consisting of five archipelagos: Windward Islands, Leeward Islands (the two island groups comprising the Society Islands), Tuamotu Archipelago (including Gambier Islands), Tubuai Islands, and Marquesas Islands; **total area** 3,940 sq km/1,521 sq mi; **capital** Papeete on Tahiti; **industries** cultivated pearls, coconut oil, vanilla tourism is important; **population** (1994) 216,600; **languages** Tahitian (official), French; **government** the French government is represented by a high commissioner (Paul Roncière). It is administered by a Council of Ministers with a president elected by the Territorial Assembly from its own members; two deputies are returned to the National Assembly in France and one senator to the Senate; **history** first visited by Europeans 1595; French protectorate 1843; annexed to France 1880–82; became an Overseas Territory changing its name from French Oceania 1958; self-governing 1977. Following demands for independence in New Caledonia 1984–85, agitation increased also in Polynesia.

**French Revolution** the period 1789–1799 that saw the end of the monarchy in France. The revolution began as an attempt to create a constitutional monarchy, but by late 1792 demands for long-overdue reforms resulted in the proclamation of the First Republic. The violence of the revolution; attacks by other nations; and bitter factional struggles, riots, and counter-revolutionary uprisings consumed the republic. This helped bring the extremists to power and the bloody Reign of Terror followed. French armies then succeeded in holding off their foreign enemies and one of the generals, Napoleon, seized power in 1799.

**frequency** in physics, the number of periodic oscillations, vibrations, or waves occurring per unit of time. The SI unit of frequency is the hertz (Hz), one hertz being equivalent to one cycle per second. Frequency is related to wavelength and velocity by the relationship $f = v/\lambda$ where $f$ is frequency, $v$ is velocity and $\lambda$ is wavelength. Frequency is the reciprocal of the period $T$ $f = 1/T$.

**fresco** mural painting technique using water-based paint on wet plaster that has been freshly applied to the wall (*fresco* is Italian for fresh). The technique is ancient and widespread; some of the earliest examples (*c.* 1750–1400 BC) were found in Knossos, Crete (now preserved in the Archaeological Museum in Heraklion). However, fresco reached its finest expression in Italy from the 13th to the 17th centuries.

**Freud, Sigmund** (1856–1939) Austrian physician who pioneered the study of the unconscious mind. He developed the methods of free association and interpretation of dreams that are basic techniques of →psychoanalysis. The influence of unconscious forces on people's thoughts and actions was Freud's discovery, as was his controversial theory of the repression of infantile sexuality as the root of neuroses in the adult. His books include *Die Traumdeutung/ The Interpretation of Dreams* (1900), *Jenseits des Lustprinzips/Beyond the Pleasure Principle* (1920), *Das Ich und das Es/The Ego and the Id* (1923), and *Das Unbehagen in der Kultur/Civilization and its Discontents* (1930). His influence has permeated the world to such an extent that it may be discerned today in almost every branch of thought.

---

**WEB SITE** > > > > > > > >

**Sigmund Freud, The Father of Psychoanalysis**

http://austriainfo.at/personen/freud/index.html

Maintained in English by the Austrian National Tourist Office, the page provides a timeline of biographical information about Freud, plus analyses of his ideas and the impact of his theories on his most notable followers.

---

**friction** in physics, the force that opposes the relative motion of two bodies in contact. The **coefficient of friction** is the ratio of the force required to achieve this relative motion to the force pressing the two bodies together.

**frog** any amphibian of the order Anura (Greek 'tailless'). There are about 24 different families of frog, containing more than 3,800 species. There are no clear rules for distinguishing between frogs and toads.

Frogs usually have squat bodies, with hind legs specialized for jumping, and webbed feet for swimming. Most live in or near water, though as adults they are air-breathing. A few live on land or even in trees. Their colour is usually greenish in the genus *Rana*, but other Ranidae are brightly coloured, for instance black and orange or yellow and white. Many use their long, extensible tongues to capture insects. The eyes are large and bulging. Frogs vary in size from the North American little grass frog *Limnaoedus ocularis*, 12 mm/0.5 in long, to the giant aquatic frog *Telmatobius culeus*, 50 cm/ 20 in long, of Lake Titicaca, South America. Frogs are widespread, inhabiting all continents except Antarctica, and they have adapted to a range of environments including deserts, forests, grasslands, and even high altitudes, with some species in the Andes and Himalayas existing above 5,000 m/ 19,600 ft.

**front** in meteorology, the boundary between two air masses of different temperature or humidity. A **cold front** marks the line of advance of a cold air mass from below, as it displaces a warm air mass; a **warm front** marks the advance of a warm air mass as it rises up over a cold one. Frontal systems define the weather of the mid-latitudes, where warm tropical air is constantly meeting cold air from the poles.

**Frost, Robert Lee** (1874–1963) US poet. His accessible, colloquial blank verse, often flavoured with New England speech patterns, is written with an individual voice and penetrating vision. His poems include 'Mending Wall' ('Something there is that does not love a wall'), 'The Road Not Taken', and 'Stopping by Woods on a Snowy Evening' and are collected in *Complete Poems* 1951.

**fruit** (from Latin *frui* 'to enjoy') in botany, the ripened ovary in flowering plants that develops from one or more seeds or carpels and encloses one or more seeds. Its function is to protect the seeds during their development and to aid in their dispersal. Fruits are often edible, sweet, juicy, and colourful When eaten they provide vitamins, minerals, and enzymes, but little protein. Most fruits are borne by perennial plants.

**fugue** (Latin 'flight') in music, a contrapuntal form with two or more subjects (principal melodies) for a number of parts, which enter in succession in direct imitation of each other or transposed to a higher or lower key, and may be combined in augmented form (larger note values). It represents the highest form of contrapuntal ingenuity in works such as Johann Sebastian Bach's *Das musikalische Opfer/The Musical Offering* (1747), on a theme of Frederick II o' Prussia, and *Die Kunst der Fuge/The Art of the Fugue* published in 1751, and Beethoven's *Grosse Fuge/Great Fugue* for string quartet (1825–26).

**Fuller, (Richard) Buckminster** (1895– 1983) US architect, engineer, and social philosopher. He embarked on an unorthodox career in an attempt to maximize energy resources through improved technology. In 1947 he invented the lightweight geodesic dome, a hemispherical space-frame of triangular components linked by rods independent of buttress or vault and capable of covering large-span areas. Within 30 years over 50,000 had been built.

**fullerene** form of carbon, discovered in 1985, based on closed cages of carbon atoms. The molecules of the most symmetrical of the fullerenes are called →buckminsterfullerenes (or buckyballs). They are perfect spheres made up of 60 carbon atoms linked together in 12 pentagons and 20 hexagons fitted together like those of a spherical football. Other fullerenes, with 28, 32, 50, 70, and 76 carbon atoms, have also been identified.

**Functionalism** in architecture and design, the principle of excluding everything that serves no practical purpose. Central to 20th-century →modernism, the Functionalist ethic developed as a reaction against the 19th-century practice of imitating and combining earlier styles. Its finest achievements are in the realms of industrial architecture and office furnishings.

**fundamentalism** in religion, an emphasis on basic principles or articles of faith. **Christian fundamentalism** emerged in the USA just after World War I (as a reaction to theological modernism and the historical criticism of the Bible) and insisted on belief in the literal truth of everything in the Bible. **Islamic fundamentalism** insists on strict observance of Muslim Shari'a law.

**fungus** (plural fungi) any of a unique group of organisms that includes moulds, yeasts, rusts, smuts, mildews, mushrooms, and toadstools. There are around 70,000 species of fungi known to science (1998), though there may be as many as 1.5 million actually in existence. They are not considered to be plants for three main reasons: they have no leaves or roots; they contain no chlorophyll (green colouring) and are therefore unable to make their own food by →photosynthesis; and they reproduce by spores. Some fungi are edible but many are highly poisonous; they often cause damage and sometimes disease to the organic matter they live and feed on, but some fungi are exploited in the production of food and drink (for example, yeasts in baking and brewing) and in medicine (for example, penicillin). (Kingdom Fungi.)

**fusion** in physics, the fusing of the nuclei of light elements, such as hydrogen, into those of a heavier element, such as helium. The resultant loss in their combined mass is converted into energy. Stars and thermonuclear weapons are powered by nuclear fusion.

**Futurism** avant-garde art movement founded in 1909 that celebrated the dynamism of the modern world. It was chiefly an Italian movement and was mainly expressed in painting, but it also embraced other arts, including literature and music, and it had extensive influence outside Italy, particularly in Russia. In Italy the movement virtually died during World War I, but in Russia it continued to flourish into the 1920s.

# Gg

**Gable, (William) Clark** (1901–1960) US actor. A star for more than 30 years, he played a range of hard-boiled, comic, and romantic roles. He won an Academy Award for his performance in Frank Capra's *It Happened One Night* (1934), and starred as Rhett Butler in *Gone With the Wind* (1939).

**Gabon** Gabonese Republic; **national name:** *République Gabonaise*; **area:** 267,667 sq km/103,346 sq mi; **capital:** Libreville; **major towns/cities:** Port-Gentil, Masuku (Franceville), Lambaréné, Mouanda; **major ports:** Port-Gentil and Owendo; **physical features:** virtually the whole country is tropical rainforest; narrow coastal plain rising to hilly interior with savanna in east and south; Ogooué River flows north–west; **head of state:** Omar Bongo from 1967; **head of government:** Jean-François Ntoutoume-Emane from 1999; **political system:** emergent democracy; **currency:** franc CFA; **GNP per capita (PPP):** (US\$) 6,660 (1998); **exports:** petroleum and petroleum products, manganese, timber and wood products, uranium. Principal market USA 67% (1997); **population:** 1,197,000 (1999 est); **language:** French (official), Bantu; **religion:** Roman Catholic, also Muslim, animist; **life expectancy:** 51 (men); 54 (women) (1995–2000).

**Gaddafi** alternative form of →Khaddhafi, Libyan leader.

**Gaia hypothesis** theory that the Earth's living and nonliving systems form an inseparable whole that is regulated and kept adapted for life by living organisms themselves. The planet therefore functions as a single organism, or a giant cell. The hypothesis was elaborated by British scientist James Lovelock and first published in 1968.

**Gainsborough, Thomas** (1727–1788) English landscape and portrait painter. In 1760 he settled in Bath, where his elegant and subtly characterized society portraits brought great success. In 1774 he went to London, becoming one of the original members of the Royal Academy and the principal rival of Joshua Reynolds. He was one of the first British artists to follow the Dutch example in painting realistic landscapes rather than imaginative Italianate scenery, as in *Mr and Mrs Andrews* (about 1750; National Gallery, London).

**Galápagos Islands** (official name *Archipiélago de Colón*) group of 12 large and several hundred smaller islands in the Pacific about 800 km/

500 mi from the mainland, belonging to Ecuador; area 7,800 sq km/3,000 sq mi; population (1990) 9,800. The capital is San Cristóbal. The islands are a nature reserve; their unique fauna (including giant tortoises, iguanas, penguins, flightless cormorants, and Darwin's finches, which inspired Charles →Darwin to formulate the principle of evolution by natural selection) is under threat from introduced species. The marine ecosystem surrounding the island supports 437 species of fish, 41 of which are unique to the Galápagos. The main industry is tuna and lobster fishing.

**galaxy** congregation of millions or billions of stars, held together by gravity.

**Spiral galaxies**, such as the →Milky Way, are flattened in shape, with a central bulge of old stars surrounded by a disc of younger stars, arranged in spiral arms like a Catherine wheel.

**Barred spirals** are spiral galaxies that have a straight bar of stars across their centre, from the ends of which the spiral arms emerge. The arms of spiral galaxies contain gas and dust from which new stars are still forming.

**Elliptical galaxies** contain old stars and very little gas. They include the most massive galaxies known, containing a trillion stars. At least some elliptical galaxies are thought to be formed by mergers between spiral galaxies. There are also irregular galaxies. Most galaxies occur in clusters, containing anything from a few to thousands of members.

**Galen** (c. 129–c. 200) Greek physician and anatomist whose ideas dominated Western medicine for almost 1,500 years. Central to his thinking were the theories of humours and the threefold circulation of the blood. He remained the highest medical authority until Andreas Vesalius and William →Harvey exposed the fundamental errors of his system.

**Galileo** (1564–1642) properly Galileo Galilei, Italian mathematician, astronomer, and physicist. He developed the astronomical telescope and was the first to see sunspots, the four main satellites of Jupiter, and the appearance of Venus going through phases, thus proving it was orbiting the Sun. Galileo discovered that freely falling bodies, heavy or light, have the same, constant acceleration and that this acceleration is due to gravity. He also determined that a body moving on a perfectly smooth horizontal surface would neither speed up nor slow down. He invented a thermometer, a hydrostatic balance, and a compass, and discovered that the path of a projectile is a parabola.

**Gallipoli** port in European Turkey, giving its name to the peninsula (ancient name **Chersonesus**) on which it stands. In World War I, at the instigation of Winston Churchill, an unsuccessful attempt was made in February 1915–January 1916 by Allied troops to force their way through the Dardanelles and link up with Russia. The campaign was fought mainly by Australian and New Zealand (Anzac) forces, who suffered heavy losses. An estimated 36,000 Commonwealth troops died during the nine-month campaign.

**gallstone** pebblelike, insoluble accretion formed in the human gall bladder or bile ducts from cholesterol or calcium salts present in bile. Gallstones may be symptomless or they may cause pain, indigestion, or jaundice. They can be dissolved with medication or removed, either by means of an endoscope or, along with the gall bladder, in an operation known as cholecystectomy.

**Gama, Vasco da** (*c.* 1469–1524) Portuguese navigator. He commanded an expedition in 1497 to discover the route to India around the Cape of Good Hope (in modern South Africa). On Christmas Day 1497 he reached land, which he named Natal. He then crossed the Indian Ocean, arriving at Calicut (now Kozhikode in Kerala) in May 1498, and returned to Portugal in September 1499.

**Gambia, The** Republic of; **area:** 10,402 sq km/4,016 sq mi; **capital:** Banjul; **major towns/cities:** Serekunda, Birkama, Bakau, Farafenni, Sukuta, Gunjur, Georgetown; **physical features:** consists of narrow strip of land along the River Gambia; river flanked by low hills; **head of state and government:** (interim) Yahya Jammeh from 1994; **political system:** transitional; **currency:** dalasi; **GNP per capita (PPP):** (US$) 1,430 (1998); **exports:** groundnuts and related products, cotton lint, fish and fish preparations, hides and skins. Principal market Belgium–Luxembourg 78% (1997 est); **population:** 1,268,000 (1999 est); **language:** English (official), Mandinka, Fula, and other indigenous tongues; **religion:** Muslim 90%, with animist and Christian minorities; **life expectancy:** 45 (men); 49 (women) (1995–2000).

**gamete** cell that functions in sexual reproduction by merging with another gamete to form a zygote. Examples of gametes include sperm and egg cells. In most organisms, the gametes are haploid (they contain half the number of chromosomes of the parent), owing to reduction division or meiosis.

**Gandhi, Indira Priyadarshani** (1917–1984) born Nehru, Indian politician, prime minister of India 1966–77 and 1980–84, and leader of the Congress Party 1966–77 and subsequently of the Congress (I) party. She was assassinated in 1984 by members of her Sikh bodyguard, resentful of her use of troops to clear malcontents from the Sikh temple at →Amritsar.

**Gandhi, Mahatma** (1869–1948) Sanskrit 'Great Soul', honorific name of Mohandas Karamchand Gandhi, Indian nationalist leader. A pacifist, he led the struggle for Indian independence from the UK by advocating nonviolent noncooperation (*satyagraha*, defence of and by truth) from 1915. He was imprisoned several times by the British authorities and was influential in the nationalist Congress Party and in the independence negotiations in 1947. He was assassinated by a Hindu nationalist in the violence that followed the partition of British India into India and Pakistan.

**Ganges** (Hindi *Ganga*) major river of India and Bangladesh; length 2,510 km/

1,560 mi. It is the most sacred river for Hindus.

**gangrene** death and decay of body tissue (often of a limb) due to bacterial action; the affected part gradually turns black and causes blood poisoning.

**García Lorca, Federico** Spanish poet. See →Lorca, Federico García.

**García Márquez, Gabriel (Gabo)** (1928–   ) Colombian novelist. His sweeping novel *Cien años de soledad/One Hundred Years of Solitude* (1967) (which tells the story of a family over a period of six generations) is an example of magic realism, a technique used to heighten the intensity of realistic portrayal of social and political issues by introducing grotesque or fanciful material. Nobel Prize for Literature 1982.

**garlic** perennial Asian plant belonging to the lily family, whose strong-smelling and sharp-tasting bulb, made up of several small segments, or cloves, is used in cooking. The plant has white flowers. It is widely cultivated and has been used successfully as a fungicide in the cereal grass sorghum. It also has antibacterial properties. (*Allium sativum*, family Liliaceae.)

**Garvey, Marcus (Moziah)** (1887–1940) Jamaican political thinker and activist, an early advocate of black nationalism. He led a Back to Africa movement for black Americans to establish a black-governed country in Africa. The Jamaican cult of →Rastafarianism is based largely on his ideas.

**gas** in physics, a form of matter, such as air, in which the molecules move randomly in otherwise empty space, filling any size or shape of container into which the gas is put.

**Gaskell, Elizabeth** (1810–1865) (Cleghorn, born Stevenson) English novelist. Her most popular book, *Cranford* (1853), is the study of a small, close-knit circle in a small town, modelled on Knutsford, Cheshire, where she was brought up. Her other books, which often deal with social concerns, include *Mary Barton* (1848), *North and South* (1855), *Sylvia's Lovers* (1863–64), and the unfinished *Wives and Daughters* (1866). She wrote a frank and sympathetic biography of her friend Charlotte →Brontë (1857).

**Gauguin, (Eugène Henri) Paul** (1848–1903) French post-Impressionist painter. Going beyond the Impressionists' concern with ever-changing appearances, he developed a heavily symbolic and decorative style characterized by his sensuous use of pure colours. In his search for a more direct and intense experience of life, he moved to islands in the South Pacific, where he created many of his finest works. Among his paintings is *The Yellow Christ* (1889; Albright-Knox Art Gallery, Buffalo, New York State).

**Gaulle, Charles de** French politician, see Charles →de Gaulle.

**Gaza Strip** strip of land on the Mediterranean sea, 10 km/6 mi wide and 40 km/25 mi long, extending northeast from the Egyptian border; area 363 sq km/140 sq mi; population (1997 est)

987,900, mainly Palestinians, plus about 2,500 Israeli settlers. It was occupied by Israel from 1967 till 1994, when responsibility for its administration was transferred to the Palestine National Authority. The capital is Gaza; other main centres of population are Khan Yunis and Rafah. The area is dependent on Israel for the supply of electricity. Agriculture is the main activity, producing citrus fruit, wheat, and olives. Prior to the great influx of Palestinian refugees in 1948 the area was rural, and is geographically part of the Negev. Industry is on a small scale, including handmade goods, for example olive wood carvings for Israel's tourist industry.

**gazelle** any of a number of lightly built, fast-running antelopes found on the open plains of Africa and southern Asia. (Especially species of the genus *Gazella*.)

**gear** toothed wheel that transmits the turning movement of one shaft to another shaft. Gear wheels may be used in pairs, or in threes if both shafts are to turn in the same direction. The gear ratio – the ratio of the number of teeth on the two wheels – determines the torque ratio, the turning force on the output shaft compared with the turning force on the input shaft. The ratio of the angular velocities of the shafts is the inverse of the gear ratio.

**Geiger counter** any of a number of devices used for detecting nuclear radiation and/or measuring its intensity by counting the number of ionizing particles produced (see →radioactivity). It detects the momentary current that passes between electrodes in a suitable gas when a nuclear particle or a radiation pulse causes the ionization of that gas. The electrodes are connected to electronic devices that enable the number of particles passing to be measured. The increased frequency of measured particles indicates the intensity of radiation. The device is named after the German physicist Hans Geiger.

**gel** solid produced by the formation of a three-dimensional cage structure,

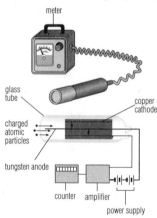

**Geiger counter** A Geiger–Müller counter detects and measures ionizing radiation (alpha, beta, and gamma particles) emitted by radioactive materials. Any incoming radiation creates ions (charged particles) within the counter, which are accelerated by the anode and cathode to create a measurable electric current.

commonly of linked large-molecular-mass polymers, in which a liquid is trapped. It is a form of colloid. A gel may be a jellylike mass (pectin, gelatin) or have a more rigid structure (silica gel).

**gene** unit of inherited material, encoded by a strand of →DNA and transcribed by →RNA. In higher organisms, genes are located on the →chromosomes. A gene consistently affects a particular character in an individual – for example, the gene for eye colour. Also termed a Mendelian gene, after Austrian biologist Gregor Mendel, it occurs at a particular point, or locus, on a particular chromosome and may have several variants, or →alleles, each specifying a particular form of that character – for example, the alleles for blue or brown eyes. Some alleles show dominance. These mask the effect of other alleles, known as →recessive.

### WEB SITE > > > > > > > >

**Introduction to Chromosomes**

http://raven.umnh.utah.edu/review/disease/chromosomes.html

Introduction to chromosomes that is part of a much larger site on genetic science based in Utah. A 'clickable' diagram of two chromosomes is used to show how geneticists tell chromosomes apart. The page also contains links to information on DNA and proteins.

**genetically modified foods** (or GM foods) foods produced using genetic engineering technology. Individual genes can be copied or transferred from one living organism to another, to incorporate specific characteristics into the organism or remove undesirable characteristics. The technology, developed in the 1980s, may be used, for example, to produce crops with higher yields, enhanced taste, resistance to pests, or a longer growing season. The first genetically modified (GM) food, the 'Flavr Savr' tomato, went on sale in the USA in 1994. GM ingredients appearing in foods on the market today include tomatoes, soya, and maize, however there remain some reservations about GM products, and some companies and countries, including Britain, have taken steps to delay the growing of GM crops until risks have been assessed, and to introduce legislation forcing GM products to be declared as such.

**genetic engineering** manipulation of genetic material by biochemical techniques. It is often achieved by the introduction of new →DNA, usually by means of a virus or plasmid. This can be for pure research, gene therapy, or to breed functionally specific plants, animals, or bacteria. These organisms with a foreign gene added are said to be transgenic. At the beginning of 1995 more than 60 plant species had been genetically engineered, and nearly 3,000 transgenic crops had been field-tested.

**genetics** branch of biology concerned with the study of →heredity and variation; it attempts to explain how characteristics of living organisms are passed on from one generation to the next. The science of genetics is based on the work of Austrian biologist Gregor Mendel whose experiments with the cross-breeding (hybridization) of peas showed that the inheritance of characteristics and traits takes place by means of discrete 'particles' ( →genes). These are present in the cells of all organisms, and are now recognized as being the basic units of heredity. All organisms possess →genotypes (sets of variable genes) and →phenotypes (characteristics produced by certain genes). Modern geneticists investigate the structure, function, and transmission of genes.

**Geneva Convention** international agreement 1864 regulating the treatment of those wounded in war, and later extended to cover the types of weapons allowed, the treatment of prisoners and the sick, and the protection of civilians in wartime. The rules were revised at conventions held 1906, 1929, and 1949, and by the 1977 Additional Protocols.

**Genghis Khan** (c. 1155–1227) also known as Chingiz Khan (Greek 'World Conqueror') Mongol conqueror, ruler of all Mongol peoples from 1206. He conquered the empires of northern China 1211–15 and Khwarazm 1219–21, and invaded northern India in 1221, while his lieutenants advanced as far as the Crimea. When he died, his empire ranged from the Yellow Sea to the Black Sea; it continued to expand after his death to extend from Hungary to Korea. Genghis Khan controlled probably a larger area than any other individual in history. He was not only a great military leader, but the creator of a stable political system.

**genocide** deliberate and systematic destruction of a national, racial, religious, or ethnic group defined by the exterminators as undesirable. The term is commonly applied to the policies of the Nazis during World War II (what they called the 'final solution' – the extermination of all 'undesirables' in occupied Europe, particularly the Jews). See →Holocaust.

**genome** the full complement of →genes carried by a single (haploid) set of →chromosomes. The term may be applied to the genetic information carried by an individual or to the range of genes found in a given species. The human genome is made up of approximately 100,000 genes (though there may be as many as 140,000 acording to a 1999 estimate from the →Human Genome Project).

**genotype** particular set of →alleles

(variants of genes) possessed by a given organism. The term is usually used in conjunction with →phenotype, which is the product of the genotype and all environmental effects.

**genus** (plural genera) group of species with many characteristics in common. Thus all doglike species (including dogs, wolves, and jackals) belong to the genus *Canis* (Latin 'dog'). →Species of the same genus are thought to be descended from a common ancestor species. Related genera are grouped into families.

**geological time** time scale embracing the history of the Earth from its physical origin to the present day. Geological time is traditionally divided into eons (Archaean or Archaeozoic, Proterozoic, and Phanerozoic in ascending chronological order), which in turn are subdivided into eras, periods, epochs, ages, and finally chrons.

**geometry** branch of mathematics concerned with the properties of space, usually in terms of plane (two-dimensional) and solid (three-dimensional) figures. The subject is usually divided into **pure geometry**, which embraces roughly the plane and solid geometry dealt with in Greek mathematician →Euclid's *Stoicheia/Elements*, and **analytical** or →**coordinate geometry**, in which problems are solved using algebraic methods. A third, quite distinct, type includes the non-Euclidean geometries.

**George VI** (1895–1952) King of Great Britain and Northern Ireland from 1936, when he succeeded after the abdication of his brother Edward VIII, who had succeeded their father George V. Created Duke of York in 1920, he married in 1923 Lady Elizabeth Bowes-Lyon (1900–  ), and their children are Elizabeth II and Princess Margaret. During World War II, he visited the Normandy and Italian battlefields.

**George, St** (died *c.* 303) patron saint of England. The story of St George rescuing a woman by slaying a dragon, evidently derived from the Greek Perseus legend, first appears in the 6th century. The cult of St George was introduced into western Europe by the Crusaders. His feast day is 23 April.

**Georgia** state in southeastern USA. It is nicknamed the Empire State of the South or the Peach State. Georgia ratified the US Constitution in 1788, becoming the 4th state to join the Union. Historically it was a cotton-producing state associated with slavery; as the birthplace of Martin Luther King, Jr, it also has strong links with the history of the civil-rights movement. Georgia is bordered to the northeast by South Carolina, to the north by North Carolina and Tennessee, to the west by Alabama, and to the south by Florida. In the southeast, Georgia has a coastline some 145 km/90 mi long on the Atlantic, off which are many of the Sea Islands; **population:** (1996 est) 7,353,000; **area:** 152,600 sq km/ 58,904 sq mi; **capital:** Atlanta; **towns and cities:** Columbus, Savannah, Macon, Albany; **industries and products:** poultry, livestock, tobacco, maize, peanuts, cotton, soybeans, china clay, crushed granite, marble, clothing and textiles, carpets, aircraft, paper products, lumber, turpentine, finance sector, tourism.

**Georgia** Republic of; **area:** 69,700 sq km/26,911 sq mi; **capital:** Tbilisi; **major towns/cities:** Kutaisi, Rustavi, Batumi, Sukhumi; **physical features:** largely mountainous with a variety of landscape from the subtropical Black Sea shores to the ice and snow of the crest line of the Caucasus; chief rivers are Kura and Rioni; **head of state:** Eduard Shevardnadze from 1992; **head of government:** Otar Patsatsia from 1993; **political system:** transitional; **currency:** lari; **GNP per capita (PPP):** (US$) 2,620 (1998 est); **exports:** metal products, machinery, tea, beverages, food and tobacco products. Principal market Russia 27.4% (1997); **population:** 5,005,000 (1999 est); **language:** Georgian; **religion:** Georgian Orthodox, also Muslim; **life expectancy:** 69 (men); 77 (women) (1995–2000).

**geothermal energy** energy extracted for heating and electricity generation from natural steam, hot water, or hot dry rocks in the Earth's crust. Water is pumped down through an injection well where it passes through joints in the hot rocks. It rises to the surface through a recovery well and may be converted to steam or run through a heat exchanger. Dry steam may be directed through turbines to produce electricity. It is an important source of energy in volcanically active areas such as Iceland and New Zealand.

**German measles** (or rubella) mild, communicable virus disease, usually caught by children. It is marked by a sore throat, pinkish rash, and slight fever, and has an incubation period of two to three weeks. If a woman contracts it in the first three months of pregnancy, it may cause serious damage to the unborn child.

**Germany** Federal Republic of; **national name:** *Bundesrepublik Deutschland*; **area:** 357,041 sq km/137,853 sq mi; **capital:** Berlin (government offices moving in phases from Bonn back to Berlin); **major towns/cities:** Cologne, Hamburg, Munich, Essen, Frankfurt am Main, Dortmund, Stuttgart, Düsseldorf, Leipzig, Dresden, Bremen, Duisburg, Hannover; **major ports:** Hamburg, Kiel, Bremerhaven, Rostock; **physical features:** flat in north, mountainous in south with Alps; rivers Rhine, Weser, Elbe flow north, Danube flows southeast, Oder and Neisse flow north along Polish frontier; many lakes, including Müritz; Black Forest, Harz Mountains, Erzgebirge (Ore Mountains), Bavarian Alps, Fichtelgebirge, Thüringer Forest; **head of state:** Johannes Rau from 1999; **head of government:** Gerhard Schroeder from 1998; **political system:** liberal democratic federal republic; **currency:** Deutschmark; **GNP per capita (PPP):** (US$) 20,810 (1998); **exports:** road vehicles, electrical machinery, metals and metal products, textiles, chemicals. Principal market France 11.7% (1998); **population:** 82,177,000 (1999 est); **language:** German; **religion:** Protestant (mainly

Lutheran) 43%, Roman Catholic 36%; **life expectancy:** 74 (men); 80 (women) (1995–2000).

**germination** in botany, the initial stages of growth in a seed, spore, or pollen grain. Seeds germinate when they are exposed to favourable external conditions of moisture, light, and temperature, and when any factors causing dormancy have been removed.

**Gestapo** (contraction of *Geheime Staatspolizei*) Nazi Germany's secret police, formed 1933, and under the direction of Heinrich Himmler from 1934.

**gestation** in all mammals except the →monotremes (platypus and spiny anteaters), the period from the time of implantation of the embryo in the uterus to birth. This period varies among species; in humans it is about 266 days, in elephants 18–22 months, in cats about 60 days, and in some species of marsupial (such as opossum) as short as 12 days.

**Gettysburg** site of one of the decisive battles of the American →Civil War: a Confederate defeat by Union forces 1–3 July 1863, at Gettysburg, Pennsylvania, 80 km/50 mi northwest of Baltimore. The site is now a national cemetery, at the dedication of which President Lincoln delivered the **Gettysburg Address** 19 November 1863, a speech in which he reiterated the principles of freedom, equality, and democracy embodied in the US Constitution.

**geyser** natural spring that intermittently discharges an explosive column of steam and hot water into the air due to the build-up of steam in underground chambers. One of the most remarkable geysers is Old Faithful, in Yellowstone National Park, Wyoming, USA. Geysers also occur in New Zealand and Iceland.

**g-force** force that pilots and astronauts experience when their craft accelerate or decelerate rapidly. One g is the ordinary pull of gravity.

Early astronauts were subjected to launch and reentry forces of up to six g or more; in the space shuttle, more than three g is experienced on liftoff. Pilots and astronauts wear g-suits that prevent their blood pooling too much under severe g-forces, which can lead to unconsciousness.

**Ghana** Republic of (formerly the Gold Coast); **area:** 238,305 sq km/92,009 sq mi; **capital:** Accra; **major towns/cities:** Kumasi, Tamale, Tema, Sekondi-Takoradi, Cape Coast, Sunyani, Koforidua, Ho, Yendi, Tarkwa, Wa, Bolgatanga; **major ports:** Sekondi, Tema; **physical features:** mostly tropical lowland plains; bisected by River Volta; **head of state and government:** Jerry Rawlings from 1981; **political system:** emergent democracy; **currency:** cedi; **GNP per capita (PPP):** (US$) 1,610 (1998 est); **exports:** gold, cocoa and related products, timber. Principal market Togo 13% (1997); **population:** 19,678,000 (1999 est); **language:** English (official) and African languages; **religion:** Christian 62%, Muslim 16%, animist;

**life expectancy:** 58 (men); 62 (women) (1995–2000).

**Ghent** (Flemish *Gent*; French *Gand*) port city and capital of East Flanders province, northwest Belgium, situated at the junction of the rivers Lys and Schelde, 55 km/34 mi northwest of Brussels; population (1997) 225,500. Industries include textiles, chemicals, electronics, metallurgy, and motor-vehicle manufacturing. The cathedral of St Bavon (12th–14th centuries) has paintings by van Eyck and Rubens.

**Gibraltar** (Arabic *Jebel Tariq*, 'Mountain of Tariq') British dependency, situated on a narrow rocky promontory at the southern tip of Spain; the **Rock of Gibraltar** formed one of the Pillars of →Hercules with Mount Acho, near Ceuta, across the Strait of Gibraltar on the north African coast.; **area:** 6.5 sq km/2.5 sq mi; **features:** strategic naval and air base, with NATO underground headquarters and communications centre; there are numerous caverns and galleries cut out in the rock, the largest of which is 70 m/230 ft long; colony of Barbary apes; the frontier zone is adjoined by the Spanish port of La Linea; **exports:** mainly a trading centre for the import and re-export of goods; **population:** (1993) 29,000; **history:** the fortress was taken by the Moors in 711 who finally ceded it to Spain in 1462. Captured from Spain in 1704 by English admiral George Rooke (1650–1709), it was ceded to Britain under the Treaty of Utrecht (1713). A referendum in 1967 confirmed the wish of the people to remain in association with the UK, but Spain continues to claim sovereignty and closed the border from 1969 to 1985. In 1989, the UK government announced it would reduce the military garrison by half. Ground troops were withdrawn in 1991, but navy and airforce units remained.

**Gide, André Paul Guillaume** (1869–1951) French novelist. His work is largely autobiographical and concerned with the conflict between desire and conventional morality. It includes *Les Nourritures terrestres/Fruits of the Earth* (1897), *L'Immoraliste/The Immoralist* (1902), *La Porte étroite/Strait is the Gate* (1909), *Les Caves du Vatican/The Vatican Cellars* (1914), and also *Les Faux-monnayeurs/The Counterfeiters* (1926). He was a cofounder of the influential literary periodical *Nouvelle Revue française* (1908), and kept an almost lifelong *Journal*. Nobel Prize for Literature 1947.

**gigabyte** in computing, a measure of memory capacity, equal to 1,024 megabytes. It is also used, less precisely, to mean 1,000 billion →bytes.

**Gilgamesh** hero of Sumerian, Hittite, Akkadian, and Assyrian legend, and lord of the Sumerian city of Uruk. The 12 verse books of the *Epic of Gilgamesh* were recorded in a standard version on 12 cuneiform tablets by the Assyrian king Ashurbanipal's scholars in the 7th century BC, and the epic itself is older than Homer's *Iliad* by at least 1,500 years.

**Gillespie, Dizzy (John Birks)** (1917–1993) US jazz trumpeter. With

Charlie Parker, he was the chief creator and exponent of the bebop style (*Groovin' High* is a CD re-issue of their seminal 78-rpm recordings). Gillespie influenced many modern jazz trumpeters, including Miles Davis.

**ginkgo** (or maidenhair tree) tree belonging to the →gymnosperm (or naked-seed-bearing) division of plants. It may reach a height of 30 m/100 ft by the time it is 200 years old. (*Ginkgo biloba*.)

**Ginsberg, (Irwin) Allen** (1926–1997) US poet and political activist. His reputation as a visionary, overtly political poet was established by *Howl* (1956), which expressed and shaped the spirit of the →Beat Generation and criticized the materialism of contemporary US society. Ginsberg, like many of his generation of poets, found his authorial voice via experimentation with drugs, alternative religion, and the hippie culture; his poetry drew, for example, on Oriental philosophies and utilized mantric breath meditations.

**ginseng** plant with a thick forked aromatic root used in alternative medicine as a tonic. (*Panax ginseng*, family Araliaceae.)

**glacier** tongue of ice, originating in mountains in snowfields above the snowline, which moves slowly downhill and is constantly replenished from its source. The geographic features produced by the erosive action of glaciers (glacial erosion) are characteristic and include glacial troughs (U-shaped valleys), corries, and arêtes. In lowlands,

the laying down of rocky debris carried by glaciers (glacial deposition) produces a variety of landscape features, such as moraines, eskers, and drumlins.

---

### WEB SITE > > > > > > > >

**Glaciers**

http://www-nsidc.colorado.edu/glaciers/

Comprehensive information about glaciers from the US National Snow and Ice Data Centre. There are explanations of why glaciers form, different kinds of glaciers, and what they may tell us about climate change. There are a number of interesting facts and a bibliography about the compacted tongues of ice which cover 10% of the land surface of our planet.

---

**Gladstone, William Ewart** (1809–1898) British Liberal politician, four times prime minister. He entered Parliament as a Tory in 1833 and held ministerial office, but left the party in 1846 and after 1859 identified himself with the Liberals. He was chancellor of the Exchequer 1852–55 and 1859–66, and prime minister 1868–74, 1880–85, 1886, and 1892–94. He introduced elementary education in 1870 and vote by secret ballot in 1872 and many reforms in Ireland, although he failed in his efforts to get a Home Rule Bill passed.

**gland** specialized organ of the body that manufactures and secretes enzymes, hormones, or other chemicals. In animals, glands vary in size from small (for example, tear glands) to large (for example, the pancreas), but in plants they are always small, and may consist of a single cell. Some glands discharge their products internally, →endocrine glands, and others externally, exocrine glands. Lymph nodes are sometimes wrongly called glands.

**glandular fever** (or infectious mononucleosis) viral disease characterized at onset by fever and painfully swollen lymph nodes (in the neck); there may also be digestive upset, sore throat, and skin rashes. Lassitude persists for months and even years, and recovery can be slow. It is caused by the Epstein–Barr virus.

**Glasgow** city and, as **Glasgow City**, unitary authority in west-central Scotland; the unitary authority formed in 1995 from the majority of land from Glasgow District Council of Strathclyde Region; **area:** 176 sq km/68 sq mi; **industries:** engineering, chemicals, printing, whisky blending, brewing, electronics, textiles, light manufacturing; **population:** (1996) 618,400.

**glasnost** (Russian 'openness') Soviet leader Mikhail →Gorbachev's policy of liberalizing various aspects of Soviet life, such as introducing greater freedom of expression and information and opening up relations with Western countries. *Glasnost* was introduced and adopted by the Soviet government in 1986.

**glass** transparent or translucent substance that is physically neither a solid nor a liquid. Although glass is easily shattered, it is one of the strongest substances known. It is made by fusing certain types of sand (silica); this fusion occurs naturally in volcanic glass.

**Glass, Philip** (1937– ) US composer. As a student of Nadia Boulanger, he was strongly influenced by Indian music; his work is characterized by repeated rhythmic figures that are continually expanded and modified. His compositions include the operas *Einstein on the Beach* (1976), *Akhnaten* (1984), *The Making of the Representative for Planet 8* (1988), and the *'Low' Symphony* (1992) on themes from David Bowie's *Low* album.

**glaucoma** condition in which pressure inside the eye (intraocular pressure) is raised abnormally as excess fluid accumulates. It occurs when the normal outflow of fluid within the chamber of the eye (aqueous humour) is interrupted. As pressure rises, the optic nerve suffers irreversible damage, leading to a reduction in the field of vision and, ultimately, loss of eyesight.

**Glendower, Owen** (c. 1350–1416) also known as Owain Glyndwr, Welsh nationalist leader. He led a rebellion against Henry IV of England, taking the title 'Prince of Wales' in 1400, and successfully led the Welsh defence against English invasions in 1400–02, although Wales was reconquered 1405–13. He gained control of most of the country and established an independent Welsh parliament, but from 1405 onwards suffered repeated defeats at the hands of Prince Hal, later →Henry V.

**global warming** an increase in average global temperature of approximately 1°F/0.5°C over the past century. Global temperature has been highly variable in

Earth history and many fluctuations in global temperature have occurred in historical times, but this most recent episode of warming coincides with the spread of industralization, prompting the hypothesis that it is the result of an accelerated →greenhouse effect caused by atmospheric pollutants, especially carbon dioxide gas. Recent melting and collapse of the Larsen Ice Shelf, Antarctica, is a consequence of global warming. Melting of ice is expected to raise sea level in the coming decades.

**glucose** (or dextrose or grape sugar) $C_6H_{12}O_6$, sugar present in the blood and manufactured by green plants during →photosynthesis. The →respiration reactions inside cells involves the oxidation of glucose to produce →ATP, the 'energy molecule' used to drive many of the body's biochemical reactions.

**glycerol** (or glycerine or propan-1,2,3-triol) $HOCH_2CH(OH)CH_2OH$, thick, colourless, odourless, sweetish liquid. It is obtained from vegetable and animal oils and fats (by treatment with acid, alkali, superheated steam, or an enzyme), or by fermentation of glucose, and is used in the manufacture of high explosives, in antifreeze solutions, to maintain moist conditions in fruits and tobacco, and in cosmetics.

**gneiss** coarse-grained →metamorphic rock, formed under conditions of high temperature and pressure, and often occurring in association with schists and granites. It has a foliated, or layered, structure consisting of thin bands of micas and/or amphiboles (rock-forming silicate minerals) dark in colour alternating with bands of granular quartz and feldspar that are light in colour. Gneisses are formed during regional metamorphism; **paragneisses** are derived from metamorphism of sedimentary rocks and **orthogneisses** from metamorphism of granite or similar igneous rocks.

**Gnosticism** esoteric cult of divine knowledge (a synthesis of Christianity, Greek philosophy, Hinduism, Buddhism, and the mystery cults of the Mediterranean), which flourished during the 2nd and 3rd centuries and was a rival to, and influence on, early Christianity. The medieval French Cathar heresy and the modern Mandean sect (in southern Iraq) descend from Gnosticism.

**Gobi** vast desert region of Central Asia in the independent state of Mongolia, and Inner Mongolia, China. It covers an area of 1,280,000 sq km/500,000 sq mi (800 km/500 mi north–south and 1,600 km/1,000 mi east–west), and lies on a high plateau 900–1,500 m/ 2,950–4,920 ft above sea level. It is mainly rocky, with shifting sands and salt marshes at lower levels. The desert is sparsely populated, mainly by nomadic herders. It is rich in the fossil remains of extinct species, and Stone Age implements.

**Gobind Singh** (1666–1708) Indian religious leader, the tenth and last guru (teacher) of Sikhism, 1675–1708, and founder of the Sikh brotherhood known as the Khalsa. On his death, the Sikh holy book, the *Guru Granth Sahib*, replaced the line of human gurus as the teacher and guide of the Sikh community.

**Goebbels, (Paul) Joseph** (1897–1945) German Nazi leader. As minister of propaganda from 1933, he brought all cultural and educational activities under Nazi control and built up sympathetic movements abroad to carry on the 'war of nerves' against Hitler's intended victims. On the capture of Berlin by the Allies, he committed suicide.

**Goethe, Johann Wolfgang von** (1749–1832) German poet, novelist, dramatist, and scholar. He is generally considered the founder of modern German literature, and was the leader of the Romantic *Sturm und Drang* movement. His masterpiece is the poetic play *Faust* (1808 and 1832). His other works include the partly autobiographical *Die Leiden des Jungen Werthers/The Sorrows of the Young Werther* (1774); the classical dramas *Iphigenie auf Tauris/Iphigenia in Tauris* (1787), *Egmont* (1788), and *Torquato Tasso* (1790); the *Wilhelm Meister* novels (1795–1829); the short novel *Die Wahlverwandschaften/Elective Affinities* (1809); and scientific treatises including *Farbenlehre/Treatise on Colour* (1810).

**Gogh, Vincent (Willem) van** (1853–1890) Dutch post-Impressionist painter. He began painting in the 1880s, his early works often being sombre depictions of peasant life, such as *The Potato Eaters* (1885; Van Gogh Museum, Amsterdam). Influenced by the Impressionists and by Japanese prints, he developed a freer style characterized by intense colour and expressive brushwork, as seen in his *Sunflowers* series (1888). His influence on modern art, particularly on expressionism, has been immense.

**goitre** enlargement of the thyroid gland seen as a swelling on the neck. It is most pronounced in simple goitre, which is caused by iodine deficiency. More common is toxic goitre or hyperthyroidism, caused by overactivity of the thyroid gland.

**gold** heavy, precious, yellow, metallic element; symbol Au (from Latin *aurum*, 'gold'), atomic number 79, relative atomic mass 197.0. It occurs in nature frequently as a free metal and is highly resistant to acids, tarnishing, and corrosion. Pure gold is the most malleable of all metals and is used as gold leaf or powder, where small amounts cover vast surfaces, such as gilded domes and statues.

The elemental form is so soft that it is alloyed for strength with a number of other metals, such as silver, copper, and platinum. Its purity is then measured in →carats on a scale of 24 (24 carats is pure gold). It is used mainly for decorative purposes (jewellery, gilding) but also for coinage, dentistry, and conductivity in electronic devices.

**Golding, William Gerald** (1911–1993) English novelist. His work is often principally concerned with the fundamental corruption and evil inherent in human nature. His first book, *Lord of the Flies* (1954; filmed in 1962), concerns the degeneration into savagery of a group of English schoolboys marooned on a Pacific island after their plane crashes; it is a chilling allegory about the savagery lurking beneath the thin veneer of modern 'civilized' life. *Pincher Martin* (1956) is a study of greed and self-delusion. Later novels include *The Spire* (1964). He was awarded the Nobel Prize for Literature in 1983 and knighted in 1988.

**Goldsmith, Oliver** (1728–1774) Irish playwright, novelist, poet, and essayist. His works include the novel *The Vicar of Wakefield* (1766), an outwardly artless and gentle story which is also social and political satire, and in which rural honesty, kindness, and patience triumph over urban values; it became one of the most popular works of fiction in English. Other works include the poem 'The Deserted Village' (1770) and the play *She Stoops to Conquer* (1773). In 1761 Goldsmith met Samuel →Johnson and became a member of his circle.

**golf** outdoor game in which a small rubber-cored ball is hit with a wooden- or iron-faced club into a series of holes using the least number of shots. On the first shot for each hole, the ball is hit from a tee, which elevates the ball slightly off the ground; subsequent strokes are played off the ground. Most courses have 18 holes and are approximately 5,500 m/6,000 yd in length. Golf developed in Scotland in the 15th century.

**Good Hope, Cape of** South African headland forming a peninsula between Table Bay and False Bay, Cape Town. The first European to sail around it was Bartolomeu →Diaz 1488. Formerly named Cape of Storms, it was given its present name by King John II of Portugal.

**Gorbachev, Mikhail Sergeyevich** (1931– ) Soviet president, in power 1985–91. He was a member of the Politburo from 1980. As general secretary of the Communist Party (CPSU) 1985–91 and president of the Supreme Soviet 1988–91, he introduced liberal reforms at home ( →perestroika and →glasnost), proposed the introduction of multiparty democracy, and attempted to halt the arms race abroad. He became head of state in 1989. He was awarded the Nobel Peace Prize in 1990.

**gorilla** largest of the apes, found in the dense forests of West Africa and mountains of central Africa. The male stands about 1.8 m/6 ft high and weighs about 200 kg/450 lb. Females are about half this size. The body is covered with blackish hair, silvered on the back in older males. Gorillas live in family groups; they are vegetarian, highly

---

**WEB SITE** > > > > > > > >
**Gorilla**
http://www.seaworld.org/animal_bytes/gorillaab.html
Illustrated guide to the gorilla including information about genus, size, life span, habitat, gestation, diet, and a series of fun facts.

intelligent, and will attack only in self-defence. They are dwindling in numbers, being shot for food by some local people, or by poachers taking young for zoos, but protective measures are having some effect. (Species *Gorilla gorilla*.)

**Gorky, Maxim** (1868–1936) pen-name of Alexei Maximovich Peshkov, Russian writer. Born in Nizhniy-Novgorod (named Gorky 1932–90 in his honour), he was exiled 1906–13 for his revolutionary principles. His works, which include the play *The Lower Depths* (1902) and the memoir *My Childhood* (1913–14), combine realism with optimistic faith in the potential of the industrial proletariat.

**Gospel** (Middle English 'good news') in the New Testament generally, the message of Christian salvation; in particular the four written accounts of the life of Jesus by Matthew, Mark, Luke, and John. Although the first three give approximately the same account or synopsis (thus giving rise to the name 'Synoptic Gospels'), their differences from John have raised problems for theologians.

**Goth** East Germanic people who settled near the Black Sea around AD 2nd century. There are two branches, the eastern Ostrogoths and the western Visigoths. The **Ostrogoths** were conquered by the Huns 372. They regained their independence in 454 and under Theodoric the Great conquered Italy 488–93; they disappeared as a nation after the Byzantine emperor Justinian I reconquered Italy 535–55.

The **Visigoths** migrated to Thrace. Under Alaric they raided Greece and Italy 395–410, sacked Rome, and established a kingdom in southern France. Expelled from there by the Franks, they established a Spanish kingdom which lasted until the Moorish conquest of 711.

**Gothic architecture** style of architecture that flourished in Europe from the mid-12th century to the end of the 15th century. It is characterized by the vertical lines of tall pillars and spires, greater height in interior spaces, the pointed arch, rib vaulting, and the flying buttress.

**Goya, Francisco José de Goya y Lucientes** (1746–1828) Spanish painter and engraver. One of the major figures of European art, Goya depicted all aspects of Spanish life – portraits, including those of the royal family, religious works, scenes of war and of everyday life. Towards the end of his life, he created strange, nightmarish works, the 'Black Paintings', with such horrific images as *Saturn Devouring One of His Sons* (about 1822; Prado, Madrid). His series of etchings include *The Disasters of War* (1810–14), depicting the horrors of the French invasion of Spain.

**Grace, W(illiam) G(ilbert)** (1848–1915) English cricketer. By profession a doctor, he became the most famous sportsman in Victorian England. A right-handed batsman, he began playing first-class cricket at the age of 16, scored 152 runs in his first Test match, and scored the first triple century in

1876. Throughout his career, which lasted nearly 45 years, he scored 54,896 runs and took 2,876 wickets.

**career highlights: all first-class cricket:** runs: 54,896; average: 39.55; best: 344 (MCC v. Kent 1876); wickets: 2,876; average: 17.92; best: 10–49 (MCC v. Oxford University 1886); **Test cricket:** runs: 1,098; average: 32.29; best: 170 (v. Australia 1886); wickets: 9; average: 26.22; best: 2–12 (v. Australia 1890).

**Grahame, Kenneth** (1859–1932) Scottish-born writer. The early volumes of sketches of childhood, *The Golden Age* (1895) and *Dream Days* (1898), were followed by his masterpiece *The Wind in the Willows* (1908) which became a children's classic. Begun as a bedtime story for his son, it is a charming tale of life on the river bank, with its blend of naturalistic style and fantasy, and its memorable animal characters, the practical Rat, Mole, Badger, and conceited, bombastic Toad. It was dramatized by A A Milne as *Toad of Toad Hall* (1929) and by Alan Bennett in 1990.

**Grand Canyon** gorge in northwestern Arizona, USA, containing the Colorado River. It is 350 km/217 mi long, 6–29 km/4–18 mi wide, and reaches depths of over 1.7 km/1.1 mi. The gorge cuts through a multicoloured series of rocks – mainly limestones, sandstones, and shales, and ranging in age from the Precambrian to the Cretaceous – and various harder strata stand out as steps on its slopes. It is one of the country's most popular national parks and millions of tourists visit it each year.

**granite** coarse-grained intrusive →igneous rock, typically consisting of the minerals quartz, feldspar, and biotite mica. It may be pink or grey, depending on the composition of the feldspar. Granites are chiefly used as building materials.

**Grant, Cary** (1904–1986) stage name of Archibald Alexander Leach, English-born actor, a US citizen from 1942. His witty, debonair personality made him a screen favourite for more than three decades. Among his many films are *She Done Him Wrong* (1933), *Bringing Up Baby* (1938), *The Philadelphia Story* (1940), *Notorious* (1946), *To Catch a Thief* (1955), *North by Northwest* (1959), and *Charade* (1963).

**graphical user interface** (GUI) in computing, a type of user interface in which programs and files appear as icons (small pictures), user options are selected from pull-down menus, and data are displayed in windows (rectangular areas), which the operator can manipulate in various ways. The operator uses a pointing device, typically a mouse, to make selections and initiate actions.

**grass** any of a very large family of plants, many of which are economically important because they provide grazing for animals and food for humans in the form of cereals. There are about 9,000 species distributed worldwide except in the Arctic regions. Most are perennial, with long, narrow leaves and jointed, hollow stems; flowers with both male and female reproductive organs are borne on spikelets; the fruits are grain-like. Included in the family are blue-grass, wheat, rye, maize, sugarcane, and bamboo. (Family Gramineae.)

**gravity** force of attraction that arises between objects by virtue of their masses. On Earth, gravity is the force of attraction between any object in the Earth's gravitational field and the Earth itself. It is regarded as one of the four fundamental →forces of nature, the other three being the →electromagnetic force, the strong nuclear force, and the weak nuclear force. The gravitational force is the weakest of the four forces, but it acts over great distances. The particle that is postulated as the carrier of the gravitational force is the graviton.

---

### WEB SITE > > > > > > > >
#### Exploring Gravity
http://www.curtin.edu.au/curtin/dept/phys-sci/gravity/index2.html

Interactive tour of all things related to gravity. The site includes quizzes and photos and covers 'Introductory', 'Intermediate', and 'Advanced' stages of study.

---

**Great Barrier Reef** chain of coral reefs and islands over 2,000 km/1,250 mi long, in the Coral Sea, off the east coast of Queensland, Australia, about 16–241 km/10–150 mi offshore. The Great Barrier Reef is made up of 3,000 individual reefs, and is believed to be the world's largest living organism. Only ten navigable channels break through the reef. The

most valuable products of the reef are pearls, pearl shells, trepangs (edible sea slugs), and sponges. The reef is popular with tourists. In 1976 it became a Marine Park and was declared a World Heritage Site by UNESCO in 1981.

**Great Lakes** series of five freshwater lakes along the USA–Canadian border: Superior, Michigan, Huron, →Erie, and →Ontario; total area 245,000 sq km/94,600 sq mi. Interconnected by a network of canals and rivers, the lakes are navigable by large ships, and they are connected with the Atlantic Ocean via the St Lawrence River and by the St Lawrence Seaway (completed in 1959), which is navigable by medium-sized ocean-going ships. In March 1998 a bill was passed through Congress designating Lake Champlain the sixth Great Lake, although controversy over this continues.

**Great Rift Valley** volcanic valley formed 10–20 million years ago owing to rifting of the Earth's crust and running about 8,000 km/5,000 mi from the Jordan Valley through the Red Sea to central Mozambique in southeast Africa. It is marked by a series of lakes, including Lake Turkana (formerly Lake Rudolf), and volcanoes, such as Mount Kilimanjaro. The rift system associated with the Rift Valley extends into northern Botswana, with geological faults controlling the location of the Okavango Delta.

**Great Trek** in South African history, the movement of 12,000–14,000 Boer (Dutch) settlers from Cape Colony

1835 and 1845 to escape British rule. They established republics in Natal and the Transvaal. It is seen by many white South Africans as the main event in the founding of the present republic and was cited as a justification for whites-only rule.

**Greco, El** (1541–1614) name given to Doménikos Theotokopoulos, Spanish painter called 'the Greek' because he was born in Crete. He studied in Italy, worked in Rome from about 1570, and by 1577 had settled in Toledo. He painted elegant portraits and intensely emotional religious scenes with increasingly distorted figures and unearthly light, such as *The Burial of Count Orgaz* (1586, Church of S Tomé, Toledo).

**Greece** Hellenic Republic; **national name:** *Elliniki Dimokratia*; **area:** 131,957 sq km/50,948 sq mi; **capital:** Athens; **major towns/cities:** Thessaloníki, Piraeus, Patras, Irákleion, Larissa, Volos; **major ports:** Piraeus, Thessaloníki, Patras, Irákleion; **physical features:** mountainous (Mount Olympus); a large number of islands, notably Crete, Corfu, and Rhodes, and Cyclades and Ionian Islands; **head of state:** Costis Stephanopoulos from 1995; **head of government:** Costas Simitis from 1996; **political system:** democracy; **currency:** drachma; **GNP per capita (PPP):** (US$) 13,010 (1998); **exports:** fruit and vegetables, clothing, mineral fuels and lubricants, textiles, iron and steel, aluminium and aluminium alloys. Principal market Germany 25.2% (1997); **population:** 10,626,000 (1999 est); **language:** Greek (official), Macedonian

(100,000–200,000 est); **religion:** Greek Orthodox; also Roman Catholic; **life expectancy:** 76 (men); 81 (women) (1995–2000).

**Greece, ancient** ancient civilization that flourished 2,500 years ago on the shores of the Ionian and Aegean Seas (modern Greece and the west coast of Turkey). Although its population never exceeded 2 million, ancient Greece made great innovations in philosophy, politics, science, architecture, and the arts, and Greek culture forms the basis of western civilization to this day.

**Greek architecture** the architecture of ancient Greece is the base for virtually all architectural developments in Europe. The Greeks invented the entablature, which allowed roofs to be hipped (inverted V-shape), and perfected the design of arcades with support columns. There were three styles, or orders, of columns: Doric (with no base), Ionic (with scrolled capitals), and Corinthian (with acanthus-leafed capitals).

**Greek language** member of the Indo-European language family, which has passed through at least five distinct phases since the 2nd millennium BC: **ancient Greek** 14th–12th centuries BC; **Archaic Greek**, including Homeric epic language, until 800 BC; **classical Greek** until 400 BC; **hellenistic Greek**, the common language of Greece, Asia Minor, West Asia, and Egypt to the 4th century AD, and **Byzantine Greek**, used until the 15th century and still the ecclesiastical language of the Greek Orthodox Church. **Modern Greek** is principally divided into the general vernacular (**demotic Greek**) and the language of education and literature (**Katharevousa**).

**Greek Orthodox Church** see →Orthodox Church.

**Greene, Maurice** (1974–  ) US athlete who in Athens, Greece, set a new 100 metres world record of 9.79 seconds (July 1999). A month later at the World Championships in Seville, Spain, he became the first person to win gold medals in both the men's 100 and 200 metres, and he won a third gold as a member of the US sprint relay team.
**career highlights:  World Championship:** gold 100 metres 1997, 1999; gold 200 metres 1999; gold 4 × 100 metres relay 1999; **World Indoor Games:** gold 60 metres 1999.

**greenhouse effect** phenomenon of the Earth's atmosphere by which solar radiation, trapped by the Earth and re-emitted from the surface as infrared radiation, is prevented from escaping by various gases in the air. Greenhouse gases trap heat because they readily absorb infrared radiation. The result is a rise in the Earth's temperature ( →global warming). The main greenhouse gases are carbon dioxide, methane, and →chlorofluorocarbons (CFCs) as well as water vapour. Fossil-fuel consumption and forest fires are the principal causes of carbon dioxide build-up; methane is a by product of agriculture (rice, cattle, sheep).

**Greenwich Mean Time** (GMT) local time on the zero line of longitude (the **Greenwich meridian**), which passes through the Old Royal Observatory at Greenwich, London. It was replaced in 1986 by coordinated universal time (UTC), but continued to be used to measure longitudes and the world's standard time zones.

**Gregorian chant** any of a body of plainsong choral chants associated with Pope Gregory the Great (540–604), which became standard in the Roman Catholic Church.

**Gregory (I) the Great** (c. 540–604) St Gregory, pope from 590 who asserted Rome's supremacy and exercised almost imperial powers. In 596 he sent St Augustine to England. He introduced the choral **Gregorian chant** into the liturgy. Feast day 12 March.

**Grenada** area: (including the southern Grenadine Islands, notably Carriacou and Petit Martinique) 344 sq km 133 sq mi; **capital:** St George's; **major**

---

**WEB SITE** > > > > > > > >

**The Greenhouse Effect**
**How the Earth Stays Warm**

http://www.enviroweb.org/edf/
ishappening/greeneffect/index.html

Explanation of the greenhouse effect, the process by which atmospheric gases trap heat. This page links to a description of how this perfectly normal and essential process is being turned into something harmful by the pollutants humans put into the atmosphere. It also explains that related phenomenon, the hole in the ozone layer.

---

**towns/cities:** Grenville, Sauteurs, Victoria, Hillsborough (Carriacou); **physical features:** southernmost of the Windward Islands; mountainous; Grand-Anse beach; Annandale Falls; the Great Pool volcanic crater; **head of state:** Elizabeth II from 1974, represented by governor general Daniel Williams from 1996; **head of government:** Keith Mitchell from 1995; **political system:** emergent democracy; **currency:** Eastern Caribbean dollar; **GNP per capita (PPP):** (US$) 4,720 (1998); **exports:** cocoa, bananas, mace, fresh fruit. Principal market UK, USA, France 18.5% each (1995); **population:** 97,000 (1999 est); **language:** English (official); some French-African patois spoken; **religion:** Roman Catholic 53%, Anglican, Seventh Day Adventist, Pentecostal; **life expectancy:** 69 (men); 74 (women) (1998 est).

**Grey, Lady Jane** (1537–1554) Queen of England for nine days, 10–19 July 1553, the great-granddaughter of Henry VII. She was married in 1553 to Lord Guildford Dudley (died 1554), son of the Duke of Northumberland. Edward VI was persuaded by Northumberland to set aside the claims to the throne of his sisters Mary and Elizabeth. When Edward died on 6 July 1553, Jane reluctantly accepted the crown and was proclaimed queen four days later. Mary, although a Roman Catholic, had the support of the populace, and the Lord Mayor of London announced that she was queen on 19 July. Grey was executed on Tower Green.

**Grieg, Edvard Hagerup** (1843–1907)

Norwegian nationalist composer. Much of his music is small-scale, particularly his songs, dances, sonatas, and piano works, strongly identifying with Norwegian folk music. Among his orchestral works are the piano concerto in A minor (1869) and the incidental music for Henrik Ibsen's drama *Peer Gynt* (1876), commissioned by Ibsen and the Norwegian government.

**Grimm brothers** Jakob Ludwig Karl (1785–1863) and Wilhelm (1786–1859), philologists and collectors of German fairy tales such as 'Hansel and Gretel' and 'Rumpelstiltskin'. Joint compilers of an exhaustive dictionary of German, they saw the study of language and the collecting of folk tales as strands in a single enterprise.

**Gropius, Walter Adolf** (1883–1969) German architect, in the USA from 1937. He was an early exponent of the international style, defined by glass curtain walls, cubic blocks, and unsupported corners. A founder director of the Bauhaus school in Weimar 1919–28, he advocated teamwork in design and artistic standards in industrial production. He was responsible for the new Bauhaus premises in Dessau 1925–26.

**gross domestic product** (GDP) value of the output of all goods and services produced within a nation's borders, normally given as a total for the year. It thus includes the production of foreign-owned firms within the country, but excludes the income from domestically owned firms located abroad. See also →gross national product.

**gross national product** (GNP) the most commonly used measurement of the wealth of a country. GNP is defined as the total value of all goods and services produced by firms owned by the country concerned. It is measured as the →gross domestic product plus income from abroad, minus income earned during the same period by foreign investors within the country.

**Guadeloupe** group of seven islands in the Leeward Islands, West Indies, an overseas *département* of France. The main islands are Basse-Terre and Grande-Terre; **area:** 1,705 sq km/658 sq mi; **chief town:** The chief town and seat of government is Basse-Terre (on the island of the same name), population (1988) 14,000; **population:** (1997 est) 411,800 (77% mulatto, 10% black, and 10% mestizo). The people of St Barthélemy and Les Saintes are mainly descended from 17th century Norman and Breton settlers; **languages:** French (official); Creole (the main language); **industries:** sugar refining and rum distilling; agriculture (major crops include sugar cane, bananas, aubergines, and sweet potatoes).

**Guatemala** Republic of; **national name:** *República de Guatemala*; **area:** 108,889 sq km/42,042 sq mi; **capital:** Guatemala City; **major towns/cities:** Quezaltenango, Escuintla, Puerto Barrios (naval base), Retalhuleu, Chiquimula; **physical features:** mountainous; narrow coastal plains; limestone tropical plateau in north; frequent earthquakes; **head of state and government:** Alfonso Portillo from 1999; **political system:** democracy; **currency:** quetzal; **GNP per capita (PPP):** (US$) 4,070 (1998); **exports:** coffee, bananas, sugar, cardamoms, shellfish, tobacco. Principal market USA 35.8% (1997); **population:** 11,090,000 (1999 est); **language:** Spanish (official) 45% speak Mayan languages; **religion:** Roman Catholic 70%, Protestant 30%; **life expectancy:** 61 (men); 67 (women) (1995–2000).

**Guatemala City** capital of Guatemala situated in the **Guatemalan Highlands** at an altitude of 1,500 m/4,921 ft; population (1990 est) 1,675,600. A group of volcanoes overlooks the city: Acatenango (3,976 m/13,044 ft); Fuego (3,763 m, 12,346 ft); Agua (3,760 m/12,336 ft). Industries include textiles, tyres, silverware, footwear, and cement. Half of the industrial output of Guatemala emanate from Guatemala City. It was founded in 1776 as Guatemala's third capital after earthquakes destroyed the earlier capital of Antigua and Cuidad Vieja in 1773 and 1542 respectively. It was itself severely damaged by subsequent earthquakes in 1917–18, and 1976.

**Guevara, Che (Ernesto)** (1928–1967) Latin American revolutionary. He was born in Resario, Argentina, and trained there as a doctor, but left his homeland in 1953 because of his opposition to the right-wing president Juan Perón. In effecting the Cuban revolution of 1959 against the Cuban dictator Fulgencio Batista, he was second only to Castro and Castro's brother Raúl. Between 1961 and 1965, he served as Cuba's ministry of industry. In 1965 he went to the Congo to fight against white mercenaries, and then to Bolivia, where he was killed in an unsuccessful attempt to lead a peasant rising near Vallegrande. He was an orthodox Marxist and renowned for his guerrilla techniques.

**guild** (or gild) medieval association, particularly of artisans or merchants, formed for mutual aid and protection and the pursuit of a common purpose, religious or economic. Guilds became politically powerful in Europe but after the 16th century their position was undermined by the growth of capitalism.

**Guinea** Republic of; **national name:** *République de Guinée;* **area:** 245,857 sq km/94,925 sq mi; **capital:** Conakry; **major towns/cities:** Labé, Nzérékoré, Kankan, Kindia; **physical features:** flat coastal plain with mountainous interior; sources of rivers Niger, Gambia, and Senegal; forest in southeast; Fouta Djallon, area of sandstone plateaux, cut by deep valleys; **head of state:** Lansana Conté from 1984; **head of government:** Lamine Sidime from 1999; **political system:** emergent democracy; **currency:** Guinean franc; **GNP per capita (PPP):** (US$) 1,760 (1998); **exports:** bauxite, alumina, diamonds, coffee. Principal market Russia 16.7% (1997); **population:** 7,359,000 (1999 est); **language:** French (official), African languages (of which eight are official); **religion:** Muslim 95%, Christian; **life expectancy:** 46 (men); 47 (women) (1995–2000).

**Guinea-Bissau** Republic of (formerly Portuguese Guinea); **national name:** *República da Guiné-Bissau;* **area:** 36,125 sq km/13,947 sq mi; **capital:** Bissau (main port); **major towns/cities:** Mansôa, São Domingos, Bolama/Bijagós, Catio, Buba, Butata, Farim, Cacine; **physical features:** flat coastal plain rising to savanna in east; **head of state:** Malan Bacai Sanha from 1999; **head of government:** Francisco Fadul from 1998; **political system:** emergent democracy; **currency:** Guinean peso; **GNP per capita (PPP):** (US$) 750 (1998); **exports:** cashew nuts, palm kernels, groundnuts, fish and shrimp, timber. Principal market India 59.1% (1997); **population:** 1,187,000 (1999 est); **language:** Portuguese (official); Crioulo (Cape Verdean dialect of Portuguese), African languages; **religion:** animist 65%, Muslim 38%, Christian 5% (mainly Roman Catholic); **life expectancy:** 44 (men); 47 (women) (1995–2000).

**guitar** flat-bodied musical instrument with six or twelve strings which are plucked or strummed with the fingers. The fingerboard is usually fretted, although some modern electric guitars are fretless. The Hawaiian guitar is laid across the player's lap, and uses a metal bar to produce a distinctive gliding tone. The solid-bodied electric guitar, developed in the 1950s by Les Paul and Leo Fender, mixes and amplifies vibrations from electromagnetic pickups at different points to produce a range of tone qualities.

**Gujarat** (or Gujerat) state of west India, formed from north and west Mumbai state in 1960; bordered to the north by Pakistan and the Rajasthan state, with

Madhya Pradesh and Maharashtra states to the east and southeast; **area:** 196,000 sq km/75,656 sq mi; **capital:** Gandhinagar (founded 1961); **major towns:** →Ahmadabad, Vadodara; main port Kandla; **physical:** includes most of the arid Rann of Kutch and the peninsula of Kathiawar, a low basalt plateau; the more fertile southwestern plain watered by the Tapti and Narmada rivers, which have contributed to the silting and decline in trading importance of the Gulf of Khambhat; the Gir Forest (the last home of the wild Asian lion); **features:** heavily industrialized; there are six universities in the state; **agriculture:** wheat, millet, cotton, rice, maize, tobacco, groundnuts, fishing; irrigation schemes such as the Kakrapara canal have allowed a food surplus to be produced in most areas; **industries:** petrochemicals, oil (from Kalol, refined at Koyali near Baroda), gas, textiles, coal, limestone, pharmaceuticals, soda ash, electrical engineering, machine tools, cement, fertilizers; dairy industry using imported and local milk; **language:** Gujarati (or Gujerati) (20 million speakers), Hindi; **population:** (1995 est) 44,568,000 (90% Hindu); **history:** →Indus valley civilization settlements dating from the 3rd and 2nd millennia BC have been found at Lothal on the Gulf of Khambhat and more recently at Kuntasi near Morvi; subsequently there was a succession of ruling groups until the British took control in 1818; after independence the area was part of the former Mumbai state, but demands for a separate Gujarati-speaking state were met in 1960.

**Gulf States** oil-rich countries sharing the coastline of the →Gulf (Bahrain, Iran, Iraq, Kuwait, Oman, Qatar, Saudi Arabia, and the United Arab Emirates). In the USA, the term refers to those states bordering the Gulf of Mexico (Alabama, Florida, Louisiana, Mississippi, and Texas).

**Gulf Stream** warm ocean →current that flows north from the warm waters of the Gulf of Mexico along the east coast of America, from which it is separated by a channel of cold water originating in the southerly Labrador current. Off Newfoundland, part of the current is diverted east across the Atlantic, where it is known as the **North Atlantic Drift**, dividing to flow north and south, and warming what would otherwise be a colder climate in the British Isles and northwest Europe.

**Gulf War** war 16 January–28 February 1991 between Iraq and a coalition of 28 nations led by the USA. The invasion and annexation of Kuwait by Iraq on 2 August 1990 provoked a build-up of US troops in Saudi Arabia, eventually totalling over 500,000. The UK subsequently deployed 42,000 troops, France 15,000, Egypt 20,000, and other nations smaller contingents.

An air offensive lasting six weeks, in which 'smart' weapons came of age, destroyed about one-third of Iraqi equipment and inflicted massive casualties. A 100-hour ground war followed which effectively destroyed the remnants of the 500,000-strong Iraqi army in or near Kuwait.

***Guru Granth Sahib*** the holy book of Sikhism, a collection of nearly 6,000 hymns by the first five and the ninth Sikh gurus, but also including the writings of some Hindus and Muslims. It is regarded as a living guru and treated with the respect that this implies.

**Gutenberg, Johannes** (*c.* 1398–1468) (Gensfleisch) German printer, the inventor of European printing from movable metal type (although Laurens Janszoon Coster has a rival claim).

**Guyana** Cooperative Republic of; **area:** 214,969 sq km/82,999 sq mi; **capital:** Georgetown (and port); **major towns/cities:** Linden, New Amsterdam, Rose Hall, Corriverton; **major ports:** New Amsterdam; **physical features:** coastal plain rises into rolling highlands with savanna in south; mostly tropical rainforest; Mount Roraima; Kaietur National Park, including Kaietur Falls on the Potaro (tributary of Essequibo) 250 m/821 ft; **head of state:** Janet Jagan from 1997; **head of government:** Samuel Hinds from 1992; **political system:** democracy; **currency:** Guyana dollar; **GNP per capita (PPP):** (US$) 2,680 (1998); **exports:** sugar, bauxite, alumina, rice, gold, rum, timber, molasses, shrimp. Principal market Canada 24.2% (1997); **population:** 855,000 (1999 est); **language:** English (official), Hindi, American Indian languages; **religion:** Hindu 54%, Christian 27%, Sunni Muslim 15%; **life

expectancy:** 61 (men); 68 (women) (1995–2000).

**gymnastics** physical exercises, originally for health and training (so called from the way in which men of ancient Greece trained: *gymnos* 'naked'). The *gymnasia* were schools for training competitors for public games.

**Men's gymnastics** includes high bar, parallel bars, horse vault, rings, pommel horse, and floor exercises. **Women's gymnastics** includes asymmetrical bars, side horse vault, balance beam, and floor exercises. Also popular are **sports acrobatics**, performed by gymnasts in pairs, trios, or fours to music, where the emphasis is on dance, balance, and timing, and **rhythmic gymnastics**, choreographed to music and performed by individuals or six-girl teams, with small hand apparatus such as a ribbon, ball, or hoop.

**gymnosperm** (Greek 'naked seed') in botany, any plant whose seeds are exposed, as opposed to the structurally more advanced →angiosperms, where they are inside an ovary. The group includes conifers and related plants such as cycads and ginkgos, whose seeds develop in →cones. Fossil gymnosperms have been found in rocks about 350 million years old.

**gynaecology** medical speciality concerned with disorders of the female reproductive system.

# Hh

**Haarlem** industrial city and capital of the province of North Holland, the Netherlands, 20 km/12 mi west of Amsterdam; population (1997) 147,400. At Velsea, to the north, a road and rail tunnel runs under the North Sea Canal, linking North and South Holland. Industries include chemicals, pharmaceuticals, textiles, and printing. Haarlem is in an area of flowering bulbs and has a 15th–16th-century cathedral and a Frans Hals museum.

**Haber, Fritz** (1868–1934) German chemist whose conversion of atmospheric nitrogen to ammonia opened the way for the synthetic fertilizer industry. His study of the combustion of hydrocarbons led to the commercial 'cracking' or fractional distillation of natural oil (petroleum) into its components (for example, diesel, petrol, and paraffin). In electrochemistry, he was the first to demonstrate that oxidation and reduction take place at the electrodes; from this he developed a general electrochemical theory.

**hacking** unauthorized access to a computer, either for fun or for malicious or fraudulent purposes. Hackers generally use microcomputers and telephone lines to obtain access. In computing, the term is used in a wider sense to mean using software for enjoyment or self-education, not necessarily involving unauthorized access. The most destructive form of hacking is the introduction of a computer virus.

**Hades** in Greek mythology, the underworld where spirits (shades) went after death, usually depicted as a cavern or pit underneath the Earth, the entrance of which was guarded by the three-headed dog Cerberus. It was presided over by the god →Pluto, originally also known as Hades (Roman Dis). Pluto was the brother of Zeus and married Persephone, daughter of Demeter and Zeus.

**Hadrian, Publius Aelius Hadrianus** (AD 76–138) Roman emperor 117–138. He was adopted by the emperor Trajan, whom he succeeded. He pursued a policy of non-expansion and consolidation after the vast conquests of Trajan's reign. His defensive policy aimed at fixing the boundaries of the empire, which included the building of Hadrian's Wall in Britain. He travelled more widely than any other emperor, and consolidated both the army and Roman administration.

**Hadrian's Wall** line of fortification built by the Roman emperor Hadrian (reigned AD 117–38) across northern Britain from the Cumbrian coast on the west to the North Sea on the east. The wall itself ran from Bowness on the Solway Firth to Wallsend on the river Tyne, a distance of 110 km/68 mi. It was defended by 16 forts and smaller intermediate fortifications. It was breached by the Picts on several occasions and finally abandoned in about 383.

**haemophilia** any of several inherited diseases in which normal blood clotting is impaired. The sufferer experiences prolonged bleeding from the slightest wound, as well as painful internal bleeding without apparent cause.

**haemorrhage** loss of blood from the circulatory system. It is 'manifest' when the blood can be seen, as when it flows from a wound, and 'occult' when the bleeding is internal, as from an ulcer or internal injury.

**Haile Selassie, Ras (Prince) Tafari** (1892–1975) 'the Lion of Judah', emperor of Ethiopia 1930–74. He pleaded unsuccessfully to the League of Nations against the Italian conquest of his country 1935–36, and was then deposed and fled to the UK. He went to Egypt in 1940 and raised an army, which he led into Ethiopia in January 1941 alongside British forces and was restored to the throne on 5 May. He was deposed by a military coup in 1974 and died in captivity the following year. Followers of the Rastafarian religion (see →Rastafarianism) believe that he was the Messiah, the incarnation of God (Jah).

**half-life** during radioactive decay, the time in which the strength of a radioactive source decays to half its original value. In theory, the decay process is never complete and there is always some residual radioactivity. For this reason, the half-life of a radioactive isotope is measured, rather than the total decay time. It may vary from millionths of a second to billions of years.

**Haiti** Republic of; **national name:** *République d'Haïti;* **area:** 27,750 sq km/ 10,714 sq mi; **capital:** Port-au-Prince; **major towns/cities:** Cap-Haïtien, Gonaïves, Les Cayes, Port-de-Paix, Jérémie, Jacmée, St Marc; **physical features:** mainly mountainous and tropical; occupies western third of Hispaniola Island in Caribbean Sea; **head of state:** René Préval from 1996; **head of government:** Jacques Edouard Alexis from 1998; **political system:** transitional; **currency:** gourde; **GNP per capita (PPP):** (US$) 1,250 (1998 est); **exports:** manufactured articles, coffee, essential oils, sisal. Principal market USA 81.4% (1997); **population:** 8,087,000 (1999 est); **language:** French (official, spoken by literate 10% minority), Creole (official); **religion:** Christian 95% (of which 80% are Roman Catholic), voodoo 4%; **life expectancy:** 51 (men); 56 (women) (1995–2000).

**Halley, Edmond** (1656–1742) English astronomer. He not only identified the comet that was later to be known by his name, but also compiled a star catalogue, detected the proper motion of stars using historical records, and began a line of research that, after his death, resulted in a reasonably accurate calculation of the astronomical unit.

**halogen** any of a group of five non-metallic elements with similar chemical bonding properties: fluorine, chlorine, bromine, iodine, and astatine. They form a linked group in the →periodic table of the elements, descending from fluorine, the most reactive, to astatine, the least reactive. They combine directly with most metals to form salts, such as common salt (NaCl). Each halogen has seven electrons in its valence shell, which accounts for the chemical similarities displayed by the group.

**Hamburg** largest inland port of Europe, in Germany, on the Elbe and Alster rivers, 103 km/64 mi from the mouth of the Elbe; population (1995) 1,706,800. Industries include marine engineering, ship-repairing, oil-refining, printing, publishing, and the production of chemicals, electronics, processed foods, and cosmetics. It is the capital of the *Land* of Hamburg, and has been an archbishopric since 834. In alliance with Lübeck, it founded the →Hanseatic League. The city suffered extensive bomb damage during World War II.

**hammerhead** any of several species of shark found in tropical seas, characterized by having eyes at the ends of flattened hammerlike extensions of the skull. Hammerheads can grow to 4 m/13 ft in length. (Genus *Sphyrna*, family Sphyrnidae.)

**Hampshire** county of south England (since April 1997 Portsmouth and

**hammerhead** The hammerhead shark's name derives from the flattened projections at the side of its head. The eyes are on the outer edges of the projections. The advantages of this head design are not known; it may be that the shark's vision is improved by the wide separation of the eyes, or the head may provide extra lift by acting as an aerofoil.

Southampton have been separate unitary authorities); **area:** 3,679 sq km/1,420 sq mi; **towns and cities:** Winchester (administrative headquarters), Aldershot, Andover, Basingstoke, Eastleigh, Gosport, Romsey, and Lymington; **physical:** New Forest (area 373 sq km/144 sq mi), in the southeast of the county, a Saxon royal hunting ground; rivers Avon, Ichen, and Test (which has trout fishing); **features:** Hampshire Basin, where Britain has onshore and offshore oil; Danebury 2,500-year-old Celtic hill fort; Beaulieu (including National Motor Museum); Broadlands (home of Lord Mountbatten); Highclere castle (home of the Earl of Carnarvon, with gardens by Capability Brown); Hambledon, where the first cricket club was founded in

1750; site of the Roman town of Silchester; Jane Austen's cottage at Chawton (1809–17), now a museum; Twyford Down section of the M3 motorway was completed in 1994 despite protests; **agriculture:** market gardening (watercress); **industries:** aeronautics, brewing, chemicals, electronics, light engineering (at Basingstoke), oil from refineries at Fawley, perfume, pharmaceuticals; **population:** (1996) 1,627,400; **famous people:** Jane Austen, Charles Dickens, Gilbert White.

**Handel, George Frideric** (1685–1759) originally Georg Friedrich Händel, German composer, a British subject from 1726. His first opera, *Almira*, was performed in Hamburg in 1705. In 1710 he was appointed Kapellmeister to the elector of Hannover (the future George I of England). In 1712 he settled in England, where he established his popularity with such works as the *Water Music* (1717), written for George I. His great choral works include the *Messiah* (1742) and the later oratorios *Samson* (1743), *Belshazzar* (1745), *Judas Maccabaeus* (1747), and *Jephtha* (1752).

**Hannibal** (247–182 BC) 'the Great', Carthaginian general from 221 BC, son of Hamilcar Barca. His siege of Saguntum (now Sagunto, near Valencia) precipitated the Second →Punic War with Rome. Following a campaign in Italy (after crossing the Alps in 218), Hannibal was the victor at Trasimene in 217 and Cannae in 216, but he failed to take Rome. In 203 he returned to Carthage to meet a Roman invasion but was defeated at Zama in 202 and exiled in 196 at Rome's insistence.

**Hannover** (or Hanover) industrial city and capital of Lower Saxony, Germany, on the rivers Leine and Ihme; population (1995) 524,600. Industries include mechanical engineering, telecommunications, and the manufacture of electrical goods, rubber, and textiles. From 1386 it was a member of the →Hanseatic League, and from 1692 capital of the electorate of Hannover (created a kingdom in 1815). George I of Great Britain and Ireland was also Elector of Hannover.

**Hanoi** capital of Vietnam, on the Red River; population (1995 est) 2,242,000. Central Hanoi has one of the highest population densities in the world: 1,300 people per hectare/3,250 per acre. Industries include tanning and food processing, especially rice milling.

**Hanseatic League** (German *Hanse* 'group, society') confederation of northern European trading cities from the 12th century to 1669. At its height in the late 14th century the Hanseatic League included over 160 cities and towns, among them Lübeck, Hamburg, Cologne, Breslau, and Kraków. The basis of the league's power was its monopoly of the Baltic trade and its relations with Flanders and England. The decline of the Hanseatic League from the 15th century was caused by the closing and moving of trade routes and the development of nation states.

**haploid** having a single set of →chromosomes in each cell. Most higher organisms are →diploid – that is, they have two sets – but their gametes (sex cells) are haploid. Some plants, such as mosses, liverworts, and many seaweeds, are haploid, and male honey bees are haploid because they develop from eggs that have not been fertilized.

**Harare** (formerly Salisbury) capital of Zimbabwe, in Mashonaland East Province, about 1,525 m/5,000 ft above sea level; population (1992) 1,184,200. It is the centre of a rich farming area producing tobacco and maize. The city's industries include milling, textiles, electrical and mechanical engineering, motor assembly, railway rolling stock, chemicals, furniture, consumer goods, and metallurgical and food processing.

**hard disk** in computing, a storage device usually consisting of a rigid metal →disk coated with a magnetic material. Data are read from and written to the disk by means of a disk drive. The hard disk may be permanently fixed into the drive or in the form of a disk pack that can be removed and exchanged with a different pack. Hard disks vary from large units with capacities of more than 3,000 megabytes, intended for use with mainframe computers, to small units with capacities as low as 20 megabytes, intended for use with microcomputers.

**Hardie, (James) Keir** (1856–1915) Scottish socialist, the first British Labour politician, member of Parliament 1892–95 and 1900–15. He worked in the mines as a boy and in 1886 became secretary of the Scottish Miners' Federation.

In 1888 he was the first Labour candidate to stand for Parliament; he entered Parliament independently as a Labour member in 1892, he became chair of the Labour party 1906–08 and 1909–10, and in 1893 was a chief founder of the Independent Labour Party.

**hardware** mechanical, electrical, and electronic components of a computer system, as opposed to the various programs, which constitute software.

**Hardy, Thomas** (1840–1928) English novelist and poet. His novels, set in rural 'Wessex' (his native West Country), portray intense human relationships played out in a harshly indifferent natural world. They include *Far From the Madding Crowd* (1874), *The Return of the Native* (1878), *The Mayor of Casterbridge* (1886), *The Woodlanders* (1887), *Tess of the d'Urbervilles* (1891), and *Jude the Obscure* (1895). His poetry includes the *Wessex Poems* (1898), the blank-verse epic of the Napoleonic Wars *The Dynasts* (1903–08), and several volumes of lyrics. Many of his books have been successfully dramatized for film and television.

**Harold (II) Godwinson** (*c.* 1020–1066) last Anglo-Saxon king of England, January to October 1066. He was defeated and killed by William of Normandy (William (I) the Conqueror) at the Battle of Hastings.

**harp** plucked musical string instrument, with the strings stretched vertically and parallel to one member of a triangular framework. A second member of the triangle is a wood and brass soundbox of triangular shape; the third member locates pegs by means of which the strings are tensioned. The orchestral harp is the largest instrument of its type. It has up to 47 diatonically tuned strings, in the range B0–C7 (seven octaves), and seven double-action pedals to alter pitch. Before the pedals are depressed, the strings sound the diatonic scale of C♭ major, but each note can be raised a semitone or a whole tone by one of the pedals. Thus all the notes of the chromatic scale can be sounded.

**Harvey, William** (1578–1657) English physician who discovered the circulation of blood. In 1628 he published his book *De motu cordis/On the Motion of the Heart and the Blood in Animals*. He also explored the development of chick and deer embryos.

**Hastings, Battle of** battle on 14 October 1066 at which William, Duke of Normandy ('the Conqueror') defeated King Harold of England, and himself took the throne. The site is 10 km/6 mi inland from Hastings, at Senlac, Sussex; it is marked by Battle Abbey.

**Haute-Normandie** (English Upper Normandy) coastal region of northwest France lying between Basse-Normandie and Picardy and bisected by the River Seine; area 12,300 sq km/4,757 sq mi; population (1990) 1,737,200. It comprises the *départements* of Eure and Seine-Maritime; its administrative centre is Rouen. Ports include Le Havre, Dieppe and Fécamp. The area is fertile and has many beech forests. There is dairy-farming and fishing, cars are manufactured, and the region is a petro-chemical centre.

**Havana** capital and port of Cuba, on the northwest coast of the island; population (1995 est) 2,219,000. Products include cigars and tobacco, sugar, coffee, and fruit. The old city centre is a world heritage site, and the oldest building in the city and in Cuba is La Fuerza, a fortress built in 1538.

**Hawaii** Pacific state of the USA. It is nicknamed the Aloha State. Hawaii was admitted to the Union in 1959 as the 50th US state. The only state not part of North America, Hawaii, variously described as part of Oceania or Polynesia, comprises a west-north-west–east-southeast oriented island chain 2,700km/1,700 mi in length, the east end of which lies some 3,400km/2,100 mi southwest of California. The Tropic of Cancer passes through the islands; **population:** (1995) 1,186,800 (34% of European descent, 25% Japanese, 14% Filipino, 12% Hawaiian, 6% Chinese); **area:** 16,800 sq km/6,485 sq mi; **capital:** →Honolulu on Oahu; **towns and cities:** Hilo, Kailua, Kaneohe; **industries and products:** tourism is the chief source of income; other industries include sugar, coffee, pineapples, macadamia nuts, orchids and other flowers, livestock, poultry, dairy goods, clothing.

**hawk** any of a group of small to medium-sized birds of prey, belonging to the same family as eagles, kites, ospreys, and vultures. Hawks have short, rounded wings and a long tail compared with falcons, and keen eye-sight; the sparrow hawk and goshawk are examples. (Especially genera *Accipiter* and *Buteo*, family Accipitridae.)

**Hawking, Stephen William** (1942– ) English physicist whose work in general →relativity – particularly gravitational field theory – led to a search for a quantum theory of gravity to explain →black holes and the →Big Bang, singularities that classical relativity theory does not adequately explain. His book *A Brief History of Time* (1988) gives a popular account of cosmology and became an international best-seller. His latest book is *The Nature of Space and Time* (1996), written with Roger Penrose.

**Haydn, (Franz) Joseph** (1732–1809) Austrian composer. He was a major exponent of the classical sonata form in his numerous chamber and orchestral works (he wrote more than 100 symphonies). He also composed choral music, including the oratorios *The Creation* (1798) and *The Seasons* (1801). He was the first great master of the string quartet, and was a teacher of Mozart and Beethoven.

**hay fever** allergic reaction to pollen, causing sneezing, with inflammation of the nasal membranes and conjunctiva of the eyes. Symptoms are due to the release of histamine. Treatment is by antihistamine drugs. An estimated 25% of Britons, 33% of Americans, and 40% of Australians suffer from hayfever.

**H-bomb** abbreviation for **hydrogen bomb**.

**Heaney, Seamus Justin** (1939– ) Irish poet and critic. Born near Castledawsen, County Londonderry, he has written powerful verse about the political situation in Northern Ireland and reflections on Ireland's cultural heritage. Collections include *Death of a Naturalist* (1966), *Field Work* (1979), *The Haw Lantern* (1987), *The Spirit Level* (1996; Whitbread Book of the Year), and *Opened Ground: Poems 1966–1996* (1998). Critical works include *The Redress of Poetry* (1995). His *Beowulf: A New Translation* (1999), a modern version of the Anglo-Saxon epic, also won the Whitbread Book of the Year award. He was professor of poetry at Oxford 1989–94 and was awarded the Nobel Prize for Literature in 1995.

**heart** muscular organ that rhythmically contracts to force blood around the body of an animal with a circulatory system. Annelid worms and some other invertebrates have simple hearts consisting of thickened sections of main blood vessels that pulse regularly. An earthworm has ten such hearts. Vertebrates have one heart. A fish heart has two chambers – the thin-walled **atrium** (once called the auricle) that expands to receive blood, and the thick-walled **ventricle** that pumps it out. Amphibians and most reptiles have two atria and one ventricle; birds and mammals have two atria and two ventricles. The beating of the heart is controlled by the autonomic nervous system and an internal control centre or pacemaker, the **sinoatrial node**.

**Hebrew** member of the Semitic people

who lived in Palestine at the time of the Old Testament and who traced their ancestry to Abraham of Ur, a city of Sumer.

**Hebrides** group of more than 500 islands (fewer than 100 inhabited) off the west coast of mainland Scotland; total area 2,900 sq km/1,120 sq mi. The Hebrides were settled by Scandinavians during the 6th–9th centuries and passed under Norwegian rule from about 890 to 1266.

**Hegel, Georg Wilhelm Friedrich** (1770–1831) German philosopher who conceived of mind and nature as two abstractions of one indivisible whole, Spirit. His system, which is a type of idealism, traces the emergence of Spirit in the logical study of concepts and the process of world history.

**Heidegger, Martin** (1889–1976) German philosopher, often classed as an existentialist. He believed that Western philosophy had 'forgotten' the fundamental question of the 'meaning of Being', and his work concerns the investigation of what he thought were the different types of being appropriate to people and to things in general.

**helicopter** powered aircraft that achieves both lift and propulsion by means of a rotary wing, or rotor, on top of the fuselage. It can take off and land vertically, move in any direction, or remain stationary in the air. It can be powered by piston or jet engine. The autogiro was a precursor.

**helium** (Greek *helios* 'Sun') colourless, odourless, gaseous, nonmetallic element, symbol He, atomic number 2, relative atomic mass 4.0026. It is grouped with the →inert gases, is nonreactive, and forms no compounds. It is the second-most abundant element (after hydrogen) in the universe, and has the lowest boiling (–268.9°C/–452°F) and melting points (–272.2°C/–458°F) of all the elements. It is present in small quantities in the Earth's atmosphere from gases issuing from radioactive elements (from alpha decay) in the Earth's crust; after hydrogen it is the second lightest element.

**Helsinki** (Swedish *Helsingfors*) capital and port of Finland; population (1994) 516,000. Industries include shipbuilding, engineering, and textiles. The port is kept open by icebreakers in winter.

**Hemingway, Ernest Miller** (1899–1961) US writer. War, bullfighting, and fishing are used symbolically in his work to represent honour, dignity, and primitivism – prominent themes in his short stories and novels, which include *A Farewell to Arms* (1929), *For Whom the Bell Tolls* (1941), and *The Old Man and the Sea* (1952) (Pulitzer prize). His deceptively simple writing style attracted many imitators. Nobel Prize for Literature 1954.

**Hendrix, Jimi (James Marshall)** (1942–1970) US rock guitarist, songwriter, and singer. He was legendary for his virtuoso experimental technique and flamboyance. *Are You Experienced?* (1967) was his first album. His performance at the 1969 Woodstock festival included a memorable version of *The Star-Spangled Banner* and is recorded in the film *Woodstock* (1970). He greatly expanded the vocabulary of the electric guitar and influenced both rock and jazz musicians.

**Henry V** (1387–1422) king of England 1413–22, son of Henry IV. Invading Normandy in 1415 (during the Hundred Years' War), he captured Harfleur and defeated the French at →Agincourt. He invaded again in 1417–19, capturing Rouen. His military victory forced the French into the Treaty of Troyes in 1420, which gave Henry control of the French government. He married Catherine of Valois in 1420 and gained recognition as heir to the French throne by his father-in-law Charles VI, but died before him. He was succeeded by his son Henry VI.

**Henry VII** (1457–1509) king of England from 1485, when he overthrew Richard III at the Battle of →Bosworth. A descendant of →John of Gaunt, Henry, by his marriage to Elizabeth of York in 1486, united the houses of York and Lancaster. Yorkist revolts continued until 1497, but Henry restored order after the Wars of the Roses by the Star Chamber and achieved independence from Parliament by amassing a private fortune through confiscations. He was succeeded by his son Henry VIII.

**Henry VIII** (1491–1547) king of England from 1509, when he succeeded his father Henry VII and married Catherine of Aragón, the widow of his brother.

During the period 1513–29 Henry pursued an active foreign policy, largely under the guidance of his Lord Chancellor, Cardinal Wolsey, who shared Henry's desire to make England stronger. Wolsey was replaced by Thomas More in 1529 for failing to persuade the pope to grant Henry a divorce. After 1532 Henry broke with papal authority, proclaimed himself head of the church in England, dissolved the monasteries, and divorced Catherine. His subsequent wives were Anne Boleyn, Jane Seymour, Anne of Cleves, Catherine Howard, and Catherine Parr.

Henry VIII was succeeded by his son Edward VI.

**hepatitis** any inflammatory disease of the liver, usually caused by a virus. Other causes include alcohol, drugs, gallstones, →lupus erythematous, and →amoebic dysentery. Symptoms include weakness, nausea, and jaundice.

**Hepworth, (Jocelyn) Barbara** (1903–1975) English sculptor. She developed a distinctive abstract style, creating slender upright forms reminiscent of standing stones or totems; and round, hollowed forms with spaces bridged by wires or strings, as in *Pelagos* (1946; Tate Gallery, London). Her preferred medium was stone, but she also worked in concrete, wood, and aluminium, and many of her later works were in bronze.

**herbivore** animal that feeds on green plants (or photosynthetic single-celled organisms) or their products, including seeds, fruit, and nectar. The most numerous type of herbivore is thought to be the zooplankton, tiny invertebrates in the surface waters of the oceans that feed on small photosynthetic algae. Herbivores are more numerous than other animals because their food is the most abundant. They form a vital link in the food chain between plants and carnivores.

**Hercules** in Roman mythology, Roman form of the deified Greek hero Heracles. Possibly the first foreign cult accepted in Rome, he was popular with merchants due to his legendary travel and ability to ward off evil, and was seen as the personification of strength.

**heredity** in biology, the transmission of traits from parent to offspring. See also →genetics.

**hernia** (or rupture) protrusion of part of an internal organ through a weakness in the surrounding muscular wall, usually in the groin. The appearance is that of a rounded soft lump or swelling.

**Herod Antipas** (21 BC–AD 39) Tetrarch (governor) of the Roman province of Galilee, northern Palestine, 4 BC–AD 39, son of Herod the Great. He divorced his wife to marry his niece Herodias, and was responsible for the death of John the Baptist. Jesus was brought before him on Pontius Pilate's discovery that he was a Galilean and hence of Herod's jurisdiction, but Herod returned him without giving any verdict. In AD 38 Herod Antipas went to Rome to try to persuade Emperor Caligula to give him the title of king, but was instead banished.

**herpes** any of several infectious diseases caused by viruses of the herpes group. **Herpes simplex I** is the causative agent of a common inflammation, the cold sore. **Herpes simplex II** is responsible for genital herpes, a highly contagious, sexually transmitted disease characterized by painful blisters in the genital area. It can be transmitted in the birth canal from mother to newborn. **Herpes zoster** causes →shingles; another herpes virus causes chickenpox.

**Herschel,** **(Frederick)** **William** (1738–1822) German-born English astronomer. He was a skilled telescope-maker, and pioneered the study of binary stars and nebulae. He discovered the planet Uranus in 1781 and infrared solar rays in 1801. He catalogued over 800 double stars, and found over 2,500 nebulae, catalogued by his sister Caroline Herschel; this work was continued by his son John Herschel. By studying the distribution of stars, William established the basic form of our Galaxy, the Milky Way. Knighted 1816.

**Hertfordshire** county of southeast England; **area:** 1,630 sq km/629 sq mi; **towns and cities:** Hertford (administrative headquarters), Bishop's Stortford, Hatfield, Hemel Hempstead, Letchworth (the first garden city; followed by Welwyn in 1919), Stevenage (the first new town, designated in 1946), St Albans, Watford, Hitchin; **physical:** rivers Lea, Stort, Colne; part of the Chiltern Hills; **features:** Hatfield House; Knebworth House (home of Lord Lytton); Brocket Hall (home of Palmerston and Melbourne); home of

George Bernard →Shaw at Ayot St Lawrence; Berkhamsted Castle (Norman); Rothamsted agricultural experimental station; **agriculture:** barley for brewing industry, dairy farming, market gardening, horticulture; **industries:** aircraft, computer electronics, electrical goods, engineering, paper and printing, plastics, pharmaceuticals, tanning, sand and gravel are worked in the south; **population:** (1996) 1,015,800; **famous people:** Henry Bessemer, Graham Greene, Cecil Rhodes.

**hertz** SI unit (symbol Hz) of frequency (the number of repetitions of a regular occurrence in one second). Radio waves are often measured in megahertz (MHz), millions of hertz, and the clock rate of a computer is usually measured in megahertz. The unit is named after German physicist Heinrich Hertz.

**Hess, (Walter Richard) Rudolf** (1894–1987) German Nazi leader. Imprisoned with Adolf Hitler 1924–25, he became his private secretary, taking down *Mein Kampf* from his dictation. In 1933 he was appointed deputy *Führer* to Hitler, a post he held until replaced by Goering in September 1939. On 10 May 1941 he landed by air in the UK with his own compromise peace proposals and was held a prisoner of war until 1945, when he was tried at Nürnberg as a war criminal and sentenced to life imprisonment. He died in Spandau prison, Berlin.

**Hesse, Hermann** (1877–1962) German writer, a Swiss citizen from 1923. A conscientious objector in World War I and a pacifist opponent of Hitler, he published short stories, poetry, and novels, including *Peter Camenzind* (1904), *Siddhartha* (1922), and *Steppenwolf* (1927). Later works, such as *Das Glasperlenspiel/The Glass Bead Game* (1943), show the influence of Indian mysticism and Jungian psychoanalysis. Above all, Hesse was the prophet of individualism. Nobel Prize for Literature 1946.

**heterotroph** any living organism that obtains its energy from organic substances produced by other organisms. All animals and fungi are heterotrophs, and they include herbivores, carnivores, and saprotrophs (those that feed on dead animal and plant material).

**hieroglyphic** (Greek 'sacred carved writing') Egyptian writing system of the mid-4th millennium BC–3rd century AD, which combines picture signs with those indicating letters. The direction of writing is normally from right to left, the signs facing the beginning of the line. It was deciphered in 1822 by the French Egyptologist J F Champollion (1790–1832) with the aid of the same →Rosetta Stone, which has the same inscription carved in hieroglyphic, demotic, and Greek. The earliest hieroglyphics were discovered by German archaeologist Gunter Dreyer on clay tablets in southern Egypt in 1998 and record linen and oil deliveries and taxes paid. From the tomb of King Scorpion I, they are dated to between 3300 BC and 3200 BC and challenge the widely-held belief that Sumerians were the first people to write. Hieroglyphics were replaced for everyday use by cursive writing from about 700 BC onwards.

**Hillary, Edmund (Percival)** (1919– ) New Zealand mountaineer. In 1953, with Nepalese Sherpa mountaineer Tenzing Norgay, he reached the summit of Mount Everest, the first to climb the world's highest peak. As a member of the Commonwealth Transantarctic Expedition 1957–58, he was the first person since R F Scott to reach the South Pole overland, on 3 January 1958.

**Himalaya** vast mountain system of central Asia, extending from the Indian states of Kashmir in the west to Assam in the east, covering the southern part of Tibet, Nepal, Sikkim, and Bhutan. It is the highest mountain range in the world. The two highest peaks are Mount →Everest and K2. Other peaks include Kanchenjunga, Makalu, Annapurna, and Nanga Parbat, all over 8,000 m/26,000 ft.

**Hinduism** (Hindu *sanatana dharma* 'eternal tradition') religion originating in northern India about 4,000 years ago, which is superficially in some of its forms polytheistic, but has a concept of the supreme spirit, Brahman, above the many divine manifestations. These include the triad of chief gods (the Trimurti): →Brahma, →Vishnu, and Siva (creator, preserver, and destroyer). Central to Hinduism are the beliefs in reincarnation and karma; the oldest scriptures are the *Vedas*. Temple worship is almost universally observed and there are many festivals. There are over 805

million Hindus worldwide. Women are not regarded as the equals of men but should be treated with kindness and respect. Muslim influence in northern India led to the veiling of women and the restriction of their movements from about the end of the 12th century.

**Hippocrates** (c. 460–c. 377 BC) Greek physician, often called the founder of medicine. Important Hippocratic ideas include cleanliness (for patients and physicians), moderation in eating and drinking, letting nature take its course, and living where the air is good. He believed that health was the result of the 'humours' of the body being in balance; imbalance caused disease. These ideas were later adopted by →Galen.

**Hitchcock, Alfred Joseph** (1899–1980) English film director, a US citizen from 1955. A master of the suspense thriller, he was noted for his meticulously drawn storyboards that determined his camera angles and for his cameo walk-ons in his own films. His *Blackmail* (1929) was the first successful British talking film. *The Thirty-Nine Steps* (1935) and *The Lady Vanishes* (1938) are British suspense classics. He went to Hollywood in 1940, and his work there included *Rebecca* (1940), *Notorious* (1946), *Strangers on a Train* (1951), *Rear Window* (1954), *Vertigo* (1958), *North by Northwest* (1959), *Psycho* (1960), and *The Birds* (1963).

**Hitler, Adolf** (1889–1945) German Nazi dictator, born in Austria. He was *Führer* (leader) of the Nazi Party from 1921 and wrote *Mein Kampf/My Struggle*

1925–27. As chancellor of Germany from 1933 and head of state from 1934, he created a dictatorship by playing party and state institutions against each other and continually creating new offices and appointments. His position was not seriously challenged until the July Plot of 1944, which failed to assassinate him. In foreign affairs, he reoccupied the Rhineland and formed an alliance with the Italian Fascist Benito →Mussolini in 1936, annexed Austria in 1938, and occupied Sudeten under the →Munich Agreement. The rest of Czechoslovakia was annexed in March 1939. The Ribbentrop–Molotov pact was followed in September by the invasion of Poland and the declaration of war by Britain and France (see →World War II). He committed suicide as Berlin fell.

**Hittite** member of any of a succession of peoples who inhabited Anatolia and northern Syria from the 3rd millennium to the 1st millennium BC. The city of Hattusas (now Boğazköy in central Turkey) became the capital of a strong kingdom which overthrew the Babylonian Empire. After a period of eclipse the Hittite New Empire became a great power (about 1400–1200 BC), which successfully waged war with Egypt. The Hittite language is an Indo-European language.

**Hobbes, Thomas** (1588–1679) English political philosopher and the first thinker since Aristotle to attempt to develop a comprehensive theory of nature, including human behaviour. In *Leviathan* (1651), he advocates absolutist

government as the only means of ensuring order and security; he saw this as deriving from the social contract.

**Hockney, David** (1937– ) English painter, printmaker, and designer, resident in California. One of the best-known figures in British pop art, he developed a distinctive figurative style, as in his portrait *Mr and Mrs Clark and Percy* (1971; Tate Gallery, London). He has experimented prolifically with technique, and produced drawings; etchings, including *Six Fairy Tales from the Brothers Grimm* (1970); photo collages; and opera sets for Glyndebourne, East Sussex, La Scala, Milan, and the Metropolitan, New York.

**Holbein, Hans, the Younger** (1497–1543) German painter and woodcut artist who spent much of his career as a portrait artist at the court of Henry VIII of England. One of the finest graphic artists of his age, he executed a woodcut series *Dance of Death* about 1525, and designed title pages for Luther's New Testament and Thomas More's *Utopia*.

**Holiday, Billie** (1915–1959) stage name of Eleanora Gough McKay, US jazz singer, also known as 'Lady Day'. She made her debut in clubs in Harlem, New York, and became known for her emotionally charged delivery and idiosyncratic phrasing. Holiday brought a blues feel to her performances with swing bands. Songs she made her own include 'Stormy Weather', 'Strange Fruit', 'I Cover the Waterfront', 'That Ole Devil Called Love', and 'Lover Man (Oh, Where can You Be?)'.

**holistic medicine** umbrella term for an approach that virtually all alternative therapies profess, which considers the overall health and lifestyle profile of a patient, and treats specific ailments not primarily as conditions to be alleviated but rather as symptoms of more fundamental disease.

**Holly, Buddy** (1936–1959) stage name of Charles Hardin Holley, US rock-and-roll singer, guitarist, and songwriter. He had a distinctive, hiccuping vocal style and was an early experimenter with recording techniques. Many of his hits with his band, the Crickets, such as 'That'll Be the Day' (1957), 'Peggy Sue' (1957), and 'Maybe Baby' (1958), have become classics. His albums include *The Chirping Crickets* (1958) and *Buddy Holly* (1958). He died in a plane crash.

**Hollywood** district in the city of Los Angeles, California; the centre of the US film industry from 1911. It is the home of film studios such as Twentieth Century Fox, MGM, Paramount, Columbia Pictures, United Artists, Disney, and Warner Bros. Many film stars' homes are situated nearby in Beverly Hills and other communities adjacent to Hollywood.

**Holocaust, the** the annihilation of an estimated 16 million people by the Hitler regime between 1933 and 1945, principally in the numerous extermination and concentration camps, most notably →Auschwitz (Oświęcim), Sobibor, Treblinka, and Maidanek in Poland, and Belsen, Buchenwald, and Dachau in Germany. Of the victims around 6 million were Jews (over 67% of European Jews); around 10 million Ukrainian, Polish, and Russian civilians and prisoners of war, Romanies, socialists, homosexuals, and others (labelled 'defectives') were also imprisoned and/or exterminated. Victims were variously starved, tortured, experimented on, and worked to death. Millions were executed in gas chambers, shot, or hanged. It was euphemistically termed the final solution (of the Jewish question). The precise death toll will never be known. Holocaust museums and memorial sites have been established in Israel and in other countries.

**Holocene** epoch of geological time that began 10,000 years ago, the second and current epoch of the Quaternary period. During this epoch the glaciers retreated, the climate became warmer, and humans developed significantly.

**holography** method of producing three-dimensional (3-D) images, called holograms, by means of →laser light. Holography uses a photographic technique (involving the splitting of a laser beam into two beams) to produce a picture, or hologram, that contains 3-D information about the object photographed. Some holograms show meaningless patterns in ordinary light and produce a 3-D image only when laser light is projected through them, but reflection holograms produce images when ordinary light is reflected from them (as found on credit cards).

**Holy Grail** in medieval Christian legend, the dish or cup used by Jesus at the Last Supper; credited with supernatural powers and a symbol of Christian grace. In certain stories incorporated in Arthurian legend, it was an object of quest by King Arthur's knights, together with the spear with which Jesus was wounded at the Crucifixion. Galahad was the only knight to achieve the mission.

**Holy Roman Empire** empire of Charlemagne and his successors, and the German Empire 962–1806, both being regarded as the Christian (hence 'holy') revival of the Roman Empire. At its height it comprised much of western and central Europe.

**homeopathy** (or homoeopathy) system of alternative medicine based on the principle that symptoms of disease are part of the body's self-healing processes, and on the practice of administering extremely diluted doses of natural substances found to produce in a healthy person the symptoms manifest in the illness being treated. Developed by the German physician Samuel Hahnemann (1755–1843), the system is widely practised today as an alternative to allopathic (orthodox) medicine, and many controlled tests and achieved cures testify its efficacy.

**Homer** according to ancient tradition, the author of the Greek narrative epics, the *Iliad* and the *Odyssey* (both derived from oral tradition). Little is known about the man, but modern research suggests that both poems should be

> **WEB SITE** > > > > > > > >
> **Works by Homer**
> http://classics.mit.edu/Browse/browse-Homer.html
> Downloadable translations of Homer's works. The three files here are the complete works *The Iliad*, *The Odyssey*, and the lesser known work *Hymn to Dionysus*. The latter of these also includes some other miscellaneous writings.

assigned to the 8th century BC, with the *Odyssey* the later of the two.

**home rule, Irish** movement to repeal the Act of →Union of 1801 that joined Ireland to Britain, and to establish an Irish parliament responsible for internal affairs. In 1870 Isaac Butt formed the Home Rule Association and the movement was led in Parliament from 1880 by Charles Stewart →Parnell. After 1918 the demand for an independent Irish republic replaced that for home rule.

**homoeopathy** variant spelling of →homeopathy.

**Honduras** Republic of; **national name:** *República de Honduras*; **area:** 112,100 sq km/43,281 sq mi; **capital:** Tegucigalpa; **major towns/cities:** San Pedro Sula, La Ceiba, El Progreso, Choluteca, Juticalpa, Danlí; **major ports:** La Ceiba, Puerto Cortés; **Physical features:** narrow tropical coastal plain with mountainous interior, Bay Islands, Caribbean reefs; **head of state and government:** Carlos Flores from 1998; **political system:** democracy; **currency:**

lempira; **GNP per capita (PPP):** (US$) 2,140 (1998); **exports:** bananas, lobsters and prawns, zinc, meat. Principal market USA 73.2% (1998); **population:** 6,315,000 (1999 est); **language:** Spanish (official); English, American Indian languages; **religion:** Roman Catholic; **life expectancy:** 68 (men); 72 (women) (1995–2000).

**Hong Kong** special administrative region in the southeast of China, comprising Hong Kong Island; the Kowloon Peninsula; many other islands, of which the largest is Lantau; and the mainland New Territories. A former British crown colony, it reverted to Chinese control in July 1997; **area:** 1,070 sq km/413 sq mi; **capital:** Victoria (Hong Kong City); **towns and cities:** Kowloon, Tsuen Wan (in the New Territories); **features:** an enclave of Guangdong province, China, it has one of the world's finest natural harbours; Hong Kong Island is connected with Kowloon by undersea railway and ferries; a world financial centre, its stock market has four exchanges; **environment:** world's most densely populated city; surrounding waters heavily polluted; **exports:** textiles, clothing, electronic goods, clocks, watches, cameras, plastic products; a large proportion of the exports and imports of southern China are transshipped here; tourism is important; **currency:** Hong Kong dollar; **population:** (1995 est) 6,189,800; 57% Hong Kong Chinese, most of the remainder refugees from the mainland; **language:** English, Chinese; **religion:** Confucianist, Buddhist, Taoist, with Muslim and Christian

minorities; **government:** Hong Kong is a Special Administrative Region within China, with a chief executive, Tung Chee-hwa, from 1997. There is an executive council, which comprises a mixture of business and political figures, and, from May 1998, an elected legislative council; **history:** formerly part of China, Hong Kong Island was occupied by Britain in 1841, during the first of the →Opium Wars, and ceded by China under the 1842 Treaty of Nanking. The Kowloon Peninsula was acquired under the 1860 Beijing (Peking) Convention and the New Territories secured on a 99-year lease from 1898. The colony, which developed into a major centre for Sino-British trade during the late 19th and early 20th centuries, was occupied by Japan from 1941 to 1945.

As the date (1997) for the termination of the New Territories' lease approached, negotiations on Hong Kong's future were opened between Britain and China in 1982. These culminated in 1984 in an agreement that Britain would transfer full sovereignty of the islands and New Territories to China in 1997 in return for Chinese assurance that Hong Kong's social and economic freedom and capitalist lifestyle would be preserved for at least 50 years.

**Honolulu** (or Honolulu on Oaha (Hawaiian 'sheltered bay') state capital and port of →Hawaii, USA, on the south coast of Oahu; seat of Honolulu County; population (1994 est) 386,000. The city is the economic centre of Hawaii. It has a natural harbour (formed by a lagoon within the coral reef) with extensive shipping facilities. Honolulu is a trading centre for European and Indian goods, and is the principal point of entry to the islands. It is often called the 'Crossroads of the Pacific'. With its warm climate and tropical vegetation, Honolulu has become a holiday resort. In addition to tourism, other industries include food processing, machinery, clothing, and building materials. It was incorporated as a city in 1907.

**Honshu** principal island of Japan, lying between Hokkaido to the northeast and Kyushu to the southwest. Its landmass is approximately four-fifths of the country. **area:** 231,100 sq km/89,228 sq mi, including 382 smaller islands; **capital:** →Tokyo; **cities:** Yokohama, Osaka, Kobe, Nagoya, Hiroshima; **features:** linked by bridges and tunnels with the islands of Hokkaido, Kyushu, and Shikoku; **physical:** a chain of volcanic mountains runs along the island; frequent earthquakes; **population:** (1995) 100,995,000.

**Hooke, Robert** (1635–1703) English scientist and inventor, originator of **Hooke's law**, and considered the foremost mechanic of his time. His inventions included a telegraph system, the spirit level, marine barometer, and sea gauge. He coined the term 'cell' in biology.

**Hoover, J(ohn) Edgar** (1895–1972) US lawyer and director of the Federal Bureau of Investigation (FBI) from 1924 until his death. He built up a powerful network for the detection of organized crime, including a national fingerprint collection. His drive against alleged communist activities after World War II and his opposition to the Kennedy administration brought much criticism for abuse of power.

**Hopkins, Gerard Manley** (1844–1889) English poet and Jesuit priest. His works are marked by originality of diction and rhythm and include 'The Wreck of the Deutschland' (1876), and 'The Windhover' and 'Pied Beauty' (both 1877). His collected works were published posthumously in 1918 by his friend the poet Robert Bridges. His employment of 'sprung rhythm' (the combination of traditional regularity of stresses with varying numbers of syllables in each line) greatly influenced later 20th-century poetry.

**Hopper, Edward** (1882–1967) US painter and etcher, one of the foremost American realists. His views of life in New England and New York in the 1930s and 1940s, painted in rich, dark colours, convey a brooding sense of emptiness and solitude, as in *Nighthawks* (1942; Art Institute, Chicago).

**hops** female fruit heads of the hop plant *Humulus lupulus*, family Cannabiaceae; these are dried and used as a tonic and in flavouring beer. In designated areas in Europe, no male hops may be grown, since seedless hops produced by the unpollinated female plant contain a greater proportion of the alpha acid that gives beer its bitter taste.

**Horace** (65–8 BC) full name Quintus Horatius Flaccus, Roman lyric poet and satirist. He became a leading poet under the patronage of Emperor Augustus. His works include *Satires* (35–30 BC); the four books of *Odes*, (*c.* 25–24 BC); *Epistles*, a series of verse letters; and an influential critical work, *Ars poetica*. They are distinguished by their style, wit, discretion, and patriotism.

**hormone** in biology, chemical secretion of the ductless →endocrine glands and specialized nerve cells concerned with control of body functions. The major glands are the thyroid, parathyroid, pituitary, adrenal, pancreas, ovary, and testis. There are also hormone-secreting cells in the kidney, liver, gastrointestinal tract, thymus (in the neck), pineal (in the brain), and placenta. Hormones bring about changes in the functions of various organs according to the body's requirements. The hypothalamus, which adjoins the pituitary gland at the base of the brain, is a control centre for overall coordination of hormone secretion; the thyroid hormones determine the rate of general body chemistry; the adrenal hormones prepare the organism during stress for 'fight or flight'; and the sexual hormones such as oestrogen and testosterone govern reproductive functions.

**hormone-replacement therapy** (HRT) use of →oestrogen and progesterone to help limit the unpleasant effects of the menopause in women. The treatment was first used in the 1970s.

**Hormuz** (or Ormuz) small island in the Strait of Hormuz belonging to Iran; area 41 sq km/16 sq mi. It is strategically important because oil tankers leaving the Gulf for Japan and the West have to pass through the strait to reach the Arabian Sea.

**Horn, Cape** (Spanish *Cabo de Hornos*) southernmost point of South America, in Magallanes region, Chile; situated on Horn Island to the south of Tierra del Fuego archipelago. The cape is notorious for gales and heavy seas, and was the sea route between the Atlantic and the Pacific Oceans until the opening of the Panama Canal in 1914. Cape Horn was discovered in 1616 by Dutch explorer Willem Schouten (1580–1625), and named after his birthplace (Hoorn).

**horse** hoofed, odd-toed, grazing mammal belonging to the same family as zebras and asses. The many breeds of domestic horse of Euro-Asian origin range in colour from white to grey, brown, and black. The yellow-brown Mongolian wild horse, or Przewalski's horse (*Equus przewalskii*), named after its Polish 'discoverer' about 1880, is the only surviving species of wild horse. (Species *Equus caballus*, family Equidae.)

**horse racing** sport of racing mounted or driven horses. Two forms in Britain are flat racing, for thoroughbred horses over a flat course, and National Hunt racing, in which the horses have to clear obstacles.

**hovercraft** vehicle that rides on a cushion of high-pressure air, free from all contact with the surface beneath, invented by English engineer Christopher Cockerell in 1959. Hovercraft need a smooth terrain when operating overland and are best adapted to use on waterways. They are useful in places where harbours have not been established.

**Hubble, Edwin Powell** (1889–1953) US astronomer. He discovered the existence of →galaxies outside our own, and classified them according to their shape. His theory that the universe is expanding is now generally accepted.

**Hubble Space Telescope** (HST) space-based astronomical observing facility, orbiting the Earth at an altitude of 610 km/380 mi. It consists of a 2.4 m/94 in telescope and four complimentary scientific instruments, is roughly cylindrical, 13 m/43 ft long, and 4 m/13 ft in diameter, with two large solar panels. HST produces a wealth of scientific data, and allows astronomers to observe the birth of stars, find planets around neighbouring stars, follow the expanding remnants of exploding stars, and search for black holes in the centre of galaxies. HST is a cooperative programme between the European Space Agency (ESA) and the US agency NASA, and is the first spacecraft specifically designed to be serviced in orbit as a permanent space-based observatory. It was launched in 1990.

**Hughes, Ted (Edward James)** (1930–1998) English poet. He was the poet laureate from 1984 until his death. His work is characterized by its harsh portrayal of the crueller aspects of nature, by its reflection of the agonies of personal experience, and by the employment of myths of creation and being, as in *Crow* (1970) and *Gaudette* (1977). His free-verse renderings, *Tales from Ovid* won the 1997 Whitbread Book of the Year Award, and his collection *Birthday Letters* was awarded the 1998 Forward Prize and the 1998 Whitbread Book of the Year Award.

**Hugo, Victor Marie** (1802–1885) French novelist, poet, and dramatist. The verse play *Hernani* (1830) firmly established Hugo as the leader of French Romanticism. This was the first of a series of dramas produced in the 1830s and early 1840s, including *Le Roi s'amuse* (1832) and *Ruy Blas* (1838). His melodramatic novels include *Notre-Dame de Paris* (1831), and *Les Misérables* (1862).

**Huguenot** French Protestant in the 16th century; the term referred mainly to Calvinists. Persecuted under Francis I and Henry II, the Huguenots survived both an attempt to exterminate them (the Massacre of St Bartholomew on 24 August 1572) and the religious wars of the next 30 years. In 1598 Henry IV (himself formerly a Huguenot) granted them toleration under the Edict of Nantes. Louis XIV revoked the edict in 1685, attempting their forcible conversion, and 400,000 emigrated.

**Human Genome Project** research scheme, begun in 1988, to map the complete nucleotide sequence of human →DNA. There are approximately 100,000 (though a 1999 estimate by a participating US company was as high as 140,000) different →genes in the human genome, and one gene may contain more than 2 million nucleotides. The programme aims to collect 10–15,000 genetic specimens from 722 ethnic groups whose genetic make-up is to be preserved for future use and study. The knowledge gained is expected to help prevent or treat many crippling and lethal diseases, but there are potential ethical problems associated with knowledge of an individual's genetic make-up, and fears that it will lead to genetic discrimination.

In March 1999 the Human Genome Project announced that they aim to have a 'working draft' (about 90%) of the human genome by spring 2000. A commercial company is also racing to complete the mapping on target for this deadline.

**human species, origins of** evolution of humans from ancestral →primates. The African apes (gorilla and chimpanzee) are shown by anatomical and molecular comparisons to be the closest living relatives of humans. The oldest known hominids (of the human group), the australopithecines, found in Africa, date from 3.5–4.4 million years ago. The first to use tools came 2 million years later, and the first humanoids to use fire and move out of Africa appeared 1.7 million years ago. →Neanderthals were not direct ancestors of the human species. Modern humans are all believed to descend from one African female of 200,000 years ago, although there is a rival theory that humans evolved in different parts of the world simultaneously.

**Hundred Years' War** series of conflicts between England and France from 1337 to 1453 that finally ended any significant involvement of the kings of England in Continental Europe. Its origins lay with the English kings' possession of Gascony (southwest France), which the French kings claimed as their fief, and with trade rivalries over →Flanders. The two kingdoms had a long history of strife before 1337, and the Hundred Years' War has sometimes been interpreted as merely an intensification of these struggles. It was caused by fears of French intervention in Scotland, which the English were trying to subdue, and by the claim of England's Edward III (through his mother Isabella, daughter of Philip IV of France) to the crown of France.

**Hungary** Republic of; **national name:** *Magyar Köztársaság;* **area:** 93,032 sq km/35,919 sq mi; **capital:** Budapest; **major towns/cities:** Miskolc, Debrecen, Szeged, Pécs, Gyor, Nyiregyháza, Székesfehérvár, Kecskemét; **physical features:** Great Hungarian Plain covers eastern half of country; Bakony Forest, Lake Balaton, and Transdanubian Highlands in the west; rivers Danube, Tisza, and Raba; more than 500 thermal springs; **head of state:** Arpád Göncz from 1990; **head of government:** Viktor Orban from 1998; **political system:** emergent democracy; **currency:** forint; **GNP per capita (PPP):** (US$) 7,320 (1998 est); **exports:** raw materials, semifinished products, industrial consumer goods, food and agricultural products, transport equipment. Principal market Germany 36.6% (1998); **population:**

10,075,000 (1999 est); **language:** Hungarian (or Magyar), one of the few languages of Europe with non-Indo-European origins; it is grouped with Finnish, Estonian, and others in the Finno-Ugric family; **religion:** Roman Catholic 67%, Calvinist 20%, other Christian denominations, Jewish; **life expectancy:** 67 (men); 75 (women) (1995–2000).

**hurricane** (tropical cyclone or typhoon) a severe →depression (region of very low atmospheric pressure) in tropical regions, called **typhoon** in the North Pacific. It is a revolving storm originating at latitudes between 5° and 20° N or S of the Equator, when the surface temperature of the ocean is above 27°C/80°F. A central calm area, called the eye, is surrounded by inwardly spiralling winds (anticlockwise in the northern hemisphere) of up to 320 kph/200 mph. A hurricane is accompanied by lightning and torrential rain, and can cause extensive damage. In meteorology, a hurricane is a wind of force 12 or more on the →Beaufort scale.

**Hussein, Saddam** (1937– ) Iraqi politician, in power from 1968, president from 1979. He presided over the Iran–Iraq war 1980–88, and harshly repressed Kurdish rebels in northern Iraq. He annexed Kuwait 1990 but was driven out by a US-dominated coalition army February 1991. Defeat in the →Gulf War led to unrest, and both the Kurds in the north and Shiites in the south rebelled. His savage repression of both revolts led to charges of genocide. In 1995, to counter evidence of rifts among his closest supporters, he called a presidential election, in which he was elected (unopposed) with 99.6% of the vote. In September 1996 his involvement in Kurdish faction fighting in northern Iraq provoked air retaliation by US forces. In March 1998 a major confrontation with the UN over the inspection of weapons of mass destruction held by Iraq, was narrowly averted.

**Huxley, Aldous Leonard** (1894–1963) English writer of novels, essays, and verse. From the disillusionment and satirical eloquence of *Crome Yellow* (1921), *Antic Hay* (1923), and *Point Counter Point* (1928), Huxley developed towards the Utopianism exemplified by *Island* (1962). His most popular work, the science fiction novel *Brave New World* (1932) shows human beings mass-produced in laboratories and rendered incapable of freedom by indoctrination and drugs.

**hybrid** offspring from a cross between individuals of different species, or two

---

**WEB SITE** > > > > > > > >
**Hurricane and Tropical Storm Tracking**

http://hurricane.terrapin.com/

Follow the current paths of Pacific and mid-Atlantic hurricanes and tropical storms at this site. Java animations of storms in previous years can also be viewed, and data sets for these storms may be downloaded. Current satellite weather maps can be accessed for the USA and surrounding region.

---

inbred lines within a species. In most cases, hybrids between species are infertile and unable to reproduce sexually. In plants, however, doubling of the chromosomes can restore the fertility of such hybrids.

**hydra** in zoology, any of a group of freshwater polyps, belonging among the →coelenterates. The body is a double-layered tube (with six to ten hollow tentacles around the mouth), 1.25 cm/0.5 in long when extended, but capable of contracting to a small knob. Usually fixed to waterweed, hydras feed on minute animals that are caught and paralysed by stinging cells on the tentacles. (Genus *Hydra*, family Hydridae, phylum Coelenterata, subphylum Cnidaria.)

**hydraulics** field of study concerned with utilizing the properties of water and other liquids, in particular the way they flow and transmit pressure, and with the application of these properties in engineering. It applies the principles of hydrostatics and hydrodynamics. The oldest type of hydraulic machine is the **hydraulic press**, invented by Joseph Bramah in England in 1795. The hydraulic principle of pressurized liquid increasing a force is commonly used on vehicle braking systems, the forging press, and the hydraulic systems of aircraft and excavators.

**hydrocarbon** any of a class of chemical compounds containing only hydrogen and carbon (for example, the alkanes and alkenes). Hydrocarbons are obtained industrially principally from petroleum and coal tar.

**hydroelectric power** electricity generated by moving water. In a typical

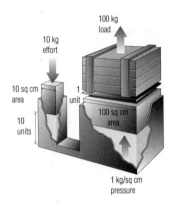

**hydraulics** The hydraulic jack transmits the pressure on a small piston to a larger one. A larger total force is developed by the larger piston but it moves a smaller distance than the small piston.

scheme, water stored in a reservoir, often created by damming a river, is piped into water →turbines, coupled to electricity generators. In pumped storage plants, water flowing through the turbines is recycled. A tidal power station exploits the rise and fall of the tides. About one-fifth of the world's electricity comes from hydroelectric power.

**hydrogen** (Greek *hydro* + *gen* 'water generator') colourless, odourless, gaseous, nonmetallic element, symbol H, atomic number 1, relative atomic mass 1.00797. It is the lightest of all the elements and occurs on Earth chiefly in combination with oxygen as water. Hydrogen is the most abundant element in the universe, where it accounts for 93% of the total number of atoms and 76% of the total mass. It is a component of most stars, including the Sun, whose heat and light are produced through the nuclear-fusion process that converts hydrogen into helium. When subjected to a pressure 500,000 times greater than that of the Earth's atmosphere, hydrogen becomes a solid with metallic properties, as in one of the inner zones of Jupiter. Hydrogen's common and industrial uses include the hardening of oils and fats by hydrogenation, the creation of high-temperature flames for welding, and as rocket fuel. It has been proposed as a fuel for road vehicles.

**hypertension** abnormally high →blood pressure due to a variety of causes, leading to excessive contraction of the smooth muscle cells of the walls of the arteries. It increases the risk of kidney disease, stroke, and heart attack.

**hypertext** system for viewing information (both text and pictures) on a computer screen in such a way that related items of information can easily be reached. For example, the program might display a map of a country; if the user clicks (with a mouse) on a particular city, the program will display information about that city.

**hypnosis** artificially induced state of relaxation or altered attention characterized by heightened suggestibility. There is evidence that, with susceptible persons, the sense of pain may be diminished, memory of past events enhanced, and illusions or hallucinations experienced. Posthypnotic amnesia (forgetting what happened during hypnosis) and posthypnotic suggestion (performing an action after hypnosis that had been suggested during it) have also been demonstrated.

**hypotenuse** the longest side of a right-angled triangle, opposite the right angle. It is of particular application in Pythagoras' theorem (the square of the hypotenuse equals the sum of the squares of the other two sides), and in trigonometry where the ratios →sine and →cosine are defined as the ratios opposite/hypotenuse and adjacent/hypotenuse respectively.

**hypothermia** condition in which the deep (core) temperature of the body falls below 35°C. If it is not discovered, coma and death ensue. Most at risk are the aged and babies (particularly if premature).

**hysterectomy** surgical removal of all or part of the uterus (womb). The operation is performed to treat fibroids (benign tumours growing in the uterus) or cancer; also to relieve heavy menstrual bleeding. A woman who has had a hysterectomy will no longer menstruate and cannot bear children.

**Ibsen, Henrik (Johan)** (1828–1906) Norwegian dramatist and poet. His realistic and often controversial plays revolutionized European theatre. Driven into voluntary exile 1864–91 by opposition to the satirical *Kjærlighedens komedie/Love's Comedy* (1862), he wrote the symbolic verse dramas *Brand* (1866) and *Peer Gynt* (1867), followed by realistic plays dealing with social issues, including *Samfundets støtter/Pillars of Society* (1877), *Et dukkehjem/A Doll's House* (1879), *Gengangere/Ghosts* (1881), *En folkefiende/An Enemy of the People* (1882), and *Hedda Gabler* (1890). By the time he returned to Norway, he was recognized as the country's greatest living writer.

**Icarus** in Greek mythology, the son of Daedalus, who with his father escaped from the labyrinth in Crete by making wings of feathers fastened with wax. Icarus plunged to his death when he flew too near the Sun and the wax melted.

**ice age** any period of glaciation occurring in the Earth's history, but particularly that in the Pleistocene epoch, immediately preceding historic times. On the North American continent, →glaciers reached as far south as the Great Lakes, and an ice sheet spread over northern Europe, leaving its remains as far south as Switzerland.

There were several glacial advances separated by interglacial stages during which the ice melted and temperatures were higher than today.

**Iceland** Republic of; **national name:** *Lýðveldið Ísland*; **area:** 103,000 sq km/ 39,768 sq mi; **capital:** Reykjavík; **major towns/cities:** Akureyri, Akranes, Kópavogur, Hafnerfjörður, Vestmannaeyjar; **physical features:** warmed by the Gulf Stream; glaciers and lava fields cover 75% of the country; active volcanoes (Hekla was once thought the gateway to Hell), geysers, hot springs, and new islands created offshore (Surtsey in 1963); subterranean hot water heats 85% of Iceland's homes; Sidujokull glacier moving at 100 metres a day; **head of state:** Ólafur Ragnar Grímsson from 1996; **head of government:** Davíd Oddsson from 1991; **political system:** democracy; **currency:** krona; **GNP per capita (PPP):** (US$) 22,830 (1998); **exports:** fish products, aluminium, ferrosilicon, diatomite, fertilizer, animal products. Principal market UK 19% (1998); **population:** 279,000 (1999 est); **language:** Icelandic, the most archaic Scandinavian language; **religion:** Evangelical Lutheran; **life expectancy:** 77 (men); 81 (women) (1995–2000).

**Iceni** ancient people of eastern England, who revolted against Roman occupation under the chieftainship of →Boudicca.

**iconography** in art history, significance attached to symbols that can help to identify subject matter (for example, a saint holding keys usually represents St Peter) and place a work of art in its historical context. The pioneer of this approach was the German art historian Erwin Panofsky.

**Idaho** state of northwestern USA. It is nicknamed Gem State. Idaho, one of the Mountain States, was admitted to the Union in 1890 as the 43rd US state. It is bordered to the east by Montana and Wyoming, to the south by Utah and Nevada, to the west by Oregon and Washington, and to the north by British Columbia, Canada; **population:** (1995) 1,163,300; **area:** 216,500 sq km/ 83,569 sq mi; **capital:** Boise; **towns and cities:** Pocatello, Idaho Falls, Nampa, Lewiston; **industries and products:** potatoes, wheat, livestock, timber, silver, lead, zinc, antimony, tourism, leisure industry.

**igneous rock** rock formed from cooling magma or lava, and solidifying from a molten state. Igneous rocks are largely composed of silica ($SiO_2$) and they are classified according to their crystal size, texture, method of formation, or chemical composition, for example by the proportions of light and dark minerals.

**Illinois** midwestern state of the USA. It is nicknamed Prairie State. Illinois was admitted to the Union in 1818 as the 21st US state. A major agricultural state, Illinois is bordered to the east by Indiana, to the southeast by Kentucky, with the Ohio River serving as a boundary, to the west by Missouri and Iowa, with the Mississippi River as a boundary, and to the north by Wisconsin. In the northeast, it has a shore of c. 100 km/60 mi on Lake Michigan, occupied by Chicago and its northern suburbs; **population:** (1995) 11,829,900; **area:** 146,100 sq km/56,395 sq mi; **capital:** Springfield; **towns and cities:** Chicago, Rockford, Peoria, Decatur, Aurora; **industries and products:** soybeans, cereals, meat and dairy products, livestock, machinery, electrical and electronic equipment.

**immunity** the protection that organisms have against foreign micro-organisms, such as bacteria and viruses, and against cancerous cells (see →cancer). The cells that provide this protection are called white blood cells, or leucocytes, and make up the immune system. They include neutrophils and macrophages, which can engulf invading organisms and other unwanted material, and natural killer cells that destroy cells infected by viruses and cancerous cells. Some of the most important immune cells are the B cells and T cells. Immune cells coordinate their activities by means of chemical messengers or lymphokines, including the antiviral messenger interferon. The lymph nodes play a major role in organizing the immune response.

**immunization** conferring immunity to infectious disease by artificial methods.

The most widely used technique is →vaccination.

Immunization is an important public health measure. If most of the population has been immunized against a particular disease, it is impossible for an epidemic to take hold.

**impeachment** judicial procedure by which government officials are accused of wrongdoing and brought to trial before a legislative body. In the USA the House of Representatives may impeach offenders to be tried before the Senate, as in the case of President Andrew Johnson in 1868. Richard →Nixon resigned the US presidency in 1974 when threatened by impeachment. President Bill →Clinton's impeachment trial took place in 1999.

**Impressionism** movement in painting that originated in France in the 1860s and had enormous influence in European and North American painting in the late 19th century. The Impressionists wanted to depict real life, to paint straight from nature, and to capture the changing effects of light. The term was first used abusively to describe Claude Monet's painting *Impression: Sunrise* (1872). The other leading Impressionists included Paul Cézanne, Edgar Degas, Edouard Manet, Camille Pissarro, Pierre-Auguste Renoir, and Alfred Sisley, but only Monet remained devoted to Impressionist ideas throughout his career.

**Inca** member of an ancient Peruvian civilization of Quechua-speaking American Indians that began in the Andean highlands about AD 1200. By the time the Spanish conquered the region in the 1530s, the Inca people ruled an area that stretched from Ecuador in the north to Chile in the south. Inca means 'king', and was the title of the ruler as well as the name of the people.

**Independence Day** public holiday in the USA, commemorating the adoption of the Declaration of Independence 4 July 1776.

**India** Republic of; **national name:** Hindi *Bharat*; **area:** 3,166,829 sq km/1,222,713 sq mi; **capital:** Delhi; **major towns/cities:** Bombay, Calcutta, Chennai (Madras), Bangalore, Hyderabad, Ahmadabad, Kanpur, Pune, Nagpur, Bhopal, Jaipur, Lucknow, Surat; **major ports:** Calcutta, Bombay, Chennai (Madras); **physical features:** Himalaya mountains on northern border; plains around rivers Ganges, Indus, Brahmaputra; Deccan peninsula south of the Narmada River forms plateau between Western and Eastern Ghats mountain ranges; desert in west; Andaman and Nicobar Islands, Lakshadweep (Laccadive Islands); **head of state:** Kocheril Raman Narayanan from 1997; **head of government:** Atal Behari Vajpayee from 1998; **political system:** liberal democratic federal republic; **currency:** rupee; **GNP per capita (PPP):** (US$) 1,700 (1998); **exports:** tea (world's largest producer), coffee, fish, iron and steel, leather, textiles, clothing, polished diamonds, handmade carpets, engineering goods, chemicals. Principal market USA 22.8% (1998); **population:** 998,056,000 (1999 est); **language:** Hindi, English, and 17 other official languages Assamese, Bengali, Gujarati, Kannada, Kashmiri, Konkani, Malayalam, Manipur, Marathi, Nepali, Oriya, Punjabi, Sanskrit, Sindhi, Tamil, Telugu, Urdu; more than 1,650 dialects; **religion:** Hindu 83%, Sunni Muslim 11%, Christian 2.5%, Sikh 2%; **life expectancy:** 62 (men); 63 (women) (1995–2000).

**Indianapolis** state capital and largest city of Indiana, on the White River, 300 km/186 mi southeast of Chicago; seat of Marion County; population (1994 est) 752,000; population of metropolitan area (1992) 1,424,000. Situated in the rich Corn Belt agricultural region, the city is an industrial centre; products include electronic components, pharmaceuticals, processed foods, machinery, plastics, and rubber. It is the venue for the Indianapolis 500 car race.

**Indian Mutiny** (also Sepoy Rebellion or Mutiny) revolt of Indian soldiers (sepoys) against the British in India from 1857 to 1858. The uprising was confined to the north, from Bengal to the Punjab, and central India. It led to the end of rule by the British East India Company and its replacement by direct British crown administration.

**Indian Ocean** ocean between Africa and Australia, with India to the north, and the southern boundary being an arbitrary line from Cape Agulhas to south Tasmania; area 73,500,000 sq km/28,371,000 sq mi; average depth 3,872 m/12,708 ft. The greatest depth is the Java Trench 7,725 m/25,353 ft. It includes two great bays on either side of the Indian peninsula, the Bay of Bengal to the east, and the Arabian Sea with the gulfs of Aden and Oman to the west.

**Indonesia** Republic of; **national name:** *Republik Indonesia*; **area:** 1,904,569 sq km/735,354 sq mi; **capital:** Jakarta; **major towns/cities:** Surabaya, Bandung, Yogyakarta (Java), Medan, Semarang (Java), Banda Aceh, Palembang (Sumatra), Ujung Pandang (Sulawesi), Denpasar (Bali), Kupang (Timor), Padang, Malang; **major ports:** Tanjung Priok, Surabaya, Semarang (Java), Ujung Pandang (Sulawesi); **physical features:** comprises 13,677 tropical islands (over 6,000 of them are inhabited) the Greater Sundas (including Java, Madura, Sumatra, Sulawesi, and Kalimantan (part of Borneo)), the Lesser Sunda Islands/ Nusa Tenggara (including Bali, Lombok, Sumbawa, Flores, Sumba, Alor, Lomblen, Timor, Roti, and Savu), Maluku/ Moluccas (over 1,000 islands including Ambon, Ternate, Tidore, Tanimbar, and Halmahera), and Irian Jaya (part of New Guinea); over half the country is tropical rainforest; it has the largest expanse of peatlands in the tropics; **head of state and government:** Abdurrahman Wahid from 1999; **political system:** authoritarian nationalist republic; **currency:** rupiah; **GNP per capita (PPP):** (US$) 2,790 (1998); **exports:** petroleum and petroleum products, natural and manufactured gas, textiles, rubber, palm oil, wood and wood products, electrical and electronic products, coffee, fishery products, coal, copper, tin, pepper, tea. Principal market Japan 18.6% (1998); **population:** 210,126,000 (1999 est);

**language:** Bahasa Indonesia (official), closely related to Malay; there are 583 regional languages and dialects; Javanese is the most widely spoken local language. Dutch is also spoken; **religion:** Muslim 88%, Christian 10%, Buddhist and Hindu 2% (the continued spread of Christianity, together with an Islamic revival, have led to greater religious tensions); **life expectancy:** 63 (men); 67 (women) (1995–2000).

**Industrial Revolution** sudden acceleration of technical and economic development that began in Britain in the second half of the 18th century. The traditional agricultural economy was replaced by one dominated by machinery and manufacturing, made possible through technical advances such as the steam engine. This transferred the balance of political power from the landowner to the industrial capitalist and created an urban working class. From 1830 to the early 20th century, the Industrial Revolution spread throughout Europe and the USA and to Japan and the various colonial empires.

**Indus Valley civilization** one of the four earliest ancient civilizations of the Old World (the other three being the →Sumerian civilization 3500 BC; Egypt 3000 BC; and China 2200 BC), developing in the northwest of the Indian subcontinent about 2500 BC.

**inert gas** (or noble gas) any of a group of six elements (helium, neon, argon, krypton, xenon, and radon), so named because they were originally thought not to enter into any chemical reactions. This is now known to be incorrect: in 1962, xenon was made to combine with fluorine, and since then, compounds of argon, krypton, and radon with fluorine and/or oxygen have been described.

**inertia** in physics, the tendency of an object to remain in a state of rest or uniform motion until an external force is applied, as described by Isaac Newton's first law of motion.

**inferiority complex** in psychology, a complex or cluster of repressed fears, described by Alfred Adler, based on physical inferiority. The term is popularly used to describe general feelings of inferiority and the overcompensation that often ensues.

**infinity** mathematical quantity that is larger than any fixed assignable quantity; symbol ∞. By convention, the result of dividing any number by zero is regarded as infinity.

**influenza** any of various viral infections primarily affecting the air passages, accompanied by systemic effects such as fever, chills, headache, joint and muscle pains, and lassitude. Treatment is with bed rest and analgesic drugs such as aspirin or paracetamol.

**information technology** (IT) collective term for the various technologies involved in processing and transmitting information. They include computing, telecommunications, and microelectronics.

**Ingres, Jean-Auguste-Dominique** (1780–1867) French painter. A leading Neo-Classicist, he was a student of Jacques

Louis →David. He studied and worked in Rome about 1807–20, where he began the *Odalisque* series of sensuous female nudes, then went to Florence, and returned to France 1824. His portraits painted in the 1840s–50s are meticulously detailed and highly polished.

**inorganic chemistry** branch of chemistry dealing with the chemical properties of the elements and their compounds, excluding the complex covalent compounds of carbon, which are considered in organic chemistry.

**insect** any of a vast group of small invertebrate animals with hard, segmented bodies, three pairs of jointed legs, and, usually, two pairs of wings; they belong among the →arthropods and are distributed throughout the world. An insect's body is divided into three segments: head, thorax, and abdomen. On the head is a pair of feelers, or antennae. The legs and wings are attached to the thorax, or middle segment of the body. The abdomen, or end segment of the body, is where food is digested and excreted and where the reproductive organs are located.

Insects vary in size from 0.02 cm/0.007 in to 35 cm/13.5 in in length. The world's smallest insect is believed to be a 'fairy fly' wasp in the family Mymaridae, with a wingspan of 0.2 mm/0.008 in. (Class Insecta.)

**insecticide** any chemical pesticide used to kill insects. Among the most effective insecticides are synthetic organic chemicals such as →DDT and dieldrin, which are chlorinated hydrocarbons. These chemicals, however, have proved persistent in the environment and are also poisonous to all animal life, including humans, and are consequently banned in many countries. Other synthetic insecticides include organic phosphorus compounds such as malathion. Insecticides prepared from plants, such as derris and pyrethrum, are safer to use but need to be applied frequently and carefully.

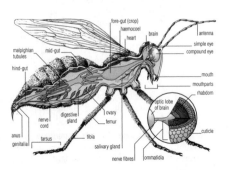

**insect** Body plan of an insect. The general features of the insect body include a segmented body divided into head, thorax, and abdomen, jointed legs, feelers or antennae, and usually two pairs of wings. Insects often have compound eyes with a large field of vision.

**insectivore** any animal whose diet is made up largely or exclusively of →insects. In particular, the name is applied to mammals of the order Insectivora, which includes the shrews, hedgehogs, moles, and tenrecs.

**instinct** in →ethology, behaviour found in all equivalent members of a given species (for example, all the males, or all the females with young) that is presumed to be genetically determined.

**insulin** protein →hormone, produced by specialized cells in the islets of Langerhans in the pancreas, that regulates the metabolism (rate of activity) of glucose, fats, and proteins. Insulin was discovered by Canadian physician Frederick Banting and Canadian physiologist Charles Best, who pioneered its use in treating →diabetes.

**integrated circuit** (IC, popularly called silicon chip) miniaturized electronic circuit produced on a single crystal, or chip, of a semiconducting material – usually silicon. It may contain many millions of components and yet measure only 5 mm/0.2 in square and 1 mm/0.04 in thick. The IC is encapsulated within a plastic or ceramic case, and linked via gold wires to metal pins with which it is connected to a →printed circuit board and the other components that make up such electronic devices as computers and calculators.

**interference** in physics, the phenomenon of two or more wave motions interacting and combining to produce a resultant wave of larger or smaller amplitude (depending on whether the combining waves are in or out of phase with each other).

**internal-combustion engine** heat engine in which fuel is burned inside the engine, contrasting with an external-combustion engine (such as the steam engine) in which fuel is burned in a separate unit. The →diesel engine and petrol engine are both internal-combustion engines. Gas →turbines and jet and rocket engines are also considered to be internal-combustion engines because they burn their fuel inside their combustion chambers.

**Internet** global computer network connecting governments, companies, universities, and many other networks and users. Electronic mail, electronic conferencing, online shopping, educational and chat services are all supported across the network, as is the ability to access remote computers and send and retrieve files. In 1997 around 60 million adults had access to the Internet in the USA alone. In 1998 the Internet generated: 301 billion in revenue, according to a report released in June 1999 by researchers at the University of Texas, USA. The Internet also created 1.2 million jobs in 1998.

**intestine** in vertebrates, the digestive tract from the stomach outlet to the anus. The human **small intestine** is 6 m/20 ft long, 4 cm/1.5 in diameter, and consists of the duodenum, jejunum, and ileum; the **large intestine** is 1.5 m/5 ft long, 6 cm/2.5 in diameter, and includes the caecum, colon, and rectum. Both are muscular tubes comprising an inner lining that secretes alkaline digestive juice, a submucous coat containing fine blood vessels and nerves, a muscular coat, and a serous coat covering all, supported by a strong peritoneum, which carries the blood and lymph vessels, and the nerves. The contents are passed along slowly by peristalsis (waves of involuntary muscular action). The term intestine is also applied to the lower digestive tract of invertebrates.

**intrauterine device** (IUD; or coil) a contraceptive device that is inserted into the womb (uterus). It is a tiny plastic object, sometimes containing copper. By causing a mild inflammation of the lining of the uterus it prevents fertilized eggs from becoming implanted.

**introversion** in psychology, preoccupation with the self, generally coupled with a lack of sociability. The opposite of introversion is extroversion.

**invertebrate** animal without a backbone. The invertebrates form all of the major divisions of the animal kingdom called phyla, with the exception of vertebrates. Invertebrates include the sponges, coelenterates, flatworms, nematodes, annelids, arthropods, molluscs, and echinoderms. Primitive aquatic chordates such as sea squirts and lancelets, which only have notochords and do not possess a vertebral column of cartilage or bone, are sometimes called invertebrate chordates, but this is misleading, since the notochord is the precursor of the backbone in advanced chordates.

**in vitro fertilization** (IVF) 'fertilization in glass' allowing eggs and sperm to unite in a laboratory to form embryos. The embryos (properly called pre-embryos in their two- to eight-celled state) are stored by cooling to the temperature of liquid air (cryopreservation) until they are implanted into the womb of the otherwise infertile mother (an extension of artificial insemination). The first baby to be produced by this method was born in 1978 in the UK. In cases where the Fallopian tubes are blocked, fertilization may be carried out by **intra-vaginal culture**, in which egg and sperm are incubated (in a plastic tube) in the mother's vagina, then transferred surgically into the uterus.

**iodine** (Greek *iodes* 'violet') greyish-black nonmetallic element, symbol I, atomic number 53, relative atomic mass 126.9044. It is a member of the →halogen group. Its crystals give off, when heated, a violet vapour with an irritating odour resembling that of chlorine. It only occurs in combination with other elements. Its salts are known as iodides, which are found in sea water. As a mineral nutrient it is vital to the proper functioning of the thyroid gland, where it occurs in trace amounts as part of the hormone thyroxine. Absence of iodine from the diet leads to →goitre. Iodine is used in photography, in medicine as an antiseptic, and in making dyes.

**ion** atom, or group of atoms, that is either positively charged (cation) or negatively charged (→anion), as a result of the loss or gain of electrons during chemical reactions or exposure to certain forms of radiation. In solution or in the molten state, ionic compounds such as salts, acids, alkalis, and metal oxides conduct electricity. These compounds are known as electrolytes.

**Ionian** member of a Hellenic people from beyond the Black Sea who crossed the Balkans around 1980 BC and invaded Asia Minor. Driven back by the →Hittites, they settled all over mainland Greece, later being supplanted by the Achaeans.

**ionic bond** (or electrovalent bond) bond produced when atoms of one element donate electrons to atoms of another element, forming positively and negatively charged ions respectively. The attraction between the oppositely charged →ions constitutes the bond. Sodium chloride ($Na^+Cl^-$) is a typical ionic compound.

**IRA** abbreviation for **Irish Republican Army**.

**Iran** Islamic Republic of (formerly Persia); **national name:** *Jomhori-e-Islami-e-Irân*; **area:** 1,648,000 sq km/636,292 sq mi; **capital:** Tehran; **major towns/cities:** Esfahan, Mashhad, Tabriz, Shiraz, Ahvaz, Bakhtaran, Qom, Kara; **major ports:** Abadan; **physical features:** plateau surrounded by mountains, including Elburz and Zagros; Lake Rezayeh; Dasht-e-Kavir desert; occupies islands of Abu Musa, Greater Tunb and Lesser Tunb in the Gulf; **head of state and government:** Seyyed Muhammad Khatami from 1997; **Leader of the Islamic Revolution:**

Seyed Ali Khamenei from 1989; **political system:** authoritarian Islamic republic; **currency:** rial; **GNP per capita (PPP):** (US$) 3,920 (1998 est); **exports:** crude petroleum and petroleum products, agricultural goods, carpets, metal ores. Principal market Japan 15.1% (1997); **population:** 66,796,000 (1999 est); **language:** Farsi (official), Kurdish, Turkish, Arabic, English,

**electron transferred**

electronic arrangement, 2.8.1 of a sodium atom

electronic arrangement, 2.8.7 of a chlorine atom

becomes a sodium ion, $Na^+$, with an electron arrangement 2.8

becomes a chloride ion, $Cl^-$, with an electron arrangement 2.8.8

**ionic bond** The formation of an ionic bond between a sodium atom and a chlorine atom to form a molecule of sodium chloride. The sodium atom transfers an electron from its outer electron shell (becoming the positive ion $Na^+$) to the chlorine atom (which becomes the negative chloride ion $Cl^-$). The opposite charges mean that the ions are strongly attracted to each other. The formation of the bond means that each atom becomes more stable, having a full quota of electrons in its outer shell.

French; **religion:** Shiite Muslim (official) 94%, Sunni Muslim, Zoroastrian, Christian, Jewish, Baha'i; **life expectancy:** 69 (men); 70 (women) (1995–2000).

**Iraq** Republic of; **national name:** al Jumhouriya al 'Iraqia; **area:** 434,924 sq km/167,924 sq mi; **capital:** Baghdad; **major towns/cities:** Mosul, Basra, Kirkuk, Hilla, Najaf, Nasiriya; **major ports:** Basra and Um Qass closed from 1980; **physical features:** mountains in north, desert in west; wide valley of rivers Tigris and Euphrates running northwest–southeast; canal linking Baghdad and Persian Gulf opened in 1992; **head of state and government:** Saddam Hussein from 1979; **political system:** one-party socialist republic; **currency:** Iraqi dinar; **GNP per capita (PPP):** N/A; **exports:** crude petroleum (accounting for more than 98% of total export earnings (1980–89), dates and other dried fruits. Principal market Jordan 95% (1995); **population:** 22,450,000 (1999 est); **language:** Arabic (official); Kurdish, Assyrian, Armenian; **religion:** Shiite Muslim 60%, Sunni Muslim 37%, Christian 3%; **life expectancy:** 61 (men); 64 (women) (1995–2000).

**Ireland** one of the British Isles, lying to the west of Great Britain, from which it is separated by the Irish Sea. It comprises the provinces of Ulster, Leinster, Munster, and Connacht, and is divided into the Republic of Ireland (which occupies the south, centre, and northwest of the island) and Northern Ireland (which occupies the northeastern corner and forms part of the United Kingdom).

**Ireland** Republic of; **national name:** Eire; **area:** 70,282 sq km/27,135 sq mi; **capital:** Dublin; **major towns/ cities:** Cork, Limerick, Galway, Waterford, Wexford; **major ports:** Cork, Dun Laoghaire, Limerick, Waterford, Galway; **physical features:** central plateau surrounded by hills; rivers Shannon, Liffey, Boyne; Bog of Allen; Macgillicuddy's Reeks, Wicklow Mountains; Lough Corrib, lakes of Killarney; Galway Bay and Aran Islands; **head of state:** Mary McAleese from 1997; **head of government:** Bertie Ahern from 1997; **political system:** democracy; **currency:** Irish pound (punt Eireannach); **GNP per capita (PPP):** (US$) 18,340 (1998); **exports:** beef and dairy products, live animals, machinery and transport equipment, electronic goods, chemicals. Principal market UK 22.2% (1998); **population:** 3,705,000 (1999 est); **language:** Irish Gaelic and English (both official); **religion:** Roman Catholic 95%, Church of Ireland, other Protestant denominations; **life expectancy:** 74 (men); 79 (women) (1995–2000).

**Irish Republican Army** (IRA) militant Irish nationalist organization formed in 1919, the paramilitary wing of →Sinn Fein. Its aim is to create a united Irish socialist republic including Ulster. To this end, the IRA has frequently carried out bombings and shootings. Despite its close association with Sinn Fein, it is not certain that the politicians have direct control of the military; the IRA usually speaks as a separate, independent organization and has, until recently, been the dominant half of the partnership. The chief common factor shared by Sinn Fein and the IRA is the aim of a united Ireland.

**iron** (Germanic *eis* 'strong') hard, malleable and ductile, silver-grey, metallic element, symbol Fe (from Latin *ferrum*), atomic number 26, relative atomic mass 55.847. It is the fourth most abundant element (the second most abundant metal, after aluminium) in the Earth's crust. Iron occurs in concentrated deposits as the ores hematite ($Fe_2O_3$), spathic ore ($FeCO_3$), and magnetite ($Fe_3O_4$). It sometimes occurs as a free metal, occasionally as fragments of iron or iron–nickel meteorites.

**Iron Age** developmental stage of human technology when weapons and tools were made from iron. Preceded by the Stone and Bronze ages, it is the last technological stage in the Three Age System framework for prehistory. Iron was produced in Thailand about 1600 BC, but was considered inferior in strength to bronze until about 1000 BC, when metallurgical techniques improved, and the alloy steel was produced by adding carbon during the smelting process.

**Irrawaddy** Myanmar (Ayeryarwady) chief river of Myanmar (Burma), flowing roughly north–south for 2,090 km/1,300 mi across the centre of the country into the Bay of Bengal. Its sources are the Mali and N'mai rivers; its chief tributaries are the Chindwin and Shweli.

**irrigation** artificial water supply for dry agricultural areas by means of dams and channels. Drawbacks are that it tends to concentrate salts at the surface, ultimately causing soil infertility, and that rich river silt is retained at dams, to the impoverishment of the land and fisheries below them.

**Islamabad** capital of Pakistan from 1967 (replacing Karachi), in the Potwar district, at the foot of the Margala Hills and immediately northwest of Rawalpindi; population (1998 est) 524,500. The city was designed by Constantinos Doxiadis in the 1960s. Landmarks include the Shahrazad Hotel and national Assembly Building. The Federal Capital Territory of Islamabad has an area of 907 sq km/350 sq mi and a population (1998 est) of 799,000. Islamabad is the centre of an agricultural region in the Vale of Kashmir.

**isobar** line drawn on maps and weather charts linking all places with the same atmospheric pressure (usually measured in millibars). When used in weather forecasting, the distance between the isobars is an indication of the barometric gradient (the rate of change in pressure). *See illustration on page 286.*

**isomer** chemical compound having the same molecular composition and mass as another, but with different physical or chemical properties owing to the different structural arrangement of its constituent atoms. For example, the organic compounds butane ($CH_3(CH_2)_2CH_3$) and methyl propane ($CH_3CH(CH_3)CH_3$) are isomers, each possessing four carbon atoms and ten hydrogen atoms but differing in the way that these are arranged with respect to each other.

**isotope** one of two or more atoms that have the same atomic number (same number of protons), but which contain a different number of neutrons, thus differing in their atomic mass (see →relative atomic mass). They may be stable or radioactive (see →radioisotope), naturally occurring, or synthesized. For example, hydrogen has the isotopes $^2$H (deuterium) and $^3$H (tritium). The term was coined by English chemist Frederick Soddy, pioneer researcher in atomic disintegration.

**Israel** State of; **national name:** *Medinat Israel*; **area:** 20,800 sq km/8,030 sq mi (as at 1949 armistice); **capital:** Jerusalem (not recognized by United Nations); **major towns/cities:** Tel Aviv-Yafo, Haifa, Bat-Yam, Holon, Ramat Gan, Petach Tikva, Rishon Leziyyon, Beersheba; **major ports:** Tel Aviv-Yafo, Haifa, 'Akko (formerly Acre), Eilat; **physical features:** coastal plain of Sharon between Haifa and Tel Aviv noted since ancient times for its fertility; central mountains of Galilee, Samaria, and Judea; Dead Sea, Lake Tiberias, and River Jordan Rift Valley along the east are below sea level; Negev Desert in the south; Israel occupies Golan Heights, West Bank, East Jerusalem, and Gaza Strip (the last was awarded limited autonomy, with West Bank town of Jericho, in 1993); **head of state:** Ezer Weizman from 1993; **head of government:** Ehud Barak from 1999; **political system:** democracy; **currency:** shekel; **GNP per capita (PPP):** (US$) 17,310 (1997); **exports:** citrus fruits, worked diamonds, machinery and parts, military hardware, food products, chemical products, textiles and clothing. Principal market USA 35.4% (1998); **population:**

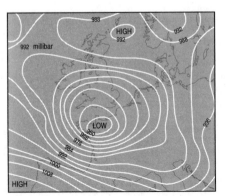

**isobar** The isobars around a low-pressure area or depression. In the northern hemisphere, winds blow anticlockwise around lows, approximately parallel to the isobars, and clockwise around highs. In the southern hemisphere, the winds blow in the opposite directions.

6,101,000 (1999 est); **language:** Hebrew and Arabic (official); English, Yiddish, European and western Asian languages; **religion:** Israel is a secular state, but the predominant faith is Judaism 85%; also Sunni Muslim, Christian, and Druze; **life expectancy:** 76 (men); 80 (women) (1995–2000).

**Italy** Republic of; **national name:** *Repubblica Italiana*; **area:** 301,300 sq km/116,331 sq mi; **capital:** Rome; **major towns/cities:** Milan, Naples, Turin, Palermo, Genoa, Bologna; **major ports:** Naples, Genoa, Palermo, Bari, Catania, Trieste; **physical features:** mountainous (Maritime Alps, Dolomites, Apennines) with narrow coastal lowlands; continental Europe's only active volcanoes Vesuvius, Etna, Stromboli; rivers Po, Adige, Arno, Tiber, Rubicon; islands of Sicily, Sardinia, Elba, Capri, Ischia, Lipari, Pantelleria; lakes Como, Maggiore, Garda; **head of state:** Carlo Azeglio Ciampi from 1999; **head of government:** Massimo d'Alema from 1998; **political system:** democracy; **currency:** lira; **GNP per capita (PPP):** (US$) 20,200 (1998); **exports:** machinery and transport equipment, textiles, clothing, footwear, wine (leading producer and exporter), metals and metal products, chemicals, wood, paper and rubber goods. Principal market Germany 16.5% (1998); **population:** 57,343,000 (1999 est); **language:** Italian; German, French, Slovene, and Albanian minorities; **religion:** Roman Catholic 100% (state religion); **life expectancy:** 75 (men); 81 (women) (1995–2000).

**Ivan (IV) the Terrible** (1530–1584) Grand Duke of Muscovy from 1533. He assumed power in 1544 and was crowned as first tsar of Russia in 1547. He conquered Kazan in 1552, Astrakhan in 1556, and Siberia in 1581. He reformed the legal code and local administration in 1555 and established trade relations with England. In his last years he alternated between debauchery and religious austerities, executing thousands and, in rage, his own son.

**IVF** abbreviation for →in vitro fertilization.

**ivory** hard white substance of which the teeth and tusks of certain mammals are made. Among the most valuable are elephants' tusks, which are of unusual hardness and density. Ivory is used in carving and other decorative work, and is so valuable that poachers continue to illegally destroy the remaining wild elephant herds in Africa to obtain it.

# Jj

**Jacobite** in Britain, a supporter of the royal house of Stuart after the deposition of James II in 1688. They include the Scottish Highlanders, who rose unsuccessfully under Claverhouse in 1689; and those who rose in Scotland and northern England in 1715 under the leadership of James Edward Stuart, the Old Pretender, and followed his son →Charles Edward Stuart in an invasion of England from 1745 to 1746 that reached Derby. After the defeat at →Culloden, Jacobitism disappeared as a political force.

**jade** semiprecious stone consisting of either jadeite, $NaAlSi_2O_6$ (a pyroxene), or nephrite, $Ca_2(Mg,Fe)_5Si_8O_{22}(OH,F)_2$ (an amphibole), ranging from colourless through shades of green to black according to the iron content. Jade ranks 5.5–6.5 on the Mohs scale of hardness.

**Jainism** (Hindi *jaina* 'person who overcomes') ancient Indian religion, sometimes regarded as an offshoot of Hinduism. Jains emphasize the importance of not injuring living beings, and their code of ethics is based on sympathy and compassion for all forms of life. They also believe in karma but not in any deity. It is a monastic, ascetic religion. There are two main sects: the Digambaras and the Swetambaras. Jainism practises the most extreme form of nonviolence (*ahimsā*) of all Indian sects, and influenced the philosophy of Mahatma →Gandhi. Jains number approximately 6 million; there are Jain communities throughout the world but the majority live in India.

**Jaipur** capital of Rajasthan, India, 240 km/150 mi southeast of Delhi; population (1991) 1,458,000. Products include textiles and metal products. Founded by Jai Singh II in 1728, it was formerly the capital of the state of Jaipur, which was merged with Rajasthan in 1949.

**Jakarta** (or Djakarta; formerly until 1949 Batavia) capital of Indonesia on the northwest coast of Java; population (1993) 9,000,000. Industries include textiles, chemicals, and plastics; a canal links it with its port of Tanjung Priok where rubber, oil, tin, coffee, tea, and palm oil are among its exports; also a tourist centre. Respiratory-tract infections caused by air pollution account for 12.6% of deaths annually. Jakarta was founded by Dutch traders 1619.

**Jamaica area:** 10,957 sq km/4,230 sq mi; **capital:** Kingston; **major towns/ cities:** Montego Bay, Spanish Town,

St Andrew, Portmore, May Pen; **physical features:** mountainous tropical island; Blue Mountains (so called because of the haze over them); **head of state:** Elizabeth II from 1962, represented by governor general Howard Felix Hanlan Cooke from 1991; **head of government:** Percival Patterson from 1992; **political system:** constitutional monarchy; **currency:** Jamaican dollar; **GNP per capita (PPP):** (US$) 3,210 (1998); **exports:** bauxite, alumina, gypsum, sugar, bananas, garments, rum. Principal market USA 33.3% (1997); **population:** 2,561,000 (1999 est); **language:** English, Jamaican creole; **religion:** Protestant 70%, Rastafarian; **life expectancy:** 73 (men); 77 (women) (1995–2000).

**James, Henry** (1843–1916) US novelist, who lived in Europe from 1875 and became a naturalized British subject in 1915. His novels deal with the social, moral, and aesthetic issues arising from the complex relationship of European to American culture. His major novels include *The Portrait of a Lady* (1881), *The Bostonians* (1886), *What Maisie Knew* (1887), *The Ambassadors* (1903), and *The Golden Bowl* (1904). He also wrote more than a hundred shorter works of fiction, notably the novella *The Aspern Papers* (1888) and the supernatural/psychological riddle *The Turn of the Screw* (1898).

**James, P(hyllis) D(orothy), Baroness James of Holland Park** (1920– ) English detective novelist. She created the characters Superintendent Adam Dalgliesh and private investigator Cordelia Gray. She was a tax official,

hospital administrator, and civil servant in the Home Office, involved with police matters, before turning to writing. Her books include *Death of an Expert Witness* (1977), *The Skull Beneath the Skin* (1982), *A Taste for Death* (1986), *Original Sin* (1994), *Certain Justice* (1997), and her memoirs, *Time to be in Earnest: A Fragment of Autobiography* (1999). Baronesss 1991.

**James I** (1566–1625) king of England from 1603 and Scotland (as **James VI**) from 1567. The son of Mary Queen of Scots and her second husband, Lord Darnley, he succeeded to the Scottish throne on the enforced abdication of his mother and assumed power in 1583. He established a strong centralized authority, and in 1589 married Anne of Denmark (1574–1619).

As successor to Elizabeth I in England, he alienated the Puritans by his High Church views and Parliament by his assertion of divine right, and was generally unpopular because of his favourites, such as Buckingham, and his schemes for an alliance with Spain. He was succeeded by his son Charles I.

**James II** (1633–1701) king of England and Scotland (as **James VII**) from 1685. The second son of Charles I, he succeeded his brother, Charles II. In 1660 James married Anne Hyde (1637–1671), mother of Mary II and Anne) and in 1673 Mary of Modena (mother of James Edward Stuart). He became a Catholic in 1671, which led first to attempts to exclude him from the succession, then to the rebellions of Monmouth and

Argyll, and finally to the Whig and Tory leaders' invitation to William of Orange to take the throne in 1688. James fled to France, then led an uprising in Ireland in 1689, but after defeat at the Battle of the →Boyne (1690) remained in exile in France.

**Janáček, Leoš** (1854–1928) Czech composer. He became director of the Conservatory at Brno in 1919 and professor at the Prague Conservatory in 1920. His music, highly original and influenced by Moravian folk music, includes arrangements of folk songs, operas (*Jenůfa*, 1904, *The Cunning Little Vixen*, 1924), and the choral *Glagolitic Mass* (1926).

**Japan** national name: *Nippon*; **area:** 377,535 sq km/145,766 sq mi; **capital:** Tokyo; **major towns/cities:** Yokohama, Osaka, Nagoya, Fukuoka, Kitakyushu, Kyoto, Sapporo, Kobe, Kawasaki, Hiroshima; **major ports:** Osaka, Nagoya, Yokohama, Kobe; **physical features:** mountainous, volcanic (Mount Fuji, volcanic Mount Aso, Japan Alps); comprises over 1,000 islands, the largest of which are Hokkaido, Honshu, Kyushu, and Shikoku; **head of state:** (figurehead) Emperor Akihito (Heisei) from 1989; **head of government:** Keizo Obuchi from 1998; **political system:** liberal democracy; **currency:** yen; **GNP per capita (PPP):** (US$) 23,180 (1998); **exports:** motor vehicles, electronic goods and components, chemicals, iron and steel products, scientific and optical equipment. Principal market USA 30.5% (1998); **population:** 126,505,000 (1999 est); **language:** Japanese; also Ainu; **religion:** Shinto, Buddhist (often combined), Christian; **life expectancy:** 77 (men); 83 (women) (1995–2000).

**Jason** in Greek mythology, the leader of the Argonauts who sailed in the *Argo* to Colchis in search of the Golden Fleece. He eloped with Medea, daughter of the king of Colchis, who had helped him achieve his goal, but later deserted her.

**jaundice** yellow discoloration of the skin and whites of the eyes caused by an excess of bile pigment in the bloodstream. Approximately 60% of newborn babies exhibit some degree of jaundice, which is treated by bathing in white, blue, or green light that converts the bile pigment bilirubin into a water-soluble compound that can be excreted in urine. A serious form of jaundice occurs in rhesus disease (see →rhesus factor).

**javelin** spear used in athletics events. The men's javelin is about 260 cm/8.5 ft long, weighing 800 g/28 oz; the women's 230 cm/7.5 ft long, weighing 600 g/21 oz. It is thrown from a scratch line at the end of a run-up. The centre of gravity on the men's javelin was altered 1986 to reduce the vast distances (90 m/100 yd) that were being thrown.

**jazz** polyphonic syncopated music, characterized by solo virtuosic improvisation, which developed in the USA at the turn of the 20th century. Initially music for dancing, often with a vocalist, it had its roots in black American and other popular music. Developing from

→blues and spirituals (religious folk songs) in the southern states, it first came to prominence in the early 20th century in New Orleans, St Louis, and Chicago, with a distinctive flavour in each city.

Traits common to all types of jazz are the modified rhythms of West Africa; the emphasis on improvisation; western European harmony emphasizing the dominant seventh and the clash of major and minor thirds; characteristic textures and timbres, first exemplified by a singer and rhythm section (consisting of a piano, bass, drums, and guitar or a combination of these instruments), and later by the addition of other instruments such as the saxophone and various brass instruments, and later still by the adoption of electrically amplified instruments.

**Jehovah's Witness** member of a religious organization originating in the USA in 1872 under Charles Taze Russell (1852–1916). Jehovah's Witnesses attach great importance to Christ's second coming, which Russell predicted would occur 1914, and which Witnesses still believe is imminent. All Witnesses are expected to take part in house-to-house preaching; there are no clergy.

**jellyfish** marine invertebrate, belonging among the →coelenterates, with an umbrella-shaped body made of a semi-transparent jellylike substance, often tinted with blue, red, or orange colours, and stinging tentacles that trail in the water. Most adult jellyfish move freely, but during parts of their life cycle many are polyplike and attached to rocks, the seabed, or another underwater surface. They feed on small animals that are paralysed by stinging cells in the jellyfish tentacles. (Phylum Coelenterata, subphylum Cnidaria.)

**Jenner, Edward** (1749–1823) English physician who pioneered vaccination. In Jenner's day, smallpox was a major killer. His discovery in 1796 that inoculation with cowpox gives immunity to smallpox was a great medical breakthrough.

**Jerome, St** (c. 340–420) one of the early Christian leaders and scholars known as the Fathers of the Church. His Latin versions of the Old and New Testaments form the basis of the Roman Catholic Vulgate. He is usually depicted with a lion. Feast day 30 September.

**Jersey** largest of the Channel Islands; capital St Helier; area 117 sq km/45 sq mi; population (1991) 85,200. It is governed by a lieutenant governor representing the English crown and an assembly. Jersey cattle were originally bred here. Jersey gave its name to a woollen garment.

**Jerusalem** (Arabic *al-Quds*; Hebrew *Yerushalayim*) ancient city of Palestine, 762 m/2,500 ft above sea level, situated in hills 55 km/34 mi from the Mediterranean, divided in 1948 between Jordan and the new republic of Israel; area (pre-1967) 37.5 sq km/14.5 sq mi, (post-1967) 108 sq km/42 sq mi, including areas of the West Bank; population (1995) 591,400. In 1950 the western New City was proclaimed as the Israeli capital, and, having captured from Jordan the eastern Old City in 1967, Israel affirmed in 1980 that the united city was the country's capital; the United Nations does not recognize East Jerusalem as part of Israel, and regards Tel Aviv as the capital.

**Jesus** (c. 4 BC–AD 29 or 30) Hebrew preacher on whose teachings →Christianity was founded. According to the accounts of his life in the four Gospels, he was born in Bethlehem, Palestine, son of God and the Virgin Mary, and brought up by Mary and her husband Joseph as a carpenter in Nazareth. After adult baptism, he gathered 12 disciples, but his preaching antagonized the Roman authorities and he was executed by crucifixion. Three days later there came reports of his →resurrection and, later, his ascension to heaven.

**Jinnah, Muhammad Ali** (1876–1948) Indian politician, Pakistan's first governor general from 1947. He was president of the Muslim League 1916 and 1934–48, and by 1940 was advocating the need for a separate state of Pakistan. At the 1946 conferences in London he insisted on the partition of British India into Hindu and Muslim states.

**Joan of Arc, St** (c. 1412–1431) also known as Jeanne d'Arc, French military leader who inspired the French at Orléans in 1428–29 and at Patay, north of Orléans, in 1429. As a young peasant girl, she was the wrong age, class, and gender to engage in warfare, yet her 'heavenly voices' instructed her to expel the occupying English from northern France and secure the coronation of Charles VII of France. Because of her strength of character, she achieved both aims. Her subsequent attempt to take Paris was overambitious, however, and she was captured May 1430 at Compiègne by the Burgundians, who sold her to the English. She was found guilty of witchcraft and heresy by a tribunal of French ecclesiastics who supported the English, and burned to death at the stake in Rouen 30 May 1431.

**Johannesburg** largest city of South Africa, situated on the Witwatersrand River in Gauteng Province; population (urban area, 1991) 1,916,100. It is the centre of a large gold-mining industry; other industries include engineering works, meat-chilling plants, and clothing factories.

**John (I) Lackland** (1167–1216) king of England from 1199 and acting king from 1189 during his brother Richard the Lion-Heart's absence on the Third Crusade.

He lost Normandy and almost all the other English possessions in France to Philip II of France by 1205. His repressive policies and excessive taxation brought him into conflict with his barons, and he was forced to seal the Magna Carta in 1215. Later repudiation of it led to the first Barons' War (1215–17), during which he died. He was succeedeed by his son Henry III.

**John of Gaunt** (1340–1399) English noble and politician, fourth (and third surviving) son of Edward III, Duke of Lancaster from 1362. He distinguished himself during the Hundred Years' War. During Edward's last years, and the years before Richard II attained the age of majority, he acted as head of government, and Parliament protested against his corrupt rule.

**Johnson, Samuel** (1709–1784) Dr Johnson, English lexicographer, author, and critic. He was also a brilliant conversationalist and the dominant figure in 18th-century London literary society. His *Dictionary* (1755), provided in its method the pedigree for subsequent lexicography and remained authoritative for over a century. In 1764 he founded, at the suggestion of the painter Joshua Reynolds, a club, known from 1779 as the Literary Club, whose members at various times included also the political philosopher Edmund Burke, the dramatist Oliver Goldsmith, the actor David Garrick, and James →Boswell, Johnson's biographer.

**John the Baptist, St** (*c.* 12 BC–*c.* AD 27) in the New Testament, an itinerant preacher. After preparation in the wilderness, he proclaimed the coming of the Messiah and baptized Jesus in the River Jordan. He was later executed by →Herod Antipas at the request of Salome, who demanded that his head be brought to her on a platter.

**joint** in any animal with a skeleton, a point of movement or articulation. In vertebrates, it is the point where two bones meet. Some joints allow no motion (the sutures of the skull), others allow a very small motion (the sacroiliac joints in the lower back), but most allow a relatively free motion. Of these, some allow a gliding motion (one vertebra of the spine on another), some have a hinge action (elbow and knee), and others allow motion in all directions (hip and shoulder joints) by means of a ball-and-socket arrangement. The ends of the bones at a moving joint are covered with cartilage for greater elasticity and smoothness, and enclosed in an envelope (capsule) of tough white fibrous tissue lined with a membrane which secretes a lubricating and cushioning synovial fluid. The joint is further strengthened by ligaments. In invertebrates with an exoskeleton, the joints are places where the exoskeleton is replaced by a more flexible outer covering, the arthrodial membrane, which allows the limb (or other body part) to bend at that point.

**Jones, Inigo** (1573–1652) English classical architect. He introduced the Palladian style to England. He was employed by James I to design scenery for Ben Jonson's masques and was appointed Surveyor of the King's Works 1615–42. He designed the Queen's House, Greenwich, 1616–35, and the Banqueting House in Whitehall, London, 1619–22.

**Jordan** Hashemite Kingdom of; **national name:** *Al Mamlaka al Urduniya al Hashemiyah*; **area:** 89,206 sq km/34,442 sq mi (West Bank 5,879 sq km/2,269 sq mi); **capital:** Amman; **major towns/cities:** Zarqa, Irbid, Saet, Ma'an; **major ports:** Aqaba; **physical**

**features:** desert plateau in east; Rift Valley separates east and west banks of River Jordan; **head of state:** King Abdullah ibn Hussein from 1999; **head of government:** Abdul-Raouf al-Rawabdeh from 1999; **political system:** constitutional monarchy; **currency:** Jordanian dinar; **GNP per capita (PPP):** (US$) 3,230 (1998); **exports:** phosphate, potash, fertilizers, foodstuffs, pharmaceuticals, fruit and vegetables, cement. Principal market India 9.2% (1998); **population:** 6,483,000 (1999 est); **language:** Arabic (official), English; **religion:** Sunni Muslim 80%, Christian 8%; **life expectancy:** 69 (men); 72 (women) (1995–2000).

**Joule, James Prescott** (1818–1889) English physicist. His work on the relations between electrical, mechanical, and chemical effects led to the discovery of the first law of →thermodynamics.

**Joyce, James Augustine Aloysius** (1882–1941) Irish writer. Joyce was born in Dublin, one of a large and poor family, and educated at University College, Dublin. His originality lies in evolving a literary form to express the complexity of the human mind, and he revolutionized the form of the English novel with his 'stream of consciousness' technique. His works include the short story collection *Dubliners* (1914), *A Portrait of the Artist as a Young Man* (1916), *Ulysses* (1922), and *Finnegans Wake* (1939).

**joystick** in computing, an input device that signals to a computer the direction and extent of displacement of a hand-held lever. It is similar to the joystick used to control the flight of an aircraft.

**Judaism** the religion of the ancient Hebrews and their descendants the Jews, based, according to the Old Testament, on a covenant between God and Abraham about 2000 BC, and the renewal of the covenant with Moses about 1200 BC. Judaism is the oldest monotheistic faith, the forebear of

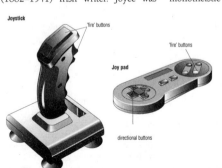

Joystick
'fire' buttons
'fire' buttons
Joy pad
directional buttons

**joystick** The directional and other controls on a conventional joystick may be translated to a joy pad, which enables all controls to be activated by buttons.

Christianity and Islam. It rests on the concept of one eternal invisible God, whose will is revealed in the Torah and who has a special relationship with the Jewish people. The Torah comprises the first five books of the Bible (the Pentateuch), which contains the history, laws, and guide to life for correct behaviour. Besides those living in Israel, there are large Jewish populations in the USA, the former USSR (mostly Russia, Ukraine, Belarus, and Moldova), the UK and Commonwealth nations, and in Jewish communities throughout the world. There are approximately 18 million Jews, with about 9 million in the Americas, 5 million in Europe, and 4 million in Asia, Africa, and the Pacific.

**judo** (Japanese *jū do*, 'gentle way') form of wrestling of Japanese origin. The two combatants wear loose-fitting, belted jackets and trousers to facilitate holds, and falls are broken by a square mat; when one has established a painful hold that the other cannot break, the latter signifies surrender by slapping the ground with a free hand. Degrees of proficiency are indicated by the colour of the belt: for novices, white, then yellow, orange (2 degrees), green (2 degrees), blue (2 degrees), brown (2 degrees), then black (Dan grades; 10 degrees, of which 1st to 5th Dan wear black belts, 6th to 9th wear red and white, and 10th wears solid red).

**Jung, Carl Gustav** (1875–1961) Swiss psychiatrist. He collaborated with Sigmund →Freud from 1907 until their disagreement 1914 over the importance of sexuality in causing psychological problems. Jung studied myth, religion, and dream symbolism, saw the unconscious as a source of spiritual insight, and distinguished between introversion and extroversion.

**Jupiter** fifth planet from the Sun, and the largest in the Solar System, with a mass equal to 70% of all the other planets combined, 318 times that of Earth's. It is largely composed of hydrogen and helium, liquefied by pressure in its interior, and probably with a rocky core larger than Earth. Its main feature is the Great Red Spot, a cloud of rising gases, 14,000 km/8,500 mi wide and 30,000 km/20,000 mi long, revolving anticlockwise; **mean distance from the Sun:** 778 million km/484 million mi; **equatorial diameter:** 142,800 km/88,700 mi; **rotation period:** 9 hr 51 min; **year:** (complete orbit) 11.86 Earth years; **atmosphere:** consists of clouds of white ammonia crystals, drawn out into belts by the planet's high speed of rotation (the fastest of any planet). Darker orange and brown clouds at lower levels may contain sulphur, as well as simple organic compounds. Further down still, temperatures are warm, a result of heat left over from Jupiter's formation, and it is this heat that drives the turbulent weather patterns of the planet. The Great Red Spot was first observed in 1664. Its top is higher than the surrounding clouds; its colour is thought to be due to red phosphorus. Jupiter's strong magnetic field gives rise to a large surrounding magnetic 'shell', or magnetosphere, from which bursts of radio waves are detected. The Southern

Equatorial Belt in which the Great Red Spot occurs is subject to unexplained fluctuation. In 1989 it sustained a dramatic and sudden fading. Jupiter's faint rings are made up of dust from its moons, particularly the four inner moons. The discovery was made in 1998 from images taken by *Galileo*. In 1995, the *Galileo* probe revealed Jupiter's atmosphere to consist of 0.2% water, less than previously estimated. **surface:** although largely composed of hydrogen and helium, Jupiter probably has a rocky core larger than Earth; **satellites:** Jupiter has 16 known moons. The four largest moons, Io, Europa (which is the size of our Moon), Ganymede, and Callisto, are the **Galilean satellites**, discovered 1610 by Galileo (Ganymede, which is larger than Mercury, is the largest moon in the Solar System). Three small moons were discovered in 1979 by the US *Voyager* space probes, as was a faint ring of dust around Jupiter's equator 55,000 km/34,000 mi above the cloud tops.

**Jupiter** (or Jove; Latin *Diovis pater* 'father of heaven') in Roman mythology, the supreme god reigning on Mount Olympus, identified with the Greek →Zeus; son of Saturn and Ops; and husband of Juno, his sister. His titles included Fulgur (thrower of lightning), Tonans (maker of thunder), Invictus (protector in battle), and Triumphator (bestower of victory). His main temple was on the Capitoline Hill in Rome; destination of the solemn triumphal processions of victorious generals. As the particular protector of Rome, he was honoured by consuls taking office.

**Jurassic** period of geological time 208–146 million years ago; the middle period of the Mesozoic era. Climates worldwide were equable, creating forests of conifers and ferns; dinosaurs were abundant, birds evolved, and limestones and iron ores were deposited.

**Jute** member of a Germanic people who originated in Jutland but later settled in Frankish territory. They occupied Kent, southeast England, in about 450, according to tradition under Hengist and Horsa, and conquered the Isle of Wight and the opposite coast of Hampshire in the early 6th century.

# Kk

**Kafka, Franz** (1883–1924) Austrian novelist. He wrote in German. His three unfinished allegorical novels *Der Prozess/The Trial* (1925), *Das Schloss/The Castle* (1926), and *Amerika/America* (1927) were posthumously published despite his instructions that they should be destroyed. His short stories include 'Die Verwandlung/The Metamorphosis' (1915), in which a man turns into a huge insect. His vision of lonely individuals trapped in bureaucratic or legal labyrinths can be seen as a powerful metaphor for modern experience.

**Kalahari Desert** arid to semi-arid desert area forming most of Botswana and extending into Namibia, Zimbabwe, and South Africa; area about 900,000 sq km/347,400 sq mi. The only permanent river, the Okavango, flows into a delta in the northwest forming marshes rich in wildlife.

**Kampala** capital of Uganda, on Lake Victoria; population (1991) 773,500. It is linked by rail with Mombasa. Products include tea, coffee, fruit, and vegetables. Industries include engineering, chemicals, paint manufacture, textiles, footwear, brewing, distilling, and food processing.

**Kandinsky, Vasily** (1866–1944) Russian-born painter. He was a pioneer of abstract art. Between 1910 and 1914 he produced the series *Improvisations* and *Compositions*, the first known examples of purely abstract work in 20th-century art. He was an originator of the expressionist *Blaue Reiter* movement (1911–12), and taught at the Bauhaus school of design in Germany (1921–33).

**Kant, Immanuel** (1724–1804) German philosopher. He believed that knowledge is not merely an aggregate of sense impressions but is dependent on the conceptual apparatus of the human understanding, which is itself not derived from experience. In ethics, Kant argued that right action cannot be based on feelings or inclinations but conforms to a law given by reason, the **categorical imperative**.

**Karachi** largest city and chief port of Pakistan, northwest of the Indus delta; population (1996 est) 10 million; 4 million live in makeshift settlements. It is the capital of Sind province. Industries include shipbuilding, engineering, chemicals, plastics, and textiles. A nuclear power plant has been developed at Paradise Point, 25 km/15 mi to the west of the city. It was the capital of

Pakistan 1947–59, when it was replaced by →Islamabad.

**Karadžić, Radovan** (1945– ) Montenegrin-born leader of the Bosnian Serbs, leader of the community's unofficial government 1992–96. He cofounded the Serbian Democratic Party of Bosnia-Herzegovina (SDS-BH) in 1990 and launched the siege of Sarajevo in 1992, plunging the country into a prolonged and bloody civil war. A succession of peace initiatives for the region failed due to his ambitious demands for Serbian territory, and he was subsequently implicated in war crimes allegedly committed in Bosnia-Herzegovina. He stepped down as party leader in July 1996. His position was further weakened when, in January 1998, the moderate Milorad Dodik became prime minister of the Bosnian Serb Republic.

**Karakoram** mountain range in central Asia, divided among China, Pakistan, and India. Peaks include K2, Masharbrum, Gasharbrum, and Mustagh Tower. **Ladakh** subsidiary range is in northeastern Kashmir on the Tibetan border.

**karate** (Japanese 'empty hand') one of the →martial arts. Karate is a type of unarmed combat derived from *kempo*, a form of the Chinese Shaolin boxing. It became popular in the West in the 1930s.

**Kashmir** area occupied by Pakistan, 78,900 sq km/30,445 sq mi, in the northwest of the former state of Kashmir, now Jammu and Kashmir.

Azad ('free') Kashmir in the west has its own legislative assembly based in Muzaffarabad while Gilgit and Baltistan regions to the north and east are governed directly by Pakistan. The Northern Areas are claimed by India and Pakistan. **population:** 1,500,000; **towns and cities:** Gilgit, Skardu; **features:** west Himalayan peak Nanga Parbat (8,126 m/26,660 ft), Karakoram Pass, Indus River, Baltoro Glacier.

**Kathmandu** (or Katmandu) capital of Nepal, situated at 1,370 m/4,500 ft in the southern Himalayas, in the Valley of Nepal, at the junction of the Baghmati and Vishnumati rivers; population (1991) 419,100. Tourism is an important economic activity.

**Kazakhstan** Republic of; **national name:** *Kazak Respublikasy*; **area:** 2,717,300 sq km/1,049,150 sq mi; **capital:** Astana (formerly called Akmola); **major towns/cities:** Karaganda, Pavlodar, Semipalatinsk, Petropavlovsk, Chimkent; **physical features:** Caspian and Aral seas, Lake Balkhash; Steppe region; natural gas and oil deposits in the Caspian Sea; **head of state:** Nursultan Nazarbayev from 1990; **head of government:** Nurlan Balgim-bayev from 1997; **political system:** authoritarian nationalist; **currency:** tenge; **GNP per capita (PPP):** (US$) 3,400 (1998); **Exports:** ferrous and nonferrous metals, mineral products (including petroleum and petroleum products), chemicals. Principal market China 29.1% (1998); **population:** 16,269,000 (1999 est); **language:** Kazakh (official), related to Turkish;

Russian; **religion:** Sunni Muslim; **life expectancy:** 63 (men); 73 (women) (1995–2000).

**Keats, John** (1795–1821) English Romantic poet. He produced work of the highest quality and promise before dying at the age of 25. *Poems* (1817), *Endymion* (1818), the great odes (particularly 'Ode to a Nightingale' and 'Ode on a Grecian Urn' written in 1819, published in 1820), and the narratives 'Isabella; or the Pot of Basil' (1818), 'Lamia' (1819), and 'The Eve of St Agnes' (1820), show his lyrical richness and talent for drawing on both classical mythology and medieval lore.

---

**WEB SITE** > > > > > > > >

**Keats, John**

http://www.bartleby.com/126/index.ht ml

Online edition of the poetical works of John Keats, indexed by title and by first line.

---

**Kelvin, William Thomson, 1st Baron Kelvin** (1824–1907) Irish physicist who introduced the **kelvin scale**, the absolute scale of temperature. His work on the conservation of energy in 1851 led to the second law of thermodynamics. Knighted 1866, Baron 1892.

**kelvin scale** temperature scale used by scientists. It begins at absolute zero (–273.15°C) and increases by the same degree intervals as the Celsius scale; that is, 0°C is the same as 273.15 K and 100°C is 373.15 K.

**Kennedy, John F(itzgerald) ('Jack')** (1917–1963) 35th president of the USA 1961–63, a Democrat; the first Roman Catholic and the youngest person to be elected president. In foreign policy he carried through the unsuccessful →Bay of Pigs invasion of Cuba, and secured the withdrawal of Soviet missiles from the island in 1962. His programme for reforms at home, called the **New Frontier**, was posthumously executed by Lyndon Johnson. Kennedy was assassinated while on a visit to Dallas, Texas, on 22 November 1963. Lee Harvey Oswald (1939–1963), who was within a few days shot dead by Jack Ruby (1911–1967), was named as the assassin.

**Kenya** Republic of; **national name:** *Jamhuri ya Kenya*; **area:** 582,600 sq km/224,941 sq mi; **capital:** Nairobi; **major towns/cities:** Mombasa, Kisumu, Nakuru, Eldoret, Nyeri; **Major ports:** Mombasa; **physical features:** mountains and highlands in west and centre; coastal plain in south; arid interior and tropical coast; semi-desert in north; Great Rift Valley, Mount Kenya, Lake Nakuru (salt lake with world's largest colony of flamingos), Lake Turkana (Rudolf); **head of state and government:** Daniel arap Moi from 1978; **political system:** authoritarian nationalist; **currency:** Kenya shilling; **GNP per capita (PPP):** (US$) 1,130 (1998); **exports:** coffee, tea, petroleum products, soda ash, horticultural products. Principal market Uganda 16.1% (1998); **population:** 29,549,000 (1999 est); **language:** Kiswahili (official), English; there are many local dialects;

**religion:** Roman Catholic, Protestant, Muslim, traditional tribal religions; **life expectancy:** 51 (men); 53 (women) (1995–2000).

**Kepler, Johannes** (1571–1630) German mathematician and astronomer. He formulated what are now called **Kepler's laws** of planetary motion: (1) the orbit of each planet is an ellipse with the Sun at one of the foci; (2) the radius vector of each planet sweeps out equal areas in equal times; (3) the squares of the periods of the planets are proportional to the cubes of their mean distances from the Sun. Kepler's laws are the basis of our understanding of the Solar System, and such scientists as Isaac →Newton built on his ideas.

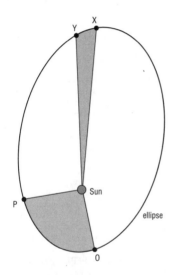

**Kepler** Kepler's second law states that the orange-shaded area equals the green-shaded area if the planet moves from P to O in the same time that it moves from X to Y. The law says, in effect, that a planet moves fastest when it is closest to the Sun.

**kerosene** thin oil obtained from the distillation of petroleum; a highly refined form is used in jet aircraft fuel. Kerosene is a mixture of hydrocarbons of the →paraffin series.

**Kerouac, Jack (Jean Louis)** (1922–1969) US novelist. He named and epitomized the →Beat Generation of the 1950s. The first of his autobiographical, myth-making books, *The Town and the City* (1950), was followed by the rhapsodic *On the Road* (1957). Other works written with similar free-wheeling energy and inspired by his interests in jazz and Buddhism include *The Dharma Bums* (1958), *Doctor Sax* (1959), and *Desolation Angels* (1965). His major contribution to poetry was *Mexico City Blues* (1959).

**Khaddafi, Moamer al** (1942– ) or Gaddafi or Qaddafi, Libyan revolutionary leader. Overthrowing King Idris in 1969, he became virtual president of a republic, although he nominally gave up all except an ideological role in 1974. He favours territorial expansion in North Africa reaching as far as the Democratic Republic of Congo (formerly Zaire), has supported rebels in Chad, and has proposed mergers with a number of countries. During the →Gulf War, however, he advocated diplomacy rather than war. Imbued with Nasserism, he was to develop afterwards his own theories (*Green Book*), based on what he called 'natural socialism' of an egalitarian nature.

**Khartoum** capital and trading centre of Sudan, in Khartoum State, at the junction of the Blue and White Nile rivers; population (1995 est) 673,000, and of Khartoum North, across the Blue Nile, 341,000. Omdurman is also a suburb of Khartoum, giving the urban area a population of over 1.3 million. It has long served as a major communications centre between the Arab countries of North Africa and central African countries. The city lies in a rich cotton growing area and an oil pipeline reached it from Port Sudan on the Red Sea. Industries include tanning, textiles, light engineering, food processing, glassware, and printing.

**Khmer Rouge** communist movement in Cambodia (Kampuchea) formed in the 1960s. Controlling the country 1974–78, it was responsible for mass deportations and executions under the leadership of →Pol Pot. Since then it has conducted guerrilla warfare, and in 1991 gained representation in the governing body.

**Khomeini, Ayatollah Ruhollah** (1900–1989) Iranian Shiite Muslim leader. Exiled from 1964 for his opposition to Shah Pahlavi, he returned when the shah left the country in 1979, and established a fundamentalist Islamic republic. His rule was marked by a protracted war with Iraq, and suppression of opposition within Iran, executing thousands of opponents.

**kidney** in vertebrates, one of a pair of organs responsible for fluid regulation, excretion of waste products, and maintaining the ionic composition of the blood. The kidneys are situated on the rear wall of the abdomen. Each one consists of a number of long tubules; the outer parts filter the aqueous components of blood, and the inner parts selectively reabsorb vital salts, leaving waste products in the remaining fluid (urine), which is passed through the ureter to the bladder. *See illustration on page 302.*

**Kierkegaard, Søren Aabye** (1813–1855) Danish philosopher and theologian, often considered to be the founder of →existentialism. He argued that no system of thought could explain the unique experience of the individual. He defended Christianity, suggesting that God cannot be known through reason, but only through a 'leap of faith'. His chief works are *Enten-Eller/Either-Or* (1843) and *Begrebet Angest/Concept of Dread* (1844).

**Kiev** (Ukrainian *Kyiv*) capital and largest city of Ukraine, situated at the confluence of the Desna and Dnieper rivers; population (1990) 2,616,000. Kiev was the capital of Russia in the Middle Ages. It is a major industrial centre, producing chemicals, clothing, leather goods, machine tools, and electrical goods, and is also a market city for the abundant agricultural produce of

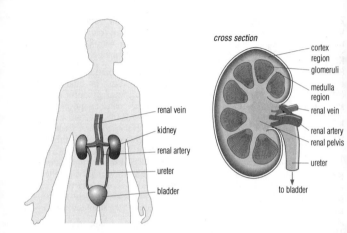

*cross section*

cortex region
glomeruli
medulla region
renal vein
renal artery
renal pelvis
ureter

to bladder

renal vein
kidney
renal artery
ureter
bladder

**kidney** Blood enters the kidney through the renal artery. The blood is filtered through the glomeruli to extract the nitrogenous waste products and excess water that make up urine. The urine flows through the ureter to the bladder; the cleaned blood then leaves the kidney via the renal vein.

the western Ukraine. Kiev University was founded in 1834. **features:** St Sophia cathedral, the oldest cathedral in Ukraine (11th century) and Kiev-Pechersky Monastery (both now museums); remains of the Golden Gate, an arched entrance to the old walled city, built in 1037. The Kiev ballet and opera companies are renowned worldwide. **history:** Kiev was founded in the 5th century by →Vikings. The Slav domination of Russia began with the rise of Kiev, the 'mother of Russian cities'; Kiev replaced Novgorod as the capital of the state of Kievan Rus in 882 and was the original centre of the Orthodox

Christian faith from 988. It was for a long time an important trading centre on the route from the Baltic to the Black Sea, but declined in importance in the 12th century. The Russian capital was moved to Vladimir in 1169, and Kiev was sacked by Mongols under Batu Khan in 1240. From the 14th–late 17th centuries, the city was successively under Tatar, Lithuanian and Polish control. It was annexed by Russia in 1686. In World War II, Kiev, then the third-largest city of the USSR, was occupied and largely destroyed by German forces 1941–43. During this period, around

200,000 of the city's inhabitants, including its entire Jewish population, were murdered.

**Kigali** capital of Rwanda, central Africa, 80 km/50 mi east of Lake Kivu; population (1993) 234,500. Products include coffee, tea, hides, textiles, cigarettes, shoes, paints, and varnishes.

**kilobyte** (K or KB) in computing, a unit of memory equal to 1,024 →bytes. It is sometimes used, less precisely, to mean 1,000 bytes.

**Kim Il Sung** (1912–1994) North Korean communist politician and marshal. He became prime minister in 1948 and led North Korea in the →Korean War 1950–53. He became president in 1972, retaining the presidency of the Communist Workers' party. He liked to be known as the 'Great Leader' and campaigned constantly for the reunification of Korea. His son **Kim Jong Il**, known as the 'Dear Leader', succeeded him.

**kinetic energy** the energy of a body resulting from motion. It is contrasted with →potential energy.

**King, Martin Luther, Jr** (1929–1968) US civil-rights campaigner, black leader, and Baptist minister. He first came to national attention as leader of the Montgomery, Alabama, bus boycott in 1955, and was one of the organizers of the march of 200,000 people on Washington, DC, in 1963 to demand racial equality. An advocate of nonviolence, he was awarded the Nobel Peace Prize 1964. On 4 April 1968 he was assassinated in Memphis, Tennessee. Although the assassination has commonly been considered to be the work of an individual, James Earl Ray, in December 1999 a civil lawsuit brought by King's family to a circuit court in Memphis, Tennessee, found that the assassination was the work of mobsters and 'several government agencies'.

**kingdom** the primary division in biological classification. At one time, only two kingdoms were recognized: animals and plants. Today most biologists prefer a five-kingdom system, even though it still involves grouping together organisms that are probably unrelated. One widely accepted scheme is as follows: **Kingdom Animalia** (all multicellular animals); **Kingdom Plantae** (all plants, including seaweeds and other algae, except blue-green); **Kingdom Fungi** (all fungi, including the unicellular yeasts, but not slime moulds); **Kingdom Protista** or **Protoctista** (protozoa, diatoms, dinoflagellates, slime moulds, and various other lower organisms with eukaryotic cells); and **Kingdom Monera** (all prokaryotes – the bacteria and cyanobacteria, or →blue-green algae). The first four of these kingdoms make up the eukaryotes.

**Kingsley, Charles** (1819–1875) English author. A rector, he was known as the 'Chartist clergyman' because of such social novels as *Yeast* (1848) and *Alton Locke* (1850). His historical novels include *Westward Hoe* (1855) and *Hereward the Wake* (1866). He also wrote, for children, *The Water Babies* (1863).

**Kipling, (Joseph) Rudyard** (1865–1936) English writer, born in India. *Plain Tales from the Hills* (1888), about Anglo-Indian society, contains the earliest of his masterly short stories. His books for children, including *The Jungle Book* (1894–95), *Just So Stories* (1902), *Puck of Pook's Hill* (1906), and the picaresque novel *Kim* (1901), reveal his imaginative identification with the exotic. Poems such as 'If–', 'Danny Deever', and 'Gunga Din', express an empathy with common experience, which contributed to his great popularity, together with a vivid sense of 'Englishness' (sometimes denigrated as a kind of jingoist imperialism).

**Kiribati** Republic of (formerly part of the Gilbert and Ellice Islands); **national name:** *Ribaberikin Kiribati;* **area:** 717 sq km/277 sq mi; **capital:** Bairiki (on Tarawa Atoll) (and port); **towns:** principal atolls North Tarawa, Gilbert group, Abaiang, Tabiteuea; **major ports:** Betio (on Tarawa); **physical features:** comprises 33 Pacific coral islands the Kiribati (Gilbert), Rawaki (Phoenix), Banaba (Ocean Island), and three of the Line Islands including Kiritimati (Christmas Island); island groups crossed by Equator and International Date Line; **head of state and government:** Teburoro Tito from 1994; **political system:** liberal democracy; **currency:** Australian dollar; **GNP per capita (PPP):** (US$) 3,480 (1998); **exports:** copra, fish, seaweed, bananas, breadfruit, taro. Principal market USA (1996); **population:** 77,000 (1999 est); **language:** English (official), Gilbertese;

**religion:** Roman Catholic, Protestan (Congregationalist); **life expectancy** 61 (men); 65 (women) (1998 est).

**Kissinger, Henry (Alfred)** (1923– German-born US diplomat. After a brilliant academic career at Harvard University, he was appointed national security adviser in 1969 by Presiden Nixon, and was secretary of state 1973–77. His missions to the USSF and China improved US relations with both countries, and he took part in negotiating US withdrawal from Vietnam in 1973 and in Arab-Israel peace negotiations 1973–75. Nobel Peace Prize 1973.

**Kitchener, Horatio (Herbert** (1850–1916) 1st Earl Kitchener of Khartoum, Irish soldier and administrator. He defeated the Sudanese at the Battle of Omdurman in 1898 and re occupied Khartoum. In South Africa, he was commander in chief 1900–02 during the Boer War, and he commanded the forces in India 1902–09. Appointed war minister on the outbreak of World War I, he was successful in his campaign calling for voluntary recruitment

**kiwi** flightless bird found only in New Zealand. It has long hairlike brown plumage, minute wings and tail, and a very long beak with nostrils at the tip. I is nocturnal and insectivorous. It lays one or two white eggs per year, each weighing up to 450 g/15.75 oz. (Species *Apteryx australis*, family Apterygidae order Apterygiformes.)

**Klee, Paul** (1879–1940) Swiss painter and graphic artist. He was one of the most original and prolific artists of the 20th century. Endlessly inventive and playful, and suggesting a childlike innocence, his works are an exploration of the potential of line, plane, and colour. *Twittering Machine* (1922; Museum of Modern Art, New York) is typical.

**Klimt, Gustav** (1862–1918) Austrian painter. He was influenced by *Jugendstil* (art nouveau) and was a founding member of the Vienna Sezession group 1897. His paintings, often sensual and erotic, have a jewelled effect similar to mosaics, for example *The Kiss* (1909; Musée des Beaux-Arts, Strasbourg). His many portraits include *Judith I* (1901; Österreichische Galerie, Vienna).

**Kong Zi** pinyin form of →Confucius, Chinese philosopher.

**Koran** (alternatively transliterated as *Quran*) the sacred book of Islam, written in Arabic. It is said to have been divinely revealed through the angel Gabriel, or Jibra'el, to the prophet Muhammad between about AD 610 and 632. The Koran is the prime source of all Islamic ethical and legal doctrines.

**Korean War** war from 1950 to 1953 between North Korea (supported by China) and South Korea, aided by the United Nations (the troops were mainly US). North Korean forces invaded South Korea on 25 June 1950, and the Security Council of the United Nations, owing to a walk-out by the USSR, voted to oppose them. The North Koreans held most of the South when US reinforcements arrived in September 1950 and forced their way through to the North Korean border with China. The Chinese retaliated, pushing them back to the original boundary by October 1950; truce negotiations began in 1951, although the war did not end until 1953.

**Kosovo** (or Kossovo) autonomous region 1945–1990 of southern Serbia; capital Priština; area 10,900 sq km/4,207 sq mi; population (1991) 2,012,500, consisting of about 210,000 Serbs and about 1.8 million Albanians. Products include wine, nickel, lead, and zinc. Since it is largely inhabited by Albanians and bordering on Albania, there have been demands for unification with that country, while in the late 1980s Serbians agitated for Kosovo to be merged with the rest of Serbia. A state of emergency was declared in February 1990 after fighting broke out between ethnic Albanians, police, and Kosovo Serbs. The parliament and government were dissolved in July 1990 and the Serbian parliament formally annexed Kosovo in September 1990. The Serbian invasion brought Kosovo to the brink of civil war; fighting and opposition efforts continued throughout the 1990s and escalated towards the end of the decade. In 1999 NATO forces moved in to keep the peace, and the UN took over the civil administration of the province.

**krill** any of several Antarctic →crustaceans, the most common species being *Euphausia superba*. Similar to a shrimp, it is up to 5 cm/ 2 in long, with two antennae, five pairs of legs, seven pairs of light organs along the body, and is coloured orange above and green beneath. It is the most abundant animal, numbering perhaps 600 trillion (million million). (Order Euphausiacea.)

**Krishna** incarnation of the Hindu god →Vishnu. The devotion of the bhakti movement is usually directed towards Krishna; an example of this is the International Society for Krishna Consciousness. Many stories are told of Krishna's mischievous youth, and he is the charioteer of Arjuna in the *Bhagavad-Gītā*.

**Kublai Khan** (*c.* 1216–1294) (also Khubilai or Kubla Khan) Mongol emperor of China from 1259. He completed his grandfather →Genghis Khan's conquest of northern China from 1240, and on his brother Mangu's death in 1259 established himself as emperor of China. He moved the capital to Khanbalik or Cambuluc (now the site of Beijing) and founded the Yuan dynasty, successfully expanding his empire into southern China, Tartary, and Tibet. He also conquered Indochina and Burma, and conducted campaigns in other neighbouring countries to secure tribute claims, but was defeated in an attempt to take Japan in 1281.

**Ku Klux Klan** US secret society dedicated to white supremacy. It was founded in 1865 to oppose Reconstruction in the Southern states after the American →Civil War and to deny political rights to the black population. Members wore hooded white robes to hide their identity, and burned crosses at their night-time meetings. In the late 20th century the Klan evolved into a paramilitary extremist group and forged loose ties with other white supremacist groups.

**kung fu** Chinese art of unarmed combat (Mandarin *ch'üan fa*), one of the martial arts. It is practised in many forms, the most popular being *wing chun*, 'beautiful springtime'. The basic principle is to use attack as a form of defence.

**Kuwait** (Arabic *Al Kuwayt* formerly Qurein) chief port and capital of the state of Kuwait, on the southern shore of Kuwait Bay; population (1993) 31,200. Kuwait is a banking and investment centre. It was heavily damaged during the Gulf War.

**Kuwait** State of; **national name:** *Dowlat al Kuwait*; **area:** 17,819 sq km/6,879 sq mi; **capital:** Kuwait (also chief port) **major towns/cities:** as-Salimiya, Hawalli, Faranawiya, Abraq Kheetan, Jahra, Ahmadi, Fahaheel; **physical features:** hot desert; islands of Failaka, Bubiyan, and Warba at northeast corner of Arabian Peninsula; **head of state** Sheikh Jabir al-Ahmad al-Jabir as-Sabah from 1977; **head of government** Crown Prince Sheikh Saad al-Abdullah al-Salinas al-Sabah from 1978; **political system:** absolute monarchy; **currency:** Kuwaiti dinar; **GNP per capita (PPP):** (US$) 24,270 (1997); **exports:** petroleum and petroleum products (accounted for more than 93% of export revenue in 1994), chemical fertilizer, gas (natural and manufactured), basic manufactures. Principal market Japan 24.1% (1997); **population:** 1,897,000

(1999 est); **language:** Arabic (official) 78%, Kurdish 10%, Farsi 4%, English; **religion:** Sunni Muslim, Shiite Muslim, Christian; **life expectancy:** 74 (men); 78 (women) (1995–2000).

**Kyoto** (or Kioto) former capital of Japan 794–1868 (when the capital was changed to Tokyo) on Honshu island, linked by canal with Lake Biwa, 510 km/317 mi west of Tokyo and 40 km/25 mi northeast of Osaka; population (1994) 1,391,000. Industries include electrical, chemical, and machinery plants; silk weaving; and the manufacture of porcelain, bronze, lacquerware, dolls, and fans.

**Kyrgyzstan** Republic of; **national name:** *Kyrgyz Respublikasy*; **area:** 198,500 sq km/76,640 sq mi; **capital:** Bishkek (formerly Frunze); **major towns/cities:** Osh, Przhevalsk, Kyzyl-Kiya, Tokmak, Djalal-Abad; **physical features:** mountainous, an extension of the Tian Shan range; **head of state:** Askar Akayev from 1990; **head of government:** Amangeldy Mursadykovich Muraliyev from 1999; **political system:** emergent democracy; **currency:** som; **GNP per capita (PPP):** (US$) 2,200 (1998); **exports:** wool, cotton yarn, tobacco, electric power, electronic and engineering products, non-ferrous metallurgy, food and beverages. Principal market Germany 37.4% (1998); **population:** 4,669,000 (1999 est); **language:** Kyrgyz, a Turkic language; **religion:** Sunni Muslim; **life expectancy:** 63 (men); 72 (women) (1995–2000).

**Labour Party** UK political party based on socialist principles, originally formed to represent workers. It was founded in 1900 and first held office in 1924. The first majority Labour government 1945–51 introduced nationalization and the National Health Service, and expanded social security. Labour was again in power 1964–70, 1974–79 and from 1997. The party leader (Tony →Blair from 1994) is elected by an electoral college, with a weighted representation of the Parliamentary Labour Party (30%), constituency parties (30%), and trade unions (40%).

**Labrador** area in northeastern Canada, part of the province of Newfoundland, lying between Ungava Bay on the northwest, the Atlantic Ocean on the east, and the Strait of Belle Isle on the southeast; area 266,060 sq km/102,699 sq mi; population (1991) 30,000. The most easterly part of the North American mainland, Labrador consists primarily of a gently sloping plateau with an irregular coastline of numerous bays, fjords, inlets, and cliffs (60–120 m/200–400 ft high). Its industries include fisheries, timber and pulp, and the mining of various minerals, especially iron ore. Hydroelectric resources include Churchill Falls, where one of the world's largest underground power houses is situated (opened in 1971). There is a Canadian Air Force base at Goose Bay on Lake Melville.

**lactation** secretion of milk in mammals, from the mammary glands. In late pregnancy, the cells lining the lobules inside the mammary glands begin extracting substances from the blood to produce milk. The supply of milk starts shortly after birth with the production of colostrum, a clear fluid consisting largely of water, protein, antibodies, and vitamins. The production of milk continues practically as long as the baby continues to suckle.

**ladybird** (or ladybug) any of various small beetles, generally red or yellow in colour, with black spots. There are more than 5,200 species worldwide. As larvae and adults, they feed on aphids and scale-insect pests. (Family Coccinellidae, order Coleoptera.)

**Lagos** chief port and former capital of Nigeria, located at the western end of an island in a lagoon and linked by bridges with the mainland via Iddo Island; population (1992 est) 1,347,000. Industries include chemicals, metal products, fish, food processing, light engineering chemicals, and brewing. Its surrounding waters are heavily polluted.

**Lahore** capital of the province of Punjab, Pakistan, situated on a tributary of the River Ravi, 50 km/30 mi west of Amritsar in India; population (1991) 3,200,000. Lahore is a commercial and banking centre, and industries include engineering, textiles, carpets, and chemicals. It is associated with the Mogul rulers Akbar, Jahangir, and Aurangzeb, whose capital it was in the 16th and 17th centuries.

**lake** body of still water lying in depressed ground without direct communication with the sea. Lakes are common in formerly glaciated regions, along the courses of slow rivers, and in low land near the sea. The main classifications are by origin: **glacial lakes**, formed by glacial scouring; **barrier lakes**, formed by landslides and glacial moraines; **crater lakes**, found in volcanoes; and **tectonic lakes**, occurring in natural fissures.

**Lamarck, Jean Baptiste de** (1744–1829) French naturalist. His theory of evolution, known as **Lamarckism**, was based on the idea that acquired characteristics (changes acquired in an individual's lifetime) are inherited by the offspring, and that organisms have an intrinsic urge to evolve into better-adapted forms. *Philosophie zoologique/Zoological Philosophy* (1809) outlined his 'transformist' (evolutionary) ideas.

**Lancashire** county of northwest England (since April 1998 Blackpool and Blackburn have been separate unitary authorities); **area:** 3,040 sq km/ 1,173 sq mi; **towns and cities:** Preston (administrative headquarters), which forms part of Central Lancashire New Town from 1970 (together with Fulwood, Bamber Bridge, Leyland, and Chorley); Lancaster, Accrington, Burnley; ports Fleetwood and Heysham; seaside resorts Morecambe and Southport; **features:** the River Ribble; the Pennines; the Forest of Bowland (moors and farming valleys); Pendle Hill; **industries:** formerly a world centre of cotton manufacture, now replaced with high-technology aerospace, nuclear fuels, and electronics industries. There is dairy farming and market gardening; **population:** (1996) 1,424,700; **famous people:** Kathleen Ferrier, Gracie Fields, George Formby, Rex Harrison.

**Landseer, Edwin Henry** (1802–1873) English painter, sculptor, and engraver of animal studies. Much of his work reflects the Victorian taste for sentimental and moralistic pictures, for example *Dignity and Impudence* (1839; Tate Gallery, London). His sculptures include the lions at the base of Nelson's Column in Trafalgar Square, London (1857–67). He was knighted in 1850.

**Languedoc-Roussillon** region of southern France, comprising the *départements* of Aude, Gard, Hérault, Lozère, and Pyrénées-Orientales; area 27,400 sq km/10,576 sq mi; population (1990) 2,115,000. The administrative centre is Montpellier. Products include fruit, vegetables, and wine.

**lanolin** sticky, purified wax obtained

from sheep's wool and used in cosmetics, soap, and leather preparation.

**Laos** Lao People's Democratic Republic; **national name:** *Saathiaranagroat Prachhathippatay Prachhachhon Lao*; **area:** 236,790 sq km/91,424 sq mi; **capital:** Vientiane; **major towns/cities:** Louangphrabang (the former royal capital), Pakse, Savannakhet; **physical features:** landlocked state with high mountains in east; Mekong River in west; rainforest covers nearly 60% of land; **head of state:** Gen Khamtay Siphandon from 1998; **head of government:** Gen Sisavath Keobounphanh from 1998; **political system:** communist, one-party state; **currency:** new kip; **GNP per capita (PPP):** (US$) 1,300 (1998 est); **exports:** timber, textiles and garments, motorcycles, electricity, coffee, tin, gypsum. Principal market Vietnam 42.7% (1997); **population:** 5,297,000 (1999 est); **language:** Lao (official), French, English; **religion:** Theravāda Buddhist 85%, animist beliefs among mountain dwellers; **life expectancy:** 52 (men); 55 (women) (1995–2000).

**lapis lazuli** rock containing the blue mineral lazurite in a matrix of white calcite with small amounts of other minerals. It occurs in silica-poor igneous rocks and metamorphic limestones found in Afghanistan, Siberia, Iran, and Chile. Lapis lazuli was a valuable pigment of the Middle Ages, also used as a gemstone and in inlaying and ornamental work.

**Lapland** region of Europe within the Arctic Circle in Norway, Sweden, Finland and the Kola Peninsula o northwest Russia, without political definition. Its chief resources are chromium, copper, iron, timber, hydroelectric power, and tourism. The indigenous population are the Saam (formerly known as Lapps), 10% o whom are nomadic, the remainder living mostly in coastal settlements Lapland has low temperatures, with two months of continuous daylight in summer and two months of continuous darkness in winter. There is summer agriculture.

**Larkin, Philip Arthur** (1922–1985 English poet. His perfectionist, pessimistic verse appeared in *The Les Deceived* (1955), and in the later volumes *The Whitsun Weddings* (1964), and *High Windows* (1974) which confirmed him as one of the most powerful and influential of 20th-century English poets. After his death, his letters and other writings, which he had instructed should be destroyed, revealed an intolerance and misanthropy not found in his published material. From 1955 until his death he was librarian at the University of Hull.

**larva** stage between hatching and adulthood in those species in which the young have a different appearance and way of life from the adults. Examples include tadpoles (frogs) and caterpillars (butterflies and moths). Larvae are typical of the invertebrates, some of which (for example, shrimps) have two or more distinct larval stages. Among vertebrates, it is only the amphibians and some fishes that have a larval stage

**larynx** in mammals, a cavity at the upper end of the trachea (windpipe) containing the vocal cords. It is stiffened with cartilage and lined with mucous membrane. Amphibians and reptiles have much simpler larynxes, with no vocal cords. Birds have a similar cavity, called the **syrinx**, found lower down the trachea, where it branches to form the bronchi. It is very complex, with well-developed vocal cords.

**Lascaux** cave system near Montignac-sur-Vézère in the Dordogne, southwestern France, with prehistoric wall art, discovered 1940. It is richly decorated with realistic and symbolic paintings of aurochs (wild cattle), horses, and red deer of the Upper Palaeolithic period (Old Stone Age, about 15,000 BC), preserved under a glaze of calcite formation.

**laser** (acronym for light amplification by stimulated emission of radiation) device for producing a narrow beam of light, capable of travelling over vast distances without dispersion, and of being focused to give enormous power densities ($10^8$ watts per $cm^2$ for high-energy lasers). The laser operates on a principle similar to that of the maser (a high-frequency microwave amplifier or oscillator). The uses of lasers include communications (a laser beam can carry much more information than can radio waves), cutting, drilling, welding, satellite tracking, medical and biological research, and surgery. Sound wave vibrations from the window glass of a room can be picked up by a reflected laser beam. Lasers are also used as entertainment in theatres, concerts, and light shows.

**Las Vegas** city in southeastern Nevada, USA; seat of Clark County; population (1994 est) 328,000. With its many nightclubs and gambling casinos, Las Vegas attracts millions of visitors each year. It is also a major convention centre. Founded in 1855 in a ranching area, the modern community developed with the coming of the railroad in 1905 and was incorporated as a city in 1911. The first casino hotel opened here in 1947. Las Vegas is the easiest place to get married in the USA, with numerous chapels along the Strip (main street) and hotel chapels.

**Latin** Indo-European language of ancient Italy. Latin has passed through four influential phases: as the language of (1) republican Rome, (2) the Roman Empire, (3) the Roman Catholic Church, and (4) Western European culture, science, philosophy, and law during the Middle Ages and the Renaissance. During the third and fourth phases, much Latin vocabulary entered the English language. It is the parent form of the Romance languages, noted for its highly inflected grammar and conciseness of expression.

**Latin America** large territory in the Western hemisphere south of the USA, consisting of Mexico, Central America, South America, and the West Indies. The main languages spoken are Spanish, Portuguese, and French.

**latitude and longitude** imaginary lines used to locate position on the globe.

Lines of latitude are drawn parallel to the Equator, with 0° at the Equator and 90° at the north and south poles. Lines of longitude are drawn at right angles to these, with 0° (the Prime Meridian) passing through Greenwich, England.

**Latvia** Republic of; **national name:** *Latvijas Republika*; **area:** 63,700 sq km/24,594 sq mi; **capital:** Riga; **major towns/cities:** Daugavpils, Leipāja, Jurmala, Jelgava, Ventspils; **major ports:** Ventspils, Leipāja; **physical features:** wooded lowland (highest point 312 m/1,024 ft), marshes, lakes; 472 km/293 mi of coastline; mild climate; **head of state:** Vaira Vike-Freiberga from 1999; **head of government:** Andris Skele from 1999; **political system:** emergent democracy; **currency:** lat; **GNP per capita (PPP):** (US$) 4,820 (1998 est); **exports:** timber and timber products, textiles, food and agricultural products, machinery and electrical equipment, metal industry products. Principal market Germany 5.6% (1998); **population:** 2,389,000 (1999 est); **language:** Latvian; **religion:** Lutheran, Roman Catholic, Russian Orthodox; **life expectancy:** 63 (men); 74 (women) (1995–2000).

**lava** molten rock (usually 800–1,100°C/1,500–2,000°F) that erupts from a →volcano and cools to form extrusive →igneous rock. It differs from magma in that it is molten rock on the surface; **magma** is molten rock below the surface. Lava that is viscous and sticky does not flow far; it forms a steep-sided conical composite volcano. Less viscous lava can flow for lon distances and forms a broad flat shiel volcano.

**law** body of rules and principles unde which is administered or orde enforced in a state or nation. In wester Europe there are two main systems Roman law and English law. US law modified form of English law.

**Lawrence, D(avid) H(erbert)** (1885–1930) English writer. His work ex presses his belief in emotion and th sexual impulse as creative and true t human nature, but his ideal of the com plete, passionate life is seen to be threat ened by the encroachment of th modern and technological world. Hi writing first received attention after th publication of the semi-autobiographi cal *The White Peacock* (1911) and *Son and Lovers* (1913). Other novels includ *The Rainbow* (1915), *Women in Lov* (1921), and *Lady Chatterley's Lover* printed privately in Italy in 1928.

**lead** heavy, soft, malleable, grey metallic element, symbol Pb (from Latin *plumbum*), atomic number 82 relative atomic mass 207.19. Usuall found as an ore (most often in galena) it occasionally occurs as a free meta (native metal), and is the final stabl product of the decay of uranium. Lea is the softest and weakest of the com monly used metals, with a low meltin point; it is a poor conductor of elec tricity and resists acid corrosion. As cumulative poison, lead enters th body from lead water pipes, lead based paints, and leaded petrol. (I humans, exposure to lead shortly after birth is associated with impaired mental health between the ages of two and four.) The metal is an effective shield against radiation and is used in batteries, glass, ceramics, and alloys such as pewter and solder.

**leaf** lateral outgrowth on the stem of a plant, and in most species the primary organ of →photosynthesis. The chief leaf types are cotyledons (seed leaves), scale leaves (on underground stems), foliage leaves, and bracts (in the axil of which a flower is produced).

**League of Nations** international organization formed after World War I

to solve international disputes by arbitration. Established in Geneva, Switzerland, 1920, the League included representatives from states throughout the world, but was severely weakened by the US decision not to become a member, and had no power to enforce its decisions. It was dissolved 1946. Its subsidiaries included the **International Labour Organization** and the **Permanent Court of International Justice** in The Hague, the Netherlands, both now under the auspices of the →United Nations (UN).

**Lear, Edward** (1812–1888) English artist and humorist. His *Book of*

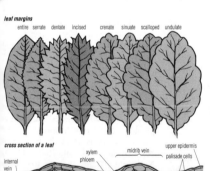

**leaf margins**

entire  serrate  dentate  incised  crenate  sinuate  scalloped  undulate

**cross section of a leaf**

internal vein

xylem
phloem

midrib vein

upper epidermis
palisade cells

spongy cells
air space
guard cells of stoma

lower epidermis

**leaf** Leaf shapes and arrangements on the stem are many and varied; in cross section, a leaf is a complex arrangement of cells surrounded by the epidermis. This is pierced by the stomata through which gases enter and leave.

*Nonsense* (1846) popularized the limerick (a five-line humorous verse). His *Nonsense Songs, Botany and Alphabets* (1871), includes two of his best-known poems, 'The Owl and the Pussycat' and 'The Jumblies'.

**Lebanon** Republic of; **national name:** *Jumhouria al-Lubnaniya*; **area:** 10,452 sq km/4,035 sq mi; **capital:** Beirut (and port); **major towns/cities:** Tripoli, Zahlé, Baabda, Baalbek, Jezzine; **major ports:** Tripoli, Tyre, Sidon, Jounie; **physical features:** narrow coastal plain; fertile Bekka valley running north–south between Lebanon and Anti-Lebanon mountain ranges; **head of state:** Emile Lahoud from 1998; **head of government:** Salim al-Hoss from 1998; **political system:** emergent democracy; **currency:** Lebanese pound; **GNP per capita (PPP):** (US$) 6,150 (1998); **exports:** paper products, textiles, fruit and vegetables, jewellery. Principal market Saudi Arabia 12.2% (1998); **population:** 3,236,000 (1999 est); **language:** Arabic (official), French, Armenian, English; **religion:** Muslim 58% (Shiite 35%, Sunni 23%), Christian 27% (mainly Maronite), Druze 3%; other Christian denominations including Orthodox, Armenian, and Roman Catholic; **life expectancy:** 68 (men); 72 (women) (1995–2000).

**Le Corbusier** (1887–1965) assumed name of Charles-Edouard Jeanneret Swiss-born French architect. He was an early and influential exponent of the Modern Movement and one of the most innovative of 20th-century architects.

His distinct brand of Functionalism firs appears in his town-planning proposal of the early 1920s, which advocate 'ver tical garden cities' with zoning of livin, and working areas and traffic separatio as solutions to urban growth and chaos From the 1940s several of his design for multistorey villas were realized notably his Unité d'habitation Marseille, 1947–52 (now demolished) using his Modulor system of standard sized units mathematically calculated according to the proportions of the human figure.

**leech** any of a group of →annelic worms. Leeches live in fresh water, an in tropical countries infest damp forests As bloodsucking animals they are inju rious to people and animals, to whom they attach themselves by means of strong mouth adapted to sucking (Class Hirudinea.)

**Leeds** industrial city and metropolitan borough in West Yorkshire, England, 40 km/25 mi southwest of York, on th River Aire; population (1991) 424,200 (city), 680,700 (district). Industrie include engineering, printing, chemi cals, glass, woollens, clothing, plastics paper, metal goods, and leather goods Notable buildings include the Town Hall (1858) designed by Cuthber Brodrick, the University of Leeds (1904), the Leeds City Art Gallery (1888), Temple Newsam House (earl 16th century, altered in about 1630) and the Cistercian Abbey of Kirkstal (1147). It is a centre of communication where road, rail, and canals (to Liverpool and Goole) meet.

**eeuwenhoek, Anton van** (1632–723) Dutch pioneer of microscopic esearch. He ground his own lenses, ome of which magnified up to 300 imes. With these he was able to see ndividual red blood cells, sperm, and acteria, achievements not repeated for nore than a century.

**eeward Islands** (1) group of islands, art of the Society Islands, in →French olynesia, South Pacific; (2) general erm for the northern half of the Lesser →Antilles in the West Indies; (3) former British colony in the West Indies 1871–1956) comprising Antigua, Montserrat, St Kitts and Nevis, Anguilla, and the Virgin Islands.

**e Havre** industrial port in the *département* of Seine-Maritime in Normandy, northwest France, on the north side of the estuary of the River Seine, 90 km/56 ni from Rouen; population (1990) 97,200, conurbation 250,000. It is the second-largest port in France, and has a cross-channel passenger links. The najor industries include engineering, chemicals, car manufacturing, and oil efining.

**eibniz, Gottfried Wilhelm** (1646–716) German mathematician, philosopher, and diplomat. Independently of, ut concurrently with, English scientist saac →Newton, he developed the branch of mathematics that is known s calculus and was one of the founders of symbolic logic. Free from all concepts of space and number, his logic vas the prototype of future abstract nathematics.

**Leicester, Robert Dudley, Earl of Leicester** (*c.* 1532–1588) English courtier. Son of the Duke of Northumberland, he was created Earl of Leicester in 1564. He led the disastrous military expedition (1585–87) sent to help the Netherlands against Spain. Despite this failure, he retained the favour of Queen Elizabeth I, who gave him command of the army prepared to resist the threat of Spanish invasion in 1588.

**Leipzig** major commercial and industrial city in west Saxony, Germany, on the Weisse Elster (a tributary of the River Elbe), 145 km/90 mi southwest of Berlin; population (1995) 478,200. Industries include printing, publishing, and the production of furs, leather goods, paper, and musical instruments. It hosts numerous trade shows, including important industrial and book fairs. The city is also a centre for the arts, culture, and education, and has a university founded in 1409.

**lemur** any of various prosimian →primates found in Madagascar and the Comoros Islands. There are about 16 species, ranging from mouse-sized to dog-sized animals; the pygmy mouse lemur (*Microcebus myoxinus*), weighing 30 g/1 oz, is the smallest primate. The diademed sifaka, weighing 7 kg/15 lb, is the largest species of lemur. Lemurs are arboreal, and some species are nocturnal. They have long, bushy tails, and feed on fruit, insects, and small animals. Many are threatened with extinction owing to loss of their forest habitat and, in some cases, from hunting. (Family Lemuridae.)

**Lenin, Vladimir Ilyich** (1870–1924) adopted name of Vladimir Ilyich Ulyanov, Russian revolutionary, first leader of the USSR, and communist theoretician. Active in the 1905 Revolution, Lenin had to leave Russia when it failed, settling in Switzerland in 1914. He returned to Russia after the February revolution of 1917 (see →Russian Revolution). He led the Bolshevik revolution of November 1917 and became leader of a Soviet government, concluded peace with Germany, and organized a successful resistance to White Russian (pro-tsarist) uprisings and foreign intervention (1918–20). His modification of traditional Marxist doctrine to fit conditions prevailing in Russia became known as **Marxism-Leninism**, the basis of communist ideology.

**Lennon, John Winston** (1940–1980) UK rock singer, songwriter, and guitarist; a founder member of the →Beatles. He lived in the USA from 1971. Both before the band's break-up in 1970 and in his solo career, he collaborated intermittently with his wife **Yoko Ono** (1933– ). 'Give Peace a Chance', a hit in 1969, became an anthem of the peace movement. His solo work alternated between the confessional and the political, as on the album *Imagine* (1971). He was shot dead by a fan.

**lens** in optics, a piece of a transparent material, such as glass, with two polished surfaces – one concave or convex, and the other plane, concave or convex – that modifies rays of light. A convex lens brings rays of light together; a concave lens makes the rays diverge. Lenses are essential to spectacles, microscopes, telescopes, cameras, and almost all optical instruments.

**lentil** annual Old World plant belonging to the pea family. The plant, which resembles vetch, grows 15–45 cm/6–1 in high and has white, blue, or purplish flowers. The seeds, contained in pods about 1.6 cm/0.6 in long, are widely used as food. (*Lens culinaris*, family Leguminosae.)

**Leo** zodiacal constellation in the northern hemisphere, represented as a lion. The Sun passes through Leo from mid-August to mid-September. Its brightest star is first-magnitude Regulus at the base of a pattern of stars called the Sickle. In astrology, the dates for Leo are

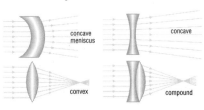

**lens** The passage of light through lenses. The concave lens diverges a beam of light from a distant source. The convex and compound lenses focus light from a distant source to a point. The distance between the focus and the lens is called the focal length. The shorter the focus, the more powerful the lens.

concave meniscus

convex

concave

compound

etween about 23 July and 22 August
ee →precession).

**eonardo da Vinci** (1452–1519) Italian
ainter, sculptor, architect, engineer,
nd scientist. One of the greatest figures
f the Italian Renaissance, he was active
1 Florence, Milan, and, from 1516,
rance. As state engineer and court
ainter to the Duke of Milan, he painted
1e *Last Supper* mural (about 1495; Sta
Iaria delle Grazie, Milan), and on his
eturn to Florence painted the *Mona
isa* (about 1503–06; Louvre, Paris).
Iis notebooks and drawings show an
nmensely inventive and enquiring
1ind, studying aspects of the natural
nd scientific world from anatomy and
otany to aerodynamics and hydraulics.

**epanto, Battle of** sea battle on 7
)ctober 1571 between the Ottoman
mpire and 'Holy League' forces from
pain, Venice, Genoa, and the Papal
tates jointly commanded by the
panish soldier Don John of Austria.
he battle took place in the
1editerranean Gulf of Corinth off
epanto (the Greek port of
Iaupaktos), then in Turkish posses-
on. It was not decisive, but the com-
ined western fleets halted Turkish
xpansion and broke Muslim sea power.

**eprosy** (or Hansen's disease) chronic,
rogressive disease caused by a bac-
erium *Mycobacterium leprae* closely
elated to that of tuberculosis. The
nfection attacks the skin and nerves.
)nce common in many countries, lep-
osy is still endemic in 28 countries and
onfined almost entirely to the tropics.

It is controlled with drugs. In 1998
there were an estimated 1.5 million
cases of leprosy, with 60% of these
being in India.

**Lesotho** Kingdom of; **area:** 30,355 sq
km/11,720 sq mi; **capital:** Maseru;
**major towns/cities:** Qacha's Nek,
Teyateyaneng, Mafeteng, Hlotse, Roma,
Quthing; **physical features:** mountainous with plateaux, forming part of
South Africa's chief watershed; **head of
state:** King Letsie III from 1996; **head
of government:** Bethuel Pakulitha
Mosisili from 1998; **political system:**
constitutional monarchy; **currency:**
loti; **GNP per capita (PPP):** (US$)
2,320 (1998 est); **exports:** clothing,
footwear, furniture, food and live animals (cattle), hides, wool and mohair,
baskets. Principal market SACU 65.1%
(1998); **population:** 2,108,000 (1999
est); **language:** Sesotho, English (official), Zulu, Xhosa; **religion:** Protestant
42%, Roman Catholic 38%, indigenous
beliefs; **life expectancy:** 55 (men); 57
(women) (1995–2000).

**Lessing, Doris May** (1919– ) born
Tayler, English novelist and short-story
writer, brought up in Rhodesia.
Concerned with social and political
themes, particularly the place of women
in society, her work includes *The Grass
is Singing* (1950), the five-novel series
*Children of Violence* (1952–69), *The
Golden Notebook* (1962), *The Good
Terrorist* (1985), *The Fifth Child* (1988),
*London Observed* (1992), and *Love
Again. Under My Skin* (1994) and
*Walking in the Shade* (1997) are volumes
of autobiography.

**leukaemia** any one of a group of cancers of the blood cells, with widespread involvement of the bone marrow and other blood-forming tissue. The central feature of leukaemia is runaway production of white blood cells that are immature or in some way abnormal. These rogue cells, which lack the defensive capacity of healthy white cells, overwhelm the normal ones, leaving the victim vulnerable to infection. Treatment is with radiotherapy and cytotoxic drugs to suppress replication of abnormal cells, or by bone-marrow transplantation.

**Levellers** democratic party in the English Civil War. The Levellers found wide support among Cromwell's New Model Army and the yeoman farmers, artisans, and small traders, and proved a powerful political force from 1647 to 1649. Their programme included the establishment of a republic, government by a parliament of one house elected by male suffrage, religious toleration, and sweeping social reforms.

**lever** simple machine consisting of a rigid rod pivoted at a fixed point called the fulcrum, used for shifting or raising a heavy load or applying force. Levers are classified into orders according to where the effort is applied, and the load-moving force developed, in relation to the position of the fulcrum.

**Lhasa** 'the Forbidden City' capital of the autonomous region of →Tibet, China, at 5,000 m/16,400 ft; population (1992) 124,000. Products include handicrafts and light industry. The holy

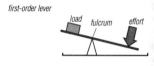

*first-order lever*

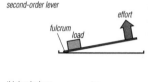

*second-order lever*

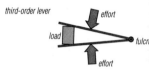

*third-order lever*

**lever** Types of lever. Practical applications of the first-order lever include the crowbar, seesaw, and scissors. The wheelbarrow is a second-order lever; tweezers or tongs are third-order levers.

city of Lamaism, Lhasa was closed to Westerners until 1904, when members of a British expedition led by C Francis E Younghusband visited the city. It was annexed with the rest of Tibet 1950–51 by China, and the spiritual and temporal head of state, the Dalai Lama, fled 1959 after a popular uprising against Chinese rule. Monasteries have been destroyed and monks killed, and an influx of Chinese settlers has generated resentment. In 1988 and 1989 nationalist demonstrators were shot by Chinese soldiers.

**iberal Democrats** in UK politics, common name for the Social and Liberal Democrats.

**Liberal Party** British political party, the successor to the Whig Party, with an ideology of liberalism. In the 19th century it represented the interests of commerce and industry. Its outstanding leaders were Palmerston, Gladstone, and Lloyd George. From 1914 it declined, and the rise of the Labour Party pushed the Liberals into the middle ground. The Liberals joined forces with the Social Democratic Party (SDP) as the Alliance for the 1983 and 1987 elections. In 1988 a majority of the SDP voted to merge with the Liberals to form the Social and Liberal Democrats.

**iberia** Republic of; **area:** 111,370 sq km/42,999 sq mi; **capital:** Monrovia (and port); **major towns/cities:** Bensonville, Saniquillie, Gbarnga, Voinjama, Buchanan; **major ports:** Buchanan, Greenville; **physical features:** forested highlands; swampy tropical coast where six rivers enter the sea; **head of state and government:** Charles Ghankay Taylor from 1997; **political system:** emergent democracy; **currency:** Liberian dollar; **GNP per capita (PPP):** (US$) N/A; **exports:** iron ore, rubber, timber, coffee, cocoa, palm-kernel oil, diamonds, gold. Principal market Belgium/Luxembourg 36.2% (1997); **population:** 2,930,000 (1999 est); **language:** English (official), over 10 Niger-Congo languages; **religion:** animist, Sunni Muslim, Christian; **life expectancy:** 46 (men); 49 (women) 1995–2000).

**Libya** Great Socialist People's Libyan Arab Republic; **national name:** *Jamahiriya al-Arabiya al-Libya al-Shabiya al-Ishtirakiya al-Uzma;* **area:** 1,759,540 sq km/679,358 sq mi; **capital:** Tripoli; **towns and cities:** Benghazi, Misurata, Az-Zaiwa, Tobruk, Ajdabiya, Derna; **major ports:** Benghazi, Misurata, Az-Zaiwa, Tobruk, Ajdabiya, Derna; **physical features:** flat to undulating plains with plateaux and depressions stretch southwards from the Mediterranean coast to an extremely dry desert interior; **head of state and government:** Moamer al-Khaddhafi from 1969; **political system:** one-party socialist state; **currency:** Libyan dinar; **GNP per capita (PPP):** (US$) 5,470 (1994 est); **exports:** crude petroleum (accounted for 94% of 1991 export earnings), chemicals and related products. Principal market Italy 41.3% (1997); **population:** 5,470,000 (1999 est); **language:** Arabic; **religion:** Sunni Muslim; **life expectancy:** 68 (men); 72 (women) (1995–2000).

**lichen** any organism of a unique group that consists of associations of a specific →fungus and a specific →alga living together in a mutually beneficial relationship. Found as coloured patches or spongelike masses on trees, rocks, and other surfaces, lichens flourish in harsh conditions. (Group Lichenes.)

**Lichtenstein, Roy** (1923–1997) US pop artist. He is best known for using advertising imagery and comic-strip techniques, often focusing on popular ideals of romance and heroism, as in *Whaam!* (1963; Tate Gallery, London).

He has also produced sculptures in brass, plastic, and enamelled metal.

**Liechtenstein** Principality of; **national name:** *Fürstentum Liechtenstein*; **area:** 160 sq km/62 sq mi; **capital:** Vaduz; **major towns/cities:** Balzers, Schaan, Ruggell, Triesen, Eschen; **physical features:** landlocked Alpine; includes part of Rhine Valley in west; **head of state:** Prince Hans Adam II from 1989; **head of government:** Mario Frick from 1993; **political system:** constitutional monarchy; **currency:** Swiss franc; **GNP per capita (PPP):** (US$) 25,100 (1995 est); **exports:** small machinery, artificial teeth and other material for dentistry, stamps, precision instruments, ceramics. Principal market Switzerland 14.5% (1996); **population:** 32,000 (1999 est); **language:** German (official); an Alemannic dialect is also spoken; **religion:** Roman Catholic (87%), Protestant; **life expectancy:** 78 (men); 83 (women) (1995–2000).

**life cycle** in biology, the sequence of developmental stages through which members of a given species pass. Most vertebrates have a simple life cycle consisting of →fertilization of sex cells or →gametes, a period of development as an →embryo, a period of juvenile growth after hatching or birth, an adulthood including →sexual reproduction, and finally death. Invertebrate life cycles are generally more complex and may involve major reconstitution of the individual's appearance (→metamorphosis) and completely different styles of life. Plants have a special type of life cycle with two distinct phases, known as alternation of generations. Many insec such as cicadas, dragonflies, an mayflies have a long larvae or pupa phase and a short adult phase Dragonflies live an aquatic life as larva and an aerial life during the adult phas In many invertebrates and protozo there is a sequence of stages in the li cycle, and in parasites different stage often occur in different host organisms

**ligament** strong, flexible connective ti sue, made of the protein →collage which joins bone to bone at moveab joints and sometimes encloses th joints. Ligaments prevent bone disloc tion (under normal circumstances) b allow joint flexion. The ligamen around the joints are composed of whi fibrous tissue. Other ligaments are com posed of yellow elastic tissue, which adapted to support a continuous b varying stress, as in the ligament con necting the various cartilages of the la ynx (voice box).

**light** →electromagnetic waves in th visible range, having a wavelength fron about 400 nanometres in the extrem violet to about 770 nanometres in th extreme red. Light is considered exhibit particle and wave propertie and the fundamental particle, or quar tum, of light is called the photon. Th speed of light (and of all electromag netic radiation) in a vacuum is approx mately 300,000 km/186,000 mi pe second, and is a universal constar denoted by $c$.

**light-emitting diode** (LED) electroni component that converts electric energy into light or infrared radiation in the range of 550 nm (green light) to 1300 nm (infrared). They are used for displaying symbols in electronic instruments and devices. An LED is a →diode made of semiconductor material, such as gallium arsenide phosphide, that glows when electricity is passed through it. The first digital watches and calculators had LED displays, but many later models use →liquid-crystal displays.

**lightning** high-voltage electrical discharge between two charged rainclouds or between a cloud and the Earth, caused by the build-up of electrical charges. Air in the path of lightning ionizes (becomes conducting) and expands; the accompanying noise is heard as thunder. Currents of 20,000 amperes and temperatures of 30,000°C/54,000°F are common. Lightning causes nitrogen oxides to form in the atmosphere and approximately 25% of the atmospheric nitrogen oxides are formed in this way.

**light year** in astronomy, the distance travelled by a beam of light in a vacuum in one year, approximately $9.4605 \times 10^{12}$ km/$5.9128 \times 10^{12}$ mi.

**Lilongwe** capital of Malawi since 1975, on the Lilongwe River; population (1993) 268,000. Products include tobacco, groundnuts, and textiles. Capital Hill, 5 km/3 mi from the old city, is the site of government buildings and offices. The city was founded in 1947.

**Lima** capital and largest city of Peru, on the River Rímac, 13 km/8 mi from its Pacific port of Callao; population (1993) 5,706,100. It comprises about one-third of the country's total population. Industries include textiles, chemicals, glass, and cement.

**lime** (or quicklime) CaO (technical name calcium oxide) white powdery substance used in making mortar and cement. It is made commercially by heating calcium carbonate ($CaCO_3$), obtained from limestone or chalk, in a lime kiln. Quicklime readily absorbs water to become calcium hydroxide $Ca(OH)_2$, known as slaked lime, which is used to reduce soil acidity.

**Limerick** county of the Republic of Ireland, in the province of Munster; county town Limerick; area 2,690 sq km/1,038 sq mi; population (1996) 165,000. The principal river is the Shannon, and towns include Abbeyfeale, Kilmallock, Newcastle West, and Rathkeale. Limerick is hilly in the southwest (Mullaghreirk Mountains) and in the northeast (Galtee Mountains). The low-lying region in the west is very fertile, and is known as the 'Golden Vale'. Dairy cattle, sheep, pigs, and poultry are reared extensively, and corn, sugar-beet, and potatoes are grown. Lace is also produced.

**limestone** sedimentary rock composed chiefly of calcium carbonate $CaCO_3$, either derived from the shells of marine organisms or precipitated from solution, mostly in the ocean. Various types of limestone are used as building stone.

**limpet** any of various marine snails belonging to several families and genera, found in the Atlantic and Pacific oceans. A limpet has a conical shell and adheres firmly to rocks by its disclike foot. Limpets leave their fixed positions only to graze on seaweeds, always returning to the same spot. The **common limpet** (*P. vulgata*) can be seen on rocks at low tide. (Especially genera *Acmaea* and *Patella*.)

**Limpopo** river in southeast Africa, rising in the Magaliesberg to the west of Pretoria in Gauteng Province, South Africa, and flowing through Mozambique to the Indian Ocean at Delagoa Bay; length 1,600 km/1,000 mi. It is also known as Crocodile River.

**Lincoln, Abraham** (1809–1865) 16th president of the USA 1861–65, a Republican. In the American →Civil War, his chief concern was the preservation of the Union from which the Confederate (Southern) slave states had seceded on his election. In 1863 he announced the freedom of the slaves with the Emancipation Proclamation. He was re-elected 1864 with victory for the North in sight, but was assassinated at the end of the war.

**Linnaeus, Carolus** (1707–1778) (Latinized form of Carl von Linné) Swedish naturalist and physician. His botanical work *Systema naturae* 1735 contained his system for classifying plants into groups depending on shared characteristics (such as the number of stamens in flowers), providing a much-needed framework for identification. He also devised the concise and precise system for naming plants and animals, using one Latin (or Latinized) word to represent the genus and a second to distinguish the species.

**lipid** any of a large number of esters of fatty acids, commonly formed by the reaction of a fatty acid with glycerol. They are soluble in alcohol but not in water. Lipids are the chief constituent of plant and animal waxes, fats, and oils.

**liquid** state of matter between a solid and a →gas. A liquid forms a level surface and assumes the shape of its container. Its atoms do not occupy fixed positions as in a crystalline solid, nor do they have freedom of movement as in a gas. Unlike a gas, a liquid is difficult to compress since pressure applied at one point is equally transmitted throughout (Pascal's principle). →Hydraulics make use of this property.

**liquid-crystal display** (LCD) display of numbers (for example, in a calculator) or pictures (such as on a pocket television screen) produced by molecules of a substance in a semiliquid state with some crystalline properties, so that clusters of molecules align in parallel formations. The display is a blank until the application of an electric field, which 'twists' the molecules so that they reflect or transmit light falling on them. There two main types of LCD are **passive matrix** and **active matrix**.

**Lisbon** (Portuguese *Lisboa*) capital of Portugal, and of the Lisboa district, in the southwest of the country, situated on a tidal lake and estuary formed by the River Tagus; population (1991

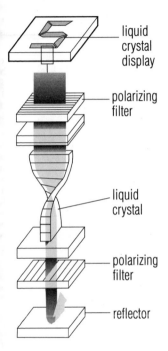

liquid crystal display

polarizing filter

liquid crystal

polarizing filter

reflector

**liquid-crystal display** A liquid-crystal display consists of a liquid crystal sandwiched between polarizing filters similar to polaroid sunglasses. When a segment of the seven-segment display is electrified, the liquid crystal twists the polarized light from the front filter, allowing the light to bounce off the rear reflector and illuminate the segment.

677,800. It is a major commercial and industrial centre, and industries include steel, textiles, chemicals, pottery, shipbuilding, and fishing. Lisbon has been Portugal's capital since 1260 and reached its peak of prosperity in the period of Portugal's empire during the 16th century. In 1755 an earthquake accompanied by a tidal wave killed 30,000–60,000 people (the estimates vary) and destroyed much of the city.

**Lister, Joseph** (1827–1912) 1st Baron Lister, English surgeon. He was the founder of antiseptic surgery, influenced by Louis →Pasteur's work on bacteria. He introduced dressings soaked in carbolic acid and strict rules of hygiene to combat wound sepsis in hospitals. Baronet 1883, Baron 1897.

**lithium** (Greek *lithos* 'stone') soft, ductile, silver-white, metallic element, symbol Li, atomic number 3, relative atomic mass 6.941. It is one of the alkali metals, has a very low density (far less than most woods), and floats on water (specific gravity 0.57); it is the lightest of all metals. Lithium is used to harden alloys, and in batteries; its compounds are used in medicine to treat manic depression.

**lithography** printmaking technique invented in 1798 by Aloys Senefelder, based on the mutual repulsion of grease and water. A drawing is made with greasy crayon on an absorbent stone, which is then wetted. The wet stone repels ink (which is greasy) applied to the surface and the crayon absorbs it, so that the drawing can be printed.

Lithographic printing is used in book production, posters, and prints, and this basic principle has developed into complex processes.

**Lithuania** Republic of; **national name:** *Lietuvos Respublika*; **area:** 65,200 sq km/25,173 sq mi; **capital:** Vilnius; **major towns/cities:** Kaunas, Klaipeda, Siauliai, Panevezys; **physical features:** central lowlands with gentle hills in west and higher terrain in southeast; 25% forested; some 3,000 small lakes, marshes, and complex sandy coastline; River Nemen; **head of state:** Valdas Adamkus from 1998; **head of government:** Andrius Kubelius from 1999; **political system:** emergent democracy; **currency:** litas; **GNP per capita (PPP):** (US$) 4,310 (1998); **exports:** textiles, machinery and equipment, non-precious metals, animal products, timber. Principal market Russia 16.5 (1998); **population:** 3,682,000 (1999 est); **language:** Lithuanian (official); **religion:** predominantly Roman Catholic; Lithuanian Lutheran Church; **life expectancy:** 64 (men); 76 (women) (1995–2000).

**litmus** dye obtained from various →lichens and used in chemistry as an indicator to test the acidic or alkaline nature of aqueous solutions; it turns red in the presence of acid, and blue in the presence of alkali.

**liver** large organ of vertebrates, which has many regulatory and storage functions. The human liver is situated in the upper abdomen, and weighs about 2 kg/4.5 lb. It is divided into four lobes. The liver receives the products of digestion, converts glucose to glycogen (a long-chain carbohydrate used for storage), and then back to glucose when needed. In this way the liver regulates the level of glucose in the blood. It removes excess amino acids from the blood, converting them to urea, which is excreted by the kidneys. The liver also synthesizes vitamins, produces bile and blood-clotting factors, and removes damaged red cells and toxins such as alcohol from the blood.

**Liverpool** city, seaport, and metropolitan borough in Merseyside, northwest England; population (1991) 481,800. Liverpool is the UK's chief Atlantic port with miles of specialized, mechanized quays on the River Mersey, and 2,100 ha/5,187 acres of dockland. The port handles 27.8 million tonnes/28.25 million tons of cargo annually. Imports include crude oil, grain, ores, edible oils, timber, and containers. There are ferries to Ireland and the Isle of Man. Traditional industries, such as ship-repairing, have declined. Present-day industries include flour-milling, sugar refining, electrical engineering, food processing, and tanning; products include chemicals, soap, margarine, and motor vehicles. There are industrial estates at Aintree, Kirkby, and Speke. A rail tunnel, and Queensway Tunnel (1934) link Liverpool and Birkenhead; Kingsway Tunnel (1971), also known as the Mersey Tunnel, links Liverpool and Wallasey. **features:** landmarks include the Bluecoat Chambers (1717); the Town Hall (1754); St George's Hall

(1838–54), the Tate Gallery in the North in the former Albert Dock (now restored as a shopping and leisure area), opened in 1987. The Walker Art Gallery (1877) and the Liverpool Philharmonic Orchestra, (founded in 1840, the Royal LPO since 1957), are here. The Grand National steeplechase takes place at Aintree. There are two universities: the University of Liverpool (opened in 1903) and John Moores University. The →Beatles were born here. The Liverpool Institute for the Performing Arts was set up by former Beatle Paul McCartney and opened in 1995. **history:** Liverpool grew in importance during the 18th century as a centre of the slave trade, and until the early 20th century through the export of the textiles from Lancashire and Yorkshire.

**Livingstone, David** (1813–1873) Scottish missionary explorer. In 1841 he went to Africa, reaching Lake Ngami in 1849. He followed the Zambezi to its mouth, saw the Victoria Falls in 1855, and went to East and Central Africa 1858–64, reaching Lakes Shirwa and Nyasa. From 1866, he tried to find the source of the River Nile, and reached Ujiji in Tanganyika in November 1871. British explorer Henry Stanley joined Livingstone in Ujiji.

**Livy** (59 BC–AD 17) adopted name of Titus Livius Roman historian. He was the author of a *History of Rome* from the city's foundation to 9 BC, based partly on legend. It was composed of 142 books, of which 35 survive, covering the periods from the arrival of Aeneas in Italy to 293 BC and from 218 to 167 BC.

**llama** South American even-toed hoofed mammal belonging to the camel family, about 1.2 m/4 ft high at the shoulder. Llamas can be white, brown, or dark, sometimes with spots or patches. They are very hardy, and require little food or water. They spit when annoyed. (Species *Lama glama*, family Camelidae.)

**Lloyd George, David, 1st Earl Lloyd-George of Dwyfor** (1863–1945) British Liberal politician, born in Manchester of Welsh parentage, prime minister 1916–22. A pioneer of social reform and the →welfare state, as chancellor of the Exchequer 1908–15 he introduced old-age pensions in 1908 and health and unemployment insurance in 1911. High unemployment, intervention in the Russian Civil War, and use of the military police force, the Black and Tans, in Ireland eroded his support as prime minister, and the creation of the Irish Free State in 1921 and his pro-Greek policy against the Turks caused the collapse of his coalition government.

**lobster** any of various large marine →crustaceans. Lobsters are grouped with freshwater crayfish in the suborder Reptantia ('walking'), although both lobsters and crayfish can also swim, using their fanlike tails. Lobsters have eyes on stalks and long antennae, and are mainly nocturnal. They scavenge and eat dead or dying fish. (Family Homaridae, order Decapoda.)

**Locarno, Pact of** series of diplomatic documents initialled in Locarno, Switzerland, 16 October 1925 and formally signed in London 1 December 1925. The pact settled the question of French security, and the signatories – Britain, France, Belgium, Italy, and Germany – guaranteed Germany's existing frontiers with France and Belgium. Following the signing of the pact, Germany was admitted to the League of Nations.

**lock** construction installed in waterways to allow boats or ships to travel from one level to another. The earliest form, the **flash lock**, was first seen in the East in 1st-century-AD China and in the West in 11th-century Holland. By this method barriers temporarily dammed a river and when removed allowed the flash flood to propel the waiting boat through or over any obstacle. This was followed in 12th-century China and 14th-century Holland by the **pound lock**. In this system the lock has gates at each end. Boats enter through one gate when the levels are the same both outside and inside. Water is then allowed in (or out of) the lock until the level rises (or falls) to the new level outside the other gate.

Locks are important to shipping where canals link oceans of differing levels, such as the Panama Canal, or where falls or rapids are replaced by these adjustable water 'steps'.

**Locke, John** (1632–1704) English philosopher. His *Essay concerning Human Understanding* (1690) maintained that experience is the only source of knowledge (empiricism), and that 'we can have knowledge no farther than we have ideas' prompted by such experience. *Two Treatises on Government* (1690) helped to form contemporary ideas of liberal democracy.

**locust** swarming grasshopper with short feelers, or antennae, and hearing organs on the abdomen (rear segment of the body). As winged adults, flying in swarms, locusts may be carried by the wind hundreds of miles from their breeding grounds; on landing they devour all vegetation. Locusts occur in nearly every continent. (Family Acrididae, order Orthoptera.)

**logarithm** (or log) the exponent or index of a number to a specified base – usually 10. For example, the logarithm to the base 10 of 1,000 is 3 because $10^3 = 1,000$; the logarithm of 2 is 0.3010 because $2 = 10^{0.3010}$. The whole-number part of a logarithm is called the **characteristic**; the fractional part is called the **mantissa**. Before the advent of cheap electronic calculators, multiplication and division could be simplified by being replaced with the addition and subtraction of logarithms.

**logic** branch of philosophy that studies valid reasoning and argument. It is also the way in which one thing may be said to follow from, or be a consequence of, another (deductive logic). Logic is generally divided into the traditional formal logic of Aristotle and the symbolic logic derived from Friedrich Frege and Bertrand Russell.

**Loire** longest river in France, rising in the Cévennes Mountains in the *département* of Ardèche at 1,350 m/4,430 ft near Mont Gerbier de Jonc, and flowing for over 1,000 km/620 mi north through Nevers to Orléans, then west through Tours and Nantes until it reaches the Bay of Biscay at St Nazaire. The Loire drains 116,550 sq km/45,000 sq mi of land, more than a fifth of France, and there are many châteaux and vineyards along its banks. The Loire gives its name to the *départements* of Loire, Haute-Loire, Loire-Atlantique, Indre-et-Loire, Maine-et-Loire, and Saône-et-Loire.

**Lombardy** (Italian *Lombardia*) region of northern Italy, between the Alps and the River Po, comprising the provinces of Bergamo, Brescia, Como, Cremona, Mantua, Milan, Pavia, Sondrio, and Varese; area 23,900 sq km/9,225 sq mi; population (1992 est) 8,882,400. Its capital is Milan. It is the country's chief industrial area with chemical, pharmaceutical, textile, and engineering operations, and its most productive agricultural region yielding wheat, maize, wine, meat, and dairy products.

**London** capital of England and the United Kingdom, located on the River Thames.

Since 1965 its metropolitan area has been known as Greater London, consisting of the City of London and 32 boroughs; total area 1,580 sq km/610 sq mi; combined population (1995) for 31 boroughs, excluding the cities of London and Westminster, 7,001,900. The **City of London**, known as the 'square mile', is the financial and commercial centre of the UK; area 2.7 sq km/1 sq mi. London is the only major European capital without a strategic authority covering the whole area. Popular tourist attractions include the **Tower of London**, St Paul's Cathedral, Buckingham Palace, and Westminster Abbey. The Millennium Dome at Greenwich is the centrepiece of Britain's millennium celebrations.

**Londonderry** (also known as Derry; until the 10th century known as **Derry-Calgaich** (Irish 'oak wood'; *Derry-Calgaich* 'the oak wood of Calgaich' (a fierce warrior) historic city and port on the River Foyle, 35 km/22 mi from Lough Foyle, county town of County Londonderry, Northern Ireland; population (1991) 95,400. Industries include textiles, chemicals, food processing, shirt manufacturing, and acetylene from naphtha. **features:** the Protestant Cathedral of St Columba dating from 1633; the Gothic revival Roman Catholic Cathedral of St Eugene (completed in 1833); the Guildhall (rebuilt in 1912), containing stained glass windows presented by livery companies of the City of London; the city walls, on which are modern iron statues by Anthony Gormley; four gates into the city still survive. **history:** Londonderry dates from the foundation of a monastery there by St Columba in AD 546. The city was subject to a number of sieges by the Danes between the 9th and 11th centuries, and by the Anglo-Normans in the 12th century; however, these were unsuccessful until

James I of England captured the city in 1608. The king granted the borough and surrounding land to the citizens of London. The Irish Society was formed to build and administer the city and a large colony of English Protestants was established. The city, then governed by Major Henry Baker and the Reverend George Walker, was unsuccessfully besieged in 1689 by the armies of James II, who had fled England when William of Orange was declared joint sovereign with James' daughter Mary. James' army was led by Richard Talbot, Earl of Tyrconnell, in a conflict known as the **Siege of Derry**, when 13 Derry apprentices and citizens loyal to William of Orange locked the city gates against the Jacobite army. The siege lasted 15 weeks, during which many of the inhabitants died of starvation and disease because of the blockade.

**Longfellow, Henry Wadsworth** (1807–1882) US poet. He is remembered for his ballads ('Excelsior', 'The Village Blacksmith', 'The Wreck of the Hesperus') and the mythic narrative epics *Evangeline* (1847), *The Song of Hiawatha* (1855), and *The Courtship of Miles Standish* (1858).

**longitude** see →latitude and longitude.

**Long March** in Chinese history, the 10,000-km/6,000-mi trek undertaken from 1934 to 1935 by →Mao Zedong and his communist forces from southeast to northwest China, under harassment from the Guomindang (nationalist) army.

**Long Parliament** English Parliament 1640–53 and 1659–60, which continued through the Civil War. After the Royalists withdrew in 1642 and the Presbyterian right was excluded in 1648, the remaining →Rump ruled England until expelled by Oliver Cromwell in 1653. Reassembled in 1659–60, the Long Parliament initiated the negotiations for the restoration of the monarchy.

**Lorca, Federico García** (1898–1936) Spanish poet and playwright. His plays include *Bodas de sangre/Blood Wedding* (1933), *Yerma* (1934), and *La casa de Bernarda Alba/The House of Bernarda Alba* (1936). His poems include the collection *Romancero gitano/Gypsy Balladbook* (1928) and the 'Lament' written for the bullfighter Ignacio Sánchez Mejías. Lorca was shot by the Falangists during the Spanish Civil War.

**Lorenz, Konrad Zacharias** (1903–1989) Austrian ethologist. He studied the relationship between instinct and behaviour, particularly in birds, and described the phenomenon of imprinting (1935). His books include *King Solomon's Ring* (1952) (on animal behaviour) and *On Aggression* (1966) (on human behaviour). In 1973 he shared the Nobel Prize for Physiology or Medicine with Nikolaas Tinbergen and Karl von Frisch.

**loris** any of a group of small prosimian →primates native to Southeast Asia. Lorises are slow-moving, tree-dwelling, and nocturnal. They have very large eyes; true lorises have no tails. They climb without leaping, gripping branches tightly and moving on or hanging below them. (Family Lorisidae.)

**Los Angeles** city and port in southwestern California, USA; population (1994) 3,449,000; Los Angeles–Riverside–Orange County consolidated metropolitan area (also known as Greater Los Angeles) (1994) 15,302,000. In size of population it is the second-largest city and the second-largest metropolitan area in the USA. The city occupies 1,204 sq km/465 sq mi. Industries include aerospace, electronics, motor vehicles, chemicals, clothing, building materials, printing, food processing, and films. Los Angeles was established as a Spanish settlement in 1781.

**Lothian** former region of Scotland (1975–96), which was replaced by East Lothian, Midlothian, West Lothian, and City of Edinburgh unitary authorities.

**loudspeaker** electromechanical device that converts electrical signals into sound waves, which are radiated into the air. The most common type of loudspeaker is the **moving-coil speaker**. Electrical signals from, for example, a radio are fed to a coil of fine wire wound around the top of a cone. The coil is surrounded by a magnet. When signals pass through it, the coil becomes an electromagnet, which by moving causes the cone to vibrate, setting up sound waves.

**Louis XIV** (1638–1715) called the Sun King, king of France from 1643, when

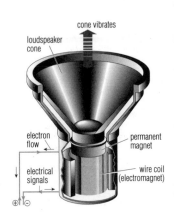

**loudspeaker** A moving-coil loudspeaker. Electrical signals flowing through the wire coil turn it into an electromagnet, which moves as the signals vary. The attached cone vibrates, producing sound waves.

he succeeded his father Louis XIII; his mother was Anne of Austria. Until 1661 France was ruled by the chief minister, Jules Mazarin, but later Louis took absolute power, summed up in his saying *L'Etat c'est moi* ('I am the state'). Throughout his reign he was engaged in unsuccessful expansionist wars – 1667–68, 1672–78, 1688–97, and 1701–13 (the War of the →Spanish Succession) – against various European alliances, always including Britain and the Netherlands. He was a patron of the arts.

**Louisiana** state in southern USA. It is nicknamed the Pelican State. Louisiana was admitted to the Union in 1818 as the 18th US state. It has been in the hands of the Spanish, French, and Americans since the 16th century, and its culture also has been influenced by African slaves and their descendants, and Caribbean and French-Canadian immigrants; the Creoles of southern parishes were originally a mix of French and Spanish descendants; the Cajuns of the southwest were originally French immigrants who had been expelled from Acadia in modern-day Nova Scotia, Canada. Musically, the state is associated with the development of jazz and the blues, particularly in the city of New Orleans. Louisiana is bordered to the north by Arkansas, to the west by Texas, with the Sabine River and Toledo Bend Reservoir forming much of the boundary, and to the east by Mississippi, with the Mississippi and Pearl rivers forming much of the boundary. To the south, the state extends into the Gulf of Mexico, its area expanding continuously through the accretional growth of the delta of the Mississippi River; much of Louisiana consists literally of fragments of other states in the Mississippi-Missouri system. **population:** (1995) 4,342,300; including Cajuns, descendants of 18th-century religious exiles from Canada, who speak a French dialect; **area:** 135,900 sq km/52,457 sq mi; **capital:** Baton Rouge; **towns and cities:** New Orleans, Shreveport, Lafayette, Metairie; **industries and products:** rice, cotton, sugar, soybeans, oil, natural gas, chemicals, sulphur, fish and shellfish, salt, processed foods, petroleum products, timber, paper, tourism, music industry.

**Louisiana Purchase** purchase by the USA from France 1803 of an area covering about 2,144,000 sq km/828,000 sq mi, including the present-day states of Louisiana, Missouri, Arkansas, Iowa, Nebraska, North Dakota, South Dakota, and Oklahoma.

**Lourdes** town in the *département* of Hautes-Pyrénées in the Midi-Pyrénées region of southwest France, on the Gave de Pau River; population (1990) 18,000. Its Christian shrine to St Bernadette has a reputation for miraculous cures, and Lourdes is an important Roman Catholic pilgrimage centre. In 1858 a young peasant girl, Bernadette Soubirous, claimed to have been shown the healing springs of the Grotte de Massabielle by a vision of the Virgin Mary.

**Lower Saxony** (German *Niedersachsen*) administrative region (German *Land*) in northern Germany, bordered to the north by Schleswig-Holstein and the city-state of Hamburg, to the northeast by Mecklenburg-West Pomerania, to the south by North Rhine-Westphalia and Hesse, on the east and southeast by Saxony-Anhalt and Thuringia respectively, and on the west by the Netherlands. **area:** 47,400 sq km/18,296 sq mi; **capital:** Hannover; **towns and cities:** Braunschweig (Brunswick), Osnabrück, Oldenburg, Göttingen, Wolfsburg, Salzgitter, Hildesheim; **physical:** Lüneburg Heath; Harz Mountains; Elbe, Weser, Jade, and Ems rivers; **industries:** cars (Volkswagen plant at Wolfsburg in the east of the state), machinery, electrical engineering, iron and steel production;

**agriculture:** cereals, oats and potatoes; **livestock farming; population:** (1995) 7,823,000; **religion:** 75% Protestant, 20% Roman Catholic; **history:** formed 1946 from Hannover, and the former Prussian provinces of Oldenburg, Braunschweig, and Schaumburg-Lippe.

**Lowry, L(aurence) S(tephen)** (1887–1976) English painter. His works depict life in the industrial towns of the north of England. In the 1920s he developed a naive style characterized by matchstick figures, often in animated groups, and gaunt simplified factories and terraced houses, painted in an almost monochrome palette. *The Pond* (1950; Tate Gallery, London) is an example.

**LSD** (abbreviation for lysergic acid diethylamide) psychedelic drug, a hallucinogen. Colourless, odourless, and easily synthesized, it is nonaddictive and nontoxic, but its effects are unpredictable. Its use is illegal in most countries.

**Luddite** one of a group of people involved in machine-wrecking riots in northern England 1811–16. The organizer of the Luddites was referred to as **General Ludd**, but may not have existed. Many Luddites were hanged or transported to penal colonies, such as Australia.

**Luftwaffe** German air force used both in World War I and (as reorganized by the Nazi leader Hermann Goering in 1933) in World War II. The Luftwaffe also covered anti-aircraft defence and the launching of the flying bombs V1 and V2.

**Luke, St** (lived 1st century AD) traditionally the compiler of the third Gospel and of the Acts of the Apostles in the New Testament. He is the patron saint of painters; his emblem is a winged ox, and his feast day 18 October.

**lung** large cavity of the body, used for gas exchange. It is essentially a sheet of thin, moist membrane that is folded so as to occupy less space. Most tetrapod (four-limbed) vertebrates have a pair of lungs occupying the thorax. The lung tissue, consisting of multitudes of air sacs and blood vessels, is very light and spongy, and functions by bringing inhaled air into close contact with the blood so that oxygen can pass into the organism and waste carbon dioxide can be passed out. The efficiency of lungs is enhanced by →breathing movements, by the thinness and moistness of their surfaces, and by a constant supply of circulating blood. *See illustration on page 332.*

**lungfish** any of a group of fleshy-finned bony fishes found in South America, Australia, and Africa. They have elongated bodies, and grow to about 2 m/6 ft, and in addition to gills have 'lungs' with which they can breathe air during periods of drought conditions. (Genera *Lepidosiren*, *Neoceratodus*, and *Protopterus*, subclass Dipnoi.)

**lupus** in medicine, any of various diseases characterized by lesions of the skin. One form (lupus vulgaris) is caused by the tubercle bacillus (see →tuberculosis). The organism produces ulcers that spread and eat away the

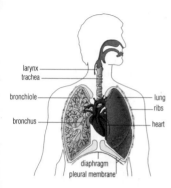

larynx
trachea
bronchiole
bronchus
lung
ribs
heart
diaphragm
pleural membrane

**lung** The human lungs contain 300,000 million tiny blood vessels which would stretch for 2,400 km/1,500 mi if laid end to end. A healthy adult at rest breathes 12 times a minute; a baby breathes at twice this rate. Each breath brings 350 millilitres of fresh air into the lungs, and expels 150 millilitres of stale air from the nose and throat.

underlying tissues. Treatment is primarily with standard antituberculous drugs, but ultraviolet light may also be used.

**Lusaka** capital of Zambia from 1964 (of Northern Rhodesia 1935–64), 370 km/230 mi northeast of Livingstone; population (1990) 982,000. It is a commercial, manufacturing, and agricultural centre. Industries include flour mills, tobacco factories, vehicle assembly, plastics, printing, cement, iron and steel, food processing, paints, plastics, fertilizers, funiture, and clothing.

**Luther, Martin** (1483–1546) German Christian church reformer, a founder of Protestantism. While he was a priest at the University of Wittenberg, he wrote an attack on the sale of indulgences (remissions of punishment for sin). The Holy Roman emperor Charles V summoned him to the Diet (meeting of dignitaries of the Holy Roman Empire) of Worms in Germany, in 1521, where he refused to retract his objections. Originally intending reform, his protest led to schism, with the emergence, following the Augsburg Confession in 1530 (a statement of the Protestant faith), of a new Protestant church. Luther is regarded as the instigator of the Protestant revolution, and Lutheranism is now the predominant religion of many N European countries, including Germany, Sweden, and Denmark.

**Luxembourg** capital of the country of Luxembourg, on the Alzette and Pétrusse rivers, south of the Ardennes uplands; population (1997) 78,300. The 16th-century Grand Ducal Palace, European Court of Justice, and European Parliament secretariat are situated here, but plenary sessions of the parliament are now held only in Strasbourg, France. Industries include steel, chemicals, textiles, and processed food.

**Luxembourg** Grand Duchy of; **national name:** *Grand-Duché de Luxembourg*; **area:** 2,586 sq km/998 sq mi; **capital:** Luxembourg; **major towns/cities:** Esch-Alzette, Differdange, Dudelange, Petange; **physical features:** on the River Moselle; part of the Ardennes

(Oesling) forest in north; **head of state:** Grand Duke Jean from 1964; **head of government:** Jean-Claude Juncker from 1995; **political system:** liberal democracy; **currency:** Luxembourg franc; **GNP per capita (PPP):** (US$) 37,420 (1998); **exports:** base metals and manufactures, mechanical and electrical equipment, rubber and related products, plastics, textiles and clothing. Principal market Germany 19% (1998); **population:** 426,000 (1999 est); **language:** French, German, local Letzeburgesch (all official); **religion:** Roman Catholic; **life expectancy:** 73 (men); 80 (women) (1995–2000).

**lymph** fluid found in the lymphatic system of vertebrates.

**lymphocyte** type of white blood cell with a large nucleus, produced in the bone marrow. Most occur in the →lymph and blood, and around sites of infection. **B lymphocytes** or B cells are responsible for producing →antibodies. **T lymphocytes** or T cells have several roles in the mechanism of →immunity.

**Lyon** (English Lyons) industrial city and administrative centre of Rhône *département* in the Rhône-Alpes region, part of which lies on the long tongue of land between the Rivers Rhône and Saône, 275 km/170 mi north of Marseille; population (1990) 422,400, conurbation 1,221,000. Lyon is France's third-largest city and most important educational centre after Paris; its main industries are textiles, chemicals, machinery, and printing. Formerly a chief fortress of France, it was the ancient **Lugdunum**, taken by the Romans in 43 BC.

# Mm

**Maastricht Treaty** treaty on European union which took effect on 1 November 1993, from which date the European Community (EC) became known as the →European Union (EU). Issues covered by the treaty included the EU's decision-making process and the establishment of closer links on foreign and military policy. A European Charter of Social Rights was approved by all member states except the UK, until a Labour government came to power in 1997.

**Macbeth** (*c.* 1005–1057) king of Scotland from 1040. The son of Findlaech, hereditary ruler of Moray and Ross, he was commander of the forces of Duncan I, King of Scotland, whom he killed in battle in 1040. His reign was prosperous until Duncan's son Malcolm III led an invasion and killed him at Lumphanan in Aberdeenshire.

**Macedonia** ancient region of Greece, forming parts of modern Greece, Bulgaria, and the Former Yugoslav Republic of Macedonia. Macedonia gained control of Greece after Philip II's victory at Chaeronea 338 BC. His son, Alexander the Great, conquered a vast empire. Macedonia became a Roman province 146 BC.

**Macedonia** Former Yugoslav Republic of (official international name); Republic of Macedon (official internal name); **national name:** *Republika Makedonija*; **area:** 25,700 sq km/9,922 sq mi; **capital:** Skopje; **major towns/cities:** Bitolj, Prilep, Kumanovo, Tetovo; **physical features:** mountainous; rivers Struma, Vardar; lakes Ohrid, Prespa; partly Mediterranean climate with hot summers; **head of state:** Kiro Gligonov from 1991; **head of government:** Ljubco Georgievski from 1998; **political system:** emergent democracy; currency: Macedonian denar; GNP per **capita (PPP):** (US$) 3,660 (1998); **exports:** manufactured goods, machinery and transport equipment, miscellaneous manufactured articles, sugar beet, vegetables, cheese, lamb, tobacco. Principal market Germany 21.4% (1998); **population:** 2,011,000 (1999 est); **language:** Macedonian, closely allied to Bulgarian and written in Cyrillic; **religion:** Christian, mainly Orthodox; Muslim 2.5%; **life expectancy:** 71 (men); 75 (women) (1995–2000).

**Machiavelli, Niccolò** (1469–1527) Italian politician and author. His name is synonymous with cunning and cynical statecraft. In his chief political writings, *Il principe*/*The Prince* (1513) and *Discorsi*/*Discourses* (1531), he discussed ways in which rulers can advance the interests of their states (and themselves) through an often amoral and opportunistic manipulation of other people.

**Machu Picchu** ruined Inca city in the Peruvian Andes, northwest of Cuzco. This settlement and stronghold stands at the top of 300-m/1,000-ft-high cliffs above the Urabamba River and covers an area of 13 sq km/5 sq mi. Built in about AD 1500, the city's remote location saved it from being found and destroyed by the Spanish conquistadors, and the remains of its houses and temples are well preserved. Machu Picchu was discovered in 1911 by the US archaeologist Hiram L Bingham.

**Macmillan, (Maurice) Harold** (1894– 1986) 1st Earl of Stockton British Conservative politician, prime minister (1957–63); foreign secretary (1955) and chancellor of the Exchequer (1955–57). In 1963 he attempted to negotiate British entry into the European Economic Community (EEC), but was blocked by the French president Charles de Gaulle. Much of his career as prime minister was spent defending the UK's retention of a nuclear weapon, and he was responsible for the purchase of US Polaris missiles in 1962.

**Madagascar** Democratic Republic of; **national name:** *Repoblika Demokratika n'i Madagaskar*; **area:** 587,041 sq km/ 226,656 sq mi; **capital:** Antananarivo; **major towns/cities:** Antsirabe, Mahajanga, Fianarantsoa, Toamasina, Ambatondrazaka; **physical features:** temperate central highlands; humid valleys and tropical coastal plains; arid in south; **head of state:** Didier Ratsiraka from 1996; **head of government:** René Tantely Gabrio Andrianarivo from 1998; **political system:** emergent democracy; **currency:** Malagasy franc; **GNP per capita (PPP):** (US$) 900 (1998); **exports:** coffee, shrimps, cloves, vanilla, petroleum products, chromium, cotton fabrics. Principal market France 39.5% (1998); **population:** 15,496,000 (1999 est); **language:** Malagasy (official); French, English; **religion:** traditional beliefs, Roman Catholic, Protestant; **life expectancy:** 56 (men); 59 (women) (1995–2000).

**mad cow disease** common name for →bovine spongiform encephalopathy, an incurable brain condition in cattle.

**Madras** former name, to 1996, of Chennai, an industrial port and capital of the state of Tamil Nadu, India.

**Madrid** autonomous community of central Spain; area 8,000 sq km/3,088 sq mi; population (1991) 4,845,900. Bounded by the Sierra de Guadarrama mountains in the northwest, and by the River Tagus in the southeast, it is arid plateau country. It is crossed by several rivers, including the Jarama, a tributary of the Tagus. Products include fruit and vegetables, grown in the south; timber from the forests in the northeast, and granite and gypsum from quarries in the mountains. The Escorial palace lies in the northwest; Aranjuez in the south has contained a royal palace since the 15th century and has luxurious gardens. The capital is Madrid.

**Mafia** (Italian 'swank') secret society

reputed to control organized crime such as gambling, loansharking, drug traffic, prostitution, and protection; connected with the Camorra of Naples. It originated in Sicily in the late Middle Ages and now operates chiefly there and in countries to which Italians have emigrated, such as the USA and Australia. During the early 1990s many centre and right-wing Italian politicians, such as the former Christian Democrat prime minister Giulio Andreotti, became discredited when it emerged that they had had dealings with the Mafia.

**Magellan, Ferdinand** (c. 1480–1521) Portuguese navigator. In 1519 he set sail in the *Victoria* from Seville with the intention of reaching the East Indies by a westerly route. He sailed through the **Strait of Magellan** at the tip of South America, crossed an ocean he named the Pacific, and in 1521 reached the Philippines, where he was killed in a battle with the islanders. His companions returned to Seville in 1522, completing the voyage under del Cano.

**magma** molten rock material beneath the Earth's (or any of the terrestrial planets) surface from which →igneous rocks are formed. →Lava is magma that has extruded on to the surface.

**Magna Carta** (Latin 'great charter') in English history, the charter granted by King John in 1215, traditionally seen as guaranteeing human rights against the excessive use of royal power. As a reply to the king's demands for excessive feudal dues and attacks on the privileges of the church, Archbishop Langton proposed to the barons the drawing-up of a binding document in 1213. John was forced to accept this at Runnymede (now in Surrey) on 15 June 1215.

**magnesium** lightweight, very ductile and malleable, silver-white, metallic element, symbol Mg, atomic number 12, relative atomic mass 24.305. It is one of the alkaline-earth metals, and the lightest of the commonly used metals. Magnesium silicate, carbonate, and chloride are widely distributed in nature. The metal is used in alloys and flash photography. It is a necessary trace element in the human diet, and green plants cannot grow without it since it is an essential constituent of the photosynthetic pigment →chlorophyll ($C_{55}H_{72}MgN_4O_5$).

**magnet** any object that forms a magnetic field (displays →magnetism), either permanently or temporarily through induction, causing it to attract materials such as iron, cobalt, nickel, and alloys of these. It always has two magnetic poles, called north and south.

**magnetic field** region around a permanent magnet, or around a conductor carrying an electric current, in which a force acts on a moving charge or on a magnet placed in the field. The field can be represented by lines of force, which by convention link north and south poles and are parallel to the directions of a small compass needle placed on them. A magnetic field's magnitude and direction are given by the magnetic flux density, expressed in teslas.

**magnetic resonance imaging** (MRI

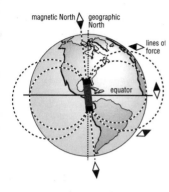

magnetic North △ geographic North

lines of force

equator

**magnetic field** The Earth's magnetic field is similar to that of a bar magnet with poles near, but not exactly at, the geographic poles. Compass needles align themselves with the magnetic field, which is horizontal near the equator and vertical at the magnetic poles.

diagnostic scanning system based on the principles of nuclear magnetic resonance. MRI yields finely detailed three-dimensional images of structures within the body without exposing the patient to harmful radiation. The technique is invaluable for imaging the soft tissues of the body, in particular the brain and the spinal cord.

**magnetism** phenomena associated with →magnetic fields. Magnetic fields are produced by moving charged particles: in electromagnets, electrons flow through a coil of wire connected to a battery; in permanent magnets, spinning electrons within the atoms generate the field.

**magnitude** in astronomy, measure of the brightness of a star or other celestial object. The larger the number denoting the magnitude, the fainter the object. Zero or first magnitude indicates some of the brightest stars. Still brighter are those of negative magnitude, such as Sirius, whose magnitude is −1.46. **Apparent magnitude** is the brightness of an object as seen from Earth; **absolute magnitude** is the brightness at a standard distance of 10 parsecs (32.616 light years).

**Magritte, René François Ghislain** (1898–1967) Belgian painter, one of the major figures in Surrealism. His work focuses on visual paradoxes and everyday objects taken out of context. Recurring motifs include bowler hats, apples, and windows, for example *Golconda* (1953; private collection), in which men in bowler hats are falling from the sky to a street below.

**Mahler, Gustav** (1860–1911) Austrian composer and conductor. His epic symphonies express a world-weary Romanticism in visionary tableaux incorporating folk music and pastoral imagery. He composed nine large-scale symphonies, many with voices, including *Symphony No 2 'Resurrection'* (1884–86, revised 1893–96) and left a tenth unfinished. He also composed orchestral lieder (songs) including *Das Lied von der Erde/The Song of the Earth* (1909) and *Kindertotenlieder/Dead Children's Songs* (1901–04).

**mahogany** timber from any of several trees found in the Americas and Africa.

Mahogany is a tropical hardwood obtained chiefly by rainforest logging. It has a warm red colour and can be highly polished. True mahogany comes mainly from *S. mahogoni* and *S. macrophylla*, but other types come from the Spanish and Australian cedars, the Indian redwood, and other trees of the mahogany family, native to Africa and the East Indies. (True mahogany genus *Swietenia*, family Meliaceae.)

**mainframe** large computer used for commercial data processing and other large-scale operations. Because of the general increase in computing power, the differences between the mainframe, supercomputer, minicomputer, and microcomputer (personal computer) are becoming less marked.

**maize** (North American corn) tall annual cereal plant that produces spikes of yellow grains which are widely used as an animal feed. Grown extensively in all subtropical and warm temperate regions, its range has been extended to colder zones by hardy varieties developed in the 1960s. (*Zea mays*.)

**Majorca** alternative spelling of →Mallorca.

**malaria** infectious parasitic disease of the tropics transmitted by mosquitoes, marked by periodic fever and an enlarged spleen. When a female mosquito of the *Anopheles* genus bites a human who has malaria, it takes in with the human blood one of four malaria protozoa of the genus *Plasmodium*. This matures within the insect and is then transferred when the mosquito bites a

**WEB SITE** > > > > > > > >

**Malaria**

http://www.malaria.org/whatismalaria.html

Page from the Malaria Foundation covering frequently asked questions on malaria. The Web site contains answers to a comprehensive list of questions regarding the disease, including thorough descriptions of the virus and its related diseases.

new victim. Malaria affects about 267 million people in 103 countries, and in 1995 around 2.1 million people died of the disease. In sub-Saharan Africa alone between 1.5 and 2 million children die from malaria and its consequences each year. In November 1998, an agreement was reached to establish a multiagency programme for research and control of the disease. The agencies involved include the World Health Organization (WHO), the World Bank, the United Nations Children's Fund, and the United Nations Development Programme. The Roll Back Malaria campaign aims to halve deaths from malaria by 2010.

**Malawi** Republic of (formerly **Nyasaland**); **national name:** *Malaŵi*; **area:** 118,484 sq km/45,735 sq mi; **capital:** Lilongwe; **major towns/cities:** Blantyre, Lilongwe, Mzuzu, Zomba; **physical features:** landlocked narrow plateau with rolling plains; mountainous west of Lake Nyasa; **head of state and government:** Bakili Muluzi from 1994; **political system:** emergent democracy; **currency:** Malawi kwacha; **GNP per**

capita (PPP): (US$) 730 (1998); exports: tobacco, tea, sugar, cotton, groundnuts. Principal market South Africa 12.8% (1997); population: 10,640,000 (1999 est); language: English, Chichewa (both official); religion: Christian 75%, Muslim 20%; life expectancy: 39 (men); 40 (women) (1995–2000).

**Malaysia** Federation of (FOM); national name: *Persekutuan Tanah Malaysia*; area: 329,759 sq km/127,319 sq mi; capital: Kuala Lumpur; major towns/cities: Johor Baharu, Ipoh, George Town (Penang), Kuala Trengganu, Kuala Baharu, Petalong Jaya, Kelang, Kuching in Sarawak, Kota Kinabalu in Sabah; major ports: Kelang; physical features: comprises peninsular Malaysia (the nine Malay states – Johore, Kedah, Kelantan, Negri Sembilan, Pahang, Perak, Perlis, Selangor, Trengganu – plus Malacca and Penang); states of Sabah and Sarawak and federal territory of Kuala Lumpur; 75% tropical rainforest; central mountain range (Mount Kinabalu, the highest peak in southeast Asia); swamps in east; Niah caves (Sarawak); head of state: Tuanku Salehuddin Abdul Aziz Shan bin al-Marhum Hisamuddin Alam Shah from 1999; head of government: Mahathir bin Muhammad from 1981; political system: liberal democracy; currency: ringgit; GNP per capita (PPP): (US$) 6,990 (1998 est); exports: palm oil, rubber, crude petroleum, machinery and transport equipment, timber, tin, textiles, electronic goods. Principal market USA 21.6% (1998);

population: 21,830,000 (1999 est); language: Malay (official), English, Chinese, Tamil, Iban; religion: Muslim (official), Buddhist, Hindu, local beliefs; life expectancy: 70 (men); 74 (women) (1995–2000).

**Maldives** Republic of the; national name: *Divehi Raajjeyge Jumhooriyaa*; area: 298 sq km/115 sq mi; capital: Malé; major towns/cities: Seenu, Kurehdhu, Kunfunadhoo, Dhiggiri, Anthimatha; physical features: comprises 1,196 coral islands, grouped into 12 clusters of atolls, largely flat, none bigger than 13 sq km/5 sq mi, average elevation 1.8 m/6 ft; 203 are inhabited; head of state and government: Maumoon Abd Gayoom from 1978; political system: authoritarian nationalist; currency: rufiya; GNP per capita (PPP): (US$) 3,100 (1998); exports: marine products (tuna bonito ('Maldive Fish'), clothing. Principal market Germany 33% (1996); population: 278,000 (1999 est); language: Divehi (Sinhalese dialect), English; religion: Sunni Muslim; life expectancy: 66 (men); 63 (women) (1995–2000).

**Mali** Republic of; national name: *République du Mali*; area: 1,240,142 sq km/478,818 sq mi; capital: Bamako; major towns/cities: Mopti, Kayes, Ségou, Timbuktu, Sikasso; physical features: landlocked state with River Niger and savannah in south; part of the Sahara in north; hills in northeast; Senegal River and its branches irrigate the southwest; head of state: Alpha Oumar Konare from 1992; head of government: Ibrahim

Boubaker Keita from 1994; **political system:** emergent democracy; **currency:** franc CFA; **GNP per capita (PPP):** (US$) 720 (1998); **exports:** cotton, livestock, gold, miscellaneous manufactured articles. Principal market Thailand 20.3% (1997); **population:** 10,960,000 (1999 est); **language:** French (official), Bambara; **religion:** Sunni Muslim 90%, animist, Christian; **life expectancy:** 52 (men); 55 (women) (1995–2000).

**Mallorca** (or Majorca) largest of the →Balearic Islands, belonging to Spain, in the western Mediterranean. **area:** 3,640 sq km/1,405 sq mi; **capital:** Palma; **features:** the highest mountain is Puig Mayor (1,445 m/4,741 ft); **industries:** olives, figs, oranges, wine, brandy, timber, sheep; tourism is the mainstay of the economy; **population:** (1990 est) 582,000.

**Malory, Thomas** (c. 1410–1471) English author. He is known for the prose romance *Le Morte D'Arthur* (c. 1470), printed in 1485, which relates the exploits of King Arthur's knights of the Round Table and the quest for the →Holy Grail. Knight of the shire from 1445.

**Malta** Republic of; **national name:** *Repubblika Ta'Malta*; **area:** 320 sq km/124 sq mi; **capital:** Valletta (and port); **major towns/cities:** Rabat, Birkirkara, Qormi, Sliema, Zetjun, Zabor; **major ports:** Marsaxlokk, Valletta; **physical features:** includes islands of Gozo 67 sq km/26 sq mi and Comino 3 sq km/1 sq mi; **head of state:** Guido de Marco from 1999; **head of government:** Edward Fenech

Adami from 1998; **political system:** liberal democracy; **currency:** Maltese lira; **GNP per capita (PPP):** (US$) 13,610 (1998); **exports:** machinery and transport equipment, manufactured articles (including clothing), beverages, chemicals, tobacco. Principal market France 20.7% (1998); **population:** 386,000 (1999 est); **language:** Maltese, English (both official); **religion:** Roman Catholic 98%; **life expectancy:** 75 (men); 79 (women) (1995–2000).

**Malthus, Thomas Robert** (1766–1834) English economist. His *Essay on the Principle of Population* (1798; revised 1803) argued for population control, since populations increase in geometric ratio and food supply only in arithmetic ratio, and influenced Charles →Darwin's thinking on natural selection as the driving force of evolution.

**mammal** any of a large group of warm-blooded vertebrate animals characterized by having mammary glands in the female; these are used for suckling the young. Other features of mammals are hair (very reduced in some species, such as whales); a middle ear formed of three small bones (ossicles); a lower jaw consisting of two bones only; seven vertebrae in the neck; and no nucleus in the red blood cells. (Class Mammalia.)

Mammals are divided into three groups:

**placental mammals**, where the young develop inside the mother's body, in the →uterus, receiving nourishment from the blood of the mother via the →placenta;

**marsupials**, where the young are born

at an early stage of development and develop further in a pouch on the mother's body where they are attached to and fed from a nipple; and **monotremes**, where the young hatch from an egg outside the mother's body and are then nourished with milk.

The monotremes are the least evolved and have been largely displaced by more sophisticated marsupials and placentals, so that there are only a few types surviving (platypus and echidna). Placentals have spread to all parts of the globe, and where placentals have competed with marsupials, the placentals have in general displaced marsupial types. However, marsupials occupy many specialized niches in South America and, especially, Australasia.

According to the Red List of endangered species published by the World Conservation Union (IUCN) for 1996, 25% of mammal species are threatened with extinction.

**Managua** capital and chief industrial city of Nicaragua, and capital of a department of the same name; it is situated on the southern shore of Lake Managua 45km/28 mi from the Pacific coast and 138 km/86 mi from the main port of Corinto; population (1995 est) 1,240,000.

**manatee** any of a group of plant-eating aquatic mammals found in marine bays and sluggish rivers, usually in thick, muddy water. They have flippers as forelimbs, no hindlimbs, and a short rounded and flattened tail used for swimming. The marine manatees can grow up to about 4.5 m/15 ft long and weigh up to 600 kg/1,323 lb. (Genus *Trichechus*, family Trichechidae, order Sirenia.)

**Manchester** metropolitan district of Greater Manchester, and city in northwest England, on the River Irwell, 50 km/31 mi east of Liverpool; population (1991) 402,900. A financial and manufacturing centre, its industries include banking and insurance; the production of cotton and man-made textiles, petrochemicals, rubber, paper, machine tools, and processed foods; and heavy, light, and electrical engineering, also printing. It is linked to the River Mersey and the Irish Sea by the **Manchester Ship Canal**, opened in 1894. Only one dock is now open.

**Mandalay** chief city of the Mandalay division of Myanmar (formerly Burma), on the River Irrawaddy, about 495 km/370 mi north of Yangon (Rangoon); population (1983) 677,000. It is a river port, with a university founded in 1964.

**Mandela, Nelson Rolihlahla** (1918– ) South African politician and lawyer, president 1994–99. He was president of the →African National Congress (ANC) 1991–97. Imprisoned from 1964, as organizer of the then banned ANC, he became a symbol of unity for the worldwide anti-→apartheid movement. In February 1990 he was released, the ban on the ANC having been lifted, and entered into negotiations with the government about a multiracial future for South Africa. In May 1994 he was sworn in as South Africa's first post-apartheid president after the ANC won 62.65% of the vote in universal-suffrage elections. He shared the Nobel Prize for Peace in 1993 with South African president F W de Klerk. In June 1999 he stepped down as president and was succeeded by ANC president, Thabo Mbeki.

**mandolin** plucked string instrument with four to six pairs of strings (courses), tuned like a violin, which flourished 1600–1800. The fingerboard is fretted to regulate intonation. It takes its name from its almond-shaped body (Italian *mandorla* 'almond'). Vivaldi composed two concertos for the mandolin about 1736.

**Manet, Edouard** (1832–1883) French painter. One of the foremost French artists of the 19th century, he is often regarded as the father of modern painting. Rebelling against the academic tradition, he developed a clear and unaffected realist style that was one of the founding forces of →Impressionism. His subjects were mainly contemporary, such as *A Bar at the Folies-Bergère* (1882; Courtauld Art Gallery, London).

**mangrove** any of several shrubs and trees, especially of the mangrove family, found in the muddy swamps of tropical and subtropical coastlines and estuaries. By sending down aerial roots from their branches, they rapidly form close-growing mangrove thickets. Their timber is resistant to water penetration and damage by marine worms. Mangrove swamps are rich breeding grounds for fish and shellfish, but these habitats are being destroyed in many countries. (Genera *Rhizophora* and *Avicennia*, families Rhizophoraceae (mangrove) and Avicenniaceae (related).)

**Manhattan** island of the city of →New York, USA, forming most of a borough; population (1990) 1,488,000. It is 20 km/12.5 mi long and 4 km/2.5 mi wide, and lies between the Hudson and East rivers. The rocks from which it is formed rise to a height of more than 73 m/240 ft in the north of the island. Manhattan Island is bounded on the north and northeast by the Harlem River and Spuyten Duyvil Creek (which separate it from the Bronx); on the south by Upper New York Bay; on the west by the Hudson River (which separates it from New Jersey); and on the east by the East River (which separates it from Queens and Brooklyn). The borough of Manhattan also includes a small port at the Bronx mainland and several islands in the East River. Manhattan is the economic hub of New York City, although there are large residential and industrial areas here also. It includes the Wall Street business centre, Broadway and its theatres, Carnegie Hall (1891), the World Trade Centre (1973), the Empire State Building (1931), the United Nations headquarters (1952), Madison Square Garden, and Central Park.

**Mann, Thomas** (1875–1955) German novelist and critic. A largely subjective artist, he drew his themes from his own experiences and inner thoughts. He was constantly preoccupied with the idea of death in the midst of life and with the position of the artist in relation to society. His first novel was *Buddenbrooks* (1901), a saga of a merchant family which traces through four generations the gradual growth of decay as culture slowly saps virility. *Der Zauberberg/The Magic Mountain* (1924), a vast symbolic work on the subject of disease in sick minds and bodies, and also the sickness of Europe, probes the question of culture in relation to life. Notable among his works of short fiction is '*Der Tod in Venedig/*Death in Venice' (1913). Nobel Prize for Literature 1929.

**Mannerism** in a general sense some idiosyncrasy, extravagance or affectation of style or manner in art, though it has more specific reference to Italian painting in the 16th century and represents a distinct phase between the art of the High Renaissance and the rise of baroque. It was largely based on an admiration for Michelangelo and a consequent exaggeration of the emphasis of his composition and the expressive distortion of his figures.

**Man Ray** US photographer, painter, and sculptor; see Man →Ray.

**Maori** (New Zealand *Maui* 'native' or 'indigenous') member of the Polynesian people of New Zealand. They number 435,000, about 15% of the total population, and around 89% live in the North Island. Maori civilization had particular strengths in warfare, cultivation, navigation, and wood- and stonework. Speechmaking and oral

history, as well as woodcarving, were the main cultural repositories before the European introduction of writing, and Maori mythology and cosmology were highly developed. Their language, Maori, belongs to the eastern branch of the Austronesian family. The Maori Language Act 1987 recognized Maori as an official language of New Zealand.

**Mao Zedong** (1893–1976) (or Mao Tsetung) Chinese communist politician and theoretician, leader of the Chinese Communist Party (CCP) 1935–76. Mao was a founder of the CCP in 1921, and became its leader in 1935. He organized the Long March 1934–35 and the war of liberation 1937–49, following which he established a People's Republic and communist rule in China. He was state president until 1959, and headed the CCP until his death. His influence diminished with the failure of his 1958–60 Great Leap Forward, but he emerged dominant again during the 1966–69 Cultural Revolution, which he launched in order to promote his own anti-bureaucratic line and to purge the party of 'revisionism'.

**map projection** ways of depicting the spherical surface of the Earth on a flat piece of paper. Traditional projections include the **conic**, **azimuthal**, and **cylindrical**. The most famous cylindrical projection is the Mercator projection, which dates from 1569. The weakness of these systems is that countries in high latitudes are shown disproportionately large, and lines of longitude and latitude appear distorted. In 1973 German historian Arno

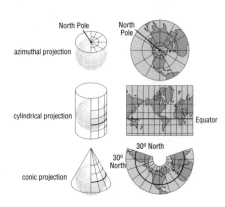

azimuthal projection

North Pole

North Pole

cylindrical projection

Equator

conic projection

30° North

30° North

**map projection** Three widely used map projections. If a light were placed at the centre of a transparent Earth, the shapes of the countries would be thrown as shadows on a sheet of paper. If the paper is flat, the azimuthal projection results; if it is wrapped around a cylinder or in the form of a cone, the cylindrical or conic projections result.

Peters devised the **Peters projection** in which the countries of the world retain their relative areas. In 1992 the US physicist Mitchell Feigenbaum devised the **optimal conformal** projection, using a computer program designed to take data about the boundary of a given area and calculate the projection that produces the minimum of inaccuracies.

**Marat, Jean Paul** (1743–1793) Swiss-born French Revolutionary leader, physician, and journalist. He was elected to the National Convention in 1792, where, as leader of the radical Montagnard faction, he carried on a long struggle with the right-wing Girondins, which resulted in their over-throw in May 1793. In July he was mur-dered in his bath by Charlotte Corday, a Girondin supporter.

**marathon** athletics endurance race over 42.195 km/26 mi 385 yd. It was first

included in the Olympic Games in Athens 1896. The distance varied until it was standardized 1924. More recently, races have been opened to wider participation, including social runners as well as those competing at senior level.

**Marathon, Battle of** battle fought in September 490 BC at the start of the Persian Wars in which the Athenians and their allies from Plataea resound-ingly defeated the Persian king Darius' invasion force. Fought on the Plain of Marathon about 40 km/25 mi northeast of Athens, it is one of the most famous battles of antiquity.

**marble** rock formed by metamorphosis of sedimentary →limestone. It takes and retains a good polish, and is used in building and sculpture. In its pure form it is white and consists almost entirely of calcite $CaCO_3$. Mineral impurities give it various colours and patterns. Carrara, Italy, is known for white marble.

**Marc, Franz** (1880–1916) German expressionist painter. He was associated with Wassily Kandinsky in founding the *Blaue Reiter* movement. Animals played an essential part in his view of the world, and bold semi-abstracts of red and blue animals, particularly horses, are characteristic of his work.

**Marconi, Guglielmo** (1874–1937) Italian electrical engineer and pioneer in the invention and development of radio. In 1895 he achieved radio communication over more than a mile, and in England 1896 he conducted successful experiments that led to the formation of the company that became Marconi's Wireless Telegraph Company Ltd. He shared the Nobel Prize for Physics 1909.

**Marco Polo** Venetian traveller and writer; see Marco →Polo.

**Mariana Trench** lowest region on the Earth's surface; the deepest part of the sea floor. The trench is 2,400 km/1,500 mi long and is situated 300 km/200 mi east of the Mariana Islands, in the northwestern Pacific Ocean. Its deepest part is the gorge known as the Challenger Deep, which extends 11,034 m/36,210 ft below sea level.

**Marie Antoinette** (1755–1793) queen of France from 1774. She was the fourth daughter of Empress Maria Theresa of Austria and the Holy Roman Emperor Francis I, and married Louis XVI of France in 1770. Her devotion to the interests of Austria, reputation for extravagance, and supposed connection with the scandal of the Diamond Necklace made her unpopular, and helped to provoke the →French Revolution of 1789. She was tried for treason in October 1793 and guillotined.

**marijuana** dried leaves and flowers of the hemp plant →cannabis, used as a drug; it is illegal in most countries. It is eaten or inhaled and causes euphoria, distortion of time, and heightened sensations of sight and sound. Mexico is the world's largest producer.

**Mark Antony** (c. 83–30 BC) (also known as Marcus Antonius) Roman politician and soldier who was the last serious rival to Octavian's (later Augustus) domination of the Roman world. He served under →Julius Caesar in Gaul and during the civil war when he commanded the left wing at the final battle of Pharsalus. He was consul with Caesar in 44 when he tried to secure for him the title of king. After Caesar's assassination, he formed the Second Triumvirate with Octavian and Lepidus. In 42 he defeated Brutus and Cassius at Philippi. He took Egypt as his share of the empire and formed a liaison with the Egyptian queen Cleopatra, but returned to Rome in 40 to marry Octavia, the sister of Octavian. In 32 the Senate declared war on Cleopatra, and Antony, who had combined forces with Cleopatra, was defeated by Octavian at Actium in 31. He returned to Egypt and committed suicide.

**Mark, St** (lived 1st century AD) in the New Testament, Christian apostle and evangelist whose name is given to the second Gospel. It was probably written AD 65–70, and used by the authors of the first and third Gospels. He is the patron saint of Venice, and his emblem is a winged lion; feast day 25 April.

**marlin** (or spearfish) any of several open-sea fishes known as billfishes. Some 2.5 m/7 ft long, they are found in warmer waters and have elongated snouts and high-standing dorsal (back) fins. Members of the family include the **sailfish** (*Istiophorus platypterus*), the fastest of all fishes over short distances – reaching speeds of 100 kph/62 mph – and the **blue marlin** (*Makaira nigricans*), highly prized as a 'game' fish. (Family Istiophoridae, order Perciformes.)

**Marlowe, Christopher** (1564–1593) English poet and dramatist. His work includes the blank-verse plays *Tamburlaine the Great* in two parts (1587–88), *The Jew of Malta* (about 1591), *Edward II* (about 1592) and *Dr Faustus* (about 1594), the poem *Hero and Leander* (1598), and a translation of parts of →Ovid's *Amores*. Marlowe transformed the new medium of English blank verse into a powerful, melodic form of expression.

**Marrakesh** (or Marrakech) historic imperial city in Morocco in the foothills of the Atlas Mountains, about 210 km/130 mi south of Casablanca; population (1982) 439,700; urban area (1993) 602,000. It is a tourist centre, and has textile, leather, and food processing industries. Founded in 1062, it has a medieval palace and mosques, and was formerly the capital of Morocco.

**Mars** fourth planet from the Sun. It is much smaller than Venus or Earth, with a mass 0.11 that of Earth. Mars is slightly pear-shaped, with a low, level northern hemisphere, which is comparatively uncratered and geologically 'young', and a heavily cratered 'ancient' southern hemisphere. **mean distance from the Sun:** 227.9 million km/141.6 million mi; **equatorial diameter:** 6,780 km/4,210 mi; **rotation period:** 24 hr 37 min; **year:** 687 Earth days; **atmosphere:** 95% carbon dioxide, 3% nitrogen, 1.5% argon, and 0.15% oxygen. Red atmospheric dust from the surface whipped up by winds of up to 450 kph/280 mph accounts for the light pink sky. The surface pressure is less than 1% of the Earth's atmospheric pressure at sea level; **surface:** The landscape is a dusty, red, eroded lava plain. Mars has white polar caps (water ice and frozen carbon dioxide) that advance and retreat with the seasons; **satellites:** two small satellites: Phobos and Deimos.

**Mars** (Mavors or Mamers in Roman mythology) the god of war (**Mars Gradivus**), depicted as a fearless warrior. The month of March is named after him. He was identified with the Greek Ares, but achieved greater status.

**Marseille** (English Marseilles) chief seaport and second city of France, and administrative centre of the *département* of Bouches-du-Rhône and of the Provence-Alpes-Côte d'Azur region, situated on the Golfe du Lion on the Mediterranean Sea; population (1990) 807,700. Industries include chemicals, metallurgy, shipbuilding, and food processing, as well as oil-refining at the massive industrial complex of Fos-sur-Mer to the west.

**Marshall Islands** Republic of the (RMI); **area:** 181 sq km/70 sq mi; **capital:** Dalap-Uliga-Darrit (on Majuro atoll); **major towns/cities:** Ebeye (the only other town); **physical features:** comprises the Ratak and Ralik island chains in the West Pacific, which together form an archipelago of 31 coral atolls, 5 islands, and 1,152 islets; **head of state and government:** Imata Kabua from 1997; **political system:** liberal democracy; **currency:** US dollar; **GNP per capita (PPP):** (US\$) 1,780 (1998 est); **exports:** coconut products, trochus shells, copra, handicrafts, fish, live animals. Principal market USA; **population:** 62,000 (1999 est); **language:** Marshallese, English (both official); **religion:** Christian (mainly Protestant) and Baha'i; **life expectancy:** 63 (men); 66 (women) (1998 est).

**Marston Moor, Battle of** battle fought in the English Civil War on 2 July 1644 on Marston Moor, 11 km/7 mi west of York. The Royalists were conclusively defeated by the Parliamentarians and Scots.

**marsupial** (Greek *marsupion* 'little purse') mammal in which the female has a pouch where she carries her young (born tiny and immature) for a considerable time after birth. Marsupials include omnivorous, herbivorous, and carnivorous species, among them the kangaroo, wombat, opossum, phalanger, bandicoot, dasyure, and wallaby.

**martial arts** any of several styles of armed and unarmed combat developed in the East from ancient techniques and arts. Common martial arts include aikido, →judo, jujitsu, →karate, kendo, and →kung fu.

**Marvell, Andrew** (1621–1678) English metaphysical poet and satirist. In 'To His Coy Mistress' (1650–52) and 'An Horatian Ode upon Cromwell's Return from Ireland' (1650) he produced, respectively, the most searching seduction and political poems in the language. He was committed to the Parliamentary cause, and was Member of Parliament for Hull from 1659. He devoted his last years mainly to verse satire and prose works attacking repressive aspects of the state and government.

**Marx, Karl Heinrich** (1818–1883) German philosopher, economist, and social theorist whose account of change through conflict is known as historical, or dialectical, materialism (see →Marxism). His *Das Kapital/Capital* (1867–95) is the fundamental text of Marxist economics, and his systematic theses on class struggle, history, and the importance of economic factors in politics have exercised an enormous influence on later thinkers and political activists.

**Marxism** philosophical system, developed by the 19th-century German social theorists →Marx and →Engels, also known as **dialectical materialism**, under which matter gives rise to mind (materialism) and all is subject to change (from dialectic; see →Hegel). As applied to history, it supposes that the succession of feudalism, capitalism, socialism, and finally the classless society is inevitable. The stubborn resistance of any existing system to change necessitates its complete overthrow in the **class struggle** – in the case of capitalism, by the proletariat – rather than gradual modification.

**Mary Queen of Scots** (1542–1587) queen of Scotland (1542–67). Also known as **Mary Stuart**, she was the daughter of James V. Mary's connection with the English royal line from Henry VII made her a threat to Elizabeth I's hold on the English throne, especially as she represented a champion of the Catholic cause. She was married three times. After her forced abdication she was imprisoned but escaped in 1568 to England. Elizabeth I held her prisoner, while the Roman Catholics, who regarded Mary as rightful queen of England, formed many conspiracies to place her on the throne, and for complicity in one of these she was executed.

**Mary I** (1516–1558) called **Bloody Mary**, queen of England from 1553. She was the eldest daughter of Henry VIII by Catherine of Aragón. When Edward VI died, Mary secured the crown without difficulty in spite of the conspiracy to substitute Lady Jane →Grey. In 1554 Mary married Philip II

of Spain, and as a devout Roman Catholic obtained the restoration of papal supremacy and sanctioned the persecution of Protestants. She was succeeded by her half-sister Elizabeth I.

**Mary Magdalene, St** (lived 1st century AD) in the New Testament, a woman whom Jesus cured of possession by evil spirits. She was present at the Crucifixion and burial, and was the first to meet the risen Jesus. She is often identified with the woman of St Luke's gospel who anointed Jesus' feet, and her symbol is a jar of ointment; feast day 22 July.

**mass** in physics, the quantity of matter in a body as measured by its inertia. Mass determines the acceleration produced in a body by a given force acting on it, the acceleration being inversely proportional to the mass of the body. The mass also determines the force exerted on a body by →gravity on Earth, although this attraction varies slightly from place to place. In the SI system, the base unit of mass is the kilogram.

**Massachusetts** state of northeast USA. It is nicknamed the Bay State or the Old Colony State. Massachusetts ratified the US Constitution in 1788, becoming the 6th state to join the Union. It is a region of great significance to US history, being the point of disembarkation for the *Mayflower* Pilgrims, as well as the site of key conflicts in the American Revolution. Massachusetts is bordered to the north by Vermont and New Hampshire, to the west by New York, to the south by Connecticut and Rhode Island, and to the southeast and east by the Atlantic Ocean. **population:** (1995) 6,073,600; **area:** 21,500 sq km/8,299 sq mi; **capital:** →Boston; **towns and cities:** Worcester, Springfield, Lowell, New Bedford, Brockton, Cambridge; **industries and products:** electronic, communications, and optical equipment, precision instruments, non-electrical machinery, fish, cranberries, dairy products, tourism, academia and research, finance sector.

**Massif Central** upland region of south-central France with mountains and plateaus; area 93,000 sq km/36,000 sq mi, highest peak Puy de Sancy, 1,886 m/6,188 ft. It is a source of hydroelectricity.

**Mata Hari** (1876–1917) stage name of Margaretha Geertruida Zelle, Dutch courtesan, dancer, and probable spy. In World War I she had affairs with highly placed military and government officials on both sides and told Allied secrets to the Germans. She may have been a double agent, in the pay of both France and Germany. She was shot by the French on espionage charges.

**materialism** philosophical theory that there is nothing in existence over and above matter and matter in motion. Such a theory excludes the possibility of deities. It also sees mind as an attribute of the physical, denying idealist theories that see mind as something independent of body; for example, Descartes' theory of 'thinking substance'.

**mathematics** science of relationships between numbers, between spatial configurations, and abstract structures. The main divisions of **pure mathematics** include geometry, arithmetic, algebra, calculus, and trigonometry. Mechanics, statistics, numerical analysis, computing, the mathematical theories of astronomy, electricity, optics, thermodynamics, and atomic studies come under the heading of **applied mathematics**.

**Matisse, Henri Emile Benoît** (1869–1954) French painter, sculptor and illustrator. Matisse was one of the most original creative forces in early 20th-century art. He was a leading figure in →fauvism and later developed a style characterized by strong, sinuous lines, surface pattern, and brilliant colour. *The Dance* (1910, The Hermitage, St Petersburg) is characteristic. Later works include pure abstracts, as in his collages of coloured paper shapes (*gouaches découpées*).

**matter** in physics, anything that has mass. All matter is made up of →atoms, which in turn are made up of →elementary particles; it ordinarily exists in one of three physical states: solid, liquid, or gas.

**Matthew, St** (lived 1st century AD) Christian apostle and evangelist, the traditional author of the first Gospel. He is usually identified with Levi, who was a tax collector in the service of Herod Antipas, and was called by Jesus to be a disciple as he sat by the Lake of Galilee receiving customs dues. His emblem is a man with wings; feast day 21 September.

## MATHEMATICAL SIGNS

| Symbol | Meaning |
|--------|---------|
| a⊂b | a implies b |
| ∞ | infinity |
| lim | limiting value |
| a≈b | a approximately equal to b |
| a=b | a equal to b |
| a>b | a greater than b |
| a<b | a smaller than b |
| a≠b | a not equal to b |
| b<a<c | a greater than b and smaller than c, that is a lies between b and c, but cannot equal either |
| a≧b | a equal to or greater than b, that is a at least as great as b |
| a≦b | a equal to or less than b, that is, a at most as great as b |
| b≦a≦c | a lies between the values of b and c and could take the values of b and c |
| \|a\| | absolute value of a; this is always positive, for example \|−5\|=5 |
| + | addition sign, positive |
| − | subtraction sign, negative |
| × | multiplication sign, times |
| : or ÷ or / | division sign, divided by |
| a+b=c | a+b, read as 'a+b', denotes the addition of a nd b. The result of the addition, c, is also known as the sum. |
| ∫ | indefinite integral |
| $\int_a^b f(x)dx$ | definite integral, or integral between x=a and x=b |
| a−b=c | a−b, read as 'a minus b', denotes subtraction of b from a. a−b, or c, is the difference. Subtraction is the opposite of addition. |
| a×b=c | a×b, read as 'a multiplied by b', denotes multiplication of a by b. a×b, or c, is the product; a and b are factors of c. |

## MATHEMATICAL SIGNS (CONTINUED)

| | |
|---|---|
| $ab=c$ <br> $a.b=c$ <br> $ab=c$ <br> $a \div b=c$ <br> $a/b=c$ | ab, read as 'a divided by b', denotes division. a is the dividend, b is the divisor. a:b, or c, is the quotient. One aspect of division – repeated subtraction, is the opposite of multiplication – repeated addition. |
| $a^b$ | $a^b$, read as 'a to the power b'. a is the base, b the exponent |
| $\sqrt[b]{a}=c$ | $\sqrt[b]{a}$ is the bth root of a, b being known as the root exponent. In the special case of $\sqrt[2]{a}=c$, $\sqrt[2]{a}$ or c is known as the square root of a, and the root exponent is usually omitted, that is $\sqrt[2]{a}=\sqrt{a}$. |
| e | exponential constant and is the base of natural (napierian) logarithms = 2.7182818284... |
| $\pi$ | ratio of the circumference of a circle to its diameter = 3.1415925535 |

**Maupassant, (Henry René Albert) Guy de** (1850–1893) French author. He established a reputation with the short story 'Boule de suif/Ball of Fat' (1880) and wrote some 300 short stories in all. His novels include Une Vie/A Woman's Life (1883) and Bel-Ami (1885). He was encouraged as a writer by Gustave →Flaubert.

**Mauritania** Islamic Republic of; **national name:** *République Islamique Arabe et Africaine de Mauritanie;* **area:** 1,030,700 sq km/397,953 sq mi; **capital:** Nouakchott (port); **major towns/cities:** Nouâdhibou, Kaédi, Zouerate, Kiffa, Rosso, Atar; **major ports:** Nouâdhibou; **physical features:** valley of River Senegal in south; remainder arid and flat; **head of state:** Maaoya Sid'Ahmed Ould Taya from 1984; **head of government:** Cheik el Avia Ould Muhammad Khouna from 1998; **political system:** emergent democracy; **currency:** ouguiya; **GNP per capita (PPP):** (US$) 1,660 (1998 est); **exports:** fish and fish products, iron ore. Principal market Japan 23.9% (1997); **population:** 2,598,000 (1999 est); **language:** French and Hasaniya Arabic (both official), African languages including Pulaar, Soninke, and Wolof; **religion:** Sunni Muslim; **life expectancy:** 52 (men); 55 (women) (1995–2000).

**Mauritius** Republic of; **area:** 1,865 sq km/720 sq mi; the island of Rodrigues is part of Mauritius; there are several small island dependencies; **capital:** Port Louis (port); **major towns/cities:** Beau Bassin-Rose Hill, Curepipe, Quatre Bornes, Vacoas-Phoenix; **physical features:** mountainous, volcanic island surrounded by coral reefs; **head of state:** Cassam Uteem from 1992; **head of government:** Navin Ramgoolam from 1995; **political system:** liberal democracy;

**currency:** Mauritian rupee; **GNP per capita (PPP):** (US$) 9,400 (1998); **exports:** raw sugar, clothing, tea, molasses, jewellery. Principal market UK 32.1% (1997); **population:** 1,149,000 (1999 est); **language:** English (official), French, Creole, Indian languages; **religion:** Hindu, Christian (mainly Roman Catholic), Muslim; **life expectancy:** 68 (men); 75 (women) (1995–2000).

**Maxwell, James Clerk** (1831–1879) Scottish physicist. His main achievement was in the understanding of →electromagnetic waves: **Maxwell's equations** bring together electricity, magnetism, and light in one set of relations. He studied gases, optics, and the sensation of colour, and his theoretical work in magnetism prepared the way for wireless telegraphy and telephony.

**Maya** member of an American Indian civilization originating in the Yucatán Peninsula in Central America about 2600 BC, with later sites in Mexico, Guatemala, and Belize, and enjoying a classical period AD 325–925, after which it declined as Toltecs from the Valley of Mexico moved south into the area, building new ceremonial centres and dominating the local people. Nevertheless, Maya sovereignty was maintained, for the most part, until late in the Spanish conquest (1560s) in some areas. Today the Maya are Roman Catholic, and number 8–9 million (1994 est). They live in Yucatán, Guatemala, Belize, and western Honduras. Many still speak Maya, a member of the Totonac-Mayan (Penutian) language family, as well as Spanish. In the 1980s more than 100,000 Maya fled from Guatemala to Mexico.

**measles** acute virus disease (rubeola), spread by airborne infection.

Symptoms are fever, severe catarrh, small spots inside the mouth, and a raised, blotchy red rash appearing for about a week after two weeks' incubation. Prevention is by vaccination.

**Mecca** (Arabic *Makkah*) city in Saudi Arabia and, as birthplace of Muhammad, the holiest city of the Islamic world; population (1991 est) 633,000. In the centre of Mecca is the Great Mosque, in the courtyard of which is the Kaaba, the sacred shrine containing the black stone believed to have been given to Abraham by the angel Gabriel.

**mechanics** branch of physics dealing with the motions of bodies and the forces causing these motions, and also with the forces acting on bodies in equilibrium. It is usually divided into →dynamics and statics.

**Medici family** noble family that ruled the Italian city-state of Florence from the 15th to the 18th centuries. The Medici arrived in Florence in the 13th century and made their fortune in banking. The first family member to control the city, from 1434 to 1464, was Cosimo de' Medici ('the Elder'); he and his grandson Lorenzo ('the Magnificent'), who ruled from 1469 to 1492, made Florence the foremost city-state in →Renaissance Italy, and were famed as patrons of the arts and humanist thought. Four Medici were elected pope, and others married into the royal families of Europe.

**medicine** the practice of preventing, diagnosing, and treating disease, both physical and mental; also any substance used in the treatment of disease. The basis of medicine is anatomy (the structure and form of the body) and physiology (the study of the body's functions).

**medicine, alternative** forms of medical treatment that do not use synthetic drugs or surgery in response to the symptoms of a disease, but aim to treat the patient as a whole (holism). The emphasis is on maintaining health (with diet and exercise) and on dealing with the underlying causes rather than just the symptoms of illness. It may involve the use of herbal remedies and techniques like →acupuncture, →homeopathy, and →chiropractic. Some alternative treatments are increasingly accepted by orthodox medicine, but the absence of enforceable standards in some fields has led to the proliferation of eccentric or untrained practitioners.

**Medina** Saudi Arabian city, about 355 km/220 mi north of Mecca; population (1991 est) 400,000. It is the second holiest city in the Islamic world, and contains the tomb of →Muhammad. It produces grain and fruit.

**Mediterranean Sea** inland sea separating Europe from north Africa, with Asia to the east; extreme length 3,700 km/ 2,300 mi; area 2,966,000 sq km/ 1,145,000 sq mi. It is linked to the Atlantic Ocean (at the Strait of Gibraltar), Red Sea and Indian Ocean (by the Suez Canal), and the Black Sea (at the Dardanelles and Sea of Marmara). The main subdivisions are the Adriatic, Aegean, Ionian, and Tyrrhenian seas. It is highly polluted.

**meerkat** (or suricate) small mammal with long soft grey fur, which is found in southern Africa, and belongs to the mongoose family. A third of its length of 35 cm/14 in is occupied by the tail. It feeds on succulent bulbs, insects, and small vertebrates, and is sociable, living in large extended family groups. Meerkat groups have a dominant breeding pair and up to 23 helpers to assist in the rearing of the babies. The dominant female produces 75% of the young.

**Melanesia** islands in the southwestern Pacific between Micronesia to the north and Polynesia to the east, embracing all the islands from the New Britain archipelago to the Fiji Islands.

**melanoma** highly malignant tumour of the melanin-forming cells (melanocytes) of the skin. It develops from an existing mole in up to two thirds of cases, but can also arise in the eye or mucous membranes.

Malignant melanoma is the most dangerous of the skin cancers; it is associated with brief but excessive exposure to sunlight. It is easily treated if caught early but deadly once it has spread. There is a genetic factor in some cases.

**melting point** temperature at which a substance melts, or changes from solid to liquid form. A pure substance under standard conditions of pressure (usually one atmosphere) has a definite melting point. If heat is supplied to a solid at its melting point, the temperature does not change until the melting process is complete. The melting point of ice is 0°C or 32°F.

**membrane** in living things, a continuous layer, made up principally of fat molecules, that encloses a →cell or organelles within a cell. Small molecules, such as water and sugars, can pass through the cell membrane by →diffusion. Large molecules, such as proteins, are transported across the membrane via special channels, a process often involving energy input. The Golgi apparatus within the cell is thought to produce certain membranes.

**Memphis** industrial city and port on the Mississippi River, in southwestern Tennessee, USA, linked by a bridge with West Memphis, Arkansas, across the river; seat of Shelby County; population (1992) 610,300. It is a major cotton market, and one of the leading centres in the USA for the production of hardwood lumber; other industries include food processing and the manufacture of pharmaceuticals, chemicals, medical supplies, furniture, and tobacco products. A 1980s industry of handmade ultramodern furniture is called Memphis style and copied by Italian and French firms.

**Mendeleyev, Dmitri Ivanovich** (1834–1907) Russian chemist who framed the periodic law in chemistry in 1869, which states that the chemical properties of the elements depend on their relative atomic masses. This law is the basis of the →periodic table of the elements, in which the elements are arranged by atomic number and organized by their related groups.

**Mendelism** in genetics, the theory of inheritance originally outlined by Austrian biologist Gregor Mendel. He suggested that, in sexually reproducing species, all characteristics are inherited through indivisible 'factors' (now identified with →genes) contributed by each parent to its offspring.

**Mendelssohn (-Bartholdy), (Jakob Ludwig) Felix** (1809–1847) German composer, also a pianist and conductor. His music has the lightness and charm of classical music, applied to Romantic and descriptive subjects. Among his best-known works are *A Midsummer Night's Dream* (1827); the *Fingal's Cave* overture (1832); and five symphonies, which include the 'Reformation' (1830), the 'Italian' (1833), and the 'Scottish' (1842). He was instrumental in promoting the revival of interest in J S Bach's music.

**meningitis** inflammation of the meninges (membranes) surrounding the brain, caused by bacterial or viral infection. Bacterial meningitis, though treatable by antibiotics, is the more serious threat. Diagnosis is by lumbar puncture.

**menopause** in women, the cessation of reproductive ability, characterized by menstruation (see →menstrual cycle) becoming irregular and eventually ceasing. The onset is at about the age of 50, but varies greatly. Menopause is usually uneventful, but some women suffer from complications such as flushing, excessive bleeding, and nervous disorders. Since the 1950s, →hormone-

# MERSEYSIDE

replacement therapy (HRT), using →oestrogen alone or with progestogen, a synthetic form of →progesterone, has been developed to counteract such effects.

**menstrual cycle** cycle that occurs in female mammals of reproductive age, in which the body is prepared for pregnancy. At the beginning of the cycle, a Graafian (egg) follicle develops in the ovary, and the inner wall of the uterus forms a soft spongy lining. The egg is released from the ovary, and the uterus lining (endometrium) becomes vascularized (filled with blood vessels). If fertilization does not occur, the corpus luteum (remains of the Graafian follicle) degenerates, and the uterine lining breaks down, and is shed. This is what causes the loss of blood that marks menstruation. The cycle then begins again. Human menstruation takes place from puberty to menopause, except during pregnancy, occurring about every 28 days.

**Mercury** in astronomy, the closest planet to the Sun. Its mass is 0.056 that of Earth. On its sunward side the surface temperature reaches over 400°C/752°F, but on the 'night' side it falls to −170°C/−274°F. **mean distance from the Sun:** 58 million km/36 million mi; **equatorial diameter:** 4,880 km/3,030 mi; **rotation period:** 59 Earth days; **year:** 88 Earth days; **atmosphere:** Mercury's small mass and high daytime temperature mean that it is impossible for an atmosphere to be retained; **surface:** composed of silicate rock often in the form of lava flows. In 1974 the US

space probe *Mariner 10* showed that Mercury's surface is cratered by meteorite impacts; **satellites:** none.

**mercury** (or quicksilver) (Latin *mercurius*) heavy, silver-grey, metallic element, symbol Hg (from Latin *hydrargyrum*), atomic number 80, relative atomic mass 200.59. It is a dense, mobile liquid with a low melting point (−38.87°C/−37.96°F). Its chief source is the mineral cinnabar, HgS, but it sometimes occurs in nature as a free metal.

**Mercury** (or Mercurius) (Latin *merx* 'merchandise') in Roman mythology, a god of commerce and gain, and messenger of the gods. He was identified with the Greek Hermes, and similarly represented with winged sandals and a winged staff entwined with snakes.

**meridian** half a great circle drawn on the Earth's surface passing through both poles and thus through all places with the same longitude. Terrestrial longitudes are usually measured from the Greenwich Meridian.

**Merseyside** metropolitan county of northwest England, created in 1974; in 1986, most of the functions of the former county council were transferred to metropolitan borough councils (The Wirral, Sefton, Liverpool, Knowsley, St Helens). **area:** 650 sq km/251 sq mi; **towns and cities:** Liverpool, Bootle, Birkenhead, St Helens, Wallasey, Southport; **physical:** River Mersey; **features:** Merseyside Innovation Centre (MIC), linked with Liverpool and John Moores Universities; Prescot Museum of clock- and watch-making; Speke Hall (Tudor), and Croxteth Hall and Country Park (a working country estate open to the public); **industries**: brewing, chemicals, electrical goods, glassmaking, metalworking, pharmaceutical products, tanning, vehicles; **population**: (1996) 1,420,400; **famous people**: the Beatles, William Ewart Gladstone, George Stubbs.

**Mesolithic** the Middle Stone Age developmental stage of human technology and of →prehistory.

**Mesopotamia** the land between the Tigris and Euphrates rivers, now part of Iraq. The civilizations of Sumer and Babylon flourished here. The →Sumerian civilization (3500 BC) may have been the earliest urban civilization.

**Mesozoic** era of geological time 245–65 million years ago, consisting of the Triassic, Jurassic, and Cretaceous periods. At the beginning of the era, the continents were joined together as Pangaea; dinosaurs and other giant reptiles dominated the sea and air; and ferns, horsetails, and cycads thrived in a warm climate worldwide. By the end of the Mesozoic era, the continents had begun to assume their present positions, flowering plants were dominant, and many of the large reptiles and marine fauna were becoming extinct.

**metabolism** the chemical processes of living organisms enabling them to grow and to function. It involves a constant alternation of building up complex molecules (**anabolism**) and breaking them down (**catabolism**). For example, green plants build up complex organic substances from water, carbon dioxide, and mineral salts (→photosynthesis); by digestion animals partially break down complex organic substances, ingested as food, and subsequently resynthesize them for use in their own bodies (see →digestive system). Within cells, complex molecules are broken down by the process of →respiration. The waste products of metabolism are removed by excretion.

**metal** any of a class of chemical elements with specific physical and chemical characteristics. Metallic elements compose about 75% of the 112 elements in the →periodic table of the elements.

Physical properties include a sonorous tone when struck, good conduction of heat and electricity, opacity but good reflection of light, malleability, which enables them to be cold-worked and rolled into sheets, ductility, which permits them to be drawn into thin wires, and the possible emission of electrons when heated (thermionic effect) or when the surface is struck by light (→photoelectric effect).

**metamorphic rock** rock altered in structure and composition by pressure, heat, or chemically active fluids after original formation. (If heat is sufficient to melt the original rock, technically it becomes an igneous rock upon cooling.) The term was coined in 1833 by Scottish geologist Charles Lyell (1797–1875).

**metamorphosis** period during the life cycle of many invertebrates, most amphibians, and some fish, during which the individual's body changes from one form to another through a major reconstitution of its tissues. For example, adult frogs are produced by metamorphosis from tadpoles, and butterflies are produced from caterpillars following metamorphosis within a pupa. In classical thought and literature, metamorphosis is the transformation of a living being into another shape, either living or inanimate (for example Niobe). The Roman poet →Ovid wrote about this theme.

**metaphor** (Greek 'transfer') figure of speech using an analogy or close comparison between two things that are not normally treated as if they had anything in common. Metaphor is a common means of extending the uses and references of words.

**metaphysical poets** group of early 17th-century English poets whose work is characterized by ingenious, highly intricate wordplay and unlikely or paradoxical imagery. They used rhetorical and literary devices, such as paradox, hyperbole, and elaborately developed conceits, in such a way as to engage the reader by their humour, strangeness, or sheer outrageousness. Among the exponents of this genre are John →Donne, George Herbert, Andrew →Marvell, Richard Crashaw, and Henry Vaughan.

**meteor** flash of light in the sky, popularly known as a **shooting** or **falling star**, caused by a particle of dust, a **meteoroid**, entering the atmosphere at speeds up to 70 kps/45 mps and burning up by friction at a height of around 100 km/60 mi. On any clear night, several **sporadic meteors** can be seen each hour.

**meteorite** piece of rock or metal from space that reaches the surface of the Earth, Moon, or other body. Most meteorites are thought to be fragments from asteroids, although some may be pieces from the heads of comets. Most are stony, although some are made of iron and a few have a mixed rock-iron composition.

**meteorology** scientific observation and study of the →atmosphere, so that weather can be accurately forecast.

Data from meteorological stations and weather satellites are collated by computer at central agencies, and forecast and weather maps based on current readings are issued at regular intervals. Modern analysis, employing some of the most powerful computers, can give useful forecasts for up to six days ahead.

**methane** $CH_4$ the simplest hydrocarbon of the paraffin series. Colourless, odourless, and lighter than air, it burns with a bluish flame and explodes when mixed with air or oxygen. It is the chief constituent of natural gas and also occurs in the explosive firedamp of coal mines. Methane emitted by rotting vegetation forms marsh gas, which may ignite by spontaneous combustion to produce the pale flame seen over marshland and known as will-o'-the-wisp.

**Methodism** evangelical Protestant Christian movement that was founded by John →Wesley in 1739 within the Church of England, but became a separate body in 1795. The Methodist Episcopal Church was founded in the

USA in 1784. There are over 50 million Methodists worldwide.

**Mexico** United States of; **national name:** *Estados Unidos Mexicanos*; **area:** 1,958,201 sq km/756,061 sq mi; **capital:** Mexico City; **major towns/cities:** Guadalajara, Monterrey, Puebla, Netzahualcóyotl, Ciudad Juárez, Tijuana; **major ports:** 49 ocean ports; **physical features:** partly arid central highlands; Sierra Madre mountain ranges east and west; tropical coastal plains; volcanoes, including Popocatepetl; Rio Grande; **head of state and government:** Ernesto Zedillo Ponce de León from 1994; **political system:** federal democracy; **currency:** Mexican peso; **GNP per capita (PPP):** (US$) 8,190 (1998 est); **exports:** petroleum and petroleum products, engines and spare parts for motor vehicles, motor vehicles, electrical and electronic goods, fresh and preserved vegetables, coffee, cotton. Principal market USA 81.9% (1998); **population:** 97,366,000 (1999 est); **language:** Spanish (official); Nahuatl, Maya, Zapoteco, Mixteco, Otomi; **religion:** Roman Catholic; **life expectancy:** 70 (men); 76 (women) (1995–2000).

**Michelangelo** (1475–1564) properly Michelangelo di Lodovico Buonarroti, Italian sculptor, painter, architect, and poet. He was active in his native Florence and in Rome. His giant talent dominated the High Renaissance. The marble *David*, 1501–04 (Accademia, Florence) set a new standard in nude sculpture. His massive figure style was translated into fresco in the Sistine Chapel, 1508–12 and 1536–41 (Vatican).

Other works in Rome include the dome of St Peter's basilica. His influence, particularly on the development of →Mannerism, was profound.

**microbiology** the study of microorganisms, mostly viruses and single-celled organisms such as bacteria, protozoa, and yeasts. The practical applications of microbiology are in medicine (since many micro-organisms cause disease); in brewing, baking, and other food and beverage processes, where the micro-organisms carry out fermentation; and in genetic engineering, which is creating increasing interest in the field of microbiology.

**Micronesia** Federated States of (FSM) **area:** 700 sq km/270 sq mi; **capital:** Kolonia, in Pohnpei state; **major towns/cities:** Weno, in Chuuk state; Lelu, in Kosrae state; **major ports:** Teketik, Lepukos, Okak; **physical features:** an archipelago of 607 equatorial, volcanic islands in the West Pacific; **head of state and government:** Jacob Nena from 1997; **political system:** democratic federal state; **currency:** US dollar; **GNP per capita (PPP):** (US$) 3,920 (1998 est); **exports:** copra, pepper, fish. Principal market Japan 84.8% (1996); **population:** 116,000 (1999 est); **language:** English (official) and eight local languages; **religion:** Christianity (mainly Roman Catholic in Yap state, Protestant elsewhere); **life expectancy:** 67 (men); 71 (women) (1995–2000).

**Micronesia** group of islands in the Pacific Ocean lying north of →Melanesia.

**micro-organism** (or microbe) living organism invisible to the naked eye but visible under a microscope. Micro-organisms include viruses and single-celled organisms such as bacteria, protozoa, yeasts, and some algae. The term has no taxonomic significance in biology. The study of micro-organisms is known as microbiology.

**microphone** primary component in a sound-reproducing system, whereby the mechanical energy of sound waves is converted into electrical signals by means of a transducer. One of the simplest is the telephone receiver mouthpiece, invented by Scottish–US inventor Alexander Graham Bell in 1876; other types of microphone are used with broadcasting and sound-film apparatus.

**microprocessor** complete computer central processing unit contained on a single →integrated circuit, or chip. The appearance of the first microprocessor in 1971 designed by Intel for a pocket calculator manufacturer heralded the introduction of the microcomputer. The microprocessor has led to a dramatic fall in the size and cost of computers, and dedicated computers can now be found in washing machines, cars, and so on. Examples of microprocessors are the Intel Pentium family and the IBM/ Motorola PowerPC, used by Apple Computer.

**microscope** instrument for forming magnified images with high resolution for detail. Optical and electron microscopes are the ones chiefly in use; other types include acoustic, scanning tunnelling, and atomic force microscopes.

**microwave** →electromagnetic wave with a wavelength in the range 0. 3 to 30 cm/0.1 in to 12 in, or 300–300,000 megahertz (between radio waves and infrared radiation). Microwaves are used in radar, in radio broadcasting, and in microwave heating and cooking.

**Midas** in Greek mythology, a king of Phrygia who was granted the ability to convert all he touched to gold by Dionysus, god of wine and excess; the gift became a curse when his food and drink also turned to metal. In another story he was given ass's ears by Apollo for preferring the music of Pan in a contest between the two gods.

**migraine** acute, sometimes incapacitating headache (generally only on one side), accompanied by nausea, that recurs, often with advance symptoms such as flashing lights. No cure has been discovered, but ergotamine normally relieves the symptoms. Some sufferers learn to avoid certain foods, such as chocolate, which suggests an allergic factor.

**Milky Way** faint band of light crossing the night sky, consisting of stars in the plane of our Galaxy. The name Milky Way is often used for the Galaxy itself. It is a spiral →galaxy, 100,000 light years in diameter and 2,000 light years thick, containing at least 100 billion →stars. The Sun is in one of its spiral arms, about 25,000 light years from the centre, not far from its central plane.

**Millais, John Everett** (1829–1896)
English painter, a founder member of
the →Pre-Raphaelite Brotherhood in
1848. Among his best known works
are *Ophelia* (1852; National Gallery,
London) and *Autumn Leaves* (1856; City
Art Galleries, Manchester). By the late
1860s he had left the Brotherhood,
developing a more fluid and conventional style which appealed strongly to
Victorian tastes.

**Miller, Arthur** (1915–  ) US dramatist.
His plays deal with family relationships
and contemporary American values,
and include *Death of a Salesman* (1949,
Pulitzer Prize), and *The Crucible* (1953),
based on the Salem witch trials and
reflecting the communist witch-hunts
of Senator Joe McCarthy. He was married 1956–61 to the film star Marilyn
Monroe, for whom he wrote the film
*The Misfits* (1960).

**millet** any of several grasses of which
the grains are used as a cereal food and
the stems as animal fodder. Species
include *Panicum miliaceum*, extensively
cultivated in the warmer parts of
Europe, and *Sorghum bicolor*, also
known as durra. (Family Gramineae.)

**millipede** any of a group of →arthro-
pods that have segmented bodies, each
segment usually bearing two pairs of
legs, and a pair of short clubbed antennae on the distinct head. Most millipedes are no more than 2.5 cm/1 in
long; a few in the tropics are 30 cm/12
in. (Class Diplopoda.)

**Milošević, Slobodan** (1941–  ) Serbian communist politician; party chief
and president of Serbia 1986–97, and
president of Yugoslavia from 1997.
Milošević wielded considerable influence over the Serb-dominated Yugoslav
federal army during the 1991–92 civil
war and continued to back Serbian militia in Bosnia-Herzegovina 1992–94,
although publicly disclaiming any
intention to 'carve up' the newly independent republic. Widely believed to be
the instigator of the conflict, Milošević
changed tactics from 1993, adopting
the public persona of peacemaker and
putting pressure on his allies, the
Bosnian Serbs, to accept negotiated
peace terms; this contributed to the
Dayton peace accord for Bosnia-
Herzegovina in November 1995.

In 1998 he faced international con-
demnation again for the brutal treatment of ethnic Albanians by Serbian
forces in the province. A peace plan was
accepted by the separatists but rejected
by Milošević.

NATO aircraft began a bombing campaign in March 1999 in an attempt to
force the Yugoslav government to end
its persecution of ethnic Albanians in
Kosovo. In June Milošević accepted
NATO's peace agreement.

**Milton, John** (1608–1674) English
poet and prose writer. His epic *Paradise
Lost* (1667) is one of the landmarks of
English literature. Early poems, including *Comus* (a masque performed 1634)
and *Lycidas* (an elegy, 1638), showed
Milton's superlative lyric gift. He also
wrote many pamphlets and prose works,
including *Areopagitica* (1644), which
opposed press censorship, and he was

Latin secretary to Oliver →Cromwell and the Council of State from 1649 until the restoration of Charles II.

**mineral** naturally formed inorganic substance with a particular chemical composition and a regularly repeating internal structure. Either in their perfect crystalline form or otherwise, minerals are the constituents of rocks. In more general usage, a mineral is any substance economically valuable for mining (including coal and oil, despite their organic origins).

**Minnesota** state in north Midwest USA. It is nicknamed the Gopher State or the North Star State. Minnesota was admitted to the Union in 1858 as the 32nd US state. One of the Great Lakes states, it is bordered to the south by Iowa, to the west by North and South Dakota, to the north by the Canadian states of Ontario and Manitoba, and to the east by Wisconsin; **population:** (1995) 4,609,500; **area:** 218,700 sq km/84,418 sq mi; **capital:** St Paul; **towns and cities:** Minneapolis, Duluth, Bloomington, Rochester; **industries and products:** cereals, soybeans, livestock, meat and dairy products, iron ore (about two-thirds of US output), non-electrical machinery, electronic equipment, pulp, finance sector.

**Miocene** ('middle recent') fourth epoch of the Tertiary period of geological time, 23.5–5.2 million years ago. At this time grasslands spread over the interior of continents, and hoofed mammals rapidly evolved.

**Miró, Joan** (1893–1983) Spanish painter and sculptor, a major figure in →surrealism. In the mid-1920s he developed an abstract style, lyrical and often witty, with amoeba shapes, some linear, some highly coloured, generally floating on a plain background. *Birth of the World* (1925; Museum of Modern Art New York) is typical of his more abstract works.

**miscarriage** spontaneous expulsion of a fetus from the womb before it is capable of independent survival. Miscarriage is believed to occur in 15% of pregnancies. Possible causes include fetal abnormality, abnormality of the uterus or cervix, infection, shock, underactive thyroid, and cocaine use.

**Mississippi** (American Indian *missi* 'big', *sipi* 'river') river in the USA, the main arm of the great river system draining the USA between the Appalachian and the Rocky mountain ranges. The length of the Mississippi is 3,778 km/2,348 mi; with its tributary the Missouri it totals 6,020 km/3,740 mi. The Mississippi rises in the lake region of northern Minnesota in the basin of Lake Itasca, and drops 20 m/65 ft over the St Anthony Falls at Minneapolis. Below the tributaries of the Minnesota, Wisconsin, Des Moines, and Illinois rivers, the confluence of the Missouri and Mississippi occurs at St Louis. Turning at the Ohio junction, it passes Memphis, and takes in the St Francis, Arkansas, Yazoo, and Red tributaries before reaching its delta on the Gulf of Mexico, beyond New Orleans. Altogether the Mississippi has 42 tributary streams and the whole Mississippi river system has a navigable length in excess of 25,900 km/16,100 mi.

**Missouri** major river in central USA, largest tributary of the →Mississippi, which it joins north of St Louis; length 3,969 km/2,466 mi; drainage area 1,370,000 sq km/529,000 sq mi. It rises among the Rocky Mountains in Montana, and passes northwards through a 366-m/1200-ft gorge known as the 'Gate of the Mountains'. The river is formed by the confluence of the Jefferson, Gallatin, and Madison rivers near Gallatin City, southwestern Montana, and flows southeast through the states of Montana, North Dakota, and South Dakota to Sioux City, Iowa. It then turns south to form the borders between Iowa and Nebraska and between Kansas and Missouri, and enters the Mississippi channel 32 km/20 mi north of St Louis. Kansas City, Missouri, is the largest city on its banks.

**mite** minute →arachnid related to the →ticks. Some mites are free-living scavengers or predators. Some are parasitic, such as the **itch mite** (*Sarcoptes scabiei*), which burrows in skin causing scabies in humans and mange in dogs, and the **red mite** (*Dermanyssus gallinae*), which sucks blood from poultry and other birds. Others parasitize plants. (Order Acarina.)

**modernism** in the arts, a general term used to describe the 20th century's conscious attempt to break with the artistic traditions of the 19th century; it is based on a concern with form and the exploration of technique as opposed to content and narrative. In the visual arts, direct representationalism gave way to abstraction (see →abstract art); in literature, writers experimented with alternatives to orthodox sequential storytelling, such as stream of consciousness; in music, the traditional concept of key was challenged by atonality; and in architecture, Functionalism ousted decorativeness as a central objective.

**Modigliani, Amedeo** (1884–1920) Italian painter and sculptor, active in France from 1906. He is best known for graceful nudes and portraits. His paintings – for example, the portrait of his mistress Jeanne Hébuterne, painted 1919 (Guggenheim Museum, New York) – have a distinctive style, the forms elongated and sensual.

**Mohammed** alternative form of →Muhammad, founder of Islam.

**Mohs scale** scale of hardness for minerals (in ascending order): 1 talc; 2 gypsum; 3 calcite; 4 fluorite; 5 apatite; 6 orthoclase; 7 quartz; 8 topaz; 9 corundum; 10 diamond.

**molar** one of the large teeth found towards the back of the mammalian mouth. The structure of the jaw, and the relation of the muscles, allows a massive force to be applied to molars. In herbivores the molars are flat with sharp ridges of enamel and are used for grinding, an adaptation to a diet of tough plant material. Carnivores have sharp powerful molars called carnassials, which are adapted for cutting meat.

## MOHS SCALE

| number | defining mineral | other substances compared |
|---|---|---|
| 1 | talc | |
| 2 | gypsum | 2½ fingernail |
| 3 | calcite | 3½ copper coin |
| 4 | fluorite | |
| 5 | apatite | 5½ steel blade |
| 6 | orthoclase | 5¾ glass |
| 7 | quartz | 7 steel file |
| 8 | topaz | |
| 9 | corundum | |
| 10 | diamond | |

*note that the scale is not regular; diamond, at number 10 the hardest natural substance, is 90 times harder in absolute terms than corundum, number 9*

**Moldova** Republic of; **national name:** *Republica Moldoveneasca*; **area:** 33,700 sq km/13,011 sq mi; **capital:** Chişinău (Kishinev); **major towns/cities:** Tiraspol, Beltsy, Bendery; **physical features:** hilly land lying largely between the rivers Prut and Dniester; northern Moldova comprises the level plain of the Beltsy Steppe and uplands; the climate is warm and moderately continental; **head of state:** Petru Lucinschi from 1997; **head of government:** Vladimir Voronin from 1999; **political system:** emergent democracy; **currency:** leu; **GNP per capita (PPP):** (US$) 1,510 (1998 est); **exports:** food and agricultural products, machinery and equipment, textiles, clothing. Principal market Russia 53% (1998); **population:** 4,379,000 (1999 est); **language:** Moldovan; **religion:** Russian Orthodox; **life expectancy:** 64 (men); 72 (women) (1995–2000).

**molecule** molecules are the smallest particles of an element or compound that can exist independently. Hydrogen

amino acids, where R is one of many possible side chains

peptide – this is one made of just three amino acid units. Proteins consist of very large numbers of amino acid units in long chains, folded up in specific ways

**molecule of protein** A protein molecule is a long chain of amino acids linked by peptide bonds. The properties of a protein are determined by the order, or sequence, of amino acids in its molecule, and by the three-dimensional structure of the molecular chain. The chain folds and twists, often forming a spiral shape.

→atoms, at room temperature, do not exist independently. They are bonded in pairs to form hydrogen molecules. A molecule of a compound consists of two or more different atoms bonded together. Molecules vary in size and complexity from the hydrogen molecule ($H_2$) to the large macromolecules of proteins. They may be held together by ionic bonds, in which the atoms gain or lose electrons to form →ions, or by covalent bonds, where electrons from each atom are shared in a new molecular orbital.

Each compound is represented by a chemical symbol, indicating the elements into which it can be broken down and the number of each type of atom present. The symbolic representation of a molecule is known as its formula. For example, one molecule of the compound water, having two atoms of hydrogen and one atom of oxygen, is shown as $H_2O$.

**mole rat, naked** small underground mammal, almost hairless, with a disproportionately large head. The mole rat is of importance to zoologists as one of the very few mammals that are eusocial, that is, living in colonies with sterile workers and one fertile female. (Species *Heterocephalus glaber*.)

**Molière** (1622–1673) pen-name of Jean-Baptiste Poquelin, French satirical dramatist and actor. Modern French comedy developed from his work. After the collapse of the Paris-based Illustre Théâtre (of which he was one of the founders), Molière performed in the provinces 1645–58. In 1655 he wrote his first play, *L'Etourdi/The Blunderer*, and on his return to Paris produced *Les Précieuses ridicules/The Affected Ladies* (1659). His satires include *L'Ecole des femmes/The School for Wives* (1662), *Le Misanthrope* (1666), *Le Bourgeois Gentilhomme/The Would-Be Gentleman* (1670), and *Le Malade imaginaire/The Imaginary Invalid* (1673). Other satiric plays include *Tartuffe* (1664) (banned for attacking the hypocrisy of the clergy; revised 1667; banned again until 1699), *Le Médecin malgré lui/Doctor in Spite of Himself* (1666), and *Les Femmes savantes/The Learned Ladies* (1672).

**mollusc** any of a group of invertebrate animals, most of which have a body divided into three parts: a head, a central mass containing the main organs, and a foot for movement; the more sophisticated octopuses and related molluscs have arms to capture their prey. The majority of molluscs are marine animals, but some live in fresh water, and a few live on dry land. They include clams, mussels, and oysters (bivalves), snails and slugs (gastropods), and cuttlefish, squids, and octopuses (cephalopods). The body is soft, without limbs (except for the cephalopods), and cold-blooded. There is no internal skeleton, but many species have a hard shell covering the body. (Phylum Mollusca.)

**Monaco** Principality of; **national name:** *Principauté de Monaco*; **area:** 1.95 sq km/0.75 sq mi; **capital:** Monaco-Ville; **major towns/cities:** Monte Carlo, La Condamine; heliport Fontvieille; **physical features:** steep and rugged; surrounded landwards by French territory; being expanded by filling in the sea; **head of state:** Prince Rainier III from 1949; **head of government:** Michel Leveque from 1998; **political system:** constitutional monarchy under French protectorate; **currency:** French franc; **GNP per capita (PPP):** (US$) 26,170 (1996 est); **population:** 32,200 (1999 est); **language:** French (official); English, Italian; **religion:** Roman Catholic; **life expectancy:** 75 (men); 82 (women) (1998 est.).

**Mondrian, Piet (Pieter Cornelis Mondriaan)** (1872–1944) Dutch painter. A founder member of the De →Stijl movement, he was the chief exponent of neoplasticism, a rigorous abstract style based on the use of simple geometric forms and pure colours. Typically his works are frameworks of horizontal and vertical lines forming rectangles of white, red, yellow, and blue, as in *Composition in Red, Yellow and Blue* (1920) (Stedelijk, Amsterdam).

**Monet, Claude** (1840–1926) French painter. He was a pioneer of Impressionism and a lifelong exponent of its ideals; his painting *Impression, Sunrise* (1872) gave the movement its name. In the 1870s he began painting the same subjects at different times of day to explore the ever-changing effects of light on colour and form; the *Haystacks* and *Rouen Cathedral* series followed in the 1890s, and from 1899 he painted a series of *Water Lilies* in the garden of his house at Giverny, Normandy (now a museum).

**Mongolia** State of (**Outer Mongolia** until 1924; **People's republic of Mongolia** until 1991); **national name:** *Mongol Uls*; **area:** 1,565,000 sq km/604,246 sq mi; **capital:** Ulaanbaatar (Ulan Bator); **major towns/cities:** Darhan, Choybalsan, Erdenet; **physical features:** high plateau with desert and steppe (grasslands); Altai Mountains in southwest; salt lakes; part of Gobi desert in southeast; contains both the world's southernmost permafrost and northernmost desert; **head of state:** Natsagiyn Bagabandi from 1997; **head of government:** Janlaviyn Narantsatsralt from 1998; **political system:** emergent democracy; **currency:** tugrik; **GNP per capita (PPP):** (US$) 1,520 (1998); **exports:** minerals and metals (primarily copper concentrate), consumer goods, foodstuffs, agricultural products. Principal market China 30.1% (1998); **population:** 2,621,000 (1999 est); **language:** Khalkha Mongolian (official); Chinese, Russian, and Turkic languages; **religion:** officially none (Tibetan Buddhist Lamaism suppressed in 1930s); **life expectancy:** 64 (men); 67 (women) (1995–2000).

**monkey** any of the various smaller, mainly tree-dwelling anthropoid →primates, excluding humans and the →apes. There are 125 species, living in Africa, Asia, and tropical Central and South America. Monkeys eat mainly leaves and fruit, and also small animals. Several species are endangered due to loss of forest habitat, for example the woolly spider monkey and black saki of the Amazonian forest.

**monolith** (Greek *monos* 'sole', *lithos* 'stone') single isolated stone or column, usually standing and of great size, used as a form of monument. Some are natural features, such as the Buck Stone in the Forest of Dean, England. Other monoliths may be quarried, resited, finished, or carved; those in Egypt of about 3000 BC take the form of obelisks. They have a wide distribution including Europe, South America, North Africa, and the Middle East.

**monomer** chemical compound composed of simple molecules from which polymers can be made. Under certain conditions the simple molecules (of the monomer) join together (polymerize) to form a very long chain molecule (macromolecule) called a polymer. For example, the polymerization of ethene (ethylene) monomers produces the polymer polyethene (polyethylene).

$$2nCH_2 = CH_2 \rightarrow (CH_2-CH_2-CH_2-CH_2)_n$$

**monotreme** any of a small group of primitive egg-laying mammals, found in Australasia. They include the echidnas (spiny anteaters) and the platypus. (Order Monotremata.)

**Monroe, Marilyn** (1926–1962) stage name of Norma Jean Mortenson or Baker, US film actor. The voluptuous blonde sex symbol of the 1950s, she made adroit comedies such as *Gentlemen Prefer Blondes* (1953), *How to Marry a Millionaire* (1953), *The Seven Year Itch* (1955), *Bus Stop* (1956), and *Some Like It Hot* (1959).

**monsoon** wind pattern that brings seasonally heavy rain to South Asia; it blows towards the sea in winter and towards the land in summer. The monsoon may cause destructive flooding all over India and Southeast Asia from April to September, leaving thousands of people homeless each year.

**Monteverdi, Claudio Giovanni Antonio** (1567–1643) Italian composer. He contributed to the development of the opera with *La favola d'Orfeo/The Legend of Orpheus* (1607) and *L'incoronazione di Poppea/The Coronation of Poppea* (1642). He also wrote madrigals, motets, and sacred music, notably the *Vespers* (1610).

**Montezuma II** (1466–1520) Aztec emperor of Mexico. He succeeded his uncle in 1502. Although he was a great warrior and legislator, heavy centralized taxation provoked resentment in outlying areas. When the Spanish conquistador Hernán Cortés landed at Veracruz in 1519 and attempted to march on Tenochtitlán, he was well received by the inhabitants and made Montezuma his prisoner. The emperor was restored to his throne as a vassal of Spain, but dissident groups among his subjects rebelled and killed him.

**Montgolfier** Joseph Michel (1740–1810) and Jacques Etienne (1745–1799) French brothers whose hot-air balloon was used for the first successful human flight 21 November 1783.

**Montréal** inland port and commercial centre of Québec, Canada, on Montréal Island at the junction of the Ottawa and St Lawrence rivers; population of metropolitan area (1996 est) 3,326,500. It is the second-largest port on the North

American east coast, the chief port of the St Lawrence–Great Lakes waterway system, and the world's farthest inland port, situated 1,600 km/1,000 mi from the Atlantic. Industries include oil-refining, engineering, food-processing, distilling, brewing, and the manufacture of steel, aircraft, ships, petrochemicals, tobacco products, clothing, pulp, and paper. Founded by the French in 1642, Montréal became a British possession in 1763.

The city was badly affected by the great ice storm of January 1998 which coated electricity pylons with ice and the weight brought many of them down, blacking out parts of Montréal and Québec.

**Moon** natural satellite of Earth, 3,476 km/2,160 mi in diameter, with a mass 0.012 (approximately one-eightieth) that of Earth.

Its surface gravity is only 0.16 (one-sixth) that of Earth. Its average distance from Earth is 384,400 km/238,855 mi, and it orbits in a west-to-east direction every 27.32 days (the **sidereal month**). It spins on its axis with one side permanently turned towards Earth. The Moon has no atmosphere and was thought to have no water till ice was discovered on its surface in 1998.

**Moore, Henry (Spencer)** (1898–1986) English sculptor. His subjects include the reclining nude, mother-and-child groups, the warrior, and interlocking abstract forms. Many of his post-1945 works are in bronze or marble, including monumental semi-abstracts such as *Reclining Figure* (1957–58), outside the UNESCO building in Paris, and are often designed to be placed in landscape settings. He is considered one of the leading artists of the 20th century.

**More, (St) Thomas** (1478–1535) English politician and author. From 1509 he was favoured by →Henry VIII and employed on foreign embassies. He was a member of the privy council from 1518 and Lord Chancellor from 1529 but resigned over Henry's break with the pope. For refusing to accept the king as head of the church, he was executed. The title of his political book *Utopia* (1516) has come to mean any supposedly perfect society.

**Mormon** (or Latter-day Saint) member of a Christian sect, the **Church of Jesus Christ of Latter-day Saints**, founded at Fayette, New York, in 1830 by Joseph Smith. According to Smith, Mormon was an ancient prophet in North America whose *Book of Mormon*, which Smith claimed was divinely revealed to him, is accepted by Mormons as part of the Christian scriptures. Originally persecuted, the Mormons migrated west to Salt Lake City, Utah, under Brigham Young's leadership and prospered; their headquarters are here. The Mormon Church is a missionary church with a worldwide membership of about 6 million.

**Morocco** Kingdom of; **national name:** *al-Mamlaka al-Maghrebia*; **area:** 458,730 sq km/177,115 sq mi (excluding Western Sahara); **capital:** Rabat; **major towns/cities:** Casablanca, Marrakesh,

Fez, Oujda, Kenitra, Tetouan, Meknès; **major ports:** Casablanca, Tangier, Agadir; **physical features:** mountain ranges, including the Atlas Mountains northeast–southwest; fertile coastal plains in west; **head of state:** Hassan II from 1961; **head of government:** Abderrahmane Youssoufi from 1998; **political system:** constitutional monarchy; **currency:** dirham (DH); **GNP per capita (PPP):** (US\$) 3,120 (1998); **exports:** phosphates and phosphoric acid, mineral products, seafoods and seafood products, citrus fruit, tobacco, clothing, hosiery. Principal market France 31.7% (1997); **population:** 27,866,000 (1999 est); **language:** Arabic (official) 75%; Berber 25%, French, Spanish; **religion:** Sunni Muslim; **life expectancy:** 65 (men); 69 (women) (1995–2000).

**Morris, William** (1834–1896) English designer, socialist, and writer. A founder of the Arts and Crafts Movement, he condemned 19th-century mechanization and sought a revival of traditional crafts, such as furnituremaking, book illustration, fabric design, and so on. He linked this to a renewal of society based on Socialist principles.

**Morse code** international code for transmitting messages by wire or radio using signals of short (dots) and long (dashes) duration, originated by US inventor Samuel Morse for use on his invention, the telegraph.

**mosaic** design or picture, usually for a floor or wall, produced by setting small pieces (*tesserae*) of marble, glass, or other materials in a cement ground. The ancient Greeks were the first to use large-scale mosaic (in the Macedonian royal palace at Pella, for example). Mosaic was commonly used by the Romans for their baths and villas (a well-known example being at Hadrian's Villa in Tivoli) and reached its highest development in the early Byzantine period (for example,in the church of San Vitale, Ravenna).

**Moscow** (Russian Moskva) industrial and commercial city, capital of the Russian Federation and of the Moscow region, and formerly (1922–91) of the USSR; population (1990) 8,801,000. Moscow lies on the Moskva River 640 km/400 mi southeast of St Petersburg, and covers an area of some 880 sq km/340 sq mi. It is the main political, economic, and cultural centre of Russia. A major manufacturing city, its industries include aerospace technology and vehicle assembly, machine and precision tool manufacture, and the production of such diverse goods as electrical equipment, textiles, chemicals, and many food products. Moscow's State University was founded in 1755; other cultural institutions include the extensive Russian State Library and the Academy of Sciences. The city is home to the renowned Bolshoi Theatre of Opera and Ballet, the Pushkin Fine Arts Museum, the Tretyakov Gallery, and the Exhibition of Economic Achievements.

**mosque** (Arabic *mesjid*) in Islam, a place of worship. Chief features are: the dome; the minaret, a balconied turret from which the faithful are called to prayer; the *mihrab*, or prayer niche, in one of the interior walls, showing the direction of the holy city of Mecca; and an open court surrounded by porticoes.

**mosquito** any of a group of flies in which the female has needlelike mouthparts and sucks blood before laying eggs. The males feed on plant juices. Some mosquitoes carry diseases such as →malaria. (Family Culicidae, order Diptera.)

**moss** small nonflowering plant of the class Musci (10,000 species), forming with the liverworts and the hornworts the order Bryophyta. The stem of each plant bears rhizoids that anchor it; there are no true roots. Leaves spirally arranged on its lower portion have sexual organs at their tips. Most mosses flourish best in damp conditions where other vegetation is thin. There are 1,000 British species of moss and more than 1,200 North American species.

**moth** any of a large number of mainly night-flying insects closely related to butterflies. Their wings are covered with microscopic scales. Most moths have a long sucking mouthpart (proboscis) for feeding on the nectar of flowers, but some have no functional mouthparts and rely instead upon stores of fat and other reserves built up during the caterpillar stage. At least 100,000 different species of moth are known. (Order Lepidoptera.)

**mould** furlike growth caused by any of a group of fungi (see →fungus) living on foodstuffs and other organic matter; a few are parasitic on plants, animals, or each other. Many moulds are of medical or industrial importance; for example, the antibiotic penicillin comes from a type of mould.

**mountain** natural upward projection of the Earth's surface, higher and steeper than a hill. Mountains are at least 330 m/1000 ft above the surrounding topography. The process of mountain building (orogeny) consists of volcanism, folding, faulting, and thrusting, resulting from the collision of two tectonic plates (see →plate tectonics) at a **convergent margin**. The existing rock is also subjected to high temperatures and pressures causing metamorphism. Plutonic activity also can accompany mountain building.

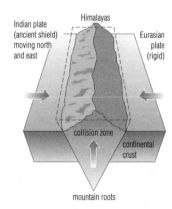

**mountain** Mountains are created when two continental plates collide and no subduction takes place, resulting in the land at the collision zone being squeezed together and thrust upwards.

## HIGHEST MOUNTAINS IN THE WORLD, AND FIRST ASCENTS

| Mountain | Location | Height m | ft | Year of first ascent | Expedition nationality (leader) |
|---|---|---|---|---|---|
| Everest | China/Nepal | 8,848 | 29,028 | 1953 | British/New Zealander (J Hunt) |
| K2 | Kashmir/Jammu | 8,611 | 28,251 | 1954 | Italian (A Desio) |
| Kangchenjunga | India/Nepal | 8,598 | 28,208 | 1955 | British (C Evans; by the southwest face) |
| Lhotse | China/Nepal | 8,511 | 27,923 | 1956 | Swiss (E Reiss) |
| Yalung Kang (formerly Kangchenjunga West Peak) | India/Nepal | 8,502 | 27,893 | 1973 | Japanese (Y Ageta) |
| Kangchenjunga South Peak | India/Nepal | 8,488 | 27,847 | 1978 | Polish (W Wróz) |
| Makalu I | China/Nepal | 8,481 | 27,824 | 1955 | French (J Couzy) |
| Kangchenjunga Middle Peak | India/Nepal | 8,475 | 27,805 | 1973 | Polish (W Wróz) |
| Lhotse Shar | China/Nepal | 8,383 | 27,503 | 1970 | Austrian (S Mayerl) |
| Dhaulagiri | Nepal | 8,172 | 26,811 | 1960 | Swiss/Austrian (K Diemberger) |
| Manaslu | Nepal | 8,156 | 26,759 | 1956 | Japanese (T Imanishi) |
| Cho Oyu | China/Nepal | 8,153 | 26,748 | 1954 | Austrian (H Tichy) |
| Nanga Parbat | Kashmir/Jammu | 8,126 | 26,660 | 1953 | German (K M Herrligkoffer) |
| Annapurna I | Nepal | 8,078 | 26,502 | 1950 | French (M Herzog) |
| Gasherbrum I | Kashmir/Jammu | 8,068 | 26,469 | 1958 | US (P K Schoening; by the southwest ridge) |
| Broad Peak | Kashmir/Jammu | 8,047 | 26,401 | 1957 | Austrian (M Schmuck) |

## HIGHLEST MOUNTAINS IN THE WORLD, AND FIRST ASCENTS (CONTINUED)

| Mountain | Location | Height m | ft | Year of first ascent | Expedition nationality (leader) |
|---|---|---|---|---|---|
| Gasherbrum II | Kashmir/Jammu | 8,034 | 26,358 | 1956 | Austrian (S Larch; by the southwest spur) |
| Gosainthan | China | 8,012 | 26,286 | 1964 | Chinese (195-strong team; accounts are inconclusive) |
| Broad Peak (Middle) | Kashmir/Jammu | 8,000 | 26,246 | 1975 | Polish (K Glazek) |
| Gasherbrum III | Kashmir/Jammu | 7,952 | 26,089 | 1975 | Polish (J Onyszkiewicz) |
| Annapurna II | Nepal | 7,937 | 26,040 | 1960 | British (C Bonington) |
| Gasherbrum IV | Kashmir/Jammu | 7,923 | 25,994 | 1958 | Italian (W Bonatti, C Mouri) |
| Gyachung Kang | Nepal | 7,921 | 25,987 | 1964 | Japanese (Y Kato, K Sakaizqwa) |
| Disteghil Shar | Kashmir | 7,884 | 25,866 | 1960 | Austrian (G Stärker, D Marchart) |
| Himalchuli | Nepal | 7,864 | 25,800 | 1960 | Japanese (M Harada, H Tanabe) |
| Nuptse | Nepal | 7,841 | 25,725 | 1961 | British (D Davis, C Bonington, L Brown) |
| Manaslu II | Nepal | 7,835 | 25,705 | 1970 | Japanese (H Watanabe, Lhakpa Tsering) |
| Masherbrum East | Kashmir | 7,821 | 25,659 | 1960 | Pakistani/US (G Bell, W Unsoeld) |
| Nanda Devi | India | 7,817 | 25,646 | 1936 | British (H W Tilman) |
| Chomo Lonzo | Nepal | 7,815 | 25,639 | 1954 | French (J Couzy, L Terry) |

**Mozambique** People's Republic of; **national name:** *República Popular de Moçambique*; **area:** 799,380 sq km/ 308,640 sq mi; **capital:** Maputo (and chief port); **major towns/cities:** Beira, Nampula, Nacala, Chimoio; **major ports:** Beira, Nacala, Quelimane; **physical features:** mostly flat tropical lowland; mountains in west; rivers Zambezi and Limpopo; **head of state:** Joaquim Alberto Chissano from 1986; **head of government:** Pascoal Mocumbi from 1994; **political system:** emergent democracy; **currency:** metical; **GNP per capita (PPP):** (US$) 850 (1998 est); **exports:** shrimps and other crustaceans, cashew nuts, raw cotton, sugar, copra, lobsters. Principal market Spain 17.1% (1996); **population:** 19,286,000 (1999 est); **language:** Portuguese (official); 16 African languages; **religion:** animist, Roman Catholic, Muslim; **life expectancy:** 44 (men); 47 (women) (1995–2000).

**Mozart, (Johann Chrysostom) Wolfgang Amadeus** (1756–1791) Austrian composer and performer who showed astonishing precocity as a child and was an adult virtuoso. He was trained by his father, **Leopold Mozart** (1719–1787). From an early age he composed prolifically, and his works include 27 piano concertos, 23 string quartets, 35 violin sonatas, and 41 symphonies including the E♭ K543, G minor K550, and C major K551 ('Jupiter') symphonies, all composed in 1788. His operas include *Idomeneo* 1780, *Entführung aus dem Serail/The Abduction from the Seraglio* (1782), *Le Nozze di Figaro/The Marriage of Figaro* (1786), *Don Giovanni*

(1787), *Così fan tutte/Thus Do All Women* (1790), and *Die Zauberflöte/The Magic Flute* (1791). Together with the work of Haydn, Mozart's music marks the height of the classical age in its purity of melody and form.

**Mugabe, Robert (Gabriel)** (1925– ) Zimbabwean politician, prime minister from 1980 and president from 1987. He was in detention in Rhodesia for nationalist activities 1964–74, then carried on guerrilla warfare from Mozambique. As leader of ZANU (Zimbabwe African National Union) he was in an uneasy alliance with Joshua Nkomo of ZAPU (Zimbabwe African People's Union) from 1976.

**Muhammad** (*c.* 570–632) also known as Mohammed or Mahomet (Arabic 'praised'), founder of Islam, born in Mecca on the Arabian peninsula. In about 616 he began to preach the worship of one God, who allegedly revealed to him the words of the Koran (it was later written down by his followers) through the angel Jibra'el (Gabriel). Muhammad fled from persecution to the town now known as Medina in 622: the flight, **Hijrah** or **Hegira**, marks the beginning of the Islamic era.

**multiple sclerosis** (MS or disseminated sclerosis) incurable chronic disease of the central nervous system, occurring in young or middle adulthood. Most prevalent in temperate zones, it affects more women than men. It is characterized by degeneration of the myelin sheath that surrounds nerves in the brain and spinal cord.

**mumps** (or infectious parotitis) virus infection marked by fever, pain, and swelling of one or both parotid salivary glands (situated in front of the ears). It is usually shortlived in children, although meningitis is a possible complication. In adults the symptoms are more serious and it may cause sterility in men.

**Munch, Edvard** (1863–1944) Norwegian painter and graphic artist, a major influence on →expressionism. His highly charged paintings, characterized by strong colours and distorted forms, often focus on intense emotional states, as in one of his best-known works *The Scream* (1893). His works brought a new urgency and power to the two themes that dominated late 19th-century decadence, death and sexuality.

**Munich** (German *München*) capital of Bavaria, Germany, on the River Isar, about 520 m/1,706 ft above sea level, some 45 km/28 mi from the edge of the Alps; population (1995) 1,240,600. The main industries are brewing, printing, precision instruments, machinery, electrical goods, computers, telecommunications, fashion, and food processing.

**Munich Agreement** pact signed on 29 September 1938 by the leaders of the UK (Neville Chamberlain), France (Edouard Daladier), Germany (Hitler), and Italy (Mussolini), under which Czechoslovakia was compelled to surrender its Sudeten-German districts (the **Sudeten**) to Germany. Chamberlain claimed it would guarantee 'peace in our time', but it did not prevent Hitler from seizing the rest of Czechoslovakia in March 1939.

**muscle** contractile animal tissue that produces locomotion and power, and maintains the movement of body substances. Muscle is made of long cells that can contract to between one-half and one-third of their relaxed length. *See illustration on page 374.*

**muscular dystrophy** any of a group of inherited chronic muscle disorders marked by weakening and wasting of muscle. Muscle fibres degenerate, to be replaced by fatty tissue, although the nerve supply remains unimpaired. Death occurs in early adult life.

**Muslim** (or Moslem), a follower of Islam.

**Mussolini, Benito Amilcare Andrea** (1883–1945) Italian dictator 1925–43. As founder of the Fascist Movement (see →fascism) in 1919 and prime minister from 1922, he became known as *Il Duce* ('the leader'). He invaded Ethiopia 1935–36, intervened in the Spanish Civil War 1936–39 in support of Franco, and conquered Albania in 1939. In June 1940 Italy entered World War II supporting Hitler. Forced by military and domestic setbacks to resign in 1943, Mussolini established a breakaway government in northern Italy 1944–45, but was killed trying to flee the country.

**Mussorgsky, Modest Petrovich** (1839–1881) Russian composer. He was a member of the group of five composers ('The Five'). His opera masterpiece *Boris Godunov* (1869), revised

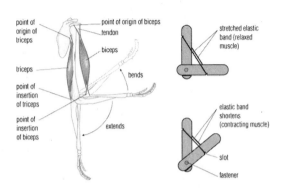

**muscle** The movements of the arm depend on two muscles, the biceps and the triceps. To lift the arm, the biceps shortens and the triceps lengthens. To lower the arm, the opposite occurs the biceps lengthens and the triceps shortens.

1871–72, touched a political nerve and employed realistic transcriptions of speech patterns. Many of his works, including *Pictures at an Exhibition* (1874) for piano, were 'revised' and orchestrated by others, including Rimsky-Korsakov, Ravel, and Shostakovich, and some have only recently been restored to their original harsh beauty.

**mutation** in biology, a change in the genes produced by a change in the →DNA that makes up the hereditary material of all living organisms. Mutations, the raw material of evolution, result from mistakes during replication (copying) of DNA molecules. Only a few improve the organism's performance and are therefore favoured by →natural selection. Mutation rates are increased by certain chemicals and by radiation.

**Myanmar** Union of (formerly **Burma**, until 1989); **national name:** *Thammada Myanmar Naingngandaw*; **area:** 676,577 sq km/261,226 sq mi; **capital:** Yangon (formerly Rangoon) (and chief port); **major towns/cities:** Mandalay, Mawlamyine, Bago, Bassein, Taunggyi, Sittwe, Manywa; **physical features:** over half is rainforest; rivers Irrawaddy and Chindwin in central lowlands ringed by mountains in north, west, and east; **head of state and government:** Than Shwe from 1992; **political system:** military republic; **currency:** kyat; **GNP per capita (PPP):** (US$) 1,280 (1996 est); **exports:** teak, rice, pulses and beans, rubber, hardwood, base metals, gems, cement. Principal market India 13.1% (1998); **population:** 45,039,000 (1999 est); **language:** Burmese (official), English; **religion:** Hinayāna Buddhist 85%, animist, Christian, Muslim; **life expectancy:** 59 (men); 62 (women) (1995–2000).

**Mycenaean civilization** Bronze Age civilization that flourished in Crete, Cyprus, Greece, the Aegean Islands, and western Anatolia about 3000–1000 BC. During this period, magnificent architecture and sophisticated artefacts were produced.

**mysticism** religious belief or spiritual experience based on direct, intuitive communion with the divine or apprehension of truths beyond the understanding. It does not always involve an orthodox deity, though it is found in all the main religions – for example, kabbalism in Judaism, Sufism in Islam, and the bhakti movement in Hinduism.

**mythology** (Greek *mythos*, *logos* 'storytelling' or a 'rationale of stories') body of traditional stories symbolically underlying a given culture. These stories describe gods and other supernatural beings with whom humans may have relationships, and are often intended to explain the workings of the universe, nature, or human history. Mythology is sometimes distinguished from legend as being entirely fictitious and imaginary, legend being woven around an historical figure or nucleus such as the tale of Troy, but such division is difficult as myth and legend are often closely interwoven.

# Nn

**Nabokov, Vladimir Vladimirovich** (1899–1977) US writer. He left his native Russia 1917 and began writing in English in the 1940s. His most widely known book is *Lolita* (1955), the story of the middle-aged Humbert Humbert's infatuation with a precocious girl of 12. His other books, remarkable for their word play and ingenious plots, include *Laughter in the Dark* (1938), *The Real Life of Sebastian Knight* (1945), *Pnin* (1957), and his memoirs *Speak, Memory* (1947).

**Nagasaki** industrial port (coal, iron, shipbuilding) on Kyushu island, Japan; population (1994) 438,000. Nagasaki was the only Japanese port open to European trade from the 16th century until 1859. The first modern Japanese shipyard opened here 1855–61. On 9 August 1945, an atom bomb was dropped on Nagasaki by the USA.

**Nairobi** capital of Kenya, in the central highlands at 1,660 m/5,450 ft; population (1993 est) 1,758,900. Industries include engineering, paints, brewing, and food processing. It is the headquarters of the United Nations Environment Programme, and has the UN Centre for Human Settlements. It is one of Africa's largest and fastest-growing cities.

**Namib Desert** coastal desert region between the Kalahari Desert and the Atlantic Ocean, extending some 2,800 km/1,740 mi from Luanda in Angola to St Helena Bay in South Africa. Its aridity is caused by the descent of dry air cooled by the cold Benguela current along the coast. The sand dunes of the Namib Desert are among the tallest in the world, reaching heights of 370 m/1,200 ft. In the most arid parts rainfall can be as little as 23 mm/0.9 in per year.

**Namibia** Republic of (formerly **South West Africa**); **area:** 824,300 sq km/318,262 sq mi; **capital:** Windhoek; **major towns/cities:** Swakopmund, Rehoboth, Rundu; **major ports:** Walvis Bay; **physical features:** mainly desert (Namib and Kalahari); Orange River; Caprivi Strip links Namibia to Zambezi River; includes the enclave of Walvis Bay (area 1,120 sq km/432 sq mi); **head of state:** Sam Nujoma from 1990; **head of government:** Hage Geingob from 1990; **political system:** democracy; **currency:** Namibia dollar; **GNP per capita (PPP):** (US$) 4,950 (1998 est); **exports:** diamonds, fish and fish products, live animals and meat, uranium, karakul pelts. Principal market UK 33% (1998); **population:** 1,695,000 (1999 est); **language:** English (official), Afrikaans, German, indigenous languages; **religion:** mainly Christian (Lutheran, Roman Catholic, Dutch Reformed Church, Anglican); **life expectancy:** 52 (men); 53 (women) (1995–2000).

**Nanak** (1469–c. 1539) Indian guru and founder of Sikhism, a religion based on the unity of God and the equality of all human beings. He was strongly opposed to caste divisions.

**nanotechnology** experimental technology using individual atoms or molecules as the components of minute machines, measured by the nanometre, or millionth of a millimetre. Nanotechnology research in the 1990s focused on testing molecular structures and refining ways to manipulate atoms using a scanning tunnelling microscope. The ultimate aim is to create very small computers and molecular machines which could perform vital engineering or medical tasks.

**Naples** (Italian *Napoli*; Greek *Neapolis* 'new city') industrial port and capital of Campania, Italy, on the Tyrrhenian Sea; population (1992) 1,071,700. Industries include shipbuilding, food-processing, and the manufacture of cars, textiles, and paper. To the south is the Isle of Capri, and behind the city is Mount Vesuvius, with the ruins of Pompeii at its foot.

**Narcissus** in late Greek mythology, a beautiful youth who rejected the love of the nymph Echo and was condemned by Nemesis, goddess of retribution, to fall in love with his reflection in a pool. He pined away, and a flower which appeared at the spot was named after him.

**narcotic** pain-relieving and sleep-inducing drug. The term is usually applied to heroin, morphine, and other opium derivatives, but may also be used for other drugs which depress brain activity, including anaesthetic agents and hypnotics.

**NASA** (acronym for National Aeronautics and Space Administration) US government agency for spaceflight and aeronautical research, founded in 1958 by the National Aeronautics and Space Act. Its headquarters are in Washington, DC, and its main installation is at the Kennedy Space Center in Florida. NASA's early planetary and lunar programmes included *Pioneer* spacecraft from 1958, which gathered data for the later crewed missions, the most famous of which took the first people to the Moon in *Apollo 11* on 16–24 July 1969.

**Naseby, Battle of** decisive battle of the English Civil War on 14 June 1645, when the Royalists, led by Prince Rupert, were defeated by the Parliamentarians ('Roundheads') under Oliver Cromwell and General Fairfax. It is named after the nearby village of Naseby, 32 km/20 mi south of Leicester.

**Nash, John** (1752–1835) English architect. His large country-house practice, established about 1796 with the landscape gardener Humphry Repton, used a wide variety of styles, and by 1798 he was enjoying the patronage of the Prince of Wales (afterwards George IV). Later he laid out Regent's Park, London, and its approaches, as well as Trafalgar Square and St James's Park. Between 1811 and 1821 he planned Regent Street (later rebuilt), repaired and enlarged Buckingham Palace (for which he designed Marble Arch), and rebuilt the Royal Pavilion, Brighton, in flamboyant oriental style.

**Natal** former province of South Africa to 1994, bounded on the east by the Indian Ocean. In 1994 it became part of KwaZulu-Natal Province. It is called Natal ('of [Christ's] birth') because the Portuguese navigator Vasco da Gama reached it on Christmas Day in 1497.

**NATO** abbreviation for →North Atlantic Treaty Organization.

**natural gas** mixture of flammable gases found in the Earth's crust (often in association with petroleum). It is one of the world's three main fossil fuels (with coal and oil). Natural gas is a mixture of →hydrocarbons, chiefly methane (80%), with ethane, butane, and propane. Natural gas is usually transported from its source by pipeline, although it may be liquefied for transport and storage and is, therefore, often used in remote areas where other fuels are scarce and expensive. Prior to transportation, butane and propane are removed and liquefied to form 'bottled gas'.

**natural selection** the process whereby gene frequencies in a population change through certain individuals producing more descendants than others because they are better able to survive and reproduce in their environment.

The accumulated effect of natural selection is to produce adaptations such as the insulating coat of a polar bear or the spadelike forelimbs of a mole. The process is slow, relying firstly on random variation in the genes of an organism being produced by →mutation and secondly on the genetic →recombination of sexual reproduction. It was recognized by Charles Darwin and English naturalist Alfred Russel Wallace as the main process driving →evolution.

**Nauru** Republic of; **national name:** *Naoero*; **area:** 21 sq km/8.1 sq mi; **capital:** (seat of government) Yaren District; **physical features:** tropical coral island in southwest Pacific; plateau encircled by coral cliffs and sandy beaches; **head of state and government:** Rene Harris from 1999; **political system:** liberal democracy; **currency:** Australian dollar; **GNP per capita (PPP):** (US$) 11,800 (1994 est); **exports:** phosphates. Principal market Australia; **population:** 11,200 (1999 est); **language:** Nauruan (official), English; **religion:** Protestant, Roman Catholic; **life expectancy:** 64 (men); 69 (women) (1998 est).

**Navarre, Kingdom of** former kingdom comprising the Spanish province of Navarre and part of what is now the French *département* of Basses-Pyrénées. It resisted the conquest of the Moors and was independent until it became French 1284 on the marriage of Philip IV to the heiress of Navarre. In 1479 Ferdinand of Aragón annexed Spanish Navarre, with French Navarre going to

Catherine of Foix (1483–1512), who kept the royal title. Her grandson became Henry IV of France, and Navarre was absorbed in the French crown lands 1620.

**Nazareth** city in Galilee, northern Israel, 30 km/19 mi southeast of Haifa; population about 64,000. According to the New Testament it was the boyhood home of Jesus.

**Nazism** ideology based on racism, nationalism, and the supremacy of the state over the individual. The German Nazi party, the *Nationalsozialistische Deutsche Arbeiterpartei* (National Socialist German Workers' Party), was formed from the German Workers' Party (founded in 1919) and led by Adolf →Hitler from 1921 to 1945.

**Neanderthal** hominid of the Mid-Late Palaeolithic, named after the Neander Tal (valley) near Düsseldorf, Germany, where a skeleton was found in 1856. *Homo sapiens neanderthalensis* lived from about 150,000 to 35,000 years ago and was similar in build to present-day people, but slightly smaller, stockier, and heavier-featured with a strong jaw and prominent brow ridges on a sloping forehead. The condition of the Neanderthal teeth that have been found suggests that they were used as clamps for holding objects with the hands.

**Nebuchadnezzar** (*c.* 630–*c.* 562 BC) or Nebuchadrezzar II, king of Babylonia from 604 BC. Shortly before his accession he defeated the Egyptians at Carchemish and brought Palestine and Syria into his empire. Judah revolted, with Egyptian assistance, 596 and 587–586 BC; on both occasions he captured Jerusalem and took many Hebrews into captivity. He largely rebuilt Babylon and constructed the hanging gardens.

**nebula** cloud of gas and dust in space. Nebulae are the birthplaces of stars, but some nebulae are produced by gas thrown off from dying stars (see →supernova). Nebulae are classified depending on whether they emit, reflect, or absorb light.

**Nehru, Jawaharlal** (1889–1964) Indian nationalist politician, prime minister from 1947 until his death. Before the partition (the division of British India into India and Pakistan), he led the socialist wing of the nationalist Congress Party, and was second in influence only to Mahatma Gandhi. He was imprisoned nine times by the British 1921–45 for political activities. As prime minister from the creation of the dominion (later republic) of India in August 1947, he originated the idea of nonalignment (neutrality towards major powers). His daughter was Prime Minister Indira Gandhi. His sister, Vijaya Lakshmi Pandit was the UN General Assembly's first female president 1953–54.

**Nelson, Horatio** (1758–1805) 1st Viscount Nelson English admiral. He joined the navy in 1770. During the Revolutionary Wars against France he lost the sight in his right eye in 1794 and lost his right arm in 1797. He became a rear admiral and a national hero after the victory off Cape St Vincent, Portugal. In 1798 he tracked the French fleet to Aboukir Bay where he almost entirely destroyed it. In 1801 he won a decisive victory over Denmark at the Battle of →Copenhagen, and in 1805, after two years of blockading Toulon, he defeated the Franco-Spanish fleet at the Battle of →Trafalgar, near Gibraltar. KB 1797, Baron 1798, Viscount 1801.

**neoclassicism** movement in art, architecture, and design in Europe and North America about 1750–1850, characterized by a revival of classical Greek and Roman styles. Leading figures of the movement were the architects Claude-Nicolas Ledoux and Robert Adam; the painters Jacques-Louis David, Jean Ingres, and Anton Mengs; the sculptors Antonio Canova, John Flaxman, Bertel Thorvaldsen, and Johann Sergel; and the designers Josiah Wedgwood, George Hepplewhite, and Thomas Sheraton.

**Neo-Impressionism** movement in French painting that developed from →Impressionism in the 1880s and flourished until the early years of the 20th century. The name was coined in 1886 in a review of the eighth and last Impressionist exhibition, held in Paris that year. Among the artists who exhibited there was Georges Seurat, who was the chief creator and outstanding exponent of Neo-Impressionism.

**Neolithic** literally 'New Stone', the last period of the →Stone Age. It was characterized by settled agricultural communities who kept domesticated animals, and made pottery and sophisticated, finely finished stone tools.

The Neolithic period began and ended at different times in different parts of the world. For example, the earliest Neolithic communities appeared about 9000 BC in the Middle East, and were followed by those in Egypt, India, and China. In Europe farming began in about 6500 BC in the Balkans and Aegean Sea areas, spreading north and east by 1000 BC. The Neolithic period ended with the start of the →Bronze Age, when people began using metals. Some Stone Age cultures persisted into the 20th century, notably in remote parts of New Guinea.

**neon** (Greek *neos* 'new') colourless, odourless, nonmetallic, gaseous element, symbol Ne, atomic number 10, relative atomic mass 20.183. It is grouped with the →inert gases, is nonreactive, and forms no compounds. It occurs in small quantities in the Earth's atmosphere.

**Nepal** Kingdom of; **national name:** *Nepal Adhirajya*; **area:** 147,181 sq km/ 56,826 sq mi; **capital:** Kathmandu; **major towns/cities:** Pátan, Moráng, Bhádgáon, Biratnagar, Lalitpur, Bhaktapur, Pokhara; **physical features:** descends from the Himalayan mountain range in the north through foothills to the River Ganges plain in the south; Mount Everest, Mount Kanchenjunga; **head of state:** King Birendra Bir Bikram Shah Dev from 1972; **head of government:** Krishna Prasad Bhattarai from 1999; **political**

**system:** constitutional monarchy; **currency:** Nepalese rupee; **GNP per capita (PPP):** (US$) 1,090 (1998); exports: woollen carpets, clothing, hides and skins, food grains, jute, timber, oil seeds, ghee, potatoes, medicinal herbs, cattle. Principal market India 32.8% (1998); **population:** (1999 est) 23,386,000; **language:** Nepali (official); 20 dialects spoken; **religion:** Hindu 90%; Buddhist, Muslim, Christian; **life expectancy:** 58 (men); 57 (women) (1995–2000).

**Neptune** in astronomy, the eighth planet in average distance from the Sun. It is a giant gas (hydrogen, helium, methane) planet, with a mass 17.2 times that of Earth. It has the highest winds in the Solar System. **mean distance from the Sun:** 4.4 billion km/2.794 billion mi; **equatorial diameter:** 48,600 km/30,200 mi; **rotation period:** 16 hr 7 min; **year:** 164.8 Earth years; **atmosphere:** methane in its atmosphere absorbs red light and gives the planet a blue colouring. Consists primarily of hydrogen (85% with helium (13%) and methane (1–2%); **surface:** hydrogen, helium and methane. Its interior is believed to have a central rocky core covered by a layer of ice; **satellites:** of Neptune's eight moons, two (Triton and Nereid) are visible from Earth. Six were discovered by the *Voyager* 2 probe in 1989, of which Proteus (diameter 415 km/260 mi) is larger than Nereid (300 km/200 mi); **rings:** there are four faint rings: Galle, Leverrier, Arago, and Adams (in order from Neptune). Galle is the widest at 1,700 km/1,060 mi. Leverrier and Arago are divided by a wide diffuse particle band called the plateau.

**Neptune** in Roman mythology, god of water, who became god of the sea only after his identification with the Greek →Poseidon.

**Nero** (AD 37–68) adopted name of Lucius Domitius Ahenobarbus, Roman emperor from 54. In 59 he had his mother Agrippina and his wife Octavia put to death. The great fire at Rome 64 was blamed on the Christians, whom he subsequently persecuted. In 65 a plot against Nero was discovered. Further revolts followed 68, and he committed suicide.

**Neruda, Pablo** (1904–1973) pen-name of Neftalí Ricardo Reyes y Basoalto, Chilean poet and diplomat. His work includes lyrics and the epic poem of the American continent *Canto General* (1950). He was awarded the 1971 Nobel Prize for Literature. He served as consul and ambassador to many countries during the period 1927–44.

**nerve** bundle of nerve cells enclosed in a sheath of connective tissue and transmitting nerve impulses to and from the brain and spinal cord. A single nerve may contain both motor and sensory nerve cells, but they function independently.

**nerve cell** (or neuron) elongated cell, the basic functional unit of the nervous system that transmits information rapidly between different parts of the body. Each nerve cell has a cell body,

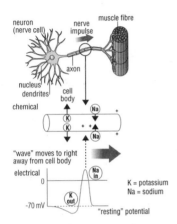

**nerve cell** The anatomy and action of a nerve cell. The nerve cell or neuron consists of a cell body with the nucleus and projections called dendrites which pick up messages. An extension of the cell, the axon, connects one cell to the dendrites of the next. When a nerve cell is stimulated, waves of sodium (Na⁺) and potassium (K⁺) ions carry an electrical impulse down the axon.

containing the nucleus, from which trail processes called dendrites, responsible for receiving incoming signals. The unit of information is the **nerve impulse**, a travelling wave of chemical and electrical changes involving the membrane of the nerve cell. The cell's longest process, the axon, carries impulses away from the cell body.

**Netherlands, the** Kingdom of (popularly referred to as **Holland**); **national name:** *Koninkrijk der Nederlanden*; **area:** 41,863 sq km/16,163 sq mi; **capital:** Amsterdam; **major towns/cities:** Rotterdam, The Hague (seat of government), Utrecht, Eindhoven, Groningen, Tilburg, Maastricht, Haarlem, Apeldoorn, Nijmegen, Enschede; **major ports:** Rotterdam; **physical features:** flat coastal lowland; rivers Rhine, Schelde, Maas; Frisian Islands; **territories:** Aruba, Netherlands Antilles (Caribbean); **head of state:** Queen Beatrix Wilhelmina Armgard from 1980; **head of government:** Wim Kok from 1994; **political system:** constitutional monarchy; **currency:** guilder; **GNP per capita (PPP):** (US$) 21,620 (1998); **exports:** machinery and transport equipment, foodstuffs, live animals, petroleum and petroleum products, natural gas, chemicals, plants and cut flowers, plant-derived products. Principal market Germany 26.5% (1997); **population:** 15,735,000 (1999 est); **language:** Dutch; **religion:** Roman Catholic, Dutch Reformed Church; **life expectancy:** 75 (men); 81 (women) (1995–2000).

**Netherlands Antilles** two groups of Caribbean islands, overseas territories of the Netherlands with full internal autonomy, comprising Curaçao and Bonaire off the coast of Venezuela (Aruba is considered separately), and St Eustatius, Saba, and the southern part of St Maarten in the Leeward Islands 800 km/500 mi to the northeast. **area:** 797 sq km/308 sq mi; **capital:** Willemstad on Curaçao; **industries:** oil from Venezuela refined here; tourism i important; rum; small manufacturing industries; **language:** Dutch (official), Papiamento, English; **population:** (1993 est) 197,100.

**network** in computing, a method of connecting computers so that they can share data and peripheral devices, such as printers. The main types are classified by the pattern of the connections – star or ring network, for example – or by the degree of geographical spread allowed; for example, local area networks (LANs) for communication within a room or building, and wide area networks (WANs) for more remote systems. Internet is the computer network that connects major English-speaking institutions throughout the world, with around 12 million users. JANET (joint academic network), a variant of the Internet, is used in Britain. SuperJANET, launched in 1992, is an extension of this that can carry 1,000 million bits of information per second.

**neuron** another name for a →nerve cell.

**neurosis** in psychology, a general term referring to emotional disorders, such as anxiety, depression, and phobias. The main disturbance tends to be one of mood; contact with reality is relatively unaffected, in contrast to psychosis.

**neutralization** in chemistry, a process occurring when the excess acid (or excess base) in a substance is reacted with added base (or added acid) so that the resulting substance is neither acidic nor basic.

**neutrino** in physics, any of three uncharged →elementary particles (and their antiparticles) of the lepton class, having a mass too close to zero to be measured. The most familiar type, the antiparticle of the electron neutrino, is emitted in the beta decay of a nucleus. The other two are the muon and tau neutrinos.

**neutron** one of the three main subatomic particles, the others being the proton and the →electron. The neutron is a composite particle, being made up of three →quarks, and therefore belongs to the baryon group of the hadrons. Neutrons have about the same mass as protons but no electric charge, and occur in the nuclei of all atoms except hydrogen. They contribute to the mass of atoms but do not affect their chemistry.

**neutron star** very small, 'superdense' star composed mostly of →neutrons. They are thought to form when massive stars explode as →supernovae, during which the protons and electrons of the star's atoms merge, owing to intense gravitational collapse, to make neutrons. A neutron star has the mass of 2-3 suns, compressed into a globe only 20 km/12 mi in diameter.

**Nevada** state in western USA. It is nicknamed the Silver State or the Sagebrush State. Nevada was admitted to the Union in 1864 as the 36th US state. It is famous as a gambling centre and, historically, especially in Reno, as a state in which marriages and divorces could be expedited. Nevada is bordered to the east by Utah and Arizona, to the west and southwest by California, and to the north by Oregon and Idaho. **population:** (1995) 1,530,100; **area:** 286,400 sq km/110,550 sq mi; **capital:** Carson City; **towns and cities:** Las Vegas, Reno; **industries and products:** mercury, barite, gold; tourism and gambling now generate more than half of the state's income.

**New Delhi** capital of India, situated in the north of the country on the Yamuna River in the Union Territory of Delhi; population (1991) 301,000. It lies near the old city of →Delhi, some 5 km/3 mi south of the Red Fort. Predominantly an administrative centre, it also produces chemicals, textiles, machine tools, electrical goods, and footwear.

**New England** region of northeast USA, comprising the states of Maine, New Hampshire, Vermont, Massachusetts, Rhode Island, and Connecticut. It is a geographic region rather than a political entity, with an area of 172,681 sq km/66,672 sq mi. Boston is the principal urban centre of the region, and Harvard and Yale are its major universities. First inhabited by the American Indian Algonquin peoples, New England was named by the explorer John Smith in 1614, and settled by Pilgrims and Puritans from England in the 17th century.

**New Model Army** army created in 1645 by Oliver →Cromwell to support the cause of Parliament during the English →Civil War. It was characterized by organization and discipline. Thomas Fairfax was its first commander.

**New Orleans** nickname 'the Big Easy', city and river port in southeast Louisiana, USA, on the Mississippi River, and the Gulf of Mexico; population (1996 est) 476,600; metropolitan area (1992) 1,303,000. It is a commercial and manufacturing centre with shipbuilding, oil-refining, and petrochemical industries. Tourism is a major activity. New Orleans is regarded as the traditional birthplace of jazz, believed to have developed from the singing and voodoo rhythms of the weekly slave gatherings in Congo Square, during the 18th and 19th centuries. The city was founded by the French in 1718.

**New South Wales** state of southeast Australia, including the dependency of Lord Howe Island; bounded by Queensland on the north, the Tasman Sea on the east, Victoria on the south, and South Australia on the west. **area:** 801,600 sq km/309,418 sq mi; **capital:** →Sydney; **towns and cities:** Newcastle, Wollongong, Wagga Wagga, Broken Hill, Goulburn, Bathurst, Armidale, Coffs Harbour, Albury, Tamworth; **physical:** Great Dividing Range (including Blue Mountains) and part of the Australian Alps (including Snowy Mountains and Mount Kosciusko); rivers Murray, Darling, and Murrumbidgee; **features:** radio telescope at Parkes; Siding Spring Mountain 859 m/2,817 ft, northwest of Sydney, with telescopes that can observe the central sector of the Galaxy; Hume Reservoir; →Canberra forms an enclave within the state; **products:** cereals, fruit, wine, sugar, tobacco, dairy products, meat, wool, gold, silver, copper, zinc, lead, coal, iron and steel, machinery, electrical appliances, cars, furniture, textiles and textile goods; **population:** (1996) 6,038,700 (about 54% in Sydney); **history:** visited by Captain James Cook in 1770; convict settlement 1788–1850; opened to free settlement by 1819; achieved self-government in 1855; became a state of the Commonwealth of Australia in 1901.

**newt** small salamander found in Europe, Asia, northwestern Africa, and North America. (Family Salamandridae, order Urodela.)

**Newton, Isaac** (1642–1727) English physicist and mathematician who laid the foundations of physics as a modern discipline. During 1665–66, he discovered the binomial theorem, differential and integral calculus, and that white light is composed of many colours. He developed the three standard laws of motion and the universal law of gravitation, set out in *Philosophiae naturalis principia mathematica* (1687), usually referred to as the *Principia*. Knighted 1705.

**New York** the most populous city in the USA, located on an inlet of the Atlantic Ocean in the far southeastern corner of New York State; population (1996 est excluding suburban metropolitan areas under separate administration) 7,380,900. New York is composed of five city boroughs that are also counties of New York State: →Manhattan (New York County); the Bronx (Bronx County); Queens (Queens County);

Brooklyn (Kings County); and Staten Island (Richmond County). As well as being the main port in North America, New York is one of the world's principal commercial and cultural centres. The many industries and services operating here include banking and other financial activities, publishing and printing, the electronic media, advertising, clothing manufacture and the fashion industry, and the production of food, chemicals, machinery, and textiles. With its great diversity of cultural institutions, places of entertainment, and sightseeing opportunities, the city also attracts a large number of tourists each year. New York is also known as the 'Big Apple'.

**New Zealand** Dominion of; **area:** 268,680 sq km/103,737 sq mi; **capital:** Wellington (and port); **major towns/cities:** Auckland, Hamilton, Palmerston North, Christchurch, Dunedin, Napier-Hastings; **major ports:** Auckland; **physical features:** comprises North Island, South Island, Stewart Island, Chatham Islands, and minor islands; mainly mountainous; Ruapehu in North Island, 2,797 m/9,180 ft, highest of three active volcanoes; geysers and hot springs of Rotorua district; Lake Taupo (616 sq km/238 sq mi), source of Waikato River; Kaingaroa state forest. In South Island are Southern Alps and Canterbury Plains; **territories:** Tokelau (three atolls transferred in 1926 from former Gilbert and Ellice Islands colony); Niue Island (one of the Cook Islands, separately administered from

1903 chief town Alafi); Cook Islands are internally self-governing but share common citizenship with New Zealand; Ross Dependency in Antarctica; **head of state:** Queen Elizabeth II from 1952, represented by governor general Catherine Tizard from 1990; **head of government:** Helen Clark from 1999; **political system:** constitutional monarchy; **currency:** New Zealand dollar; **GNP per capita (PPP):** (US$) 15,840 (1998); **exports:** meat, dairy products, wool, fish, timber and wood products, fruit and vegetables, aluminium, machinery. Principal market Australia 21.2% (1998); **population:** 3,828,000 (1999 est); **language:** English (official), Maori; **religion:** Christian; **life expectancy:** 74 (men); 80 (women) (1995–2000).

**Niagara Falls** two waterfalls on the Niagara River, on the Canada–USA border, between lakes Erie and Ontario and separated by Goat Island. The **American Falls** are 51 m/167 ft high, 330 m/1,080 ft wide; **Horseshoe Falls**, in Canada, are 49 m/160 ft high, 790 m/2,600 ft across.

**Nicaragua** Republic of; **national name:** *República de Nicaragua;* **area:** 127,849 sq km/49,362 sq mi; **capital:** Managua; **major towns/cities:** León, Chinandega, Masaya, Granada; **major ports:** Corinto, Puerto Cabezas, El Bluff; **physical features:** narrow Pacific coastal plain separated from broad Atlantic coastal plain by volcanic mountains and lakes Managua and Nicaragua; one of world's most active earthquake regions; **head of state and**

**government:** Arnoldo Aleman from 1997; **political system:** emergent democracy; **currency:** cordoba; **GNP per capita (PPP):** (US$) 1,790 (1998 est); **exports:** coffee, meat, cotton, sugar, seafood, bananas, chemical products. Principal market USA 34.8% (1998); **population:** 4,938,000 (1999 est); **language:** Spanish (official), Indian, English; **religion:** Roman Catholic 95%; **life expectancy:** 66 (men); 71 (women) (1995–2000).

**Nicholas II** (1868–1918) tsar of Russia 1894–1917. He was dominated by his wife, Tsarina Alexandra, who was under the influence of the religious charlatan →Rasputin. His mismanagement of the Russo-Japanese War and of internal affairs led to the revolution of 1905, which he suppressed, although he was forced to grant limited constitutional reforms. He took Russia into World War I in 1914, was forced to abdicate in 1917 after the →Russian Revolution, and was executed with his family.

**nickel** hard, malleable and ductile, silver-white metallic element, symbol Ni, atomic number 28, relative atomic mass 58.71. It occurs in igneous rocks and as a free metal (native metal), occasionally occurring in fragments of iron-nickel meteorites. It is a component of the Earth's core, which is held to consist principally of iron with some nickel. It has a high melting point, low electrical and thermal conductivity, and can be magnetized. It does not tarnish and therefore is much used for alloys, electroplating, and for coinage.

**nicotine** $C_{10}H_{14}N_2$ alkaloid (nitrogenous compound) obtained from the dried leaves of the tobacco plant *Nicotiana tabacum* and used as an insecticide. A colourless oil, soluble in water, it turns brown on exposure to the air.

**Nietzsche, Friedrich Wilhelm** (1844–1900) German philosopher who rejected the accepted absolute moral values and the 'slave morality' of Christianity. He argued that 'God is dead' and therefore people were free to create their own values. His ideal was the *übermensch*, or 'Superman', who would impose his will on the weak and worthless. Nietzsche claimed that knowledge is never objective but always serves some interest or unconscious purpose.

**Niger** Republic of; **national name:** *République du Niger*; **area:** 1,186,408 sq km/458,072 sq mi; **capital:** Niamey; **major towns/cities:** Zinder, Maradi, Tahoua, Agadez, Birui N'Konui; **physical features:** desert plains between hills in north and savannah in south; River Niger in southwest, Lake Chad in southeast; **head of state:** Daouda Mallam Wanke from 1999; **head of government:** Ibrahim Hassane Mayaki from 1997; **political system:** transitional; **currency:** franc CFA; **GNP per capita (PPP):** (US$) 830 (1998); **exports:** uranium ore, live animals, hides and skins, cow-peas, cotton. Principal market USA 29.7% (1997); **population:** 10,401,000 (1999 est); **language:** French (official), Hausa, Djerma, and other minority languages; **religion:** Sunni Muslim; also Christian, and traditional animist beliefs; **life expectancy:** 47 (men); 50 (women) (1995–2000).

**Niger** (Semitic *Nihal*) third-longest river in Africa, 4,185 km/2,600 mi. It rises in the highlands bordering Sierra Leone and Guinea, flows northeast through Mali, then southeast through Niger and Nigeria to an inland delta on the Gulf of Guinea. Its total catchment area is 1.5 million sq km/579,150 sq mi. The flow is sluggish and the river frequently floods its banks. It was explored by the Scot Mungo Park 1795–1806, who was drowned in the river near Bussa.

**Nigeria** Federal Republic of; **area:** 923,773 sq km/356,668 sq mi; **capital:** Abuja; **major towns/cities:** Ibadan, Lagos, Ogbomosho, Kano, Oshogbo, Ilorin, Abeokuta, Zaria, Ouitsha, Iwo, Kaduna; **major ports:** Lagos, Port Harcourt, Warri, Calabar; **physical features:** arid savannah in north; tropical rainforest in south, with mangrove swamps along coast; River Niger forms wide delta; mountains in southeast; **head of state and government:** Olusegun Obasanjo from 1999; **political system:** military republic; **currency:** naira; **GNP per capita (PPP):** (US$) 820 (1998); **exports:** petroleum, cocoa beans, rubber, palm products, urea and ammonia, fish. Principal market USA 36.9% (1997); **population:** 108,945,000 (1999 est); **language:** English (official), Hausa, Ibo, Yoruba; **religion:** Sunni Muslim 50% (in north), Christian 40% (in south), local religions 10%; **life expectancy:** 49 (men); 52 (women) (1995–2000).

**Nightingale, Florence** (1820–1910) English nurse, the founder of nursing as a profession. She took a team of nurses to Scutari (now ūskûdar, Turkey) in 1854 and reduced the →Crimean War hospital death rate from 42% to 2%. In 1856 she founded the Nightingale School and Home for Nurses in London.

**Nijinsky, Vaslav Fomich** (1890–1950) Russian dancer and choreographer. Noted for his powerful but graceful technique, he was a legendary member of →Diaghilev's Ballets Russes, for whom he choreographed Debussy's *Prélude à l'après-midi d'un faune* (1912) and *Jeux* (1913), and Stravinsky's *Le Sacre du printemps/The Rite of Spring* (1913).

**Nile** (Semitic *nihal* 'river') river in Africa, the world's longest, 6,695 km/4,160 mi. The **Blue Nile** rises in Lake Tana, Ethiopia, the **White Nile** at Lake Victoria, and they join at Khartoum, Sudan. The river enters the Mediterranean Sea at a vast delta in northern Egypt.

**Nineveh** capital of the Assyrian Empire from the 8th century BC until its destruction by the Medes under King Cyaxares in 612 BC. It was situated on the River Tigris (opposite the present city of Mosul, Iraq) and was adorned with palaces.

**nirvana** (Sanskrit 'a blowing out') in Buddhism, and other Indian religions, the ultimate religious goal characterized by the attainment of perfect serenity, compassion, and wisdom by the eradication of all desires. When nirvana is attained, the cycle of life and death, known as transmigration, is broken and a state of liberty, free from pain and desire, is reached.

**nitrate** salt or ester of nitric acid, containing the $NO_3^-$ ion. Nitrates are used in explosives, in the chemical and pharmaceutical industries, in curing meat, and as fertilizers. They are the most water-soluble salts known and play a major part in the nitrogen cycle. Nitrates in the soil, whether naturally occurring or from inorganic or organic fertilizers, can be used by plants to make proteins and nucleic acids. However, runoff from fields can result in nitrate pollution.

**nitric acid** (or aqua fortis) $HNO_3$ fuming acid obtained by the oxidation of ammonia or the action of sulphuric acid on potassium nitrate. It is a highly corrosive acid, dissolving most metals, and a strong oxidizing agent. It is used in the nitration and esterification of organic substances, and in the making of sulphuric acid, nitrates, explosives, plastics, and dyes.

**nitrogen** (Greek *nitron* 'native soda', sodium or potassium nitrate) colourless, odourless, tasteless, gaseous, nonmetallic element, symbol N, atomic number 7, relative atomic mass 14.0067. It forms almost 80% of the Earth's atmosphere by volume and is a constituent of all plant and animal tissues (in proteins and nucleic acids). Nitrogen is obtained for industrial use by the liquefaction and fractional distillation of air. Its compounds are used in the manufacture of foods, drugs, fertilizers, dyes, and explosives.

**Nixon, Richard M(ilhous)** (1913– 1994) 37th president of the USA 1969–74, a Republican. He attracted attention as a member of the House Un-American Activities Committee 1948, and was vice-president to Eisenhower 1953–61. As president he was responsible for US withdrawal from Vietnam, and the normalization of relations with communist China, but at home his culpability in the cover-up of the →Watergate scandal and the existence of a 'slush fund' for political machinations during his re-election campaign of 1972 led him to resign in 1974 when threatened with →impeachment.

**Nō** (or Noh classical) aristocratic Japanese drama which developed from the 14th to the 16th centuries and is still performed. There is a repertory of some 250 pieces, of which five, one from each of the several classes devoted to different subjects, may be put on in a performance lasting a whole day. Dance, mime, music, and chanting develop the mythical or historical themes. All the actors are men, some of whom wear masks and elaborate costumes; scenery is limited. Nō influenced kabuki drama.

**Nobel prize** annual international prize, first awarded in 1901 under the will of Alfred Nobel, Swedish chemist, who invented dynamite. The interest on the Nobel endowment fund is divided annually among the persons who have made the greatest contributions in the fields of physics, chemistry, medicine, literature, and world peace. The first four are awarded by academic committees based in Sweden, while the peace prize is awarded by a committee of the Norwegian parliament. A sixth prize, for economics, financed by the Swedish National Bank, was first awarded in 1969. The prizes have a large cash award and are given to organizations – such as the United Nations peacekeeping forces, which received the Nobel Peace Prize in 1988 – as well as individuals.

**noble gas** alternative name for inert gas.

**Norman** any of the descendants of the Norsemen (to whose chief, Rollo, Normandy was granted by Charles III of France in 911) who adopted French language and culture. During the 11th and 12th centuries they conquered England in 1066 (under William the Conqueror), Scotland in 1072, parts of Wales and Ireland, southern Italy, Sicily, and Malta, and took a prominent part in the Crusades.

**Normandy** (French *Normandie*) former duchy of northwest France now divided into two regions: →Haute-Normandie and Basse-Normandie; area 29,900 sq km/11,544 sq mi; population (both parts, 1990) 3,146,500. Normandy was named after the Viking Norsemen (Normans) who conquered and settled in the area in the 9th century. As a French duchy it reached its peak under William the Conqueror and was renowned for its centres of learning established by Lanfranc and St Anselm. Normandy was united with England from 1100 to 1135. England and France fought over it during the Hundred Years' War, England finally losing it in 1449 to Charles VII. In World War II the Normandy beaches were the site of the Allied invasion on D-day, 6 June 1944.

**North America** third largest of the continents (including Greenland and Central America), and over twice the size of Europe. **area:** 24,000,000 sq km/9,400,000 sq mi; **largest cities:** (population over 1 million) Mexico City, New York, Chicago, Toronto, Los Angeles, Montréal, Guadalajara, Monterrey, Philadelphia, Houston, Guatemala City, Vancouver, Detroit, San Diego, Dallas; **physical:** occupying the northern part of the landmass of the western hemisphere between the Arctic Ocean and the tropical southeast tip of the isthmus that joins Central America to South America; the northernmost point on the mainland is the tip of Boothia Peninsula in the Canadian Arctic; the northernmost point on adjacent islands is Cape Morris Jesup on Greenland; the most westerly point on the mainland is Cape Prince of Wales, Alaska; the most westerly point on adjacent islands is Attu Island in the Aleutians; the most easterly point on the mainland lies on the southeast coast of Labrador; the highest point is Mount McKinley, Alaska, 6,194 m/20,320 ft; the lowest point is Badwater in Death Valley −86 m/−282 ft.

Perhaps the most dominating characteristic is the western cordillera running parallel to the coast from Alaska to Panama; it is called the →Rocky Mountains in the USA and Canada and its continuation into Mexico is called the Sierra Madre. The cordillera is a series of ranges divided by intermontane plateaus and takes up about one-third of the continental area.

To the east of the cordillera lie the Great Plains, the agricultural heartland of North America, which descend in a series of steps to the depressions occupied by the →Great Lakes in the east and the Gulf of Mexico coastal lowlands in the southeast. The Plains are characterized by treeless expanses crossed by broad, shallow river valleys. To the north and east of the region lie the Laurentian Highlands of Canada, an ancient plateau or shield area. Glaciation has deeply affected its landscape. In the east are the Appalachian Mountains, flanked by the narrow coastal plain which widens further south. Erosion here has created a line of planed crests, or terraces, at altitudes between 300–1,200 m/985–3,935 ft. This has also formed a ridge-and-valley topography which was an early barrier to continental penetration. The Fall Line is the abrupt junction of plateau and coastal plain in the east; **features:** Lake Superior (the largest body of fresh water in the world); Grand Canyon on the Colorado River; Redwood National Park, California, has some of the world's tallest trees; San Andreas Fault, California; deserts: Death Valley, Mojave, Sonoran; rivers (over 1,600 km/1,000 mi) include Mississippi, Missouri, Mackenzie, Rio Grande, Yukon, Arkansas, Colorado, Saskatchewan-Bow, Columbia, Red, Peace, Snake.

**North Atlantic Treaty Organization** (NATO) association set up in April 1949 in response to the Soviet blockade of Berlin, to provide for the collective defence of the major Western European and North American states against the perceived threat from the USSR. The collapse of communism in eastern Europe from 1989 prompted the most radical review of its policy and defence strategy since its inception. After the Eastern European Warsaw Pact was disbanded in 1991, an adjunct to NATO, the **North Atlantic Cooperation Council** (NACC), was established, including all the former Soviet republics, with the aim of building greater security in Europe. In 1992 it was agreed that the Organization for Security and Cooperation in Europe would in future authorize all NATO's military responses within Europe.

At the 1994 Brussels summit a 'partnership for peace' (PFP) programme was formally launched, inviting former members of the Warsaw Pact and ex-Soviet republics to take part in a wide range of military cooperation arrangements, including training alongside NATO members.

**North Korea** People's Democratic Republic of; **national name:** *Chosun Minchu-chui Inmin Konghwa-guk*; **area:** 120,538 sq km/46,539 sq mi; **capital:** Pyongyang; **major towns/cities:** Hamhung, Chongjin, Nampo, Wonsan, Sinuiji; **physical features:** wide coastal plain in west rising to mountains cut by deep valleys in interior; **head of state:** Kim Jong Il from 1994; **head of government:** Hong Song Nam from 1997; **political system:** communism; **currency:** won; **GNP per capita (PPP):** (US$) 845 (1997 est); **exports:** base metals, textiles, vegetable products, machinery and equipment. Principal market Japan 27.9% (1995 est); **population:** 23,702,000 (1999 est); **language:** Korean; **religion:** Chondoist, Buddhist, Christian, traditional beliefs; **life expectancy:** 69 (men); 75 (women) (1995–2000).

**North Sea** sea to the east of Britain and bounded by the coasts of Belgium, The Netherlands, Germany, Denmark, and Norway; part of the Atlantic Ocean; area 523,000 sq km/202,000 sq mi; average depth 55 m/180 ft, greatest depth 660 m/2,165 ft. The Dogger Bank extends east to west with shallows of as little as 11 m/36 ft, forming a traditionally well-stocked fishing ground. A deep channel follows the coast of Scandinavia reaching as far as the Skagerrak. In the northeast the North Sea joins the Norwegian Sea, and in the south it meets the Strait of Dover. It has 300 oil platforms, 10,000 km/6,200 mi of gas pipeline (gas was discovered in 1965), and fisheries (especially mackerel and herring).

**Norway** Kingdom of; **national name:** *Kongeriket Norge*; **area:** 387,000 sq km/149,420 sq mi (includes Svalbard and Jan Mayen); **capital:** Oslo; **major towns/cities:** Bergen, Trondheim,

Stavanger, Kristiansand, Drammen; **physical features:** mountainous with fertile valleys and deeply indented coast; forests cover 25%; extends north of Arctic Circle; **territories:** dependencies in the Arctic (Svalbard and Jan Mayen) and in Antarctica (Bouvet and Peter I Island, and Queen Maud Land); **head of state:** Harald V from 1991; **head of government:** Kjell Magne Bondevik from 1997; political system: constitutional monarchy; **currency:** Norwegian krone; **GNP per capita (PPP):** (US$) 24,290 (1998); **exports:** petroleum, natural gas, fish products, non-ferrous metals, wood pulp and paper. Principal market UK 16.9% (1998); **population:** 4,442,000 (1999 est); **language:** Norwegian (official); there are Saami-(Lapp) and Finnish-speaking minorities; **religion:** Evangelical Lutheran (endowed by state); **life expectancy:** 75 (men); 81 (women) (1995–2000).

**nose** in humans, the upper entrance of the respiratory tract; the organ of the sense of smell. The external part is divided down the middle by a septum of → cartilage. The nostrils contain plates of cartilage that can be moved by muscles and have a growth of stiff hairs at the margin to prevent foreign objects from entering. The whole nasal cavity is lined with a mucous membrane that warms and moistens the air as it enters and ejects dirt. In the upper parts of the cavity the membrane contains 50 million olfactory receptor cells (cells sensitive to smell).

**nova** (plural novae) faint star that suddenly erupts in brightness by 10,000 times or more, remains bright for a few days, and then fades away and is not seen again for very many years, if at all. Novae are believed to occur in close →binary star systems, where gas from one star flows to a companion →white dwarf. The gas ignites and is thrown off in an explosion at speeds of 1,500 kps/930 mps or more. Unlike a →supernova, the star is not completely

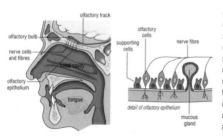

labels: olfactory track; olfactory bulb; nerve cells and fibres; nasal cavity; olfactory epithelium; tongue; olfactory cells; supporting cells; nerve fibre; detail of olfactory epithelium; mucous gland

**nose** The structure of the nose. The organs of smell are confined to a small area in the roof of the nasal cavity. The olfactory cells are stimulated when certain molecules reach them. Smell is one of our most subtle senses: tens of thousands of smells can be distinguished. By comparison, taste, although closely related to smell, is a crude sensation. All the subtleties of taste depend upon smell.

disrupted by the outburst. After a few weeks or months it subsides to its previous state; it may erupt many more times.

**Nova Scotia** maritime province of eastern Canada, comprising the peninsula of Nova Scotia, extending southeast from New Brunswick into the Atlantic Ocean, and Cape Breton Island, which is separated from the northeastern end of the mainland by the Canso Strait. **area:** 55,500 sq km/21,423 sq mi; **capital:** Halifax (chief port); **towns and cities:** Dartmouth, Sydney, Annapolis Royal, Truro; **population:** (1996 est) 942,800; **physical:** Chignecto Isthmus; Cobequid Mountains; Cape Breton Highlands; Annapolis Valley; Bay of Fundy; Northumberland Strait; numerous lakes: Bras d'Or, St Andrew's Channel; fjord coastline; **industries:** mineral extraction (coal, barite, gypsum); lumbering and paper-milling; fishing; agriculture (dairy produce, poultry, eggs, vegetables, and fruit); tourism.

**nuclear energy** (or atomic energy) energy released from the inner core, or →nucleus, of the atom. Energy produced by **nuclear fission** (the splitting of uranium or plutonium nuclei) has been harnessed since the 1950s to generate electricity, and research continues into the possible controlled use of **nuclear fusion** (the fusing, or combining, of atomic nuclei).

**nuclear physics** study of the properties of the nucleus of the →atom, including the structure of nuclei; nuclear forces; the interactions between particles and nuclei; and the study of radioactive decay. The study of elementary particles is →particle physics.

**nucleus** in biology, the central, membrane-enclosed part of a eukaryotic cell, containing threads of DNA. During cell division these coil up to form chromosomes. The nucleus controls the function of the cell by determining which proteins are produced within it (see →DNA for details of this process). Because proteins are the chief structural molecules of living matter and, as enzymes, regulate all aspects of metabolism, it may be seen that the genetic code within the nucleus is effectively responsible for building and controlling the whole organism.

**nucleus** in physics, the positively charged central part of an →atom, which constitutes almost all its mass. Except for hydrogen nuclei, which have only protons, nuclei are composed of both protons and neutrons. Surrounding the nuclei are electrons, of equal and opposite charge to that of the protons, thus giving the atom a neutral charge.

**number** symbol used in counting or measuring. In mathematics, there are various kinds of numbers. The everyday number system is the decimal ('proceeding by tens') system, using the base ten. →**Real numbers** include all rational numbers (integers, or whole numbers, and fractions) and irrational numbers (those not expressible as fractions). **Complex numbers** include the real and imaginary numbers (real-number multiples of the square root of −1). The →binary number system, used in computers, has two as its base. The natural numbers, 0, 1, 2, 3, 4, 5, 6, 7, 8, and 9, give a counting system that, in the decimal system, continues 10, 11, 12, 13, and so on. These are whole numbers (integers), with fractions represented as, for example, 1/4, 1/2, 3/4, or as decimal fractions (0.25, 0.5, 0.75). They are also **rational numbers**. **Irrational numbers** cannot be represented in this way and require symbols, such as √2, π, and e. They can be expressed numerically only as the (inexact) approximations 1.414, 3.142, and 2.718 (to three places of decimals) respectively. The symbols π and e are also examples of **transcendental numbers**, because they (unlike √2) cannot be derived by solving a polynomial equation (an equation with one →variable quantity) with rational coefficients (multiplying factors). Complex numbers, which include the real numbers as well as imaginary numbers, take the general form $a + bi$, where i = √−1 (that is, $i^2 = −1$), and $a$ is the real part and $bi$ the imaginary part.

**Nuremberg trials** after World War II, the trials of the 24 chief Nazi war criminals November 1945–October 1946 by an international military tribunal consisting of four judges and four prosecutors: one of each from the USA, UK, USSR, and France. An appendix accused the German cabinet, general staff, high command, Nazi leadership corps, SS, Sturmabteilung, and →Gestapo of criminal behaviour.

**Nureyev, Rudolf Hametovich** (1938–1993) Russian dancer and choreographer. A soloist with the Kirov Ballet, he defected to the West during a visit to Paris 1961. Mainly associated with the Royal Ballet (London) and as Margot Fonteyn's principal partner, he was one of the most brilliant dancers of the 1960s and 1970s. Nureyev danced in such roles as Prince Siegfried in *Swan Lake* and Armand in *Marguerite and Armand*, which was created especially for Fonteyn and Nureyev. He also danced and acted in films and on television and choreographed several ballets. It was due to his enormous impact on the ballet world that the male dancer's role was elevated to the equivalent of the ballerina's.

**nutrition** the strategy adopted by an organism to obtain the chemicals it needs to live, grow, and reproduce. Also, the science of food, and its effect on human and animal life, health, and disease. Nutrition involves the study of the basic nutrients required to sustain life, their bioavailability in foods and overall diet, and the effects upon them of cooking and storage. It is also concerned with dietary deficiency diseases.

**nylon** synthetic long-chain polymer similar in chemical structure to protein. Nylon was the first all-synthesized fibre, made from petroleum, natural gas, air, and water by the Du Pont firm in 1938. It is used in the manufacture of moulded articles, textiles, and medical sutures. Nylon fibres are stronger and more elastic than silk and are relatively insensitive to moisture and mildew.

Nylon is used for hosiery and woven goods, simulating other materials such as silks and furs; it is also used for carpets.

# Oo

**oak** any of a group of trees or shrubs belonging to the beech family, with over 300 known species widely distributed in temperate zones. Oaks are valuable for timber, the wood being durable and straight-grained. Their fruits are called acorns. (Genus *Quercus*, family Fagaceae.)

**oasis** area of land made fertile by the presence of water near the surface in an otherwise arid region. The occurrence of oases affects the distribution of plants, animals, and people in the desert regions of the world.

**oboe** musical instrument of the woodwind family, a refined treble shawm of narrow tapering bore and exposed double reed. The oboe was developed by the Hotteterre family of instrument-makers about 1700 and was incorporated in the court ensemble of Louis XIV. In C, with a normal compass of about 2½ octaves, it has a rich tone of elegant finish. Oboe concertos have been composed by Vivaldi, Albinoni, Richard Strauss, Martinu, and others. Heinz Holliger is a modern virtuoso oboist.

**obsessive-compulsive disorder** (OCD) in psychiatry, anxiety disorder that manifests itself in the need to check constantly that certain acts have been performed 'correctly'. Sufferers may, for example, feel compelled to repeatedly wash themselves or return home again and again to check that doors have been unlocked and appliances switched off. They may also hoard certain objects and insist in these being arranged in a precise way or be troubled by intrusive and unpleasant thoughts. In extreme cases normal life is disrupted through the hours devoted to compulsive actions. Treatment involves cognitive therapy and drug therapy with serotonin-blocking drugs such as Prozac.

**obstetrics** medical speciality concerned with the management of pregnancy, childbirth, and the immediate postnatal period.

**ocean** great mass of salt water. Strictly speaking three oceans exist – the Atlantic, Indian, and Pacific – to which the Arctic is often added. They cover approximately 70% or 363,000,000 sq km/140,000,000 sq mi of the total surface area of the Earth. Water levels recorded in the world's oceans have shown an increase of 10–15 cm/4–6 in over the past 100 years.

**October Revolution** second stage of the →Russian Revolution 1917, when, on the night of 24 October (6 November in the Western calendar), the Bolshevik forces under Trotsky, and on orders from Lenin, seized the Winter Palace and arrested members of the Provisional Government. The following day the Second All-Russian Congress of Soviets handed over power to the Bolsheviks.

**Odessa** principal seaport of Ukraine, on the Black Sea, and capital of the Odessa region (oblast); population (1990) 1,106,400. Odessa is a commercial port, naval base, and tourist resort. The principal industries here are shipbuilding, fishing, steelmaking, and food processing. Products manufactured in the city include chemicals, pharmaceuticals, and machinery. Among the main goods handled in the port are grain, sugar, timber, and oil.

**Odin** (Germanic *Woden* or *Wotan*) ('the raging one') chief god of Norse mythology, god of war, and the source of wisdom. A sky god, he lived in Asgard at the top of the world-tree Yggdrasil. From the →Valkyries, his divine maidens, he received the souls of half those heroes slain in battle, feasting with them in his great hall Valhalla; the remainder were feasted by Freya. His son was →Thor, god of thunder. Wednesday or Woden's day is named after him.

**Odysseus** (Latin Ulysses, 'son of wrath') chief character of Homer's *Odyssey*, king of the island of Ithaca (modern Thiaki or Levkas); he is also mentioned in the *Iliad* as one of the leaders of the Greek forces at the siege of Troy. Odysseus was distinguished among Greek leaders for his cleverness and cunning. He appears in other later tragedies, but his ten years' odyssey by sea after the fall of Troy is the most commonly known tradition.

**Oedipus** in Greek mythology, king of Thebes who unwittingly killed his father, Laius, and married his mother, Jocasta, in fulfilment of a prophecy. When he learned what he had done, he put out his eyes. His story was dramatized by the Greek tragedian →Sophocles.

**oestrogen** any of a group of hormones produced by the ovaries of vertebrates; the term is also used for various synthetic hormones that mimic their effects. The principal oestrogen in mammals is oestradiol. Oestrogens control female sexual development, promote the growth of female secondary sexual characteristics, stimulate egg production, and, in mammals, prepare the lining of the uterus for pregnancy.

**Offa's Dyke** defensive earthwork dyke along the English–Welsh border, of which there are remains from the mouth of the River Dee to that of the River Severn. It was built about AD 785 by King Offa of Mercia, England, and represents the boundary secured by his wars with Wales.

**Ohio** state in northern central USA. It is nicknamed the Buckeye State. It was admitted to the Union in 1803 as the 17th US state. Part of the Midwest, it is bordered to the east by Pennsylvania, to the east and southeast by West Virginia, to the southwest by Kentucky, to the west by Indiana, to the northwest by

Michigan's Lower Peninsula, and to the north by Lake Erie. Ohio comprises the eastern section of the US Corn Belt; heavily industrialized, it is also a quintessential Rust Belt state, today struggling with pollution and the need to diversify industrially. **population:** (1995) 11,150,500; **area:** 107,100 sq km/41,341 sq mi; **capital:** Columbus; **towns and cities:** Cleveland, Cincinnati, Dayton, Akron, Toledo, Youngstown, Canton; **industries and products:** coal, cereals, livestock, dairy foods, machinery, chemicals, steel, motor vehicles, automotive and aircraft parts, rubber products, office equipment, refined petroleum, tourism.

**oil** flammable substance, usually insoluble in water, and composed chiefly of carbon and hydrogen. Oils may be solids (fats and waxes) or liquids. The three main types are: **essential oils**, obtained from plants; **fixed oils**, obtained from animals and plants; and **mineral oils**, obtained chiefly from the refining of →petroleum.

**O'Keeffe, Georgia** (1887–1986) US painter. She is known chiefly for her large, semi-abstract studies of flowers and bones, such as *Black Iris* (1926; Metropolitan Museum of Art, New York) and the *Pelvis Series* of the 1940s. She was married 1924–46 to photographer and art exhibitor Alfred Stieglitz, in whose gallery her work was first shown.

**Oklahoma** state in southern central USA. It is nicknamed the Sooner State. Oklahoma was admitted to the Union in 1907 as the 46th US state. It is bordered to the south by Texas, to the west, at the extreme of the Oklahoma panhandle, by New Mexico, to the north by Colorado and Kansas, and to the east by Missouri and Arkansas. Oklahoma is the US state most associated with American Indians; its name is a Choctaw coinage meaning 'red people'. **population:** (1995) 3,277,700; **area:** 181,100 sq km/69,905 sq mi; **capital:** Oklahoma City; **towns and cities:** Tulsa, Lawton, Norman, Enid; **industries and products:** cereals, peanuts, cotton, livestock, oil, natural gas, helium, machinery and other metal products.

**Olduvai Gorge** deep cleft in the Serengeti steppe, Tanzania, where Louis and Mary Leakey found prehistoric stone tools in the 1930s. They discovered Pleistocene remains of prehumans and gigantic animals 1958–59. The gorge has given its name to the **Olduvai culture**, a simple stone-tool culture of prehistoric hominids, dating from 2–0.5 million years ago.

**Old World** the continents of the eastern hemisphere, so called because they were familiar to Europeans before the Americas. The term is used as an adjective to describe animals and plants that live in the eastern hemisphere.

**Oligocene** third epoch of the Tertiary period of geological time, 35.5–3.25 million years ago. The name, from Greek, means 'a little recent', referring to the presence of the remains of some modern types of animals existing at that time.

**Olivier, Laurence Kerr** (1907–1989) English actor and director. For many years associated with the Old Vic Theatre, he was director of the National Theatre company 1962–73. His stage roles include Henry V, Hamlet, Richard III, and Archie Rice in John Osborne's *The Entertainer* (1957; filmed 1960). He directed and starred in filmed versions of Shakespeare's plays; for example, *Henry V* (1944) and *Hamlet* (1948) (Academy Award). He was knighted in 1947 and created a baron in 1970.

**Olympic Games** sporting contests originally held in Olympia, ancient Greece, every four years during a sacred truce; records were kept from 776 BC. Women were forbidden to be present, and the male contestants were naked. The ancient Games were abolished in AD 394. The present-day games have been held every four years since 1896. Since 1924 there has been a separate winter Games programme; from 1994 the winter and summer Games are held two years apart.

**Oman** Sultanate of; **national name:** *Saltanat 'Uman*; **area:** 272,000 sq km/105,019 sq mi; **capital:** Muscat; **major towns/cities:** Salalah, Ibri, Sohar, Al-Buraimi, Nizwa; **major ports:** Mina Qaboos, Mina Raysut; **physical features:** mountains to north and south of a high arid plateau; fertile coastal strip; Jebel Akhdar highlands; Kuria Muria Islands; **head of state and government:** Qaboos bin Said from 1970; **political system:** absolute monarchy; **currency:** Omani rial; **GNP per capita (PPP):** (US$) 8,690 (1997); **exports:** petroleum, metals and metal goods, textiles, animals and products. Principal market Japan 23.3% (1997); **population:** 2,460,000 (1999 est); **language:** Arabic (official); English, Urdu, other Indian languages; **religion:** Ibadhi Muslim 75%, Sunni Muslim, Shiite Muslim, Hindu; **life expectancy:** 69 (men); 73 (women) (1995–2000).

**Omar Khayyám** (*c.* 1050–*c.* 1123) Persian astronomer, mathematician, and poet. In the West, he is chiefly known as a poet through Edward Fitzgerald's version of 'The Rubaiyat of Omar Khayyám' (1859).

**omnivore** animal that feeds on both plant and animal material. Omnivores have digestive adaptations intermediate between those of →herbivores and carnivores, with relatively unspecialized digestive systems and gut microorganisms that can digest a variety of foodstuffs. Omnivores include humans, chimpanzees, cockroaches, and ants.

**O'Neill, Eugene Gladstone** (1888–1953) US playwright. He is widely regarded as the greatest US dramatist. His plays, although tragic, are characterized by a down-to-earth quality and are often experimental in form, influenced by German expressionism, Strindberg, and Freud. They were a radical departure from the romantic and melodramatic American theatre entertainments. They include the Pulitzer prize-winning plays *Beyond the Horizon* (1920) and *Anna Christie* (1921), as well as *The Emperor Jones* (1920), *The Hairy*

*Ape* (1922), *Desire Under the Elms* (1924), *The Iceman Cometh* (1946), and the posthumously produced autobiographical drama *A Long Day's Journey into Night* (1956; written 1941), also a Pulitzer prize winner. He was awarded the Nobel Prize for Literature 1936.

**Ontario** province of southeastern–central Canada, in area the country's second largest province, and its most populous. It is bounded to the north and northeast by Hudson Bay and James Bay, to the east by Québec (with the Ottawa River forming most of the boundary), and by Manitoba to the west. On the south it borders on, and extends into, all of the Great Lakes except Lake Michigan. From west to east along Ontario's southern boundary lie the US states of Minnesota, Wisconsin, Michigan, Ohio, Pennsylvania, and New York. **area:** 1,068,600 sq km/412,480 sq mi; **capital:** →Toronto (Canada's largest city); **towns and cities:** Hamilton, Ottawa (federal capital), London, Windsor, Kitchener, St Catharines, Oshawa, Thunder Bay, Sudbury; **population:** (1996) 11,252,400; **physical:** Canadian Shield; lakes Erie, Huron, Ontario, Superior; rivers Ottawa, Albany, St Lawrence; Georgian Bay; Niagara Falls; **industries:** mining (nickel, iron, gold, copper, uranium); manufacture of cars, aircraft, iron, steel, and high-tech goods; production of pulp, paper, oil, and chemicals; agriculture includes livestock rearing, cultivation of fruit, vegetables, and cereals.

**onyx** semiprecious variety of chalcedonic silica ($SiO_2$) in which the crystals are too fine to be detected under a microscope, a state known as cryptocrystalline. It has straight parallel bands of different colours: milk-white, black, and red.

**opal** form of hydrous silica ($SiO_2 . nH_2O$), often occurring as stalactites and found in many types of rock. The common opal is translucent, milk-white, yellow, red, blue, or green, and lustrous. Precious opal is opalescent, the characteristic play of colours being caused by close-packed silica spheres diffracting light rays within the stone.

**opera** dramatic musical work in which singing takes the place of speech. In opera the music accompanying the action has paramount importance, although dancing and spectacular staging may also play their parts. Opera originated in late 16th-century Florence when the musical declamation, lyrical monologues, and choruses of classical Greek drama were reproduced in current forms.

**ophthalmology** medical speciality concerned with diseases of the eye and its surrounding tissues.

**opium** drug extracted from the unripe seeds of the opium poppy (*Papaver somniferum*) of southwestern Asia. An addictive →narcotic, it contains several alkaloids, including **morphine**, one of the most powerful natural painkillers and addictive narcotics known, and **codeine**, a milder painkiller.

**Opium Wars** two wars, the First Opium War 1839–42 and the Second Opium

War 1856–60, waged by Britain against China to enforce the opening of Chinese ports to trade in opium. Opium from British India paid for Britain's imports from China, such as porcelain, silk, and, above all, tea.

**optical fibre** very fine, optically pure glass fibre through which light can be reflected to transmit images or data from one end to the other. Although expensive to produce and install, optical fibres can carry more data than traditional cables, and are less susceptible to interference. Standard optical fibre transmitters can send up to 10 billion bits of information per second by switching a laser beam on and off.

**optics** branch of physics that deals with the study of →light and vision – for example, shadows and mirror images, lenses, microscopes, telescopes, and cameras. For all practical purposes light rays travel in straight lines, although Albert →Einstein demonstrated that they may be 'bent' by a gravitational field. On striking a surface they are reflected or refracted with some absorption of energy, and the study of this is known as geometrical optics.

**oracle** (Latin *orare* 'to speak') sacred site where a deity gives answers or oracles, through the mouth of its priest, to a supplicant's questions about personal affairs or state policy. These were often ambivalent. There were more than 250 oracular seats in the Greek world. The earliest example was probably at Dodona (in Epirus), where priests interpreted the sounds made by the sacred oaks of →Zeus, but the most celebrated was that of →Apollo, god of prophecy, at →Delphi.

**orbit** path of one body in space around another, such as the orbit of Earth around the Sun, or the Moon around Earth. When the two bodies are similar in mass, as in a →binary star, both bodies move around their common centre of mass. The movement of objects in orbit follows Johann →Kepler's laws, which apply to artificial satellites as well as to natural bodies.

**orchid** any plant of a large family that contains at least 15,000 species and 700 genera, distributed throughout the world except in the coldest areas, and most numerous in damp equatorial regions. The flowers are the most highly evolved of the plant kingdom; they have three sepals and three petals and sometimes grow singly, but more usually appear with other flowers on spikes, growing up one side of the main stem, or all around the main stem, which may be upright or drooping. (Family Orchidaceae.)

**ordinal number** in mathematics, one of the series first, second, third, fourth, . . . . Ordinal numbers relate to order, whereas →cardinal numbers (1, 2, 3, 4, . . .) relate to quantity, or count.

**Ordovician** period of geological time 510–439 million years ago; the second period of the →Palaeozoic era. Animal life was confined to the sea: reef-building algae and the first jawless fish are characteristic.

**ore** body of rock, a vein within it, or a deposit of sediment, worth mining for the economically valuable mineral it contains. The term is usually applied to sources of metals. Occasionally metals are found uncombined (native metals), but more often they occur as compounds such as carbonates, sulphides, or oxides. The ores often contain unwanted impurities that must be removed when the metal is extracted.

**Oregon** state in northwestern USA, on the Pacific coast. It is nicknamed Beaver State. Oregon was admitted to the Union in 1859 as the 33rd US state. It is bordered to the east by Idaho, to the north by Washington, to the south by California and Nevada, and to the west by the Pacific Ocean. **population:** (1995) 3,140,600; **area:** 251,500 sq km/97,079 sq mi; **capital:** Salem; **towns and cities:** Portland, Eugene, Gresham, Beaverton; **industries and products:** wheat, fruit, dairy farming, livestock, salmon and tuna, timber, electronics, tourism, leisure industry.

**organ** in biology, part of a living body that has a distinctive function or set of functions. Examples include the liver or brain in animals, or the leaf in plants. An organ is composed of a group of coordinated →tissues. A group of organs working together to perform a function is called an **organ system**, for example, the →digestive system comprises a number of organs including the stomach, the small intestine, the colon, the pancreas, and the liver.

**organic chemistry** branch of chemistry that deals with carbon compounds. Organic compounds form the chemical basis of life and are more abundant than inorganic compounds. In a typical organic compound, each carbon atom forms bonds covalently with each of its neighbouring carbon atoms in a chain or ring, and additionally with other atoms, commonly hydrogen, oxygen, nitrogen, or sulphur.

---

**WEB SITE** > > > > > > >

**Organic Chemistry →Introduction**

http://www.netcomuk.co.uk/%7Epetersl/auf1oc1.htm

Interesting essay on organic chemistry that includes explanatory diagrams.

---

**Orinoco** river in northern South America; it rises in the Sierra Parima range in southern Venezuela near the Brazilian border and flows north for about 2,400 km/1,500 mi through Venezuela, forming the boundary with Colombia for about 320 km/200 mi; tributaries include the Guaviare, Meta, Apure, Ventuari, Caura, Arauca, and Caroni rivers. It is navigable by large steamers for 1,125 km/700 mi from its Atlantic delta; rapids obstruct the upper river. The Orinoco is South America's third-largest river; its drainage basin area is 962,000 sq km/371428 sq mi.

**Orion** in astronomy, a very prominent constellation in the equatorial region of the sky, identified with the hunter of Greek mythology.

**Orkney Islands** island group and unitary authority off the northeast coast of Scotland. **area:** 1,014 sq km/391 sq mi; **towns:** Kirkwall (administrative headquarters), Stromness, both on Mainland (Pomona); **physical:** there are 90 islands and inlets in the group. The surface of the islands is irregular and indented by many arms of the sea. Next to Mainland, the most important of the islands are North and South Ronaldsay, Hoy, Rousay, Stronsay, Flotta, Shapinsay, Eday, Sanday, and Westray; **features:** Skara Brae Neolithic village, and Maes Howe burial chamber; Scapa Flow; oil terminal on Flotta; **industries:** offshore oil, woollen weaving, wind-powered electricity generation, distilling, boat-building, fish curing; **agriculture:** fishing, beef cattle, dairy products; **population:** (1996) 19,600; **famous people:** Edwin Muir, John Rae; **history:** population of Scandinavian descent; Harald I (Fairhair) of Norway conquered the islands in 876; pledged to James III of Scotland in 1468 for the dowry of Margaret of Denmark; Scapa Flow, between Mainland and Hoy, was a naval base in both world wars, the German fleet scuttled itself here on 21 June 1919.

**Orpheus** mythical Greek poet and musician of Thrace; the son of →Apollo and the Muse Calliope. Orpheus ventured into Hades, the underworld, to bring back his wife Eurydice, who had died from a snakebite. His lyre playing was so charming that Pluto granted her return to life, but on condition that Orpheus walked ahead without looking back. He turned at the entrance and Eurydice was irretrievably lost. In his grief, he offended the maenad women of Thrace, and they tore him to pieces.

**Orthodox Church** (or Eastern Orthodox Church or Greek Orthodox Church) federation of self-governing Christian churches mainly found in Eastern Europe and parts of Asia. The centre of worship is the Eucharist. There is a married clergy, except for bishops; the Immaculate Conception is not accepted. The highest rank in the church is that of ecumenical patriarch, or bishop of Istanbul. There are (1990) about 130 million adherents.

**orthopaedics** (Greek *orthos* 'straight'; *pais* 'child') medical speciality concerned with the correction of disease or damage in bones and joints.

**Orwell, George** (1903–1950) pen-name of Eric Arthur Blair, English writer. His books include the satirical fable *Animal Farm* (1945), an attack on the Soviet Union and its leader, Stalin, which includes such slogans as 'All animals are equal, but some are more equal than others'; and the prophetic *Nineteen Eighty-Four* (1949), targeting Cold War politics, which portrays the catastrophic excesses of state control over the individual. He also wrote numerous essays. Orwell was distrustful of all political parties and ideologies, and a deep sense of social conscience and antipathy towards political dictatorship characterizes his work.

**Osborne, John James** (1929–1994) English dramatist. He became one of the first Angry Young Men (anti-establishment writers of the 1950s) of British theatre with his debut play, *Look Back in Anger* (1956). Other plays include *The Entertainer* (1957), *Luther* (1960), *Inadmissible Evidence* (1964), and *A Patriot for Me* (1965).

**osmosis** movement of water through a selectively permeable membrane separating solutions of different concentrations. Water passes by →diffusion from a **weak solution** (high water concentration) to a **strong solution** (low water concentration) until the two concentrations are equal. The selectively permeable membrane allows the diffusion of water but not of the solute (for example, sugar molecules). Many cell membranes behave in this way, and osmosis is a vital mechanism in the transport of fluids in living organisms – for example, in the transport of water from soil (weak solution) into the roots of plants (stronger solution of cell sap).

**osteopathy** system of alternative medical practice that relies on physical manipulation to treat mechanical stress. It was developed over a century ago by US physician Andrew Taylor Still, who maintained that most ailments can be prevented or cured by techniques of spinal manipulation.

**osteoporosis** disease in which the bone substance becomes porous and brittle. It is common in older people, affecting more women than men. It may be treated with calcium supplements and etidronate. Approximately 1.7 million people worldwide, mostly women, suffer

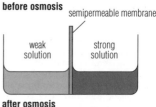

**before osmosis**

semipermeable membrane

weak solution

strong solution

**after osmosis**

equal concentrations

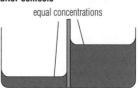

**osmosis** Apparatus for measuring osmotic pressure. In 1877 German physicist Wilhelm Pfeffer used this apparatus to make the first ever measurement of osmotic pressure and show that osmotic pressure varies according to temperature and the strength of the solute (dissolved substance).

hip fractures, mainly due to osteoporosis. A single gene was discovered in 1993 to have a major influence on bone thinning.

**Ottawa** capital of Canada, in eastern Ontario, on the hills overlooking the Ottawa River, and divided by the Rideau Canal into the Upper (western) and Lower (eastern) towns; population (1996 est) of metropolitan area (with adjoining Hull, Québec) 1,030,500. Industries include engineering, food-processing, publishing, lumber, and the manufacture of pulp, paper, textiles, and leather products. Government, and community and health services employ a large section of the workforce. Ottawa was founded 1826–32 as Bytown, in honour of John By (1781–1836), whose army engineers were building the Rideau Canal. In 1854 it was renamed after the Ottawa River; the name deriving from the Outaouac, Native Canadian Algonquin people of the area.

**Ottoman Empire** Muslim empire of the Turks from 1300 to 1920, the successor of the Seljuk Empire. It was founded by Osman I and reached its height with →Suleiman in the 16th century. Its capital was Istanbul (formerly Constantinople).

**Ouagadougou** (also Wagadugu) capital and industrial centre of Burkina Faso, and of Kadiogo Province; population (1991 est) 634,000. Products include textiles, vegetable oil, beverages, and soap. Its pre-eminence as a commercial centre is challenged by Bobo-Dioulasso. The city has the palace of Moro Naba, emperor of the Mossi people, a neo-Romanesque cathedral, and a central avenue called the Champs Elysées. It was the capital of the Mossi empire from the 15th century.

**Ovid** (43 BC–AD 17) Publius Ovidius Naso, Latin poet. His poetry deals mainly with the themes of love (*Amores* 20 BC, *Ars amatoria/The Art of Love* 1 BC), mythology (*Metamorphoses* AD 2), and exile (*Tristia* AD 9–12). Born at Sulmo, Ovid studied rhetoric in Rome in preparation for a legal career, but soon turned to literature. In AD 9 he was banished by Augustus to Tomis, on the Black Sea, where he died. Sophisticated, ironical, and self-pitying,

his work was highly influential during the Middle Ages and Renaissance.

**Owen, Wilfred Edward Salter** (1893–1918) English poet. His verse, owing much to the encouragement of Siegfried Sassoon, is among the most moving of World War I poetry; it shatters the illusion of the glory of war, revealing its hollowness and cruel destruction of beauty. Only four poems were published during his lifetime; he was killed in action a week before the Armistice. After Owen's death Sassoon collected and edited his *Poems* (1920). Among the best known are 'Dulce et Decorum Est' and 'Anthem for Doomed Youth', published in 1921. Benjamin →Britten used several of the poems in his *War Requiem* (1962).

**Owens, Jesse (James Cleveland)** (1913–1980) US track and field athlete who excelled in the sprints, hurdles, and the long jump. At the 1936 Berlin Olympics he won four gold medals.

---

**WEB SITE** > > > > > > > >

**Owens, Jesse**

http://www.cmgww.com/sports/owens

Biography and photographs of Jesse Owens, the legendary African-American athlete of the 1930s. The site also contains a list of quotes from Owens, who won four gold medals at the 1936 Berlin Olympics.

---

**owl** any of a group of mainly nocturnal birds of prey found worldwide. They have hooked beaks, heads that can turn quickly and far round on their very short necks, and forward-facing immobile eyes, surrounded by 'facial discs' of rayed feathers; they fly silently and have an acute sense of hearing. Owls comprise two families: typical owls (family Strigidae), of which there are about 120 species, and barn owls (family Tytonidae), of which there are 10 species. (Order Strigiformes.)

**oxide** compound of oxygen and another element, frequently produced by burning the element or a compound of it in air or oxygen.

**oxygen** (Greek *oxys* 'acid'; *genes* 'forming') colourless, odourless, tasteless, nonmetallic, gaseous element, symbol O, atomic number 8, relative atomic mass 15.9994. It is the most abundant element in the Earth's crust (almost 50% by mass), forms about 21% by volume of the atmosphere, and is present in combined form in water and many other substances. Oxygen is a by-product of →photosynthesis and the basis for →respiration in plants and animals.

**ozone** $O_3$ highly reactive pale-blue gas with a penetrating odour. Ozone is an allotrope of oxygen (see →allotropy), made up of three atoms of oxygen. It is formed when the molecule of the stable form of oxygen ($O_2$) is split by ultraviolet radiation or electrical discharge. It forms the ozone layer in the upper atmosphere, which protects life on Earth from ultraviolet rays, a cause of skin cancer.

# Pp

**pacemaker** (or sinoatrial node, SA node) in vertebrates, a group of muscle cells in the wall of the heart that contracts spontaneously and rhythmically, setting the pace for the contractions of the rest of the heart. The pacemaker's intrinsic rate of contraction is increased or decreased, according to the needs of the body, by stimulation from the →autonomic nervous system. The term also refers to a medical device implanted under the skin of a patient whose heart beats inefficiently. It delivers minute electric shocks to stimulate the heart muscles at regular intervals and restores normal heartbeat.

**Pacific Ocean** world's largest ocean, extending from Antarctica to the Bering Strait; area 166,242,500 sq km/64,170,000 sq mi; greatest breadth 16,000 km/9,942 mi, length 11,000 km/6,835 mi; average depth 4,188 m/13,749 ft; greatest depth of any ocean 11,524 m/37,808 ft in the Mindanao Trench, east of the Philippines.

**paediatrics** medical speciality concerned with the care of children. Paediatricians treat childhood diseases such as measles, chicken pox, and mumps, and immunize children against more serious infections such as diptheria. Their role also includes treating and identifying disorders caused by lack of proper nutrition or child abuse.

**Paine, Thomas** (1737–1809) English left-wing political writer. He was active in the American and French revolutions. His pamphlet *Common Sense* (1776) ignited passions in the American Revolution; others include *The Rights of Man* (1791) and *The Age of Reason* (1793). He advocated republicanism, deism, the abolition of slavery, and the emancipation of women.

**Pakistan** Islamic Republic of; **national name:** *Islami Jamhuriya e Pakistan*; **area:** 803,940 sq km/310,321 sq mi; one-third of Kashmir under Pakistani control; **capital:** Islamabad; **major towns/cities:** Lahore, Rawalpindi, Faisalabad, Karachi, Hyderabad, Multan, Peshawar, Gujranwala, Sialkot, Sargodha, Quetta, Islamabad; **major ports:** Karachi, Port Qasim; **physical features:** fertile Indus plain in east, Baluchistan plateau in west, mountains in north and northwest; the 'five rivers' (Indus, Jhelum, Chenab, Ravi, and Sutlej) feed the world's largest irrigation system; K2 mountain; Khyber Pass; **head of state and government:** General Pervez Musharraf from 1999;

**political system:** emergent democracy; **currency:** Pakistan rupee; **GNP per capita (PPP):** (US$) 1,560 (1998); **exports:** cotton, textiles, petroleum and petroleum products, clothing and accessories, leather, rice, food and live animals. Principal market USA 21.5% (1998–99); **population:** 152,330,000 (1999 est); **language:** Urdu (official); English, Punjabi, Sindhi, Pashto, Baluchi, other local dialects; **religion:** Sunni Muslim 75%, Shiite Muslim 20%; also Hindu, Christian, Parsee, Buddhist; **life expectancy:** 63 (men); 65 (women) (1995–2000).

**Palaeocene** (Greek 'old' + 'recent') first epoch of the Tertiary period of geological time, 65–56.5 million years ago. Many types of mammals spread rapidly after the disappearance of the great reptiles of the Mesozoic. Flying mammals replaced the flying reptiles, swimming mammals replaced the swimming reptiles, and all the ecological niches vacated by the reptiles were adopted by mammals.

**palaeontology** in geology, the study of ancient life, encompassing the structure of ancient organisms and their environment, evolution, and ecology, as revealed by their →fossils. The practical aspects of palaeontology are based on using the presence of different fossils to date particular rock strata and to identify rocks that were laid down under particular conditions; for instance, giving rise to the formation of oil.

**Palaeozoic** era of geological time 570–245 million years ago. It comprises the Cambrian, Ordovician, Silurian, Devonian, Carboniferous, and Permian periods. The Cambrian, Ordovician, and Silurian constitute the Lower or Early Palaeozoic; the Devonian, Carboniferous, and Permian make up the Upper or Late Palaeozoic. The era includes the evolution of hard-shelled multicellular life forms in the sea; the invasion of land by plants and animals; and the evolution of fish, amphibians, and early reptiles. The earliest identifiable fossils date from this era.

**Palau** Republic of (also known as **Belau**); **area:** 508 sq km/196 sq mi; **capital:** Koror (on Koror Island); **major towns/cities:** Melekeiok, Garusuun, Malakal; **physical features:** more than 350 (mostly uninhabited) islands, islets, and atolls in the west Pacific; warm, humid climate, susceptible to typhoons; **head of state and government:** Kuniwo Nakamura from 1992; **political system:** liberal democracy; **currency:** US dollar; **GNP per capita (PPP):** (US$) N/A; **exports:** copra, coconut oil, handicrafts, trochus, tuna; **population:** 19,000 (1999 est); **language:** Palauan and English; **religion:** Christian, principally Roman Catholic; **life expectancy:** 65 (men); 71 (women) (1998 est).

**Palestine** (Arabic *Falastin*, 'Philistine') historic geographical area at the eastern end of the Mediterranean sea, also known as the Holy Land because of its historic and symbolic importance for Jews, Christians, and Muslims. Early settlers included the Canaanites, Hebrews, and Philistines. Over the centuries it became part of the Egyptian,

Assyrian, Babylonian, Macedonian, Ptolemaic, Seleucid, Roman, Byzantine, Arab, Ottoman, and British empires. Today it comprises parts of modern Israel–Palestine and Jordan.

**Palestine Liberation Organization** (PLO) Arab organization founded in 1964 to bring about an independent state in Palestine. It consists of several distinct groupings, the chief of which is al-Fatah, led by Yassir →Arafat, the president of the PLO from 1969.

**Palladio, Andrea** (1508–1580) Italian architect who created harmonious and balanced classical structures. He designed numerous palaces and country houses in and around Vicenza, making use of Roman classical forms, symmetry, and proportion. The Villa Malcontenta and the Villa Rotonda are examples of houses designed from 1540 for patrician families of the Venetian Republic. He also designed churches in Venice and published his studies of classical form in several illustrated books.

**palm** any of a group of large treelike plants with a single tall stem that has a thick cluster of large palmate (five-lobed) leaves or pinnate leaves (leaflets either side of the stem) at the top. Most of the numerous species are tropical or subtropical. Some, such as the coconut, date, sago, and oil palms, are important economically. (Family Palmae.)

**Pampas** flat treeless plains in central Argentina, lying between the foothills of the Andes and the Atlantic coast, and stretching north from the Río Colorado to the Gran Chaco; area 650,000 sq km/25,097 sq mi; it incorporates the provinces of Buenos Aires, La Pampa, Santa Fé, and Cordobá. The eastern Pampas consist of grasslands which support large cattle ranches and produce flax and over half the nation's output of grain; the western Pampas are arid and unproductive. The characteristic vegetation is the **pampas grass** which grows to a height of 2–3m/6–10 ft.

**Panama** Republic of; **national name:** *República de Panamá*; **area:** 77,100 sq km/29,768 sq mi; **capital:** Panamá (or Panama City); **major towns/cities:** San Miguelito, Colón, David, La Chorrera, Santiago, Chitré; **major ports:** Colón, Cristóbal, Balboa; **physical features:** coastal plains and mountainous interior; tropical rainforest in east and northwest; Archipelago de las Perlas in Gulf of Panama; Panama Canal; **head of state and government:** Mireya Moscoso from 1999; **political system:** emergent democracy; **currency:** balboa; **GNP per capita (PPP):** (US$) 6,940 (1998); **exports:** bananas, shrimps and lobsters, sugar, clothing, coffee. Principal market USA 39.9% (1998); **population:** 2,812,000 (1999 est); **language:** Spanish (official), English; **religion:** Roman Catholic; **life expectancy:** 72 (men); 76 (women) (1995–2000).

**Panama Canal** canal across the Panama isthmus in Central America, connecting the Pacific and Atlantic oceans; length 80 km/50 mi, with 12 locks; average width 150 m/492 ft. It was built by the USA 1904–14, after an unsuccessful attempt by the French. The **Panama Canal Zone** was acquired 'in perpetuity' by the USA in 1903, comprising land extending about 5 km/3 mi on either side of the canal. The zone passed to Panama in 1979, and under a treaty signed by President Carter in 1978, control of the canal was ceded to Panama at the end of 1999. In December 1999 all US military bases in the Canal Zone were closed, and the control changeover went into effect on 31 December 1999.

**Pankhurst, Emmeline** (1858–1928) born Goulden, English →suffragette. Founder of the Women's Social and Political Union (WSPU) in 1903, she launched the militant suffragette campaign in 1905. In 1926 she joined the Conservative Party and was a prospective Parliamentary candidate for Whitechapel.

**Papua New Guinea area:** 462,840 sq km/178,702 sq mi; **capital:** Port Moresby (on East New Guinea) (also port); **major towns/cities:** Lae, Madang, Arawa, Wewak, Goroka, Rabaul, Mount Hagen; **major ports:** Rabaul; **physical features:** mountainous; swamps and plains; monsoon climate; tropical islands of New Ireland, New Britain, and Bougainville; Admiralty Islands, D'Entrecasteaux Islands, and Louisiade Archipelago; active volcanoes Vulcan and Tavurvur; **head of state:** Queen Elizabeth II, represented by governor general Silas Atopare from 1997; **head of government:** Mekere Morauta from 1999; **political system:** liberal democracy; **currency:** kina; **GNP per capita (PPP):** (US$) 2,700 (1998 est); **exports:** gold, copper ore and concentrates, crude petroleum, timber, coffee beans, coconut and copra products. Principal market Australia 19.8% (1998); **population:** 4,702,000 (1999 est); **language:** English (official); pidgin English, 715 local languages; **religion:** Protestant, Roman Catholic, local faiths; **life expectancy:** 57 (men); 59 (women) (1995–2000).

**papyrus** type of paper made by the ancient Egyptians. Typically papyrus was made by gluing together some 20 sheets of the pith of the papyrus or paper reed plant *Cyperus papyrus*, family Cyperaceae. These sheets were arranged in alternating layers aligned vertically followed by horizontally. The strips were then covered with linen and beaten with a mallet. Finally, the papyrus was polished with a stone. Papyrus was in use before the First Dynasty.

**paracetamol** analgesic, particularly effective for musculoskeletal pain. It is as effective as aspirin in reducing fever and less irritating to the stomach, but has little anti-inflammatory action. An overdose can cause severe, often irreversible or even fatal, liver and kidney damage.

**paraffin** common name for →alkane, any member of the series of hydrocarbons with the general formula $C_nH_{2n+2}$. The lower members are gases, such as methane (marsh or natural gas). The middle ones (mainly liquid) form the basis of petrol, kerosene, and lubricating oils, while the higher ones (paraffin waxes) are used in ointment and cosmetic bases.

**Paraguay** Republic of; **national name:** *República del Paraguay*; **area:** 406,752 sq km/157,046 sq mi; **capital:** Asunción (and port); **major towns/ cities:** Ciudad del Este, Pedro Juan Caballero, San Lorenzo, Fernando de la Mora, Lambare, Concepción, Villartica, Encaración; **major ports:** Concepción; **physical features:** low marshy plain and marshlands; divided by Paraguay River; Paraná River forms southeast boundary; **head of state and government:** Luis Gonzalez Macchi from 1999; **political system:** emergent democracy; **currency:** guaraní; **GNP per capita (PPP):** (US$) 3,650 (1998); **exports:** soybeans (and other oil seeds), cotton, timber and wood manufactures, hides and skins, meat. Principal market Brazil 37.1% (1998); **population:** 5,359,000 (1999 est); **language:** Spanish 6% (official), Guaraní 90%; **religion:** Roman Catholic (official religion); Mennonite, Anglican; **life expectancy:** 68 (men); 72 (women) (1995–2000).

**parallelogram** in mathematics, a quadrilateral (four-sided plane figure) with opposite pairs of sides equal in length and parallel, and opposite angles equal. The diagonals of a parallelogram bisect each other. Its area is the product of the length of one side and the perpendicular distance between this and the opposite side. In the special case when all four sides are equal in length, the parallelogram is known as a rhombus, and when the internal angles

are right angles, it is a rectangle or square.

**parallel processing** emerging computer technology that allows more than one computation at the same time. Although in the 1990s this technology enabled only a small number of computer processor units to work in parallel, in theory thousands or millions of processors could be used at the same time.

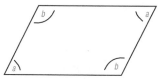

*(i) opposite sides and angles are equal*

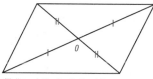

*(ii) diagonals bisect each other at 0*

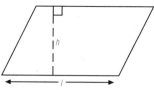

*(iii) area of a parallelogram l x h*

**parallelogram** Some properties of a parallelogram.

**paralysis** loss of voluntary movement due to failure of nerve impulses to reach the muscles involved. It may result from almost any disorder of the nervous system, including brain or spinal cord injury, poliomyelitis, stroke, and progressive conditions such as a tumour or multiple sclerosis. Paralysis may also involve loss of sensation due to sensory nerve disturbance.

**Paramaribo** chief port and capital of Suriname, on the west bank of the Suriname River near its mouth on the Atlantic coast; population (1996) 150,000. Products include coffee, fruit, timber, and bauxite.

**paranoia** mental disorder marked by delusions of grandeur or persecution. In popular usage, paranoia means baseless or exaggerated fear and suspicion.

**parasite** organism that lives on or in another organism (called the host) and depends on it for nutrition, often at the expense of the host's welfare. Parasites that live inside the host, such as liver flukes and tapeworms, are called **endoparasites**; those that live on the exterior, such as fleas and lice, are called **ectoparasites**.

**Paris** port and capital of France, on the River Seine; *département* (Ville de Paris) in the Île-de-France region; area of the *agglomération parisienne* (comprising the *Ville de Paris* and 379 *communes* surrounding it) 105 sq km/40.5 sq mi; population *Ville de Paris* (1990) 2,152,000; *agglomération parisienne* (1990) 9,300,000. The city is the core of a highly centralized national administration, a focus of European transport networks, and France's leading centre for education, research, finance, and industry. Manufactured products include metal, electrical and luxury goods, chemicals, glass, and tobacco. As one of the world's principal historic and cultural centres, Paris attracts enormous numbers of tourists throughout the year.

**Parkinson's disease** (or parkinsonism or paralysis agitans) degenerative disease of the brain characterized by a progressive loss of mobility, muscular rigidity, tremor, and speech difficulties. The condition is mainly seen in people over the age of 50.

**Parnell, Charles Stewart** (1846–1891) Irish nationalist politician. He supported a policy of obstruction and violence to attain →home rule, and became the president of the Nationalist Party in 1877. In 1879 he approved the Land League, and his attitude led to his imprisonment in 1881. His career was ruined in 1890 when he was cited as co-respondent in a divorce case. Because of his great influence over his followers, he was called 'the 'uncrowned king of Ireland'.

**parrot** tropical bird found mainly in Australia and South America. These colourful birds have been valued as pets in the Western world for many centuries. Parrots have the ability to imitate human speech. They are mainly vegetarian, and range in size from the 8.5 cm/3.5 in pygmy parrot to the 100 cm/40 in macaw. The smaller species are commonly referred to as parakeets. The plumage is often very colourful, and the call is usually a harsh screech. In most species the sexes are indistinguishable. Several species are endangered. Parrots are members of the family Psittacidae, of the order Psittaciformes.

**Parthia** ancient country in western Asia in what is now northeastern Iran, capital Ctesiphon. Parthian ascendancy began with the Arsacid dynasty in 248 BC, and reached the peak of its power under Mithridates I in the 2nd century BC; the region was annexed to Persia under the Sassanians AD 226.

**particle physics** study of the particles that make up all atoms, and of their interactions. More than 300 subatomic particles have now been identified by physicists, categorized into several classes according to their mass, electric charge, spin, magnetic moment, and interaction. Subatomic particles include the →elementary particles (→quarks, leptons, and gauge bosons), which are believed to be indivisible and so may be considered the fundamental units of matter; and the hadrons (baryons, such as the proton and neutron, and

mesons), which are composite particles, made up of two or three quarks. The proton, electron, and neutrino are the only stable particles (the neutron being stable only when in the atomic nucleus). The unstable particles decay rapidly into other particles, and are known from experiments with particle accelerators and cosmic radiation. See →atomic structure.

**Pascal, Blaise** (1623–1662) French philosopher and mathematician. He contributed to the development of hydraulics, →calculus, and the mathematical theory of →probability.

**Passchendaele, Battle of** in World War I, successful but costly British operation to capture the Passchendaele ridge in western Flanders, part of the third Battle of →Ypres October–November 1917; British casualties numbered nearly 400,000. The name is often erroneously applied to the whole of the battle of Ypres, but Passchendaele was in fact just part of that battle.

**Pasternak, Boris Leonidovich** (1890–1960) Russian poet and novelist. His novel *Dr Zhivago* (1957) was banned in the USSR as a 'hostile act', and was awarded a Nobel prize (which Pasternak declined). The ban on *Dr Zhivago* has since been lifted and Pasternak has been posthumously rehabilitated.

**Pasteur, Louis** (1822–1895) French chemist and microbiologist who discovered that fermentation is caused by micro-organisms and developed the germ theory of disease. He also created a vaccine for →rabies, which led to the foundation of the Pasteur Institute in Paris in 1888.

**pasteurization** treatment of food to reduce the number of micro-organisms it contains and so protect consumers from disease. Harmful bacteria are killed and the development of others is delayed. For milk, the method involves heating it to 72°C/161°F for 15 seconds followed by rapid cooling to 10°C/50°F or lower. The process also kills beneficial bacteria and reduces the nutritive property of milk.

**Patagonia** geographic region of South America, in southern Argentina and Chile; area 780,000 sq km/301,158 sq mi. A thinly populated vast plateau area, it stretches from the Río Colorado in central Argentina to the Magellan Straits in the south, and slopes eastwards from the Andes to the Atlantic coast. It consists of the provinces of Neuquén, Rio Negro, Chubut, and Santa Cruz. The main towns are the port of Comodoro Rivadavia (Argentina) and Punta Arenas (Chile).

**pathology** medical speciality concerned with the study of disease processes and how these provoke structural and functional changes in the body.

**Patrick, St** (*c.* 389–*c.* 461) patron saint of Ireland. Born in Britain, probably in South Wales, he was carried off by pirates to six years' slavery in Antrim, Ireland, before escaping either to Britain or Gaul – his poor Latin suggests the former – to train as a missionary. He is variously said to have landed again in Ireland 432 or 456, and his work was a vital factor in the spread of Christian influence there. His symbols are snakes and shamrocks; feast day 17 March.

**Paul, St** (*c.* AD 3–*c.* AD 68) Christian missionary and martyr; in the New Testament, one of the apostles and author of 13 epistles. Originally opposed to Christianity, he took part in the stoning of St Stephen. He is said to have been converted by a vision on the road to Damascus. After his conversion he made great missionary journeys, for example to Philippi and Ephesus, becoming known as the Apostle of the Gentiles (non-Jews). His emblems are a sword and a book; feast day 29 June.

**Pavlov, Ivan Petrovich** (1849–1936) Russian physiologist who studied conditioned reflexes in animals. His work had a great impact on behavioural theory and learning theory. Nobel Prize for Physiology or Medicine 1904.

**pearl** shiny, hard, rounded abnormal growth composed of nacre (or mother-of-pearl), a chalky substance. Nacre is secreted by many molluscs, and deposited in thin layers on the inside of the shell around a parasite, a grain of sand, or some other irritant body. After several years of the mantle (the layer of tissue between the shell and the body mass) secreting this nacre, a pearl is formed.

**Pearl Harbor** US Pacific naval base on Oahu island, Hawaii, USA, the scene of a Japanese aerial attack on 7 December

1941, which brought the USA into World War II. The attack took place while Japanese envoys were holding so-called peace talks in Washington. More than 2,000 members of the US armed forces were killed, and a large part of the US Pacific fleet was destroyed or damaged.

**Peasants' Revolt** the rising of the English peasantry in June 1381, the result of economic, social, and political disillusionment. It was sparked off by the imposition of a new poll tax, three times the rates of those imposed in 1377 and 1379. Led by Watt →Tyler and John Ball, rebels from southeast England marched on London and demanded reforms. The authorities put down the revolt by deceit and force.

**Peel, Robert** (1788–1850) British Conservative politician. As home secretary 1822–27 and 1828–30, he founded the modern police force and in 1829 introduced Roman Catholic emancipation. He was prime minister 1834–35 and 1841–46, when his repeal of the →Corn Laws caused him and his followers to break with the party. 2nd baronet 1830.

**Peloponnesian War** war fought 431–404 BC between Athens and Sparta and their respective allies, involving most of the Greek world from Asia Minor to Sicily and from Byzantium (present-day Istanbul, Turkey) to Crete. Sparked by Spartan fears about the growth of Athenian power, it continued until the Spartan general Lysander captured the Athenian fleet in 405 at Aegospotami and starved the Athenians into surrender in 404. As a result of this victory, Athens' political power collapsed.

**penguin** marine flightless bird, family Spheniscidae, order Sphenisciformes, mostly black and white, found in the southern hemisphere. They comprise 18 species in six genera. Males are usually larger than the females. Penguins range in size from 40 cm/1.6 ft to 1.2 m/4 ft tall, and have thick feathers to protect them from the intense cold. They are awkward on land (except on snow slopes down which they propel themselves at a rapid pace), but their wings have evolved into flippers, making them excellent swimmers. Penguins congregate to breed in 'rookeries', and often spend many months incubating their eggs while their mates are out at sea feeding. They feed on a mixture of fish, squid, and krill.

**penicillin** any of a group of →antibiotic (bacteria killing) compounds obtained from filtrates of moulds of the genus *Penicillium* (especially *P. notatum*) or produced synthetically. Penicillin was the first antibiotic to be discovered (by Alexander →Fleming); it kills a broad spectrum of bacteria, many of which cause disease in humans.

**penis** male reproductive organ containing the urethra, the channel through which urine and semen are voided. It transfers sperm to the female reproductive tract to fertilize the ovum. In mammals, the penis is made erect by vessels that fill with blood, and in most mammals (but not humans) is stiffened by a bone.

**Pennines, the** range of hills in northern England, known as the 'the backbone of England'; length (from the Scottish border to the Peaks in Derbyshire) 400 km/250 mi. The highest peak in the Pennines (which are sometimes referred to as mountains rather than hills) is Cross Fell (893 m/2,930 ft). It is the watershed for the main rivers of northeast England. The rocks are carboniferous limestone and millstone grit, the land high moorland and fell.

**Pennsylvania** state in northeastern USA. It is nicknamed the Keystone State. Pennsylvania ratified the US Constitution in 1787, becoming the 2nd state to join the Union. It is bordered to the north by New York, with a small coastal strip on Lake Erie, to the west by Ohio and the West Virginia panhandle, to the south, on what was the Mason-Dixon Line, by West Virginia, Maryland, and Delaware, and to the east by New Jersey, across the Delaware River. Pennsylvania was the hub of US industry in the late 19th and early 20th century. **population:** (1995) 12,071,800; **area:** 117,400 sq km/ 45,316 sq mi; **capital:** Harrisburg; **towns and cities:** Philadelphia, Pittsburgh, Erie, Allentown, Scranton; **industries and products:** hay, cereals, mushrooms, cattle, poultry, dairy products, cement, limestone, coal, steel, petroleum products, pharmaceuticals, chemicals, motor vehicles and equipment, electronic components, textiles, tourism.

**peptide** molecule comprising two or more →amino acid molecules (not necessarily different) joined by **peptide bonds**, whereby the acid group of one acid is linked to the amino group of the other (–CO.NH). The number of amino acid molecules in the peptide is indicated by referring to it as a di-, tri-, or polypeptide (two, three, or many amino acids).

**Pepys, Samuel** (1633–1703) English naval administrator and diarist. His *Diary* (1660–69) is a unique record of the daily life of the period, the historical events of the Restoration, the manners and scandals of the court, naval administration, and Pepys's own interests, weaknesses, and intimate feelings. Written in shorthand, it was not deciphered until 1825.

**percussion instrument** musical instrument played by being struck with the hand or a beater. Percussion instruments can be divided into those that can be tuned to produce a sound of definite pitch, such as the timpani, tubular bells, glockenspiel, xylophone, and piano, and those of indefinite pitch, including the bass drum, tambourine, triangle, cymbals, and castanets.

**perennial plant** plant that lives for more than two years. Herbaceous perennials have aerial stems and leaves that die each autumn. They survive the winter by means of an underground storage (perennating) organ, such as a bulb or rhizome. Trees and shrubs or woody perennials have stems that persist above ground throughout the year, and may be either →deciduous or →evergreen. See also →annual plant.

**Peres, Shimon** (1923– ) Israeli Labour politician, prime minister 1984–86 and 1995–96. He was prime minister, then foreign minister, under a power-sharing agreement with the leader of the Likud Party, Yitzhak Shamir. From 1989 to 1990 he was finance minister in a Labour–Likud coalition. As foreign minister in Yitzhak Rabin's Labour government from 1992, he negotiated the 1993 peace agreement with the Palestine Liberation Organization (PLO). He was awarded the 1994 Nobel Prize for Peace jointly with Rabin and PLO leader Yassir Arafat.

Following the assassination of Rabin in November 1995, Peres succeeded him as prime minister, and pledged to continue the peace process in which they had both been so closely involved, but in May 1996 he was defeated in Israel's first direct elections for prime minister.

*perestroika* (Russian 'restructuring') in Soviet politics, the wide-ranging economic and political reforms initiated from 1985 by Mikhail Gorbachev, finally leading to the demise of the Soviet Union. Originally, in the economic sphere, *perestroika* was conceived as involving 'intensive development' concentrating on automation and improved labour efficiency. It evolved to attend increasingly to market indicators and incentives ('market socialism') and the gradual dismantling of the Stalinist central-planning system, with decision-taking being devolved to self-financing enterprises.

**Pericles** (*c.* 495–429 BC) Athenian politician under whom Athens reached the height of power. He persuaded the Athenians to reject Sparta's ultimata in 432 BC, and was responsible for Athenian strategy in the opening years of the Peloponnesian War. His policies helped to transform the Delian League into an empire, but the disasters of the →Peloponnesian War led to his removal from office in 430 BC. Although quickly reinstated, he died soon after.

**periodic table of the elements** in chemistry, a table in which the elements are arranged in order of their atomic number. The table summarizes the major properties of the elements and enables predictions to be made about their behaviour. *See illustration on page 418.*

**Permian** period of geological time 290–245 million years ago, the last period of the Palaeozoic era. Its end was marked by a significant change in marine life, including the extinction of many corals and trilobites. Deserts were widespread, terrestrial amphibians and mammal-like reptiles flourished, and cone-bearing plants (gymnosperms) came to prominence. In the oceans, 49% of families and 72% of genera vanished in the late Permian. On land, 78% of reptile families and 67% of amphibian families disappeared.

**Persia, ancient** kingdom in southwestern Asia. The early Persians were a nomadic Aryan people who migrated through the Caucasus to the Iranian plateau. Cyrus organized the empire into provinces which were each ruled by Satraps. The royal house is known as the Achaemenids after the founder of

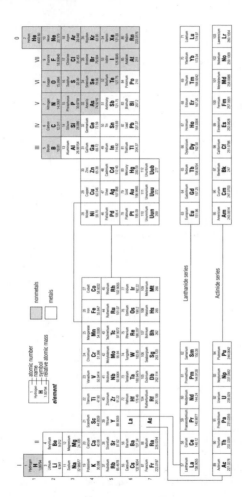

**periodic table of the elements** The periodic table of the elements arranges the elements into horizontal rows (called periods) and vertical columns (called groups) according to their atomic numbers. The elements in a group or column all have similar properties – for example, all the elements in the far right-hand column are inert gases.

the line. The administrative centre was Susa, with the royal palace at Persepolis.

Expansion led the Persians into conflicts with Greek cities, notably in the Ionian Revolt, Darius I's campaign that ended at the Athenian victory of Marathon (490 BC), and Xerxes I's full-blown invasion of the Greek mainland 480.

**Persian Gulf** (or Arabian Gulf) large shallow inlet of the Arabian Sea; area 233,000 sq km/90,000 sq mi. It divides the Arabian peninsula from Iran and is linked by the Strait of Hormuz and the Gulf of Oman to the Arabian Sea. Oilfields producing about one-third of the world's oil surround it in the Gulf States of Bahrain, Iran, Iraq, Kuwait, Oman, Qatar, Saudi Arabia, and the United Arab Emirates.

**Persian Wars** series of conflicts between Greece and Persia in 499–479 BC. Greek involvement with Persia began when Cyrus (II) the Great (reigned 559–530 BC) conquered the Greek cities of western Asia Minor and ended with →Alexander (III) the Great's conquest of Persia, but the term 'Persian Wars' usually refers to the two Persian invasions of mainland Greece in 490 and 480/79. The Greek victory marked the end of Persian domination of the ancient world and the beginning of Greek supremacy.

**Perth** capital of the state of →Western Australia; population 1,096,829 (1996). Perth is situated on the southwest coast of Australia, on the River Swan, 19 km/12 mi inland. Its port is at Fremantle, to the southwest at the mouth of the Swan. Industries include oil refining, electronics, food processing, shipbuilding, banking and finance, and tourism; products include textiles, nickel, alumina, fertilizers, cement, furniture, and motor vehicles. Perth is an important centre for the export of primary products: refined oil, minerals, wool, wheat, meat, fruit, timber, and dairy produce. Perth has four universities: the University of Western Australia (founded 1911); Murdoch University (1975); Curtin University of Technology (1987); Edith Cowan University (1990).

**Peru** Republic of; **national name:** *República del Perú;* **area:** 1,285,200 sq km/496,216 sq mi; **capital:** Lima; **major towns/cities:** Arequipa, Iquitos, Chiclayo, Trujillo, Cuzco, Piura, Chimbote; **major ports:** Callao, Chimbote, Salaverry; **physical features:** Andes mountains running northwest–southeast cover 27% of Peru, separating Amazon river-basin jungle in northeast from coastal plain in west; desert along coast north–south (Atacama Desert); Lake Titicaca; **head of state:** Alberto Fujimori from 1990; **head of government:** Alberto Pandolfi from 1998; **political system:** democracy; **currency:** nuevo sol; **GNP per capita (PPP):** (US$) 4,910 (1998 est); **exports:** copper, fishmeal, zinc, gold, refined petroleum products. Principal market USA 24.9% (1997); **population:** 25,230,000 (1999 est); **language:** Spanish, Quechua (both official), Aymara; **religion:** Roman Catholic (state religion); **life expectancy:** 66 (men); 71 (women) (1995–2000).

**pesticide** any chemical used in farming, gardening, or indoors to combat pests. Pesticides are of three main types: **insecticides** (to kill insects), **fungicides** (to kill fungal diseases), and **herbicides** (to kill plants, mainly those considered weeds). Pesticides cause a number of pollution problems through spray drift on to surrounding areas, direct contamination of users or the public, and as residues on food. The World Health Organization (WHO) estimated in 1999 that 20,000 people die annually worldwide from pesticide poisoning incidents.

The safest pesticides include those made from plants, such as the insecticides pyrethrum and derris.

**Peter (I) the Great** (1672–1725) tsar of Russia from 1682 on the death of his half-brother Tsar Feodor III; he assumed control of the government in 1689. He attempted to reorganize the country on Western lines. He modernized the army, had a fleet built, remodelled the administrative and legal systems, encouraged education, and brought the Russian Orthodox Church under state control. On the Baltic coast, where he had conquered territory from Sweden, Peter built a new city, St Petersburg, and moved the capital there from Moscow.

**Peterloo massacre** the events in St Peter's Fields in Manchester, England, on 16 August 1819, when an open-air meeting in support of parliamentary reform was charged by yeomanry (voluntary cavalry soldiers) and hussars (regular cavalry soldiers). Eleven people were killed and 500 wounded. The name was given in analogy with the Battle of Waterloo.

**Peter, St** (lived 1st century) Christian martyr, the author of two epistles in the New Testament and leader of the apostles. He is regarded as the first bishop of Rome, whose mantle the pope inherits. His real name was Simon, but he was nicknamed Kephas ('Peter', from the Greek for 'rock') by Jesus, as being the rock upon which he would build his church. His emblem is two keys; feast day 29 June.

**Petrarch, Francesco** (1304–1374) Italian Petrarca Italian poet, humanist, and leader of the revival of classical learning. His *Il canzoniere/Songbook* (also known as *Rime Sparse/Scattered Lyrics*) contains madrigals, songs, and →sonnets in praise of his idealized love, 'Laura', whom he first saw in 1327 (she was a married woman and refused to become his mistress). These were Petrarch's greatest contributions to Italian literature; they shaped the lyric poetry of the Renaissance and greatly influenced French and English love poetry. Although he did not invent the sonnet form, he was its finest early practitioner and the 'Petrarchan sonnet' was admired as an ideal model by later poets.

**petrol** mixture of hydrocarbons derived from petroleum, mainly used as a fuel for internal-combustion engines. It is colourless and highly volatile. **Leaded petrol** contains antiknock (a mixture of tetraethyl lead and dibromoethane), which improves the combustion of petrol and the performance of a car engine. The lead from the exhaust fumes enters the atmosphere, mostly as simple lead compounds. There is strong evidence that it can act as a nerve poison on young children and cause mental impairment. This has prompted a gradual switch to the use of **unleaded petrol** in the UK.

**petroleum** (or crude oil) natural mineral oil, a thick greenish-brown flammable liquid found underground in permeable rocks. Petroleum consists of hydrocarbons mixed with oxygen, sulphur, nitrogen, and other elements in varying proportions. It is thought to be derived from ancient organic material that has been converted by, first, bacterial action, then heat, and pressure (but its origin may be chemical also).

From crude petroleum, various products are made by distillation and other processes; for example, fuel oil, petrol, kerosene, diesel, and lubricating oil. Petroleum products and chemicals are used in large quantities in the manufacture of detergents, artificial fibres, plastics, insecticides, fertilizers, pharmaceuticals, toiletries, and synthetic rubber.

**pH** scale from 0 to 14 for measuring acidity or alkalinity. A pH of 7.0 indicates neutrality, below 7 is acid, while above 7 is alkaline. Strong acids, such as those used in car batteries, have a pH of about 2; strong alkalis such as sodium hydroxide are pH 13.

**Phanerozoic** (Greek *phanero* 'visible') eon in Earth history, consisting of the most recent 570 million years. It comprises the Palaeozoic, Mesozoic, and

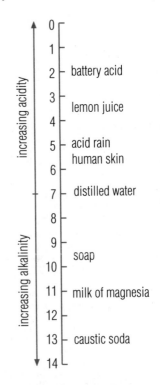

**pH** The pHs of some common substances. The lower the pH is, the more acidic the substance; the higher the pH, the more alkaline the substance.

Cenozoic eras. The vast majority of fossils come from this eon, owing to the evolution of hard shells and internal skeletons. The name means 'interval of well-displayed life'.

**Pharisee** (Hebrew 'separatist') member of a conservative Jewish sect that arose in Roman-occupied Palestine in the 2nd century BC in protest against all movements favouring compromise with Hellenistic culture. The Pharisees were devout adherents of the law, both as found in the Torah and in the oral tradition known as the Mishnah.

**phenotype** in genetics, visible traits, those actually displayed by an organism. The phenotype is not a direct reflection of the →genotype because some alleles are masked by the presence of other, dominant alleles. The phenotype is further modified by the effects of the environment (for example, poor nutrition stunts growth).

**pheromone** chemical signal (such as an odour) that is emitted by one animal and affects the behaviour of others. Pheromones are used by many animal species to attract mates.

**Philip II** (1165–1223) (also known as Philip Augustus) king of France from 1180. As part of his efforts to establish a strong monarchy and evict the English from their French possessions, he waged war in turn against the English kings Henry II, Richard (I) the Lionheart (with whom he also went on the Third Crusade), and John (1167–1216).

**Philippines** Republic of the; **national name:** *Republika ng Pilipinas*; **area:** 300,000 sq km/115,830 sq mi; **capital:** Manila (on Luzon) (and chief port); **major towns/cities:** Quezon City (on Luzon), Davao, Caloocan, Cebu, Zamboanga; **major ports:** Cebu, Davao (on Mindanao), Iloilo, Zamboanga (on Mindanao); **physical features:** comprises over 7,000 islands; volcanic mountain ranges traverse main chain north–south; 50% still forested. The largest islands are Luzon 108,172 sq km/41,754 sq mi and Mindanao 94,227 sq km/36,372 sq mi; others include Samar, Negros, Palawan, Panay, Mindoro, Leyte, Cebu, and the Sulu group; Pinatubo volcano (1,759 m/5,770 ft); Mindanao has active volcano Apo (2,954 m/9,690 ft) and mountainous rainforest; **head of state and government:** Joseph Ejercito Estrada from 1998; **political system:** emergent democracy; **currency:** peso; **GNP per capita (PPP):** (US$) 3,540 (1998); **exports:** electronic products (notably semiconductors and microcircuits), garments, agricultural products (particularly fruit and seafood), woodcraft and furniture, lumber, chemicals, coconut oil. Principal market USA 34.2% (1998); **population:** 74,454,000 (1999 est); **language:** Tagalog (Filipino, official); English and Spanish; Cebuano, Ilocano, and more than 70 other indigenous languages; **religion:** mainly Roman Catholic; Protestant, Muslim, local religions; **life expectancy:** 67 (men); 70 (women) (1995–2000).

**Philistine** member of a seafaring people of non-Semitic origin who founded city-states on the Palestinian coastal plain in the 12th century BC, adopting a Semitic language and religion.

**philosophy** (Greek 'love of wisdom') systematic analysis and critical examination of fundamental problems such as the nature of reality, mind, perception, self, free will, causation, time and space, and moral judgements. Traditionally, philosophy has three branches: metaphysics (the nature of being), epistemology (theory of knowledge), and logic (study of valid inference). Modern philosophy also includes ethics, aesthetics, political theory, the philosophy of science, and the philosophy of religion.

**phloem** tissue found in vascular plants whose main function is to conduct sugars and other food materials from the leaves, where they are produced, to all other parts of the plant.

**Phnom Penh** capital of Cambodia, on the Mekong River, 210 km/130 mi northwest of Saigon; population (1994) 920,000. Industries include textiles and food-processing. It has been Cambodia's capital since the 15th century, and has royal palaces, museums, and pagodas.

**phoenix** in Egyptian and Oriental mythology, a sacred bird born from the sun. The Egyptians believed it was also connected with the soul and the obelisk. In China the phoenix signified good and its appearance prosperity; its departure boded calamity. According to the Greek historian Herodotus, the creature visited the temple of the sun at Heliopolis every 500 years to bury its dead father, embalmed in a ball of myrrh. In another version, the phoenix placed itself on the city's burning altar or built a nest as a funeral pyre, and rose rejuvenated from the ashes. Only one phoenix existed at a time.

**photoelectric effect** in physics, the emission of →electrons from a substance (usually a metallic surface) when it is struck by photons (quanta of electromagnetic radiation), usually those of visible light or ultraviolet radiation.

**photography** process for reproducing images on sensitized materials by various forms of radiant energy, including visible light, ultraviolet, infrared, X-rays, atomic radiations, and electron beams.

Photography was developed in the 19th century; among the pioneers were Louis →Daguerre in France and Fox Talbot in the UK. Colour photography dates from the early 20th century.

**photosynthesis** process by which green plants trap light energy from the Sun. This energy is used to drive a series of chemical reactions which lead to the formation of carbohydrates. The carbohydrates occur in the form of simple sugar, or glucose, which provides the basic food for both plants and animals. For photosynthesis to occur, the plant must possess →chlorophyll and must have a supply of carbon dioxide and water. Photosynthesis takes place inside chloroplasts which are found mainly in the leaf cells of plants.

The by-product of photosynthesis, oxygen, is of great importance to all living organisms, and virtually all atmospheric oxygen has originated by photosynthesis.

### WEB SITE > > > > > > > >
#### Introduction to Photosynthesis and its Applications

http://photoscience.la.asu.edu/
photosyn/education/photointro.html

Good general introduction to photosynthesis, written by a professor at Arizona State University, USA. A discussion of the basics – illustrated with photographs and diagrams, is followed by an explanation of photosynthetic electron transfer, carbon fixation, and the effects of increasing exposure to carbon dioxide.

**physical chemistry** branch of chemistry concerned with examining the relationships between the chemical compositions of substances and the physical properties that they display. Most chemical reactions exhibit some physical phenomenon (change of state, temperature, pressure, or volume, or the use or production of electricity), and the measurement and study of such phenomena has led to many chemical theories and laws.

**physics** branch of science concerned with the laws that govern the structure of the universe, and the investigation of the properties of matter and energy and their interactions. For convenience, physics is often divided into branches such as atomic physics, nuclear physics,

### WEB SITE > > > > > > > >
#### PhysicsTutor.com

http://www.physicstutor.com/

Search for help with physics problems with this online 'teacher'.

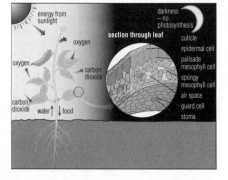

**photosynthesis** Process by which green plants and some bacteria manufacture carbohydrates from water and atmospheric carbon dioxide, using the energy of sunlight. Photosynthesis depends on the ability of chlorophyll molecules within plant cells to trap the energy of light to split water molecules, giving off oxygen as a by-product. The hydrogen of the water molecules is then used to reduce carbon dioxide to simple carbohydrates.

particle physics, solid-state physics, molecular physics, electricity and magnetism, optics, acoustics, heat, thermodynamics, quantum theory, and relativity. Before the 20th century, physics was known as natural philosophy.

**physiology** branch of biology that deals with the functioning of living organisms, as opposed to anatomy, which studies their structures.

**physiotherapy** treatment of injury and disease by physical means such as exercise, heat, manipulation, massage, and electrical stimulation.

**pi** symbol $\pi$, the ratio of the circumference of a circle to its diameter. Pi is an irrational number; it cannot be expressed as the ratio of two integers, and its expression as a decimal never terminates and never starts recurring. The value of pi is 3.1415926, correct to seven decimal places. Common approximations to pi are 22/7 and 3.14, although the value 3 can be used as a rough estimation.

**piano** (or pianoforte; originally fortepiano) stringed musical instrument played by felt-covered hammers activated from a keyboard. It is therefore a form of mechanized dulcimer, a percussion instrument, unlike the earlier harpsichord, a mechanized harp in which the strings are plucked. It is capable of dynamic gradation between soft (Italian *piano*) and loud (Italian *forte*) tones, hence its name. The first piano was constructed in 1704 and introduced in 1709 by Bartolommeo Cristofori, a

harpsichord maker from Padua. It uses a clever mechanism to make the keyboard touch-sensitive. Extensively developed during the 18th century, the piano attracted admiration among many composers, although it was not until 1768 that Johann Christian Bach gave one of the first public recitals on the instrument.

**Picasso, Pablo Ruiz y** (1881–1973) Spanish artist, chiefly active in France. He was one of the most inventive and prolific talents in 20th-century art. His Blue Period 1901–04 and Rose Period 1905–06 preceded the revolutionary *Les Demoiselles d'Avignon* (1907; Museum of Modern Art, New York), which paved the way for →cubism. In the early 1920s he was considered a leader of the surrealist movement. From the 1930s his work included sculpture, ceramics, and graphic works in a wide variety of media. Among his best-known paintings is *Guernica* (1937; Prado, Madrid), a comment on the bombing of civilians in the Spanish Civil War.

**Pict** Roman term for a member of the peoples of northern Scotland, possibly meaning 'painted' (tattooed). Of pre-Celtic origin, and speaking a Celtic language which died out in about the 10th century, the Picts are thought to have inhabited much of England before the arrival of the Celtic Britons. They were united with the Celtic Scots under the rule of Kenneth MacAlpin in 844. Their greatest monument is a series of carved stones, whose symbols remain undeciphered.

**piezoelectric effect** property of some crystals (for example, quartz) to develop an electromotive force or voltage across opposite faces when subjected to tension or compression, and, conversely, to expand or contract in size when subjected to an electromotive force. Piezoelectric crystal oscillators are used as frequency standards (for example, replacing balance wheels in watches), and for producing ultrasound.

**Pigs, Bay of** inlet on the south coast of Cuba about 145 km/90 mi southwest of Havana. It was the site of an unsuccessful invasion attempt by 1,500 US-sponsored Cuban exiles 17–20 April 1961; 1,173 were taken prisoner.

**Pilate, Pontius** (died *c.* AD 36) Roman procurator of Judea AD 26–36. The New Testament Gospels describe his reluctant ordering of Jesus' crucifixion, but there has been considerable debate about his actual role in it.

**Pilgrims** (or Pilgrim Fathers) the emigrants who sailed from Plymouth, Devon, England, in the *Mayflower* on 16 September 1620. They founded the first colony in New England, North America, at New Plymouth, Massachusetts. Of the 102 passengers about a third were Puritan refugees.

**Pill, the** commonly used term for the contraceptive pill, based on female hormones. The combined pill, which contains synthetic hormones similar to oestrogen and progesterone, stops the production of eggs, and makes the mucus produced by the cervix hostile to sperm. It is the most effective form of contraception apart from sterilization, being more than 99% effective.

**Pinochet (Ugarte), Augusto** (1915– ) Chilean military dictator from 1973, when a coup backed by the US Central Intelligence Agency ousted and killed President Salvador Allende, until 1989. Pinochet took over the presidency as the result of the coup and governed ruthlessly, crushing all political opposition (including more than 3,000 people who 'vanished' or were killed) but also presiding over the country's economic expansion in the 1980s, stimulated further by free-market reforms. In 1988 he called and lost a plebiscite to ratify him as sole nominee for the presidency. He was voted out of power when general elections were held in December 1989 but remained head of the armed forces until March 1998 when he became senator for life, which gave him instant legal immunity. An attempt was made to force Pinochet to stand trial in 1999 by arresting him while he was visiting the UK. However, a team of British doctors declared him unfit to stand trial and he was returned to Chile.

**Pinter, Harold** (1930– ) English dramatist, originally an actor. He specializes in the tragicomedy of the breakdown of communication, broadly in the tradition of the Theatre of the Absurd – for example, *The Birthday Party* (1958) and *The Caretaker* (1960). Later plays include *The Homecoming* (1965), *Old Times* (1971), *Betrayal* (1978), and *Moonlight* (1993). His *Various Voices: Prose, Poetry, Politics, 1948–1998* was published in 1998.

**piranha** any South American freshwater fish of the genus *Serrusalmus*, in the same order as cichlids. They can grow to 60 cm/2 ft long, and have razor-sharp teeth; some species may rapidly devour animals, especially if attracted by blood.

**Pisa** (ancient Pisae) town in Tuscany, Italy, on the River Arno, 70 km/43 mi southwest of Florence; population (1991) 101,000. Industries include tourism, engineering, and the production of glass and textiles. Its famous campanile (bell-tower), the **Leaning Tower of Pisa** (repaired 1990), is 55 m/180 ft high and about 5 m/16.5 ft out of perpendicular, the foundations being only about 3 m/10 ft deep and built on unstable ground.

**piston** barrel-shaped device used in reciprocating engines (steam, petrol, diesel oil) to harness power. Pistons are driven up and down in cylinders by expanding steam or hot gases. They pass on their motion via a connecting rod and crank to a crankshaft, which turns the driving wheels. In a pump or compressor, the role of the piston is reversed, being used to move gases and liquids. See also →internal-combustion engine.

**pitcher plant** any of various insectivorous plants, the leaves of which are shaped like a pitcher and filled with a fluid that traps and digests insects. (Genera especially *Nepenthes* and *Sarracenia*, family Sarraceniaceae.)

**Pitt, William, the Elder** (1708–1778) 1st Earl of Chatham, British Whig politician, 'the Great Commoner'. As paymaster of the forces 1746–55, he broke with tradition by refusing to enrich himself; he was dismissed for attacking the Duke of Newcastle, the prime minister. He served effectively as prime minister in coalition governments 1756–61 (successfully conducting the Seven Years' War) and 1766–68. He was created an earl in 1766.

**Pitt, William, the Younger** (1759–1806) British Tory prime minister 1783–1801 and 1804–06. He raised the

**piranha** Red piranhas swim in shoals so large that they can devour even large animals by their combined efforts. Their razor sharp teeth and strong jaws can chop off pieces of flesh with great speed.

importance of the House of Commons, clamped down on corruption, carried out fiscal reforms, and effected the union with Ireland. He attempted to keep Britain at peace but underestimated the importance of the French Revolution and became embroiled in wars with France from 1793; he died on hearing of Napoleon's victory at Austerlitz.

**Pittsburgh** (nickname 'City of Bridges') second-largest city in Pennsylvania, USA, at the confluence of the Allegheny and Monongahela rivers, forming the Ohio River; population (1996 est) 350,400; metropolitan area (1992) 2,406,000. It is a business and financial centre with one of the largest river ports in the world. High technology and healthcare services dominate an economy formerly based on iron, steel, heavy engineering, and glass industries.

**pituitary gland** major →endocrine gland of vertebrates, situated in the centre of the brain. It is attached to the hypothalamus by a stalk. The pituitary consists of two lobes. The posterior lobe is an extension of the hypothalamus, and is in effect nervous tissue. It stores

two hormones synthesized in the hypothalamus: ADH and oxytocin. The anterior lobe secretes six hormones, some of which control the activities of other glands (thyroid, gonads, and adrenal cortex); others are direct-acting hormones affecting milk secretion and controlling growth.

**pixel** derived from picture element single dot on a computer screen. All screen images are made up of a collection of pixels, with each pixel being either off (dark) or on (illuminated, possibly in colour). The number of pixels available determines the screen's resolution. Typical resolutions of microcomputer screens vary from 320 x 200 pixels to 800 x 600 pixels, but screens with 1,024 x 768 pixels or more are now common for high-quality graphic (pictorial) displays.

**placenta** organ that attaches the developing →embryo or →fetus to the →uterus in placental mammals (mammals other than marsupials, platypuses, and echidnas). Composed of maternal and embryonic tissue, it links the blood supply of the embryo to the blood supply of the mother, allowing the

**pixel** Computer screen images are made of a number of pixels ('dots'). The greater the number of pixels the greater the resolution of the image; most computer screens are set at 640 × 480 pixels, although higher resolutions are available.

exchange of oxygen, nutrients, and waste products. The two blood systems are not in direct contact, but are separated by thin membranes, with materials diffusing across from one system to the other. The placenta also produces hormones that maintain and regulate pregnancy. It is shed as part of the afterbirth.

**plague** term applied to any epidemic disease with a high mortality rate, but it usually refers to the bubonic plague. This is a disease transmitted by fleas (carried by the black rat) which infect the sufferer with the bacillus *Yersinia pestis*. An early symptom is swelling of lymph nodes, usually in the armpit and groin; such swellings are called 'buboes'. It causes virulent blood poisoning and the death rate is high.

**Planck, Max Karl Ernst** (1858–1947) German physicist who framed the →quantum theory in 1900. His research into the manner in which heated bodies radiate energy led him to report that energy is emitted only in indivisible amounts, called 'quanta', the magnitudes of which are proportional to the frequency of the radiation. His discovery ran counter to classical physics and is held to have marked the commencement of the modern science. He was awarded the Nobel Prize for Physics in 1918.

**planet** (Greek 'wanderer') large celestial body in orbit around a star, composed of rock, metal, or gas. There are nine planets in the →Solar System: Mercury, Venus, Earth, Mars, Jupiter, Saturn, Neptune, Uranus, and Pluto. The inner four, called the **terrestrial planets**, are small and rocky, and include the planet Earth. The outer planets, with the exception of Pluto, are called the **major planets**, and consist of large balls of rock, liquid, and gas; the largest is Jupiter, which contains a mass equivalent to 70% of all the other planets combined. Planets do not produce light, but reflect the light of their parent star. *See table on page 430.*

**plankton** small, often microscopic, forms of plant and animal life that live in the upper layers of fresh and salt water, and are an important source of food for larger animals. Marine plankton is concentrated in areas where rising currents bring mineral salts to the surface.

**plant** organism that carries out →photosynthesis, has cellulose cell walls and complex cells, and is immobile. A few parasitic plants have lost the ability to photosynthesize but are still considered to be plants.

---

### WEB SITE > > > > > > > >

#### Plants and their Structure

http:\\gened.emc.maricopa.edu/ bio/bio181/ BIOBK/BioBookPLANTANAT.html

Informative guide to the structure of plants. The page begins with a hypertext exploration of the general organization of plant species, then moves on to a discussion of plant cells and tissue types. Diagrams and microscopic images accompany the text.

## THE PLANETS

(– = not applicable.)

| Planet | Main constituents | Atmosphere | Average distance from the Sun | | Orbital period (Earth yrs) | Diameter | | Average density (water = 1 unit) | |
|--------|-------------------|------------|---------|---------|---------|---------|---------|---------|---------|
| | | | km (millions) | mi (millions) | | km (thousands) | mi (thousands) | | |
| Mercury | rock, ferrous | – | 58 | 36 | 0.241 | 4.88 | 3.03 | 5.4 | |
| Venus | rock, ferrous | carbon dioxide | 108 | 67 | 0.615 | 12.10 | 7.51 | 5.2 | |
| Earth | rock, ferrous | nitrogen, oxygen | 150 | 93 | 1.00 | 12.76 | 7.92 | 5.5 | |
| Mars | rock | carbon dioxide | 228 | 141 | 1.88 | 6.78 | 4.21 | 3.9 | |
| Jupiter | liquid hydrogen, helium | – | 778 | 483 | 11.86 | 142.80 | 88.73 | 1.3 | |
| Saturn | hydrogen, helium | – | 1,427 | 886 | 29.46 | 120.00 | 74.56 | 0.7 | |
| Uranus | ice, hydrogen, helium | hydrogen, helium | 2,870 | 1,783 | 84.00 | 50.80 | 31.56 | 1.3 | |
| Neptune | ice, hydrogen, helium | hydrogen, helium | 4,497 | 2,794 | 164.80 | 48.60 | 30.20 | 1.6 | |
| Pluto | ice, rock | methane | 5,900 | 3,666 | 248.50 | 2.27 | 1.41 | ~2 | |

Plants are →autotrophs, that is, they make carbohydrates from water and carbon dioxide, and are the primary producers in all food chains, so that all animal life is dependent on them. They play a vital part in the carbon cycle, removing carbon dioxide from the atmosphere and generating oxygen. The study of plants is known as →botany.

**Plantagenet** English royal house, which reigned from 1154 to 1399, and whose name comes from the nickname of Geoffrey, Count of Anjou (1113–1151), father of Henry II, who often wore in his hat a sprig of broom, *planta genista*. In the 1450s, Richard, Duke of York, took 'Plantagenet' as a surname to emphasize his superior claim to the throne over that of Henry VI.

**plasma** in biology, the liquid component of the →blood. It is a straw-coloured fluid, largely composed of water (around 90%), in which a number of substances are dissolved. These include a variety of proteins (around 7%) such as fibrinogen (important in →blood clotting), inorganic mineral salts such as sodium and calcium, waste products such as →urea, traces of →hormones, and →antibodies to defend against infection.

**plasma** in physics, an ionized gas produced at extremely high temperatures, as in the Sun and other stars, which contains positive and negative charges in equal numbers. It is a good electrical conductor. In thermonuclear reactions the plasma produced is confined through the use of magnetic fields.

**plastic** any of the stable synthetic materials that are fluid at some stage in their manufacture, when they can be shaped, and that later set to rigid or semi-rigid solids. Plastics today are chiefly derived from petroleum. Most are polymers, made up of long chains of identical molecules.

**plate tectonics** theory formulated in the 1960s to explain the phenomena of →continental drift and seafloor spreading, and the formation of the major physical features of the Earth's surface. The Earth's outermost layer, the lithosphere, is regarded as a jigsaw puzzle of rigid major and minor plates that move relative to each other, probably under the influence of convection currents in the mantle beneath. At the margins of the plates, where they collide or move apart, major landforms such as →mountains, →volcanoes, ocean trenches, and **ocean ridges** are created. The rate of plate movement is at most 15 cm/6 in per year.

**Plath, Sylvia** (1932–1963) US poet and novelist. Her powerful, highly personal poems, often expressing a sense of desolation, are distinguished by their intensity and sharp imagery. Her *Collected Poems* (1981) was awarded a Pulitzer prize. Her autobiographical novel *The Bell Jar* (1961) deals with the events surrounding a young woman's emotional breakdown.

**Plato** (*c.* 427–347 BC) Greek philosopher. He was a pupil of Socrates, teacher of Aristotle, and founder of the Academy school of philosophy. He was the author of philosophical dialogues on such topics as metaphysics, ethics, and politics. Central to his teachings is the notion of Forms, which are located outside the everyday world – timeless, motionless, and absolutely real.

**Pleistocene** first epoch of the Quaternary period of geological time, beginning 1.64 million years ago and ending 10,000 years ago. The polar ice caps were extensive and glaciers were abundant during the ice age of this period, and humans evolved into modern *Homo sapiens sapiens* about 100,000 years ago.

**Pliny the Elder** (c. AD 23–79) Gaius Plinius Secundus, Roman scientific encyclopedist and historian. Many of his works have been lost, but in *Historia naturalis/Natural History*, probably completed AD 77, Pliny surveys all the known sciences of his day, notably astronomy, meteorology, geography, mineralogy, zoology, and botany.

**Pliocene** ('almost recent') fifth and last epoch of the Tertiary period of geological time, 5.2–1.64 million years ago. The earliest hominid, the humanlike ape *Australopithecines*, evolved in Africa.

**Plutarch** (c. AD 46–c. 120) Greek biographer and essayist. He is best remembered for his *Lives*, a collection of short biographies of famous figures from Greek and Roman history arranged in contrasting pairs (for example, Alexander the Great and Julius Caesar are paired). He also wrote *Moralia*, a collection of essays on moral and social themes.

**Pluto** in astronomy, the smallest and, usually, outermost planet of the Solar System. The existence of Pluto was predicted by calculation by Percival Lowell and the planet was located by Clyde Tombaugh in 1930. Its highly elliptical orbit occasionally takes it within the orbit of Neptune, as in 1979–99. Pluto has a mass about 0.002 of that of Earth. **mean distance from the Sun:** 5.8 billion km/3.6 billion mi; **equatorial diameter:** 2,300 km/1,438 mi; **rotation period:** 6.39 Earth days; **year:** 248.5 Earth years; **atmosphere:** thin atmosphere with small amounts of methane gas; **surface:** low density, composed of rock and ice, primarily frozen methane; there is an ice cap at Pluto's north pole; **satellites:** one moon, Charon.

**Pluto** (or Hades) in Greek mythology, lord of →Hades, the underworld. His Roman counterpart was **Dis** (also Orcus). He was the son of the Titans Kronos and Rhea; and brother of Zeus, Poseidon, Hera, Hestia, and Demeter. He abducted and married Persephone, daughter of the goddess of agriculture Demeter, causing winter on Earth; Persephone was eventually allotted six months of each year in Hades, and six with her mother.

**plutonium** silvery-white, radioactive, metallic element of the actinide series, symbol Pu, atomic number 94, relative atomic mass 239.13. It occurs in nature in minute quantities in pitchblende and other ores, but is produced in quantity only synthetically. It has six allotropic forms (see →allotropy) and is one of three fissile elements (elements capable of splitting into other elements – the others are thorium and uranium). Plutonium dioxide, $PuO_2$, a yellow crystalline solid, is the compound most widely used in the nuclear industry. It was believed to be inert until US researchers discovered in 1999 that it reacts very slowly with oxygen and water to form a previously unknown green crystalline compound that is soluble in water.

**pneumonia** inflammation of the lungs, generally due to bacterial or viral infection but also to particulate matter or gases. It is characterized by a build-up of fluid in the alveoli, the clustered air sacs (at the ends of the air passages) where oxygen exchange takes place.

**Poe, Edgar Allan** (1809–1849) US writer and poet. His short stories are renowned for their horrific atmosphere, as in 'The Fall of the House of Usher' (1839) and 'The Masque of the Red Death' (1842), and for their acute reasoning (ratiocination), as in 'The Gold Bug' (1843) and 'The Murders in the Rue Morgue' (1841) (in which the investigators Legrand and Dupin anticipate Conan Doyle's Sherlock Holmes). His poems include 'The Raven' (1845). His novel *The Narrative of Arthur Gordon Pym of Nantucket* (1838) has attracted critical attention.

**poetry** the imaginative expression of emotion, thought, or narrative, frequently in metrical form and often using figurative language. Poetry has traditionally been distinguished from prose (ordinary written language) by rhyme or the rhythmical arrangement of words (metre), the employment of the line as a formal unit, heightened vocabulary, and freedom of syntax. Poetic images are presented using a variety of techniques, of which the most universal is the use of metaphor and simile to evoke a range of associations through implicit or explicit comparison. Although not frequently encountered in modern verse, alliteration has been used, chiefly for rhetoric or emphasis, in works dating back to Old English.

**Poland** Republic of; **national name:** *Rzeczpospolita Polska*; **area:** 312,683 sq km/120,726 sq mi; **capital:** Warsaw; **major towns/cities:** Łódź, Kraków (Cracow), Wrocław (Breslau), Poznań (Posen), Gdańsk (Danzig), Szczecin (Stettin), Katowice (Kattowitz), Bydgoszcz (Bromberg), Lublin; **major ports:** Gdańsk (Danzig), Szczecin (Stettin), Gdynia (Gdingen); **physical features:** part of the great plain of Europe; Vistula, Oder, and Neisse rivers; Sudeten, Tatra, and Carpathian mountains on southern frontier; **head of state:** Aleksander Kwaśniewski from 1995; **head of government:** Jerzy Buzek from 1997; **political system:** emergent democracy; **currency:** złoty; **GNP per capita (PPP):** (US$) 6,740 (1998); **exports:** machinery and transport equipment, textiles, chemicals, coal, coke, copper, sulphur, steel, food and agricultural products, clothing and leather products, wood and paper products. Principal market Germany 36% (1998); **population:** 38,741,000

(1999 est); **language:** Polish; **religion:** Roman Catholic 95%; **life expectancy:** 68 (men); 77 (women) (1995–2000).

**Polaris** (or Pole Star or North Star) bright star closest to the north celestial pole, and the brightest star in the constellation →Ursa Minor. Its position is indicated by the 'pointers' in →Ursa Major. Polaris is a yellow →supergiant about 500 light years away from the Sun. It is also known as **Alpha Ursae Minoris**.

**pole** either of the geographic north and south points of the axis about which the Earth rotates. The geographic poles differ from the magnetic poles, which are the points towards which a freely suspended magnetic needle will point.

**polio** (short for poliomyelitis) viral infection of the central nervous system affecting nerves that activate muscles. The disease used to be known as infantile paralysis since children were most often affected. Two kinds of vaccine are available, one injected and one given by mouth. The Americas were declared to be polio-free by the Pan American Health Organization in 1994. In 1997 the World Health Organization (WHO) reported that causes of polio had dropped by nearly 90% since 1988 when the organization began its programme to eradicate the disease by the year 2000. Most remaining cases were in Africa and southeast Asia in early 2000.

**pollen** the grains of seed plants that contain the male gametes. In →angiosperms (flowering plants) pollen is produced within anthers; in most →gymnosperms (cone-bearing plants) it is produced in male cones. A pollen grain is typically yellow and, when mature, has a hard outer wall. Pollen of insect-pollinated plants is often sticky and spiny and larger than the smooth, light grains produced by wind-pollinated species.

**Pollock, (Paul) Jackson** (1912–1956) US painter. He was a pioneer of abstract expressionism and one of the foremost exponents of action painting. His style is characterized by complex networks of swirling, interwoven lines of great delicacy and rhythmic subtlety.

**Polo, Marco** (1254–1324) Venetian traveller and writer. He joined his father (Niccolo) and uncle (Maffeo), who had travelled to China as merchants (1260–69), when they began a journey overland back to China (1271). Once there, he learned Mongolian and served the emperor Kubla Khan until he returned to Europe by sea 1292–95.

**Pol Pot** (c. 1925–1998) also known as Saloth Sar and Tol Saut, Cambodian politician and leader of the Khmer Rouge communist movement that overthrew the government in 1975. After widespread atrocities against the civilian population, his regime was deposed by a Vietnamese invasion in 1979. Pol Pot continued to help lead the Khmer Rouge despite officially resigning from all positions in 1989. He was captured in 1997 but escaped from Cambodia, reportedly to Thailand, in January 1998 to avoid facing an international court for his crimes against humanity. The Cambodian government announced mid-April 1998 that he had been captured inside Thailand. However, a few days later reports of Pol Pot's death were confirmed. He died following a heart attack, in a Cambodian village two miles from the Thai border.

**Polynesia** islands of Oceania east of 170° E latitude, including Hawaii, Kiribati, Tuvalu, Fiji Islands, Tonga, Tokelau, Samoa, Cook Islands, and French Polynesia.

**Pompeii** ancient city in Italy, near the volcano →Vesuvius, 21 km/13 mi southeast of Naples.

In AD 63 an earthquake destroyed much of the city, which had been a Roman port and pleasure resort; it was completely buried beneath volcanic ash when Vesuvius, a composite – and therefore explosive – volcano erupted in AD 79. Over 2,000 people were killed. Pompeii was rediscovered in 1748 and the systematic excavation begun in 1763 still continues.

**Pompey the Great** (106–48 BC) Gnaeus Pompeius Magnus, Roman soldier and politician. From 60 BC to 53 BC, he was a member of the First Triumvirate with Julius Caesar and Marcus Livius Crassus. Originally a supporter of Sulla, Pompey became consul with Crassus in 70 BC. He defeated Mithridates VI Eupator of Pontus, and annexed Syria and Palestine. He married Caesar's daughter Julia (died 54 BC) in 59 BC. When the Triumvirate broke down after 53 BC, Pompey was

drawn into leadership of the senatorial faction. On the outbreak of civil war 49 BC he withdrew to Greece, was defeated by Caesar at Pharsalus 48 BC, and was murdered in Egypt.

**pop art** movement in modern art that took its imagery from the glossy world of advertising and from popular culture such as comic strips, films, and television; it developed in the 1950s and flourished in the 1960s, notably in Britain and the USA. The term was coined by the British critic Lawrence Alloway (1926–1990) in about 1955, to refer to works of art that drew upon popular culture. Richard Hamilton, one of the leading British pioneers and exponents of pop art, defined it in 1957 as 'popular, transient, expendable, low-cost, mass-produced, young, witty, sexy, gimmicky, glamorous, and Big Business'. In its eclecticism and sense of irony and playfulness, pop art helped to prepare the way for the →postmodernism that has been a feature of Western culture since the 1970s.

**Pope, Alexander** (1688–1744) English poet and satirist. He established his poetic reputation with the precocious *Pastorals* (1709) and *An Essay on Criticism* (1711), which were followed by a parody of the heroic epic, *The Rape of the Lock* (1712–14), *The Temple of Fame* (1715), and 'Eloisa to Abelard' (1717). The highly neoclassical translations of Homer's *Iliad* and *Odyssey* (1715–26) were very successful but his edition of Shakespeare (1725) attracted scholarly ridicule, which led Pope to write a satire on scholarly dullness, *The*

*Dunciad* (1728). His finest mature works are his *Imitations of the Satires of Horace* (1733–38) and his personal letters.

**Popper, Karl Raimund** (1902–1994) British philosopher of science, who was born in Austria and became a naturalized British subject in 1945. His theory of falsificationism states that although scientific generalizations cannot be conclusively verified, they can be conclusively falsified by a counterinstance; therefore, science is not certain knowledge but a series of 'conjectures and refutations', approaching, though never reaching, a definitive truth. For Popper, psychoanalysis and Marxism are falsifiable and therefore unscientific.

**Port-of-Spain** port and capital of Trinidad and Tobago, on the island of Trinidad; population (1990) 58,400. It has a cathedral (1813–28) and the San Andres Fort (1785).

**Portugal** Republic of; **national name:** *República Portuguesa*; **area:** 92,000 sq km/35,521 sq mi (including the Azores and Madeira); **capital:** Lisbon; **major towns/cities:** Porto, Coimbra, Amadora, Setúbal, Guarde, Portalegre; **major ports:** Porto, Setúbal; **physical features:** mountainous in the north (Serra da Estrêla mountains); plains in the south; rivers Minho, Douro, Tagus (Tejo), Guadiana; **head of state:** Jorge Sampaio from 1996; **head of government:** Antonio Guterres from 1995; **political system:** democracy; **currency:** escudo; **GNP per capita (PPP):** (US\$) 14,380 (1998); **exports:** textiles, clothing, footwear, pulp and waste paper, wood and cork manufactures, tinned fish, electrical equipment, wine, refined petroleum. Principal market Germany 19.8% (1998); **population:** 9,873,000 (1999 est); **language:** Portuguese; **religion:** Roman Catholic 97%; **life expectancy:** 72 (men); 79 (women) (1995–2000).

**Portuguese man-of-war** any of a genus *Physalia* of phylum *Coelenterata* (see →coelenterate). They live in the sea, in colonies, and have a large air-filled bladder (or 'float') on top and numerous hanging tentacles made up of feeding, stinging, and reproductive individuals. The float can be 30 cm/1 ft long.

**Poseidon** (Roman Neptune) in Greek mythology, the chief god of the sea, brother of Zeus and Pluto. The brothers dethroned their father, Kronos, and divided his realm, Poseidon taking the sea. Husband of Amphitrite, his sons were the merman sea god Triton and the Cyclops Polyphemus.

**positivism** theory that confines genuine knowledge within the bounds of science and observation. The theory is associated with the French philosopher Auguste Comte and empiricism. **Logical positivism** developed in the 1920s. It rejected any metaphysical world beyond everyday science and common sense, and confined statements to those of formal logic or mathematics.

**post-Impressionism** broad term covering various developments in French painting that developed out of →Impressionism in the period from about 1880 to about 1905. Some of these developments built on the achievements of Impressionism, but others were reactions against its concentration on surface appearances, seeking to reintroduce a concern with emotional and symbolic values.

**postmodernism** late 20th-century movement in architecture and the arts that rejects the preoccupation of →modernism with purity of form and technique. Postmodernists use an amalgam of style elements from the past, such as the classical and the baroque, and apply them to spare modern forms, often with ironic effect. Their slightly off-key familiarity creates a more immediate appeal than the austerities of modernism. Exponents include the architects Robert Venturi and Michael Graves and the novelists David Lodge and Thomas Pynchon. In literary criticism and critical theory, postmodernism denotes a differently conceived resumption rather than a repudiation of modernist radicalism.

**potassium** (Dutch *potassa* 'potash') soft, waxlike, silver-white, metallic element, symbol K (Latin *kalium*), atomic number 19, relative atomic mass 39.0983. It is one of the alkali metals and has a very low density – it floats on water, and is the second lightest metal (after lithium). It oxidizes rapidly when exposed to air and reacts violently with water. Of great abundance in the Earth's crust, it is widely distributed with other elements and found in salt and mineral deposits

in the form of potassium aluminium silicates.

**potential difference** (pd) difference in the electrical potential (see →potential, electric) of two points, being equal to the electrical energy converted by a unit electric charge moving from one point to the other. The SI unit of potential difference is the volt (V). The potential difference between two points in a circuit is commonly referred to as voltage.

**potential, electric** in physics, the relative electrical state of an object. The potential at a point is equal to the energy required to bring a unit electric charge from infinity to the point. The SI unit of potential is the volt (V). Positive electric charges will flow 'downhill' from a region of high potential to a region of low potential.

**potential energy** (PE) in physics, →energy possessed by an object by virtue of its relative position or state (for example, as in a compressed spring or a muscle). It is contrasted with kinetic energy, the form of energy possessed by moving bodies. An object that has been raised up is described as having gravitational potential energy.

**Potter, (Helen) Beatrix** (1866–1943) English writer and illustrator of children's books. Her first book was *The Tale of Peter Rabbit* (1900), followed by *The Tailor of Gloucester* (1902), based on her observation of family pets and wildlife. Other books in the series include *The Tale of Mrs Tiggy-Winkle* (1904), *The Tale of Jeremy Fisher* (1906), and a sequel to Peter Rabbit, *The Tale of* *the Flopsy Bunnies* (1909). Her tales are told with a childlike wonder, devoid of sentimentality, and accompanied by delicate illustrations.

**pottery and porcelain** ceramics in domestic and ornamental use, including earthenware, stoneware, and bone china (or softpaste porcelain). Made of 5% bone ash and china clay, bone china was first made in the West in imitation of Chinese porcelain. The standard British bone china was developed about 1800, with a body of clay mixed with ox bones; a harder version, called parian, was developed in the 19th century and was used for figurine ornaments.

Hardpaste porcelain is characterized by its hardness, ringing sound when struck, translucence, and shining finish, like that of a cowrie shell (Italian *porcellana*). It is made of kaolin and petuntse (fusible feldspar consisting chiefly of silicates reduced to a fine white powder); it is high-fired at 1,400°C/2,552°F. Porcelain first evolved from stoneware in China in about the 6th century AD. A formula for making porcelain was developed in the 18th century in Germany, also in France, Italy, and Britain. It was first produced in the USA in the early 19th century.

**Pound, Ezra Loomis** (1885–1972) US poet and cultural critic. He is regarded as one of the most important figures of 20th-century literature, and his work revolutionized modern poetry. His *Personae* and *Exultations* (1909) established and promoted the principles of Imagism, and influenced numerous poets, including T S →Eliot. His largest work was his series of *Cantos* (1925–69), a highly complex, eclectic collage that sought to create a unifying, modern cultural tradition.

**power** in physics, the rate of doing work or consuming energy. It is measured in watts (joules per second) or other units of work per unit time.

**Prague** (Czech *Praha*) city and capital of the Czech Republic on the River Vltava; population (1993) 1,217,300. Industries include cars, aircraft, chemicals, paper and printing, clothing, brewing, and food processing. It was the capital of Czechoslovakia 1918–93.

**Prague Spring** the 1968 programme of liberalization, begun under a new Communist Party leader in Czechoslovakia. In August 1968 Soviet tanks invaded Czechoslovakia and entered the capital Prague to put down the liberalization movement initiated by the prime minister Alexander Dubček, who had earlier sought to assure the Soviets that his planned reforms would not threaten socialism. Dubček was arrested but released soon afterwards. Most of the Prague Spring reforms were reversed.

**Precambrian** in geology, the time from the formation of Earth (4.6 billion years ago) up to 570 million years ago. Its boundary with the succeeding Cambrian period marks the time when animals first developed hard outer parts (exoskeletons) and so left abundant fossil remains. It comprises about 85% of geological time and is divided into two periods: the Archaean, in which no life existed, and the Proterozoic, in which there was life in some form.

**precession** slow wobble of the Earth on its axis, like that of a spinning top. The gravitational pulls of the Sun and Moon on the Earth's equatorial bulge cause the Earth's axis to trace out a circle on the sky every 25,800 years. The position of the celestial poles is constantly changing owing to precession, as are the positions of the equinoxes (the points at which the celestial equator intersects the Sun's path around the sky). The **precession of the equinoxes** means that there is a gradual westward drift in the ecliptic – the path that the Sun appears to follow – and in the coordinates of objects on the celestial sphere.

**precipitation** in chemistry, the formation of an insoluble solid in a liquid as a result of a reaction within the liquid between two or more soluble substances. If the solid settles, it forms a precipitate; if the particles of solid are very small, they will remain in suspension, forming a colloidal precipitate.

**pregnancy** in humans, the process during which a developing embryo grows within the woman's womb. It begins at conception and ends at birth, and the normal length is 40 weeks, or around nine months.

**prehistory** human cultures before the use of writing. The study of prehistory is mainly dependent on archaeology. General chronological dividing lines between prehistoric eras, or history and

prehistory, are difficult to determine because communities have developed at differing rates. The Three Age System of classification (published in 1836 by the Danish archaeologist Christian Thomsen) is based on the predominant materials used by early humans for tools and weapons: →Stone Age, →Bronze Age, and →Iron Age.

**premenstrual tension** (PMT or premenstrual syndrome) medical condition caused by hormone changes and comprising a number of physical and emotional features that occur cyclically before menstruation and disappear with its onset. Symptoms include mood changes, breast tenderness, a feeling of bloatedness, and headache.

**Pre-Raphaelite Brotherhood** (PRB) group of British painters (1848–53); Dante Gabriel →Rossetti, John Everett →Millais, and Holman Hunt – at this time young students at the Royal Academy – were the leading figures among the seven founders. They aimed to paint serious subjects, to study nature closely, and to return to the sincerity of spirit of painters before the time of Raphael Sanzio (1483–1520). Their subjects were mainly biblical and literary, painted with obsessive naturalism and attention to detail. The group was short-lived but added a new realism to the art of the 1850s, and influenced many painters.

In his later work only Hunt remained true to Pre-Raphaelite ideals, but the name stuck to Rossetti, the least committed of the original group, and was applied to his later dreamily romantic pictures, although these had moved away from the movement's founding ideas. There was a 'second wave' of Pre-Raphaelitism in the late 19th century, stimulated by Ruskin and Rossetti, and associated with the revival of handicrafts and the art of design. William Morris and Edward Burne-Jones were among the many artists influenced at this time.

**Presbyterianism** system of Christian Protestant church government that was expounded during the Reformation by John Calvin in Geneva, Switzerland, which gives its name to the established Church of Scotland, and is also practised in England, Wales, Ireland, Switzerland, North America, and elsewhere. There is no compulsory form of worship and each congregation is governed by presbyters or elders (clerical or lay), who are of equal rank. Congregations are grouped in presbyteries, synods, and general assemblies.

**Presley, Elvis Aron** (1935–1977) US singer and guitarist, the most influential performer of the rock-and-roll era. With his recordings for Sun Records in Memphis, Tennessee, 1954–55, and early hits such as 'Heartbreak Hotel', 'Hound Dog' and 'Love Me Tender' (all 1956), he created an individual vocal style, influenced by Southern blues, gospel music, country music, and rhythm and blues. His records continue to sell in their millions.

**Priestley, J(ohn) B(oynton)** (1894–1984) English novelist and dramatist. His first success was a novel about

travelling theatre, *The Good Companions* (1929). He followed it with a realist novel about London life, *Angel Pavement* (1930). His career as a dramatist began with *Dangerous Corner* (1932), one of several plays in which time is a preoccupation. His best-known plays are the enigmatic *An Inspector Calls* (1945) and *The Linden Tree* (1948), a study of postwar social issues.

**primate** in zoology, any member of the order of mammals that includes monkeys, apes, and humans (together called anthropoids), as well as lemurs, bushbabies, lorises, and tarsiers (together called prosimians).

Generally, they have forward-directed eyes, gripping hands and feet, opposable thumbs, and big toes. They tend to have nails rather than claws, with gripping pads on the ends of the digits, all adaptations to the arboreal, climbing mode of life.

**prime number** number that can be divided only by 1 and itself, that is, having no other factors. There is an infinite number of primes, the first ten of which are 2, 3, 5, 7, 11, 13, 17, 19, 23, and 29 (by definition, the number 1 is excluded from the set of prime numbers). The number 2 is the only even prime because all other even numbers have 2 as a factor.

**printed circuit board** (PCB) electrical circuit created by laying (printing) 'tracks' of a conductor such as copper on one or both sides of an insulating board. The PCB was invented in 1936 by Austrian scientist Paul Eisler, and was first used on a large scale in 1948.

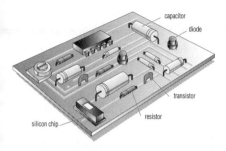

**printed circuit board** A typical microcomputer printed circuit board (PCB). The PCB contains sockets for the integrated circuits, or chips, and the connecting tracks.

capacitor

diode

transistor

resistor

silicon chip

**printmaking** creating a picture or design by printing from a plate (woodblock, stone, or metal sheet) that holds ink or colour. The oldest form of print is the woodcut, common in medieval Europe, followed by line engraving (from the 15th century), and etching (from the 17th century); coloured woodblock prints flourished in Japan from the 18th century. →Lithography was invented in 1796.

**prism** in optics, a triangular block of transparent material (plastic, glass, silica) commonly used to 'bend' a ray of light or split a beam into its spectral colours. Prisms are used as mirrors to define the optical path in binoculars, camera viewfinders, and periscopes. The dispersive property of prisms is used in the →spectroscope.

**probability** likelihood, or chance, that an event will occur, often expressed as odds, or in mathematics, numerically as a fraction or decimal.

In general, the probability that $n$ particular events will happen out of a total of $m$ possible events is $n/m$. A certainty has a probability of 1; an impossibility has a probability of 0. Empirical probability is defined as the number of successful events divided by the total possible number of events.

**progesterone** steroid hormone that occurs in vertebrates. In mammals, it regulates the menstrual cycle and pregnancy. Progesterone is secreted by the corpus luteum (the ruptured Graafian follicle of a discharged ovum).

**programming language** in computing, a special notation in which instructions for controlling a computer are written. Programming languages are designed to be easy for people to write and read, but must be capable of being mechanically translated (by a compiler or an interpreter) into the machine code that the computer can execute. Programming languages may be classified as high-level languages or low-level languages.

**Prohibition** in US history, the period 1920–33 when the 18th Amendment to the US Constitution was in force, and the manufacture, transportation, and sale of alcohol was illegal. This led to bootlegging (the illegal distribution of liquor, often illicitly distilled), to the financial advantage of organized crime.

**prokaryote** in biology, an organism whose cells lack organelles (specialized segregated structures such as nuclei, mitochondria, and chloroplasts). Prokaryote DNA is not arranged in chromosomes but forms a coiled structure called a nucleoid. The prokaryotes comprise only the bacteria and cyanobacteria (see →blue-green algae); all other organisms are eukaryotes.

**Prokofiev, Sergey Sergeyevich** (1891–1953) Russian composer. His music includes operas such as *The Love for Three Oranges* (1921); ballets for Sergei Diaghilev, including *Romeo and Juliet* (1935); seven symphonies including the *Classical Symphony* (1916–17); music for film, including Eisenstein's *Alexander Nevsky* (1938); piano and violin concertos; songs and cantatas (for example, that composed for the 30th anniversary of the October Revolution); and *Peter and the Wolf* (1936) for children, to his own libretto after a Russian folk tale.

**propeller** screwlike device used to propel some ships and aeroplanes. A propeller has a number of curved blades that describe a helical path as they rotate with the hub, and accelerate fluid (liquid or gas) backwards during rotation. Reaction to this backward movement of fluid sets up a propulsive thrust forwards. The marine screw propeller

was developed by Francis Pettit Smith in the UK and Swedish-born John Ericson in the USA and was first used in 1839.

**prostaglandin** any of a group of complex fatty acids present in the body that act as messenger substances between cells. Effects include stimulating the contraction of smooth muscle (for example, of the womb during birth), regulating the production of stomach acid, and modifying hormonal activity. In excess, prostaglandins may produce inflammatory disorders such as arthritis. Synthetic prostaglandins are used to induce labour in humans and domestic animals.

**prostate gland** gland surrounding and opening into the urethra at the base of the →bladder in male mammals.

**protein** complex, biologically important substance composed of amino acids joined by →peptide bonds. Proteins are essential to all living organisms. As →enzymes they regulate all aspects of metabolism. Structural proteins such as keratin and collagen make up the skin, claws, bones, tendons, and ligaments; muscle proteins produce movement; haemoglobin transports oxygen; and membrane proteins regulate the movement of substances into and out of cells. For humans, protein is an essential part of the diet, and is found in greatest quantity in soybeans and other grain legumes, meat, eggs, and cheese.

**Proterozoic** eon of geological time, 3.5 billion to 570 million years ago, the second division of the Precambrian. It is defined as the time of simple life, since many rocks dating from this eon show traces of biological activity, and some contain the fossils of bacteria and algae.

**Protestantism** one of the main divisions of Christianity, which emerged from Roman Catholicism at the →Reformation. The chief denominations are the Anglican Communion (Church of England in the UK and Episcopal Church in the USA), Baptists, Christian Scientists, Congregationalists (United Church of Christ), Lutherans, Methodists, Pentecostals, and Presbyterians, with a total membership of about 300 million.

**protist** in biology, a single-celled organism which has a eukaryotic cell, but which is not a member of the plant, fungal, or animal kingdoms. The main protists are →protozoa.

**protozoa** group of single-celled organisms without rigid cell walls. Some, such as amoeba, ingest other cells, but most are saprotrophs or parasites. The group is polyphyletic (containing organisms which have different evolutionary origins).

**Proust, Marcel** (1871–1922) French novelist and critic. His immense autobiographical work *A la Recherche du temps perdu/Remembrance of Things Past* (1913–27) consisting of a series of novels, is the expression of his childhood memories coaxed from his subconscious; it is also a precise reflection of life in France at the end of the 19th century.

**Prussia** northern German state 1618–1945 on the Baltic coast. It was an independent kingdom until 1867, when it became, under Otto von →Bismarck, the military power of the North German Confederation and part of the German Empire 1871 under the Prussian king Wilhelm I. West Prussia became part of Poland under the Treaty of Versailles, and East Prussia was largely incorporated into the USSR after 1945.

**pseudocarp** in botany, a fruitlike structure that incorporates tissue that is not derived from the ovary wall. The additional tissues may be derived from floral parts such as the receptacle and →calyx. For example, the coloured, fleshy part of a strawberry develops from the receptacle and the true fruits are small achenes – the 'pips' embedded in its outer surface. Rose hips are a type of pseudocarp that consists of a hollow, fleshy receptacle containing a number of achenes within. Different types of pseudocarp include pineapples, figs, apples, and pears.

**psoriasis** chronic, recurring skin disease characterized by raised, red, scaly patches, on the scalp, elbows, knees, and elsewhere. Tar preparations, steroid creams, and ultraviolet light are used to treat it, and sometimes it disappears spontaneously. Psoriasis may be accompanied by a form of arthritis (inflammation of the joints). Psoriasis affects 100 million people worldwide.

**psychiatry** branch of medicine dealing with the diagnosis and treatment of mental disorder, normally divided into the areas of **neurotic conditions**, including anxiety, depression, and hysteria, and **psychotic disorders**, such as schizophrenia. Psychiatric treatment consists of drugs, analysis, or electro-convulsive therapy.

**psychoanalysis** theory and treatment method for neuroses, developed by →Sigmund Freud in the 1890s. Psychoanalysis asserts that the impact of early childhood sexuality and experiences, stored in the unconscious, can lead to the development of adult emotional problems. The main treatment method involves the free association of ideas, and their interpretation by patient and analyst, in order to discover these long-buried events and to grasp their significance to the patient, linking aspects of the patient's historical past with the present relationship to the analyst. Psychoanalytic treatment aims to free the patient from specific symptoms and from irrational inhibitions and anxieties.

**psychology** systematic study of human and animal behaviour. The first psychology laboratory was founded in 1879 by Wilhelm Wundt at Leipzig, Germany. The subject includes diverse areas of study and application, among them the roles of instinct, heredity, environment, and culture; the processes of sensation, perception, learning, and memory; the bases of motivation and emotion; and the functioning of thought, intelligence, and language. Significant psychologists have included Gustav Fechner, founder of psychophysics; Wolfgang Köhler, one of the Gestalt or 'whole' psychologists; Sigmund Freud and his associates Carl Jung and Alfred Adler; William James, Jean Piaget; Carl Rogers; Hans Eysenck; J B Watson; and B F Skinner.

**psychotherapy** any treatment for psychological problems that involves talking rather than surgery or drugs. Examples include cognitive therapy and →psychoanalysis.

**Ptolemy** (c. AD 100–c. AD 170) Claudius Ptolemaeus, Egyptian astronomer and geographer. His *Almagest* developed the theory that Earth is the centre of the universe, with the Sun, Moon, and stars revolving around it. In 1543 the Polish astronomer →Copernicus proposed an alternative to the Ptolemaic system. Ptolemy's *Geography* was a standard source of information until the 16th century.

**Puccini, Giacomo (Antonio Domenico Michele Secondo Maria)** (1858–1924) Italian opera composer. His music shows a strong gift for melody and dramatic effect and his operas combine exotic plots with elements of *verismo* (realism). They include *Manon Lescaut* (1893), *La Bohème* (1896), *Tosca* (1900), *Madam Butterfly* (1904), and the unfinished *Turandot* (1926).

**Puerto Rico** the Commonwealth of: easternmost island of the Greater Antilles, situated between the US Virgin Islands and the Dominican Republic. Residents are US citizens, represented in US Congress by an elected Resident Commissioner with a seat in the House of Representatives. **area:** 9,000 sq km

3,475 sq mi; **capital:** San Juan; **towns and cities:** ports Mayagüez, Ponce; **features:** volcanic mountains run east–west; the islands of Vieques and Culebra belong to Puerto Rico; **exports:** sugar, tobacco, rum, pineapples, textiles, plastics, chemicals, processed foods, vegetables, coffee; **currency:** US dollar; **population:** (1992 est) 3,336,000; **language:** Spanish and English (official); **religion:** Roman Catholic; **history:** visited in 1493 by Columbus; annexed by Spain in 1509; ceded to the USA after the Spanish-American War in 1898; known as **Porto Rico** ('Rich Port') 1898–1932; achieved commonwealth status with local self-government in 1952.

**Pugin, Augustus Welby Northmore** (1812–1852) English architect and designer. He collaborated with Charles Barry in the detailed design of the New Palace of Westminster (Houses of Parliament). He did much to instigate the Gothic Revival in England, largely through his books *Contrasts: or a Parallel between the Architecture of the 15th and 19th Centuries* (1836) and *Gothic Ornaments from Ancient Buildings in England and France* (1828–31).

**pulley** simple machine consisting of a fixed, grooved wheel, sometimes in a block, around which a rope or chain can be run. A simple pulley serves only to change the direction of the applied effort (as in a simple hoist for raising loads). The use of more than one pulley results in a mechanical advantage, so that a given effort can raise a heavier load.

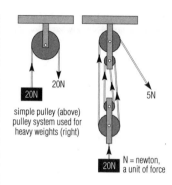

simple pulley (above)
pulley system used for heavy weights (right)

20N

20N

5N

20N    N = newton, a unit of force

**pulley** The mechanical advantage of a pulley increases with the number of rope strands. If a pulley system has four ropes supporting the load, the mechanical advantage is four, and a 5 newton force will lift a 20 newton load.

**pulsar** celestial source that emits pulses of energy at regular intervals, ranging from a few seconds to a few thousandths of a second. Pulsars are thought to be rapidly rotating →neutron stars, which flash at radio and other wavelengths as they spin. They were discovered in 1967 by Jocelyn Bell-Burnell and Antony Hewish at the Mullard Radio Astronomy Observatory, Cambridge, England. By 1998 1,000 pulsars had been discovered since the initial identification in 1967.

**Punic Wars** three wars between →Rome and →Carthage: **First Punic War** 264–241 BC, resulted in the defeat of the Carthaginians under Hamilcar Barca and the cession of Sicily to Rome;

**Second Punic War** 218–201 BC, Hannibal invaded Italy, defeated the Romans at Trebia, Trasimene, and at Cannae (under Fabius Maximus), but was finally defeated himself by Scipio Africanus Major at Zama (now in Algeria); **Third Punic War** 149–146 BC, ended in the destruction of Carthage, and its possessions becoming the Roman province of Africa.

**Punjab** (Sanskrit 'five rivers': the Indus tributaries Jhelum, Chenab, Ravi, Beas, and Sutlej) former state of British India, now divided between India and Pakistan. Punjab was annexed by Britain 1849 after the Sikh Wars (1845–46 and 1848–49), and formed into a province with its capital at Lahore. Under the British, West Punjab was extensively irrigated, and land was granted to Indians who had served in the British army.

**Punjab massacres** in the violence occurring after the partition of India 1947, more than a million people died while relocating in the Punjab. The eastern section became an Indian state, while the western area, dominated by the Muslims, went to Pakistan. Violence occurred as Muslims fled from eastern Punjab, and Hindus and Sikhs moved from Pakistan to India.

**pupa** nonfeeding, largely immobile stage of some insect life cycles, in which larval tissues are broken down, and adult tissues and structures are formed.

**Purcell, Henry** (c. 1659–1695) English baroque composer. His music balances high formality with melodic expression of controlled intensity, for example, the opera *Dido and Aeneas* (1689) and music for Dryden's *King Arthur* (1691) and for *The Fairy Queen* (1692). He wrote more than 500 works, ranging from secular operas and incidental music for plays to cantatas and church music.

---

### WEB SITE > > > > > > > >
**Purcell, Henry**

http://portico.bl.uk/exhibitions/purcell/overview.html

Audio clip of funeral march composed by Purcell, and images of the manuscripts displayed by the British library on the 300th anniversary of his death, including a page from a newly discovered volume of music composed by him.

---

**Puritan** from 1564, a member of the Church of England who wished to eliminate Roman Catholic survivals in church ritual, or substitute a presbyterian for an episcopal form of church government. The term also covers the separatists who withdrew from the church altogether.

**Pushkin, Aleksandr Sergeyevich** (1799–1837) Russian poet and writer. His works include the novel in verse *Eugene Onegin* (1823–31) and the tragic drama *Boris Godunov* (1825). Pushkin's range was wide, and his willingness to experiment freed later Russian writers from many of the archaic conventions of the literature of his time.

**pyramid** four-sided building with tri-angular sides. Pyramids were used in ancient Egypt to enclose a royal tomb; for example, the Great Pyramid of Khufu/Cheops at El Gîza, near Cairo, 230 m/755 ft square and 147 m/481 ft high. The three pyramids at Gîza were considered one of the →Seven Wonders of the World. In Babylon and Assyria, broadly stepped pyramids (ziggurats) were used as the base for a shrine to a god: the Tower of Babel was probably one of these.

**Pyrenees** (French *Pyrénées*; Spanish *Pirineos*) mountain range in southwest Europe between France and Spain; length about 435 km/270 mi; highest peak Aneto (French *Néthon*) 3,404 m/11,172 ft. Andorra lies entirely within the range. Hydroelectric power has encouraged industrial development in the foothills.

**Pythagoras** (*c.* 580–500 BC) Greek mathematician and philosopher who formulated →Pythagoras' theorem.

**Pythagoras' theorem** in geometry, a theorem stating that in a right-angled

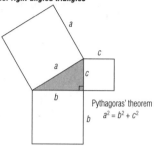

*for right-angled triangles*

Pythagoras' theorem
$$a^2 = b^2 + c^2$$

**Pythagoras' theorem** Pythagoras' theorem for right-angled triangles is likely to have been known long before the time of Pythagoras. It was probably used by the ancient Egyptians to lay out the pyramids.

triangle, the area of the square on the hypotenuse (the longest side) is equal to the sum of the areas of the squares drawn on the other two sides. If the hypotenuse is $a$ units long and the lengths of the other sides are $b$ and $c$, then $a^2 = b^2 + c^2$.

# Qq

**Qatar** State of; **national name:** *Dawlat Qatar*; **area:** 11,400 sq km/4,401 sq mi; **capital:** Doha (and chief port); **major towns/cities:** Dukhan, centre of oil production; Halul, terminal for offshore oilfields; Umm Said, Ruwais, Wakra, Al-Khour; **physical features:** mostly flat desert with salt flats in south; **head of state and government:** Sheikh Hamad bin Khalifa al-Thani from 1995; **political system:** absolute monarchy; **currency:** Qatari riyal; **GNP per capita (PPP):** (US\$) 20,100 (1997 est); **exports:** petroleum. Principal market Japan 49.7% (1997); **population:** 589,000 (1999 est); **language:** Arabic (official); English; **religion:** Sunni Muslim; **life expectancy:** 70 (men); 75 (women) (1995–2000).

**Quaker** popular name, originally derogatory, for a member of the Society of Friends.

**quantum theory** (or quantum mechanics) in physics, the theory that →energy does not have a continuous range of values, but is, instead, absorbed or radiated discontinuously, in multiples of definite, indivisible units called quanta. Just as earlier theory showed how light, generally seen as a wave motion, could also in some ways be seen as composed of discrete particles, quantum theory shows how atomic particles such as electrons may also be seen as having wavelike properties. Quantum theory is the basis of particle physics, modern theoretical chemistry, and the solid-state physics that describes the behaviour of the silicon chips used in computers.

**quark** in physics, the →elementary particle that is the fundamental constituent of all hadrons (subatomic particle that experiences the strong nuclear force and divided into baryons, such as neutrons and protons, and mesons). Quarks have electric charges that are fractions of the electronic charge (+2/3 or –1/3 of the electronic charge). There are six types, or 'flavours': up, down, top, bottom, strange, and charmed, each of which has three varieties, or 'colours': red, green, and blue (visual colour is not meant, although the analogy is useful in many ways). To each quark there is an antiparticle, called an antiquark.

**quartz** crystalline form of silica $SiO_2$, one of the most abundant minerals of the Earth's crust (12% by volume). Quartz occurs in many different kinds of rock, including sandstone and granite. It ranks 7 on the Mohs scale of hardness and is resistant to chemical or mechanical breakdown. Quartzes vary according to the size and purity of their crystals. Crystals of pure quartz are coarse, colourless, transparent, show no cleavage, and fracture unevenly; this form is usually called rock crystal. Impure coloured varieties, often used as gemstones, include →agate, citrine quartz, and →amethyst. Quartz is also used as a general name for the cryptocrystalline and noncrystalline varieties of silica, such as chalcedony, chert, and opal.

Quartz is used in ornamental work and industry, where its reaction to electricity makes it valuable in electronic instruments (see →piezoelectric effect). Quartz can also be made synthetically.

**quasar** (from 'quasi-stellar object' or QSO) one of the most distant extragalactic objects known, discovered in 1963. Quasars appear starlike, but each emits more energy than 100 giant galaxies. They are thought to be at the centre of galaxies, their brilliance emanating from the stars and gas falling towards an immense →black hole at their nucleus. Most quasars are found in elliptical galaxies.

**Quaternary** period of geological time that began 1.64 million years ago and is still in process. It is divided into the →Pleistocene and →Holocene epochs.

**Québec** (Iroquois *Kebec*, 'a place where waters narrow') capital and port of Québec province, Canada, at the junction of the Saint-Charles and St Lawrence rivers, Canada; population (1991) 167,500, metropolitan area (1996) 697,600. It is a major inland seaport, and a commercial, financial, and administrative centre. Industries include printing and publishing; and the production of paper, pulp, wood products, electronic goods, textiles, and leather. Lumber and wheat are exported. It is a centre of French culture, and most of its inhabitants are French-speaking.

**Queensland** state in northeast Australia, including the adjacent islands in the Pacific Ocean and in the Gulf of Carpentaria; bordered on the west by Northern Territory, on the southwest by South Australia, on the south by New South Wales, on the east by the Pacific Ocean, and on the extreme northwest by the Gulf of Carpentaria. **area:** 1,727,200 sq km/666,699 sq mi; **capital:** Brisbane; **towns and cities:** Toowoomba, Townsville, Cairns, Rockhampton, Bundaberg, Mackay, Ipswich, Maryborough; **features:** second-largest of the Australian states; Great Dividing Range; Great Barrier Reef (collection of coral reefs and islands about 2,000 km/1,250 mi long, off the east coast); Mount Isa mining area; Gold Coast, south of Brisbane; Sunshine Coast, north of Brisbane; **products:** sugar, wheat, pineapples, beef, cotton, wool, tobacco, copper, gold, silver, lead, zinc, coal, nickel, bauxite, uranium, natural gas, oil, fish; **population:** (1996) 3,368,850, concentrated in the southeast; **history:** visited by Captain Cook in 1770; first settlement a penal colony at Moreton Bay in 1824; opened to free settlers in 1842; part of New South Wales from 1788 to 1859, when it became self-governing.

# Rr

**Rabat** capital and industrial port of Morocco, on the Atlantic coast, 177 km/110 mi west of Fès; population (urban area, 1991) 519,000; Rabat-Salé 1,494,000. It is situated on the Bou Regreg River, opposite Salé. Industries include textiles, asbestos, carpets, pottery, leather goods, fishing; other exports include skins, wax, cork, slippers, and beans. Founded in 1190, it is named after its original *ribat* or fortified monastery.

**Rabelais, François** (c. 1495–1553) French satirist, monk, and physician. His name has become synonymous with bawdy humour. He was educated in the humanist tradition and was the author of satirical allegories, including a cycle known as Gargantua and Pantagruel which included *La Vie estimable du grand Gargantua, père de Pantagruel*/*The Inestimable Life of the Great Gargantua, Father of Pantagruel*, the first to be written, but published in 1534, two years after *Les Horribles et épouvantables Faits et prouesses du très renommé Pantagruel*/*The Horrible and Dreadful Deeds and Prowess of the Very Renowned Pantagruel* (1532).

**rabies** (or hydrophobia, Greek 'fear of water') viral disease of the central nervous system that can afflict all warm-blooded creatures. It is caused by a lyssavirus. It is almost invariably fatal once symptoms have developed. Its transmission to humans is generally by a bite from an infected animal. Rabies continues to kill hundreds of thousands of people every year; almost all these deaths occur in Asia, Africa, and South America.

**Rabin, Yitzhak** (1922–1995) Israeli Labour politician, prime minister 1974–77 and 1992–95. As a former soldier, he was a national hero in the Arab-Israeli Wars. His policy of favouring Palestinian self-government in the occupied territories contributed to the success of the centre-left party in the 1992 elections. In September 1993 he signed a historic peace agreement with the Palestinian Liberation Organization (PLO), providing for a phased withdrawal of Israeli forces. He was awarded the 1994 Nobel Prize for Peace jointly with Israeli foreign minister Shimon Peres and PLO leader Yassir Arafat. He was shot and killed by a young Israeli extremist while attending a peace rally in Tel Aviv in November 1995.

**Rachmaninov, Sergei Vasilevich** (1873–1943) Russian composer, conductor, and pianist. After the 1917 Revolution he emigrated to the USA.

His music is melodious and emotional and includes operas, such as *Francesca da Rimini* (1906), three symphonies, four piano concertos, piano pieces, and songs. Among his other works are the *Prelude in C-Sharp Minor* (1892) and *Rhapsody on a Theme of Paganini* (1934) for piano and orchestra.

**radar astronomy** bouncing of radio waves off objects in the Solar System, with reception and analysis of the 'echoes'. Radar contact with the Moon was first made in 1945 and with Venus in 1961. The travel time for radio reflections allows the distances of objects to be determined accurately. Analysis of the reflected beam reveals the rotation period and allows the object's surface to be mapped. The rotation periods of Venus and Mercury were first determined by radar. Radar maps of Venus were obtained first by Earth-based radar and subsequently by orbiting space probes.

**radiation** in physics, emission of radiant →energy as particles or waves – for example, heat, light, alpha particles, and beta particles (see →electromagnetic waves and →radioactivity).

**radio** transmission and reception of radio waves. In radio transmission a microphone converts sound waves (pressure variations in the air) into →electromagnetic waves that are then picked up by a receiving aerial and fed to a loudspeaker, which converts them back into sound waves.

**radioactivity** spontaneous alteration of the nuclei of radioactive atoms,

accompanied by the emission of radiation. It is the property exhibited by the radioactive →isotopes of stable elements and all isotopes of radioactive elements, and can be either natural or induced.

---

**WEB SITE** > > > > > > > >

**Radiation and Radioactivity**

http://www.iso.utah.edu/train/cover.htm

Online tutorial on the basics of this subject of study. The sections covered include 'The atom', 'Half-life', and 'Measures of radiation and radioactivity'.

---

**radio astronomy** study of radio waves emitted naturally by objects in space, by means of a radio telescope. Radio emission comes from hot gases (thermal radiation); electrons spiralling in magnetic fields (synchrotron radiation); and specific wavelengths (lines) emitted by atoms and molecules in space, such as the 21-cm/8.3-in line emitted by hydrogen gas.

**radiocarbon dating** (or carbon dating) method of dating organic materials (for example, bone or wood), used in archaeology. Plants take up carbon dioxide gas from the atmosphere and incorporate it into their tissues, and some of that carbon dioxide contains the radioactive isotope of carbon, $^{14}C$ or carbon-14. As this decays at a known rate (half of it decays every 5,730 years), the time elapsed since the plant died can be measured in a laboratory. Animals take carbon-14 into their bodies from eating plant tissues and their remains can be similarly dated. After

120,000 years so little carbon-14 is left that no measure is possible (see →half-life).

**radiography** branch of science concerned with the use of radiation (particularly →X-rays) to produce images on photographic film or fluorescent screens. X-rays penetrate matter according to its nature, density, and thickness. In doing so they can cast shadows on photographic film, producing a radiograph. Radiography is widely used in medicine for examining bones and tissues and in industry for examining solid materials; for example, to check welded seams in pipelines.

**radioisotope** (contraction of radioactive isotope) in physics, a naturally occurring or synthetic radioactive form of an element. Most radioisotopes are made by bombarding a stable element with neutrons in the core of a nuclear reactor. The radiations given off by radioisotopes are easy to detect (hence their use as tracers), can in some instances penetrate substantial thicknesses of materials, and have profound effects (such as genetic →mutation) on living matter.

**radiotherapy** treatment of disease by →radiation from X-ray machines or radioactive sources. Radiation, which reduces the activity of dividing cells, is of special value for its effect on malignant tissues, certain nonmalignant tumours, and some diseases of the skin.

**radium** (Latin *radius* 'ray') white, radioactive, metallic element, symbol Ra, atomic number 88, relative atomic mass 226.02. It is one of the alkaline-earth metals, found in nature in pitchblende and other uranium ores. Of the 16 isotopes, the commonest, Ra-226, has a half-life of 1,620 years. The element was discovered and named in 1898 by Pierre and Marie →Curie, who were investigating the residues of pitchblende.

**rafflesia** (or stinking corpse lily) any of a group of parasitic plants without stems, native to Malaysia, Indonesia, and Thailand. There are 14 species, several of which are endangered by the destruction of the forests where they grow. The fruit is used locally for medicine. The largest flowers in the world are produced by *R. arnoldiana*. About 1 m/3 ft across, they exude a smell of rotting flesh, which attracts flies to pollinate them. (Genus *Rafflesia*, family Rafflesiaceae.)

**railway** method of transport in which trains convey passengers and goods along a twin rail track. Following the work of British steam pioneers such as the Scottish engineer James →Watt, the English engineer George →Stephenson built the first public steam railway, from Stockton to Darlington, England, in 1825. This heralded extensive railway building in Britain, continental Europe, and North America, providing a fast and economical means of transport and communication. After World War II, steam engines were replaced by electric and diesel engines. At the same time, the growth of road building, air services, and car ownership brought to an end the supremacy of the railways.

**rainforest** dense forest usually found on or near the →Equator where the climate is hot and wet. Moist air brought by the converging tradewinds rises because of the heat producing heavy rainfall. Over half the tropical rainforests are in Central and South America, primarily the lower Amazon and the coasts of Ecuador and Columbia. The rest are in Southeast Asia (Malaysia, Indonesia, and New Guinea) and in West Africa and the Congo.

Tropical rainforest once covered 14% of the Earth's land surface, but is now being destroyed at an increasing rate as valuable timber is harvested and the land cleared for agriculture, causing problems of →deforestation. Although by 1991 over 50% of the world's rainforest had been removed, they still comprise about 50% of all growing wood on the planet, and harbour at least 40% of the Earth's species (plants and animals).

**Raleigh, Walter** (*c.* 1552–1618) (or Ralegh) English adventurer, writer, and courtier to Queen Elizabeth I. He organized expeditions to colonize North America 1584–87, all unsuccessful, and made exploratory voyages to South America 1595 and 1616. His aggressive actions against Spanish interests, including attacks on Spanish ports, brought him into conflict with the pacific James I. He was imprisoned for treason 1603–16 and executed on his return from an unsuccessful final expedition to South America. He is traditionally credited with introducing the potato to Europe and popularizing the use of tobacco.

**Rama** incarnation of →Vishnu, the supreme spirit of Hinduism. He is the hero of the epic poem the *Rāmāyana*, and he is regarded as an example of morality and virtue.

**Ramadan** in the Muslim calendar, the ninth month of the year. Throughout Ramadan a strict fast is observed during the hours of daylight; Muslims are encouraged to read the whole Koran in commemoration of the Night of Power (which falls during the month) when, it is believed, Muhammad first received his revelations from the angel Gabriel.

**Rambert, Marie** (1888–1982) adopted name of Cyvia Myriam Rambam, Polish-born British ballet dancer and teacher. One of the major innovative and influential figures in modern ballet, she worked with Vaslav Nijinsky on *The Rite of Spring* for the Diaghilev ballet in Paris 1912–13, opened the Rambert School in London in 1920, and in 1926 founded the Ballet Rambert which she directed. It became a modern-dance company from 1966 and was renamed the Rambert Dance Company in 1987. Rambert became a British citizen in 1918. She was created a DBE in 1962.

**Rangoon** former name (to 1989) of Yangon, the capital of Myanmar (Burma).

**Rasputin** (1871–1916) Russian 'dissolute'; born Grigory Efimovich Novykh, Siberian Eastern Orthodox mystic. He acquired influence over the Tsarina Alexandra, wife of →Nicholas II, and was able to make political and ecclesiastical appointments. His abuse of power and notorious debauchery (reputedly including the tsarina) led to his murder by a group of nobles.

**Rastafarianism** religion originating in the West Indies, based on the ideas of →Marcus Garvey, who called on black people to return to Africa and set up a black-governed country there. When Haile Selassie (**Ras Tafari**, 'Lion of Judah') was crowned emperor of Ethiopia 1930, this was seen as a fulfilment of prophecy and some Rastafarians acknowledged him as an incarnation of God (**Jah**), others as a prophet. The use of ganja (marijuana) is a sacrament. There are no churches. There were about 1 million Rastafarians by 1990.

**ratio** measure of the relative size of two quantities or of two measurements (in similar units), expressed as a proportion. For example, the ratio of vowels to consonants in the alphabet is 5:21; the ratio of 500 m to 2 km is 500:2,000, or 1:4. Ratios are normally expressed as whole numbers, so 2:3.5 would become 4:7 (the ratio remains the same provided both numbers are multiplied or divided by the same number).

**rationalism** in theology, the belief that human reason rather than divine revelation is the correct means of ascertaining truth and regulating behaviour. In philosophy, rationalism takes the view that self-evident a priori propositions (deduced by reason alone) are the sole basis of all knowledge. It is usually contrasted with empiricism, which argues that all knowledge must ultimately be derived from the senses.

**Rauschenberg, Robert** (1925– ) born Milton Rauschenberg, US pop artist. He has created happenings and multimedia works, called 'combined painting', such as *Monogram* (1959, Moderna Museet, Stockholm), a stuffed goat daubed with paint and wearing a car tyre around its body. In the 1960s he returned to painting and used the silk-screen printing process to transfer images to canvas.

**raven** any of several large →crows, genus *Corvus*, of the Corvidae family, order Passeriformes. The common raven *C. corax* is about 60 cm/2 ft long with a wingspan of nearly 1 m/3 ft, and has black, lustrous plumage; the beak and mouth, tongue, legs, and feet are also black. It is a scavenger, and is found only in the northern hemisphere.

**Ray, Man** (1890–1976) adopted name of Emmanuel Rabinovich Rudnitsky, US photographer, painter, and sculptor. He was active mainly in France and was associated with the →Dada movement and then →surrealism. One of his best-known sculptures is *Gift* (1921), a surrealist ready-made consisting of an iron on to which a row of nails has been glued.

**reaction** in chemistry, the coming together of two or more atoms, ions, or molecules with the result that a chemical change takes place; that is, a change that occurs when two or more substances interact with each other, resulting in the production of different substances with different chemical compositions. The nature of the reaction is portrayed by a chemical equation.

**realism** in the arts and literature generally, an unadorned, naturalistic approach to subject matter. More specifically, realism refers to a movement in mid-19th-century European art and literature, a reaction against Romantic and classical idealization and a rejection of conventional academic themes (such as mythology, history, and sublime landscapes) in favour of everyday life and carefully observed social settings. The movement was particularly important in France, where it had political overtones; the painters Gustave →Courbet and Honoré Daumier, two leading realists, both used their art to expose social injustice.

**real number** in mathematics, any of the rational numbers (which include the integers) or irrational numbers. Real numbers exclude imaginary numbers, found in complex numbers of the general form $a + bi$ where $i = \sqrt{-1}$, although these do include a real component $a$.

**recessive gene** in genetics, an →allele (alternative form of a gene) that will show in the →phenotype (observed characteristics of an organism) only if its partner allele on the paired chromosome is similarly recessive. Such an allele will not show if its partner is dominant, that is if the organism is heterozygous for a particular characteristic. Alleles for blue eyes in humans, and for shortness in pea plants, are recessive. Most mutant alleles are recessive and therefore are only rarely expressed (see →haemophilia).

**recombination** in genetics, any process that recombines, or 'shuffles', the genetic material, thus increasing genetic variation in the offspring. The two main processes of recombination both occur during meiosis (reduction division of cells). One is **crossing over**, in which chromosome pairs exchange segments; the other is the random reassortment of chromosomes that occurs when each gamete (sperm or egg) receives only one of each chromosome pair.

**rectifier** in electrical engineering, a device used for obtaining one-directional current (DC) from an alternating source of supply (AC). (The process is necessary because almost all electrical power is generated, transmitted, and supplied as alternating current, but many devices, from television sets to electric motors, require direct current.) Types include plate rectifiers, thermionic →diodes, and semiconductor diodes.

**red blood cell** (or erythrocyte) the most common type of blood cell, responsible for transporting oxygen around the body. It contains haemoglobin, which combines with oxygen from the lungs to form oxyhaemoglobin. When transported to the tissues, these cells are able to release the oxygen because the oxyhaemoglobin splits into its original constituents.

**red dwarf** any star that is cool, faint, and small (about one-tenth the mass and diameter of the Sun). Red dwarfs burn slowly, and have estimated lifetimes of 100 billion years. They may be the most abundant type of star, but are difficult to see because they are so faint. Two of the closest stars to the Sun,

Proxima Centauri and Barnard's Star, are red dwarfs.

**red giant** any large bright star with a cool surface. It is thought to represent a late stage in the evolution of a star like the Sun, as it runs out of hydrogen fuel at its centre and begins to burn heavier elements, such as helium, carbon, and silicon. Because of more complex nuclear reactions that then occur in the red giant's interior, it eventually becomes gravitationally unstable and begins to collapse and heat up. The result is either explosion of the star as a →supernova, leaving behind a →neutron star, or loss of mass by more gradual means to produce a →white dwarf.

**Red Sea** branch of the Indian Ocean, formed from a submerged section of the Great →Rift Valley, extending northwest from the Gulf of Aden. It is 2,000 km/1,200 mi long and up to 320 km/200 mi wide, reaching depths of over 2,300 km/7,545 ft. Egypt, Sudan, Ethiopia, and Eritrea (in Africa) and Saudi Arabia (Asia) are on its shores. At its northern end, it divides into the gulfs of Suez and Aqaba, separated by the Sinai peninsula.

**red shift** in astronomy, the lengthening of the wavelengths of light from an object as a result of the object's motion away from us. It is an example of the →Doppler effect. The red shift in light from galaxies is evidence that the universe is expanding.

**refining** any process that purifies or converts something into a more useful form. Metals usually need refining after

they have been extracted from their ores by such processes as →smelting. Petroleum, or crude oil, needs refining before it can be used; the process involves fractional distillation, the separation of the substance into separate components or 'fractions'.

**reflection** the throwing back or deflection of waves, such as →light or sound waves, when they hit a surface. The **law of reflection** states that the angle of incidence (the angle between the ray and a perpendicular line drawn to the surface) is equal to the angle of reflection (the angle between the reflected ray and a perpendicular to the surface).

**reflex** in animals, a very rapid involuntary response to a particular stimulus. It is controlled by the nervous system. A reflex involves only a few nerve cells, unlike the slower but more complex responses produced by the many processing nerve cells of the brain.

**Reformation** religious and political movement in 16th-century Europe to reform the Roman Catholic Church, which led to the establishment of Protestant churches. Anticipated from the 12th century by the Waldenses, Lollards, and Hussites, it was set off by German priest Martin →Luther in 1517, and became effective when the absolute monarchies gave it support by challenging the political power of the papacy and confiscating church wealth.

**refraction** the bending of a wave when it passes from one medium into another. It is the effect of the different speeds of wave propagation in two substances that have different densities. The amount of refraction depends on the densities of the media, the angle at which the wave strikes the surface of the second medium, and the amount of bending and change of velocity corresponding to the wave's frequency (dispersion). Refraction occurs with all types of progressive waves – →electromagnetic waves, sound waves, and water waves – and differs from →reflection, which involves no change in velocity.

**refrigeration** use of technology to transfer heat from cold to warm, against the normal temperature gradient, so that a body is able to remain substantially colder than its surroundings. Refrigeration equipment is used for the chilling and deep-freezing of food in food technology, and in air conditioners and industrial processes.

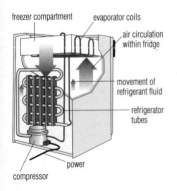

**refrigeration** The constituent parts of a refrigerator and the flow of air and refrigerant fluid around the system.

**Regency** in Britain, the years 1811–20 during which George IV (then Prince of Wales) acted as regent for his father George III, who was finally declared insane and unfit to govern in December 1810. The Regency was marked by the Prince Regent's turbulent private life, his dissolute public image, and the fashionable society he patronized.

**Regency style** style of architecture and interior furnishings popular in England during the late 18th and early 19th centuries. It is characterized by restrained simplicity and the imitation of ancient classical elements, often Greek.

**Reims** (English Rheims) city in the *département* of Marne, and largest commercial centre of the Champagne-Ardenne region, France, situated 130 km/80 mi northeast of Paris on the right bank of the River Vesle, a tributary of the Aisne; population (1990) 185,200, conurbation 206,000. From 987 all but six French kings were crowned here. The western facade of its cathedral, Notre Dame, is one of the masterpieces of the Middle Ages. In World War II the German High Command formally surrendered here to US general Eisenhower on 7 May 1945. Reims is the centre of the champagne trade, and has textile, chemical, mechanical, metallurgical, and foodstuff manufactures.

**reincarnation** (or transmigration or metempsychosis) belief that after death the human soul or the spirit of a plant or animal may live again in another human or animal. It is part of the teachings of many religions and philosophies; for example, ancient Egyptian and Greek (the philosophies of Pythagoras and Plato), Buddhism, Hinduism, Jainism, Sikhism, certain Christian heresies (such as the Cathars), and theosophy.

**relative atomic mass** the mass of an atom relative to one-twelfth the mass of an atom of carbon-12. It depends primarily on the number of protons and neutrons in the atom, the electrons having negligible mass. If more than one →isotope of the element is present, the relative atomic mass is calculated by taking an average that takes account of the relative proportions of each isotope, resulting in values that are not whole numbers. The term **atomic weight**, although commonly used, is strictly speaking incorrect.

**relativity** in physics, the theory of the relative rather than absolute character of motion and mass, and the interdependence of matter, time, and space, as developed by German-born US physicist Albert →Einstein in two phases.

**special theory of relativity** (1905): Starting from the premises that (1) the laws of nature are the same for all observers in unaccelerated motion, and (2) the speed of light is independent of the motion of its source, Einstein arrived at some rather unexpected consequences. Intuitively familiar concepts, like mass, length, and time, had to be modified. For example, an object moving rapidly past the observer will appear to be both shorter and heavier than when it is at rest (that is, at rest relative

to the observer), and a clock moving rapidly past the observer will appear to be running slower than when it is at rest. These predictions of relativity theory seem to be foreign to everyday experience merely because the changes are quite negligible at speeds less than about 1,500 km s$^{-1}$, and they only become appreciable at speeds approaching the speed of light.

**general theory of relativity** (1915): The geometrical properties of space-time were to be conceived as modified locally by the presence of a body with mass. A planet's orbit around the Sun (as observed in three-dimensional space) arises from its natural trajectory in modified space-time; there is no need to invoke, as Isaac →Newton did, a force of →gravity coming from the Sun and acting on the planet. Einstein's general theory accounts for a peculiarity in the behaviour of the motion of the perihelion of the orbit of the planet Mercury that cannot be explained in Newton's theory. The new theory also said that light rays should bend when they pass by a massive object. The predicted bending of starlight was observed during the eclipse of the Sun 1919. A third corroboration is found in the shift towards the red in the spectra of the Sun and, in particular, of stars of great density – white dwarfs such as the companion of Sirius.

**Rembrandt, Harmensz van Rijn** (1606–1669) Dutch painter and etcher. He was one of the most prolific and significant artists in Europe of the 17th century. Between 1629 and 1669 he painted about 60 penetrating self-portraits. He also painted religious subjects, and produced about 300 etchings and over 1,000 drawings. His major group portraits include *The Anatomy Lesson of Dr Tulp* (1632; Mauritshuis, The Hague) and *The Night Watch* (1642; Rijksmuseum, Amsterdam).

**Renaissance** (or Revival of Learning) period in European cultural history that began in Italy around 1400 and lasted there until the end of the 1500s. Elsewhere in Europe it began later, and lasted until the 1600s. One characteristic of the Renaissance was the rediscovery of classical literature, led by the writers Giovanni →Boccaccio and Francesco →Petrarch. A central theme of the Renaissance was humanism, the belief in the active rather than the contemplative life, and a faith in the republican ideal. The greatest expression of the Renaissance was in the arts and learning. The term 'Renaissance' (French 'rebirth') to describe this period of cultural history was invented by historians in the 1800s.

**Renoir, Pierre-Auguste** (1841–1919) French Impressionist painter. He met Claude →Monet and Alfred Sisley in the early 1860s, and together they formed the nucleus of →Impressionism. He developed a lively, colourful painting style with feathery brushwork (known as his 'rainbow style') and painted many scenes of everyday life, such as *The Luncheon of the Boating Party* (1881; Phillips Collection, Washington, DC), and also female nudes, such as *The Bathers* (about 1884–87; Philadelphia Museum of Art).

**repetitive strain injury** (RSI) inflammation of tendon sheaths, mainly in the hands and wrists, which may be disabling. It is found predominantly in factory workers involved in constant repetitive movements, and in those who work with computer keyboards. The symptoms include aching muscles, weak wrists, tingling fingers and in severe cases, pain and paralysis. Some victims have successfully sued their employers for damages. In 1999 RSI affected more than a million people annually in Britain and the USA.

**replication** in biology, production of copies of the genetic material DNA; it occurs during cell division (mitosis and meiosis). Most mutations are caused by mistakes during replication.

**reproduction** in biology, the process by which a living organism produces other organisms more or less similar to itself. The ways in which species reproduce differ, but the two main methods are by →asexual reproduction and →sexual reproduction. Asexual reproduction involves only one parent without the formation of →gametes: the parent's cells divide by mitosis to produce new cells with the same number and kind of →chromosomes as its own. Thus offspring produced asexually are clones of the parent and there is no variation. Sexual reproduction involves two parents, one male and one female. The parents' sex cells divide by meiosis producing gametes, which contain only half the number of chromosomes of the parent cell. In this way, when two sets of chromosomes combine during →fertilization, a new combination of genes is produced. Hence the new organism will differ from both parents, and variation is introduced. The ability to reproduce is considered one of the fundamental attributes of living things.

**reptile** any member of a class (Reptilia) of vertebrates. Unlike amphibians, reptiles have hard-shelled, yolk-filled eggs that are laid on land and from which fully formed young are born. Some snakes and lizards retain their eggs and give birth to live young. Reptiles are cold-blooded, and their skin is usually covered with scales. The metabolism is slow, and in some cases (certain large snakes) intervals between meals may be months. Reptiles date back over 300 million years.

**resistance** in physics, that property of a conductor that restricts the flow of electricity through it, associated with the conversion of electrical energy to heat; also the magnitude of this property. Resistance depends on many factors, such as the nature of the material, its temperature, dimensions, and thermal properties; degree of impurity; the nature and state of illumination of the surface; and the frequency and magnitude of the current. The SI unit of resistance is the ohm.

resistance = voltage/current

This is known as Ohm's law.

**respiration** metabolic process in organisms in which food molecules are broken down to release energy. The cells of all living organisms need a continuous supply of energy, and in most plants and animals this is obtained by **aerobic** respiration. In this process, oxygen is used to break down the glucose molecules in food. This releases energy in the form of energy-carrying molecules (→ATP), and produces carbon dioxide and water as by-products. Respiration sometimes occurs without oxygen, and this is called **anaerobic** respiration. In this case, the end products are energy and either lactose acid or ethanol (alcohol) and carbon dioxide; this process is termed fermentation.

---

### WEB SITE > > > > > > > >

**Respiratory System**

http://library.advanced.org/10348/find/content/respiratory.html

Detailed description of how respiration occurs in humans. The text is accompanied by useful graphics.

---

**Restoration comedy** style of English theatre, dating from the Restoration (1660). It witnessed the first appearance of women on the English stage, most notably in the 'breeches part', specially created in order to costume the actor in male attire, thus revealing her figure to its best advantage. The genre placed much emphasis on wit and sexual intrigues. Examples include Wycherley's *The Country Wife* (1675), Congreve's *The Way of the World* (1700), and Farquhar's *The Beaux' Stratagem* (1707).

**resurrection** in Christian, Jewish, and Muslim belief, the rising from the dead that all souls will experience at the Last Judgement. The Resurrection also refers to Jesus rising from the dead on the third day after his crucifixion, a belief central to Christianity and celebrated at Easter.

**retrovirus** any of a family of →viruses (Retroviridae) containing the genetic material →RNA rather than the more usual →DNA.

**revolutions of 1848** series of revolts in various parts of Europe against monarchical rule. Although some of the revolutionaries had republican ideas, many more were motivated by economic grievances. The revolution began in France with the overthrow of Louis Philippe and then spread to Italy, the Austrian Empire, and Germany, where the short-lived Frankfurt Parliament put forward ideas about political unity in Germany. None of the revolutions enjoyed any lasting success, and most were violently suppressed within a few months.

**Reynolds, Joshua** (1723–1792) English painter. One of the greatest portraitists of the 18th century, he displayed a facility for striking and characterful compositions in the 'Grand Manner', a style based on classical and Renaissance art. He often borrowed classical poses, for example *Mrs Siddons as the Tragic Muse* (1784; San Marino, California). His elegant portraits are mostly of wealthy patrons, though he also painted such figures as the writers Laurence Sterne and Dr Johnson, and the actor David Garrick. Active in London from 1752, he became the first president of

the Royal Academy in 1768 and founded the Royal Academy schools. He was knighted in 1769.

**rhesus factor** group of →antigens on the surface of red blood cells of humans which characterize the rhesus blood group system. Most individuals possess the main rhesus factor (Rh+), but those without this factor (Rh−) produce →antibodies if they come into contact with it. The name comes from rhesus monkeys, in whose blood rhesus factors were first found.

**Rhine** (German Rhein, French Rhin, Dutch Rijn) European river rising in Switzerland and reaching the North Sea via Germany and the Netherlands; length 1,320 km/820 mi. It drains an area of some 220,000 sq km/85,000 sq mi and is navigable for 805 km/500 mi. Tributaries include the Moselle and the Ruhr. The Rhine is linked with the Mediterranean by the Rhine–Rhône Waterway, and with the Black Sea by the Rhine–Main–Danube Waterway.

**Rhode Island** smallest state of the USA, located in New England. It is nicknamed Little Rhody or the Ocean State, and is officially known as **Rhode Island and Providence Plantations**. Rhode Island ratified the US Constitution in 1790, becoming the 13th state to join the Union. It is bordered to the north and east by Massachusetts, to the west by Connecticut, and to the south by the Atlantic Ocean. **population:** (1995) 989,800; **area:** 3,100 sq km/1,197 sq mi; **capital:** Providence; **towns and cities:** Warwick, Cranston, Newport,

Woonsocket; **industries and products:** electronics, machine tools, jewellery, textiles, silverware, rubber, and plastics. Agriculture is limited by the rocky terrain but is important in rural areas, the main crops being apples and potatoes. Rhode Island Red hens were developed here from the 19th century.

**Rhodes, Cecil John** (1853–1902) South African politician, born in the UK, prime minister of Cape Colony 1890–96. Aiming at the formation of a South African federation and the creation of a block of British territory from the Cape to Cairo, he was responsible for the annexation of Bechuanaland (now Botswana) in 1885. He formed the British South Africa Company in 1889, which occupied Mashonaland and Matabeleland, thus forming **Rhodesia** (now Zambia and Zimbabwe).

**Rhône** river of southern Europe; length 810 km/500 mi. It rises at the Rhône Glacier (altitude 1,825 m/5,987 ft) in the canton of Valais in Switzerland and flows through Lake Geneva to Lyon in France, where, at its confluence with the Saône, the upper limit of navigation is reached. The river then turns due south and passes Vienne and Avignon. Near Arles it divides into the **Grand** and **Petit Rhône**, flowing respectively southeast and southwest into the Mediterranean west of Marseille. Here it forms a two-armed delta; the area between the tributaries is the marshy region known as the Camargue.

**riboflavin** (or vitamin B$_2$) →vitamin of the B complex important in cell respiration. It is obtained from eggs, liver, and milk. A deficiency in the diet causes stunted growth.

**ribonucleic acid** full name of →RNA.

**Richard (I) the Lion-Heart** (1157–1199) French *Coeur-de-Lion*, king of England 1189–99. He spent all but six months of his reign abroad. He was the third son of Henry II, against whom he twice rebelled. In the third →Crusade 1191–92 he won victories at Cyprus, Acre, and Arsuf (against →Saladin), but failed to recover Jerusalem. While returning overland he was captured by the Duke of Austria, who handed him over to the emperor Henry VI, and he was held prisoner until a large ransom was raised. He then returned briefly to England, where his brother John had been ruling in his stead. His later years were spent in warfare in France, where he was killed by a crossbow bolt while besieging Châlus-Chabrol in 1199. He left no heir.

**Richard III** (1452–1485) king of England from 1483. The son of Richard, Duke of York, he was created Duke of Gloucester by his brother Edward IV, and distinguished himself in the Wars of the →Roses. On Edward's death 1483 he became protector to his nephew Edward V, and soon secured the crown for himself on the plea that Edward IV's sons were illegitimate. He proved a capable ruler, but the suspicion that he had murdered Edward V and his brother undermined his popularity. In 1485 Henry, Earl of Richmond (later →Henry VII), raised a rebellion, and

Richard III was defeated and killed at →Bosworth.

**Richardson, Samuel** (1689–1761) English novelist. He was one of the founders of the modern novel. *Pamela* (1740–41), written in the form of a series of letters and containing much dramatic conversation, was sensationally popular all across Europe, and was followed by *Clarissa* (1747–48) and *Sir Charles Grandison* (1753–54).

**Richelieu, Armand Jean du Plessis de** (1585–1642) French cardinal and politician, chief minister from 1624. He aimed to make the monarchy absolute; he ruthlessly crushed opposition by the nobility and destroyed the political power of the →Huguenots, while leaving them religious freedom. Abroad, he sought to establish French supremacy by breaking the power of the Habsburgs; he therefore supported the Swedish king Gustavus Adolphus and the German Protestant princes against Austria and in 1635 brought France into the Thirty Years' War.

**Richter scale** scale based on measurement of seismic waves, used to determine the magnitude of an →earthquake at its epicentre. The magnitude of an earthquake differs from its intensity, measured by the Mercalli scale, which is subjective and varies from place to place for the same earthquake. The scale is named after US seismologist Charles Richter. *See table on page 464.*

**Rift Valley, Great** longest 'split' in the Earth's surface; see →Great Rift Valley.

**Rimbaud, (Jean Nicolas) Arthur** (1854–1891) French Symbolist poet. His verse was chiefly written before the age of 20, notably *Les Illuminations* published 1886. From 1871 he lived with the poet Paul Verlaine.

**Rimsky-Korsakov, Nikolai Andreievich** (1844–1908) Russian composer. He composed many operas and works for orchestra, He also wrote an influential text on orchestration. His opera *The Golden Cockerel* (1907) was a satirical attack on despotism that was banned until 1909. He also completed works by other composers, for example, Mussorgsky's *Boris Godunov*.

**ringworm** any of various contagious skin infections due to related kinds of fungus, usually resulting in circular, itchy, discoloured patches covered with scales or blisters. The scalp and feet (athlete's foot) are generally involved. Treatment is with antifungal preparations.

**Rio de Janeiro** (Portuguese 'river of January') port and resort in southeast Brazil; capital of Rio de Janeiro federal unit (state), and former national capital (1763–1960); population 5,480,800 (1991) (metropolitan area 10,389,400). It is situated on the southwest shore of Guanabara Bay, an inlet of the Atlantic Ocean; Sugar Loaf Mountain (a huge cone-shaped rock outcrop, composed of granite, quartz and fedspar) stands at the entrance to the harbour, and the city is dominated by the 30 m/100 ft-high figure of Christ on the top of Corcovado, a jagged peak 690 m/2,264 ft high. Industries include ship-repair, sugar refining, textiles, and the

## THE RICHTER SCALE

The Richter scale is based on measurement of seismic waves, used to determine the magnitude of an earthquake at its epicentre. The magnitude of an earthquake differs from its intensity, measured by the Mercalli scale, which is subjective and varies from place to place for the same earthquake. The Richter scale was named after US seismologist Charles Richter (1900–1985). The relative amount of energy released indicates the ratio of energy between earthquakes of different magnitude.

| Magnitude | Relative amount of energy released | Examples | Year |
|---|---|---|---|
| 1 | 1 | | |
| 2 | 31 | | |
| 3 | 960 | | |
| 4 | 30,000 | Carlisle, England (4.7) | 1979 |
| 5 | 920,000 | Wrexham, Wales (5.1) | 1990 |
| 6 | 29,000,000 | San Fernando (CA), USA (6.5) | 1971 |
| | | northern Armenia (6.8) | 1988 |
| 7 | 890,000,000 | Loma Prieta (CA), USA (7.1) | 1989 |
| | | Kobe, Japan (7.2) | 1995 |
| | | Izmit, Turkey (7.4) | 1999 |
| | | Taichung and Nantou counties, Taiwan (7.6) | 1999 |
| | | Rasht, Iran (7.7) | 1990 |
| | | San Francisco (CA), USA (7.7–7.9)[1] | 1906 |
| 8 | 28,000,000,000 | Tangshan, China (8.0) | 1976 |
| | | Gansu, China (8.6) | 1920 |
| | | Lisbon, Portugal (8.7) | 1955 |
| 9 | 850,000,000,000 | Prince William Sound (AK), USA (9.2) | 1964 |

[1] Richter's original estimate of a magnitude of 8.3 was revised by two studies carried out by the California Institute of Technology and the US Geological Survey.

manufacture of foodstuffs; coffee, sugar, and iron ore are exported.

**Rio Grande** (Mexican Río Bravo del Norte) river of the USA and Mexico, rising in the Rocky Mountains in southern Colorado, it flows southeast, through New Mexico and Texas, to the Gulf of Mexico near Brownsville; length 3,050 km/1,900 mi. From El Paso, the river forms the US–Mexican border for the last 2,400 km/1,500 mi of its course. Insufficient water is carried for the demands of irrigation both sides of the border, and the Rio Grande is eventually reduced to a trickle in its lower reaches. Its rate of flow is subject to international agreements.

**river** large body of water that flows down a slope along a channel restricted by adjacent banks and levées. A river originates at a point called its source, and enters a sea or lake at its mouth. Along its length it may be joined by smaller rivers called tributaries; a river and its tributaries are contained within a drainage basin. The point at which two rivers join is called the confluence. *See table on pages 466–67.*

**RNA** (abbreviation for ribonucleic acid) nucleic acid involved in the process of translating the genetic material →DNA into proteins. It is usually single-stranded, unlike the double-stranded DNA, and consists of a large number of nucleotides strung together, each of which comprises the sugar ribose, a phosphate group, and one of four bases (uracil, cytosine, adenine, or guanine). RNA is copied from DNA by the

formation of →base pairs, with uracil taking the place of thymine.

**Robert (I) the Bruce** (1274–1329) king of Scots from 1306, successful guerrilla fighter, and grandson of Robert de Bruce. In 1307 he displayed his tactical skill in the Battle of Loudun Hill against the English under Edward I, and defeated the English again under Edward II at Bannockburn in 1314. In 1328 the Treaty of Northampton recognized Scotland's independence and Robert the Bruce as king.

Large English expeditions of 1322 and 1327 were beaten by Robert's 'scorched earth' policy, apparently his deathbed advice on how best to conduct warfare.

**Robespierre, Maximilien François Marie Isidore de** (1758–1794) French politician in the →French Revolution. As leader of the Jacobins in the National Convention (1792), he supported the execution of Louis XVI and the overthrow of the right-wing republican Girondins, and in July 1793 was elected to the Committee of Public Safety. A year later he was guillotined; many believe that he was a scapegoat for the Reign of Terror since he ordered only 72 executions personally.

**Rocky Mountains** (or Rockies) largest North American mountain system, extending for 4,800 km/3,000 mi from the Mexican plateau near Sante Fe, north through the west-central states of the USA, and through Canada to the Alaskan border. It forms part of the Continental Divide, which separates

## LONGEST RIVERS IN THE WORLD

| River | Location | Approximate length | |
|---|---|---|---|
| | | km | mi |
| Nile | Africa | 6,695 | 4,160 |
| Amazon | South America | 6,570 | 4,083 |
| Chang Jiang (Yangtze) | China | 6,300 | 3,915 |
| Mississippi–Missouri–Red Rock | USA | 6,020 | 3,741 |
| Huang He (Yellow River) | China | 5,464 | 3,395 |
| Ob–Irtysh | China/Kazakhstan/Russian Federation | 5,410 | 3,362 |
| Amur–Shilka | Asia | 4,416 | 2,744 |
| Lena | Russian Federation | 4,400 | 2,734 |
| Congo | Africa | 4,374 | 2,718 |
| Mackenzie–Peace–Finlay | Canada | 4,241 | 2,635 |
| Mekong | Asia | 4,180 | 2,597 |
| Niger | Africa | 4,100 | 2,548 |
| Yenisei | Russian Federation | 4,100 | 2,548 |
| Paraná | Brazil | 3,943 | 2,450 |
| Mississippi | USA | 3,779 | 2,348 |
| Murray–Darling | Australia | 3,751 | 2,331 |
| Missouri | USA | 3,726 | 2,315 |
| Volga | Russian Federation | 3,685 | 2,290 |
| Madeira | Brazil | 3,241 | 2,014 |
| Purus | Brazil | 3,211 | 1,995 |
| São Francisco | Brazil | 3,199 | 1,988 |
| Yukon | USA/Canada | 3,185 | 1,979 |

(continued)

## LONGEST RIVERS IN THE WORLD (CONTINUED)

| River | Location | Approximate length | |
|---|---|---|---|
| | | km | mi |
| Rio Grande | USA/Mexico | 3,058 | 1,900 |
| Indus | Tibet/Pakistan | 2,897 | 1,800 |
| Danube | central and eastern Europe | 2,858 | 1,776 |
| Japura | Brazil | 2,816 | 1,750 |
| Salween | Myanmar/China | 2,800 | 1,740 |
| Brahmaputra | Asia | 2,736 | 1,700 |
| Euphrates | Iraq | 2,736 | 1,700 |
| Tocantins | Brazil | 2,699 | 1,677 |
| Zambezi | Africa | 2,650 | 1,647 |
| Orinoco | Venezuela | 2,559 | 1,590 |
| Paraguay | Paraguay | 2,549 | 1,584 |
| Amu Darya | Tajikistan/Turkmenistan/Uzbekistan | 2,540 | 1,578 |
| Ural | Russian Federation/Kazakhstan | 2,535 | 1,575 |
| Kolyma | Russian Federation | 2,513 | 1,562 |
| Ganges | India/Bangladesh | 2,510 | 1,560 |
| Arkansas | USA | 2,344 | 1,459 |
| Colorado | USA | 2,333 | 1,450 |
| Dnieper | Russian Federation/Belarus/Ukraine | 2,285 | 1,420 |
| Syr Darya | Asia | 2,205 | 1,370 |
| Irrawaddy | Myanmar | 2,152 | 1,337 |
| Orange | South Africa | 2,092 | 1,300 |

rivers draining into the Atlantic or Arctic oceans from those flowing toward the Pacific Ocean. To the east lie the Great Plains, and to the west, the plateaux separating the Rocky Mountains from parallel Pacific coast ranges. Mount Elbert is the highest peak, 4,400 m/14,433 ft. Some geographers consider the Yukon and Alaskan ranges as part of the system, making the highest point Mount McKinley (Denali) 6,194 m/20,320 ft, and its total length 5,150 km/3,219 mi.

**rococo** movement in the arts and architecture in 18th-century Europe, tending towards lightness, elegance, delicacy, and decorative charm. The term 'rococo' is derived from the French *rocaille* (rock- or shell-work), a style of interior decoration based on S-curves and scroll-like forms. Jean-Antoine Watteau's paintings and Sèvres porcelain belong to the French rococo vogue. In the 1730s the movement became widespread in Europe, notably in the churches and palaces of southern Germany and Austria. Chippendale furniture is an English example of the French rococo style.

**rodent** any mammal of the worldwide order Rodentia, making up nearly half of all mammal species. Besides ordinary 'cheek teeth', they have a single front pair of incisor teeth in both upper and lower jaw, which continue to grow as they are worn down.

**Rodin, (René François) Auguste** (1840–1917) French sculptor. He is considered the greatest of his day. He freed sculpture from the idealizing conventions of the time by his realistic treatment of the human figure, introducing a new boldness of style and expression. Examples are *Le Penseur/ The Thinker* (1904; Musée Rodin, Paris), *Le Baiser/The Kiss* (1886; marble version in the Louvre, Paris), and *The Burghers of Calais* (1884–86; copy in Embankment Gardens, Westminster, London).

**Rolling Stones, the** British band formed in 1962, once notorious as the 'bad boys' of rock. Original members were Mick Jagger (1943– ), Keith Richards (1943– ), Brian Jones (1942–1969), Bill Wyman (1936– ), Charlie Watts (1941– ), and the pianist Ian Stewart (1938–1985). A rock-and-roll institution, the Rolling Stones were still performing and recording in the 1990s.

**ROM** (acronym for read-only memory) in computing, a memory device in the form of a collection of integrated circuits (chips), frequently used in microcomputers. ROM chips are loaded with data and programs during manufacture and, unlike RAM (random-access memory) chips, can subsequently only be read, not written to, by computer. However, the contents of the chips are not lost when the power is switched off, as happens in RAM.

**Roman Britain** period in British history from the two expeditions by Julius Caesar in 55 and 54 BC to the early 5th century AD. Roman relations with Britain began with Caesar's expeditions, but the actual conquest was not begun until

AD 43. During the reign of the emperor Domitian, the governer of the province, Agricola, campaigned in Scotland. After several unsuccessful attempts to conquer Scotland, the northern frontier was fixed between the Solway and the Tyne at →Hadrian's Wall.

**Roman Catholicism** one of the main divisions of the Christian religion, separate from the Eastern Orthodox Church from 1054, and headed by the pope. For history and beliefs, see →Christianity. Membership is concentrated in southern Europe, Latin America, and the Philippines. In February 2000, Rome reported the number of baptized Roman Catholics to be 1.045 billion, an increase of 40 million since 1998.

**Roman Empire** from 27 BC to the 5th century AD; see →Rome, ancient.

**Romanesque architecture** style of Western European →architecture of the 10th to 12th centuries, marked by rounded arches, solid volumes, and emphasis on perpendicular elements. In England the style is also known as Norman architecture.

**Romania** national name: *România*; area: 237,500 sq km/91,698 sq mi; capital: Bucharest; major towns/cities: Braşov, Timişoara, Cluj-Napoca, Iaşl, Constanţi, Galaţi, Craiova, Ploieşti; major ports: Galaţi, Constanţa, Brăila; physical features: mountains surrounding a plateau, with river plains in south and east. Carpathian Mountains, Transylvanian Alps; River Danube; Black Sea coast; mineral springs; head of state: Emil Constantinescu from 1996; head of government: Mugur Isarescu from 1999; political system: emergent democracy; currency: leu; GNP per capita (PPP): (US$) 3,970 (1998); exports: base metals and metallic articles, textiles and clothing, machinery and equipment, mineral products, foodstuffs. Principal market Italy 19.5% (1997); population: 22,402,000 (1999 est); language: Romanian (official), Hungarian, German; religion: mainly Romanian Orthodox; life expectancy: 66 (men); 74 (women) (1995–2000).

**Romanticism** in literature and the visual arts, a style that emphasizes the imagination, emotions, and creativity of the individual artist. Romanticism also refers specifically to late-18th- and early-19th-century European culture, as contrasted with 18th-century →classicism.

**Romanticism** in music, a preoccupation with subjective emotion expressed primarily through melody, a use of folk idioms, and a cult of the musician as visionary artist and hero (virtuoso). Often linked with nationalistic feelings, the Romantic movement reached its height in the late 19th century, as in the works of Robert Schumann and Richard Wagner.

**Rome** (Italian *Roma*) capital of Italy and of Lazio region, on the River Tiber, 27 km/17 mi from the Tyrrhenian Sea; population (1992) 2,723,300.

Rome is an important road, rail, and cultural centre. A large section of the population finds employment in government and other offices: the headquarters of the Roman Catholic church (the Vatican City State, a separate sovereign area within Rome) and other international bodies, such as the Food and Agriculture Oranization (FAO), are here; it is also a destination for many tourists and pilgrims. Industries have developed, mainly to the south and east of the city; these include engineering, printing, food-processing, electronics, and the manufacture of chemicals, pharmaceuticals, plastics, and clothes. The city is a centre for the film and fashion industries. Among the remains of the ancient city (see →Rome, ancient) are the Forum, Colosseum, and Pantheon.

**Rome, ancient history** Ancient Rome was a civilization based on the city of Rome. It lasted for about 800 years. Traditionally founded as a kingdom in 753 BC, Rome became a republic in 510 BC following the expulsion of its last king, Tarquinius Superbus. From then, its history is one of almost continual expansion until the murder of Julius Caesar and the foundation of the empire in 27 BC under →Augustus and his successors. At its peak under Trajan, the Roman Empire stretched from Britain to Mesopotamia and the Caspian Sea. A long line of emperors ruling by virtue of military, rather than civil, power marked the beginning of Rome's long decline; under Diocletian the empire was divided into two parts – East and West – although it was temporarily reunited under Constantine, the first emperor to formally adopt Christianity.

The end of the Roman Empire is generally dated by the deposition of the last emperor in the west in AD 476. The Eastern Empire continued until 1453 with its capital at Constantinople (modern Istanbul).

**Rommel, Erwin Johannes Eugen** (1891–1944) German field marshal. He served in World War I, and in World War II he played an important part in the invasions of central Europe and France. He was commander of the North African offensive from 1941 (when he was nicknamed 'Desert Fox') until defeated in the Battles of El Alamein and he was expelled from Africa in March 1943.

**Röntgen, Wilhelm Konrad** (1845–1923) (or Roentgen) German physicist. He discovered →X-rays 1895. While investigating the passage of electricity through gases, he noticed the fluorescence of a barium platinocyanide screen. This radiation passed through some substances opaque to light, and affected photographic plates. Developments from this discovery revolutionized medical diagnosis. He won the Nobel Prize for Physics 1901.

**rook** gregarious European →crow *Corvus frugilegus*. The plumage is black and lustrous and the face bare; the legs, toes, and claws are also black. A rook can grow to 45 cm/18 in long. Rooks nest in colonies (rookeries) at the tops of trees. They feed mainly on invertebrates found just below the soil surface. The last 5 mm/0.2 in of beak tip is mostly cartilage containing lots of nerve endings to enable the rook to feel for hidden food.

**Roosevelt, Franklin D(elano)** (1882–1945) 32nd president of the USA 1933–45, a Democrat. He served as governor of New York 1929–33. Becoming president during the Great Depression, he launched the **New Deal** economic and social reform programme, which made him popular with the people. After the outbreak of World War II he introduced lend-lease for the supply of war materials and services to the Allies and drew up the Atlantic Charter of solidarity. Once the USA had entered the war in 1941, he spent much time in meetings with Allied leaders.

**Roosevelt, Theodore** (1858–1919) 26th president of the USA 1901–09, a Republican. After serving as governor of New York 1898–1900 he became vice president to McKinley, whom he succeeded as president on McKinley's assassination in 1901. He campaigned against the great trusts (associations of enterprises that reduce competition), while carrying on a jingoist foreign policy designed to enforce US supremacy over Latin America.

**root** the part of a plant that is usually underground, and whose primary functions are anchorage and the absorption of water and dissolved mineral salts. Roots usually grow downwards and towards water (that is, they are positively geotropic and hydrotropic; see →tropism). Plants such as epiphytic orchids, which grow above ground, produce aerial roots that absorb moisture from the atmosphere. Others, such as ivy, have climbing roots arising from the stems, which serve to attach the plant to trees and walls. *See illustration on page 472.*

**root** of an equation, a value that satisfies the equality. For example, $x = 0$ and $x = 5$ are roots of the equation $x^2 - 5x = 0$.

**Roses, Wars of the** civil wars in England 1455–85 between the houses of Lancaster (badge, red rose) and York (badge, white rose), both of whom claimed the throne through descent from the sons of Edward III. As a result of Henry VI's lapse into insanity in 1453, Richard, Duke of York, was installed as protector of the realm. Upon his recovery, Henry forced York to take up arms in self-defence.

**Rosetta Stone** slab of basalt with inscriptions from 197 BC, found near the town of Rosetta, Egypt, 1799. Giving the same text in three versions – Greek, hieroglyphic, and demotic script – it became the key to deciphering other Egyptian inscriptions.

**Rosh Hashanah** two-day holiday that marks the start of the Jewish New Year (first new Moon after the autumn equinox), traditionally announced by blowing a ram's horn (a shofar).

**Ross Dependency** all the Antarctic islands and territories between 160° east and 150° west longitude, and situated south of 60° south latitude; it includes Edward VII Land, Ross Sea and its islands (including the Balleny Isles),

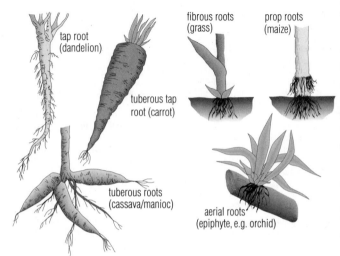

**root** Types of root. Many flowers (dandelion) and vegetables (carrot) have swollen tap roots with smaller lateral roots. The tuberous roots of the cassava are swollen parts of an underground stem modified to store food. The fibrous roots of the grasses are of equal size. Prop roots grow out from the stem and then grow down into the ground to support a heavy plant. Aerial roots grow from stems but do not grow into the ground; many absorb moisture from the air.

and parts of Victoria Land. It is claimed by New Zealand. **area:** 450,000 sq km/173,745 sq mi; **features:** the **Ross Ice Shelf** (or Ross Barrier), a permanent layer of ice across the Ross Sea about 425 m/1,394 ft thick; **population:** scientific personnel only; **history:** claimed by the UK in 1923, with the claim subsequently transferred to New Zealand. It is probable that marine organisms beneath the ice shelf had been undisturbed from the Pleistocene period until drillings were made in 1976.

**Rossetti, Christina Georgina** (1830–1894) English poet and a devout High Anglican. Her best-known work is *Goblin Market and Other Poems* (1862); among others are *The Prince's Progress* (1866), *Annus Domini* (1874), and *A Pageant* (1881). She was the sister of Dante Gabriel →Rossetti.

**Rossetti, Dante Gabriel** (1828–1882) English painter and poet. He was a founding member of the →Pre-Raphaelite Brotherhood in 1848. As well as romantic medieval scenes, he produced many idealized portraits of women, including the *Beata Beatrix* (1864). His verse includes 'The Blessed Damozel' (1850). His sister was the poet Christina →Rossetti.

**Rossini, Gioacchino Antonio** (1792–1868) Italian composer. His first success was the opera *Tancredi* in 1813. In 1816 his opera buffa (humorous opera) *Il barbiere di Siviglia/The Barber of Seville* was produced in Rome. He was the most successful opera composer of his time, producing 20 operas in the period 1815–23. He also created (with Gaetano Donizetti and Bellini) the 19th-century Italian operatic style.

**Rothko, Mark** (1903–1970) adopted name of Marcus Rothkovich, Russian-born US painter. He was a leading exponent of abstract expressionism and a pioneer, towards the end of his life, of Colour Field painting. Typically, his works are canvases covered in large hazy rectangles of thin paint, the colours subtly modulated, as in *Light Red over Black* (1957; Tate Gallery, London).

**Roundhead** member of the Parliamentary party during the English →Civil War 1640–60, opposing the Royalist Cavaliers. The term referred to the short hair then worn only by men of the lower classes.

**Rousseau, Henri Julien Félix** (1844–1910) 'Le Douanier', French painter. A self-taught naive artist, he painted scenes of the Parisian suburbs, portraits, and exotic scenes with painstaking detail, as in *Tropical Storm with a Tiger* (1891; National Gallery, London). He was much admired by artists such as Gauguin and Picasso, and writers such as the poet Apollinaire.

**Rousseau, Jean-Jacques** (1712–1778) French social philosopher and writer. His book *Du Contrat social/Social Contract* (1762), emphasizing the rights of the people over those of the government, was a significant influence on the French Revolution. In the novel *Emile* (1762), he outlined a new theory of education.

**Royalist** term often used to describe monarchist factions. In England, it is used especially for those who supported Charles I during the English →Civil War. They are also known as 'Cavaliers', and their opponents as 'Parliamentarians' or →Roundheads.

**rubber** coagulated latex of a variety of plants, mainly from the New World. Most important is Para rubber, which comes from the tree *Hevea brasiliensis*, belonging to the spurge family. It was introduced from Brazil to Southeast Asia, where most of the world supply is now produced, the chief exporters being Peninsular Malaysia, Indonesia, Sri Lanka, Cambodia, Thailand, Sarawak, and Brunei. At about seven years the tree, which may grow to 20 m/60 ft, is ready for tapping. Small cuts are made in the trunk and the latex drips into collecting cups. In pure form, rubber is white and has the formula $(C_5H_8)_n$.

**rubella** technical term for →German measles.

**Rubens, Peter Paul** (1577–1640) Flemish painter. He was one of the greatest figures of the →baroque. Bringing the exuberance of Italian baroque to northern Europe, he created innumerable religious and allegorical paintings for churches and palaces. These show mastery of drama and movement in large compositions, and a love of rich colour and texture. He also painted portraits and, in his last years, landscapes. *The Rape of the Daughters of Leucippus* (1617; Alte Pinakothek, Munich) is typical.

**Rubicon** ancient name of the small river flowing into the Adriatic that, under the Roman Republic, marked the boundary between Italy proper and Cisalpine Gaul. When Caesar led his army across it in 49 BC, he therefore declared war on the Republic; hence to 'cross the Rubicon' means to take an irrevocable step.

**ruby** the red transparent gem variety of the mineral corundum $Al_2O_3$, aluminium oxide. Small amounts of chromium oxide, $Cr_2O_3$, substituting for aluminium oxide, give ruby its colour. Natural rubies are found mainly in Myanmar (Burma), but rubies can also be produced artificially and such synthetic stones are used in →lasers.

**Rugby League** professional form of rugby football founded in England in 1895 as the Northern Union when a dispute about pay caused northern clubs to break away from the Rugby Football Union. The game is similar to →Rugby Union, but the number of players was reduced from 15 to 13 in 1906, and other rule changes have made the game more open and fast-moving.

**Rugby Union** form of rugby in which there are 15 players on each side. Points are scored by 'tries', scored by 'touching down' the ball beyond the goal line or by kicking goals from penalties. The Rugby Football Union was formed in 1871 and has its headquarters in England (Twickenham, Middlesex). Formerly an amateur game, the game's status was revoked in August 1995 by the International Rugby Football Board, which lifted restrictions on players moving between Rugby Union and Rugby League.

**Ruhr** river in Germany, length 235 km/146 mi. It rises in the Rotha-argebirge Mountains at the eastern boundary of North Rhine-Westphalia, and flows west to join the Rhine at Duisburg. The **Ruhr Valley**, a metropolitan industrial area produces petrochemicals, cars, iron, and steel at Duisburg and Dortmund; it is also a coal-mining area.

**ruminant** any even-toed hoofed mammal with a rumen, the 'first stomach' of its complex digestive system. Plant food is stored and fermented before being brought back to the mouth for chewing (chewing the cud) and then is swallowed to the next stomach. Ruminants include cattle, antelopes, goats, deer, and giraffes, all with a four-chambered stomach. Camels are also ruminants, but they have a three-chambered stomach.

**Rump, the** English parliament formed between December 1648 and November 1653 after Pride's purge of the →Long Parliament to ensure a majority in favour of trying Charles I. It was dismissed in 1653 by Cromwell, who replaced it with the →Barebones Parliament.

**rush** any of a group of grasslike plants found in wet places in cold and temperate regions. The round stems and flexible leaves of some species have been used for making mats and baskets since ancient times. (Genus *Juncus*, family Juncaceae.)

**Rushdie, (Ahmed) Salman** (1947– ) British writer. He was born in India of a Muslim family. His book *Midnight's Children* (1981) deals with India from the date of independence and won the Booker Prize. His novel *The Satanic Verses* (1988) (the title refers to verses deleted from the Koran) offended many Muslims with alleged blasphemy. In 1989 the Ayatollah Khomeini of Iran placed a religious *fatwa* on Rushdie, calling for him and his publishers to be killed.

**Russell, Bertrand Arthur William** (1872–1970) 3rd Earl Russell, English philosopher, mathematician, and peace campaigner. He contributed to the development of modern mathematical logic and wrote about social issues. His works include *Principia Mathematica* (1910–13; with A N Whitehead), in which he attempted to show that mathematics could be reduced to a branch of logic; *The Problems of Philosophy* (1912); and *A History of Western Philosophy* (1946). He was an outspoken liberal pacifist. He was awarded the Nobel Prize for Literature in 1950. Earl 1931.

**Russian Federation** formerly to 1991 **Russian Soviet Federal Socialist Republic (RSFSR); national name:** *Rossiskaya Federatsiya;* **area:** 17,075,400 sq km/6,592,811 sq mi; **capital:** Moscow; **major towns/cities:** St Petersburg (Leningrad), Nizhniy Novgorod (Gorky), Rostov-na-Donu, Samara (Kuibyshev), Tver (Kalinin), Volgograd, Vyatka (Kirov), Yekaterinburg (Sverdlovsk), Novosibirsk, Chelyabinsk, Kazan, Omsk, Perm, Ufa; **physical features:** fertile Black Earth district; extensive forests; the Ural Mountains with large mineral resources; Lake Baikal, world's deepest lake; **head of state:** Vladimir Putin acting president 1999; presidential elections scheduled for 2000; **head of government:** Vladimir Putin from 1999; **political system:** emergent democracy; **currency:** rouble; **GNP per capita (PPP):** (US$) 3,950 (1998); **exports:** mineral fuels, ferrous and non-ferrous metals and derivatives, precious stones, chemical products, machinery and transport equipment, weapons, timber and paper products. Principal market Ukraine 9.1% (1998); **population:** 147,195,000 (1999 est); **language:** Russian; **religion:** traditionally Russian Orthodox; **life expectancy:** 61 (men); 73 (women) (1995–2000).

**Russian Orthodox Church** another name for the →Orthodox Church.

**Russian Revolution** two revolutions of February and October 1917 (Julian calendar) that began with the overthrow of the Romanov dynasty and ended with the establishment of a communist soviet (council) state, the Union of Soviet Socialist Republics (USSR). In October Bolshevik workers and sailors, led by Vladimir Ilyich →Lenin, seized government buildings and took over power.

**Russo-Japanese War** war between Russia and Japan 1904–05, which arose from conflicting ambitions in Korea and Manchuria, specifically, the Russian occupation of Port Arthur (modern Lüshun) 1897 and of the Amur province 1900. Japan successfully besieged Port Arthur May 1904–January 1905, took Mukden (modern Shenyang) on 29 February–10 March, and on 27 May defeated the Russian Baltic fleet, which had sailed halfway around the world to Tsushima Strait. A peace was signed 23 August 1905. Russia surrendered its lease on Port Arthur, ceded southern Sakhalin to Japan, evacuated Manchuria, and recognized Japan's interests in Korea.

**rust** reddish-brown oxide of iron formed by the action of moisture and oxygen on the metal. It consists mainly of hydrated iron(III) oxide ($Fe_2O_3.H_2O$) and iron(III) hydroxide ($Fe(OH)_3$). Rusting is the commonest form of →corrosion.

**Rutherford, Ernest, 1st Baron Rutherford of Nelson** (1871–1937) New Zealand-born British physicist. He was a pioneer of modern atomic science. His main research was in the field of →radioactivity, and he discovered alpha, beta, and gamma rays. He was the first to recognize the nuclear nature of the atom in 1911. He was awarded a Nobel prize in 1908.

**Rwanda** Republic of; **national name:** *Republika y'u Rwanda*; **area:** 26,338 sq km/10,169 sq mi; **capital:** Kigali; **major towns/cities:** Butare, Ruhengeri, Gisenyi; **physical features:** high savanna and hills, with volcanic mountains in northwest; part of lake Kivu; highest peak Mount Karisimbi 4,507 m/14,792 ft; Kagera River (whose headwaters are the source of the Nile); **head of state:** Pasteur Bizimungu from 1994; **head of government:** Pierre Celestin Rwigema from 1995; **political system:** transitional; **currency:** Rwanda franc; **GNP per capita (PPP):** (US$) 690 (1998); **exports:** coffee, tea, tin ores and concentrates, pyrethrum, quinquina. Principal market Belgium–Luxembourg 36.1% (1997); **population:** 7,235,000 (1999 est); **language:** Kinyarwanda, French (official); Kiswahili; **religion:** Roman Catholic 54%, animist 23%, Protestant 12%, Muslim 9%; **life expectancy:** 39 (men); 42 (women) (1995–2000).

## Ss

**Sabah** self-governing state of the federation of Malaysia, occupying northeast Borneo, forming (with Sarawak) East Malaysia. **area:** 73,613 sq km/28,415 sq mi; **capital:** Kota Kinabalu (formerly Jesselton); **physical:** chiefly mountainous (highest peak Mount Kinabalu 4,098 m/13,450 ft) and forested; **industries:** hardwoods (25% of the world's supplies), rubber, fish, cocoa, palm oil, copper, copra, and hemp; **population:** (1990) 1,736,900, of which the Kadazans form the largest ethnic group at 30%; also included are 250,000 immigrants from Indonesia and the Philippines; **language:** Malay (official) and English; **religion:** Sunni Muslim and Christian (the Kadazans, among whom there is unrest about increasing Muslim dominance); **government:** consists of a constitutional head of state with a chief minister, cabinet, and legislative assembly; **history:** in 1877–78 the sultan of Sulu made concessions to the North Borneo Company, which was eventually consolidated with Labuan as a British colony 1946, and became the state of Sabah within Malaysia 1963. The Philippines advanced territorial claims on Sabah 1962 and 1968 on the grounds that the original cession by the sultan was illegal, Spain having then been sovereign in the area.

**Sabine** member of an ancient people of central Italy, conquered by the Romans and amalgamated with them in the 3rd century BC. The so-called **rape of the Sabine women** – a mythical attempt by Romulus in the early days of Rome to carry off the Sabine women to colonize the new city – is frequently depicted in art.

**saccharin** (or ortho-sulpho benzimide) $C_7H_5NO_3S$ sweet, white, crystalline solid derived from coal tar and substituted for sugar. Since 1977 it has been regarded as potentially carcinogenic. Its use is not universally permitted and it has been largely replaced by other sweetening agents.

**sacrament** in Christian usage, observances forming the visible sign of inward grace. In the Roman Catholic Church there are seven sacraments: baptism, Holy Communion (Eucharist or Mass), confirmation, rite of reconciliation (confession and penance), holy orders, matrimony, and the anointing of the sick.

**sadism** tendency to derive pleasure (usually sexual) from inflicting physical or mental pain on others. The term is derived from the Marquis de Sade.

**saffron** crocus plant belonging to the iris family, probably native to southwestern Asia, and formerly widely cultivated in Europe; also the dried orange-yellow stigmas of its purple flowers, used for colouring and flavouring in cookery. (*Crocus sativus*, family Iridaceae.)

**saga** prose narrative written down in the 11th–13th centuries in Norway and Iceland. The sagas range from family chronicles, such as the *Landnamabok* of Ari (1067–1148), to legendary and anonymous works such as *Njal's Saga*.

**Sahara** (Arabic *Sahra* 'wilderness') largest desert in the world, occupying around 9,000,000 sq km/3,500,000 sq mi of north Africa from the Atlantic to the Nile, covering: west Egypt; part of west Sudan; large parts of Mauritania, Mali, Niger, and Chad; and southern parts of Morocco, Algeria, Tunisia, and Libya. Small areas in Algeria and Tunisia are below sea level, but it is mainly a plateau with a central mountain system, including the Ahaggar Mountains in Algeria, the Aïr Massif in Niger, and the Tibesti Massif in Chad, of which the highest peak is Emi Koussi, 3,415 m/11,208 ft.

**Sahel** (Arabic *sahil* 'coast') marginal area to the south of the Sahara, from Senegal to Somalia, which experiences desert-like conditions during periods of low rainfall. The desertification is partly due to climatic fluctuations but has also been caused by the pressures of a rapidly expanding population, which has led to overgrazing and the destruction of trees and scrub for fuelwood. In recent years many famines have taken place in the area.

**Saigon** former name (to 1976) of Ho Chi Minh City, Vietnam.

**saint** holy man or woman respected for his or her wisdom, spirituality, and dedication to their faith. Within the Roman Catholic Church a saint is officially recognized through canonization by the pope. Many saints are associated with miracles and canonization usually occurs after a thorough investigation of the lives and miracles attributed to them. For individual saints, see under forename; for example, →Paul, St.

**St Christopher–Nevis** alternate form of St Kitts and Nevis.

**St Kitts and Nevis** (or St Christopher and Nevis) Federation of; **area:** 262 sq km/101 sq mi (St Kitts 168 sq km/65 sq mi, Nevis 93 sq km/36 sq mi); **capital:** Basseterre (on St Kitts) (and chief port); **major towns/cities:** Charlestown (largest on Nevis), Newcastle, Sandy Point Town, Dieppe Bay Town; **physical features:** both islands are volcanic; fertile plains on coast; black beaches; **head of state:** Queen Elizabeth II from 1983, represented by Governor General Dr Cuthbert Montraville Sebastian from 1996; **head of government:** Denzil Douglas from 1995; **political system:** federal constitutional monarchy; **currency:** East Caribbean dollar; **GNP per capita (PPP):** (US$) 7,940 (1998); **exports:** sugar, manufactures, postage stamps; sugar and sugar products accounted for approximately 40% of export earnings in 1992. Principal market USA 46.6% (1996); **population:** 42,000 (1999 est); **language:** English (official); **religion:** Anglican 36%, Methodist 32%, other Protestant 8%, Roman Catholic 10%; **life expectancy:** 65 (men); 71 (women) (1998 est).

**St Lucia area:** 617 sq km/238 sq mi; **capital:** Castries; **major towns/cities:** Soufrière, Vieux-Fort, Laborie; **major ports:** Vieux-Fort; **physical features:** mountainous island with fertile valleys; mainly tropical forest; volcanic peaks; Gros and Petit Pitons; **head of state:** Queen Elizabeth II from 1979, represented by Governor General Dr Perlette Louisy from 1997; **head of government:** Kenny Anthony from 1997; **political system:** constitutional monarchy; **currency:** East Caribbean dollar; **GNP per capita (PPP):** (US$) 4,610 (1998); **exports:** bananas, coconut oil, cocoa beans, copra, beverages, tobacco, miscellaneous articles. Principal market UK 50% (1995); **population:** 154,000 (1999 est); **language:** English; French patois; **religion:** Roman Catholic 90%; **life expectancy:** 68 (men); 75 (women) (1998 est).

**St Vincent and the Grenadines area:** 388 sq km/150 sq mi, including islets of the Northern Grenadines 43 sq km/17 sq mi; **capital:** Kingstown; **major towns/cities:** Georgetown, Châteaubelair, Layon, Baronallie; **physical features:** volcanic mountains, thickly forested; La Soufrière volcano; **head of state:** Queen Elizabeth II from 1979, represented by governor general David Jack from 1989; **head of government:** James Mitchell from 1984; **political system:**

constitutional monarchy; **currency:** East Caribbean dollar; **GNP per capita (PPP):** (US$) 4,090 (1998); **exports:** bananas, eddoes, dasheen, sweet potatoes, flour, ginger, tannias, plantains. Principal market UK 38.5% (1996); **population:** 120,000 (1999 est); **language:** English; French patois; **religion:** Anglican, Methodist, Roman Catholic; **life expectancy:** 72 (men); 76 (women) (1998 est).

**St Petersburg** capital of the St Petersburg region, Russian Federation, at the head of the Gulf of Finland; population (1994) 4,883,000. Industries include shipbuilding, machinery, chemicals, and textiles. It was renamed **Petrograd** 1914 and was called **Leningrad** 1924–91, when its original name was restored.

Built on a low and swampy site, St Petersburg is split up by the mouths of the River Neva, which connects it with Lake Ladoga. The climate is severe. The city became a seaport when it was linked with the Baltic by a ship canal built 1875–93. It is also linked by canal and river with the Caspian and Black seas, and in 1975 a seaway connection was completed via lakes Onega and Ladoga with the White Sea near Belomorsk, allowing naval forces to reach the Barents Sea free of NATO surveillance.

**Saladin** (c. 1138–1193) (or Salah al-Din Yusuf ibn Ayyub Kurdish) conqueror of the Kingdom of Jerusalem. He was tutored in the military arts by his uncle, a general in Aleppo, before becoming the ruler of Egypt in 1169 and Aleppo in 1183. He recovered Jerusalem from the Christians in 1187, precipitating the Third →Crusade, but was later defeated by Richard (I) the Lionheart. Renowned for knightly courtesy, Saladin made peace with Richard in 1192.

**Salamis, Battle of** in the Persian Wars, sea battle fought in the Strait of Salamis west of Athens, Greece, in 480 BC between the Greeks and the invading Persians. Despite being heavily outnumbered, the Greeks inflicted a crushing defeat on the invading Persians which effectively destroyed their fleet.

**Salinger, J(erome) D(avid)** (1919–   ) US writer. He wrote the classic novel of mid-20th-century adolescence *The Catcher in the Rye* (1951). He developed his lyrical Zen themes in *Franny and Zooey* (1961) and *Raise High the Roof Beam, Carpenters* and *Seymour: An Introduction* (1963), short stories about a Jewish family named Glass, after which he stopped publishing. He also wrote *For Esmé – With Love and Squalor* (1953).

**salmonella** any of a very varied group of bacteria, genus *Salmonella*, that colonize the intestines of humans and some animals. Some strains cause typhoid and paratyphoid fevers, while others cause salmonella →food poisoning, which is characterized by stomach pains, vomiting, diarrhoea, and headache. It can be fatal in elderly people, but others usually recover in a few days without antibiotics. Most cases are caused by contaminated animal products, especially poultry meat.

**salt** in chemistry, any compound formed from an acid and a base through the replacement of all or part of the hydrogen in the acid by a metal or electropositive radical. **Common salt** is sodium chloride (see →salt, common).

**salt, common** (or sodium chloride) NaCl white crystalline solid, found dissolved in sea water and as rock salt (the mineral halite) in large deposits and salt domes. Common salt is used extensively in the food industry as a preservative and for flavouring, and in the chemical industry in the making of chlorine and sodium.

**Salzburg** capital of the federal state of Salzburg, west Austria, on the River Salzach; population (1995) 142,000. There are textile industries, and stock rearing, dairy farming, forestry, tourism, and the manufacture of musical instruments all contribute to the local economy. The city is dominated by the Hohensalzburg fortress (founded 1077, present buildings 1465–1519). It is the seat of an archbishopric founded by St Boniface in about 700 and has a 17th-century cathedral. It is also a conference centre. There are numerous fine Romanesque, Gothic, and baroque churches. It is the birthplace of the composer Wolfgang Amadeus Mozart and an annual music festival in August has been held here since 1920. The Mozart Museum of Sound and Film opened in 1991.

**Samara** (formerly (1935–91) Kuibyshev) capital city and river port of Samara oblast (region), west-central Russian Federation; population (1996 est) 1,175,000. Samara is located on the River Volga and the main Trans-Siberian Railway, 820 km/510 mi southeast of Moscow. It is a major industrial centre, with large heavy-engineering industries (producing road vehicles and railway rolling stock), as well as chemical, oil-processing, wood-processing, and light industries.

**Samarkand** (Uzbek Samarqand) city in eastern Uzbekistan, capital of Samarkand wiloyat (oblast), near the River Zerafshan, 217 km/135 mi east of Bukhara; population (1996) 370,000. Industries include cotton-ginning, silk manufacture, production of foodstuffs, and engineering. Samarkand is one of the oldest cities in Central Asia, dating from the 3rd or 4th millennium BC. The Registan – a collection of mosques, courtyards and former Muslim theological seminaries ('madrasahs') – forms the centrepiece of the historic town. A university is situated here.

**Samoa** Independent State of; **national name:** *Malotutu'atasi o Samoa i Sisifo*; **area:** 2,830 sq km/1,092 sq mi; **capital:** Apia (on Upolu island) (and chief port); **major towns/cities:** Lalomanu, Falevai, Tuasivi, Falealupo; **physical features:** comprises South Pacific islands of Savai'i and Upolu, with two smaller tropical islands and uninhabited islets; mountain ranges on main islands; coral reefs; over half forested; **head of state:** King Malietoa Tanumafili II from 1962; **head of government:** Tuila'epa Sa'ilele

Malielegaoi from 1998; **political system:** liberal democracy; **currency:** tala, or Samoa dollar; **GNP per capita (PPP):** (US$) 3,440 (1998); **exports:** coconut cream, beer, cigarettes, taro, copra, cocoa, bananas, timber. Principal market Australia 69.8% (1997); **population:** 177,000 (1999 est); **language:** English, Samoan (official); **religion:** Congregationalist; also Roman Catholic, Methodist; **life expectancy:** 69 (men); 74 (women) (1995–2000).

**Samoa** volcanic island chain in the southwestern Pacific. It is divided into Samoa and American Samoa.

**samurai** (or bushi, Japanese 'one who serves') Japanese term for the warrior class which became the ruling military elite for almost 700 years. A samurai was an armed retainer of a *daimyō* (large landowner) with specific duties and privileges and a strict code of honour. The system was abolished in 1869 and all samurai were pensioned off by the government.

**San Andreas fault** geological fault stretching for 1,125 km/700 mi northwest–southeast through the state of California, USA. It marks a conservative plate margin, where two plates slide past each other (see →plate tectonics).

**sand** loose grains of rock, sized 0.0625–2.00 mm/0.0025–0.08 in in diameter, consisting most commonly of →quartz, but owing their varying colour to mixtures of other minerals. Sand is used in cement-making, as an abrasive, in glass-making, and for other purposes.

**Sandinista** member of a Nicaraguan left-wing organization (Sandinist National Liberation Front, FSLN) named after Augusto César Sandino, a guerrilla leader killed 1934. It was formed 1962 and obtained widespread support from the trade unions, the church, and the middle classes, which enabled it to overthrow the regime of General Anastasio Somoza in July 1979.

The FSLN dominated the Nicaraguan government and fought a civil war against US-backed Contra guerrillas until 1988. The FSLN was defeated in elections of 1990 by a US-backed coalition, but remained the party with the largest number of seats.

**San Francisco** chief Pacific port in California, USA, on the tip of a peninsula in San Francisco Bay; population (1996 est) 735,300, metropolitan area of San Francisco and Oakland 3,686,600. The entrance channel from the Pacific to San Francisco Bay was named the Golden Gate in 1846; its strait was crossed in 1937 by the world's second-longest single-span bridge, 1,280 m/4,200 ft in length. Manufactured goods include textiles, machinery and metalware, electrical equipment, petroleum products, and pharmaceuticals. San Francisco is also a financial, trade, corporate, and diversified service centre. Tourism is a major industry. A Spanish fort (the Presidio) and the San Francisco de Asis Mission were established here in 1776. San Francisco has the largest Chinese community outside Asia.

**San Marino** Most Serene Republic of; **national name:** *Serenissima Repubblica di San Marino*; **area:** 61 sq km/24 sq mi; **capital:** San Marino; **major towns/cities:** Serravalle (industrial centre), Faetano, Fiorentino, Monte Giardino; **physical features:** the slope of Mount Titano; **head of state and government:** two captains regent, elected for a six-month period; **political system:** direct democracy; **currency:** Italian lira; **GNP per capita (PPP):** (US$) 20,000 (1997 est); **exports:** wood machinery, chemicals, wine, olive oil, textiles, tiles, ceramics, varnishes, building stone, lime, chestnuts, hides. Principal market Italy; **population:** 25,000 (1999 est); **language:** Italian; **religion:** Roman Catholic 95%; **life expectancy:** 78 (men); 85 (women) (1998 est).

**Sanskrit** the dominant classical language of the Indian subcontinent, a member of the Indo-Iranian group of the Indo-European language family, and the sacred language of Hinduism. The oldest form of Sanskrit is Vedic, the variety used in the *Vedas* and *Upanishads* (about 1500–700 BC).

**São Tomé and Príncipe** Democratic Republic of; **national name:** *República Democrática de São Tomé e Príncipe*; **area:** 1,000 sq km/386 sq mi; **capital:** São Tomé; **major towns/cities:** São António, Santana, Porto-Alegre; **physical features:** comprises two main islands and several smaller ones, all volcanic; thickly forested and fertile; **head of state:** Miguel Trovoada from 1991; **head of government:** Carlos da Graca from 1994; **political system:** emergent democracy; **currency:** dobra; **GNP per capita (PPP):** (US$) 1,350 (1998); **exports:** cocoa, copra, coffee, bananas, palm oil. Principal market the Netherlands 50.9% (1997); **population:** 154,000 (1999 est); **language:** Portuguese (official); Fang (a Bantu language); **religion:** Roman Catholic 80%, animist; **life expectancy:** 63 (men); 66 (women) (1998 est).

**sapphire** deep-blue, transparent gem variety of the mineral corundum $Al_2O_3$, aluminium oxide. Small amounts of iron and titanium give it its colour. A corundum gem of any colour except red (which is a ruby) can be called a sapphire; for example, yellow sapphire.

**Sappho** (*c.* 610–*c.* 580 BC) Greek lyric poet. A native of Lesbos and contemporary of the poet Alcaeus, she was famed for her female eroticism (hence lesbianism). The surviving fragments of her poems express a keen sense of loss, and delight in the worship of the goddess →Aphrodite.

**Sarajevo** capital of Bosnia-Herzegovina; population (1991) 526,000. Industries include engineering, brewing, chemicals, carpets, and ceramics. A Bosnian, Gavrilo Princip, assassinated Archduke Franz Ferdinand here 1914, thereby precipitating World War I. From April 1992 the city was the target of a siege by Bosnian Serb forces in their fight to carve up the newly independent republic. A United Nations ultimatum and the threat of NATO bombing led to a ceasefire February 1994 and the effective end of the siege as Serbian heavy weaponry was withdrawn from the high points surrounding the city.

**Sarawak** state of Malaysia, on the northwest corner of the island of Borneo; **area:** 124,400 sq km/48,018 sq mi; **capital:** Kuching; **physical:** mountainous; the rainforest, which may be 10 million years old, contains several thousand tree species; **industries:** timber, oil, rice, pepper, rubber, coconuts, and natural gas; **population:** (1991) 1,669,000; 24 ethnic groups make up almost half this number; **history:** Sarawak was granted by the Sultan of Brunei to English soldier James Brooke 1841, who became 'Rajah of Sarawak'. It was a British protectorate from 1888 until captured by the Japanese in World War II. It was a crown colony 1946–63, when it became part of Malaysia.

**Sartre, Jean-Paul** (1905–1980) French author and philosopher. He was a leading proponent of →existentialism. He published his first novel, *La Nausée/Nausea* (1937), followed by the trilogy *Les Chemins de la liberté/Roads to Freedom* (1944–45) and many plays, including *Les Mouches/The Flies* (1943), *Huis clos/In Camera* (1944), and *Les Séquestrés d'Altona/The Condemned of Altona* (1960). *L'Etre et le néant/Being and Nothingness* (1943), his first major philosophical work, sets out a radical doctrine of human freedom. In the later work *Critique de la raison dialectique/Critique of Dialectical Reason* (1960) he tried to produce a fusion of existentialism and Marxism.

**satellite** any small body that orbits a larger one, either natural or artificial. Natural satellites that orbit planets are called moons. The first artificial satellite, *Sputnik 1*, was launched into orbit around the Earth by the USSR in 1957. Artificial satellites are used for scientific purposes, communications, weather forecasting, and military applications. The brightest artificial satellites can be seen by the naked eye.

**Satie, Erik (Alfred Leslie)** (1866–1925) French composer. His piano pieces, such as the three *Gymnopédies* 1888, are precise and tinged with melancholy, and parody romantic expression with surreal commentary. His aesthetic of ironic simplicity, as in the *Messe des pauvres/Poor People's Mass* 1895, acted as a nationalist antidote to the perceived excesses of German Romanticism.

**Saturn** in astronomy, the second-largest planet in the Solar System, sixth from the Sun, and encircled by bright and easily visible equatorial rings. Viewed through a telescope it is ochre. Its polar diameter is 12,000 km/7,450 mi smaller than its equatorial diameter, a result of its fast rotation and low density, the lowest of any planet. Its mass is 95 times that of Earth, and its magnetic field 1,000 times stronger. **mean distance from the Sun:** 1.427 billion km/0.886 billion mi; **equatorial diameter:** 120,000 km/75,000 mi; **rotational period:** 10 hr 14 min at equator, 10 hr 40 min at higher latitudes; **year:** 29.46 Earth years; **atmosphere:** visible surface consists of swirling clouds, probably made of frozen ammonia at a temperature of −170°C/−274°F, although the markings in the clouds are not as prominent as Jupiter's. The space probes *Voyager 1* and 2 found winds reaching 1,800 kph/1,100 mph; **surface:** Saturn is believed to have a small core of rock and iron, encased in ice and topped by a deep layer of liquid hydrogen; **satellites:** 18 known moons, more than for any other planet. The largest moon, →Titan, has a dense atmosphere. Other satellites include Epimetheus, Janus, Pandor, and Prometheus; **rings:** The rings visible from Earth begin about 14,000 km/9,000 mi from the planet's cloudtops and extend out to about 76,000 km/47,000 mi. Made of small chunks of ice and rock (averaging 1 m/3.3 ft across), they are 275,000 km/170,000 mi rim to rim, but only 100 m/300 ft thick. The Voyager probes showed that the rings actually consist of thousands of closely spaced ringlets, looking like the grooves in a gramophone record.

**Saturn** (or Saturnus) in Roman mythology, the god of agriculture, identified by the Romans with the Greek god Kronos. His period of rule was the ancient Golden Age, when he introduced social order and the arts of civilization. Saturn was dethroned by his sons Jupiter, Neptune, and Dis. At the **Saturnalia**, his festival in December, gifts were exchanged, and slaves were briefly treated as their masters' equals.

**Saudi Arabia** Kingdom of; **national name:** *Mamlaka al-'Arabiya as-Sa'udiya*; **area:** 2,200,518 sq km/849,620 sq mi; **capital:** Riyadh; **major towns/cities:**

Jiddah, Mecca, Medina, Taif, Dammam, Hufuf; **major ports:** Jiddah, Dammam, Jubail, Jizan, Yanbu; **physical features:** desert, sloping to the Persian Gulf from a height of 2,750 m/9,000 ft in the west; **head of state and government:** King Fahd Ibn Abdul Aziz from 1982; **political system:** absolute monarchy; **currency:** rial; **GNP per capita (PPP):** (US$) 9,200 (1998 est); **exports:** crude and refined petroleum, petrochemicals, wheat. Principal market Japan 17% (1997); **population:** 20,899,000 (1999 est); **language:** Arabic; **religion:** Sunni Muslim; there is a Shiite minority; **life expectancy:** 70 (men); 73 (women) (1995–2000).

**Saul** (lived 11th century BC) in the Old Testament, the first king of Israel. He was anointed by Samuel and warred successfully against the neighbouring Ammonites and Philistines, but fell from God's favour in his battle against the Amalekites. He became jealous and suspicious of David and turned against him and Samuel. After being wounded in battle with the Philistines, in which his three sons died, he committed suicide.

**savanna** (or savannah) extensive open tropical grasslands, with scattered trees and shrubs. Savannas cover large areas of Africa, North and South America, and northern Australia. The soil is acidic and sandy and generally considered suitable only as pasture for low-density grazing.

**Savonarola, Girolamo** (1452–1498) Italian reformer, a Dominican friar and an eloquent preacher. His crusade against political and religious corruption won him popular support, and in 1494 he led a revolt in Florence that expelled the ruling Medici family and established a democratic republic. His denunciations of Pope Alexander VI led to his excommunication 1497, and in 1498 he was arrested, tortured, hanged, and burned for heresy.

**scabies** contagious infection of the skin caused by the parasitic itch mite *Sarcoptes scabiei*, which burrows under the skin to deposit eggs. Treatment is by antiparasitic creams and lotions.

**scale** in music, a sequence of pitches that establishes a key, and in some respects the character of a composition. A scale is defined by its starting note and may be major or minor depending on the order of intervals. A **chromatic scale** is the full range of 12 notes: it has no key because there is no fixed starting point. *See illustration on page 486.*

**Scandinavia** peninsula in northwestern Europe, comprising Norway and Sweden; politically and culturally it also includes Denmark, Iceland, the Faroe Islands, and Finland. (See separate entries for all of these.)

**scarab** any of a family Scarabaeidae of beetles, often brilliantly coloured, and including cockchafers, June beetles, and dung beetles. The *Scarabeus sacer* was revered by the ancient Egyptians as the symbol of resurrection.

**scepticism** ancient philosophical view that absolute knowledge of things is ultimately unobtainable, hence the only proper attitude is to suspend judgement.

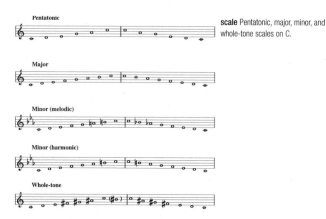

**scale** Pentatonic, major, minor, and whole-tone scales on C.

Its origins lay in the teachings of the Greek philosopher Pyrrho, who maintained that peace of mind lay in renouncing all claims to knowledge.

**Schiele, Egon** (1890–1918) Austrian artist. Strongly influenced by →art nouveau, and in particular Gustav →Klimt, he developed an angular, contorted style, employing garish colours, that made him an important pioneer of →expressionism. His subject matter includes portraits and openly erotic nudes.

**schist** →metamorphic rock containing mica or another platy or elongate mineral, whose crystals are aligned to give a foliation (planar texture) known as schistosity. Schist may contain additional minerals such as garnet.

**schizophrenia** mental disorder, a psychosis of unknown origin, which can lead to profound changes in personality, behaviour, and perception, including delusions and hallucinations. It is more common in males and the early-onset form is more severe than when the illness develops in later life. Modern treatment approaches include drugs, family therapy, stress reduction, and rehabilitation.

**Schrödinger, Erwin** (1887–1961) Austrian physicist. He advanced the study of wave mechanics to describe the behaviour of electrons in atoms. He produced in 1926 a solid mathematical explanation of the →quantum theory and the structure of the atom. Nobel prize 1933.

**Schubert, Franz Peter** (1797–1828) Austrian composer. His ten symphonies include the incomplete eighth in B minor (the 'Unfinished') and the 'Great' in C major. He wrote chamber and piano music, including the 'Trout

Quintet', and over 600 lieder (songs) combining the Romantic expression of emotion with pure melody. They include the cycles *Die schöne Müllerin/ The Beautiful Maid of the Mill* (1823) and *Die Winterreise/The Winter Journey* (1827).

**Schumann, Robert Alexander** (1810– 1856) German composer and writer. His songs and short piano pieces portray states of emotion with great economy. Among his compositions are four symphonies, a violin concerto, a piano concerto, sonatas, and song cycles, such as *Dichterliebe/Poet's Love* (1840). Mendelssohn championed many of his works.

**sciatica** persistent pain in the back and down the outside of one leg, along the sciatic nerve and its branches. Causes of sciatica include inflammation of the nerve or pressure of a displaced disc on a nerve root leading out of the lower spine.

**scorpion** any arachnid of the order Scorpiones, common in the tropics and subtropics. Scorpions have four pairs of walking legs, large pincers, and long tails ending in upcurved poisonous stings, though the venom is not usually fatal to a healthy adult human. Some species reach 25 cm/10 in. There are about 600 different species.

**Scorsese, Martin** (1942– ) US director, screenwriter, and producer. One of the most influential figures in modern American cinema, he has made such contemporary classics as *Mean Streets* (1973), *Taxi Driver* (1976), *Raging Bull* (1980), *GoodFellas* (1990), and *The Age of Innocence* (1993).

**Scott, Robert Falcon** (1868–1912) known as Scott of the Antarctic, English explorer who commanded two Antarctic expeditions, 1901–04 and 1910– 12. On 18 January 1912 he reached the South Pole, shortly after the Norwegian Roald →Amundsen, but on the return journey he and his companions died in a blizzard only a few miles from their base camp. His journal was recovered and published in 1913.

**Scott, Walter** (1771–1832) Scottish novelist and poet. His first works were translations of German ballads and collections of Scottish ballads, which he followed with narrative poems of his own, such as *The Lay of the Last Minstrel* (1805), *Marmion* (1808), and *The Lady of the Lake* (1810). He gained a European reputation for his historical novels such as *Waverley* (1814), *Rob Roy* (1817), *The Heart of Midlothian* (1818), and *Ivanhoe* (1819), all published anonymously.

**scrapie** fatal disease of sheep and goats that attacks the central nervous system, causing deterioration of the brain cells, and leading to the characteristic staggering gait and other behavioural abnormalities, before death. It is caused by the presence of an abnormal version of the brain protein PrP and is related to →bovine spongiform encephalopathy, the disease of cattle known as 'mad cow disease', and Creutzfeldt–Jakob disease in humans. It is a transmissible spongiform encephalopathy.

**scuba** (acronym for self-contained underwater breathing apparatus) another name for →aqualung.

**sculpture** artistic shaping of materials such as wood, stone, clay, metal, and, more recently, plastic and other synthetics. The earliest prehistoric human artefacts include sculpted stone figurines, and all ancient civilizations have left behind examples of sculpture. Many indigenous cultures have maintained rich traditions of sculpture. Those of Africa, South America, and the Caribbean in particular have been influential in the development of contemporary Western sculpture.

Historically, most sculpture has been religious in intent. Chinese, Japanese, and Indian sculptures are usually Buddhist or Hindu images. African, American Indian, and Oceanic sculptures reflect spirit cults and animist beliefs.

There are two main techniques traditionally employed in sculpture: **carving**, involving the cutting away of hard materials such as wood or stone to reveal an image; and **modelling**, involving the building up of an image from malleable materials, such as clay or wax, which may then be cast in bronze. In the 20th century various techniques for 'constructing' sculptures have been developed, for example metal welding and assemblage.

**scurvy** disease caused by deficiency of vitamin C (ascorbic acid), which is contained in fresh vegetables and fruit. The signs are weakness and aching joints and muscles, progressing to bleeding of the gums and other spontaneous haemorrhage, and drying-up of the skin and hair. It is reversed by giving the vitamin.

**seafloor spreading** growth of the ocean crust outwards (sideways) from ocean ridges. The concept of seafloor spreading has been combined with that of continental drift and incorporated into →plate tectonics.

**seal** aquatic carnivorous mammal of the families Otariidae and Phocidae (sometimes placed in a separate order, the Pinnipedia). The eared seals or sea lions (Otariidae) have small external ears, unlike the true seals (Phocidae). Seals have a streamlined body with thick blubber for insulation, and front and hind flippers. They are able to close their nostrils as they dive, and obtain oxygen from their blood supply while under water. They feed on fish, squid, and crustaceans, and are commonly found in Arctic and Antarctic seas, but also in Mediterranean, Caribbean, and Hawaiian waters.

**sea slug** any of an order (Nudibranchia) of marine gastropod molluscs in which the shell is reduced or absent. The order includes some very colourful forms, especially in the tropics. They are largely carnivorous, feeding on hydroids and sponges.

**seaweed** any of a vast group of simple multicellular plant forms belonging to the →algae and found growing in the sea, brackish estuaries, and salt marshes, from about the high-tide mark to depths of 100–200 m/300–600 ft. Many seaweeds have holdfasts (attaching them to rocks or other surfaces),

Chemical precipitates include some limestones and evaporated deposits such as gypsum and halite (rock salt). Coal, oil shale, and limestone made of fossil material are examples of organic sedimentary rocks.

**seed** the reproductive →structure of higher plants (angiosperms and →gymnosperms). It develops from a fertilized ovule and consists of an embryo and a food store, surrounded and protected by an outer seed coat, called the testa.

sea slug Sea slugs are molluscs related to snails, with a reduced or absent shell. Their bright coloration warns predators that they contain poisons and are distasteful.

stalks, and fronds, sometimes with air bladders to keep them afloat, and are green, blue-green, red, or brown.

**secretary of state** in the UK, a title held by a number of ministers; for example, the secretary of state for foreign and commonwealth affairs.

**sedimentary rock** rock formed by the accumulation and cementation of deposits that have been laid down by water, wind, ice, or gravity. Sedimentary rocks cover more than two-thirds of the Earth's surface and comprise three major categories: clastic, chemically precipitated, and organic (or biogenic). Clastic sediments are the largest group and are composed of fragments of pre-existing rocks; they include clays, sands, and gravels.

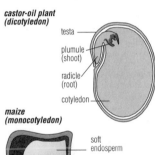

*castor-oil plant (dicotyledon)*

- testa
- plumule (shoot)
- radicle (root)
- cotyledon

*maize (monocotyledon)*

- soft endosperm
- hard endosperm
- scutellum
- plumule
- radicle

seed The structure of seeds. The castor is a dicotyledon, a plant in which the developing plant has two leaves, developed from the cotyledon. In maize, a monocotyledon, there is a single leaf developed from the scutellum.

The food store is contained either in a specialized nutritive tissue, the endosperm, or in the →cotyledons of the embryo itself. In angiosperms the seed is enclosed within a →fruit, whereas in gymnosperms it is usually naked and unprotected, once shed from the female cone.

Following →germination the seed develops into a new plant.

**Seine** French river rising on the Langres plateau in the *département* of Côte d'Or, 30 km/19 mi northwest of Dijon, and flowing 774 km/472 mi northwest through →Paris and Rouen to join the English Channel at Le Havre. It is the third longest, but economically the most important, river in the country.

**seismology** study of earthquakes and how their shock waves travel through the Earth. By examining the global pattern of waves produced by an earthquake, seismologists can deduce the nature of the materials through which they have passed. This leads to an understanding of the Earth's internal structure.

**semantics** branch of linguistics dealing with the meaning of words and sentences. Semantics asks how we can use language to express things about the real world and how the meanings of linguistic expressions can reflect people's thoughts. Semantic knowledge is compositional; the meaning of a sentence is based on the meanings of the words it contains and the order they appear in. For example, the sentences 'Teachers love children' and 'Children love teachers' both involve people loving other people but because of the different order of words they mean different things.

**semaphore** visual signalling code in which the relative positions of two moveable pointers or hand-held flags stand for different letters or numbers. The system is used by ships at sea and for railway signals.

**Senate** in ancient Rome, the 'council of elders'. Originally consisting of the heads of patrician families, it was recruited from ex-magistrates and persons who had rendered notable public service, but was periodically purged by the censors. Although nominally advisory, it controlled finance and foreign policy. Sulla doubled its size to 600.

**Seneca, Lucius Annaeus** (c. 4 BC–AD c. 65) Roman Stoic playwright, author of essays and nine tragedies. He was tutor to the future emperor Nero but lost favour after Nero's accession to the throne and was ordered to commit suicide. His tragedies were accepted as classical models by 16th-century dramatists.

**Senegal** Republic of; **national name:** *République du Sénégal*; **area:** 196,200 sq km/75,752 sq mi; **capital:** Dakar (and chief port); **major towns/cities:** Thiès, Kaolack, Saint-Louis, Ziguinchor, Diourbel; **physical features:** plains rising to hills in southeast; swamp and tropical forest in southwest; River Senegal; The Gambia forms an enclave within Senegal; **head of state:** Abdou Diouf from 1981; **head of government:** Mamadou Lamine Loum from 1998; **political system:** emergent socialist democracy; **currency:** franc CFA; **GNP per capita (PPP):** (US$) 1,710 (1998); **exports:** fresh and processed fish, refined petroleum products, chemicals, groundnuts and related products, calcium phosphates and related products. Principal market India 25.6% (1997); **population:** 9,240,000 (1999 est); **language:** French (official); Wolof; **religion:** mainly Sunni Muslim; **life expectancy:** 51 (men); 54 (women) (1995–2000).

**senile dementia** →dementia associated with old age, often caused by →Alzheimer's disease.

**sensitivity** in biology, the ability of an organism, or part of an organism, to detect changes in the environment. All living things are capable of some sensitivity, and any change detected by an organism is called a stimulus. Plant response to stimuli (for example, light, heat, moisture) is by directional growth (→tropism). In animals, the body cells that detect the stimuli are called receptors, and these are often contained within a sense organ. For example, the eye is a sense organ, within which the retina contains rod and cone cells which are receptors. The part of the body that responds to a stimulus, such as a muscle, is called an effector, and the communication of stimuli from receptors to effectors is termed 'coordination'; messages are passed from receptors to effectors either via the →nerves or by means of chemicals called →hormones. Rapid communication and response to stimuli, such as light, sound, and scent, can be essential to an animal's well-being

and survival, and evolution has led to the development of highly complex mechanisms for this purpose.

**Seoul** (or Sŏul) capital of South Korea (Republic of Korea), near the Han River, and with its chief port at Inchon; population (1994) 11,500,000. Industries include engineering, textiles, food processing, electrical and electronic equipment, chemicals, and machinery.

**Sepoy Rebellion** alternative name for the →Indian Mutiny, a revolt of Indian soldiers against the British in India 1857–58.

**septicaemia** general term for any form of blood poisoning.

**sequencing** in biochemistry, determining the sequence of chemical subunits within a large molecule. Techniques for sequencing amino acids in proteins were established in the 1950s, insulin being the first for which the sequence was completed. The →Human Genome Project is attempting to determine the sequence of the 3 billion base pairs within human →DNA.

**sequoia** either of two species of →conifer tree belonging to the redwood family, native to the western USA. The **redwood** (*Sequoia sempervirens*) is a long-living timber tree, and one specimen, the Howard Libbey Redwood, is the world's tallest tree at 110 m/361 ft, with a trunk circumference of 13.4 m/44 ft. The giant sequoia (*Sequoiadendron giganteum*) reaches up to 30 m/100 ft in circumference at the base of the trunk, and grows almost as tall as the redwood.

It is also (except for the bristlecone pine) the oldest living tree, some specimens being estimated at over 3,500 years of age. (Family Taxodiaceae.)

**Serbia** (Serbo-Croatian *Srbija*) constituent republic of Yugoslavia, which includes Kosovo and Vojvodina. **area:** 88,400 sq km/34,122 sq mi; **capital:** Belgrade; **physical:** fertile Danube plains in the north, mountainous in the south (Dinaric Alps, Sar Mountains, northern Albanian Alps, Balkan Mountains); rivers Sava, Tisza, Morava; **features:** includes the former autonomous provinces of →Kosovo, capital Priština, of which the predominantly Albanian population demands unification with Albania, and Vojvodina, capital Novi Sad, largest town Subotica, with a predominantly Serbian population and a large Hungarian minority; **population:** (1991) 9,791,400; **language:** the Serbian variant of Serbo-Croatian; **religion:** Serbian Orthodox; **history:** The Serbs settled in the Balkans in the 7th century and became Christians in the 9th century. They were united as one kingdom in about 1169; the Serbian hero Stephan Dushan (1331–1355) founded an empire covering most of the Balkans. After their defeat at Kosovo in 1389 they came under the domination of the Turks, who annexed Serbia in 1459. Uprisings of 1804–16, led by Kara George and Miloš Obrenović, forced the Turks to recognize Serbia as an autonomous principality under Miloš. The assassination of Kara George on Obrenović's orders gave rise to a long feud between the two houses. After a war with Turkey in 1876–78, Serbia became an independent kingdom. On the assassination of the last Obrenovic in 1903 the Karageorgević dynasty came to the throne.

The two Balkan Wars in 1912–13 greatly enlarged Serbia's territory at the expense of Turkey and Bulgaria. Serbia's designs on Bosnia-Herzegovina, backed by Russia, led to friction with Austria, culminating in the outbreak of war in 1914. Serbia was overrun in 1915–16 and was occupied until 1918, when it became the nucleus of the new kingdom of the Serbs, Croats, and Slovenes, and subsequently Yugoslavia. Rivalry between Croats and Serbs continued within the republic. During World War II Serbia was under a puppet government set up by the Germans (94% of Serbian Jews were killed in 1941–44); after the war it became a constituent republic of Yugoslavia.

From 1986 Slobodan →Milošević as Serbian communist party chief and president waged a populist campaign to end the autonomous status of the provinces of Kosovo and Vojvodina.

The 1991 civil war in Yugoslavia arose from the Milošević nationalist government attempting the forcible annexation of Serb-dominated regions making use of the largely Serbian federal army. A successor Yugoslavia, announced by Serbia and Montenegro in April 1992, was rejected by the USA and EC because of concerns over serious human rights violations in Kosovo and Serbia's continued backing of Bosnian Serbs in their fight to partition Bosnia-Herzegovina.

Despite continued civil unrest,

Milošević was elected in July 1997 to the Yugoslav presidency.

Early 1998 saw fighting between Serb paramilitary forces and ethnic Albanians in Kosovo.

In March 1999, NATO aircraft began a bombing campaign in an attempt to force the Yugoslav government to end its persecution of ethnic Albanians in Kosovo.

At the end of June the Serbian parliament accepted a peace plan put forward by the Group of Eight (G8) nations.

**serfdom** the legal and economic status of peasants under feudalism. Serfs could not be sold like slaves, but they were not free to leave their master's estate without his permission. They had to work the lord's land without pay for a number of days every week and pay a percentage of their produce to the lord every year. They also served as soldiers in the event of conflict. Serfs also had to perform extra labour at harvest time and other busy seasons; in return they were allowed to cultivate a portion of the estate for their own benefit.

**set** (or class) in mathematics, any collection of defined things (elements), provided the elements are distinct and that there is a rule to decide whether an element is a member of a set. It is usually denoted by a capital letter and indicated by curly brackets {}.

**Seurat, Georges Pierre** (1859–1891) French artist. One of the major post-Impressionists, he originated, with Paul Signac, the technique of pointillism (painting with small dabs rather than long brushstrokes). One of his best-known works is *A Sunday Afternoon on the Island of La Grande Jatte* (1886; Art Institute of Chicago).

**Seven Wonders of the World** in antiquity, the →pyramids of Egypt, the Hanging Gardens of Babylon, the temple of Artemis at Ephesus, the Greek sculptor Phidias' chryselephantine statue of Zeus at Olympia, the Mausoleum at Halicarnassus, the Colossus of Rhodes, and the lighthouse on the island of Pharos in the Bay of Alexandria.

**Seven Years' War** fighting in North America (known as the French and Indian war) 1756–63 arising from the conflict between Austria and Prussia, and between France and Britain over colonial supremacy. Britain and Prussia defeated France, Austria, Spain, and Russia; Britain gained control of India and many of France's colonies, including Canada.

Spain ceded Florida to Britain in exchange for Cuba. Fighting against great odds, Prussia was eventually successful in becoming established as one of the great European powers. The war ended with the Treaty of Paris 1763, signed by Britain, France, and Spain.

**sex determination** process by which the sex of an organism is determined. In many species, the sex of an individual is dictated by the two sex chromosomes (X and Y) it receives from its parents. In mammals, some plants, and a few insects, males are XY, and females XX; in birds, reptiles, some amphibians, and butterflies the reverse is the case. In bees and wasps, males are produced from unfertilized eggs, females from fertilized eggs.

Environmental factors can affect some fish and reptiles, such as turtles, where sex is influenced by the temperature at which the eggs develop. In 1991 it was shown that maleness was caused by a single gene, 14 base pairs long, on the Y chromosome.

**sexual reproduction** reproductive process in organisms that requires the union, or →fertilization, of gametes (such as eggs and sperm). These are usually produced by two different individuals, although self-fertilization occurs in a few hermaphrodites such as tapeworms. Most organisms other than bacteria and cyanobacteria →(blue-green algae) show some sort of sexual process. Except in some lower organisms, the gametes are of two distinct types called eggs and sperm. The organisms producing the eggs are called females, and those producing the sperm, males. The fusion of a male and female gamete produces a zygote, from which a new individual develops. See →reproduction.

**Seychelles** Republic of; **area:** 453 sq km/174 sq mi; **capital:** Victoria (on Mahé island) (and chief port); **major towns/cities:** Cascade, Port Glaud, Misere; **physical features:** comprises two distinct island groups one, the Granitic group, concentrated, the other, the Outer or Coralline group, widely scattered; totals over 100 islands and islets; **head of state and government:** France-Albert René from 1977; **political system:** emergent democracy; **currency:** Seychelles rupee; **GNP per capita (PPP):** (US$) 10,530 (1998); **exports:** fresh and frozen fish, canned tuna, shark fins, cinnamon bark, refined petroleum products. Principal market France 18.7% (1997); **population:** 79,000 (1999 est); **language:** creole (Asian, African, European mixture) 95%, English, French (all official); **religion:** Roman Catholic; **life expectancy:** 66 (men); 76 (women) (1998 est).

**Seymour, Jane** (c. 1509–1537) English noble, third wife of Henry VIII, whom she married 1536. She died soon after the birth of her son Edward VI.

**Shackleton, Ernest Henry** (1874–1922) Irish Antarctic explorer. In 1908–09, he commanded the British Antarctic expedition that reached 88° 23′ S latitude, located the magnetic South Pole, and climbed Mount Erebus. He was knighted in 1909.

**Shaftesbury, Anthony Ashley Cooper, 1st Earl of Shaftesbury** (1621–1683) English politician, a supporter of the Restoration of the monarchy. He became Lord Chancellor in 1672, but went into opposition in 1673 and began to organize the Whig Party. He headed the Whigs' demand for the exclusion of the future James II from the succession, secured the passing of the Habeas Corpus Act of 1679, then, when accused of treason in 1681, fled to Holland. He became baronet in 1631, baron in 1661, and was created earl in 1672.

**Shakespeare, William** (1564–1616) English dramatist and poet. He is considered the greatest English dramatist. His plays, written in blank verse with some prose, can be broadly divided into lyric plays, including *Romeo and Juliet* and *A Midsummer Night's Dream*; comedies, including *The Comedy of Errors*, *As You Like It*, *Much Ado About Nothing*, and *Measure For Measure*; historical plays, such as *Henry VI* (in three parts), *Richard III*, and *Henry IV* (in two parts), which often showed cynical political wisdom; and tragedies, including *Hamlet*, *Othello*, *King Lear*, and *Macbeth*. He also wrote numerous sonnets.

## SHAKESPEARE'S PLAYS

| Title | First performed/ written (approximate) |
| --- | --- |
| **Early Plays** | |
| *Henry VI Part I* | 1589–92 |
| *Henry VI Part II* | 1590–91 |
| *Henry VI Part III* | 1590–92 |
| *The Comedy of Errors* | 1591–93 |
| *The Taming of the Shrew* | 1593–94 |
| *Titus Andronicus* | 1593–94 |
| *The Two Gentlemen of Verona* | 1590–95 |
| *Love's Labour's Lost* | 1593–95 |
| *Romeo and Juliet* | 1594–95 |
| **Histories** | |
| *Richard III* | 1592–93 |
| *Richard II* | 1595–97 |
| *King John* | 1595–97 |
| *Henry IV Part I* | 1596–97 |
| *Henry IV Part II* | 1596–97 |
| *Henry V* | 1599 |
| **Roman Plays** | |
| *Julius Caesar* | 1599 |
| *Antony and Cleopatra* | 1606–07 |
| *Coriolanus* | 1608 |
| **The 'Great' or 'Middle' Comedies** | |
| *A Midsummer Night's Dream* | 1594–95 |
| *The Merchant of Venice* | 1596–98 |
| *Much Ado About Nothing* | 1598 |
| *As You Like It* | 1599–1600 |
| *The Merry Wives of Windsor* | 1597 |
| *Twelfth Night* | 1600–02 |
| **The Great Tragedies** | |
| *Hamlet* | 1601–02 |
| *Othello* | 1604 |
| *King Lear* | 1605–06 |
| *Macbeth* | 1606 |
| *Timon of Athens* | 1607–08 |
| **The 'Dark' Comedies** | |
| *Troilus and Cressida* | 1601–02 |
| *All's Well That Ends Well* | 1602–03 |
| *Measure for Measure* | 1604 |
| **Late Plays** | |
| *Pericles* | 1606–08 |
| *Cymbeline* | 1609–10 |
| *The Winter's Tale* | 1611 |
| *The Tempest* | 1611 |
| *Henry VIII* | 1613 |

**Shanghai** largest urban settlement and mainland port in China, in Jiangsu province, on the Huangpu and Wusong rivers, 24 km/15 mi from the Chang Jiang estuary; population (1993) 8,760,000. The municipality of Shanghai has an area of 5,800 sq km/2,239 sq mi; population (1996) 14,190,000. Shanghai is China's principal commercial and financial centre. Textiles, paper, chemicals, steel, vehicles, agricultural machinery, precision instruments, shipbuilding, and flour are produced; other industries include vegetable-oil milling and oil-refining. Administratively independent of Jiangsu, Shanghai answers directly to the central government.

**share** in finance, that part of the capital of a company held by a member (shareholder). Shares may be numbered and are issued as units of definite face value; shareholders are not always called on to pay the full face value of their shares, though they bind themselves to do so.

**Shari'a** the law of Islam believed by Muslims to be based on divine revelation, and drawn from a number of sources, including the Koran, the Hadith, and the consensus of the Muslim community. Under this law, *qisās*, or retribution, allows a family to exact equal punishment on an accused; *diyat*, or blood money, is payable to a dead person's family as compensation.

**shark** any member of various orders of cartilaginous fishes (class Chondrichthyes), found throughout the oceans of the world. There are about 400 known species of shark. They have tough, usually grey skin covered in denticles (small toothlike scales). A shark's streamlined body has side pectoral fins, a high dorsal fin, and a forked tail with a large upper lobe. Five open gill slits are visible on each side of the generally pointed head. They shed and replace their teeth continually, even before birth. Teeth may be replaced as frequently as every week. Most sharks are fish-eaters, and a few will attack humans. They range from several feet in length to the great white shark *Carcharodon carcharias*, 9 m/30 ft long, and the harmless plankton-feeding whale shark *Rhincodon typus*, over 15 m/50 ft in length.

**Shaw, George Bernard** (1856–1950) Irish dramatist, critic, and novelist, and an early member of the socialist Fabian Society, although he resigned in 1911. His plays combine comedy with political, philosophical, and polemic aspects, aiming to make an impact on his

**shark** The great white shark of the Atlantic, Pacific, and Indian oceans is a large and aggressive fish. It has a reputation for eating humans. Like all sharks, the great white has a skeleton made of cartilage, not bone.

audience's social conscience as well as their emotions. They include *Arms and the Man* (1894), *The Devil's Disciple* (1897), *Man and Superman* (1903), *Pygmalion* (1913), and *St Joan* (1923). He was awarded the Nobel Prize for Literature in 1925.

**Shelley, Mary Wollstonecraft** (1797–1851) born Mary Godwin, English writer. She is best known as the author of the Gothic horror story *Frankenstein* (1818), which is considered to be the origin of modern science fiction, and her other novels include *The Last Man* (1826) and *Valperga* (1823). In 1814 she eloped to Switzerland with the poet Percy Bysshe Shelley, whom she married in 1816 on the death of his first wife Harriet. She was the daughter of Mary Wollstonecraft and William Godwin.

---

**WEB SITE** > > > > > > > >

**Mary Shelley Resource Page**

http://www.desert-fairy.com/maryshel.shtml

Resource on this English writer, most famed for her creation of *Frankenstein*. There is illustrated hypertext on her life, the literary sources of *Frankenstein*, and the events of the pivotal summer of 1816. The site also includes wide-ranging information about her contemporaries and parents, including Lord Byron, Percy Shelley, and Mary Wollstonecraft.

---

**Shelley, Percy Bysshe** (1792–1822) English lyric poet and critic. With his skill in poetic form and metre, his intellectual capacity and searching mind, his rebellious but constructive nature, and his notorious moral nonconformity, he is a commanding figure of the Romantic movement. He fought all his life against religion and for political freedom. This is reflected in his early poems such as *Queen Mab* (1813). He later wrote tragedies including *The Cenci* (1818), lyric dramas such as *Prometheus Unbound* (1820), and lyrical poems such as 'Ode to the West Wind'. He drowned while sailing in Italy.

**Shetland Islands** (Old Norse *Hjaltland* 'high land' or 'Hjalte's land') islands and unitary authority off the north coast of Scotland, 80 km/50 mi north-east of the Orkney Islands, an important centre of the North Sea oil industry, and the most northerly part of the UK. **area:** 1,452 sq km/560 sq mi; **towns:** Lerwick (administrative headquarters), on Mainland, largest of 12 inhabited islands; **physical:** the 100 islands are mostly bleak, hilly, and clad in moorland. The climate is moist, cool, and windy; in summer there is almost perpetual daylight, whilst winter days are very short. On clear winter nights, the aurora borealis ('northern lights') can frequently be seen in the sky; **industries:** processed fish, handknits from Fair Isle and Unst, herring fishing, salmon farming, cattle and sheep farming; large oil and gas fields west of Shetland; Europe's largest oil port is Sullom Voe, Mainland; production at Foinaven oilfield, the first to be developed in Atlantic waters; tourism;

**population:** (1996) 22,500; **history:** dialect derived from Norse, the islands having been a Norse dependency from the 9th century until 1472 when they were annexed by Scotland.

**Shiite** (or Shiah) member of a sect of Islam that believes that →Ali was →Muhammad's first true successor. The Shiites are doctrinally opposed to the Sunni Muslims. They developed their own law differing only in minor directions, such as inheritance and the status of women. In Shi'ism, the clergy are empowered to intervene between God and humans, whereas among the Sunni, the relationship with God is direct and the clergy serve as advisers.

The Shiites are prominent in Iran, the Lebanon, and Indo-Pakistan, and are also found in Iraq and Bahrain.

**shingles** common name for →herpes zoster, a disease characterized by infection of sensory nerves, with pain and eruption of blisters along the course of the affected nerves.

**ship** large seagoing vessel. The Greeks, Phoenicians, Romans, and Vikings used ships extensively for trade, exploration, and warfare. The 14th century was the era of European exploration by sailing ship, largely aided by the invention of the compass. In the 15th century Britain's Royal Navy was first formed, but in the 16th–19th centuries Spanish and Dutch fleets dominated the shipping lanes of both the Atlantic and Pacific.

The ultimate sailing ships, the fast US and British tea clippers, were built in the 19th century. Also in the 19th century, iron was first used for some shipbuilding instead of wood. Steam-propelled ships of the late 19th century were followed by compound engine and turbine-propelled vessels from the early 20th century.

**shogun** Japanese term for military dictator and abbreviation for 'seii tai shogun' – 'great barbarian-conquering general'. Technically an imperial appointment, the office was treated as hereditary and was held by a series of clans, the Minamoto 1192–1219, the Ashikaga 1336–1573, and the Tokugawa 1603–1868. The shogun held legislative, judicial, and executive power.

**Short Parliament** the English Parliament that was summoned by Charles I on 13 April 1640 to raise funds for his war against the Scots. It was succeeded later in the year by the →Long Parliament.

**shot put** (or putting the shot) in athletics, the sport of throwing (or putting) overhand from the shoulder a metal ball (or shot). Standard shot weights are 7.26 kg/16 lb for men and 4 kg/8.8 lb for women.

**Sibelius, Jean Julius Christian** (1865–1957) Finnish composer. His works include nationalistic symphonic poems such as *En saga* (1893) and *Finlandia* (1900), a violin concerto (1904), and seven symphonies. In 1940 he abruptly ceased composing and spent the rest of his life as a recluse. Restoration of many works to their original state has helped to dispel his conservative image and reveal unexpectedly radical features.

**Siberia** Asian region of Russia, extending from the Ural Mountains to the Pacific Ocean. **area:** 12,050,000 sq km/4,650,000 sq mi; **towns:** Novosibirsk, Omsk, Krasnoyarsk, Irkutsk, Tomsk; **features:** continental climate, bringing long and extremely cold winters; the world's largest remaining native forests (*taiga*); Lake Baikal; volcanoes (on the Kamchatka Peninsula); Ussuriland, domain of the world's largest cat, the Siberian tiger; **industries:** hydroelectric power from rivers Lena, Ob, and Yenisey; forestry and agriculture; vast mineral resources, including coal (in the Kuznetsk Basin), gold, diamonds, oil, natural gas, iron, copper, nickel, cobalt.

**Sicily** (Italian *Sicilia*) the largest Mediterranean island and an autonomous region of Italy, divided from the Italian mainland by the Strait of Messina; area 25,700 sq km/9,920 sq mi; population (1992) 4,997,700. It consists of nine provinces: Agrigento, Caltanissetta, Catania, Enna, Messina, Palermo, Ragusa, Syracuse, and Trapani; its capital is Palermo. Exports include Marsala wine, olives, citrus, refined oil and petrochemicals, pharmaceuticals, potash, asphalt, and marble. The region also incorporates the islands of Lipari, Egadi, Ustica, and Pantelleria. Etna, 3,323 m/10,906 ft high, is the highest volcano in Europe; its last major eruption was in 1993.

**Sickert, Walter Richard** (1860–1942) English artist. His works, broadly Impressionist in style, capture subtleties of tone and light, often with a melancholic atmosphere, their most familiar subjects being the rather shabby cityscapes and domestic and music-hall interiors of late Victorian and Edwardian London. *Ennui* (about 1913; Tate Gallery, London) is a typical interior painting. His work inspired the Camden Town Group.

**Sidney, Philip** (1554–1586) English poet and incompetent soldier. He wrote the sonnet sequence *Astrophel and Stella* (1591), *Arcadia* (1590), a prose romance, and *Apologie for Poetrie* (1595). Politically, Sidney became a charismatic, but hardly powerful, figure supporting a 'forward' foreign policy that would help the Protestant Netherlands against the Spanish.

**Sierra Leone** Republic of; **area:** 71,740 sq km/27,698 sq mi; **capital:** Freetown; **major towns/cities:** Koidu, Bo, Kenema, Makeni; **major ports:** Bonthe-Sherbro; **physical features:** mountains in east; hills and forest; coastal mangrove swamps; **head of state and government:** Ahmad Tejan Kabbah from 1998; **political system:** transitional; **currency:** leone; **GNP per capita (PPP):** (US$) 390 (1998); **exports:** rutile, diamonds, bauxite, gold, coffee, cocoa beans. Principal market Belgium – Luxembourg 48.9% (1997); **population:** 4,717,000 (1999 est); **language:** English (official), Krio (a creole language); **religion:** animist 52%, Muslim 39%, Protestant 6%, Roman Catholic 2% (1980 est); **life**

**expectancy:** 36 (men); 39 (women) (1995–2000).

**Sikhism** religion professed by 14 million Indians, living mainly in the Punjab. Sikhism was founded by Nanak (1469–c. 1539). Sikhs believe in a single God who is the immortal creator of the universe and who has never been incarnate in any form, and in the equality of all human beings; Sikhism is strongly opposed to caste divisions.

Their holy book is the *Guru Granth Sahib*. Guru Gobind Singh (1666–1708) instituted the *Khanda-di-Pahul*, the baptism of the sword, and established the Khalsa ('pure'), the company of the faithful. The Khalsa wear the five Ks: *kes*, long hair; *kangha*, a comb; *kirpan*, a sword; *kachh*, short trousers; and *kara*, a steel bracelet. Sikh men take the last name 'Singh' ('lion') and women 'Kaur' ('princess').

**Sikh Wars** two wars in India between the Sikhs and the British.

The **First Sikh War 1845–46** followed an invasion of British India by Punjabi Sikhs. The Sikhs were defeated and part of their territory annexed.

The **Second Sikh War 1848–49** arose from a Sikh revolt in Multan. They were defeated, and the British annexed the Punjab.

**silicon chip** →integrated circuit with microscopically small electrical components on a piece of silicon crystal only a few millimetres square.

**silk** fine soft thread produced by the larva of the silkworm moth when making its cocoon. It is soaked, carefully unwrapped, and used in the manufacture of textiles. The introduction of synthetics originally harmed the silk industry, but rising standards of living have produced an increased demand for real silk. It is manufactured in China, India, Japan, and Thailand.

**Silurian** period of geological time 439–409 million years ago, the third period of the Palaeozoic era. Silurian sediments are mostly marine and consist of shales and limestone. Luxuriant reefs were built by coral-like organisms. The first land plants began to evolve during this period, and there were many ostracoderms (armoured jawless fishes). The first jawed fishes (called acanthodians) also appeared.

**silver** white, lustrous, extremely malleable and ductile, metallic element, symbol Ag (from Latin *argentum*), atomic number 47, relative atomic mass 107.868. It occurs in nature in ores and as a free metal; the chief ores are sulphides, from which the metal is extracted by smelting with lead. It is one of the best metallic conductors of both heat and electricity; its most useful compounds are the chloride and bromide, which darken on exposure to light and are the basis of photographic emulsions.

**Sinai** Egyptian peninsula, largely desert, at the head of the Red Sea; area 65,000 sq km/25,000 sq mi. Resources include oil, natural gas, manganese, and coal; irrigation water from the River Nile is carried under the Suez Canal. The main towns are Al-Arish (the capital of South Sinai governorate) and Al-Tur (capital of North Sinai governorate). It is the ancient source of turquoise. Tourism is of increasing importance.

**Sinatra, Frank (Francis Albert)** (1915–1998) US singer and film actor. Celebrated for his phrasing and emotion, especially on love ballads, he was particularly associated with the song 'My Way'. His films included *From Here to Eternity* (1953), for which he won an Academy Award, *Some Came Running* (1959), and the political thriller *The Manchurian Candidate* (1963).

**sine** in trigonometry, a function of an angle in a right-angled triangle which is defined as the ratio of the length of the side opposite the angle to the length of the hypotenuse (the longest side).

**Singapore** capital of Singapore, on the southeast coast of the island of Singapore; population (1993) 2,874,000. Major industries include trade, shipping, banking, electronics, shipbuilding, and oil refining. Formerly a British colonial town, it was occupied by Japanese forces during World War II.

**Singapore** Republic of; **area:** 622 sq km/240 sq mi; **capital:** Singapore City; **major towns/cities:** Jurong, Changi; **physical features:** comprises Singapore Island, low and flat, and 57 small islands; Singapore Island is joined to the mainland by causeway across Strait of Johore; **head of state:** Ong Teng Cheong from 1993; **head of government:** Goh Chok Tong from 1990; **political system:** liberal democracy with strict limits on dissent; **currency:** Singapore dollar; **GNP per capita (PPP):** (US$) 28,260 (1998); **exports:** electrical and nonelectrical machinery, transport equipment, petroleum products, chemicals, rubber, foodstuffs, clothing, metal products, iron and steel, orchids and other

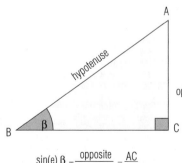

**sine** The sine is a function of an angle in a right-angled triangle found by dividing the length of the side opposite the angle by the length of the hypotenuse (the longest side). Sine (usually abbreviated sin) is one of the fundamental trigonometric ratios.

$$\sin(e)\ \beta = \frac{\text{opposite}}{\text{hypotenuse}} = \frac{AC}{AB}$$

plants, aquarium fish. Principal market USA 19.9% (1998); **population:** 3,522,000 (1999 est); **language:** Malay (national tongue), Chinese, Tamil, English (all official); **religion:** Buddhist, Taoist, Muslim, Hindu, Christian; **life expectancy:** 75 (men); 80 (women) (1995–2000).

**Sinn Fein** (Gaelic 'we ourselves') Irish political party founded in 1905, whose aim is the creation of a united republican Ireland. The driving political force behind Irish nationalism between 1916 and 1921, Sinn Fein returned to prominence with the outbreak of violence ('the Troubles') in Northern Ireland in the late 1960s, when it split into 'Provisional' and 'Official' wings at the same time as the →Irish Republican Army (IRA), with which it is closely associated. From the late 1970s 'Provisional' Sinn Fein assumed a more active political role, putting up candidates to stand in local and national elections. Sinn Fein won two seats in the 1997 UK general election and one seat in the 1997 Irish general election. Gerry →Adams became party president in 1978. Sinn Fein participated in the multiparty negotiations (known as the Stormont Talks) and became a signatory of the agreement reached on Good Friday, 10 April 1998. The party gained 17.6% of votes in the June 1998 elections to the 108-seat Belfast assembly. In September a historic meeting between Gerry Adams and the Ulster Unionist leader, David Trimble, took place at Stormont; Sinn Fein also agreed to appoint a contact with the international body overseeing the decommissioning of arms – the party's chief negotiator, Martin McGuinness.

**Sino-Japanese Wars** two wars waged by Japan against China 1894–95 and 1931–45 to expand to the mainland. Territory gained in the First Sino-Japanese War (Korea) and in the 1930s (Manchuria, Shanghai) was returned at the end of World War II.

**Sirius** (or the Dog Star or Alpha Canis Majoris) brightest star in the night sky, 8.6 light years from the Sun in the constellation Canis Major. Sirius is a double star: Sirius A is a white star with a mass 2.3 times that of the Sun, a diameter 1.8 times that of the Sun, and a true luminosity of 23 Suns. It is orbited every 50 years by a →white dwarf, Sirius B, also known as the Pup.

**SI units** (French *Système International d'Unités*) standard system of scientific units used by scientists worldwide.

Originally proposed in 1960, it replaces the m.k.s., c.g.s., and f.p.s. systems. It is based on seven basic units: the metre (m) for length, kilogram (kg) for mass, second (s) for time, ampere (A) for electrical current, kelvin (K) for temperature, mole (mol) for amount of substance, and candela (cd) for luminosity.

**Six-Day War** another name for the third Arab-Israeli War.

**skeleton** the rigid or semirigid framework that supports and gives form to an animal's body, protects its internal organs, and provides anchorage points for its muscles. The skeleton may be composed of bone and cartilage (vertebrates), chitin (arthropods), calcium carbonate (molluscs and other invertebrates), or silica (many protists). The human skeleton is composed of 206 bones, with the vertebral column (spine) forming the central supporting structure.

**skiing** self-propulsion on snow by means of elongated runners (skis) for the feet, slightly bent upward at the tip. It is a popular recreational sport, as cross-country ski touring or as downhill runs on mountain trails; events include downhill; slalom, in which a series of turns between flags have to be negotiated; cross-country racing; and ski jumping, when jumps of over 150 m/490 ft are achieved from ramps up to 90 m/295 ft high. Speed-skiing uses skis approximately one-third longer and wider than normal with which speeds of up to 200 kph/125 mph have been recorded. Recently, **snowboarding** (or monoboarding), the use of a single, very broad ski, similar to a surf board, used with the feet facing the front and placed together, has become increasingly popular.

**skin** the covering of the body of a vertebrate. In mammals, the outer layer (epidermis) is dead and its cells are constantly being rubbed away and replaced from below; it helps to protect the body from infection and to prevent dehydration. The lower layer (dermis) contains blood vessels, nerves, hair roots, and

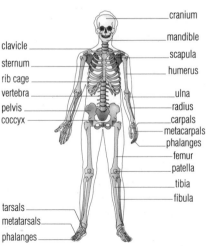

cranium
mandible
clavicle
scapula
sternum
humerus
rib cage
vertebra
ulna
pelvis
radius
coccyx
carpals
metacarpals
phalanges
femur
patella
tibia
fibula
tarsals
metatarsals
phalanges

**skeleton** The human skeleton is made up of 206 bones and provides a strong but flexible supportive framework for the body.

sweat and sebaceous glands, and is supported by a network of fibrous and elastic cells. The medical speciality concerned with skin diseases is called dermatology.

**slash and burn** simple agricultural method whereby natural vegetation is cut and burned, and the clearing then farmed for a few years until the soil loses its fertility, whereupon farmers move on and leave the area to regrow. Although this is possible with a small, widely dispersed population, it becomes unsustainable with more people and is now a cause of →deforestation.

**slavery** the enforced servitude of one person (a slave) to another or one group to another. A slave has no personal rights and is the property of another person by birth, purchase, or capture. Slavery goes back to prehistoric times but declined in Europe after the fall of the Roman Empire. During the imperialism of Spain, Portugal, and Britain in the 16th to 18th centuries and in the American South in the 17th to 19th centuries, slavery became a mainstay of an agricultural factory economy, with millions of Africans sold to work on plantations in North and South America. Millions more died in the process, but the profits from this trade were enormous. Slavery was abolished in the British Empire in 1833 and in the USA at the end of the Civil War (1863–65), but continues illegally in some countries.

**sloth** slow-moving South American mammal, about 70 cm/2.5 ft long, family Bradypodidae, order Edentata. Sloths are greyish brown and have small rounded heads, rudimentary tails, and prolonged forelimbs. Each foot has long curved claws adapted to clinging upside down from trees. On the ground the animals cannot walk, but drag themselves along. They are vegetarian.

**Slovak Republic** national name: *Slovenská Republika*; **area:** 49,035 sq km/18,932 sq mi; **capital:** Bratislava; **major towns/cities:** Košice, Nitra, Prešov, Banská Bystrica, Žilina, Trnava; **physical features:** Western range of Carpathian Mountains, including Tatra and Beskids in north; Danube plain in south; numerous lakes and mineral springs; **head of state:** Rudolf Schuster from 1999; **head of government:** Mikulas Dzurinda from 1998; **political system:** emergent democracy; **currency:** Slovak koruna (based on Czechoslovak koruna); **GNP per capita (PPP):** (US$) 6,600 (1998 est); **exports:** basic manufactures, machinery and transport equipment, miscellaneous manufactured articles. Principal market Germany 28.9% (1998); **population:** 5,381,000 (1999 est); **language:** Slovak (official); **religion:** Roman Catholic (over 50%), Lutheran, Reformist, Orthodox; **life expectancy:** 69 (men); 77 (women) (1995–2000).

**Slovakia** one of the two republics that formed the Federative Republic of Czechoslovakia. Settled in the 5th–6th centuries by Slavs; it was occupied by the Magyars in the 10th century, and was part of the kingdom of Hungary until 1918, when it became a province of Czechoslovakia. Slovakia was a puppet state under German domination 1939–45, and was abolished as an administrative division in 1949. Its capital and chief town was Bratislava. It was re-established as a sovereign state, the Slovak Republic, after the break-up of Czechoslovakia 1993.

**Slovenia** Republic of; **national name:** *Republika Slovenija*; **area:** 20,251 sq km/7,818 sq mi; **capital:** Ljubljana; **major towns/cities:** Maribor, Kranj, Celji, Velenje, Koper (Capodistria); **major ports:** Koper; **physical features:** mountainous; Sava and Drava rivers; **head of state:** Milan Kučan from 1990; **head of government:** Janez Drnovšek from 1992; **political system:** emergent democracy; **currency:** tolar; **GNP per capita (PPP):** (US$) 12,730 (1998 est); **exports:** raw materials, semi-finished goods, machinery, electric motors, transport equipment, foodstuffs, clothing, pharmaceuticals, cosmetics. Principal market Germany 28.4% (1998); **population:** 1,989,000 (1999 est); **language:** Slovene, resembling Serbo-Croat, written in Roman characters; **religion:** Roman Catholic; **life expectancy:** 71 (men); 78 (women) (1995–2000).

**smallpox** acute, highly contagious viral disease, marked by aches, fever, vomiting, and skin eruptions leaving pitted scars. Widespread vaccination programmes have wiped out this often fatal disease.

**smart weapon** programmable bomb or missile that can be guided to its target by laser technology, TV homing technology, or terrain-contour matching (TERCOM). A smart weapon relies on its pinpoint accuracy to destroy a target rather than on the size of its warhead.

**smell** sense that responds to chemical molecules in the air. It works by having receptors for particular chemical groups, into which the airborne chemicals must fit to trigger a message to the brain.

**smelting** processing a metallic ore in a furnace to produce the metal. Oxide ores such as iron ore are smelted with coke (carbon), which reduces the ore into metal and also provides fuel for the process.

**Smith, Adam** (1723–1790) Scottish economist. He is often regarded as the founder of political economy. His *The Wealth of Nations* (1776) defined national wealth in terms of consumable goods and the labour that produces them, rather than in terms of bullion, as prevailing economic theories assumed. The ultimate cause of economic growth is explained by the division of labour – dividing a production process into several repetitive operations, each carried out by different workers, is more efficient. Smith advocated the free working of individual enterprise, and the necessity of 'free trade'.

**snooker** indoor game derived from →billiards (via pool). It is played with 22 balls: 15 red, one each of yellow, green, brown, blue, pink, and black, and one white cueball. A tapered pole (cue) is used to move the balls across the table. Red balls are worth one point when sunk, while the coloured balls have ascending values from two points for the yellow to seven points for the black. The world professional championship was first held in 1927. The world amateur championship was first held in 1963. A snooker World Cup team event was inaugurated at Bangkok, Thailand, in 1996. The International Olympic Committee recognized snooker as an Olympic sport in 1998; snooker is likely to make its Olympic debut at the Athens games in 2004.

**Sobers, Garry (Garfield St Auburn)** (1936–   ) West Indian Test cricketer, arguably the world's finest ever all rounder. He held the world individual record for the highest Test innings with 365 not out, until beaten by Brian Lara in 1994. He played county cricket for Nottinghamshire and, in a match against Glamorgan at Swansea in 1968, he became the first to score six sixes in an over in first-class cricket. He played for the West Indies on 93 occasions, and was captain 39 times. He was knighted for services to cricket in 1975.

**socialism** movement aiming to establish a classless society by substituting public for private ownership of the means of production, distribution, and exchange. The term has been used to describe positions as widely apart as anarchism and social democracy. Socialist ideas appeared in classical times; in early Christianity; among later Christian sects such as the Anabaptists and Diggers; and, in the 18th and early 19th centuries, were put forward as systematic political aims by Jean-Jacques Rousseau, Claude Saint-Simon, François Fourier, and Robert Owen, among others. See also Karl →Marx and Friedrich →Engels.

**sociobiology** study of the biological basis of all social behaviour, including the application of population genetics to the evolution of behaviour. It builds on the concept of inclusive fitness, contained in the notion of the 'selfish gene'. Contrary to some popular interpretations, it does not assume that all behaviour is genetically determined.

**sociology** systematic study of the origin and constitution of human society, in particular of social order and social change, social conflict and social problems. It studies institutions such as the family, law, and the church, as well as concepts such as norm, role, and culture. Sociology attempts to study people in their social environment according to certain underlying moral, philosophical, and political codes of behaviour.

**Socrates** (c. 469–399 BC) Athenian philosopher. He wrote nothing but was immortalized in the dialogues of his pupil Plato. In his desire to combat the scepticism of the sophists, Socrates asserted the possibility of genuine knowledge. In ethics, he put forward the view that the good person never knowingly does wrong. True knowledge emerges through dialogue and systematic questioning and an abandoning of uncritical claims to knowledge.

**sodium** soft, waxlike, silver-white, metallic element, symbol Na (from

Latin *natrium*), atomic number 11, relative atomic mass 22.989. It is one of the alkali metals and has a very low density, being light enough to float on water. It is the sixth-most abundant element (the fourth-most abundant metal) in the Earth's crust. Sodium is highly reactive, oxidizing rapidly when exposed to air and reacting violently with water. Its most familiar compound is sodium chloride (common salt), which occurs naturally in the oceans and in salt deposits left by dried-up ancient seas.

**sodium chloride** (or common salt or table salt) NaCl white, crystalline compound found widely in nature. It is a typical ionic solid with a high melting point (801°C/1,474°F); it is soluble in water, insoluble in organic solvents, and is a strong electrolyte when molten or in aqueous solution. Found in concentrated deposits, it is widely used in the food industry as a flavouring and preservative, and in the chemical industry in the manufacture of sodium, chlorine, and sodium carbonate.

**soil** loose covering of broken rocky material and decaying organic matter overlying the bedrock of the Earth's surface. It is comprised of minerals, organic matter (called humus) derived from decomposed plants and organisms, living organisms, air, and water. Soils differ according to climate, parent material, rainfall, relief of the bedrock, and the proportion of organic material. The study of soils is **pedology**.

**solar energy** energy derived from the Sun's radiation. The amount of energy falling on just 1 sq km/0.3861 sq mi is about 4,000 megawatts, enough to heat and light a small town. In one second the Sun gives off 13 million times more energy than all the electricity used in the USA in one year. Solar heaters have industrial or domestic uses. They usually consist of a black (heat-absorbing) panel containing pipes through which air or water, heated by the Sun, is circulated, either by thermal convection or by a pump.

Solar energy may also be harnessed indirectly using **solar cells** (photovoltaic cells) made of panels of semiconductor material (usually silicon), which generate electricity when illuminated by sunlight. Although it is difficult to generate a high output from solar energy compared to sources such as nuclear or fossil fuels, it is a major nonpolluting and renewable energy source used as far north as Scandinavia as well as in the southwestern USA and in Mediterranean countries.

**solar radiation** radiation given off by the Sun, consisting mainly of visible light, →ultraviolet radiation, and infrared radiation, although the whole spectrum of →electromagnetic waves is present, from radio waves to X-rays. High-energy charged particles, such as electrons, are also emitted, especially from solar flares. When these reach the Earth, they cause magnetic storms (disruptions of the Earth's magnetic field), which interfere with radio communications.

**Solar System** the →Sun (a star) and all the bodies orbiting it: the nine →planets (Mercury, Venus, Earth, Mars, Jupiter, Saturn, Uranus, Neptune, and

Pluto), their moons, the asteroids, and the comets. The Sun contains 99.86% of the mass of the Solar System.

**WEB SITE** > > > > > > > >

**Solar System**

http://www.hawastsoc.org/solar/eng/homepage.htm

Educational tour of the Solar System. It contains information and statistics about the Sun, Earth, planets, moons, asteroids, comets, and meteorites found within the Solar System, supported by images.

**solenoid** coil of wire, usually cylindrical, in which a magnetic field is created by passing an electric current through it. This field can be used to move an iron rod placed on its axis.

Mechanical valves attached to the rod can be operated by switching the current on or off, so converting electrical energy into mechanical energy. Solenoids are used to relay energy from the battery of a car to the starter motor by means of the ignition switch.

**Solomon** (*c.* 974–*c.* 922 BC) in the Old Testament, third king of Israel, son of David by Bathsheba. During a peaceful

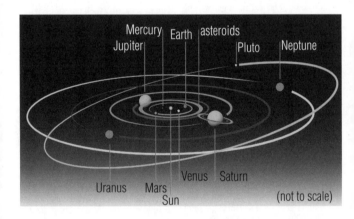

**Solar System** Most of the objects in the Solar System lie close to the plane of the ecliptic. The planets are tiny compared to the Sun. If the Sun were the size of a basketball, the planet closest to the Sun, Mercury, would be the size of a mustard seed 15 m/48 ft from the Sun. The most distant planet, Pluto, would be a pinhead 1.6 km/1 mi away from the Sun. The Earth, which is the third planet out from the Sun, would be the size of a pea 32 m/100 ft from the Sun.

reign, he was famed for his wisdom and his alliances with Egypt and Phoenicia. The much later biblical Proverbs, Ecclesiastes, and Song of Songs are attributed to him. He built the temple in Jerusalem with the aid of heavy taxation and forced labour, resulting in the revolt of northern Israel.

**Solomon Islands** area: 27,600 sq km/10,656 sq mi; **capital:** Honiara (on Guadalcanal) (and chief port); **major towns/cities:** Gizo, Kieta, Auki; **major ports:** Yandina; **physical features:** comprises all but the northernmost islands (which belong to Papua New Guinea) of a Melanesian archipelago stretching nearly 1,500 km/900 mi. The largest is Guadalcanal (area 6,500 sq km/2,510 sq mi); others are Malaita, San Cristobal, New Georgia, Santa Isabel, Choiseul; mainly mountainous and forested; **head of state:** Queen Elizabeth II, represented by governor general Moses Pitakaka from 1994; **head of government:** Bartholomew Ulufa'alu from 1997; **political system:** constitutional monarchy; **currency:** Solomon Island dollar; **GNP per capita (PPP):** (US$) 2,080 (1998); **exports:** timber, fish products, oil palm products, copra, cocoa, coconut oil. Principal market Japan 59.2% (1997); **population:** 430,000 (1999 est); **language:** English (official); there are some 120 Melanesian dialects spoken by 85% of the population, and Papuan and Polynesian languages; **religion:** Anglican, Roman Catholic, South Sea Evangelical, other Protestant; **life expectancy:** 70 (men); 74 (women) (1995–2000).

**solstice** either of the days on which the Sun is farthest north or south of the celestial equator each year. The summer solstice, when the Sun is farthest north, occurs around 21 June; the winter solstice around 22 December.

**solution** two or more substances mixed to form a single, homogenous phase. One of the substances is the solvent and the others (solutes) are said to be dissolved in it.

**solvent** substance, usually a liquid, that will dissolve another substance (see →solution). Although the commonest solvent is water, in popular use the term refers to low-boiling-point organic liquids, which are harmful if used in a confined space. They can give rise to respiratory problems, liver damage, and neurological complaints.

**Solzhenitsyn, Alexander Isayevich** (1918– ) Soviet novelist. He became a US citizen in 1974. He was in prison and exile 1945–57 for anti-Stalinist comments. Much of his writing is semiautobiographical and highly critical of the system, including *One Day in the Life of Ivan Denisovich* (1962), which deals with the labour camps under Stalin, and *The Gulag Archipelago* (1973), an exposé of the whole Soviet labour-camp network. This led to his expulsion from the USSR (1974). He was awarded a Nobel prize (1970).

**Somalia** Somali Democratic Republic; **national name:** *Jamhuriyadda Dimugradiga ee Soomaliya*; **area:** 637,700 sq km/246,215 sq mi; **capital:** Mogadishu (and port); **major towns/cities:**

Hargeysa, Berbera, Kismayo, Marka; **major ports:** Berbera, Marka, Kismayo; **physical features:** mainly flat, with hills in north; **head of state and government (interim):** Hussein Aidid from 1996; **political system:** transitional; **currency:** Somali shilling; **GNP per capita (PPP):** (US$) 620 (1996 est); **exports:** livestock, skins and hides, bananas, fish and fish products, myrrh. Principal market Saudi Arabia 57.9% (1997); **population:** 9,672,000 (1999 est); **language:** Somali, Arabic (both official), Italian, English; **religion:** Sunni Muslim; **life expectancy:** 45 (men); 49 (women) (1995–2000).

**Somme, Battle of the** Allied offensive in World War I during July–November 1916 on the River Somme in northern France, during which severe losses were suffered by both sides. It was planned by the Marshal of France, Joseph Joffre, and UK commander in chief Douglas Haig; the Allies lost over 600,000 soldiers and advanced 13 km/8 mi. It was the first battle in which tanks were used. The German offensive around St Quentin during March–April 1918 is sometimes called the Second Battle of the Somme.

**sonnet** fourteen-line poem of Italian origin introduced to England by Thomas Wyatt in the form used by Petrarch (rhyming *abba abba cdcdcd* or *cdecde*) and followed by Milton and Wordsworth; Shakespeare used the form *abab cdcd efef gg*.

**Sophocles** (*c.* 496–406 BC) Athenian dramatist. He is attributed with having developed tragedy by introducing a third actor and scene-painting, and ranked with →Aeschylus and →Euripides as one of the three great tragedians. He wrote some 120 plays, of which seven tragedies survive. These are *Antigone* (443), *Oedipus the King* (429), *Electra* (410), *Ajax*, *Trachiniae*, *Philoctetes* (409), and *Oedipus at Colonus* (401) (produced after his death).

**soprano** the highest range of the female voice, stretching from around D4 to A6. Some operatic roles require the extended upper range of a coloratura soprano, reaching to around F6, for example Kiri →Te Kanawa. Some instruments use the prefix soprano for those models which sound in the compass of the soprano voice.

**soul music** emotionally intense style of rhythm and blues sung by, among others, Sam Cooke, Aretha Franklin, and Al Green. A synthesis of blues, gospel music, and jazz, it emerged in the 1950s. Sometimes all popular music made by African-Americans is labelled soul music.

**South Africa** Republic of; **national name:** *Republiek van Suid-Afrika*; **area:** 1,222,081 sq km/471,845 sq mi; **capital:** Cape Town (legislative) (and port), Pretoria (administrative), Bloemfontein (judicial); **major towns/cities:** Johannesburg, Durban, Port Elizabeth, Vereeniging, East London, Pietermaritzburg, Kimberley; **major ports:** Durban, Port Elizabeth, East London; **physical features:** southern end of large plateau, fringed by mountains and lowland coastal margin; Drakensberg Mountains, Table Mountain; Limpopo and Orange rivers; **territories:** Marion Island and Prince Edward Island in the Antarctic; **head of state and government:** Thabo Mbeki from 1999; **political system:** liberal democracy; **currency:** rand; **GNP per capita (PPP):** (US$) 6,990 (1998 est); **exports:** metals and metal products, gold, precious and semiprecious stones, mineral products and chemicals, natural cultured pearls, machinery and mechanical appliances, wool, maize, fruit, sugar. Principal market UK 10.1% (1997); **population:** 39,900,000 (1999 est); **language:** English and Afrikaans (both official); main African languages Xhosa, Zulu, and Sesotho (all official); **religion:** Dutch Reformed Church and other Christian denominations, Hindu, Muslim; **life expectancy:** 52 (men); 58 (women) (1995–2000).

**South African Wars** two wars between the Boers (settlers of Dutch origin) and the British; essentially fought for the gold and diamonds of the Transvaal.

The **War of 1881** was triggered by the attempt of the Boers of the Transvaal to reassert the independence surrendered in 1877 in return for British aid against African peoples. The British were defeated at Majuba, and the Transvaal again became independent.

The **War of 1899–1902**, also known as the **Boer War**, was preceded by the armed Jameson Raid into the Boer Transvaal; a failed attempt, inspired by the Cape Colony prime minister Cecil Rhodes, to precipitate a revolt against Paul Kruger, the Transvaal president. The *uitlanders* (non-Boer immigrants) were still not given the vote by the Boers, negotiations failed, and the Boers invaded British territory, besieging Ladysmith, Mafeking (now Mafikeng), and Kimberley. The war ended with the Peace of Vereeniging following the Boer defeat.

**South America** fourth largest of the continents, nearly twice as large as Europe (13% of the world's land surface), extending south from Central America; **area:** 17,864,000 sq km/ 6,900,000 sq mi; **largest cities:** (population over 3.5 million) Buenos Aires, São Paulo, Rio de Janeiro, Bogotá, Santiago, Lima, Caracas; **features:** Lake Titicaca (the world's highest navigable lake); La Paz (highest capital city in the world); Atacama Desert; Inca ruins at Machu Picchu; rivers include the Amazon (world's largest and second longest), Paraná, Madeira, São Francisco, Purús, Paraguay, Orinoco, Araguaia, Negro, Uruguay; **physical:** occupying the southern part of the landmass of the western hemisphere, the South American continent stretches from Point Gallinas on the Caribbean coast of Colombia to Cape Horn at the southern tip of Horn Island, which lies adjacent to Tierra del Fuego; the most southerly point on the mainland is Cape Froward on the Brunswick peninsula, southern Chile; at its maximum width (5,120 km/3,200 mi) the continent stretches from Point Pariñas, Peru, in the extreme west to Point Coqueiros, just north of Recife, Brazil, in the east; five-sixths of the continent lies in the southern hemisphere and two-thirds within the tropics.

**South Australia** state of south-central Australia, including Kangaroo Island and other islands in the Indian Ocean; bounded on the northeast by Queensland, on the east by New South Wales, on the southeast by Victoria, on the south by the Indian Ocean, and on the west by Western Australia; **area:** 984,381 sq km/379,971 sq mi; **capital:** →Adelaide (chief port); **towns:** Whyalla, Mount Gambier, Port Pirie, Port Augusta; **features:** Murray Valley irrigated area, including wine-growing Barossa Valley; salt lakes Eyre and Torrens; Mount Lofty, Musgrave, and Flinders ranges; parts of the Nullarbor Plain, and Great Victoria and Simpson deserts; experimental rocket range in the arid north at Woomera (Woomera Prohibited Area); **products:** meat, wool, wine, wheat, barley, almonds, oranges and other citrus fruits, dried and canned fruit, coal, copper, uranium, silver, zinc, gold, steel, jade, slate, opals, marble, granite, household and electrical goods, vehicles, oil, natural gas; **population:** (1996) 1,428,000; **history:** possibly known to the Dutch in the 16th century; surveyed by Dutch navigator Abel Tasman in 1644; first European settlement in 1834; became a province in 1836 and a state in 1901.

**South Korea** Republic of Korea; **national name:** *Daehan Min-kuk;* **area:** 98,799 sq km/38,146 sq mi; **capital:** Seoul; **major towns/cities:** Pusan,

Taegu, Inchon, Kwangju, Taejon; **major ports:** Pusan, Inchon; **physical features:** southern end of a mountainous peninsula separating the Sea of Japan from the Yellow Sea; **head of state:** Kim Dae Jung from 1998; **head of government:** Kim Jong Pil from 1998; **political system:** emergent democracy; **currency:** won; **GNP per capita (PPP):** (US$) 12,270 (1998); **exports:** electrical machinery, textiles, clothing, footwear, telecommunications and sound equipment, chemical products, ships ('invisible export' – overseas construction work). Principal market USA 17.2% (1998); **population:** 46,479,000 (1999 est); **language:** Korean; **religion:** Shamanist, Buddhist, Confucian, Protestant, Roman Catholic; **life expectancy:** 69 (men); 76 (women) (1995–2000).

**Soviet Union** alternative name for the former Union of Soviet Socialist Republics (USSR).

**Soweto** (acronym for South West Township) urban settlement in South Africa, southwest of Johannesburg; population (1991) 597,000. It experienced civil unrest during the →apartheid regime. Industries include wood pulp and paper manufacturing.

**soybean** leguminous plant, native to East Asia, in particular Japan and China. Originally grown as a food crop for animals, it is increasingly used for human consumption in cooking oils and margarine, as a flour, soya milk, soy sauce, or processed into tofu, miso, or textured vegetable protein (TVP). (Genus *Glycine max.*)

**Soyinka, Wole** (1934–   ) pen-name of

Akinwande Oluwole Soyinka, Nigerian author and dramatist, who founded a national theatre in Nigeria. His plays explore Yoruba myth, ritual, and culture, with the early *Swamp Dwellers* (1958) and *The Lion and the Jewel* (1959), culminating with *A Dance of the Forests* (1960), written as a tragic vision of Nigerian independence. Tragic inevitability is the theme of *Madmen and Specialists* (1970) and of *Death and the King's Horseman* (1976), but he has also written sharp satires, from *The Jero Plays* (1960 and 1973) to the indictment of African dictatorship in *A Play of Giants* (1984). His plays have also been produced in London, England, and New York. He was the first African to receive the Nobel Prize for Literature, in 1986. A volume of poetry, *From Zia with Love*, appeared in 1992.

**space** or outer space void that exists beyond Earth's atmosphere. Above 120 km/75 mi, very little atmosphere remains, so objects can continue to move quickly without extra energy. The space between the planets is not entirely empty, but filled with the tenuous gas of the solar wind as well as dust specks.

**space shuttle** reusable crewed spacecraft. The first was launched 12 April 1981 by the USA. It was developed by NASA to reduce the cost of using space for commercial, scientific, and military purposes. After leaving its payload in space, the space-shuttle orbiter can be flown back to Earth to land on a runway, and is then available for reuse.

**space-time** in physics, combination of space and time used in the theory of →relativity. When developing relativity, Albert Einstein showed that time was in many respects like an extra dimension (or direction) to space. Space and time can thus be considered as entwined into a single entity, rather than two separate things.

**Spain** Kingdom of; **national name:** *Reino de España*; **area:** 504,750 sq km/194,883 sq mi; **capital:** Madrid; **major towns/cities:** Barcelona, Valencia, Zaragoza, Seville, Málaga, Bilbao, Las Palmas de Gran Canarias, Murcia, Córdoba, Palma de Mallorca, Granada; **major ports:** Barcelona, Valencia, Cartagena, Málaga, Cádiz, Vigo, Santander, Bilbao; **physical features:** central plateau with mountain ranges, lowlands in south; rivers Ebro, Douro, Tagus, Guadiana, Guadalquivir; Iberian Plateau (Meseta); Pyrenees, Cantabrian Mountains, Andalusian Mountains, Sierra Nevada; **territories:** Balearic and Canary Islands; in North Africa Ceuta, Melilla, Alhucemas, Chafarinas Islands, Peñón de Vélez; **head of state:** King Juan Carlos I from 1975; **head of government:** José Maria Aznar from 1996; **political system:** constitutional monarchy; **currency:** peseta; **GNP per capita (PPP):** (US$) 16,060 (1998); **exports:** motor vehicles, machinery and electrical equipment, vegetable products, metals and their manufactures, foodstuffs. Principal market France 19.6% (1998); **population:** 39,633,000 (1999 est); **language:** Spanish (Castilian, official), Basque, Catalan, Galician; **religion:** Roman

Catholic; **life expectancy:** 75 (men); 82 (women) (1995–2000).

**Spanish Armada** fleet sent by Philip II of Spain against England in 1588. Consisting of 130 ships, it sailed from Lisbon and carried on a running fight up the Channel with the English fleet of 197 small ships under Howard of Effingham and Francis →Drake. The Armada anchored off Calais but fire ships forced it to put to sea, and a general action followed off Gravelines. What remained of the Armada escaped around the north of Scotland and west of Ireland, suffering many losses by storm and shipwreck on the way. Only about half the original fleet returned to Spain.

**Spanish Civil War** 1936–39. See →Civil War, Spanish.

**Spanish Main** common term for the Caribbean Sea in the 16th–17th centuries, but more properly the South American mainland between the River Orinoco and Panama.

**Spanish Succession, War of the** war 1701–14 of Britain, Austria, the Netherlands, Portugal, and Denmark (the Allies) against France, Spain, and Bavaria. It was caused by Louis XIV's acceptance of the Spanish throne on behalf of his grandson, Philip, in defiance of the Partition Treaty of 1700, under which it would have passed to Archduke Charles of Austria (later Holy Roman Emperor Charles VI).

**spark plug** plug that produces an electric spark in the cylinder of a petrol engine to ignite the fuel mixture. It consists essentially of two electrodes insulated from one another. High-voltage (18,000 V) electricity is fed to a central electrode via the distributor. At the base of the electrode, inside the cylinder, the electricity jumps to another electrode earthed to the engine body, creating a spark.

**sparrow** any of a family (Passeridae) of small Old World birds of the order Passeriformes with short, thick bills, but applied particularly to the different members of the genus *Passer* in the family Ploceidae, order Passeriformes.

Many numbers of the New World family Emberizidae, which includes warblers, orioles, and buntings, are also called sparrows; for example, the North American song sparrow *Melospize melodia*.

**species** in biology, a distinguishable group of organisms that resemble each other or consist of a few distinctive types (as in polymorphism), and that can all interbreed to produce fertile offspring. Species are the lowest level in the system of biological classification.

**spectroscopy** study of spectra (see →spectrum) associated with atoms or molecules in solid, liquid, or gaseous phase. Spectroscopy can be used to identify unknown compounds and is an invaluable tool in science, medicine, and industry (for example, in checking the purity of drugs).

**spectrum** (plural spectra) in physics, an arrangement of frequencies or wavelengths when electromagnetic radiations are separated into their constituent parts.

Visible light is part of the electromagnetic spectrum and most sources emit waves over a range of wavelengths that can be broken up or 'dispersed'; white light can be separated into red, orange, yellow, green, blue, indigo, and violet. The visible spectrum was first studied by Isaac →Newton, who showed in 1672 how white light could be broken up into different colours.

**Spender, Stephen (Harold)** (1909–1995) English poet and critic. His early poetry has a left-wing political content. With Cyril Connolly he founded the magazine *Horizon* (of which he was co-editor 1939–41), and Spender was co-editor of *Encounter* (1953–66). His *Journals (1939–83)* and *Collected Poems (1928–1985)* were published in 1985. He was knighted in 1983.

**Spenser, Edmund** (*c.* 1552–1599) English poet. His major work is the allegorical epic *The Faerie Queene*, of which six books survive (three published in 1590 and three in 1596). Other books include *The Shepheard's Calendar* (1579), *Astrophel* (1586), the love sonnets *Amoretti*, and the marriage poem *Epithalamion* (1595).

**sperm** (or spermatozoon) in biology, the male →gamete of animals. Each sperm cell has a head capsule containing a nucleus, a middle portion containing mitochondria (which provide energy), and a long tail (flagellum). See →sexual reproduction.

**spider** any arachnid (eight-legged animal) of the order Araneae. There are about 30,000 known species, mostly a few centimetres in size, although a few tropical forms attain great size, for example, some bird-eating spiders attain a body length of 9 cm/3.5 in. Spiders produce silk, and many spin webs to trap their prey. They are found everywhere in the world except Antarctica. Many species are found in woods and dry commons; a few are aquatic. Spiders are predators; they bite their prey, releasing a powerful toxin from poison glands which causes paralysis, together with digestive juices. They then suck out the juices and soft parts.

**Spielberg, Steven** (1947– ) US film director, writer, and producer. Immensely popular, Spielberg's films often combine heartfelt sentimentality and a childlike sensibility. His credits include such phenomenal box-office successes as *Jaws* (1975), *Close Encounters of the Third Kind* (1977), *Raiders of the Lost Ark* (1981), *ET The Extra-Terrestrial* (1982), *Jurassic Park* (1992), the multi-award-winning *Schindler's List* (1993), and *Saving Private Ryan* (1998). He was the recipient of the American Film Institute's life achievement award in 1995. The US financial magazine *Forbes* listed him in 1997 as the biggest earner in showbusiness.

**spina bifida** congenital defect in which part of the spinal cord and its membranes are exposed, due to incomplete development of the spine (vertebral column). It is a neural tube defect.

**spinal cord** major component of the →central nervous system in vertebrates. It consists of bundles of nerves enveloped in three layers of membrane (the meninges) and is bathed in cerebrospinal fluid. The spinal cord is encased and protected by the vertebral column, lying within the vertebral canal formed by the posterior arches of successive vertebrae.

**spine** backbone of vertebrates. In most mammals, it contains 26 small bones called vertebrae, which enclose and protect the spinal cord (which links the peripheral nervous system to the brain). The spine articulates with the skull, ribs, and hip bones, and provides attachment for the back muscles.

**Spinoza, Benedict** (1632–1677) (or Baruch) Dutch philosopher. He believed in a rationalistic pantheism that owed much to René →Descartes's mathematical appreciation of the universe. Mind and matter are two modes of an infinite substance that he called God or Nature, good and evil being relative. He was a determinist, believing that human action was motivated by self-preservation.

**spiritualism** belief in the survival of the human personality and in communication between the living and those who have died. The spiritualist movement originated in the USA in 1848. Adherents practise mediumship, which claims to allow clairvoyant knowledge of distant events and spirit healing. The writer Arthur Conan →Doyle and the Victorian prime minister William →Gladstone were converts.

**spleen** organ in vertebrates, part of the reticuloendothelial system, which helps to process →lymphocytes. It

also regulates the number of red blood cells in circulation by destroying old cells, and stores iron. It is situated on the left side of the body, behind the stomach.

**Spode, Josiah** (1754–1827) English potter. Around 1800, he developed bone porcelain (made from bone ash, china stone, and china clay), which was produced at all English factories in the 19th century. He became potter to King George III in 1806.

**spreadsheet** in computing, a program that mimics a sheet of ruled paper, divided into columns down the page, and rows across. The user enters values into cells within the sheet, then instructs the program to perform some operation on them, such as totalling a column or finding the average of a series of numbers. Highly complex numerical analyses may be built up from these simple steps.

**spring** in geology, a natural flow of water from the ground, formed at the point of intersection of the water table and the ground's surface. The source of water is rain that has percolated through the overlying rocks. During its underground passage, the water may have dissolved mineral substances that may then be precipitated at the spring (hence, a mineral spring).

**springbok** South African antelope *Antidorcas marsupialis* about 80 cm/30 in at the shoulder, with head and body 1.3 m/4 ft long. It may leap 3 m/10 ft or more in the air when startled or playing, and has a fold of skin along the middle of the back which is raised to a crest in alarm. Springboks once migrated in herds of over a million, but are now found only in small numbers where protected.

**square root** in mathematics, a number that when squared (multiplied by itself) equals a given number. For example, the square root of 25 (written √25) is ± 5, because 5 × 5 = 25, and (−5) × (−5) = 25. As an exponent, a square root is represented by 1/2, for example, $16^{1/2} = 4$.

**Sri Lanka** Democratic Socialist Republic of (formerly to 1972 **Ceylon**); **national name:** *Sri Lanka Prajathanthrika Samajawadi Janarajaya*; **area:** 65,610 sq km/25,332 sq mi; **capital:** Colombo (and chief port); **major towns/cities:** Kandy, Dehiwala-Mount Lavinia, Moratuwa, Jaffna, Kotte, Kandy; **major ports:** Jaffna, Galle, Negombo, Trincomalee; **physical features:** flat in north and around coast; hills and mountains in south and central interior; **head of state:** Chandrika Bandaranaike Kumaratunga from 1994; **head of government:** Sirimavo Bandaranaike from 1994; **political system:** liberal democracy; **currency:** Sri Lankan rupee; **GNP per capita (PPP):** (US$) 2,300 (1998 est); **exports:** clothing and textiles, tea (world's largest exporter and third-largest producer), precious and semi-precious stones, coconuts and coconut products, rubber. Principal market USA 39.9% (1998); **population:** 18,639,000 (1999 est); **language:** Sinhala, Tamil, English; **religion:** Buddhist 69%, Hindu 15%, Muslim 8%, Christian 7%; **life expectancy:** 71 (men); 75 (women) (1995–2000).

**stainless steel** widely used →alloy of iron, chromium, and nickel that resists rusting. Its chromium content also gives it a high tensile strength. It is used for cutlery and kitchen fittings, and in surgical instruments. Stainless steel was first produced in the UK in 1913 and in Germany in 1914.

**stalactite and stalagmite** cave structures formed by the deposition of calcite dissolved in ground water. **Stalactites** grow downwards from the roofs or walls and can be icicle-shaped, straw-shaped, curtain-shaped, or formed as terraces. **Stalagmites** grow upwards from the cave floor and can be conical, fir-cone-shaped, or resemble a stack of saucers. Growing stalactites and stalagmites may meet to form a continuous column from floor to ceiling.

**stamen** male reproductive organ of a flower. The stamens are collectively referred to as the androecium. A typical stamen consists of a stalk, or filament, with an anther, the pollen-bearing organ, at its apex, but in some primitive plants, such as *Magnolia*, the stamen may not be markedly differentiated. *See illustration on page 518.*

**Stanley, Henry Morton** (1841–1904) adopted name of John Rowlands, Welsh-born US explorer and journalist who made four expeditions to Africa. He and David →Livingstone met at Ujiji in 1871 and explored Lake Tanganyika. He traced the course of the Congo River to the sea 1874–77, established

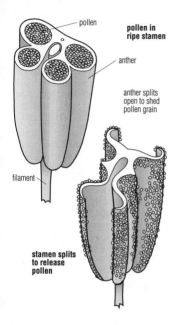

pollen

**pollen in ripe stamen**

anther

anther splits open to shed pollen grain

filament

**stamen splits to release pollen**

**stamen** The stamen is the male reproductive organ of a flower. It has a thin stalk called a filament with an anther at the tip. The anther contains pollen sacs, which split to release tiny grains of pollen.

the Congo Free State (Democratic Republic of Congo) 1879–84, and charted much of the interior 1887–89.

**star** luminous globe of gas, mainly hydrogen and helium, which produces its own heat and light by nuclear reactions. Although stars shine for a very long time – many billions of years – they are not eternal, and have been found to change in appearance at different stages in their lives.

---

**WEB SITE** > > > > > > > >

**Stars and Constellations**

http://www.astro.wisc.edu/~dolan/
constellations/constellations.html

Hugely informative site on stars and constellations. It includes star charts of all major stars and constellations, details of the origins of the various names, photographs of the galaxy and the Milky Way, and details on what stars can be seen at any given time.

---

**starch** widely distributed, high-molecular-mass →carbohydrate, produced by plants as a food store; main dietary sources are cereals, legumes, and tubers, including potatoes. It consists of varying proportions of two →glucose polymers (polysaccharides): straight-chain (amylose) and branched (amylopectin) molecules.

**starling** any member of a large widespread Old World family (Sturnidae) of chunky, dark, generally gregarious birds of the order Passeriformes. The European starling *Sturnus vulgaris*, common in northern Eurasia, has been naturalized in North America from the late 19th century. The black, speckled plumage is glossed with green and purple. The feathers on the upper parts are tipped with buff, and the wings are greyish-black, with a reddish-brown fringe.

The female is less glossy and lustrous than the male. Its own call is a bright whistle, but it is a mimic of the songs of other birds. It is about 20 cm/8 in long.

**statistics** branch of mathematics concerned with the collection and interpretation of data. For example, to determine the mean age of the children in a school, a statistically acceptable answer might be obtained by calculating an average based on the ages of a representative sample, consisting, for example, of a random tenth of the pupils from each class. →Probability is the branch of statistics dealing with predictions of events.

**steady-state theory** in astronomy, a rival theory to that of the →Big Bang, which claims that the universe has no origin but is expanding because new matter is being created continuously throughout the universe. The theory was proposed in 1948 by Austrian-born British cosmologist Hermann Bondi, Austrian-born US astronomer Thomas Gold, and English astronomer, cosmologist, and writer Fred Hoyle, but it was dealt a severe blow in 1965 by the discovery of cosmic background radiation (radiation left over from the formation of the universe) and is now largely rejected.

**steam engine** engine that uses the power of steam to produce useful work. It was the principal power source during the British Industrial Revolution in the 18th century. The first successful steam engine was built 1712 by English inventor Thomas Newcomen at Dudley, West Midlands; it was developed further by Scottish mining engineer James Watt from 1769 and by English mining engineer Richard Trevithick, whose high-pressure steam engine of 1802 led to the development of the steam locomotive.

**Stein, Gertrude** (1874–1946) US writer. She influenced authors Ernest →Hemingway, Sherwood Anderson, and F Scott →Fitzgerald with her radical prose style. Drawing on the stream-of-consciousness psychology of William James and on the geometry of Cézanne and the cubist painters in Paris, she evolved a 'continuous present' style made up of constant repetition and variation of simple phrases. Her work includes the self-portrait *The Autobiography of Alice B Toklas* (1933).

**Steinbeck, John Ernst** (1902–1968) US novelist. His realist novels, such as *In Dubious Battle* (1936), *Of Mice and Men* (1937), and *The Grapes of Wrath* (1939; Pulitzer prize; filmed 1940), portray agricultural life in his native California, where migrant farm labourers from the Oklahoma dust bowl struggled to survive. He was awarded the Nobel Prize for Literature in 1962.

**Stendhal** (1783–1842) pen-name of Marie Henri Beyle, French novelist. His novels *Le Rouge et le Noir/The Red and the Black* (1830) and *La Chartreuse de Parme/The Charterhouse of Parma* (1839) were pioneering works in their treatment of disguise and hypocrisy and outstanding for their psychological analysis; a review of the latter by fellow novelist →Balzac (1840) furthered

Stendhal's reputation, but he was not fully understood during his lifetime.

**Stephen** (c. 1097–1154) king of England from 1135. A grandson of William the Conqueror, he was elected king in 1135, although he had previously recognized Henry I's daughter Matilda as heiress to the throne. Matilda landed in England in 1139, and civil war disrupted the country until 1153, when Stephen acknowledged Matilda's son, Henry II, as his own heir.

**Stephenson, George** (1781–1848) English engineer. He built the first successful steam locomotive. He also invented a safety lamp independently of Humphrey →Davy in 1815. He was appointed engineer of the Stockton and Darlington Railway, the world's first public railway, in 1821, and of the Liverpool and Manchester Railway in 1826. In 1829 he won a prize with his locomotive *Rocket*.

**Stephenson, Robert** (1803–1859) English civil engineer. He constructed railway bridges such as the high-level bridge at Newcastle-upon-Tyne, England, and the Menai and Conway tubular bridges in Wales. He was the son of George →Stephenson.

**steppe** the temperate grasslands of Europe and Asia. Sometimes the term refers to other temperate grasslands and semi-arid desert edges.

**sterilization** any surgical operation to terminate the possibility of reproduction. In women, this is normally achieved by sealing or tying off the →Fallopian tubes (tubal ligation) so that fertilization can no longer take place. In men, the transmission of sperm is blocked by →vasectomy.

**Sterne, Laurence** (1713–1768) Irish writer. Sterne was born in Clonmel, County Tipperary, and ordained in 1737. He created the comic anti-hero Tristram Shandy in *The Life and Opinions of Tristram Shandy, Gent* (1759–67). An eccentrically whimsical and bawdy novel, its associations of ideas on the philosophic principles of John Locke, and other devices, foreshadow in part some of the techniques associated with the 20th-century novel, such as stream-of-consciousness. His other works include *A Sentimental Journey through France and Italy* (1768).

**Stevenson, Robert Louis Balfour** (1850–1894) Scottish novelist and poet. He wrote the adventure stories *Treasure Island* (1883), *Kidnapped* (1886), and *The Master of Ballantrae* (1889), notable for their characterization as well as their action. He was a master also of shorter fiction such as *The Strange Case of Dr Jekyll and Mr Hyde* (1886), and of stories of the supernatural such as *Thrawn Janet* (1881).

**Stijl, De** (Dutch 'the style') influential movement in art, architecture, and design founded in 1917 in the Netherlands. Attempting to bring art and design together in a single coherent system, the members of De Stijl developed an austere simplification of style, based on simple geometrical shapes and primary colour. Its best-known member was the abstract painter Piet →Mondrian. The group's main theorist and publicist was Theo van Doesburg (1883–1931), and his death effectively marked its end.

**stock exchange** institution for the buying and selling of stocks and shares (securities). The world's largest stock exchanges are London, New York (Wall Street), and Tokyo. The oldest stock exchanges are Antwerp (1460), Hamburg (1558), Amsterdam (1602), New York (1790), and London (1801). The former division on the London Stock Exchange between brokers (who bought shares from jobbers to sell to the public) and jobbers (who sold them only to brokers on commission, the 'jobbers' turn') was abolished in 1986.

**Stockhausen, Karlheinz** (1928– ) German composer of avant-garde music. He has continued to explore new musical sounds and compositional techniques since the 1950s. His major works include *Gesang der Jünglinge* (1956), *Kontakte* (1960; electronic music), and *Sirius* (1977).

**Stoicism** (Greek *stoa* 'porch') Greek school of philosophy, founded about 300 BC by Zeno of Citium. The Stoics were pantheistic materialists who believed that happiness lay in accepting the law of the universe. They emphasized human brotherhood, denounced slavery, and were internationalist. The name is derived from the porch on which Zeno taught.

**stomach** the first cavity in the digestive system of animals. In mammals it is a bag of muscle situated just below the diaphragm. Food enters it from the oesophagus, is digested by the acid and →enzymes secreted by the stomach lining, and then passes into the duodenum. Some plant-eating mammals have

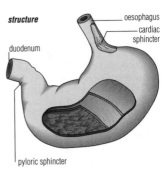

*structure*

oesophagus
cardiac sphincter
duodenum
pyloric sphincter

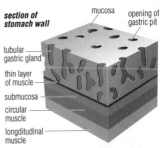

*section of stomach wall*

mucosa
opening of gastric pit
tubular gastric gland
thin layer of muscle
submucosa
circular muscle
longditudinal muscle

**stomach** The human stomach can hold about 1.5 l/2.6 pt of liquid. The digestive juices are acidic enough to dissolve metal. To avoid damage, the cells of the stomach lining are replaced quickly – 500,000 cells are replaced every minute, and the whole stomach lining every three days.

multichambered stomachs that harbour bacteria in one of the chambers to assist in the digestion of →cellulose.

The gizzard is part of the stomach in birds.

**Stone Age** the developmental stage of humans in →prehistory before the use of metals, when tools and weapons were made chiefly of stone, especially flint. The Stone Age is subdivided into the Old or **Palaeolithic**, when flint implements were simply chipped into shape; the Middle or **Mesolithic**; and the New or **Neolithic**, when implements were ground and polished. Palaeolithic people were hunters and gatherers; by the Neolithic period people were taking the first steps in agriculture, the domestication of animals, weaving, and pottery.

**Stonehenge** (Old English 'hanging stones') megalithic monument on Salisbury Plain, 3 km/1.9 mi west of Amesbury in Wiltshire, England. The site developed over various periods from a simple henge (earthwork circle and ditch), dating from about 3000 BC, to a complex stone structure, from about 2100 BC, which included a circle of 30 upright stones, their tops linked by lintel stones to form a continuous circle about 30 m/100 ft across.

**Stoppard, Tom** (1937– ) originally Thomas Straussler, Czechoslovak-born British dramatist. His works use wit and wordplay to explore logical and philosophical ideas. His play *Rosencrantz and Guildenstern are Dead* (1967) was followed by comedies including *The Real Inspector Hound* (1968), *Jumpers* (1972),

*Travesties* (1974), *Dirty Linen* (1976), *The Real Thing* (1982), *Hapgood* (1988), *Arcadia* (1993), and *Indian Ink* (1995). He has also written for radio, television, and the cinema.

**Strachey, (Giles) Lytton** (1880–1932) English critic and biographer. He was a member of the →Bloomsbury Group of writers and artists. His *Landmarks in French Literature* was written in 1912. The mocking and witty treatment of Cardinal Manning, Florence Nightingale, Thomas Arnold, and General Gordon in *Eminent Victorians* (1918) won him recognition. His biography of *Queen Victoria* (1921) was more affectionate.

**Stradivari, Antonio** (c. 1644–1737) (Latin form *Stradivarius*) Italian stringed instrument maker, generally considered the greatest of all violin makers. He produced more than 1,100 instruments from his family workshops, over 600 of which survive; they have achieved the status (and sale-room prices) of works of art.

**Strasbourg** (German *Strassburg*) administrative centre of the Bas-Rhin *département* and of →Alsace region, northeast France, situated near the German border on the River Ill, 3 km/1.9 mi west of the Rhine near its confluence with the Rhine–Rhône and Rhine and Marne canals; population (1990) 255,900, conurbation 388,000. Industries include car manufacture, tobacco, printing and publishing, and preserves. The town was selected as the headquarters for the →Council of

Europe in 1949, and sessions of the European Parliament alternate between here and Luxembourg. It has an 11th–15th-century cathedral.

**stratosphere** that part of the atmosphere 10–40 km/6–25 mi from the Earth's surface, where the temperature slowly rises from a low of −55°C/−67°F to around 0°C/32°F. The air is rarefied and at around 25 km/15 mi much →ozone is concentrated.

**Strauss, Richard Georg** (1864–1949) German composer and conductor. He followed the German Romantic tradition but had a strongly personal style, characterized by his bold, colourful orchestration. He first wrote tone poems such as *Don Juan* (1889), *Till Eulenspiegel's Merry Pranks* (1895), and *Also sprach Zarathustra/Thus Spake Zarathustra* (1896). He then moved on to opera with *Salome* (1905) and *Elektra* (1909), both of which have elements of polytonality. He reverted to a more traditional style with *Der Rosenkavalier/ The Knight of the Rose* (1909–10).

**Stravinsky, Igor Fyodorovich** (1882– 1971) Russian composer, later of French (1934) and US (1945) nationality. He studied under →Rimsky-Korsakov and wrote the music for the Diaghilev ballets *The Firebird* (1910), *Petrushka* (1911), and *The Rite of Spring* (1913) (controversial at the time for their unorthodox rhythms and harmonies). His works also include symphonies, concertos (for violin and piano), chamber music, and operas; for example, *The Rake's Progress* (1951) and *The Flood* (1962).

**strike** stoppage of work by employees, often as members of a trade union, to obtain or resist change in wages, hours, or conditions. A lockout is a weapon of an employer to thwart or enforce such change by preventing employees from working. Another measure is work to rule, when production is virtually brought to a halt by strict observance of union rules.

**Strindberg, (Johan) August** (1849– 1912) Swedish dramatist and novelist. His plays are in a variety of styles including historical dramas, symbolic dramas (the two-part *Dödsdansen/The Dance of Death* 1901), and 'chamber plays' such as *Spöksonaten/The Ghost [Spook] Sonata* (1907). *Fadren/The Father* (1887) and *Fröken Julie/Miss Julie* (1888) are among his best-known works.

**stroke** (or cerebrovascular accident or apoplexy) interruption of the blood supply to part of the brain due to a sudden bleed in the brain (cerebral haemorrhage) or embolism or →thrombosis. Strokes vary in severity from producing almost no symptoms to proving rapidly fatal. In between are those (often recurring) that leave a wide range of impaired function, depending on the size and location of the event.

**structuralism** 20th-century philosophical movement that has influenced such areas as linguistics, anthropology, and literary criticism. Inspired by the work of the Swiss linguist Ferdinand de Saussure, structuralists believe that objects should be analysed as systems of relations, rather than as positive entities.

**Stubbs, George** (1724–1806) English artist. He is renowned for his paintings of horses, such as *Mares and Foals* (about 1763; Tate Gallery, London). After the publication of his book of engravings *The Anatomy of the Horse* (1766), he was widely commissioned as an animal painter. The dramatic *Lion Attacking a Horse* (1770; Yale University Art Gallery, New Haven, Connecticut) and the peaceful *Reapers* (1786; Tate Gallery, London) show the variety of mood in his painting.

**subatomic particle** in physics, a particle that is smaller than an atom. Such particles may be indivisible →elementary particles, such as the →electron and →quark, or they may be composites, such as the proton, →neutron, and alpha particle. See also →particle physics.

**subduction zone** region where two plates of the Earth's rigid lithosphere collide, and one plate descends below the other into the weaker asthenosphere. Subduction occurs along ocean trenches, most of which encircle the Pacific Ocean; portions of the ocean plate slide beneath other plates carrying continents.

**sublimation** in chemistry, the conversion of a solid to vapour without passing through the liquid phase.

**submarine** underwater warship. The first underwater boat was constructed in 1620 for James I of England by the Dutch scientist Cornelius van Drebbel (1572–1633). A naval submarine, or submersible torpedo boat, the *Gymnote*, was launched by France in 1888. The conventional submarine of World War I was driven by diesel engine on the surface and by battery-powered electric motors underwater. The diesel engine also drove a generator that produced electricity to charge the batteries.

**succession** in ecology, a series of changes that occur in the structure and composition of the vegetation in a given area from the time it is first colonized by plants (primary succession), or after it has been disturbed by fire, flood, or clearing (secondary succession).

**sucrose** (or cane sugar or beet sugar) $C_{12}H_{22}O_{11}$ a sugar found in the pith of sugar cane and in sugar beets. It is popularly known as →sugar.

**Sudan** Democratic Republic of; **national name:** *Jamhuryat es-Sudan;* **area:** 2,505,800 sq km/967,489 sq mi; **capital:** Khartoum; **major towns/ cities:** Omdurman, Port Sudan, Juba, Wadi Medani, al-Obeid, Kassala, Atbara, al-Qadarif, Kosti; **major ports:** Port Sudan; **physical features:** fertile Nile valley separates Libyan Desert in west from high rocky Nubian Desert in east; **head of state and government:** Gen Omar Hassan Ahmed al-Bashir from 1989; **political system:** emergent democracy; **currency:** Sudanese dinar; **GNP per capita (PPP):** (US$) 1,360 (1998); **exports:** cotton, sesame seed, gum arabic, sorghum, livestock, hides and skins. Principal market Saudi Arabia 21.3% (1997); **population:** 28,882,000 (1999 est); **language:** Arabic 51% (official), local languages; **religion:** Sunni Muslim; also animist

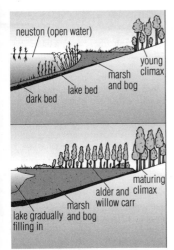

**succession** The succession of plant types along a lake. As the lake gradually fills in, a mature climax community of trees forms inland from the shore. Extending out from the shore, a series of plant communities can be discerned with small, rapidly growing species closest to the shore.

and Christian; **life expectancy:** 54 (men); 56 (women) (1995–2000).

**Sudeten** mountainous region in northeast Bohemia, Czech Republic, extending eastwards along the border with Poland. Sudeten was annexed by Germany under the →Munich Agreement 1938; it was returned to Czechoslovakia in 1945.

Germany and the Czech Republic sought to bury decades of mutual antagonism in January 1997 by signing a joint declaration aimed at drawing a line under the vexed issue of the Sudetenland. Germany apologised for the suffering caused during the Nazi occupation. For their part, the Czechs expressed regret over the 'injustices' that took place during the expulsion of more than 2.5 million Sudetenland Germans after World War II. It took over two years to reach agreement.

**Suez Canal** artificial waterway from Port Said to Suez, linking the Mediterranean and Red Seas; 160 km/100 mi long. It separates Africa from Asia and provides the shortest eastwards sea route from Europe. It was opened in 1869, nationalized in 1956, blocked by Egypt during the Arab-Israeli War in 1967, and not reopened until 1975.

**Suez Crisis** military confrontation from October to December 1956 following the nationalization of the Suez Canal by President Nasser of Egypt. In an attempt to reassert international control of the canal, Israel launched an attack, after which British and French troops landed. Widespread international censure forced the withdrawal of the British and French. The crisis resulted in the resignation of British prime minister Anthony Eden.

**Suffolk** county of eastern England. **area:** 3,800 sq km/1,467 sq mi; **towns:** Ipswich (administrative headquarters), Aldeburgh, Beccles, Bury St Edmunds, Felixstowe, Lowestoft, Sudbury, Southwold; **physical:** undulating lowlands in the south and west; flat coastline; rivers Waveney (the boundary with Norfolk),

Alde, Deben, Orwell, Stour (the boundary with Essex), Little Ouse; part of the Norfolk Broads; **agriculture:** cereals (barley, oats, wheat), sugar beet; cattle, sheep, and pig rearing; fishing (for which Lowestoft is the main centre); **industries:** agricultural machinery; chemicals; coconut matting; electronics; fertilizers; food processing; motor vehicle components; North Sea oil and gas exploration; printing; telecommunications research; silk; timber; brewing; **population:** (1996) 661,600; **famous people:** Benjamin Britten, John Constable, George Crabbe, Thomas Gainsborough, Elizabeth Garrett Anderson.

**suffragette** (or suffragist) woman fighting for the right to vote. In the UK, women's suffrage bills were repeatedly introduced and defeated in Parliament between 1886 and 1911, and a militant campaign was launched in 1906 by Emmeline →Pankhurst and her daughters. In 1918 women were granted limited franchise; in 1928 it was extended to all women over 21. In the USA the 19th amendment to the constitution in 1920 gave women the vote in federal and state elections.

**Sufism** mystical movement of Islam that originated in the 8th century. Sufis believe that deep intuition is the only real guide to knowledge. The movement has a strong strain of asceticism. The name derives from Arabic *suf*, a rough woollen robe worn as an indication of disregard for material things. There are a number of groups or brotherhoods within Sufism, each with its own method of meditative practice, one of which is the whirling dance of the dervishes.

**sugar** (or sucrose) sweet, soluble, crystalline carbohydrate found in the pith of sugar cane and in sugar beet. It is a disaccharide sugar, each of its molecules being made up of two simple-sugar (monosaccharide) units: glucose and fructose. Sugar is easily digested and forms a major source of energy in humans, being used in cooking and in the food industry as a sweetener and, in high concentrations, as a preservative. A high consumption is associated with obesity and tooth decay. In the UK, sucrose may not be used in baby foods.

**Sulawesi** (formerly Celebes) island in eastern Indonesia, one of the Sunda Islands; area (with dependent islands) 190,000 sq km/73,000 sq mi; population (1990) 12,520,700. It is mountainous and forested and produces copra and nickel.

**Suleiman** (*c.* 1494–1566) (or Solyman Ottoman) sultan from 1520, known as the Magnificent and the Lawgiver. Under his rule, the Ottoman Empire flourished and reached its largest extent. He made conquests in the Balkans, the Mediterranean, Persia, and North Africa, but was defeated at Vienna in 1529 and Valletta (on Malta) in 1565. He was a patron of the arts, a poet, and an administrator.

**sulphur** brittle, pale-yellow, nonmetallic element, symbol S, atomic number 16, relative atomic mass 32.064. It occurs in three allotropic forms: two crystalline (called rhombic and monoclinic, following the arrangements of the atoms within the crystals) and one amorphous. It burns in air with a blue flame and a stifling odour. Insoluble in water but soluble in carbon disulphide, it is a good electrical insulator. Sulphur is widely used in the manufacture of sulphuric acid (used to treat phosphate rock to make fertilizers) and in making paper, matches, gunpowder and fireworks, in vulcanizing rubber, and in medicines and insecticides.

**sulphuric acid** (or oil of vitriol) $H_2SO_4$ a dense, viscous, colourless liquid that is extremely corrosive. It gives out heat when added to water and can cause severe burns. Sulphuric acid is used extensively in the chemical industry, in the refining of petrol, and in the manufacture of fertilizers, detergents, explosives, and dyes. It forms the acid component of car batteries.

**Sumatra** (or Sumatera) second-largest island of Indonesia, one of the Sunda Islands; area 473,600 sq km/182,800 sq mi; population (1990) 36,505,700. East of a longitudinal volcanic mountain range is a wide plain; both are heavily forested. Products include rubber, rice, tobacco, tea, timber, tin, and petroleum.

**Sumerian civilization** the world's earliest civilization, dating from about 3500 BC and located at the confluence of the Tigris and Euphrates rivers in lower Mesopotamia (present-day Iraq). It was a city-state with priests as secular rulers. After 2300 BC, Sumer declined.

**Sun** the →star at the centre of the Solar System. Its diameter is 1.4 million km/865,000 mi; its temperature at the surface is about 5,800 K/5,530°C/9,986°F, and at the centre 15 million K/about 15 million°C/about 27 million°F. It is composed of about 70% hydrogen and 30% helium, with other elements making up less than 1%. The Sun's energy is generated by nuclear fusion reactions that turn hydrogen into helium at its centre. The gas core is far denser than mercury or lead on Earth. The Sun is about 4.6 billion years old, with a predicted lifetime of 10 billion years.

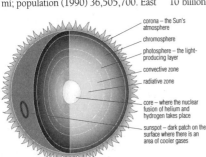

corona – the Sun's atmosphere
chromosphere
photosphere – the light-producing layer
convective zone
radiative zone
core – where the nuclear fusion of helium and hydrogen takes place
sunspot – dark patch on the surface where there is an area of cooler gases

**Sun** The structure of the Sun. Nuclear reactions at the core releases vast amounts of energy in the form of light and heat that radiate out to the photosphere and corona. Surges of glowing gas rise as prominences from the surface of the Sun and cooler areas, known as sunspots, appear as dark patches on the giant star's surface.

**Sunni** member of the larger of the two main sects of Islam, with about 680 million adherents. Sunni Muslims believe that the first three caliphs were all legitimate successors of the prophet Muhammad, and that guidance on belief and life should come from the Koran and the Hadith, and from the Shari'a, not from a human authority or spiritual leader. Imams in Sunni Islam are educated lay teachers of the faith and prayer leaders.

**sunspot** dark patch on the surface of the Sun, actually an area of cooler gas, thought to be caused by strong magnetic fields that block the outward flow of heat to the Sun's surface. Sunspots consist of a dark central umbra, about 4,000 K (3,700°C/6,700°F), and a lighter surrounding penumbra, about 5,500 K (5,200°C/9,400°F). They last from several days to over a month, ranging in size from 2,000 km/1,250 mi to groups stretching for over 100,000 km/62,000 mi.

**superconductivity** in physics, increase in electrical conductivity at low temperatures. The resistance of some metals and metallic compounds decreases uniformly with decreasing temperature until at a critical temperature (the superconducting point), within a few degrees of absolute zero (0 K/−273.15°C/−459.67°F), the resistance suddenly falls to zero. The phenomenon was discovered by Dutch scientist Heike Kamerlingh Onnes in 1911.

**supergiant** largest and most luminous type of star known, with a diameter of up to 1,000 times that of the Sun and apparent magnitudes of between 0.4 and 1.3. Supergiants are likely to become →supernovae.

**supernova** explosive death of a star, which temporarily attains a brightness of 100 million Suns or more, so that it can shine as brilliantly as a small galaxy for a few days or weeks. Very approximately, it is thought that a supernova explodes in a large galaxy about once every 100 years. Many supernovae – astronomers estimate some 50% – remain undetected because of obscuring by interstellar dust.

**superstring theory** in physics, a mathematical theory developed in the 1980s to explain the properties of →elementary particles and the forces between them (in particular, gravity and the nuclear forces) in a way that combines →relativity and →quantum theory.

In string theory, the fundamental objects in the universe are not pointlike particles but extremely small stringlike objects. These objects exist in a universe of ten dimensions, although, for reasons not yet understood, only three space dimensions and one dimension of time are discernible.

**surface tension** in physics, the property that causes the surface of a liquid to behave as if it were covered with a weak elastic skin; this is why a needle can float on water. It is caused by the exposed surface's tendency to contract to the smallest possible area because of cohesive forces between →molecules at the surface. Allied phenomena include the formation of droplets, the concave profile of a meniscus, and the capillary action by which water soaks into a sponge.

**Suriname** Republic of (formerly **Dutch Guiana**); **national name:** *Republiek Suriname*; **area:** 163,820 sq km/63,250 sq mi; **capital:** Paramaribo; **major towns/cities:** Nieuw Nickerie, Moengo, Pontoetoe, Brokopondo, Nieuw Amsterdam; **physical features:** hilly and forested, with flat and narrow coastal plain; Suriname River; **head of state:** Jules Wijdenbosch from 1996; **head of government:** Prataapnarain Shawh Radhecheran Radhakishun from 1996; **political system:** emergent democracy; **currency:** Suriname guilder; **GNP per capita (PPP):** (US$) 3,680 (1997 est); **exports:** alumina, aluminium, shrimps, bananas, plantains, rice, wood and wood products. Principal market USA 16.4% (1997); **population:** 416,000 (1998 est); **language:** Dutch (official), Sranan (creole), English, Hindi, Javanese, Chinese. Spanish is the main working language; **religion:** Christian, Hindu, Muslim; **life expectancy:** 68 (men); 73 (women) (1995–2000).

**surrealism** movement in art, literature, and film that developed out of →dada around 1922. Led by André →Breton, who produced the *Surrealist Manifesto* (1924), the surrealists were inspired by the thoughts and visions of the subconscious mind. They explored varied styles and techniques, and the movement became the dominant force in Western art between World Wars I and II.

---

**WEB SITE** > > > > > > > >

**Surrealism**

http://www.surrealist.com/surrealist

Introduction to the surrealist world. It is currently divided into the sections 'History', 'Art', and 'Artists'. The section of art is currently very limited, but there are good biographies on the major members of this literary and artistic movement. The site also includes André Breton's famous essay, 'What is surrealism?'.

---

**suspension** mixture consisting of small solid particles dispersed in a liquid or gas, which will settle on standing. An example is milk of magnesia, which is a suspension of magnesium hydroxide in water.

**Sussex** former county of England, on the south coast, now divided into East Sussex and West Sussex.

**swan** large water bird, with a long slender neck and webbed feet, closely related to ducks and geese. The four species of swan found in the northern hemisphere are white; the three species found in the southern hemisphere are all or partly black. The male (cob) and female (pen) are similar in appearance, and they usually pair for life. They nest on or near water in every continent, except Africa and Antarctica. Swans produce a clutch of 4–6 greenish coloured eggs and their young are known as cygnets. Cygnets are covered with a grey down and only become fully feathered and able to fly after 14–16 weeks.

Swans feed mainly on aquatic plants. They are among the largest and heaviest birds that can fly and because of this require large areas of water to take off. They fly with a slow, graceful wing beat and when migrating, fly in a distinctive V-shaped flock.

The **mute swan** is the most common species. It is native to northern Europe and Asia, but has been introduced and is now widespread in North America. The mute swan has white feathers, black legs and a bright orange flattened bill with a black knob on the upper bill, near the eyes. It may be as long as 150 cm/5 ft in length and weigh as much as 14 kg/30 lb. It hisses loudly when angry.

**Swaziland** Kingdom of; **national name:** *Umbuso we Swatini*; **area:** 17,400 sq km/6,718 sq mi; **capital:** Mbabane; **major towns/cities:** Manzini, Big Bend, Mhlume, Havelock Mine, Nhlangano; **physical features:** central valley; mountains in west (Highveld); plateau in east (Lowveld and Lubombo plateau); **head of state:** King Mswati III from 1986; **head of government:** Barnabas Sibusiso Dlamini from 1996; **political system:** transitional absolute monarchy; **currency:** lilangeni; **GNP per capita (PPP):** (US$) 3,580 (1998); **exports:** sugar, wood pulp, cotton yarn, canned fruits, asbestos, coal, diamonds, gold. Principal market South Africa 74% (1997); **population:** 980,000 (1999

est); **language:** Swazi, English (both official); **religion:** Christian, animist; **life expectancy:** 58 (men); 63 (women) (1995–2000).

**Sweden** Kingdom of; **national name:** *Konungariket Sverige*; **area:** 450,000 sq km/173,745 sq mi; **capital:** Stockholm (and chief port); **major towns/cities:** Göteborg, Malmö, Uppsala, Norrköping, Västerås, Linköping, Orebro, Jönköping, Helsingborg, Borås; **major ports:** Helsingborg, Malmö, Göteborg; **physical features:** mountains in west; plains in south; thickly forested; more than 20,000 islands off the Stockholm coast; lakes, including Vänern, Vättern, Mälaren, and Hjälmaren; **head of state:** King Carl XVI Gustaf from 1973; **head of government:** Goran Persson from 1996; **political system:** constitutional monarchy; **currency:** Swedish krona; **GNP per capita (PPP):** (US$) 19,480 (1998); **exports:** forestry products (wood, pulp, and paper), machinery, motor vehicles, power-generating non-electrical machinery, chemicals, iron and steel. Principal market Germany 11.2% (1998); **population:** 8,892,000 (1999 est); **language:** Swedish; there are Finnish- and Saami-speaking minorities; **religion:** Evangelical Lutheran (established national church); **life expectancy:** 76 (men); 81 (women) (1995–2000).

**Swift, Jonathan** (1667–1745) Irish satirist and Anglican cleric. Born in Dublin, he was educated there at Trinity College, and ordained in 1694. He wrote *Gulliver's Travels* (1726), an allegory describing travel to lands inhabited by giants, miniature people, and intelligent horses. His other works include *The Tale of a Tub* (1704), attacking corruption in religion and learning; and the satirical pamphlet *A Modest Proposal* (1729); written in protest of the on-going famine in Ireland, it suggested that children of the poor should be eaten. His lucid prose style is simple and controlled and he imparted his views with fierce indignation and wit.

**Switzerland** Swiss Confederation; **national name:** German *Schweiz*, French *Suisse*, Romansch *Svizra*; **area:** 41,300 sq km/15,945 sq mi; **capital:** Bern (Berne); **major towns/cities:** Zürich, Geneva, Basel, Lausanne, Luzern, St Gallen, Winterthur; **major ports:** river port Basel (on the Rhine); **physical features:** most mountainous country in Europe (Alps and Jura mountains); highest peak Dufourspitze 4,634 m/15,203 ft in Apennines; **head of state and government:** Ruth Dreifuss from 1999; **government:** federal democracy; **currency:** Swiss franc; **GNP per capita (PPP):** (US$) 26,620 (1998); **exports:** machinery and equipment, pharmaceutical and chemical products, foodstuffs, precision instruments, clocks and watches, metal products. Principal market Germany 23.6% (1998); **population:** 7,345,000 (1999 est); **language:** German 64%, French 19%, Italian 8%, Romansch 0.6% (all official); **religion:** Roman Catholic 50%, Protestant 48%;

**life expectancy:** 75 (men); 82 (women) (1995–2000).

**swordfish** marine bony fish *Xiphias gladius*, the only member of its family (Xiphiidae), characterized by a long swordlike beak protruding from the upper jaw. It may reach 4.5 m/15 ft in length and weigh 450 kg/1,000 lb.

**Sydney** principal port of Australia and capital of the state of →New South Wales; population (1996) 3,276,500. Founded in 1788, Sydney is situated on Port Jackson inlet on the southeast coast of Australia, and is built around a number of bays and inlets that form an impressive natural harbour. Industries include financial services, oil refining, engineering, electronics, and the manufacture of scientific equipment, chemicals, clothing, and furniture. Notable architectural landmarks are the Harbour Bridge, the nearby Sydney Opera House, and Centre Point Tower. There are many parks, as well as coastal beaches ideal for surfing, such as Bondi and Manly. In 1994 Sydney was chosen to host the Olympic Games in the year 2000.

**symbiosis** any close relationship between two organisms of different species, and one where both partners benefit from the association. A well-known example is the pollination relationship between insects and flowers, where the insects feed on nectar and carry pollen from one flower to another. This is sometimes known as mutualism.

**symmetry** exact likeness in shape about a given line (axis), point, or plane. A figure has symmetry if one half can be rotated and/or reflected onto the other. (Symmetry preserves length, angle, but not necessarily orientation.) In a wider sense, symmetry exists if a change in the system leaves the essential features of

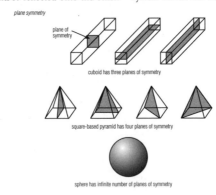

*plane symmetry*

plane of symmetry

cuboid has three planes of symmetry

square-based pyramid has four planes of symmetry

sphere has infinite number of planes of symmetry

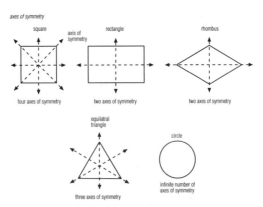

*axes of symmetry*

square

axis of symmetry

four axes of symmetry

rectangle

two axes of symmetry

rhombus

two axes of symmetry

equilatral triangle

three axes of symmetry

circle

infinite number of axes of symmetry

**symmetry** Planes and axes of symmetry.

the system unchanged; for example, reversing the sign of electric charges does not change the electrical behaviour of an arrangement of charges.

**symphony** abstract musical composition for orchestra, traditionally in four separate but closely related movements. It developed from the smaller sonata form, the Italian overture, and the concerto grosso.

**synagogue** in Judaism, a place of worship; in the USA a synagogue is also called a temple by the non-Orthodox. As an institution it dates from the destruction of the Temple in Jerusalem in AD 70, though it had been developing from the time of the Babylonian exile as a substitute for the Temple. In antiquity it was a public meeting hall where the Torah was also read, but today it is used primarily for prayer and services. A service requires a quorum (*minyan*) of ten adult Jewish men.

**synapse** junction between two →nerve cells, or between a nerve cell and a muscle (a neuromuscular junction), across which a nerve impulse is transmitted. The two cells are separated by a narrow gap called the synaptic cleft. The gap is bridged by a chemical neurotransmitter, released by the nerve impulse.

**synthesis** in chemistry, the formation of a substance or compound from more elementary compounds. The synthesis of a drug can involve several stages from the initial material to the final product; the complexity of these stages is a major factor in the cost of production.

**syphilis** sexually transmitted disease caused by the spiral-shaped bacterium (spirochete) *Treponema pallidum*. Untreated, it runs its course in three stages over many years, often starting with a painless hard sore, or chancre, developing within a month on the area of infection (usually the genitals). The second stage, months later, is a rash with arthritis, hepatitis, and/or meningitis. The third stage, years later, leads eventually to paralysis, blindness, insanity, and death. The Wassermann test is a diagnostic blood test for syphilis.

**Syria** Syrian Arab Republic; **national name:** *al-Jamhuriya al-Arabya as-Suriya*; **area:** 185,200 sq km/71,505 sq mi; **capital:** Damascus; **major towns/ cities:** Aleppo, Homs, Latakia, Hama; **major ports:** Latakia; **physical features:** mountains alternate with fertile plains and desert areas; Euphrates River; **head of state and government:** Bashar al-Assad is son and likely successor of Hafez al-Assad, who died in June 2000; **political system:** socialist republic; **currency:** Syrian pound; **GNP per capita (PPP):** (US$) 3,000 (1998); **exports:** crude petroleum, textiles, vegetables, fruit, raw cotton, natural phosphate. Principal market Italy 17.5% (1997); **population:** 15,725,000 (1999 est); **language:** Arabic 89% (official); Kurdish 6%, Armenian 3%; **religion:** Sunni Muslim 90%; other Islamic sects, Christian; **life expectancy:** 67 (men); 71 (women) (1995–2000).

# Tt

**Tacitus, Publius Cornelius** (*c.* AD 56–*c.* 120) Roman historian. A public orator in Rome, he was consul under Nerva 97–98 and proconsul of Asia 112–113. He wrote histories of the Roman empire, *Annales* and *Historiae*, covering the years AD 14–68 and 69–97 respectively. He also wrote a *Life of Agricola* (97; he married Agricola's daughter 77) and a description of the Germanic tribes, *Germania* (98).

**Tagore, Rabindranath** (1861–1941) Bengali Indian writer. He translated into English his own verse *Gitanjali/Song Offerings* (1912) and his verse play *Chitra* (1896). He was awarded the Nobel Prize for Literature in 1913.

**Taiwan** (Republic of China) **national name:** *Chung Hua Min Kuo*; **area:** 36,179 sq km/13,968 sq mi; **capital:** Taipei; **major towns/cities:** Kaohsiung, Taichung, Tainan,. Panchiao, Yunlin; **major ports:** Kaohsiung, Keelung; **physical features:** island (formerly Formosa) off People's Republic of China; mountainous, with lowlands in west; Penghu (Pescadores), Jinmen (Quemoy), Mazu (Matsu) islands; **head of state:** Lee Teng-hui from 1988; **head of government:** Vincent Siew from 1997; **political system:** emergent democracy; **currency:** New Taiwan dollar; **GNP per capita (PPP):** (US$) 18,950 (1998 est);

**exports:** electronic products, base metals and metal articles, textiles and clothing, machinery, information and communication products, plastic and rubber products, vehicles and transport equipment, footwear, headwear, umbrellas, toys, games, sports equipment. Principal market USA 26.6% (1998); **population:** 22,113,000 (1999 est); **language:** Mandarin Chinese (official); Taiwan, Hakka dialects; **religion:** officially atheist; Taoist, Confucian, Buddhist, Christian; **life expectancy:** 74 (men); 80 (women) (1998 est).

**Tajikistan** Republic of; **national name:** *Respublika i Tojikiston*; **area:** 143,100 sq km/55,250 sq mi; **capital:** Dushanbe; **major towns/cities:** Khodzhent (formerly Leninabad), Kurgan-Tyube, Kulyab; **physical features:** mountainous, more than half of its territory lying above 3,000 m/10,000 ft; huge mountain glaciers, which are the source of many rapid rivers; **head of state:** Imamali Rakhmanov from 1994; **head of government:** Yahya Azimov from 1996; **political system:** authoritarian nationalist; **currencies:** Tajik and Russian rouble; **GNP per capita (PPP):** (US$) 1,310 (1998 est); **exports:** aluminium, cotton lint. Principal market Uzbekistan 36.8% (1997); **population:** 6,104,000 (1999 est); **language:**

Tajik (official), similar to Farsi (Persian); **religion:** Sunni Muslim; **life expectancy:** 64 (men); 70 (women) (1995–2000).

**Taj Mahal** white marble mausoleum built 1630–53 on the River Yamuna near Agra, India. Erected by Shah Jahan to the memory of his favourite wife, it is a celebrated example of Indo-Islamic architecture, the fusion of Muslim and Hindu styles.

**Talmud** the two most important works of post-biblical Jewish literature. The Babylonian and the Palestinian (or Jerusalem) Talmud provide a compilation of ancient Jewish law and tradition. The Babylonian Talmud was edited at the end of the 5th century AD and is the more authoritative version for later Judaism; both Talmuds are written in a mix of Hebrew and Aramaic. They contain the commentary (*gemara*) on the *Mishnah* (early rabbinical commentaries compiled about AD 200), and the material can be generally divided into *halakhah*, consisting of legal and ritual matters, and *aggadah* (or *haggadah*), concerned with ethical, theological, and folklorist matters.

**Tamerlane** (1335–1405) also known as Timur Leng or Timur the Lame, Turco-Mongol ruler of Samarkand, in Uzbekistan, from 1369 who conquered Persia, Azerbaijan, Armenia, and Georgia. He defeated the Golden Horde in 1395, sacked Delhi in 1398, invaded Syria and Anatolia, and captured the Ottoman sultan Bayezid I (*c.* 1360–1403) in Ankara in 1402; he died invading China.

**Tamil Nadu** formerly (until 1968) Madras State, state of southeast India bounded on the north by Karnataka and Andhra Pradesh, Kerala on the west, and the Bay of Bengal and Indian Ocean on the east and south; **area:** 130,100 sq km/50,219 sq mi; **capital:** Chennai (formerly Madras); **physical:** coastal plains, including the Cauvery delta; inland the Nilgiri Hills and extensions of the Western Ghats; rainfall is unreliable, derived mainly from the northeast monsoon; **features:** hydroelectric power schemes at Mettur and Moyar; coal-powered power stations at Neyveli and Ennore; **industries:** the state has a good deal of mineral wealth including coal, chromite, bauxite, limestone, and manganese; **agriculture:** tea, coffee, spices, sugar cane, coconuts as cash crops; rice, millet, groundnuts, frequently dependent on tank and well irrigation; fishing; **population:** (1995 est) 60,225,000; **language:** Tamil; Telugu spoken in the north by 10%; **history:** the present state was formed 1956. Tamil Nadu comprises part of the former British Madras presidency (later province) formed from areas taken from France and Tipu Sahib, the sultan of Mysore, in the 18th century, which became a state of the Republic of India in 1950. The northeast was detached to form Andhra Pradesh in 1953; in 1956 other areas went to Kerala and Mysore (now Karnataka), and the Laccadive Islands (now Lakshadweep) became a separate Union Territory.

**Tanganyika, Lake** lake 772 m/2,534 ft above sea level in the Great Rift Valley,

East Africa, with the Democratic Republic of Congo to the west, Zambia to the south, and Tanzania and Burundi to the east. It is about 645 km/400 mi long, with an area of about 31,000 sq km/12,000 sq mi, and is the deepest lake (1,435 m/4,710 ft) in Africa, and the second-deepest freshwater lake in the world. The mountains around its shores rise to about 2,700 m/8,860 ft. The chief ports on the lake are Bujumbura (Burundi), Kigoma (Tanzania), and Kalémié (Democratic Republic of Congo).

**tangent** in geometry, a straight line that touches a curve and gives the gradient of the curve at the point of contact. At a maximum, minimum, or point of inflection, the tangent to a curve has zero gradient. Also, in trigonometry, a function of an acute angle in a right-angled triangle, defined as the ratio of the length of the side opposite the angle to the length of the side adjacent to it; a way of expressing the gradient of a line.

**tank** armoured fighting vehicle that runs on tracks and is fitted with weapons systems capable of defeating other tanks and destroying life and property. The term was originally a code name for the first effective tracked and armoured fighting vehicle, invented by the British soldier and scholar Ernest Swinton, and first used in the Battle of the Somme 1916.

**Tanzania** United Republic of; **national name:** *Jamhuri ya Muungano wa Tanzania*; **area:** 945,000 sq km/364,864 sq mi; **capital:** Dodoma (since 1983);

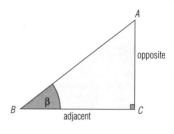

$$\text{tangent } \beta = \frac{\sin \beta}{\cos \beta} = \frac{\text{opposite}}{\text{adjacent}} = \frac{AC}{BC}$$

**tangent** The tangent of an angle is a mathematical function used in the study of right-angled triangles. If the tangent of an angle $\beta$ is known, then the length of the opposite side can be found given the length of the adjacent side, or vice versa.

**major towns/cities:** Zanzibar Town, Mwanza, Tabora, Mbeya, Tanga; **major ports:** (former capital) Dar es Salaam; **physical features:** central plateau; lakes in north and west; coastal plains; lakes Victoria, Tanganyika, and Nyasa; half the country is forested; comprises islands of Zanzibar and Pemba; Mount Kilimanjaro, 5,895 m/19,340 ft, the highest peak in Africa; Olduvai Gorge; Ngorongoro Crater, 14.5 km/9 mi across, 762 m/2,500 ft deep; **head of state:** Benjamin Mkapa from 1995; **head of government:** Cleoopa Msuya from 1994; **political system:** emergent democracy; **currency:** Tanzanian shilling; **GNP per capita (PPP):** (US$) 490 (1998); **exports:** coffee beans, raw cotton, tobacco, tea, cloves, cashew nuts, minerals, petroleum products. Principal market India 11.6% (1997); **population:** 32,793,000 (1999 est); **language:** Kiswahili, English (both official); **religion:** Muslim, Christian, traditional religions; **life expectancy:** 50 (men); 53 (women) (1995–2000).

**tapeworm** any of various parasitic flatworms of the class Cestoda. They lack digestive and sense organs, can reach 15 m/50 ft in length, and attach themselves to the host's intestines by means of hooks and suckers. Tapeworms are made up of hundreds of individual segments, each of which develops into a functional hermaphroditic reproductive unit capable of producing numerous eggs. The larvae of tapeworms usually reach humans in imperfectly cooked meat or fish, causing anaemia and intestinal disorders.

**tapioca** granular starch used in cooking, produced from the cassava root. The cassava plant belongs to the spurge family and, although native to South America, is now widely grown throughout the tropics.

**tarantula** wolf spider *Lycosa tarantula* (family Lycosidae) with a 2.5 cm/1 in body. It spins no web, relying on its speed in hunting to catch its prey. The name 'tarantula' is also used for any of the numerous large, hairy spiders of the family Theraphosidae, with large poison fangs, native to the southwestern USA and tropical America.

**Tarquinius Superbus** (lived 6th century BC) Tarquin the Proud, last king of Rome 534–510 BC. He abolished certain rights of Romans, and made the city powerful. According to legend, he was deposed when his son Sextus raped Lucretia.

**tarsier** any of three species of the prosimian primates, genus *Tarsius*, of the East Indies and the Philippines. These survivors of early primates are about the size of a rat with thick, light-brown fur, very large eyes, and long feet and hands. They are nocturnal, arboreal, and eat insects and lizards.

**Tasmania** (formerly (1642–1856) Van Diemen's Land) island in the Indian Ocean, southeast of Australia, separated from the mainland by Bass Strait; state of Australia; **area:** about 68,000 sq km/26,248 sq mi; **capital:** Hobart; **towns and cities:** Launceston (chief port), Devonport, Burnie, Queenstown; **features:** the smallest of the Australian states; territory includes numerous smaller islands; World Heritage Area in the southwest; unique flora and fauna, including the Huon pine and the Tasmanian devil (a marsupial found only in Tasmania); **products:** wool, dairy products, apples and other fruit, processed foods, timber, paper, iron, tungsten, copper, silver, coal, cement; **population:** (1996) 459,700; **history:** the first European to visit was Abel Tasman in 1642; British penal colony established at Risdon Cove in 1803; part of New South Wales until 1825; name changed to Tasmania in 1856; became a state of the Australian Commonwealth in 1901.

**taste** sense that detects some of the

chemical constituents of food. The human tongue can distinguish only four basic tastes (sweet, sour, bitter, and salty) but it is supplemented by the sense of smell. What we refer to as taste is really a composite sense made up of both taste and smell.

**taxonomy** another name for the classification of living organisms.

**Tbilisi** (formerly Tiflis) capital and cultural centre of Georgia, located on the Kura River in the Caucasus Mountains; population (1996) 1,200,000. It is a major economic, transportation and industrial centre. Industries include the manufacture of textiles, machinery, ceramics, and tobacco. In the lead-up to the collapse of the USSR in 1989 and Georgian independence, the city was the scene of bloody clashes between Russian security forces and nationalist demonstrators.

**Tchaikovsky, Pyotr Il'yich** (1840– 1893) Russian composer. His strong sense of melody, personal expression, and brilliant orchestration are clear throughout his many Romantic works, which include six symphonies, three piano concertos, a violin concerto, operas (including *Eugene Onegin* 1879), ballets (including *The Nutcracker* 1891–92), orchestral fantasies (including *Romeo and Juliet* 1870), and chamber and vocal music.

**tea** evergreen shrub or small tree whose fermented, dried leaves are soaked in hot water to make a refreshing drink. Known in China as early as 2737 BC, tea was first brought to Europe AD 1610 and rapidly became a popular drink. In 1823 the shrub was found growing wild in northern India, and plantations were later established in Assam and Sri Lanka; producers today include Africa, South America, Georgia, Azerbaijan, Indonesia, and Iran. (*Camellia sinensis*, family Theaceae.)

**technology** the use of tools, power, and materials, generally for the purposes of production. Almost every human process for getting food and shelter depends on complex technological systems, which have been developed over a 3-million-year period. Significant milestones include the advent of the →steam engine in 1712, the introduction of →electricity and the →internal combustion engine in the mid-1870s, and recent developments in communications, →electronics, and the nuclear and space industries. The **advanced technology** (highly automated and specialized) on which modern industrialized society depends is frequently contrasted with the **low technology** (labour-intensive and unspecialized) that characterizes some developing countries. Intermediate technology is an attempt to adapt scientifically advanced inventions to less developed areas by using local materials and methods of manufacture. Appropriate technology refers to simple and small-scale tools and machinery of use to developing countries.

**Tecumseh** (1768–1813) American Indian chief of the Shawnee. He attempted to unite the Indian peoples from Canada to Florida against the encroachment of white settlers, but the defeat of his brother Tenskwatawa, 'the Prophet', at the battle of Tippecanoe in November 1811 by W H Harrison, governor of the Indiana Territory, largely destroyed the confederacy built up by Tecumseh.

**Teflon** trade name for polytetrafluoroethene (PTFE), a tough, waxlike, heat-resistant plastic used for coating nonstick cookware and in gaskets and bearings.

**Te Kanawa, Kiri Janette** (1944– ) New Zealand soprano. Te Kanawa's first major role was the Countess in Mozart's *The Marriage of Figaro* at Covent Garden, London, 1971. Her voice combines the purity and intensity of the upper range with an extended lower range of great richness and resonance. Apart from classical roles, she has also featured popular music in her repertoire, such as the 1984 recording of Leonard Bernstein's *West Side Story*. DBE 1982.

**Tel Aviv-Yafo** (or Tel Aviv-Jaffa) city in Israel, situated on the coast of Sharon Plain, 77 km/48 mi northwest of Jerusalem; population (1995) 355,900. Industries include textiles, chemicals, sugar, printing, publishing, and tourism. Tel Aviv was founded in 1909 as a Jewish residential area in the Arab town of Jaffa, with which it was combined in 1949; their ports were superseded in 1965 by Ashdod to the south. During the →Gulf War of 1991, Tel Aviv became a target for Iraqi missiles as part of Saddam Hussein's strategy to break up the Arab alliance against him. It is regarded by the UN as the capital of Israel.

**telephone** instrument for communicating by voice along wires, developed by Scottish inventor Alexander Graham →Bell in 1876. The transmitter (mouthpiece) consists of a carbon microphone, with a diaphragm that vibrates when a person speaks into it. The diaphragm vibrations compress grains of carbon to a greater or lesser extent, altering their resistance to an electric current passing through them. This sets up variable electrical signals, which travel along the telephone lines to the receiver of the person being called. There they cause the magnetism of an electromagnet to vary, making a diaphragm above the electromagnet vibrate and give out sound waves, which mirror those that entered the mouthpiece originally.

**telescope** optical instrument that magnifies images of faint and distant objects; any device for collecting and focusing light and other forms of electromagnetic radiation. It is a major research tool in astronomy and is used to sight over land and sea; small telescopes can be attached to cameras and rifles. A telescope with a large aperture, or opening, can distinguish finer detail and fainter objects than one with a small aperture. The refracting telescope uses lenses, and the reflecting telescope uses mirrors. A third type, the catadioptric telescope, is a combination of lenses and mirrors. *See illustration on page 540.*

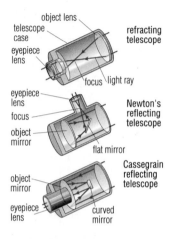

**telescope** Three kinds of telescope. The refracting telescope uses a large objective lens to gather light and form an image which the smaller eyepiece lens magnifies. A reflecting telescope uses a mirror to gather light. The Cassegrain telescope uses a corrective lens to achieve a wide field of view. It is one of the most widely used tools of astronomy.

**television** (TV) reproduction of visual images at a distance using radio waves. For transmission, a television camera converts the pattern of light it takes in into a pattern of electrical charges. This is scanned line by line by a beam of electrons from an electron gun, resulting in variable electrical signals that represent the picture. These signals are combined with a radio carrier wave and broadcast as electromagnetic waves. The TV aerial picks up the wave and feeds it to the receiver (TV set). This separates out the vision signals, which pass to a cathode-ray tube where a beam of electrons is made to scan across the screen line by line, mirroring the action of the electron gun in the TV camera. The result is a recreation of the pattern of light that entered the camera.

**Telford, Thomas** (1757–1834) Scottish civil engineer. He opened up northern Scotland by building roads and waterways. He constructed many aqueducts and canals, including the Caledonian Canal (1802–23), and erected the Menai road suspension bridge between Wales and Anglesey 1819–26, a type of structure scarcely tried previously in the UK. In Scotland he constructed over 1,600 km/1,000 mi of road and 1,200 bridges, churches, and harbours.

**temperature** degree or intensity of heat of an object and the condition that determines whether it will transfer heat to another object or receive heat from it, according to the laws of →thermodynamics. The temperature of an object is a measure of the average kinetic energy possessed by the atoms or molecules of which it is composed. The SI unit of temperature is the kelvin (symbol K) used with the Kelvin scale. Other measures of temperature in common use are the Celsius scale and the Fahrenheit scale.

**Ten Commandments** in the Old Testament, the laws given by God to the Hebrew leader Moses on Mount Sinai, engraved on two tablets of stone.

They are: to have no other gods

besides Jehovah; to make no idols; not to misuse the name of God; to keep the sabbath holy; to honour one's parents; not to commit murder, adultery, or theft; not to give false evidence; and not to be covetous. They form the basis of Jewish and Christian moral codes; the 'tablets of the Law' given to Moses are also mentioned in the Koran. The giving of the Ten Commandments is celebrated in the Jewish festival of *Shavuot*.

**tendon** (or sinew) in vertebrates, a cord of very strong, fibrous connective tissue that joins muscle to bone. Tendons are largely composed of bundles of fibres made of the protein collagen, and because of their inelasticity are very efficient at transforming muscle power into movement.

**Tenerife** largest of the →Canary Islands, in the province of Santa Cruz de Tenerife, Spain; area 2,060 sq km/795 sq mi; population (1991) 706,900. Fruit and vegetables are produced, especially bananas and tomatoes, and the island is a popular tourist resort. Santa Cruz is the main town here, and Pico de Teide, an active volcano, is the highest peak in Spain (3,713 m/12,186 ft high).

**Tennessee** state in eastern central USA. It is nicknamed the Volunteer State. Tennessee was admitted to the Union in 1796 as the 16th US state. It is bordered to the east by North Carolina, to the south by Georgia, Alabama, and Mississippi, to the west by Arkansas and Missouri, across the Mississippi River, and to the north by Kentucky and Virginia. Historically, Tennessee was a plantation state, associated with slavery. Culturally, it is one of the centres of country music. **population:** (1995) 5,256,100; **area:** 109,200 sq km/ 42,151 sq mi; **capital:** Nashville; **towns and cities:** Memphis, Knoxville, Chattanooga, Clarksville; **industries and products:** cereals, cotton, tobacco, soybeans, livestock, timber, coal, zinc, copper, chemicals, power generation, automobiles, aluminium, music industry, tourism.

**tennis** racket-and-ball game invented towards the end of the 19th century. Although played on different surfaces (grass, wood, shale, clay, concrete), it is also called 'lawn tennis'. The aim of the two or four players (in singles or doubles matches) is to strike the ball into the prescribed area of the court, with oval-headed rackets (strung with gut or nylon), in such a way that it cannot be returned. The game is won by those first winning four points (called 15, 30, 40, game), unless both sides reach 40 (deuce), when two consecutive points are needed to win. A set is won by winning six games with a margin of two over opponents, though a tie-break system operates, that is at six games to each side (or in some cases eight) except in the final set. A match lasts a maximum of five sets for men, three for women.

**Tennyson, Alfred** (1809–1892) 1st Baron Tennyson, English poet. He was poet laureate from 1850–92. His verse has a majestic, musical quality, and few poets have surpassed his precision and delicacy of language. His works include

'The Lady of Shalott' (1833), 'The Lotus Eaters' (1833), 'Ulysses' (1842), 'Break, Break, Break' (1842), and 'The Charge of the Light Brigade' (1854); the longer narratives *Locksley Hall* (1832) and *Maud* (1855); the elegy *In Memoriam* (1850); and a long series of poems on the Arthurian legends, *The Idylls of the King* (1859–89).

**termite** any member of the insect order Isoptera. Termites are soft-bodied social insects living in large colonies which include one or more queens (of relatively enormous size and producing an egg every two seconds), much smaller kings, and still smaller soldiers, workers, and immature forms. Termites build galleried nests of soil particles that may be 6 m/20 ft high.

**Terror, Reign of** phase of the →French Revolution when the Jacobins were in power (October 1793 to July 1794) under →Robespierre and began systematically to murder their political opponents. The Terror was at its height in the early months of 1794. Across France, it is thought that between 17,000 and 40,000 people were executed, mainly by guillotine, until public indignation rose and Robespierre was overthrown and guillotined in July 1794.

**Tertiary** period of geological time 65–1.64 million years ago, divided into five epochs: Palaeocene, Eocene, Oligocene, Miocene, and Pliocene. During the Tertiary period, mammals took over all the ecological niches left vacant by the extinction of the dinosaurs, and became the prevalent land animals. The continents took on their present positions, and climatic and vegetation zones as we know them became established. Within the geological time column the Tertiary follows the Cretaceous period and is succeeded by the Quaternary period.

**testosterone** in vertebrates, hormone secreted chiefly by the testes, but also by the ovaries and the cortex of the adrenal glands. It promotes the development of secondary sexual characteristics in males. In animals with a breeding season, the onset of breeding behaviour is accompanied by a rise in the level of testosterone in the blood.

**tetanus** (or lockjaw) acute disease caused by the toxin of the bacillus *Clostridium tetani*, which usually enters the body through a wound. The bacterium is chiefly found in richly manured soil. Untreated, in seven to ten days tetanus produces muscular spasm and rigidity of the jaw spreading to other parts of the body, convulsions, and death. There is a vaccine, and the disease may be treatable with tetanus antitoxin and antibiotics.

**tetrahedron** (plural tetrahedra) in geometry, a solid figure (polyhedron) with four triangular faces; that is, a pyramid on a triangular base. A regular tetrahedron has equilateral triangles as its faces.

**Texas** state in southwestern USA. It is nicknamed the Lone Star State. Texas was admitted to the Union in 1845 as the 28th US state. One of the Great Plains states, it is bordered to the east by Louisiana, to the northeast by Arkansas, to the north by Oklahoma, to the west by New Mexico, to the southwest by the Mexican states of Chihuahua, Coahuil, Nuevo Léon, and Tamaulipas, and to the southeast by the Gulf of Mexico. Texas is the largest state in the lower 48 US states. **population:** (1995) 18,724,000; **area:** 691,200 sq km/266,803 sq mi; **capital:** Austin; **towns and cities:** Houston, Dallas, Fort Worth, San Antonio, El Paso, Corpus Christi, Lubbock; **industries and products:** rice, cotton, sorghum, wheat, hay, livestock, shrimps, meat products, lumber, wood and paper products, petroleum (nearly one-third of US production), natural gas, sulphur, salt, uranium, chemicals, petrochemicals, nonelectrical machinery, fabricated metal products, transportation equipment, electric and electronic equipment, aerospace equipment, computer and high-tech machinery, finance sector, tourism.

**Thackeray, William Makepeace** (1811–1863) English novelist and essayist. He was a regular contributor to *Fraser's Magazine* and *Punch*. His first novel was *Vanity Fair* (1847–48), significant for the breadth of its canvas as well as for the depth of the characterization. This was followed by *Pendennis* (1848), *Henry Esmond* (1852) (and its sequel *The Virginians*, 1857–59), and *The Newcomes* (1853–55), in which Thackeray's tendency to sentimentality is most marked.

**Thailand** Kingdom of; **national name:** *Prathet Thai* or *Muang Thai*; **area:** 513,115 sq km/198,113 sq mi; **capital:** Bangkok (and chief port); **major towns/cities:** Chiangmai, Hat Yai, Khon Kaen, Songkhla, Chon Buri, Nakhon Si Thammarat, Lampang, Phitsannlok, Ratchasima; **major ports:** Nakhon Sawan; **physical features:** mountainous, semi-arid plateau in northeast, fertile central region, tropical isthmus in south; rivers Chao Phraya, Mekong, and Salween; **head of state:** King Bhumibol Adulyadej from 1946; **head of government:** Chavalit Yongchaiyudh from 1996; **political system:** military-controlled emergent democracy; **currency:** baht; **GNP per capita (PPP):** (US$) 5,840 (1998); **exports:** textiles and clothing, electronic goods, rice, rubber, gemstones, sugar, cassava (tapioca), fish (especially prawns), machinery and manufactures, chemicals. Principal market USA 22.3% (1998); **population:** 60,858,000 (1999 est); **language:** Thai and Chinese (both official); Lao, Chinese, Malay, Khmer; **religion:**

Buddhist; **life expectancy:** 66 (men); 72 (women) (1995–2000).

**theatre** a place or building in which dramatic performances for an audience take place; these include drama, dancing, music, mime, opera, ballet, and puppets. Theatre history can be traced to Egyptian religious ritualistic drama as long ago as 3200 BC. The first known European theatres were in Greece from about 600 BC.

The earliest theatres were natural amphitheatres. By the Hellenistic period came the development of the stage, a raised platform on which the action took place. In medieval times, temporary stages of wood and canvas, one for every scene, were set up in churches and market squares for the performance of mimes and miracle plays. With the Renaissance came the creation of scenic illusion, with the actors appearing within a proscenium arch; in the 19th century the introduction of the curtain and interior lighting further heightened this illusion. In the 20th century, alternative types of theatre were developed, including open stage, thrust stage, theatre-in-the-round, and studio theatre.

Famous theatre companies include the Comédie Française in Paris (founded by Louis XIV in 1690 and given a permanent home in 1792), the first national theatre. The Living Theater was founded in New York in 1947 by Julian Beck and Judith Malina. In Britain the National Theatre company was established in 1963; other national theatres exist in Stockholm, Moscow, Athens, Copenhagen, Vienna, Warsaw, and elsewhere.

For traditional Japanese theatre, see →Nō.

**theology** study of God or gods, either by reasoned deduction from the natural world (natural theology) or through divine revelation (revealed theology), as in the scriptures of Christianity, Islam, or other religions.

**Theravāda** one of the two major forms of →Buddhism, common in Southeast Asia (Sri Lanka, Thailand, Cambodia, and Myanmar); the other is the later Mahāyāna.

**thermal conductivity** in physics, the ability of a substance to conduct heat. Good thermal conductors, like good electrical conductors, are generally materials with many free electrons (such as metals).

**thermodynamics** branch of physics dealing with the transformation of heat into and from other forms of energy. It is the basis of the study of the efficient working of engines, such as the steam and internal combustion engines. The three laws of thermodynamics are: (1) energy can be neither created nor destroyed, heat and mechanical work being mutually convertible; (2) it is impossible for an unaided self-acting machine to convey heat from one body to another at a higher temperature; and (3) it is impossible by any procedure, no matter how idealized, to reduce any system to the absolute zero of temperature (0 K/–273°C/–459°F) in a finite number of operations. Put into mathematical form, these laws have widespread applications in physics and chemistry.

**thermometer** instrument for measuring temperature. There are many types, designed to measure different temperature ranges to varying degrees of

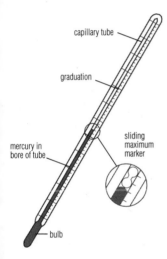

capillary tube

graduation

mercury in
bore of tube

sliding
maximum
marker

bulb

**thermometer** Maximum and minimum
thermometers are universally used in weather-
reporting stations. The maximum thermometer,
shown here, includes a magnet that fits tightly
inside a capillary tube and is moved up it by the
rising mercury. When the temperature falls, the
magnet remains in position, thus enabling the
maximum temperature to be recorded.

accuracy. Each makes use of a different physical effect of temperature. Expansion of a liquid is employed in common liquid-in-glass thermometers, such as those containing mercury or alcohol. The more accurate gas thermometer uses the effect of temperature on the pressure of a gas held at constant volume. A resistance thermometer takes advantage of the change in resistance of a conductor (such as a platinum wire) with variation in temperature. Another electrical thermometer is the thermocouple. Mechanically, temperature change can be indicated by the change in curvature of a bimetallic strip (as commonly used in a thermostat).

**Thermopylae, Battle of** battle between the Greeks under the Spartan king Leonidas and the invading Persians under Xerxes I. They clashed at the narrow mountain pass of Thermopylae, leading from Thessaly to Locrish in central Greece. Although the Greeks were defeated, the heroism of those who fought to the last against the Persians boosted Greek morale.

**Third World** (or developing world) those countries that are less developed than the industrialized free-market countries of the West (First World) and the industrialized former communist countries (Second World). Third World countries are the poorest, as measured by their income per head of population, and are concentrated in Asia, Africa, and Latin America.

The early 1970s saw the beginnings of attempts by Third World countries to act together in confronting the powerful industrialized countries over such matters as the level of prices of primary products, with the nations regarding themselves as a group that had been exploited in the past by the developed nations and that had a right to catch up with them.

**Thirty Years' War** major war 1618–48 in central Europe. Beginning as a German conflict between Protestants and Catholics, it was gradually transformed into a struggle to determine whether the ruling Austrian Habsburg family could gain control of all Germany. The war caused serious economic and demographic problems in central Europe. Under the Peace of Westphalia the German states were granted their sovereignty and the emperor retained only nominal control.

**Thomas, Dylan Marlais** (1914–1953) Welsh poet. His poems, characterized by complex imagery and a strong musicality, include the celebration of his 30th birthday 'Poem in October' and the evocation of his youth 'Fern Hill' (1946). His 'play for voices' *Under Milk Wood* (1954) describes with humour and compassion a day in the life of the residents of a small Welsh fishing village, Llareggub. The short stories of *Portrait of the Artist as a Young Dog* (1940) are autobiographical.

**Thomas à Kempis** (*c.* 1380–1471) adopted name of Thomas Hämmerken, German Augustinian monk, author of *De Imitatio Christi/Imitation of Christ* (1441), a devotional handbook of the *devotio moderna*. The work proved quickly popular, being translated into Dutch and French.

**Thomson, J(oseph) J(ohn)** (1856–1940) English physicist. He discovered the →electron in 1897. His work inaugurated the electrical theory of the atom, and his elucidation of positive rays and their application to an analysis of neon led to the discovery of →isotopes. He was awarded a Nobel prize in 1906 and was knighted in 1908.

**Thor** in Norse and Teutonic mythology, the god of thunder (his hammer), represented as a man of enormous strength defending humanity against demons and the frost giants. He was the son of Odin and Freya, and one of the Aesir (warrior gods). Thursday is named after him.

**thorax** in four-limbed vertebrates, the part of the body containing the heart and lungs, and protected by the ribcage; in arthropods, the middle part of the body, between the head and abdomen.

**Thrace** (Greek Thráki) ancient region of the Balkans, southeastern Europe, formed by parts of modern Greece and Bulgaria. It was held successively by the Greeks, Persians, Macedonians, and Romans.

**thrombosis** condition in which a blood clot forms in a vein or artery, causing loss of circulation to the area served by the vessel. If it breaks away, it often travels to the lungs, causing pulmonary embolism.

**thrush** any bird of the large family Turdidae, order Passeriformes, found worldwide and known for their song. Thrushes are usually brown with speckles of other colours. They are 12–30 cm/5–12 in long.

**thrush** in medicine, infection usually of the mouth (particularly in infants), but also sometimes of the vagina, caused by a yeastlike fungus (*Candida*). It is seen as white patches on the mucous membranes.

**thyroid** endocrine gland of vertebrates, situated in the neck in front of the →trachea. It secretes several hormones, principally thyroxine, an iodine-containing hormone that stimulates growth, metabolism, and other functions of the body. The thyroid gland may be thought of as the regulator gland of the body's metabolic rate. If it is overactive, as in hyperthyroidism, the sufferer feels hot and sweaty, has an increased heart rate, diarrhoea, and weight loss. Conversely, an underactive thyroid leads to myxoedema, a condition characterized by sensitivity to the cold, constipation, and weight gain. In infants, an underactive thyroid leads to cretinism, a form of mental retardation.

**Tibet** autonomous region of southwestern China (Pinyin form Xizang); **area:** 1,221,600 sq km/471,538 sq mi; **capital:** Lhasa; **features:** Tibet occupies a barren plateau bounded to the south and southwest by the Himalayas and north by the Kunlun Mountains, traversed west to east by the Bukamagna, Karakoram, and other mountain ranges, and having an average elevation of 4,000–4,500 m/13,000–15,000 ft. The Sutlej, Brahmaputra, and Indus rivers rise in Tibet, which has numerous lakes, many of which are salty. The →yak is the main domestic animal; **government:** Tibet is an autonomous region of China, with its own People's Government and People's Congress. The controlling force in Tibet is the Communist Party of China, represented locally by First Secretary Wu Jinghua from 1985. Tibetan nationalists regard the province as being under colonial rule. There is a government-in-exile in Dharmsala, Himachel Pradesh, India, where the →Dalai Lama lives; **industries:** wool, borax, salt, horn, musk, herbs, furs, gold, iron pyrites, lapis lazuli, mercury, textiles, chemicals, agricultural machinery. Tibet has the largest uranium reserves in the world: uranium processing and extraction is causing pollution, and human and animal birth deformities; **population:** (1993) 2,290,000; many Chinese have settled in Tibet; 2 million Tibetans live in China outside Tibet; **religion:** traditionally Lamaist (a form of Mahāyāna Buddhism); **history:** Tibet was an independent kingdom from the 5th century AD. It came under nominal Chinese rule about 1700. From 1910–13 the capital, Lhasa, was occupied by Chinese troops, after which independence was re-established. China regained control 1951 when the historic ruler and religious leader, the Dalai Lama, was driven from the country and the monks (who formed 25% of the population) were forced out of the monasteries. The Chinese People's

Liberation Army (PLA) controlled Tibet 1951–59, although the Dalai Lama returned as nominal spiritual and temporal head of state. In 1959 a Tibetan uprising spread from bordering regions to Lhasa and was supported by Tibet's local government. The rebellion was suppressed by the PLA, prompting the Dalai Lama and 9,000 Tibetans to flee to India. The Chinese proceeded to dissolve the Tibet local government, abolish serfdom, collectivize agriculture, and suppress Lamaism. In 1965 Tibet became an autonomous region of China. Chinese rule continued to be resented, however, and the economy languished.

**tibia** the anterior of the pair of bones in the leg between the ankle and the knee. In humans, the tibia is the shinbone. It articulates with the femur above to form the knee joint, the fibula externally at its upper and lower ends, and with the talus below, forming the ankle joint.

**tick** any of the arachnid family Ixodoidae, order Acarina, of large bloodsucking mites. They have flat bodies protected by horny shields. Many carry and transmit diseases to mammals (including humans) and birds.

**tide** the rhythmic rise and fall of the sea level in the Earth's oceans and their inlets and estuaries due to the gravitational attraction of the Moon and, to a lesser extent, the Sun, affecting regions of the Earth unequally as it rotates. Water on the side of the Earth nearest the Moon feels the Moon's pull and accumulates directly below it producing high tide.

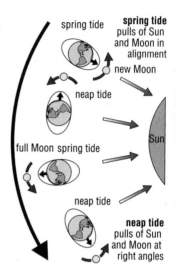

**tide** The gravitational pull of the Moon is the main cause of the tides. Water on the side of the Earth nearest the Moon feels the Moon's pull and accumulates directly under the Moon. When the Sun and the Moon are in line, at new and full moon, the gravitational pull of the Sun and Moon are in line and produce a high spring tide. When the Sun and Moon are at right angles, lower neap tides occur.

**Tigré** (or Tigray) region in the northern highlands of Ethiopia; area 65,900 sq km/25,444 sq mi; population (1995 est) 3,307,000. The chief town is Mek'elē. A mountainous region in the west; the highest point is Mokada, rising to 2295 m/7529 ft. The east of the region is much lower; some of the Danakil Depression is below sea level. Most of the population live by cultivation in the south and by nomadic herding in the north, but the area suffers from periodic severe droughts. In 1978 a guerrilla group known as the Tigré People's Liberation Front (TPLF) began fighting for regional autonomy. In 1989 government troops were forced from the province, and the TPLF advanced towards Addis Ababa, playing the key role in the fall of the Ethiopian government in May 1991.

**Timor** largest and most easterly of the Lesser Sunda Islands, part of Indonesia; area 33,610 sq km/12,973 sq mi. Its indigenous people were the Atoni; successive migrants have included the Malay, Melanesian, Chinese, Arab, and Gujerati.

The Dutch were established in Kupang 1613, with the Portuguese in the north and east. Portugal established a colonial administration in Timor 1702, but the claim was disputed by the Dutch, as well as by the Timorese, who frequently rebelled. Timor was divided into West Timor and →East Timor by treaties of 1859 and 1913 and subjected to Dutch and Portuguese control respectively; during World War II both parts were occupied by Japan. West Timor (capital Kupang) became part of Indonesia 1949. East Timor (capital Dili) comprises the enclave on the northwest coast, and the islands of Atauro and Jaco. It was seized by Indonesia 1975, and became an Indonesian province 1976 (East Timor is the English name for the

Indonesian province of Timor Timur). The annexation is not recognized by the United Nations, and guerrilla warfare by local people seeking independence continues. Since 1975 over 500,000 Timorese have been killed by Indonesian troops or have resettled in West Timor. East Timor is handed over to UN peacekeepers in 2000 as a move towards independence.

Products include coffee, maize, rice, and coconuts.

**tin** soft, silver-white, malleable and somewhat ductile, metallic element, symbol Sn (from Latin *stannum*), atomic number 50, relative atomic mass 118.69. Tin exhibits →allotropy, having three forms: the familiar lustrous metallic form above 13.2°C/55.8°F; a brittle form above 161°C/321.8°F; and a grey powder form below 13.2°C/55.8°F (commonly called tin pest or tin disease). The metal is quite soft (slightly harder than lead) and can be rolled, pressed, or hammered into extremely thin sheets; it has a low melting point. In nature it occurs rarely as a free metal. It resists corrosion and is therefore used for coating and plating other metals.

**tinnitus** in medicine, constant buzzing or ringing in the ears. The phenomenon may originate from prolonged exposure to noisy conditions (drilling, machinery, or loud music) or from damage to or disease of the middle or inner ear. The victim may become overwhelmed by the relentless noise in the head.

**Tintoretto** (1518–1594) adopted name of Jacopo Robusti, Venetian painter who produced portraits and religious works of great intensity. Outstanding among his many works is a series of religious works in the Scuola di S Rocco in Venice (1564–88), the dramatic figures lit by a flickering, unearthly light, the space around them distorted into long perspectives. Among his best-known works is *St George and the Dragon* (*c.*1570, National Gallery, London).

**Tipperary** county of the Republic of Ireland, in the province of Munster, divided into North and South Ridings; county town Clonmel; area 4,255 sq km/1,643 sq mi; population (1996) 133,500. It includes part of the Golden Vale, a fertile dairy-farming region. Agriculture is the chief industry; barley and oats are the main crops, but potatoes and turnips are also grown. Cattle are reared in large numbers, and there are flour mills and butter factories. There is also horse and greyhound breeding. Other main towns are Cahir, Carrick-on-Suir, Cashel, Templemore, Tipperary, Thurles, Nenagh, and Roscrea. Major tourist attractions in the county include the Rock of Cashel and Cahir Castle.

**tissue** in biology, any kind of cellular fabric that occurs in an organism's body. Several kinds of tissue can usually be distinguished, each consisting of cells of a particular kind bound together by cell walls (in plants) or extracellular matrix (in animals). Thus, nerve and muscle are different kinds of tissue in animals, as are parenchyma and sclerenchyma in plants.

**Titan** in astronomy, the largest moon of the planet Saturn, with a diameter of 5,150 km/3,200 mi and a mean distance from Saturn of 1,222,000 km/759,000 mi. It was discovered in 1655 by Dutch mathematician and astronomer Christiaan Huygens, and is the second-largest moon in the Solar System (Ganymede, of Jupiter, is larger).

**Titian** (*c.* 1487–1576) anglicized form of Tiziano Vecellio, Italian painter. He was one of the greatest artists of the High Renaissance. During his long career he was court painter to Charles V, Holy Roman Emperor, and to his son, Philip II of Spain. He produced a vast number of portraits, religious paintings, and mythological scenes, including *Bacchus and Ariadne* (1520–23; National Gallery, London) and *Venus and Adonis* (1554; Prado, Madrid).

**Titicaca, Lake** lake in the Andes, 3,810 m/12,500 ft above sea level and 1,220 m/4,000 ft above the tree line; area 8,300 sq km/3,200 sq mi, the largest lake in South America, and the world's highest navigable body of water. It is divided between Bolivia (port at Guaqui) and Peru (ports at Puno (principal port) and Huancane). The lake is fed by several streams which originate in the snow-capped surrounding mountains. The lake contains enormous frogs, which are farmed, the legs being an edible delicacy, and there is some trout farming. The herding of alpacas and llamas is also common. It is one of the few places in the world where reed boats are still made, by the Uru tribal peoples (Lake Tana in Ethiopia is another). The lake is also used for irrigation.

**Togo** Republic of (formerly **Togoland**); **national name:** *République Togolaise*; **area:** 56,800 sq km/21,930 sq mi; **capital:** Lomé; **major towns/cities:** Sokodé, Kpalimé, Kara, Atakpamé, Bassar, Tsévié; **physical features:** two savanna plains, divided by range of hills northeast–southwest; coastal lagoons and marsh; Mono Tableland, Oti Plateau, Oti River; **head of state:** Etienne Gnassingbé Eyadéma from 1967; **head of government:** Kwasi Klutse from 1996; **political system:** emergent democracy; **currency:** franc CFA; **GNP per capita (PPP):** (US$) 1,390 (1998); **exports:** phosphates (mainly calcium phosphates), ginned cotton, green coffee, cocoa beans. Principal market Canada 7.6% (1997); **population:** 4,512,000 (1999 est); **language:** French (official), Ewe, Kabre, Gurma; **religion:** animist, Catholic, Muslim, Protestant; **life expectancy:** 48 (men); 50 (women) (1995–2000).

**Tokyo** capital of Japan, on Honshu island; population (1994) 7,874,000. It is Japan's main cultural, financial and industrial centre (engineering, chemicals, textiles, electrical goods).

Founded in the 16th century as Yedo (or Edo), it was renamed when the emperor moved his court here from Kyoto in 1868. By the end of the 18th century, Yedo, with 1 million people, was the largest city in the world. An earthquake in 1923 killed 58,000 people and destroyed much of the city, which was again severely damaged by Allied bombing in World War II when 60% of Tokyo's housing was destroyed; US firebomb raids of 1945 were particularly destructive with over 100,000 people killed in just one night of bombing on 9 March. The subsequent rebuilding has made it into one of the world's most modern cities.

**Tolpuddle Martyrs** six farm labourers of Tolpuddle, a village in Dorset, southwest England, who were transported to Australia in 1834 after being sentenced for 'administering unlawful oaths' – as a 'union', they had threatened to withdraw their labour unless their pay was guaranteed, and had been prepared to put this in writing. They were pardoned two years later, after nationwide agitation. They returned to England and all but one migrated to Canada.

**Tolstoy, Leo Nikolaievich** (1828–1910) Russian novelist. He wrote *War and Peace* (1863–69) and *Anna Karenina* (1873–77). He was offended by the materialism of western Europe and in the 1860s and 1870s he became a pioneer of 'free education'. From 1880 he underwent a profound spiritual crisis and took up various moral positions, including passive resistance to evil, rejection of authority (religious or civil) and private ownership, and a return to basic mystical Christianity. He was excommunicated by the Orthodox Church, and his later works were banned.

**Toltec** ('builder') member of an ancient American Indian people who ruled much of Mexico and Central America in the 10th–12th centuries, with their capital and religious centre at Tula or Tollán, northeast of Mexico City. They also occupied and extended the ancient Maya city of Chichen Itzá in Yucatán. After the fall of the Toltecs the Aztecs took over much of their former territory, except for the regions regained by the Maya.

**Tonga** Kingdom of (or **Friendly Islands**); **national name:** *Pule'anga Fakatu'i 'o Tonga*; **area:** 750 sq km/ 290 sq mi; **capital:** Nuku'alofa (on Tongatapu Island); **major towns/cities:** Pangai, Neiafu; **physical features:** three groups of islands in southwest Pacific, mostly coral formations, but actively volcanic in west; of the 170 islands in the Tonga group, 36 are inhabited; **head of state:** King Taufa'ahau Tupou IV from 1965; **head of government:** Baron Vaea of Houma from 1991; **political system:** constitutional monarchy; **currency:** Tongan dollar or pa'anga; **GNP per capita (PPP):** (US$) 3,860 (1998); **exports:** vanilla beans, pumpkins, coconut oil and other coconut products, watermelons, knitted clothes, cassava, yams, sweet potatoes, footwear. Principal market Japan 52.9% (1997); **population:** 98,000 (1999 est); **language:** Tongan (official); English; **religion:** Free Wesleyan Church; **life expectancy:** 68 (men); 72 (women) (1998 est).

**tonsils** in higher vertebrates, masses of lymphoid tissue situated at the back of the mouth and throat (palatine tonsils), and on the rear surface of the tongue (lingual tonsils). The tonsils contain many →lymphocytes and are part of the body's defence system against infection.

**tooth** in vertebrates, one of a set of hard, bonelike structures in the mouth, used for biting and chewing food, and in defence and aggression. In humans, the first set (20 milk teeth) appear from age six months to two and a half years. The permanent →dentition replaces these from the sixth year onwards, the wisdom teeth (third molars) sometimes not appearing until the age of 25 or 30. Adults have 32 teeth: two incisors, one canine (eye tooth), two premolars, and

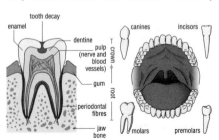

**tooth** Adults have 32 teeth: two incisors, one canine, two premolars, and three molars on each side of each jaw. Each tooth has three parts: crown, neck, and root. The crown consists of a dense layer of mineral, the enamel, surrounding hard dentine with a soft centre, the pulp.

three molars on each side of each jaw. Each tooth consists of an enamel coat (hardened calcium deposits), dentine (a thick, bonelike layer), and an inner pulp cavity, housing nerves and blood vessels. Mammalian teeth have roots surrounded by cementum, which fuses them into their sockets in the jaw-bones.

The neck of the tooth is covered by the gum, while the enamel-covered crown protrudes above the gum line.

**topaz** mineral, aluminium fluorosilicate, $Al_2(F_2SiO_4)$. It is usually yellow, but pink if it has been heated, and is used as a gemstone when transparent. It ranks 8 on the Mohs scale of hardness.

**topography** the surface shape and composition of the landscape, comprising both natural and artificial features, and its study. Topographical features include the relief and contours of the land; the distribution of mountains, valleys, and human settlements; and the patterns of rivers, roads, and railways.

**topology** branch of geometry that deals with those properties of a figure that remain unchanged even when the figure is transformed (bent, stretched) – for example, when a square painted on a rubber sheet is deformed by distorting the sheet.

Topology has scientific applications, as in the study of turbulence in flowing fluids.

**Torah** in Judaism, the first five books of the Hebrew Bible (Christian Old Testament). It contains a traditional history of the world from the Creation to the death of Moses; it also includes the Hebrew people's covenant with their one God, rules for religious observance, and guidelines for social conduct, including the Ten Commandments.

**tornado** extremely violent revolving storm with swirling, funnel-shaped clouds, caused by a rising column of warm air propelled by strong wind. A tornado can rise to a great height, but with a diameter of only a few hundred metres or less. Tornadoes move with wind speeds of 160–480 kph/100–300 mph, destroying everything in their path. They are common in the central USA and Australia.

**Toronto** (Huron 'place of meeting') port and capital of →Ontario, Canada, at the mouths of the Humber and Don rivers on Lake Ontario; population (1991) 635,400, metropolitan area (1996) 4,444,700. It is a major shipping point on the St Lawrence Seaway, and Canada's main financial, business, commercial, and manufacturing centre. Industries include shipbuilding, food-processing, publishing, and the production of fabricated metals, aircraft, farm machinery, cars, chemicals, and clothing. It is also a tourist and cultural centre, with theatres and a film industry.

**torpedo** self-propelled underwater missile, invented 1866 by British engineer Robert Whitehead. Modern torpedoes are homing missiles; some resemble mines in that they lie on the seabed until activated by the acoustic signal of a passing ship. A television camera enables them to be remotely controlled, and in the final stage of attack they lock on to the radar or sonar signals of the target ship.

**tortoise** reptile of the order Chelonia, family Testudinidae, with the body enclosed in a hard shell. Tortoises are related to the terrapins and turtles, and range in length from 10 cm/4 in to 150 cm/5 ft. The shell consists of a curved upper carapace and flattened lower plastron joined at the sides; it is generally more domed than that of turtles. The head and limbs is withdrawn into it when the tortoise is in danger. Most land tortoises are herbivorous, feeding on plant material, and have no teeth. The mouth forms a sharp-edged beak. They occur in the warmer regions of all continents except Australia. Tortoises have been known to live for 150 years.

**totemism** (Algonquin Indian 'mark of my family') the belief in individual or clan kinship with an animal, plant, or object. This totem is sacred to those concerned, and they are forbidden to eat or desecrate it; marriage within the clan is usually forbidden. Totemism occurs among Pacific Islanders and Australian Aborigines, and was formerly prevalent throughout Europe, Africa, and Asia. Most American Indian societies had totems as well.

**Toulouse-Lautrec, Henri (Marie Raymond de)** (1864–1901) French artist. He was active in Paris, where he painted entertainers and prostitutes in a style characterized by strong colours, bold design, and brilliant technical skill.

From 1891 his lithographic posters were a great success, skilfully executed and yet retaining the spontaneous character of sketches. His later work was to prove vital to the development of poster art.

**tour de France** French road race for professional cyclists held annually over approximately 4,800 km/3,000 mi of primarily French roads. The race takes about three weeks to complete and the route varies each year, often taking in adjoining countries, but always ending in Paris. A separate stage is held every day, and the overall leader at the end of each stage wears the coveted 'yellow jersey' (French *maillot jaune*).

**trace element** chemical element necessary in minute quantities for the health of a plant or animal. For example, magnesium, which occurs in chlorophyll, is essential to photosynthesis, and iodine is needed by the thyroid gland of mammals for making hormones that control growth and body chemistry.

**trachea** tube that forms an airway in air-breathing animals. In land-living vertebrates, including humans, it is also known as the windpipe and runs from the larynx to the upper part of the chest. Its diameter is about 1.5 cm/0.6 in and its length 10 cm/4 in. It is strong and flexible, and reinforced by rings of →cartilage. In the upper chest, the trachea branches into two tubes: the left and right bronchi, which enter the lungs. Insects have a branching network of tubes called tracheae, which conduct air from holes (spiracles) in the body surface to all the body tissues. The finest

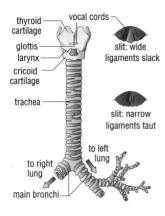

**trachea** The human trachea, or windpipe. The larynx, or voice box, lies at the entrance to the trachea. The two vocal cords are membranes that normally remain open and still. When they are drawn together, the passage of air makes them vibrate and produce sounds.

branches of the tracheae are called tracheoles.

**trade wind** prevailing wind that blows towards the Equator from the northeast and southeast. Trade winds are caused by hot air rising at the Equator and the consequent movement of air from north and south to take its place. The winds are deflected towards the west because of the Earth's west-to-east rotation.

The unpredictable calms known as the →doldrums lie at their convergence.

**Trafalgar, Battle of** during the Napoleonic Wars, victory of the British fleet, commanded by Admiral Horatio Nelson, over a combined French and Spanish fleet on 21 October 1805; Nelson was mortally wounded during the action. The victory laid the foundation for British naval supremacy throughout the 19th century. It is named after Cape Trafalgar, a low headland in southwest Spain, near the western entrance to the Straits of Gibraltar.

**tragedy** in the theatre, a play dealing with a serious theme, traditionally one in which a character meets disaster as a result either of personal failings or circumstances beyond his or her control. Historically the classical view of tragedy, as expressed by the Greek tragedians Aeschylus, Euripides, and Sophocles, and the Roman tragedian Seneca, has been predominant in the Western tradition. In the 20th century tragedies dealing with exalted or heroic figures in an elevated manner have virtually died out. Tragedy has been replaced by dramas with 'tragic' implications or overtones, as in the work of Ibsen, O'Neill, Tennessee Williams, and Osborne, for example, or by the problem plays of Pirandello, Brecht, and Beckett.

**tranquillizer** common name for any drug for reducing anxiety or tension (anxiolytic), such as benzodiazepines, barbiturates, antidepressants, and beta-blockers. The use of drugs to control anxiety is becoming much less popular, because most of the drugs available are capable of inducing dependence.

**transformer** device in which, by electromagnetic induction, an alternating current (AC) of one voltage is transformed to another voltage, without change of →frequency. Transformers are widely used in electrical apparatus of all kinds, and in particular in power transmission where high voltages and low currents are utilized.

**transistor** solid-state electronic component, made of semiconductor material, with three or more electrodes, that can regulate a current passing through it. A transistor can act as an amplifier, oscillator, photocell, or switch, and (unlike earlier thermionic valves) usually operates on a very small amount of power. Transistors commonly consist of a tiny sandwich of germanium or silicon, alternate layers having different electrical properties because they are impregnated with minute amounts of different impurities.

**transpiration** the loss of water from a plant by evaporation. Most water is lost from the leaves through pores known as stomata, whose primary function is to allow gas exchange between the plant's internal tissues and the atmosphere. Transpiration from the leaf surfaces causes a continuous upward flow of water from the roots via the →xylem, which is known as the transpiration stream.

**transplant** in medicine, the transfer of a tissue or organ from one human being to another or from one part of the body to another (skin grafting). In most organ transplants, the operation is for life-saving purposes, although the immune system tends to reject foreign tissue.

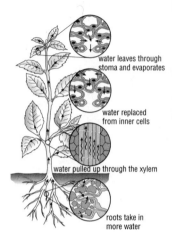

water leaves through stoma and evaporates

water replaced from inner cells

water pulled up through the xylem

roots take in more water

**transpiration** The loss of water from a plant by evaporation is known as transpiration. Most of the water is lost through the surface openings, or stomata, on the leaves. The evaporation produces what is known as the transpiration stream, a tension that draws water up from the roots through the xylem, water-carrying vessels in the stem.

Careful matching and immunosuppressive drugs must be used, but these are not always successful.

**Trans-Siberian Railway** the world's longest single-service railway, connecting the cities of European Russia with Omsk, Novosibirsk, Irkutsk, and Khabarovsk, terminating at Nakhodka on the Pacific coast east of Vladivostok. The line was built between 1891 and 1915, and has a total length of

9,289 km/5,772 mi, from Moscow to Vladivostok.

**transuranic element** (or transuranium element) chemical element with an atomic number of 93 or more – that is, with a greater number of protons in the nucleus than has uranium. All transuranic elements are radioactive. Neptunium and plutonium are found in nature; the others are synthesized in nuclear reactions.

**Transylvania** mountainous area of central and northwestern Romania, bounded to the south by the Transylvanian Alps (an extension of the Carpathian Mountains). Formerly a principality, with its capital at Cluj-Napoca, it was part of Hungary from about 1000 until its people voted to unite with Romania 1918. It is the home of the vampire legends. In a 1996 treaty Hungary renounced its claims on Transylvania.

**trapezium** (US trapezoid) in geometry, a

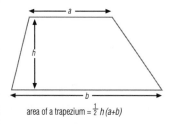

area of a trapezium $= \frac{1}{2} h(a+b)$

**trapezium** A trapezium is a four-sided plane figure with two of its sides parallel.

four-sided plane figure (quadrilateral) with two of its sides parallel. If the parallel sides have lengths $a$ and $b$ and the perpendicular distance between them is $h$ (the height of the trapezium), its area $A=\frac{1}{2}h(a + b)$.

**tree** perennial plant with a woody stem, usually a single stem (trunk), made up of wood and protected by an outer layer of bark. It absorbs water through a root system. There is no clear dividing line between shrubs and trees, but sometimes a minimum achievable height of 6 m/20 ft is used to define a tree.

**triangle** in geometry, a three-sided plane figure, the sum of whose interior angles is 180°. Triangles can be classified by the relative lengths of their sides. A scalene triangle has three sides of unequal length; an isosceles triangle has at least two equal sides; an equilateral triangle has three equal sides (and three equal angles of 60°).

**Triassic** period of geological time 245–208 million years ago, the first period of the Mesozoic era. The continents were fused together to form the world continent Pangaea. Triassic sediments contain remains of early dinosaurs and other reptiles now extinct. By late Triassic times, the first mammals had evolved.

There was a mass extinction of 95% of plants at the end of the Triassic caused by rising temperatures.

**trigonometry** branch of mathematics that solves problems relating to plane and spherical triangles. Its principles are based on the fixed proportions of

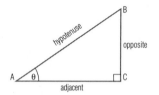

for any right-angled triangle with angle θ as shown the
trigonometrical ratios are

$$\sin(e) \; \theta = \frac{BC}{AB} = \frac{opposite}{hypotenuse}$$

$$\cos \theta = \frac{AC}{AB} = \frac{adjacent}{hypotenuse}$$

$$\tan \theta = \frac{BC}{AC} = \frac{opposite}{adjacent}$$

**trigonometry** At its simplest level, trigonometry
deals with the relationships between the sides and
angles of triangles. Unknown angles or lengths are
calculated by using trigonometrical ratios such as
sine, cosine, and tangent. The earliest applications
of trigonometry were in the fields of navigation,
surveying, and astronomy, and usually involved
working out an inaccessible distance such as the
distance of the Earth from the Moon.

sides for a particular angle in a right-
angled triangle, the simplest of which
are known as the →sine, →cosine,
and →tangent (so-called trigonometrical ratios). Trigonometry is of practical importance in navigation, surveying,
and simple harmonic motion in
physics.

**trilobite** any of a large class (Trilobita)
of extinct, marine, invertebrate arthropods of the Palaeozoic era, with a
flattened, oval body, 1–65 cm/0.4–26 in
long. The hard-shelled body was
divided by two deep furrows into three
lobes. Some were burrowers, others
were swimming and floating forms.
Their worldwide distribution, many
species, and the immense quantities of
their remains make them useful in geological dating.

**Trinidad and Tobago** Republic of; **area:**
5,130 sq km/1,980 sq mi including

smaller islands (Trinidad 4,828 sq
km/1,864 sq mi and Tobago 300 sq km/
115 sq mi); **capital:** Port-of-Spain (and
port); **major towns/cities:** San
Fernando, Arima, Point Fortin; **major
ports:** Scarborough, Point Lisas; **physical features:** comprises two main
islands and some smaller ones in
Caribbean Sea; coastal swamps and hills
east–west; **head of state:** A N R

Robinson from 1997; **head of government:** Basdeo Panday from 1995; **political system:** democracy; Movement for Social Transformation (Motion), left of centre; **currency:** Trinidad and Tobago dollar; **GNP per capita (PPP):** (US$) 6,720 (1998); **exports:** mineral fuels and lubricants, chemicals, basic manufactures, food. Principal market USA 39.7% (1997); **population:** 1,288,000 (1999 est); **language:** English (official); Hindi, French, Spanish; **religion:** Roman Catholic, Anglican, Hindu, Muslim; **life expectancy:** 72 (men); 76 (women) (1995–2000).

**Trinity** in Christianity, the union of three persons – Father, Son, and Holy Ghost/Spirit – in one godhead. The precise meaning of the doctrine has been the cause of unending dispute, and was the chief cause of the split between the Eastern Orthodox and Roman Catholic churches. Trinity Sunday occurs on the Sunday after Pentecost (Whitsun).

**Triple Alliance** pact from 1882 between Germany, Austria-Hungary, and Italy to offset the power of Russia and France. It was last renewed 1912, but during World War I Italy's initial neutrality gradually changed and it denounced the alliance in 1915. The term also refers to other alliances: 1668 – England, Holland, and Sweden; 1717 – Britain, Holland, and France (joined 1718 by Austria); 1788 – Britain, Prussia, and Holland; 1795 – Britain, Russia, and Austria.

**Triple Entente** alliance of Britain, France, and Russia 1907–17. In 1911 this became a military alliance and formed the basis of the Allied powers in World War I against the Central Powers, Germany and Austria-Hungary.

**Trojan horse** seemingly innocuous but treacherous gift from an enemy. In Greek mythology, during the siege of Troy, an enormous wooden horse was left by the Greek army outside the gates of the city. When the Greeks had retreated, the Trojans, believing it to be a religious offering, brought the horse in. Greek soldiers then emerged from within the hollow horse and opened the city gates to enable Troy to be captured.

**trombone** brass wind instrument of mainly cylindrical bore, incorporating a movable slide which allows a continuous glissando (slide) in pitch over a span of half an octave. The longer the tube length, the lower the note. All the notes of the chromatic scale are therefore available by placing the slide in any of seven basic positions, and blowing a harmonic series of notes built upon each basic note. A descendant of the Renaissance sackbut, the baroque trombone has a shallow cup mouthpiece and modestly flared bell giving a firm, noble tone, to which the modern wide bell adds a brassy sheen. The tenor and bass trombones are staple instruments of the orchestra and brass band, also of Dixieland and jazz bands, either separately or as a tenor-bass hybrid. The hybrid has a switch which lowers the pitch a fourth from B♭ to F.

**tropics** the area between the tropics of Cancer and Capricorn, defined by the parallels of latitude approximately 23°30′ north and south of the Equator. They are the limits of the area of Earth's surface in which the Sun can be directly overhead. The mean monthly temperature is over 20°C/68°F.

**tropism** (or tropic movement) the directional growth of a plant, or part of a plant, in response to an external stimulus such as gravity or light. If the movement is directed towards the stimulus it is described as positive; if away from it, it is negative. Geotropism for example, the response of plants to gravity, causes the root (positively geotropic) to grow downwards, and the stem (negatively geotropic) to grow upwards.

**Trotsky, Leon** (1879–1940) adopted name of Lev Davidovitch Bronstein, Russian revolutionary. He joined the Bolshevik party and took a leading part in the seizure of power in 1917 and in raising the Red Army that fought the Civil War 1918–20. In the struggle for power that followed →Lenin's death in 1924, Stalin defeated Trotsky, and this and other differences with the Communist Party led to his exile in 1929. He settled in Mexico, where he was assassinated at Stalin's instigation. Trotsky believed in world revolution and in permanent revolution, and was an uncompromising, if liberal, idealist.

**Troy** (also known as Ilium) ancient city in Asia Minor (modern Hissarlik in Turkey), just south of the Dardanelles. It has a long and complex history dating from about 3000 BC to AD 1200. In 1820 the city was identified as Troy, the site of the legendary ten-year Trojan War described in Homer's epic *Iliad*, but its actual name is unknown.

**trumpet** member of an ancient family of lip-reed instruments existing worldwide in a variety of forms and materials, and forming part of the brass section in a modern orchestra. Its distinguishing features are a generally cylindrical bore and straight or coiled shape, producing a penetrating tone of stable pitch for signalling and ceremonial use. Valve trumpets were introduced around 1820, giving access to the full range of chromatic pitches.

**tsetse fly** any of a number of blood-feeding African flies of the genus *Glossina*, some of which transmit the disease nagana to cattle and sleeping sickness to human beings. Tsetse flies may grow up to 1.5 cm/0.6 in long.

**tsunami** (Japanese 'harbour wave') ocean wave generated by vertical movements of the sea floor resulting from earthquakes or volcanic activity. Unlike waves generated by surface winds, the entire depth of water is involved in the wave motion. In the open ocean the tsunami takes the form of several successive waves, rarely in excess of 1 m/ 3 ft in height but travelling at speeds of 650–800 kph/400–500 mph. In the coastal shallows tsunamis slow down and build up producing huge swells over 15 m/45 ft high in some cases and over 30 m/90 ft in rare instances. The waves sweep inland causing great loss of life and property. On 26 May 1983, an earthquake in the Pacific Ocean caused tsunamis up to 14 m/42 ft high, which killed 104 people along the west coast of Japan near Minehama, Honshu.

**tuber** swollen region of an underground stem or root, usually modified for storing food. The potato is a stem tuber, as shown by the presence of terminal and lateral buds, the 'eyes' of the potato. Root tubers, for example dahlias, developed from adventitious roots (growing from the stem, not from other roots), lack these. Both types of tuber can give rise to new individuals and so provide a means of vegetative reproduction.

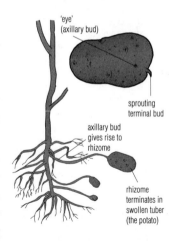

'eye' (axillary bud)

sprouting terminal bud

axillary bud gives rise to rhizome

rhizome terminates in swollen tuber (the potato)

**tuber** Tubers are produced underground from stems, as in the potato, or from roots, as in the dahlia. Tubers can grow into new plants.

**tuberculosis** (TB, formerly known as consumption or phthisis) infectious disease caused by the bacillus *Mycobacterium tuberculosis*. It takes several forms, of which pulmonary tuberculosis is by far the most common. A vaccine, BCG, was developed around 1920 and the first antituberculosis drug, streptomycin, in 1944. The bacterium is mostly kept in check by the body's immune system; about 5% of those infected develop the disease. Treatment of patients with a combination of anti-TB medicines for 6–8 months produces a cure rate of 80%. In 1999 there were 8 million new cases of TB and 2 million deaths. Only 5% of cases are in developed countries. Worldwide there are 16 million people with TB and 2 billion (a third of the global population) are infected with *Mycobacterium tuberculosis*.

**Tudor dynasty** English dynasty 1485–1603, founded by Henry VII, who became king by overthrowing Richard III (the last of the York dynasty) at the Battle of Bosworth. Henry VII reigned from 1485 to 1509, and was succeeded by Henry VIII (reigned 1509–47); Edward VI (reigned 1547–53); Mary (reigned 1553–58); and Elizabeth I (reigned 1558–1603). Elizabeth died childless and the throne of England passed to her cousin James VI of Scotland, who thus became James I of England and the first of the Stuart line.

**tundra** region of high latitude almost devoid of trees, resulting from the presence of permafrost. The vegetation consists mostly of grasses, sedges, heather, mosses, and lichens. Tundra stretches in a continuous belt across northern North America and Eurasia. Tundra is also used to describe similar conditions at high altitudes.

**tungsten** (Swedish *tung sten* 'heavy stone') hard, heavy, grey-white, metallic element, symbol W (from German *Wolfram*), atomic number 74, relative atomic mass 183.85. It occurs in the minerals wolframite, scheelite, and hubertite. It has the highest melting point of any metal (3,410°C/6,170°F) and is added to steel to make it harder, stronger, and more elastic; its other uses include high-speed cutting tools, electrical elements, and thermionic couplings. Its salts are used in the paint and tanning industries.

**Tunis** capital and chief port of Tunisia; population (1994) 674,100. Industries include chemicals, textiles, engineering, lead smelting, and distilling. Velvets, silks, linen, and fez caps are also manufactured. Exports include phosphates, iron ore, fruit, and vegetables. Founded by the Arabs, it was captured by the Turks in 1533, then occupied by the French in 1881 and by the Axis powers 1942–43. The ruins of ancient →Carthage are to the northeast.

**Tunisia** Tunisian Republic; **national name:** *al-Jumhuriya at-Tunisiya*; **area:** 164,150 sq km/63,378 sq mi; **capital:** Tunis (and chief port); **major towns/cities:** Sfax, Ariana, Bizerte, Djerba, Gabès, Sousse, Kairouan, Bardo, La Goulette; **major ports:** Sfax, Sousse, Bizerte; **physical features:** arable and forested land in north graduates towards desert in south; fertile island of Jerba, linked to mainland by causeway (identified with island of lotus-eaters); Shott el Jerid salt lakes; **head of state:** Zine el-Abidine Ben Ali from 1987; **head of government:** Hamed Karoui from 1989; **political system:** emergent democracy; **currency:** Tunisian dinar; **GNP per capita (PPP):** (US\$) 5,160 (1998); **exports:** textiles and clothing, crude petroleum, phosphates and fertilizers, olive oil, fruit, leather and shoes, fishery products, machinery and electrical appliances. Principal market France 27% (1998); **population:** 9,460,000 (1999 est); **language:** Arabic (official); French; **religion:** Sunni Muslim; Jewish, Christian; **life expectancy:** 68 (men); 71 (women) (1995–2000).

**turbine** engine in which steam, water, gas, or air is made to spin a rotating shaft by pushing on angled blades, like a fan. Turbines are among the most powerful machines. Steam turbines are used to drive the generators in power stations and ships' propellers; water turbines spin the generators in hydroelectric power plants; and gas turbines (as jet engines) power most aircraft and drive machines in industry.

**Turin shroud** ancient piece of linen bearing the image of a body, claimed to be that of Jesus. Independent tests carried out 1988 by scientists in Switzerland, the USA, and the UK showed that the cloth of the shroud dated from between 1260 and 1390. The shroud, property of the pope, is kept in Turin Cathedral, Italy. A more detailed 20-year study published in 1997 revealed that the shroud was made, around 1325, by daubing a man in red ochre paint and then wrapping him tightly in the linen sheet. Vermillion paint was then splashed on the head and wrists to suggest blood stains. Why it was made, and by whom, remains a mystery.

**Turkey** Republic of; **national name:** *Türkiye Cumhuriyeti*; **area:** 779,500 sq km/300,964 sq mi; **capital:** Ankara; **major towns/cities:** Istanbul, Izmir, Adana, Bursa, Antakya, Gaziantep, Konya, Mersin, Kayseri, Edirne, Antalya; **major ports:** Istanbul and Izmir; **physical features:** central plateau surrounded by mountains, partly in Europe (Thrace) and partly in Asia (Anatolia); Bosporus and Dardanelles; Mount Ararat (highest peak Great Ararat, 5,137 m/16,854 ft); Taurus Mountains in southwest (highest peak Kaldi Dag, 3,734 m/12,255 ft); sources of rivers Euphrates and Tigris in east; **head of state:** Suleiman Demirel from 1993; **head of government:** Bülent Ecevit from 1999; **political system:** democracy; **currency:** Turkish lira; **GNP per capita (PPP):** (US$) 5,830 (1998 est); **exports:** textiles and clothing, agricultural products and foodstuffs (including figs, nuts, and dried fruit), tobacco, leather, glass, refined petroleum and petroleum products. Principal market Germany 20.3% (1998); **population:** 65,546,000 (1999 est); **language:** Turkish (official); Kurdish, Arabic; **religion:** Sunni Muslim;

Orthodox, Armenian churches; **life expectancy:** 67 (men); 72 (women) (1995–2000).

**Turkmenistan** Republic of; **area:** 488,100 sq km/188,455 sq mi; **capital:** Ashgabat; **major towns/cities:** Chardzhov, Mary (Merv), Nebit-Dag, Krasnovodsk; **major ports:** Turkmenbashi; **physical:** about 90% of land is desert including the Kara Kum 'Black Sands' desert (area 310,800 sq km/120,000 sq mi); **head of state and government:** Saparmurad Niyazov from 1990; **political system:** authoritarian nationalist; **currency:** manat; **GNP per capita (PPP):** (US$) 1,480 (1998 est); **exports:** natural gas, cotton yarn, electric energy, petroleum and petroleum products. Principal market Ukraine 43.6% (1997); **population:** 4,384,000 (1999 est); **language:** West Turkic, closely related to Turkish; **religion:** Sunni Muslim; **life expectancy:** 62 (men); 69 (women) (1995–2000).

**Turner, Joseph Mallord William** (1775–1851) English painter. He was one of the most original artists of his day. He travelled widely in Europe, and his landscapes became increasingly Romantic, with the subject often transformed in scale and flooded with brilliant, hazy light. Many later works anticipate Impressionism, for example *Rain, Steam and Speed* (1844; National Gallery, London).

**Turpin, Dick (Richard)** (1705–1739) English highwayman. The son of an innkeeper, he turned to highway robbery, cattle-thieving, and smuggling, and was hanged at York, England.

**Tuscany** (Italian *Toscana*; Roman *Etruria*) region of north central Italy, on the west coast, comprising the provinces of Massa e Carrara, Arezzo, Florence, Grosseto, Livorno, Lucca, Pisa, Pistoia, and Siena; area 23,000 sq km/8,878 sq mi; population (1992 est) 3,528,700. Its capital is Florence, and cities include Pisa, Livorno, and Siena. The area is mainly agricultural, producing cereals, wine (Chianti hills), olives (Lucca) and tobacco (plain of Arno); it also has mining of lignite (upper Arno) and iron (Elba) and marble quarries (Carrara, Apuan Alps). The Tuscan dialect has been adopted as the standard form of Italian.

**Tutankhamen** king (pharaoh) of ancient Egypt of the 18th dynasty, 1333–1323 BC. A son of Akhenaton (also called Amenhotep IV), he was about 11 at his accession. In 1922 his tomb was discovered by the British archaeologists Lord Carnarvon and Howard Carter in the Valley of the Kings at Luxor, almost untouched by tomb robbers. The contents included many works of art and his solid-gold coffin, which are now displayed in a Cairo museum.

**Tutu, Desmond Mpilo** (1931– ) South African priest, Anglican archbishop of Cape Town 1986–96 and general secretary of the South African Council of Churches 1979–84. One of the leading figures in the struggle against →apartheid in the Republic of South Africa, he was awarded the 1984 Nobel Peace Prize for encouraging peaceful reconciliation between the black and white communities.

**Tuvalu** South West Pacific State of (formerly **Ellice Islands**); **area:** 25 sq km/9.6 sq mi; **capital:** Fongafale (on Funafuti atoll); **major towns/cities:** Vaitupu, Niutao, Nanumea; **physical features:** nine low coral atolls forming a chain of 579 km/650 mi in the Southwest Pacific; **head of state:** Queen Elizabeth II from 1978, represented by governor general Tulaga Manuella from 1994; **head of government:** Ionatana Ionatana from 1999; **political system:** liberal democracy; **currency:** Australian dollar; **GNP per capita (PPP):** (US$) 1,435 (1996); **exports:** copra. Principal market Australia; **population:** 11,000 (1999 est); **language:** Tuvaluan, English; **religion:** Christian (mainly Protestant); **life expectancy:** 63 (men), 66 (women) (1998 est).

**Twain, Mark** (1835–1910) pen-name of Samuel Langhorne Clemens, US

---

### WEB SITE > > > > > > >

**Mark Twain in His Times**

http://etext.virginia.edu/railton/index2.html

In-depth look at the life and work of Mark Twain. This site contains many photographs and illustrations from his most popular works, not to mention detailed copies of original editions. All this is placed in the context of the period, with illuminating information on stage adaptations and the unusual marketing techniques he used to sell his books.

---

writer. He established his reputation with the comic masterpiece *The Innocents Abroad* (1869) and two classic American novels, in dialect, *The Adventures of Tom Sawyer* (1876) and *The Adventures of Huckleberry Finn* (1885). He also wrote satire, as in *A Connecticut Yankee at King Arthur's Court* (1889). He is recognized as one of America's finest and most characteristic writers.

**twin** one of two young produced from a single pregnancy. Human twins may be genetically identical (monozygotic), having been formed from a single fertilized egg that splits into two cells, both of which became implanted. Non-identical (fraternal or dizygotic) twins are formed when two eggs are fertilized at the same time.

**two-stroke cycle** operating cycle for internal combustion piston engines. The engine cycle is completed after just two strokes (up or down) of the piston, which distinguishes it from the more common →four-stroke cycle. Power mowers and lightweight motorcycles use two-stroke petrol engines, which are cheaper and simpler than four-strokes.

**Tyler, Wat** (died 1381) English leader of the →Peasants' Revolt of 1381. He was probably born in Kent or Essex, and may have served in the French wars. After taking Canterbury, he led the peasant army to Blackheath, outside London, and went on to invade the city. King Richard II met the rebels at Mile End and promised to redress their grievances, which included the imposition of a poll tax. At a further conference at Smithfield, London, Tyler was murdered.

**typhoid fever** acute infectious disease of the digestive tract, caused by the bacterium *Salmonella typhi*, and usually contracted through a contaminated water supply. It is characterized by bowel haemorrhage and damage to the spleen. Treatment is with antibiotics.

**typhoon** violent revolving storm, a →hurricane in the western Pacific Ocean.

**typhus** any one of a group of infectious diseases caused by bacteria transmitted by lice, fleas, mites, and ticks. Symptoms include fever, headache, and rash. The most serious form is epidemic typhus, which also affects the brain, heart, lungs, and kidneys and is associated with insanitary overcrowded conditions. Treatment is by antibiotics.

# Uu

**Uganda** Republic of; **area:** 236,600 sq km/91,351 sq mi; **capital:** Kampala; **major towns/cities:** Jinja, Mbale, Entebbe, Masaka, Bugembe; **physical features:** plateau with mountains in west (Ruwenzori Range, with Mount Margherita, 5,110 m/16,765 ft); forest and grassland; 18% is lakes, rivers, and wetlands (Owen Falls on White Nile where it leaves Lake Victoria; Lake Albert in west); arid in northwest; **head of state:** Yoweri Museveni from 1986; **head of government:** Apolo Nsibambi from 1999; **political system:** emergent democracy; **currency:** Uganda new shilling; **GNP per capita (PPP):** (US$) 1,170 (1998 est); **exports:** coffee, cotton, tea, tobacco, oil seeds and oleaginous fruit; hides and skins, textiles. Principal market Spain 14.4% (1997); **population:** 21,143,000 (1999 est); **language:** English (official), Kiswahili, Bantu and Nilotic languages; **religion:** Christian 50%, animist 40%, Muslim 10%; **life expectancy:** 39 (men); 40 (women) (1995–2000).

**Ukraine area:** 603,700 sq km/233,088 sq mi; **capital:** Kiev; **major towns/cities:** Kharkov, Donetsk, Dnepropetrovsk, Lugansk (Voroshilovgrad), Lviv (Lvov), Mariupol (Zhdanov), Krivoy Rog, Zaporozhye, Odessa; **physical features:** Russian plain; Carpathian and Crimean Mountains; rivers Dnieper (with the Dnieper dam 1932), Donetz, Bug; **head of state:** Leonid Kuchma from 1994; **head of government:** Valery Pustovoitenko from 1997; **political system:** emergent democracy; **currency:** hryvna; **GNP per capita (PPP):** (US$) 2,420 (1998 est); **exports:** grain, coal, oil, various minerals. Principal market Russia 23% (1998); **population:** 50,658,000 (1999 est); **language:** Ukrainian (a Slavonic language); **religion:** traditionally Ukrainian Orthodox; also Ukrainian Catholic; **life expectancy:** 64 (men); 74 (women) (1995–2000).

**ulcer** any persistent breach in a body surface (skin or mucous membrane). It may be caused by infection, irritation, or tumour and is often inflamed. Common ulcers include aphthous (mouth), gastric (stomach), duodenal, decubitus ulcers (pressure sores), and those complicating varicose veins.

**Ulster** a former kingdom and province in the north of Ireland, annexed by England in 1461. From Jacobean times it was a centre of English, and later Scottish, settlement on land confiscated from its owners; divided in 1921 into Northern Ireland (counties Antrim, Armagh, Down, Fermanagh, Londonderry, and Tyrone) and the

Republic of Ireland (counties Cavan, Donegal, and Monaghan).

**ultrasonics** branch of physics dealing with the theory and application of ultrasound: sound waves occurring at frequencies too high to be heard by the human ear (that is, above about 20 kHz).

**ultraviolet radiation** electromagnetic radiation invisible to the human eye, of wavelengths from about 400 to 4 nm (where the →X-ray range begins). Physiologically, ultraviolet radiation is extremely powerful, producing sunburn and causing the formation of vitamin D in the skin.

**Ulysses** Roman name for →Odysseus, the Greek mythological hero.

**uncertainty principle** (or indeterminacy principle) in quantum mechanics, the principle that it is impossible to know with unlimited accuracy the position and momentum of a particle. The principle arises because in order to locate a particle exactly, an observer must bounce light (in the form of a photon) off the particle, which must alter its position in an unpredictable way.

**Underground Railroad** in US history, a network established in the North before the →American Civil War to provide sanctuary and assistance for escaped black slaves. Safe houses, transport facilities, and 'conductors' existed to lead the slaves to safety in the North and Canada, although the number of fugitives who secured their freedom by these means may have been exaggerated.

**UNESCO** (acronym for United Nations Educational, Scientific, and Cultural Organization) specialized agency of the United Nations, established in 1946, to promote international cooperation in education, science, and culture, with its headquarters in Paris.

**ungulate** general name for any hoofed mammal. Included are the odd-toed ungulates (perissodactyls) and the even-toed ungulates (artiodactyls), along with subungulates such as elephants.

**unicellular organism** animal or plant consisting of a single cell. Most are invisible without a microscope but a few, such as the giant →amoeba, may be visible to the naked eye. The main groups of unicellular organisms are bacteria, protozoa, unicellular algae, and unicellular fungi or yeasts. Some become disease-causing agents and may then be called pathogens.

**unified field theory** in physics, the theory that attempts to explain the four fundamental forces (strong nuclear, weak nuclear, electromagnetic, and gravity) in terms of a single unified force (see →particle physics).

**Union, Acts of** act of Parliament of 1707 that brought about the union of England and Scotland; that of 1801 united England and Ireland.

**United Arab Emirates** (UAE) federatión of the emirates of Abu Dhabi, Ajman, Dubai, Fujairah, Ras al Khaimah, Sharjah, Umm al Qaiwain; **national name:** *Ittihad al-Imarat al-Arabiyah*; **area:** 83,657 sq km/32,299 sq mi; **capital:** Abu Dhabi; **major towns/cities:** Dubai, Sharjah, Ras al-Khaimah, Ajman, Fujairah; **major ports:** Dubai; **physical features:** desert and flat coastal plain; mountains in east; **head of state:** Sheikh Zayed bin Sultan al-Nahayan of Abu Dhabi from 1971; **head of government:** Maktum bin Rashid al-Maktum of Dubai from 1990; **political system:** absolutism; **currency:** UAE dirham; **GNP per capita (PPP):** (US$) 19,720 (1998); **exports:** crude petroleum, natural gas, re-exports (mainly machinery and transport equipment). Principal market Japan 36.3% (1997); **population:** 2,397,000 (1999 est); **language:** Arabic (official), Farsi, Hindi, Urdu, English; **religion:** Muslim 96%; Christian, Hindu; **life expectancy:** 74 (men); 77 (women) (1995–2000).

**United Kingdom** of Great Britain and Northern Ireland (UK); **area:** 244,100 sq km/94,247 sq mi; **capital:** London; **major towns/cities:** Birmingham, Glasgow, Leeds, Sheffield, Liverpool, Manchester, Edinburgh, Bradford, Bristol, Coventry, Belfast, Newcastle upon Tyne, Cardiff; **major ports:** London, Grimsby, Southampton, Liverpool; **physical features:** became separated from European continent in about 6000 BC; rolling landscape, increasingly mountainous towards the north, with Grampian Mountains in Scotland, Pennines in northern England, Cambrian Mountains in Wales; rivers include Thames, Severn, and Spey; **territories:** Anguilla, Bermuda, British Antarctic Territory, British Indian Ocean Territory, British Virgin Islands, Cayman Islands, Falkland Islands, Gibraltar, Montserrat, Pitcairn Islands, St Helena and Dependencies (Ascension, Tristan da Cunha), Turks and Caicos Islands; the Channel Islands and the Isle of Man are not part of the UK but are direct dependencies of the crown; **head of state:** Queen Elizabeth II from 1952; **head of government:** Tony Blair from 1997; **political system:** liberal democracy; **currency:** pound sterling (£); **GNP per capita (PPP):** (US$) 20,640 (1998); **exports:** industrial and electrical machinery, chemicals, automatic data-processing equipment, motor vehicles, petroleum, finished and semi-finished manufactured products, agricultural products and foodstuffs. Principal market USA 13.3% (1998); **population:** 58,744,000 (1999 est) **language:** English, Welsh, Gaelic; **religion:** Church of England (established Church); other Protestant denominations, Roman Catholic, Muslim, Jewish, Hindu, Sikh; **life expectancy:** 75 (men); 80 (women) (1995–2000).

**United Nations** (UN) association of states for international peace, security, and cooperation, with its headquarters in New York. The UN was established in 1945 by 51 states as a successor to the →League of Nations, and has played a role in many areas, such as refugees, development assistance, disaster relief, cultural cooperation, and peacekeeping. Its membership in 1996 stood at 185 states, and the total proposed budget for 1995–96 (raised by the member states) was $2,600 million supporting more than 50,000 staff. Kofi Annan became secretary-general in 1997 and in January 1998 Louise Frechette was elected its first deputy secretary-general. There are six official working languages: English, French, Russian, Spanish, Chinese, and Arabic. The name 'United Nations' was coined by the US president Franklin D Roosevelt.

The principal institutions are the General Assembly, the Security Council, the Economic and Social Council, the Trusteeship Council, all based in New York; and the International Court of Justice in The Hague, Netherlands. At a July 1998 UN conference in Rome, attended by 160 countries, a treaty was agreed to set up a permanent international criminal court to try individuals accused of war crimes, genocide, and crimes against humanity.

The UN operates many specialized agencies, involved either in promoting communication between states (such as the International Telecommunication Union, ITU), or concerned with welfare of states, such as the World Health Organization (WHO), the UN Educational, Scientific and Cultural Organization (UNESCO), and the International Bank for Reconstruction and Development (World Bank). Much of the work of the specialized welfare agencies concerns the developing countries, and consists mainly of research and field work. However, they also provide international standards relevant to all countries in their respective fields.

Though autonomous, the specialized agencies are related to the UN by special arrangements and work with the UN and each other through the coordinating machinery of the Economic and Social Council.

**United States of America** area: 9,372,615 sq km/3,618,766 sq mi; **capital:** Washington DC; **major towns/ cities:** New York, Los Angeles, Chicago, Philadelphia, Detroit, San Francisco, Washington, Dallas, San Diego, San Antonio, Houston, Boston, Baltimore, Phoenix, Indianapolis, Memphis, Honolulu, San José; **physical features:** topography and vegetation from tropical (Hawaii) to arctic (Alaska); mountain ranges parallel with east and west coasts; the Rocky Mountains separate rivers emptying into the Pacific from those flowing into the Gulf of Mexico; Great Lakes in north; rivers include Hudson, Mississippi, Missouri, Colorado, Columbia, Snake, Rio Grande, Ohio; **territories:** the commonwealths of Puerto Rico and Northern Marianas; Guam, the US Virgin Islands, American Samoa, Wake Island, Midway Islands, and Johnston and Sand Islands; **head of state and government:** Bill Clinton from 1993; **Political system:** liberal democracy; **currency:** US dollar; **GNP per capita (PPP):** (US$) 29,340 (1998); **exports:** machinery, motor vehicles, agricultural products and foodstuffs, aircraft, weapons, chemicals, electronics. Principal market Canada 23.3% (1998); **population:** 276,219,000 (1999 est); **language:** English, Spanish; **religion:** Christian 86.5% (Roman Catholic 26%, Baptist 19%, Methodist 8%, Lutheran 5%); Jewish 1.8%; Muslim 0.5%;

**UNITED STATES OF AMERICA: STATES**

| State | Nickname(s) | Abbreviation | Capital | Area sq km | Area sq mi | Population (1998) | Joined the Union |
|---|---|---|---|---|---|---|---|
| Alabama | Heart of Dixie/Camellia State | AL | Montgomery | 134,700 | 51,994 | 4,352,000 | 1819 |
| Alaska | Mainland State/The Last Frontier | AK | Juneau | 1,531,100 | 591,005 | 614,000 | 1959 |
| Arizona | Grand Canyon State/Apache State | AZ | Phoenix | 294,100 | 113,523 | 4,669,000 | 1912 |
| Arkansas | Bear State/Land of Opportunity | AR | Little Rock | 137,800 | 53,191 | 2,538,000 | 1836 |
| California | Golden State | CA | Sacramento | 411,100 | 158,685 | 32,667,000 | 1850 |
| Colorado | Centennial State | CO | Denver | 269,700 | 104,104 | 3,971,000 | 1876 |
| Connecticut | Constitution State/Nutmeg State | CT | Hartford | 13,000 | 5018 | 3,274,000 | 1788 |
| Delaware | First State/Diamond State | DE | Dover | 5,300 | 2,046 | 744,000 | 1787 |
| Florida | Sunshine State/Everglade State | FL | Tallahassee | 152,000 | 58,672 | 14,916,000 | 1845 |
| Georgia | Empire State of the South/ Peach State | GA | Atlanta | 152,600 | 58,904 | 7,642,000 | 1788 |
| Hawaii | Aloha State | HI | Honolulu | 16,800 | 6,485 | 1,193,000 | 1959 |
| Idaho | Gem State | ID | Boise | 216,500 | 83,569 | 1,229,000 | 1890 |
| Illinois | Inland Empire/Prairie State/ Land of Lincoln | IL | Springfield | 146,100 | 56,395 | 12,045,000 | 1818 |
| Indiana | Hoosier State | IN | Indianapolis | 93,700 | 36,168 | 5,899,000 | 1816 |
| Iowa | Hawkeye State/Corn State | IA | Des Moines | 145,800 | 56,279 | 2,862,000 | 1846 |
| Kansas | Sunflower State/Jayhawker State | KS | Topeka | 213,200 | 82,295 | 2,629,000 | 1861 |
| Kentucky | Bluegrass State | KY | Frankfort | 104,700 | 40,414 | 3,936,000 | 1792 |

(continued)

## UNITED STATES OF AMERICA: STATES (CONTINUED)

| State | Nickname(s) | Abbreviation | Capital | Area sq km | Area sq mi | Population (1998) | Joined the Union |
|---|---|---|---|---|---|---|---|
| Louisiana | Pelican State/Sugar State/Creole State | LA | Baton Rouge | 135,900 | 52,457 | 4,369,000 | 1792 |
| Maine | Pine Tree State | ME | Augusta | 86,200 | 33,273 | 1,244,000 | 1812 |
| Maryland | Old Line State/Free State | MD | Annapolis | 31,600 | 12,198 | 5,135,000 | 1788 |
| Massachusetts | Bay State/Old Colony | MA | Boston | 21,500 | 8,299 | 6,147,000 | 1788 |
| Michigan | Great Lakes State/Wolverine State | MI | Lansing | 151,600 | 58,518 | 9,817,000 | 1837 |
| Minnesota | North Star State/Gopher State | MN | St Paul | 218,700 | 84,418 | 4,725,000 | 1858 |
| Mississippi | Magnolia State | MS | Jackson | 123,600 | 47,710 | 2,752,000 | 1817 |
| Missouri | Show Me State/Bullion State | MO | Jefferson City | 180,600 | 69,712 | 5,439,000 | 1821 |
| Montana | Treasure State/Big Sky Country | MT | Helena | 381,200 | 147,143 | 880,000 | 1889 |
| Nebraska | Cornhusker State/Beef State | NE | Lincoln | 200,400 | 77,354 | 1,663,000 | 1867 |
| Nevada | Sagebrush State/Silver State/ Battleborn State | NV | Carson City | 286,400 | 110,550 | 1,747,000 | 1864 |
| New Hampshire | Granite State | NH | Concord | 24,000 | 9,264 | 1,185,000 | 1788 |
| New Jersey | Garden State | NJ | Trenton | 20,200 | 7,797 | 8,115,000 | 1787 |
| New Mexico | Land of Enchantment/Sunshine State | NM | Santa Fé | 315,000 | 121,590 | 1,737,000 | 1912 |
| New York | Empire State | NY | Albany | 127,200 | 49,099 | 18,175,000 | 1788 |
| North Carolina | Tar Heel State/Old North State | NC | Raleigh | 136,400 | 52,650 | 7,546,000 | 1789 |
| North Dakota | Peace Garden State | ND | Bismarck | 183,100 | 70,677 | 638,000 | 1889 |
| Ohio | Buckeye State | OH | Columbus | 107,100 | 41,341 | 11,209,000 | 1803 |

(continued)

## UNITED STATES OF AMERICA: STATES (CONTINUED)

| State | Nickname(s) | Abbreviation | Capital | Area sq km | Area sq mi | Population (1998) | Joined the Union |
|---|---|---|---|---|---|---|---|
| Oklahoma | Sooner State | OK | Oklahoma City | 181,100 | 69,905 | 3,347,000 | 1907 |
| Oregon | Beaver State/Sunset State | OR | Salem | 251,500 | 97,079 | 3,282,000 | 1859 |
| Pennsylvania | Keystone State | PA | Harrisburg | 117,400 | 45,316 | 12,001,000 | 1787 |
| Rhode Island | Little Rhody/Ocean State | RI | Providence | 3,100 | 1,197 | 988,000 | 1790 |
| South Carolina | Palmetto State | SC | Columbia | 80,600 | 31,112 | 3,836,000 | 1788 |
| South Dakota | Coyote State/Mount Rushmore State | SD | Pierre | 199,800 | 77,123 | 738,000 | 1889 |
| Tennessee | Volunteer State | TN | Nashville | 109,200 | 42,151 | 5,431,000 | 1796 |
| Texas | Lone Star State | TX | Austin | 691,200 | 266,803 | 19,760,000 | 1845 |
| Utah | Beehive State/Mormon State | UT | Salt Lake City | 219,900 | 84,881 | 2,100,000 | 1896 |
| Vermont | Green Mountain State | VT | Montpelier | 24,900 | 9,611 | 591,000 | 1791 |
| Virginia | Old Dominion State/Mother of Presidents | VA | Richmond | 105,600 | 40,762 | 6,791,000 | 1788 |
| Washington | Evergreen State/Chinook State | WA | Olympia | 176,700 | 68,206 | 5,689,000 | 1889 |
| West Virginia | Mountain State/Panhandle State | WV | Charleston | 62,900 | 24,279 | 1,811,000 | 1863 |
| Wisconsin | Badger State/America's Dairyland | WI | Madison | 145,500 | 56,163 | 5,224,000 | 1848 |
| Wyoming | Equality State | WY | Cheyenne | 253,400 | 97,812 | 481,000 | 1890 |
| District of Columbia (Federal District) – established by Act of Congress 1790–91 | | DC | Washington | 180 | 69 | 523,000 | – |

Buddhist and Hindu less than 0.5%; **life expectancy:** 73 (men); 80 (women) (1995–2000).

**universe** all of space and its contents, the study of which is called →cosmology. The universe is thought to be between 10 billion and 20 billion years old, and is mostly empty space, dotted with →galaxies for as far as telescopes can see. The most distant detected galaxies and →quasars lie 10 billion light years or more from Earth, and are moving farther apart as the universe expands. Several theories attempt to explain how the universe came into being and evolved; for example, the →Big Bang theory of an expanding universe originating in a single explosive event, and the contradictory →steady-state theory.

**UNIX** multiuser operating system designed for minicomputers but becoming increasingly popular on microcomputers, workstations, mainframes, and supercomputers.

**unsaturated compound** chemical compound in which two adjacent atoms are linked by a double or triple covalent bond.

**Upanishad** one of a collection of Hindu sacred treatises, written in Sanskrit, connected with the Vedas but composed later, about 800–200 BC. Metaphysical and ethical, their doctrine equated the atman (self) with the Brahman (supreme spirit) – 'Tat tvam asi' ('Thou art that') – and developed the theory of the transmigration of souls.

**Ur** ancient city of the →Sumerian civilization, in modern Iraq. Excavations by the British archaeologist Leonard Woolley show that it was inhabited from about 3500 BC. He discovered evidence of a flood that may have inspired the *Epic of Gilgamesh* as well as the biblical account, and remains of ziggurats, or step pyramids.

**Ural Mountains** (Russian *Ural'skiy Khrebet*) mountain system extending for over 2,000 km/1,242 mi from the Arctic Ocean to the Caspian Sea, and traditionally regarded as separating Europe from Asia. The highest peak is Naradnaya, 1,894 m/6,214 ft. The mountains hold vast mineral wealth.

**Uranus** seventh planet from the Sun, discovered by German-born British astronomer William →Herschel in 1781. It is twice as far out as the sixth planet, Saturn. Uranus has a mass 14.5 times that of Earth. The spin axis of Uranus is tilted at 98°, so that one pole points towards the Sun, giving extreme seasons. **mean distance from the Sun:** 2.9 billion km/1.8 billion mi; **equatorial diameter:** 50,800 km/ 31,600 mi; **rotation period:** 17.2 hr; **year:** 84 Earth years; **atmosphere:** deep atmosphere composed mainly of hydrogen and helium; **surface:** composed primarily of rock and various ices with only about 15% hydrogen and helium, but may also contain heavier elements, which might account for Uranus' mean density being higher than Saturn's; **satellites:** 17 moons (two discovered in 1997); 11 thin rings around the planet's equator were discovered in 1977; **rings:**

11 rings, composed of rock and dust, around the planet's equator, were detected by the US space probe *Voyager 2*. The rings are charcoal black and may be debris of former 'moonlets' that have broken up. The ring furthest from the planet centre (51,000 km/31,800 mi), Epsilon, is 100 km/62 mi at its widest point. In 1995, US astronomers determined that the ring particles contained long-chain hydrocarbons. Looking at the brightest region of Epsilon, they were also able to calculate the precession of Uranus as 264 days, the fastest known precession in the Solar System.

**urea** $CO(NH_2)_2$ waste product formed in the mammalian liver when nitrogen compounds are broken down. It is filtered from the blood by the kidneys, and stored in the bladder as urine prior to release. When purified, it is a white, crystalline solid. In industry it is used to make urea-formaldehyde plastics (or resins), pharmaceuticals, and fertilizers.

**urinary system** system of organs that removes nitrogenous waste products and excess water from the bodies of animals. In vertebrates, it consists of a pair of kidneys, which produce urine; ureters, which drain the kidneys; and (in bony fishes, amphibians, some reptiles, and mammals) a bladder that stores the urine before its discharge. In mammals, the urine is expelled through the urethra; in other vertebrates, the urine drains into a common excretory chamber called a cloaca, and the urine is not discharged separately.

**Ursa Major** (Latin 'Great Bear')

third-largest constellation in the sky, in the north polar region. Its seven brightest stars make up the familiar shape or asterism of the Big Dipper or Plough. The second star of the handle of the dipper, called Mizar, has a companion star, Alcor.

Two stars forming the far side of the dipper bowl act as pointers to the north pole star, →Polaris. Dubhe, one of them, is the constellation's brightest star.

**Ursa Minor** (Latin 'Little Bear') small constellation of the northern hemisphere, popularly known as the Little Dipper. It is shaped like a dipper, with the bright north pole star →Polaris at the end of the handle.

**Uruguay** Oriental Republic of; **national name:** *República Oriental del Uruguay*; **area:** 176,200 sq km/68,030 sq mi; **capital:** Montevideo; **major towns/ cities:** Salto, Paysandú, Las Piedras; **physical features:** grassy plains (pampas) and low hills; rivers Negro, Uruguay, Río de la Plata; **head of state and government:** Jorge Batlle from 1999; **political system:** democracy; **currency:** Uruguayan peso; **GNP per capita (PPP):** (US$) 9,480 (1998); **exports:** textiles, meat (chiefly beef), live animals and by-products (mainly hides and leather products), cereals, footwear. Principal market Brazil 34.7% (1998); **population:** 3,313,000 (1999 est); **language:** Spanish (official); **religion:** mainly Roman Catholic; **life expectancy:** 71 (men); 78 (women) (1995–2000).

**Utah** state in western USA. It is nicknamed the Beehive State or the

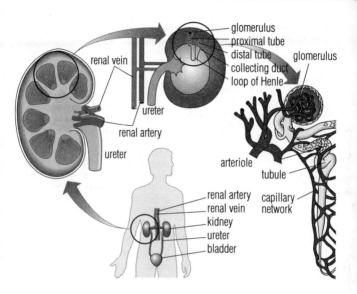

**urinary system** The human urinary system. At the bottom, the complete system in outline; on the left, the arrangement of blood vessels connected to the kidney; at the top right, a detail of the network of vessels within a kidney.

Mormon State. Utah was admitted to the Union in 1896 as the 45th US state. One of the Mountain States, it is bordered to the east by Colorado, to the north by Wyoming, to the west by Nevada, and to the south by Arizona. At the 'Four Corners', in the southeast, it also touches New Mexico; **population:** (1995) 1,951,400; **area:** 219,900 sq km/84,881 sq mi; **capital:** Salt Lake City; **towns and cities:** Provo, Ogden, West Valley City; **industries and products:** wool, gold, silver, copper, coal, oil, potash, salt, steel, aerospace and military-dependent industries, tourism.

**uterus** hollow muscular organ of female mammals, located between the bladder and rectum, and connected to the Fallopian tubes above and the vagina below. The embryo develops within the uterus, and in placental mammals is attached to it after implantation via the →placenta and umbilical cord. The lining of the uterus changes during the →menstrual cycle. In humans and other higher primates, it is a single structure, but in other mammals it is paired.

**Utrecht** province of the Netherlands, lying southeast of Amsterdam, and south of the IJsselmeer, on the Kromme Rijn (Crooked Rhine). **area:** 1,330 sq km/514 sq mi; **capital:** Utrecht; **towns and cities:** Amersfoort, Zeist, Nieuwegeun, Veenendaal; **physical:** sandy, barren soil in the east; more fertile in the west; **industries:** petrochemicals, textiles, electrical goods, engineering, steelworks, railway workshops, furniture; **agriculture:** livestock, dairy products, fruit, vegetables, cereals; **population:** (1997) 1,079,400; **history:** ruled by the bishops of Utrecht in the Middle Ages; sold to the emperor Charles V of Spain 1527; became a centre of Protestant resistance to Spanish rule; with the signing of the Treaty of Utrecht, became one of the seven United Provinces of the Netherlands in 1579.

**Uttar Pradesh** state of north India, bordered by Nepal and China to the northeast, and Indian states to the south and west. **area:** 294,400 sq km/113,638 sq mi; **capital:** Lucknow; **towns and cities:** Kanpur, Varanasi, Agra, Allahabad, Meerut, Haridwar; **physical:** Gangetic plain covers three-quarters of the state, which rises to the Himalayas in the northwest (Nanda Devi, 7,818 m/25,655 ft); the Ganges rises in the northwest, and flows southeast; the Yamuna and Ghaghara rivers also drain southeastwards; to the south are the Shiwalik hills; **features:** most populous state in India; Tehri Dam project; **industries:** sugar, oil refining, textiles, leather-work, cement, chemicals, coal, silica, handicrafts (Varanasi, Lucknow); **agriculture:** wheat, rice, millet, barley, sugar cane, groundnuts, peas, cotton, oilseed, potatoes, livestock, fruit; new strains of wheat have increased yields since the 1960s; **population:** (1994 est) 150,695,000; **famous people:** Indira Gandhi, Ravi Shankar; **language:** Hindi; **religion:** 80% Hinduism; religious sites in the state include Varanasi, Haridwar, Allahabad; 15% Muslim; **history:** formerly the heart of the Mogul Empire and generating point of the →Indian Mutiny in 1857 and subsequent opposition to British rule; see also →Agra. There are secessionist demands for a new hill state to be created out of the territory of Uttar Pradesh.

**Uzbekistan** Republic of; **national name:** *Ozbekistan Respublikasy*; **area:** 447,400 sq km/172,741 sq mi; **capital:** Tashkent; **major towns/cities:** Samarkand, Bukhara, Namangan, Andizhan; **physical features:** oases in deserts; rivers Amu Darya, Syr Darya; Ferghana Valley; rich in mineral deposits; **head of state:** Islam Karimov from 1990; **head of government:** Otkir Sultonov from 1995; **political system:** authoritarian nationalist; **currency:** som; **GNP per capita (PPP):** (US$) 2,900 (1998); **exports:** cotton fibre, textiles, machinery, food and energy products, gold. Principal market Russia 14.9% (1998); **population:** 23,941,000 (1999 est); **language:** Uzbek, a Turkic language; **religion:** Sunni Muslim; **life expectancy:** 64 (men); 71 (women) (1995–2000).

# Vv

**vaccine** any preparation of modified pathogens (viruses or bacteria) that is introduced into the body, usually either orally or by a hypodermic syringe, to induce the specific →antibody reaction that produces →immunity against a particular disease.

**vacuum** in general, a region completely empty of matter; in physics, any enclosure in which the gas pressure is considerably less than atmospheric pressure (101,325 pascals).

**vacuum flask** (or Dewar flask or Thermos flask) container for keeping things either hot or cold. It has two silvered glass walls with a vacuum between them, in a metal or plastic outer case. This design reduces the three forms of heat transfer: radiation (prevented by the silvering), conduction, and convection (both prevented by the vacuum). A vacuum flask is therefore equally efficient at keeping cold liquids cold or hot liquids hot. It was invented by the Scottish chemist James Dewar in about 1872, to store liquefied gases.

**vagina** the lower part of the reproductive tract in female mammals, linking the uterus to the exterior. It admits the penis during sexual intercourse, and is the birth canal down which the baby passes during delivery.

screw top

silvered on inside

contents

vacuum

outer container

**vacuum flask** The vacuum flask allows no heat to escape from or enter its contents. It has double walls with a vacuum between to prevent heat loss by conduction. Radiation is prevented by silvering the walls. The vacuum flask was invented by Scottish chemist James Dewar in about 1872.

**Valencia** city and capital of Valencia province in the Valencian Community, eastern Spain, on the estuary of the Guadalaviar River; population (1991) 752,900. It is the centre of a very rich agricultural plain noted for the high quality of its citrus fruits, particularly oranges; industries include textiles, chemicals, ship repair, and wine.

**valency** in chemistry, the measure of an element's ability to combine with other elements, expressed as the number of atoms of hydrogen (or any other standard univalent element) capable of uniting with (or replacing) its atoms. The number of electrons in the outermost shell of the atom dictates the combining ability of an element.

**Valkyrie** (Old Norse *valr* 'slain', *kjosa* 'choose') in Norse mythology, any of the female attendants of →Odin. They directed the course of battles and selected the most valiant warriors to die; half being escorted to Valhalla, and the remainder to Sessrumnir, the hall of Freya.

**Valley of the Kings** burial place of kings in ancient Egypt opposite Thebes, Egypt, on the left bank of the Nile. It was established as a royal cemetery during the reign of Thotmes I (*c.* 1500 BC) and abandoned during the reign of Ramses XI (*c.* 1100 BC).

**value-added tax** (VAT) tax on goods and services. VAT is imposed by the European Union (EU) on member states. The tax varies from state to state. An agreed proportion of the tax money is used to fund the EU.

**valve** in animals, a structure for controlling the direction of the blood flow. In humans and other vertebrates, the contractions of the beating heart cause the correct blood flow into the arteries because a series of valves prevents back flow. Diseased valves, detected as 'heart murmurs', have decreased efficiency. The tendency for low-pressure venous blood to collect at the base of limbs under the influence of gravity is counteracted by a series of small valves within the veins. It was the existence of these valves that prompted the 17th-century physician William Harvey to suggest that the blood circulated around the body.

**vampire bat** South and Central American bat of the family Desmodontidae, of which there are three species. The common vampire *Desmodus rotundus* is found from northern Mexico to central Argentina; its head and body grow to 9 cm/3.5 in. Vampire bats feed on the blood of birds and mammals; they slice a piece of skin from a sleeping animal with their sharp incisor teeth and lap up the flowing blood. They chiefly approach their prey by flying low then crawling and leaping.

**van der Waals' law** modified form of the gas laws that includes corrections for the non-ideal behaviour of real gases (the molecules of ideal gases occupy no space and exert no forces on each other). It is named after Dutch physicist J D van der Waals (1837–1923).

**vanilla** any of a group of climbing orchids native to tropical America but now cultivated elsewhere, with large, fragrant white or yellow flowers. The dried and fermented fruit, or podlike capsules, of the species *V. planifolia* are the source of the vanilla flavouring used in cookery and baking. (Genus *Vanilla*.)

**Vanuatu** Republic of; **national name:** *Ripablik blong Vanuatu;* **area:** 14,800 sq km/5,714 sq mi; **capital:** (and chief port) Port-Vila (on Efate); **major towns/cities:** Luganville (on Espíritu Santo); **major ports:** Santo; **physical features:** comprises around 70 inhabited islands, including Espíritu Santo, Malekula, and Efate; densely forested, mountainous; three active volcanoes; cyclones on average twice a year; **head of state:** John Bernard Bani from 1999; **head of government:** Donald Kalpokas from 1998; **political system:** democracy; **currency:** vatu; **GNP per capita (PPP):** (US$) 3,160 (1998 est); **exports:** copra, beef, timber, cocoa, shells. Principal market Japan 32.1% (1997); **population:** 186,000 (1999 est); **language:** Bislama 82%, English, French (all official); **religion:** Christian 80%, animist; **life expectancy:** 66 (men); 70 (women) (1995–2000).

**Vatican City State; national name:** *Stato della Città del Vaticano;* **area:** 0.4 sq km/0.2 sq mi; **physical features:** forms an enclave in the heart of Rome, Italy; **head of state:** John Paul II from 1978; **head of government:** Cardinal Sebastiano Baggio; **political system:** absolute Catholicism; **currency:** Vatican City lira; Italian lira; **GNP per capita (PPP):** see Italy; **population:** 1,000 (1999 est); **language:** Latin (official), Italian; **religion:** Roman Catholic; **life expectancy:** see Italy.

**vapour density** density of a gas, expressed as the mass of a given volume of the gas divided by the →mass of an equal volume of a reference gas (such as hydrogen or air) at the same temperature and pressure. It is equal approximately to half the relative molecular weight (mass) of the gas.

**Varanasi** (or Benares or Banaras) city in Uttar Pradesh, India, one of the seven holy cities of Hinduism, on the River Ganges; population (1991) 932,000. There are 1,500 golden shrines, and a 5 km/3 mi frontage to the Ganges with sacred stairways (ghats) for purification by bathing. Varanasi is also a sacred centre of →Jainism, →Sikhism, and →Buddhism: Buddha came to Varanasi from Gaya and is believed to have preached in the Deer Park. One-third of its inhabitants are Muslim.

**variable** in mathematics, a changing quantity (one that can take various values), as opposed to a constant. For example, in the algebraic expression $y = 4x^3 + 2$, the variables are $x$ and $y$, whereas 4 and 2 are constants.

**variable star** in astronomy, a star whose brightness changes, either regularly or irregularly, over a period ranging from a few hours to months or years. The Cepheid variables regularly expand and contract in size every few days or weeks.

**varicose veins** (or varicosis) condition where the veins become swollen and twisted. The veins of the legs are most often affected; other vulnerable sites include the rectum (haemorrhoids) and testes.

**vasectomy** male sterilization; an operation to cut and tie the ducts that carry sperm from the testes to the penis. Vasectomy does not affect sexual performance, but the semen produced at ejaculation no longer contains sperm.

**Vaughan Williams, Ralph** (1872–1958) English composer. His style was tonal and often evocative of the English countryside through the use of folk themes. Among his works are the orchestral *Fantasia on a Theme by Thomas Tallis* (1910); the opera *Sir John in Love* (1929), featuring the Elizabethan song 'Greensleeves'; and nine symphonies (1909–57).

**vein** in animals with a circulatory system, any vessel that carries blood from the body to the heart. Veins contain valves that prevent the blood from running back when moving against gravity. They carry blood at low pressure, so their walls are thinner than those of arteries. They always carry deoxygenated blood, with the exception of the pulmonary vein, leading from the lungs to the heart in birds and mammals, which carries newly oxygenated blood.

**veldt** subtropical grassland in South Africa, equivalent to the →Pampas of South America.

**velocity** speed of an object in a given direction. Velocity is a vector quantity, since its direction is important as well as its magnitude (or speed).

**vena cava** either of the two great veins of the trunk, returning deoxygenated blood to the right atrium of the →heart. The superior vena cava, beginning where the arches of the two innominate veins join high in the chest, receives blood from the head, neck, chest, and arms; the inferior vena cava, arising from the junction of the right and left common iliac veins, receives blood from all parts of the body below the diaphragm.

**venereal disease** (VD) any disease mainly transmitted by sexual contact, although commonly the term is used specifically for gonorrhoea and syphilis, both occurring worldwide, and chancroid ('soft sore') and lymphogranuloma venerum, seen mostly in the tropics. The term sexually transmitted disease (STD) is more often used to encompass a growing list of conditions passed on primarily, but not exclusively, by sexual contact.

**Venezuela** Republic of; **national name:** *República de Venezuela*; **area:** 912,100 sq km/352,161 sq mi; **capital:** Caracas; **major towns/cities:** Maracaibo, Maracay, Barquisimeto, Valencia, Ciudad Guayana, San Cristóbal; **major ports:** Maracaibo; **physical features:** Andes Mountains and Lake Maracaibo in northwest; central plains (llanos); delta of River Orinoco in east; Guiana Highlands in southeast; **head of state and government:** Hugo Chávez Frías from 1998; **political system:** federal democracy; **currency:** bolívar; **GNP per capita (PPP):** (US\$) 8,190 (1998); **exports:** petroleum and petroleum products, metals (mainly aluminium and iron ore), natural gas, chemicals, basic manufactures, motor vehicles and parts. Principal market USA 56.7% (1997); **population:** 23,706,000 (1999 est); **language:** Spanish (official), Indian languages 2%; **religion:** Roman Catholic; **life expectancy:** 70 (men); 76 (women) (1995–2000).

**Venice** (Italian *Venezia*) city, port, and naval base on the northeast coast of Italy; population (1992) 305,600. It is the capital of Veneto region.

The old city is built on piles on low-lying islands in a salt-water lagoon, sheltered from the Adriatic Sea by the Lido and other small strips of land. There are about 150 canals crossed by some 400 bridges. Apart from tourism (it draws 8 million tourists a year), industries include glass, jewellery, textiles, and lace. Venice was an independent trading republic from the 10th century, ruled by a doge, or chief magistrate, and was one of the centres of the Italian Renaissance. It was renowned as a centre of early publishing; 15% of all printed books before 1500 were printed in Venice.

**Venn diagram** in mathematics, a diagram representing a →set or sets and the logical relationships between them. The sets are drawn as circles. An area of overlap between two circles (sets) contains elements that are common to both sets, and thus represents a third set. Circles that do not overlap represent sets with no elements in common

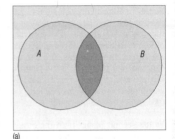

(a)

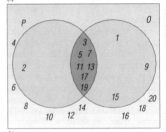

(b)

$\xi$ = *set of whole numbers from 1 to 20*
*O* = *set of odd numbers*
*P* = *set of prime numbers*

**Venn diagram** Sets and their relationships are often represented by Venn diagrams. The sets are drawn as circles – the area of overlap between the circles shows elements that are common to each set, and thus represent a third set. Here (a) is a Venn diagram of two intersecting sets and (b) a Venn diagram showing the set of whole numbers from 1 to 20 and the subsets P and O of prime and odd numbers, respectively. The intersection of P and O contains all the prime numbers that are also odd.

(disjoint sets). The method is named after the English logician John Venn.

**Venus** in Roman mythology, the goddess of love and beauty, equivalent to the Greek →Aphrodite. The patricians of Rome claimed descent from her son, the Trojan prince Aeneas, and she was consequently venerated as the guardian of the Roman people. Venus was also worshipped as a goddess of military victory and patroness of spring.

**Venus** second planet from the Sun. It can approach Earth to within 38 million km/24 million mi, closer than any other planet. Its mass is 0.82 that of Earth. Venus rotates on its axis more slowly than any other planet, from east to west, the opposite direction to the other planets (except Uranus and possibly Pluto). **mean distance from the Sun:** 108.2 million km/67.2 million mi; **equatorial diameter:** 12,100 km/7,500 mi; **rotation period:** 243 Earth days; **year:** 225 Earth days; **atmosphere:** Venus is shrouded by clouds of sulphuric acid droplets that sweep across the planet from east to west every four days. The atmosphere is almost entirely carbon dioxide, which traps the Sun's heat by the →greenhouse effect and raises the surface temperature of the planet to 480°C/900°F, with an atmospheric pressure of 90 times that at the surface of the Earth; **surface:** consists mainly of silicate rock and may have an interior structure similar to that of Earth: an iron–nickel core, a mantle composed of more mafic rocks (rocks made of one or more ferromagnesian, dark-coloured minerals), and a thin siliceous outer crust. The surface is dotted with deep impact craters. Some of Venus

volcanoes may still be active; **satellites:** no moons.

**Verdi, Giuseppe Fortunino Francesco** (1813–1901) Italian opera composer of the Romantic period. He took his native operatic style to new heights of dramatic expression. In 1842 he wrote the opera *Nabucco*, followed by *Ernani* (1844) and *Rigoletto* (1851). Other works include *Il trovatore* and *La traviata* (both 1853), *Aïda* (1871), and the masterpieces of his old age, *Otello* (1887) and *Falstaff* (1893). His *Requiem* (1874) commemorates the poet and novelist Alessandro Manzoni.

**Vermeer, Jan** (1632–1675) Dutch painter, active in Delft. He painted quiet, everyday scenes that are characterized by an almost abstract simplicity, subtle colour harmonies, and a remarkable ability to suggest the fall of light on objects. Examples are *The Lacemaker* (about 1655; Louvre, Paris) and *Maidservant Pouring Milk* (about 1658; Rijksmuseum, Amsterdam).

**Verne, Jules** (1828–1905) French author. He wrote tales of adventure that anticipated future scientific developments: *Five Weeks in a Balloon* (1862), *Journey to the Centre of the Earth* (1864), *Twenty Thousand Leagues under the Sea* (1870), and *Around the World in Eighty Days* (1873).

**vertebrate** any animal with a backbone. The 41,000 species of vertebrates include mammals, birds, reptiles, amphibians, and fishes. They include most of the larger animals, but in terms of numbers of species are only a tiny proportion of the world's animals. The zoological taxonomic group Vertebrata is a subgroup of the phylum Chordata.

**Vespasian** (9–79) also known as Titus Flavius Vespasianus, Roman emperor from AD 69. Proclaimed emperor by his soldiers while he was campaigning in Palestine, he reorganized the eastern provinces, and was a capable administrator. He was responsible for the construction of the Colosseum in Rome, which was completed by his son Titus.

**Vesuvius** (Italian *Vesuvio*) active volcano in Campania, Italy, 15 km/9 mi southeast of Naples, Italy; height 1,277 m/4,190 ft. In AD 79 it destroyed the cities of Pompeii, Herculaneum, and Stabiae.

**Victoria** (1819–1901) queen of the UK from 1837, when she succeeded her uncle William IV, and Empress of India from 1877. In 1840 she married Prince →Albert of Saxe-Coburg and Gotha. Her relations with her prime ministers ranged from the affectionate (Melbourne and Disraeli) to the stormy (Peel, Palmerston, and Gladstone). Her golden jubilee in 1887 and diamond jubilee in 1897 marked a waning of republican sentiment, which had developed with her withdrawal from public life on Albert's death in 1861.

**Vienna** (German *Wien*) capital of Austria, on the River Danube at the foot of the Wiener Wald (Vienna Woods); population (1995) 1,531,200. Although within the territory of Lower Austria, it is a separate province. Industries include engineering, electrical goods, electronics, clothing, precision and musical instruments, and beer. It is a major cultural and tourist centre.

**Vietnam** Socialist Republic of; **national name:** *Công Hòa Xã Hội Chu Nghia Việt Nam*; **area:** 329,600 sq km/127,258 sq mi; **capital:** Hanoi; **major towns/cities:** Ho Chi Minh City (formerly Saigon), Haiphong, Da Nang, Can Tho, Nha Trang, Nam Dinh; **major ports:** Ho Chi Minh City (formerly Saigon), Da Nang, Haiphong; **physical features:** Red River and Mekong deltas, centre of cultivation and population; tropical rainforest; mountainous in north and northwest; **head of state:** Tran Duc Luong from 1997; **head of government:** Phan Van Khai from 1997; **political system:** communism; **currency:** dong; **GNP per capita (PPP):** (US$) 1,690 (1998); **exports:** rice (leading exporter), crude petroleum, coal, coffee, marine products, handicrafts, light industrial goods, rubber, nuts, tea, garments, tin. Principal market Japan 18.2% (1997); **population:** 78,705,000 (1999 est); **language:** Vietnamese (official); French, English, Khmer, Chinese, local languages; **religion:** Taoist, Buddhist, Roman Catholic; **life expectancy:** 65 (men); 70 (women) (1995–2000).

**Viking** (or Norseman) the inhabitants of Scandinavia in the period 800–1100. They traded with, and raided, much of Europe, and often settled there. In their narrow, shallow-draught, highly manoeuvrable longships, the Vikings penetrated far inland along rivers. They plundered for gold and land, and were equally energetic as colonists – with colonies stretching from North America to central Russia – and as traders, with main trading posts at Birka (near Stockholm) and Hedeby (near Schleswig). The Vikings had a sophisticated literary culture, with →sagas and runic inscriptions, and an organized system of government with an assembly ('thing'). Their kings and chieftains were buried with their ships, together with their possessions.

**vine** (or grapevine) any of a group of climbing woody plants, especially *V. vinifera*, native to Asia Minor and cultivated from antiquity. The fruits (grapes) are eaten or made into wine or other fermented drinks; dried fruits of certain varieties are known as raisins and currants. Many other species of climbing plant are also called vines. (Genus *Vitis*, family Vitaceae.)

**viola** bowed, stringed musical instrument, the alto member of the violin family. Its four strings are tuned C3, G3, D4, and A5. With its dark, vibrant tone, it is often used for music of reflective character, as in Stravinsky's *Elegy* (1944) or Britten's *Lachrymae* (1950). Its principal function is harmonic in string quartets and orchestras. Concertos have been written for the viola by composers such as Telemann, Berlioz, Walton, Hindemith, and Bartók.

**violin** bowed, four-stringed musical instrument, the smallest and highest pitched (treble) of the violin family.

The strings are tuned in fifths (G3, D4, A5, and E5).

**Virgil** (70–19 BC) Publius Vergilius Maro, Roman poet. He wrote the *Eclogues* (37 BC), a series of pastoral poems; the *Georgics* (30 BC), four books on the art of farming; and his epic masterpiece, the *Aeneid* (30–19 BC). He was patronized by Maecenas on behalf of Octavian (later the emperor Augustus).

**Virginia** state in eastern USA. It is nicknamed Old Dominion. Officially known as the **Commonwealth of Virginia**, it ratified the US Constitution in 1788, becoming the 10th US state. It is bordered to the north by Maryland and the District of Columbia, to the west by Kentucky and West Virginia, and to the south by North Carolina and Tennessee. In the east it occupies the southern tip of the Delamarva Peninsula and is bordered by the Atlantic Ocean. Virginia was the northeasternmost state of the Confederacy. **population:** (1995) 6,618,400; **area:** 105,600 sq km/40,762 sq mi; **capital:** Richmond; **towns and cities:** Norfolk, Virginia Beach, Newport News, Hampton, Chesapeake, Portsmouth; **industries and products:** sweet potatoes, maize, tobacco, apples, peanuts, coal, ships, lorries, paper, chemicals, processed food, textiles, tourism, leisure industry.

**virtual reality** advanced form of computer simulation, in which a participant has the illusion of being part of an artificial environment. The participant views the environment through two tiny television screens (one for each eye) built into a visor. Sensors detect movements of the participant's head or body, causing the apparent viewing position to change. Gloves (datagloves) fitted with sensors may be worn, which allow the participant seemingly to pick up and move objects in the environment.

**virus** infectious particle consisting of a core of nucleic acid (DNA or RNA) enclosed in a protein shell. Viruses are acellular and able to function and reproduce only if they can invade a living cell to use the cell's system to replicate themselves. In the process they may disrupt or alter the host cell's own DNA. The healthy human body reacts by producing an antiviral protein, interferon, which prevents the infection spreading to adjacent cells.

There are around 5,000 species of virus known to science (1998), though there may be as many as 0.5 million actually in existence.

**Vishnu** in Hinduism, the second in the triad of gods (with Brahma and Siva) representing three aspects of the supreme spirit. He is the Preserver, and is believed to have assumed human appearance in nine *avatāras*, or incarnations, in such forms as Rama and Krishna. His worshippers are the Vaishnavas.

**Visigoth** member of the western branch of the →Goths, an East Germanic people.

**vitamin** any of various chemically unrelated organic compounds that are necessary in small quantities for the normal functioning of the human body. Many act as coenzymes, small molecules that enable →enzymes to function effectively. Vitamins must be supplied by the diet because the body cannot make them.

They are normally present in adequate amounts in a balanced diet. Deficiency of a vitamin may lead to a metabolic disorder ('deficiency disease'), which can be remedied by sufficient intake of the vitamin. They are generally classified as water-soluble (B and C) or fat-soluble (A, D, E, and K).

**Vivaldi, Antonio Lucio** (1678–1741) Italian baroque composer, violinist, and conductor. One of the most prolific composers of his day, he was particularly influential through his concertos, several of which were transcribed by Johann Sebastian Bach. He wrote 23 symphonies; 75 sonatas; over 400 concertos, including *The Four Seasons* (1725) for violin and orchestra; over 40 operas; and much sacred music. His work was largely neglected until the 1930s.

**vivisection** literally, cutting into a living animal. Used originally to mean experimental surgery or dissection practised on a live subject, the term is often used by antivivisection campaigners to include any experiment on animals, surgical or otherwise.

**Vladivostok** city on the western shore of the Sea of Japan, on a peninsula extending into Peter the Great Bay; population (1996 est) 627,000. It is the capital of the Primorski (Maritime) Krai of the Russian Federation, and one of the most important economic and cultural centres of the Russian Far East, where it is the largest city. Vladivostok is a terminus of the Trans-Siberian Railway (9,289 km/5,772 mi from Moscow) and the Northern Sea Route, centre of communications for the Pacific territories, the largest Russian port on the Pacific, and the chief base of the Pacific Fleet. The port is kept open by icebreakers during winter.

**volatile** in chemistry, term describing a substance that readily passes from the liquid to the vapour phase. Volatile substances have a high vapour pressure.

**volcano** crack in the Earth's crust through which hot magma (molten rock) and gases well up. The magma is termed lava when it reaches the surface. A volcanic mountain, usually cone shaped with a crater on top, is formed around the opening, or vent, by the build-up of solidified lava and ashes (rock fragments). Most volcanoes arise on plate margins (see →plate tectonics), where the movements of plates generate magma or allow it to rise from the mantle beneath. However, a number are found far from plate-margin activity, on 'hot spots' where the Earth's crust is thin.

**WEB SITE** > > > > > > > >

**Volcanoes**

http://www.learner.org/exhibits
/volcanoes/

Dramatic site that opens with a picture of an erupting volcano, and asks whether volcanic catastrophes – which threaten millions of people in an increasingly densely-populated world – can be predicted. With the help of video clips and interactive tasks, the well-written text goes on to answer important questions about volcanic activity; how volcanoes form and what the forces are that cause solid rock to melt and burst through the surface of the Earth.

**Volga** (ancient Rha) longest river in Europe, entirely within the territory of the Russian Federation. The Volga has a total length 3,685 km/2,290 mi, 3,540 km/2,200 mi of which are navigable. It rises in the Valdai plateau northwest of Moscow, and flows into the Caspian Sea

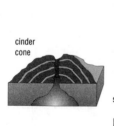

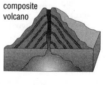

**volcano** There are two main types of volcano, but three distinctive cone shapes. Composite volcanoes emit a stiff, rapidly solidifying lava which forms high, steep-sided cones. Volcanoes that regularly throw out ash build up flatter domes known as cinder cones. The lava from a shield volcano is not ejected violently, flowing over the crater rim forming a broad low profile.

88 km/55 mi below the city of Astrakhan. The Volga basin drains most of the central and eastern parts of European Russia, its total drainage area being 1,360,000 sq km/525,100 sq mi.

**volt** SI unit of electromotive force or electric potential (see →potential, electric), symbol V. A small battery has a potential of 1.5 volts, whilst a high-tension transmission line may carry up to 765,000 volts. The domestic electricity supply in the UK is 230 volts (lowered from 240 volts in 1995); it is 110 volts in the USA.

**Voltaire** (1694–1778) pen-name of François-Marie Arouet, French writer. He is the embodiment of the 18th-century →Enlightenment. He wrote histories, books of political analysis and philosophy, essays on science and literature, plays, poetry, and the satirical fable *Candide* (1759), his best-known work. A trenchant satirist of social and political evils, he was often forced to flee from his enemies and was twice imprisoned. His works include *Lettres philosophiques sur les Anglais/Philosophical Letters on the English* (1733) (essays in favour of English ways, thought, and political practice), *Le Siècle de Louis XIV/The Age of Louis XIV* (1751), and *Dictionnaire philosophique/Philosophical Dictionary* (1764).

**voodoo** set of magical beliefs and practices, followed in some parts of Africa, South America, and the West Indies, especially Haiti. It arose in the 17th century on slave plantations as a combination of Roman Catholicism and West African religious traditions; believers retain membership in the Roman Catholic church. It was once practiced in New Orleans and other areas of southern USA by African-Americans. Beliefs include the existence of loa, spirits who closely involve themselves in human affairs, and some of whose identities mesh with those of Christian saints. The loa are invoked by the priest (*houngan*) or priestess (*manbo*) at ceremonies, during which members of the congregation become possessed by the spirits and go into a trance.

**vulture** any of various carrion-eating birds of prey in the order Falconiformes, with naked heads and necks, strong hooked bills, and keen senses of sight and smell. Vultures are up to 1 m/3.3 ft long, with wingspans of up to 3.7 m/12 ft. The plumage is usually dark, and the head brightly coloured.

# Ww

**Wagner, (Wilhelm) Richard** (1813–1883) German opera composer. He revolutionized the 19th-century conception of opera, envisaging it as a wholly new art form in which musical, poetic, and scenic elements should be unified through such devices as the leitmotif. His operas include *Tannhäuser* (1845), *Lohengrin* (1848), and *Tristan und Isolde* (1865). In 1872 he founded the Festival Theatre in Bayreuth; his masterpiece *Der Ring des Nibelungen/The Ring of the Nibelung*, a sequence of four operas, was first performed there 1876. His last work, *Parsifal*, was produced 1882.

**Wailing Wall** (or in Judaism, Western Wall) the remaining part of the Temple in Jerusalem, a sacred site of pilgrimage and prayer for Jews. There they offer prayers either aloud ('wailing') or on pieces of paper placed between the stones of the wall.

**Wales** (Welsh Cymru) Principality of; constituent part of the UK, in the west between the British Channel and the Irish Sea. **area:** 20,780 sq km/8,021 sq mi; **capital:** Cardiff; **towns and cities:** Swansea, Wrexham, Newport, Carmarthen; **features:** Snowdonia Mountains (Snowdon 1,085 m/3,560 ft, the highest point in England and Wales) in the northwest and in the southeast the Black Mountains, Brecon Beacons, and Black Forest ranges; rivers Severn, Wye, Usk, and Dee; **industries:** traditional industries have declined, but varied modern and high-technology ventures are being developed. There are oil refineries and open-cast coal mining. The last deep coal mine in north Wales closed in 1996. Wales has the largest concentration of Japanese-owned plants in the UK. It also has the highest density of sheep in the world and a dairy industry; tourism is important; **currency:** pound sterling; **population:** (1993 est) 2,906,000; **language:** English, 19% Welsh-speaking; **religion:** Nonconformist Protestant denominations; Roman Catholic minority; **government:** returns 40 members to the UK Parliament; in April 1996, the 8 counties were replaced by 22 county and county borough unitary authorities; devolved National Assembly for Wales (approved by referendum in 1997) began sitting in Cardiff from 1999.

**Wałęsa, Lech** (1943– ) Polish trade-union leader, president of Poland 1990–95. One of the founding members of the Solidarity free-trade-union movement, which emerged to challenge the communist government during strikes in the Gdańsk shipyards in August 1980. Wałęsa led the movement to become a national force. He was awarded the Nobel Prize for Peace in 1983. After his election as president, he gradually became estranged from Solidarity. In 1997 he formed a Christian Democratic party, which was, however, unlikely to make a significant impact on Polish political life.

**Walker, Alice Malsenior** (1944– ) US poet, novelist, critic, and essay writer. She has been active in the US civil-rights movement since the 1960s and, as a black woman, wrote about the double burden of racist and sexist oppression, about colonialism, and the quest for political and spiritual recovery. Her novel *The Color Purple* (1982, filmed 1985), told in the form of letters, won a Pulitzer prize. Her other works include *Possessing the Secret of Joy* (1992), which deals passionately with female circumcision, and *By the Light of My Father's Smile* (1998).

**waltz** ballroom dance in moderate triple time (3/4) that developed in Germany and Austria during the late 18th century from the Austrian *Ländler* (traditional peasants' country dance). Associated particularly with Vienna and the Strauss family, the waltz has remained popular up to the present day and has inspired composers including Chopin, Brahms, and Ravel.

**WAP** (acronym for wireless application protocol) initiative started in the 1990s by Unwired Planet, Motorola, Nokia, and Ericsson to develop a standard for delivering Web-like applications on a new generation of mobile phones. It is possible to use the phones for e-mail and messaging, reading Web pages, shopping, booking tickets, and making other financial transactions, as well as for phone calls. It has been claimed that WAP mobile phones, rather than PCs, will become the most popular tool for surfing the Web within the next few years.

**Warhol, Andy** (1928–1987) adopted name of Andrew Warhola, US pop artist and film-maker. He made his name 1962 with paintings of Campbell's soup cans, Coca-Cola bottles, and film stars. In his New York studio, the Factory, he and his assistants produced garish silk-screen prints. His films include *Chelsea Girls* (1966) and *Trash* (1970).

**Warsaw** (Polish *Warszawa*) capital of Poland, on the River Vistula; population (1993) 1,653,300. Industries include engineering, food processing, printing, clothing, and pharmaceuticals.

**Washington, George** (1732–1799) commander of the American forces during the American Revolutionary War and 1st president of the USA 1789–97; known as 'the father of his country'. An experienced soldier, he had fought in campaigns against the French during the French and Indian War. He was elected to the Virginia House of Burgesses 1759 and was a leader of the Virginia militia, gaining valuable exposure to wilderness fighting. As a strong opponent of the British government's policy, he sat in the Continental Congresses of 1774 and

1775, and on the outbreak of the American Revolution was chosen to be commander in chief of the Continental army. After many setbacks, he accepted the surrender of British general Cornwallis at Yorktown in 1781.

After the war Washington retired to his Virginia estate, Mount Vernon, but in 1787 he re-entered politics as president of the Constitutional Convention in Philadelphia, and was elected US president in 1789. He attempted to draw his ministers from all factions, but his aristocratic outlook and acceptance of the fiscal policy championed by Alexander Hamilton alienated his secretary of state, Thomas Jefferson, who resigned in 1793, thus creating the two-party system.

Washington was re-elected president in 1793 but refused to serve a third term, setting a precedent that stood until 1940. He died and was buried at Mount Vernon.

**Washington, DC** (District of Columbia) capital of the USA, on the Potomac River; the world's first planned national capital. It was named Washington, DC, to distinguish it from Washington state, and because it is coextensive with the District of Columbia, hence DC; population (1996 est) 543,200; metropolitan area extending outside the District of Columbia (1990) 3,923,600. The District of Columbia, the federal district of the USA, is an area of 174 sq km/69 sq mi. Its site was chosen by President George Washington, and the first structures date from 1793. Washington, DC, operates the national executive, legislative, and judicial government of the USA, and is a centre for international diplomacy and finance. Federal and district government are key employers, though numbers employed by both are decreasing. Public, trade, business, and social organizations maintain a presence, as well as law and other service agencies. Tourism is a major industry.

**wasp** any of several families of winged stinging insects of the order Hymenoptera, characterized by a thin stalk between the thorax and the abdomen. Wasps can be social or solitary. Among social wasps, the queens devote themselves to egg laying, the fertilized eggs producing female workers; the males come from unfertilized eggs and have no sting. The larvae are fed on insects, but the mature wasps feed mainly on fruit and sugar. In winter, the fertilized queens hibernate, but the other wasps die.

**waterfall** cascade of water in a river or stream. It occurs when a river flows over a bed of rock that resists erosion; weaker rocks downstream are worn away, creating a steep, vertical drop and a plunge pool into which the water falls. Over time, continuing erosion causes the waterfall to retreat upstream forming a deep valley, or gorge.

**Watergate** US political scandal, named after the building in Washington, DC, which housed the headquarters of the Democratic National Committee in the 1972 presidential election. Five men, hired by the Republican Committee for the Re-election of the President (popularly known as CREEP), were caught after breaking into the Watergate with complex electronic surveillance equipment. Investigations revealed that the White House was implicated in the break-in, and that there was a 'slush fund', used to finance unethical activities, including using the CIA and the Internal Revenue Service for political ends, setting up paramilitary operations against opponents, altering and destroying evidence, and bribing defendants to lie or remain silent. In August 1974, President →Nixon was forced by the Supreme Court to surrender to Congress tape recordings of conversations he had held with administration officials, which indicated his complicity in a cover-up. Nixon resigned rather than face impeachment for obstruction of justice and other crimes.

**Waterloo, Battle of** final battle of the Napoleonic Wars on 18 June 1815 in which a coalition force of British, Prussian, and Dutch troops under the Duke of Wellington defeated Napoleon near the village of Waterloo, 13 km/8 mi south of Brussels, Belgium. Napoleon found Wellington's army isolated from his allies and began a direct offensive to smash them, but the British held on until joined by the Prussians under Marshal Gebhard von Blücher. Four days later Napoleon abdicated for the second and final time.

**Watson, James Dewey** (1928– ) US biologist. His research on the molecular structure of →DNA and the genetic code, in collaboration with Francis →Crick, earned him a shared Nobel prize in 1962. Based on earlier works, they were able to show that DNA formed a double helix of two spiral strands held together by base pairs.

**Watt, James** (1736–1819) Scottish engineer who developed the steam engine in the 1760s, making Thomas Newcomen's engine vastly more efficient by cooling the used steam in a condenser separate from the main cylinder. He eventually made a double-acting machine that supplied power with both directions of the piston and developed rotary motion. He also invented devices associated with the steam engine, artistic instruments and a copying process, and devised the horsepower as a description of an engine's rate of working. The modern unit of power, the watt, is named after him.

**Waugh, Evelyn (Arthur St John)** (1903–1966) English novelist. His humorous social satires include *Decline and Fall* (1928), *Vile Bodies* (1930), *Scoop* (1938), and *The Loved One* (1948). He developed a serious concern with religious issues in *Brideshead Revisited* (1945) (successfully dramatized for television in the 1980s). *The Ordeal of Gilbert Pinfold* (1957) is largely autobiographical.

**wave** in the oceans, a ridge or swell formed by wind or other causes. The power of a wave is determined by the strength of the wind and the distance of open water over which the wind blows (the fetch). Waves are the main agents of →coastal erosion and deposition: sweeping away or building up beaches, creating spits and berms, and wearing down cliffs by their hydraulic action and by the corrosion of the sand and shingle that they carry. A →tsunami (misleadingly called a 'tidal wave') is formed after a submarine earthquake.

**wave** in physics, waves are oscillations that are propagated from a source. Mechanical waves require a medium through which to travel. Electromagnetic waves do not; they can travel through a vacuum. Waves carry energy but they do not transfer matter. There are two types: in a longitudinal wave, such as a sound wave, the disturbance is parallel to the wave's direction of travel; in a transverse wave, such as an electromagnetic wave, it is perpendicular. The medium (for example the Earth, for seismic waves) is not permanently displaced by the passage of a wave.

**wavelength** the distance between successive crests of a →wave. The wavelength of a light wave determines its colour; red light has a wavelength of about 700 nanometres, for example. The complete range of wavelengths of electromagnetic waves is called the electromagnetic →spectrum.

**wax** solid fatty substance of animal, vegetable, or mineral origin.

Waxes are composed variously of →esters, fatty acids, free →alcohols, and solid hydrocarbons.

**Wayne, John** (1907–1979) 'Duke', stage name of Marion Michael Morrison, US actor. He played the archetypal western hero: plain-speaking, brave, and solitary. His films include *Stagecoach* (1939), *Red River* (1948), *She*

*Wore a Yellow Ribbon* (1949), *The Searchers* (1956), *Rio Bravo* (1959), *The Man Who Shot Liberty Valance* (1962), and *True Grit* (1969; Academy Award).

**weevil** any of a superfamily (Curculionoidea) of →beetles, usually less than 6 mm/0.25 in long, and with a head prolonged into a downward beak, which is used for boring into plant stems and trees for feeding.

**Weill, Kurt Julian** (1900–1950) German composer; a US citizen from 1943. He wrote chamber and orchestral music and collaborated with Bertolt →Brecht on operas such as *Die Dreigroschenoper/The Threepenny Opera* (1928) and *Aufstieg und Fall der Stadt Mahagonny/The Rise and Fall of the City of Mahagonny* (1929), both of which attacked social corruption (*Mahagonny*, which satirized US frontier values, caused a riot at its premiere in Leipzig). He tried to evolve a new form of music theatre, using subjects with a contemporary relevance and the simplest musical means. In 1933 he left Germany, and from 1935 was in the USA, where he wrote a number of successful scores for Broadway, among them the antiwar musical *Johnny Johnson* (1936), *Knickerbocker Holiday* (1938, including the often covered 'September Song'), and *Street Scene* (1947), based on an Elmer Rice play set in the Depression.

**Weimar Republic** constitutional republic in Germany from 1919 to 1933, which was crippled by the election of antidemocratic parties to the Reichstag (parliament), and then subverted by the Nazi leader Hitler after his appointment as chancellor in 1933. It took its name from the city where in February 1919 a constituent assembly met to draw up a democratic constitution.

**welfare state** political system under which the state (rather than the individual or the private sector) has responsibility for the welfare of its citizens. Services such as unemployment and sickness benefits, family allowances and income supplements, pensions, medical care, and education may be provided and financed through state insurance schemes and taxation.

**Welles, (George) Orson** (1915–1985) US actor, screenwriter, and film and theatre director. His first and greatest film was *Citizen Kane* (1941), which he produced, directed, and starred in. Later work includes the *films noirs The Lady from Shanghai* (1948) and *Touch of Evil* (1958). As an actor, he created the character of Harry Lime in the film *The Third Man* (1949).

**Wellington, Arthur Wellesley, 1st Duke of Wellington** (1769–1852) Irish-born British soldier and Tory politician. As commander in the Peninsular War, he expelled the French from Spain in 1814. He defeated Napoleon Bonaparte at Quatre-Bras and Waterloo in 1815, and was a member of the Congress of Vienna. As prime minister 1828–30, he was forced to concede Roman Catholic emancipation. KB 1804, Viscount 1809, Earl 1812, Marquess 1812, Duke 1814.

**Wells, H(erbert) G(eorge)** (1866–1946) English writer. He was a pioneer of science fiction with such novels as *The Time Machine* (1895) and *The War of the Worlds* (1898), which describes a Martian invasion of Earth and brought him nationwide recognition. His later novels had an anti-establishment, anti-conventional humour remarkable in its day, for example *Kipps* (1905) and *Tono-Bungay* (1909). He was originally a Fabian and later became a Labour party supporter. He was a Labour candidate for London University in 1921 and 1922.

**Wesley, John** (1703–1791) English founder of Methodism. When the pulpits of the Church of England were closed to him and his followers, he took the gospel to the people. For 50 years he rode about the country on horseback, preaching daily, largely in the open air. His sermons became the doctrinal standard of the Wesleyan Methodist Church.

**West Bank** area (5,879 sq km/2,270 sq mi) on the west bank of the River Jordan; population (1994) 1,122,900. The area has been occupied by Israel since 1967; Israel refers to the area as Judaea and Samaria.

**Western Australia** state of Australia, bounded on the north and west by the Indian Ocean, on the east by Northern Territory and South Australia, on the south by the Southern Ocean. **area:** 2,525,500 sq km/974,843 sq mi; **capital:** Perth; **towns and cities:** Fremantle (main port), Bunbury, Geraldton, Kalgoorlie-Boulder, Albany, Broome;

**features:** largest state in Australia, occupying nearly one-third of the continent; territory includes the Monte Bello Islands; Cocos Islands; Christmas Island; Nullarbor Plain; Gibson, Sandy, and Great Victoria deserts; Ningaloo Reef; Purnululu National Park; Shark Bay World Heritage Area; many unusual flora and fauna (karri, jarrah, and tingle trees; more than 8,000 species of wildflowers; black swan); **products:** wheat, fresh and dried fruit, beef, dairy products, wool, wine, natural gas, oil, iron, gold, nickel, diamonds, bauxite, cultured and freshwater pearls, timber, fish; **population:** (1996) 1,726,100; **history:** first European to land was Dutch navigator Dirck Hartog in 1616; visited by Englishman William Dampier in 1688; a short-lived convict settlement at King George Sound in 1826; first non-convict settlement founded on Swan River (at Perth) in 1829; governed at first by New South Wales; became self-governing in 1890; became a state in 1901.

**West Indies** archipelago of about 1,200 islands, dividing the Atlantic Ocean from the Gulf of Mexico and the Caribbean Sea. The islands are divided into Bahamas; Greater Antilles Cuba, Hispaniola (Haiti, Dominican Republic), Jamaica, and Puerto Rico; **Lesser Antilles** Aruba, Netherlands Antilles, Trinidad and Tobago, the Windward Islands (Grenada, Barbados, St Vincent, St Lucia, Martinique, Dominica, Guadeloupe), the Leeward Islands (Montserrat, Antigua, St Kitts and Nevis, Barbuda, Anguilla, St Martin, British

and US Virgin Islands), and many smaller islands.

**wetland** permanently wet land area or habitat. Wetlands include areas of marsh, fen, bog, flood plain, and shallow coastal areas. Wetlands are extremely fertile. They provide warm, sheltered waters for fisheries, lush vegetation for grazing livestock, and an abundance of wildlife. Estuaries and seaweed beds are more than 16 times as productive as the open ocean.

**whale** any marine mammal of the order Cetacea. The only mammals to have adapted to living entirely in water, they have front limbs modified into flippers and no externally visible traces of hind limbs. They have horizontal tail flukes. When they surface to breathe, the hot air they breathe out condenses to form a 'spout' through the blowhole (single or double nostrils) in the top of the head. Whales are intelligent and have a complex communication system, known as 'songs'. They occur in all seas of the world.

The order is divided into two groups: the toothed whales (Odontoceti) and the baleen whales (Mysticeti). Toothed whales are predators, feeding on fish and squid. They include →dolphins and porpoises, along with large forms such as sperm whales. The largest whales are the baleen whales, with plates of modified mucous membrane called baleen (whalebone) in the mouth; these strain the food, mainly microscopic plankton, from the water. Baleen whales include the finback and right whales, and the blue whale, the largest animal that has ever lived, of length up to 30 m/100 ft.

Whales have been hunted for hundreds of years; today they are close to extinction. Of the 11 great whale species, 7 were listed as either endangered or vulnerable in the late 1990s. Whale-watching, as an economic alternative to whaling, generated $121 million worldwide in 1994.

**wheat** cereal plant derived from the wild *Triticum*, a grass native to the Middle East. It is the chief cereal used in breadmaking and is widely cultivated in temperate climates suited to its growth. Wheat is killed by frost, and damp makes the grains soft, so warm, dry regions produce the most valuable grain.

**white blood cell** (or leucocyte) one of a number of different cells that play a part in the body's defences and give immunity against disease. Some (neutrophils and macrophages) engulf invading micro-organisms, others kill infected cells, while →lymphocytes produce more specific immune responses. White blood cells are colourless, with clear or granulated cytoplasm, and are capable of independent amoeboid movement. They occur in the blood, →lymph, and elsewhere in the body's tissues.

**white dwarf** small, hot star, the last stage in the life of a →star such as the Sun. White dwarfs make up 10% of the stars in the Galaxy; most have a mass 60% of that of the Sun, but only 1% of the Sun's diameter, similar in size to the Earth. Most have surface temperatures of 8,000°C/14,400°F or more, hotter than

the Sun. Yet, being so small, their overall luminosities may be less than 1% of that of the Sun. The Milky Way contains an estimated 50 billion white dwarfs.

**Whitman, Walt(er)** (1819–1892) US poet. He published *Leaves of Grass* (1855), which contains the symbolic 'Song of Myself'. It used unconventional free verse (with no rhyme or regular rhythm) and scandalized the public by its frank celebration of sexuality.

**Whittle, Frank** (1907–1996) British engineer. He patented the basic design for the turbojet engine in 1930. In the Royal Air Force he worked on jet propulsion (1937–46). In May 1941 the Gloster E 28/39 aircraft first flew with the Whittle jet engine. Both the German (first operational jet planes) and the US jet aircraft were built using his principles. He was knighted in 1948.

**WHO** (acronym for →World Health Organization) agency of the United Nations established to prevent the spread of diseases.

**whooping cough** (or pertussis) acute infectious disease, seen mainly in children, caused by colonization of the air passages by the bacterium *Bordetella pertussis*. There may be catarrh, mild fever, and loss of appetite, but the main symptom is violent coughing, associated with the sharp intake of breath that is the characteristic 'whoop', and often followed by vomiting and severe nose bleeds. The cough may persist for weeks.

**Wilberforce, William** (1759–1833) English reformer. He was instrumental in abolishing slavery in the British Empire. He entered Parliament in 1780; in 1807 his bill banning the trade in slaves from the West Indies was passed, and in 1833, largely through his efforts, slavery was eradicated throughout the empire. He died shortly before the Slavery Abolition Act was passed.

**Wilde, Oscar (Fingal O'Flahertie Wills)** (1854–1900) Irish writer. With his flamboyant style and quotable conversation, he dazzled London society and, on his lecture tour in 1882, the USA. He published his only novel, *The Picture of Dorian Gray*, in 1891, followed by a series of sharp comedies, including *A Woman of No Importance* (1893) and *The Importance of Being Earnest* (1895). In 1895 he was imprisoned for two years for homosexual offences; he died in exile.

**wildebeest** (or gnu) either of two species of African →antelope, with a cowlike face, a beard and mane, and heavy curved horns in both sexes. The body is up to 1.3 m/4.2 ft high at the shoulder and slopes away to the hindquarters. (Genus *Connochaetes*.)

**William (I) the Conqueror** (c. 1027–1087) king of England from 1066. He was the illegitimate son of Duke Robert the Devil and succeeded his father as duke of Normandy in 1035. Claiming that his relative King Edward the Confessor had bequeathed him the English throne, William invaded the country 1066, defeating →Harold II at Hastings, Sussex, and was crowned king of England.

**William (III) of Orange** (1650–1702) king of Great Britain and Ireland from 1688, the son of William II of Orange and Mary, daughter of Charles I. He was offered the English crown by the parliamentary opposition to James II. He invaded England in 1688 and in 1689 became joint sovereign with his wife, Mary II. He spent much of his reign campaigning, first in Ireland, where he defeated James II at the Battle of the Boyne in 1690, and later against the French in Flanders. He died childless and was succeeded by Mary's sister, Anne.

**Williams, Tennessee (Thomas Lanier)** (1911–1983) US dramatist. His work is characterized by fluent dialogue and searching analysis of the psychological deficiencies of his characters. His plays, usually set in the Deep South against a background of decadence and degradation, include *The Glass Menagerie* (1945), *A Streetcar Named Desire* (1947), and *Cat on a Hot Tin Roof* (1955), the last two of which earned Pulitzer prizes.

**Windows** in computing, originally Microsoft's →graphical user interface (GUI) for IBM PCs and clones running MS-DOS. Windows has developed into a family of operating systems that run on a wide variety of computers from pen-operated palmtop organizers to large, multi-processor computers in corporate data centres.

**wind power** the harnessing of wind energy to produce power. The wind has long been used as a source of energy: sailing ships and windmills are ancient inventions. After the energy crisis of the 1970s wind turbines began to be used to produce electricity on a large scale.

**wing** in biology, the modified forelimb of birds and bats, or the membranous outgrowths of the exoskeleton of insects, which give the power of flight. Birds and bats have two wings. Bird wings have feathers attached to the fused digits ('fingers') and forearm bones, while bat wings consist of skin stretched between the digits. Most insects have four wings, which are strengthened by wing veins.

**Winnipeg** nickname 'Gateway to the West' (Cree *win-nipuy* 'muddy water'), capital of Manitoba, Canada, at the confluence of the Red and Assiniboine rivers, 65 km/40 mi south of Lake Winnipeg, 30 km/20 mi north of the US border; population (1991) 616,800, metropolitan area (1996) 676,700. It is a focus for trans-Canada and Canada–US traffic, and a market and transhipment point for wheat and other produce from the prairie provinces: Manitoba, Alberta, and Saskatchewan. Processed foods, textiles, farming machinery, and transport equipment are manufactured. Established as Winnipeg in 1870 on the site of earlier forts, the city expanded with the arrival of the Canadian Pacific Railroad in 1881.

**Wisconsin** state in northern central USA. It is nicknamed the Badger State. Wisconsin was admitted to the Union in 1848 as the 30th US state. Part of the Midwest, it is bordered to the south by Illinois, to the west by Iowa and

**wing** Birds can fly because of the specialized shape of their wings: a rounded leading edge, flattened underneath and round on top. This aerofoil shape produces lift in the same way that an aircraft wing does. The outline of the wing is related to the speed of flight. Fast birds of prey have a streamlined shape. Larger birds, such as the eagle, have large wings with separated tip feathers which reduce drag and allow slow flight. Insect wings are not aerofoils. They push downwards to produce lift, in the same way that oars are used to push through water.

Minnesota, to the north by Lake Superior and the Upper Peninsula of Michigan, and to the east by Lake Michigan. **population:** 5,122,900 (1995); **area:** 145,500 sq km/56,163 sq mi; **capital:** Madison; **towns and cities:** Milwaukee, Green Bay, Racine; **industries and products:** leading US dairy state; maize, hay, industrial and agricultural machinery, engines and turbines, precision instruments, paper products, cars and lorries, plumbing equipment, research, and tourism.

**Wittgenstein, Ludwig Josef Johann** (1889–1951) Austrian philosopher. His *Tractatus Logico-Philosophicus* (1922) postulated the 'picture theory' of language: that words represent things according to social agreement. He subsequently rejected this idea, and developed the idea that usage was more important than convention.

**Wodehouse, P(elham) G(renville)** (1881–1975) English novelist. He became a US citizen in 1955. His humorous novels and stories portray the accident-prone world of such characters as the socialite Bertie Wooster and his invaluable and impeccable manservant Jeeves, and Lord Emsworth of Blandings Castle with his prize pig, the Empress of Blandings.

**wolf** any of two species of large wild dogs of the genus *Canis*. The grey or timber wolf *C. lupus*, of North America and Eurasia, is highly social, measures up to 90 cm/3 ft at the shoulder, and weighs up to 45 kg/100 lb. It has been greatly reduced in numbers except for isolated wilderness regions. The red wolf *C. rufus*, generally more slender and smaller (average weight about 15 kg/35 lb) and tawnier in colour, may not be a separate species, but a grey wolf–coyote hybrid. It used to be restricted to southern central USA, but is now thought to be extinct in the wild.

**Wolfe, James** (1727–1759) English soldier. He served in Canada and commanded a victorious expedition against the French general Montcalm in Quebec on the Plains of Abraham, during which both commanders were killed. The British victory established their supremacy over Canada.

**Wollstonecraft, Mary** (1759–1797) British feminist. She was a member of a group of radical intellectuals called the English Jacobins. Her book *A Vindication of the Rights of Women* (1792) demanded equal educational opportunities for women. She married William Godwin in 1797 and died giving birth to a daughter, Mary (later Mary →Shelley).

**Wolsey, Thomas** (c. 1475–1530) English cleric and politician. In Henry VIII's service from 1509, he became archbishop of York in 1514, cardinal and lord chancellor in 1515, and began the dissolution of the monasteries.

His reluctance to further Henry's divorce from Catherine of Aragon led to his downfall in 1529. He was charged with high treason in 1530 but died before being tried.

**wolverine** *Gulo gulo*, largest land member of the weasel family (Mustelidae), found in Europe, Asia, and North America.

It is stocky in build, and about 1 m/3.3 ft long. Its long, thick fur is dark brown on the back and belly and lighter on the sides. It covers food that it cannot eat with an unpleasant secretion. Destruction of habitat and trapping for its fur have greatly reduced its numbers.

**women's movement** campaign for the rights of women, including social, political, and economic equality with men. Early European campaigners of the 17th–19th centuries fought for women's right to own property, to have access to higher education, and to vote (see →suffragette). Once women's suffrage was achieved in the 20th century, the emphasis of the movement shifted to the goals of equal social and economic opportunities for women, including employment. A continuing area of concern in industrialized countries is the contradiction between the now generally accepted principle of equality and the inequalities that remain between the sexes in state policies and in everyday life.

**woodlouse** crustacean of the order Isopoda. Woodlice have segmented bodies, flattened undersides, and 14 legs. The eggs are carried by the female in a pouch beneath the thorax. They often live in high densities: up to as many as 8,900 per square metre.

**woodworm** common name for the larval stage of certain wood-boring beetles. Dead or injured trees are their natural target, but they also attack structural timber and furniture.

**Woolf, (Adeline) Virginia** (1882–1941) born Stephen, English novelist and critic. In novels such as *Mrs Dalloway* (1925), *To the Lighthouse* (1927), and *The Waves* (1931), she used a 'stream of consciousness' technique to render inner experience. In *A Room of One's Own* (1929) (nonfiction), *Orlando* (1928), and *The Years* (1937), she examines the importance of economic independence for women and other feminist principles.

**Wordsworth, William** (1770–1850) English Romantic poet. In 1797 he moved with his sister Dorothy Wordsworth to Somerset, where he lived near Samuel Taylor →Coleridge and collaborated with him on *Lyrical Ballads* (1798) (which included 'Tintern Abbey', a meditation on his response to nature. From 1799 he lived in the Lake District. His most notable individual poems were published in *Poems* (1807) (including 'Intimations of Immortality'). At intervals between then and 1839 he revised *The Prelude* (posthumously published in 1850), the first part of his uncompleted philosophical, creative, and spiritual autobiography in verse. He was appointed poet laureate in 1843.

**World Health Organization** (WHO) specialized agency of the United Nations established in 1946 to prevent the spread of diseases and to eradicate them. In 1996–97 it had a budget of $842.654 million. Its headquarters are in Geneva, Switzerland. The WHO's greatest achievement to date has been the eradication of smallpox.

**World War I** 1914–18 war between the Central European Powers (Germany, Austria-Hungary, and allies) on one side and the Triple Entente (Britain and the British Empire, France, and Russia) and their allies, including the USA (which entered 1917), on the other side. An estimated 10 million lives were lost and twice that number were wounded. It was fought on the eastern and western fronts, in the Middle East, in Africa, and at sea.

**World War II** 1939–45 war between Germany, Italy, and Japan (the Axis powers) on one side, and Britain, the Commonwealth, France, the USA, the USSR, and China (the Allied powers) on the other. An estimated 55 million lives were lost (20 million of them citizens of the USSR), and 60 million people in Europe were displaced because of bombing raids. The war was fought in the Atlantic and Pacific theatres.

It is estimated that, during the course of the war, for every tonne of bombs dropped on the UK, 315 fell on Germany. In 1945, Germany surrendered (May) but Japan fought on until the USA dropped atomic bombs on Hiroshima and Nagasaki (August).

**worm** any of various elongated limbless invertebrates belonging to several phyla. Worms include flatworms, such as flukes and →tapeworms; roundworms or nematodes, such as eelworm and the hookworm; marine ribbon worms

---

**WEB SITE** > > > > > > > >
**Worm World**

http://www.nj.com/yucky/worm/

Lively guide for children, with information on topics such as worms' bodies, how to make a worm bin, and different types of worm, plus an art gallery and some worm jokes.

---

or nemerteans; and segmented worms or →annelids.

**Wounded Knee** site on the Oglala Sioux Reservation, South Dakota, USA, of a confrontation between the US Army and American Indians; the last 'battle' of America's Indian Wars. On 15 December 1890 Chief Sitting Bull was killed, supposedly resisting arrest, and on 29 December a group of Indians involved in the Ghost Dance Movement (aimed at resumption of Indian control of North America with the aid of the spirits of dead braves) were surrounded by the 7th Cavalry; 153 Indians were gunned down.

**W particle** in physics, an →elementary particle, one of the weakons responsible for transmitting the weak nuclear force.

**Wren, Christopher** (1632–1723) English architect. His ingenious use of a refined and sober baroque style can be seen in his best-known work, St Paul's Cathedral, London (1675–1711), and in the many churches he built in London including St Mary-le-Bow, Cheapside (1670–77), and St Bride's, Fleet Street (1671–78). His other works include the Sheldonian Theatre, Oxford (1664–69), Greenwich Hospital, London (begun 1694), and Marlborough House, London (1709–10; now much altered).

**Wright, Frank Lloyd** (1869–1959) US architect. He is known for 'organic architecture', in which buildings reflect their natural surroundings. From the 1890s, he developed his celebrated prairie house style, a series of low, spreading houses with projecting roofs.

He later diversified, employing reinforced concrete to explore a variety of geometric forms. Among his buildings are his Wisconsin home, Taliesin East (1925), in prairie-house style; Falling Water, near Pittsburgh, Pennsylvania (1936), a house of cantilevered terraces straddling a waterfall; and the Guggenheim Museum, New York (1959), a spiral ramp rising from a circular plan.

**Wright brothers** Orville (1871–1948) and Wilbur (1867–1912) US inventors; brothers who pioneered piloted, powered flight. Inspired by Otto Lilienthal's gliding, they perfected their piloted glider in 1902. In 1903 they built a powered machine, a 12-hp 341-kg/750-lb plane, and became the first to make a successful powered flight, near Kitty Hawk, North Carolina. Orville flew 36.6 m/120 ft in 12 seconds; Wilbur, 260 m/852 ft in 59 seconds.

**Wrocław** (formerly Breslau) industrial river port in Poland, on the River Oder; population (1993) 643,600. Industries include shipbuilding, engineering, textiles, and electronics. It was the capital of the German province of Lower Silesia until 1945.

**Wyclif, John** (*c.* 1320–1384) (or Wycliffe) English religious reformer. Allying himself with the party of John of Gaunt, which was opposed to ecclesiastical influence at court, he attacked abuses in the church, maintaining that the Bible rather than the church was the supreme authority. He criticized such fundamental doctrines as priestly absolution, confession, and indulgences, and set disciples to work on translating the Bible into English.

**Wyoming** state in western USA. It is nicknamed the Equality State. Wyoming was admitted to the Union in 1890 as the 44th US state. One of the Mountain States, it is bordered to the east by Nebraska and South Dakota, to the north by Montana, to the west by Montana, Idaho, and Utah, and to the south by Utah and Colorado. **population:** (1995) 480,200; **area:** 253,400 sq km/97,812 sq mi; **capital:** Cheyenne; **towns and cities:** Casper, Laramie; **industries and products:** oil, natural gas, sodium salts, coal, uranium, sheep, beef.

**X chromosome** larger of the two sex chromosomes, the smaller being the →Y chromosome. These two chromosomes are involved in sex determination. Females have two X chromosomes, males have an X and a Y. Genes carried on the X chromosome produce the phenomenon of sex linkage.

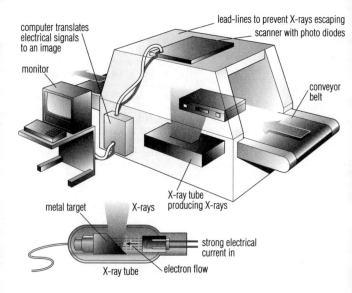

computer translates electrical signals to an image

lead-lines to prevent X-rays escaping

scanner with photo diodes

monitor

conveyor belt

metal target

X-rays

X-ray tube producing X-rays

strong electrical current in

X-ray tube

electron flow

**X-ray** A X-ray image. The X-rays are generated by high-speed electrons impinging on a tungsten target. The rays pass through the specimen and on to a photographic plate or imager.

**xerophyte** plant adapted to live in dry conditions. Common adaptations to reduce the rate of →transpiration include a reduction of leaf size, sometimes to spines or scales; a dense covering of hairs over the leaf to trap a layer of moist air (as in edelweiss); water storage cells; sunken stomata; and permanently rolled leaves or leaves that roll up in dry weather (as in marram grass). Many desert cacti are xerophytes.

**X-ray** band of electromagnetic radiation in the wavelength range $10^{-11}$ to $10^{-9}$ m (between gamma rays and ultraviolet radiation; see →electromagnetic waves). Applications of X-rays make use of their short wavelength (as in X-ray diffraction) or their penetrating power (as in medical X-rays of internal body tissues). X-rays are dangerous and can cause cancer.

**xylem** tissue found in vascular plants, whose main function is to conduct water and dissolved mineral nutrients from the roots to other parts of the plant. Xylem is composed of a number of different types of cell, and may include long, thin, usually dead cells known as tracheids; fibres (schlerenchyma); thin-walled parenchyma cells; and conducting vessels.

**xylophone** musical →percussion instrument of African and Indonesian origin, consisting of a series of hardwood bars of varying lengths, each with its own distinct pitch, arranged in sequence over a resonator or resonators, and played with hard sticks. It first appeared as an orchestral instrument in Saint-Saëns's *Danse macabre* (1874), illustrating dancing skeletons.

# Yy

**yak** species of cattle *Bos grunniens*, family Bovidae, which lives in wild herds at high altitudes in Tibet. It stands about 2 m/6 ft at the shoulder and has long shaggy hair on the underparts. It has large, upward-curving horns and humped shoulders. It is in danger of becoming extinct.

**Y chromosome** smaller of the two sex chromosomes. In male mammals it occurs paired with the other type of sex chromosome (X), which carries far more genes. The Y chromosome is the smallest of all the mammalian chromosomes and is considered to be largely inert (that is, without direct effect on the physical body). There are only 20 genes discovered so far on the human Y chromosome, much fewer than on all other human chromosomes. See also →sex determination.

**yeast** one of various single-celled fungi (see →fungus) that form masses of tiny round or oval cells by budding. When placed in a sugar solution the cells multiply and convert the sugar into alcohol and carbon dioxide. Yeasts are used as fermenting agents in baking, brewing, and the making of wine and spirits. Brewer's yeast (*S. cerevisiae*) is a rich source of vitamin B. (Especially genus *Saccharomyces*; also other related genera.)

**Yeats, W(illiam) B(utler)** (1865–1939) Irish poet, dramatist, and scholar. He was a leader of the Irish literary revival and a founder of the Abbey Theatre in Dublin. His early work was romantic and lyrical, as in the poem 'The Lake Isle of Innisfree' and the plays *The Countess Cathleen* (1892) and *The Land of Heart's Desire* (1894). His later poetry, which includes *The Wild Swans at Coole* (1917) and *The Winding Stair* (1929), was also much influenced by European and Eastern thought. He was a senator of the Irish Free State 1922–28, and won the Nobel Prize for Literature in 1923.

---

## WEB SITE > > > > > > > >
### Yeats, W B

http://www.lit.kobe-u.ac.jp/~hishika/
yeats.htm

Appreciation of the life and work of the Irish poet as well as links to more than 300 poems, class notes for teaching on the poet, newsletters, and Yeats fan clubs.

---

**yellow fever** (or yellow jack) acute tropical viral disease, prevalent in the Caribbean area, Brazil, and on the west coast of Africa. The yellow fever virus is an arbovirus transmitted by the mosquito. Its symptoms include a high fever, headache, joint and muscle pains, vomiting, and yellowish skin (jaundice, possibly leading to liver failure); the heart and kidneys may also be affected. The mortality rate is 25%, with 91% of all cases occurring in Africa.

**Yeltsin, Boris Nikolayevich** (1931– ) Russian politician, president of the Russian Soviet Federative Socialist Republic (RSFSR) 1990–91, and president of the newly independent Russian Federation 1991–99. He directed the Federation's secession from the USSR and the formation of a new, decentralized confederation, the Commonwealth of Independent States (CIS), with himself as the most powerful leader. A referendum in 1993 supported his policies of price deregulation and accelerated privatization, despite severe economic problems and civil unrest. He survived a coup attempt later the same year, but was subsequently forced to compromise on the pace of his reforms after far-right electoral gains, and lost considerable public support. He suffered two heart attacks, in October and November 1995, yet still contested the June 1996 presidential elections, in which he secured re-election by defeating Communist Party leader Gennady Zyuganov in the second round run-off. Yeltsin resigned as president on 31 December 1999. Announcing that he was bowing out to give a younger generation a chance, he apologized to his country for failing to fulfil their hopes. He relinquished his power six months early to his chosen successor, Vladimir Putin, in return for receiving guarantees of immunity from any future prosecution for any of his actions in the Kremlin.

**Yemen** Republic of; **national name:** *Jamhuriya al Yamaniya*; **area:** 531,900 sq km/205,366 sq mi; **capital:** San'a; **major towns/cities:** Aden, Ta'izz, Al Mukalla, Hodeida, Ibb, Dhamar; **major ports:** Aden; **physical features:** hot, moist coastal plain, rising to plateau and desert; **head of state:** Ali Abdullah Saleh from 1990; **head of government:** Abdul Ali al-Rahman al-Iryani from 1998; **political system:** emergent democracy; **currency:** riyal (North); dinar (South), both legal currency throughout the country; **GNP per capita (PPP):** (US$) 740 (1998); **exports:** petroleum and petroleum products, cotton, basic manufactures, clothing, live animals, hides and skins, fish, rice, coffee. Principal market China 30.9% (1997); **population:** 17,488,000 (1999 est); **language:** Arabic; **religion:** Sunni Muslim 63%, Shiite Muslim 37%; **life expectancy:** 57 (men); 58 (women) (1995–2000).

**Yevtushenko, Yevgeny Aleksandrovich** (1933– ) Soviet poet. He aroused controversy with his anti-Stalinist 'Stalin's Heirs' (1956), published with Khrushchev's support, and 'Babi Yar' (1961), which attacked Russian as well as Nazi anti-Semitism. His other works include the long poem *Zima Junction* (1956), the novel *Berries* (1981), and *Precocious Autobiography* (1963).

**yoga** (Sanskrit 'union') Hindu philosophical system attributed to Patanjali, who lived about 150 BC at Gonda, Uttar Pradesh, India. He preached mystical union with a personal deity through the practice of self-hypnosis and a rising above the senses by abstract meditation, adoption of special postures, and ascetic practices. As practised in the West, yoga is more a system of mental and physical exercise, and of induced relaxation as a means of relieving stress.

**Yom Kippur** the Jewish Day of →Atonement.

**York** cathedral and industrial city and administrative headquarters of York unitary authority in northern England, on the River Ouse; population (1991) 127,700. It was the administrative headquarters of the county of North Yorkshire until 1996. Industries include tourism and the manufacture of scientific instruments, sugar, chocolate, and glass. Founded in AD 71 as the Roman provincial capital Eboracum, York retains many of its medieval streets and buildings and much of its 14th-century city wall; the Gothic York Minster, England's largest medieval cathedral, includes fine 15th-century stained glass. The city is visited by some 3 million tourists a year.

**Yugoslavia** Federal Republic of; **national name:** *Federativna Republika Jugoslavija*; **area:** 58,300 sq km/22,509 sq mi; **capital:** Belgrade; **major towns/cities:** Priština, Novi Sad, Niš,

Rijeka, Kragujevac, Podgorica (formerly Titograd), Subotica; **physical features:** federation of republics of Serbia and Montenegro and two former autonomous provinces, Kosovo and Vojvodina; **head of state:** Slobodan Milošević from 1997; **head of government:** Momir Bulatović from 1998; **political system:** socialist pluralist republic; **currency:** new Yugoslav dinar; **GNP per capita (PPP):** (US$) 5,880 (1997 est); **exports:** basic manufactures, machinery and transport equipment, clothing, miscellaneous manufactured articles, food and live animals. Principal market Italy 11.5% (1997); **population:** 10,637,000 (1999 est); **language:** Serbo-Croatian; Albanian (in Kosovo); **religion:** Serbian and Montenegrin Orthodox; Muslim in southern Serbia; **life expectancy:** 70 (men); 76 (women) (1995–2000).

**Ypres, Battles of** (Flemish Ieper) in World War I, three major battles 1914–17 between German and Allied forces near Ypres, a Belgian town in western Flanders, 40 km/25 mi south of Ostend. Neither side made much progress in any of the battles, despite heavy casualties, but the third battle in particular (also known as Passchendaele) July–November 1917 stands out as an enormous waste of life for little return. The Menin Gate (1927) is a memorial to British soldiers lost in these battles.

# Zz

**Zambezi** (or Zambesi) river in central and southeast Africa; length 2,650 km/1,650 mi from northwest Zambia through Mozambique to the Indian Ocean, with a wide delta near Chinde. Major tributaries include the Kafue in Zambia. It is interrupted by rapids, and includes on the Zimbabwe–Zambia border the Victoria Falls (Mosi-oa-tunya) and Kariba Dam, which forms the reservoir of Lake Kariba with large fisheries. Its drainage area is about 1,347,000 sq km/520,077 sq mi.

**Zambia** Republic of (formerly **Northern Rhodesia**); **area:** 752,600 sq km/290,578 sq mi; **capital:** Lusaka; **major towns/cities:** Kitwe, Ndola, Kabwe, Mufulira, Chingola, Luanshya, Livingstone; **physical features:** forested plateau cut through by rivers; Zambezi River, Victoria Falls, Kariba Dam; **head of state and government:** Frederick Chiluba from 1991; **political system:** emergent democracy; **currency:** Zambian kwacha; **GNP per capita (PPP):** (US$) 860 (1998); **exports:** copper, zinc, lead, cobalt, tobacco. Principal market Japan 11.6% (1997); **population:** 8,976,000 (1999 est); **language:** English (official); Bantu languages; **religion:** Christian, animist, Hindu,

Muslim; **life expectancy:** 40 (men); 41 (women) (1995–2000).

**Zeebrugge** small Belgian ferry port on the North Sea, linked to Bruges by a canal (built 1896–1907), 14 km/9 mi long. It was occupied by the Germans in World War I and developed as a major naval base. In March 1987 it was the scene of a disaster in which over 180 passengers lost their lives when the car ferry *Herald of Free Enterprise* put to sea from Zeebrugge with its car-loading doors still open.

**Zen** (abbreviation of Japanese *zenna* 'quiet mind concentration') form of Buddhism introduced from India to Japan via China in the 12th century. *Kōan* (paradoxical questions), intense meditation, and sudden enlightenment are elements of Zen practice. Soto Zen was spread by the priest Dōgen (1200–1253), who emphasized work, practice, discipline, and philosophical questions to discover one's Buddha-nature in the 'realization of self'.

**Zeppelin, Ferdinand Adolf August Heinrich, Count von Zeppelin** (1838–1917) German airship pioneer. His first airship was built and tested in 1900. During World War I a number of zeppelins bombed England. They were also used for luxury passenger transport but the construction of hydrogen-filled airships with rigid keels was abandoned after several disasters in the 1920s and 1930s. Zeppelin also helped to pioneer large multi-engine bomber planes.

**Zeus** in Greek mythology, the chief of the Olympian gods (Roman →Jupiter). He was the son of Kronos, whom he overthrew; his brothers included Pluto and Poseidon, his sisters Demeter, Hestia, and Hera. As the supreme god he dispensed good and evil and was the father and ruler of all humankind, the fount of kingly power and law and order. His emblems were the thunderbolt and aegis (shield), representing the thundercloud. The colossal ivory and gold statue of the seated god, made by Phidias for the temple of Zeus in the Peloponnese, was one of the →Seven Wonders of the World.

**Zhou Enlai** (1898–1976) (or Chou Enlai) Chinese communist politician. Zhou, a member of the Chinese Communist Party (CCP) from the 1920s, was prime minister 1949–76 and foreign minister 1949–58. He was a moderate Maoist and weathered the Cultural Revolution. He played a key role in foreign affairs.

**Zimbabwe** Republic of (formerly **Southern Rhodesia**); **area:** 390,300 sq km/150,694 sq mi; **capital:** Harare; **major towns/cities:** Bulawayo, Gweru, Kwekwe, Mutare, Chitungwiza, Hwange; **physical features:** high plateau with central high veld and mountains in east; rivers Zambezi, Limpopo; Victoria Falls; **head of state and government:** Robert

Mugabe from 1987; **political system:** effectively one-party socialist republic; **currency:** Zimbabwe dollar; **GNP per capita (PPP):** (US$) 2,150 (1998); **exports:** tobacco, metals and metal alloys, textiles and clothing, cotton lint. Principal market South Africa 12.1% (1997); **population:** 11,529,000 (1999 est); **language:** English (official), Shona, Sindebele; **religion:** Christian, Muslim, Hindu, animist; **life expectancy:** 44 (men); 45 (women) (1995–2000).

**zinc** (Germanic *zint* 'point') hard, brittle, bluish-white, metallic element, symbol Zn, atomic number 30, relative atomic mass 65.37. The principal ore is sphalerite or zinc blende (zinc sulphide, ZnS). Zinc is hardly affected by air or moisture at ordinary temperatures; its chief uses are in alloys such as brass and in coating metals (for example, galvanized iron). Its compounds include zinc oxide, used in ointments (as an astringent) and cosmetics, paints, glass, and printing ink.

Zinc is an essential trace element in most animals; adult humans have 2–3 g/0.07–0.1 oz zinc in their bodies. There are more than 300 known enzymes that contain zinc.

**Zion** Jebusite (Amorites of Canaan) stronghold in Jerusalem captured by King David, and the hill on which he built the Temple, symbol of Jerusalem and of Jewish national life.

**Zionism** national liberation movement advocating the re-establishment of a Jewish homeland (the *Eretz Israel*) in

Palestine. Here, in the 'promised land' of the Bible, its adherents called for the Jewish people to be granted a sovereign state with its capital at Jerusalem, the 'city of Zion'. The movement was founded by the Hungarian writer Theodor Herzl, who in 1897 convened the First Zionist Congress in the Swiss city of Basel. Zionism was the driving force behind the creation of the state of Israel in 1948.

**zither** member of a family of musical instruments consisting of one or more strings stretched over a resonating frame or soundbox, played horizontally. The modern concert zither has up to 45 strings of which five, passing over frets, are plucked with a plectrum for melody, and the remainder are plucked with the fingers for harmonic accompaniment.

**zodiac** zone of the heavens containing the paths of the Sun, Moon, and planets. When this was devised by the ancient Greeks, only five planets were known, making the zodiac about 16° wide. In astrology, the zodiac is divided into 12 signs, each 30° in extent: Aries, Taurus, Gemini, Cancer, Leo, Virgo, Libra, Scorpio, Sagittarius, Capricorn, Aquarius, and Pisces. These do not cover the same areas of sky as the astronomical constellations.

**Zola, Émile Edouard Charles Antoine** (1840–1902) French novelist and social reformer. He made his name with *Thérèse Raquin* (1867), a grim, powerful story of remorse. With *La Fortune des Rougon/The Fortune of the Rougons* (1867) he began a series of some 20 naturalistic novels collectively known as *Le Rougon-Macquart*, portraying the fortunes of a French family under the Second Empire. They include *Le Ventre de Paris/The Underbelly of Paris* (1873), *Nana* (1880), and *La Débâcle/The Debacle* (1892). In 1898 he published *J'accuse/I Accuse*, a pamphlet indicting the persecutors of Alfred →Dreyfus, for which he was prosecuted for libel but later pardoned.

**zoology** branch of biology concerned with the study of animals. It includes any aspect of the study of animal form and function – description of present-day animals, the study of evolution of animal forms, anatomy, →physiology, embryology, behaviour, and geographical distribution.

**Zoroastrianism** pre-Islamic Persian religion founded by the Persian prophet Zoroaster in the 6th century BC, and still practised by the Parsees in India. The Zend-Avesta are the sacred scriptures of the faith. The theology is dualistic, Ahura Mazda or Ormuzd (the good God) being perpetually in conflict with Ahriman (the evil God), but the former is assured of eventual victory. There are approximately 100,000 (1991) Zoroastrians worldwide; membership is restricted to those with both parents belonging to the faith.

**Zurich** city and capital of Switzerland, situated at the exit of the Limmat River from Lake Zurich; population (1995) 422,700. Lying at the foot of the Alps, it is the capital of Zurich canton, the principal financial and business centre of Switzerland, and one of the world's leading international banking and insurance centres (the 'Gnomes of Zurich'). Manufactured goods include machinery, electrical goods, textiles, and printed works. It is the largest city in Switzerland.

# Appendix

# Appendix

## IMPERIAL AND METRIC CONVERSION FACTORS

| Imperial to metric | | Metric to imperial | |
| --- | --- | --- | --- |
| **To convert from** | **Multiply by** | **To convert from** | **Multiply by** |
| **Length** | | | |
| inches to millimetres | 25.4 | millimetres to inches | 0.0393701 |
| feet to metres | 0.3048 | metres to feet | 3.28084 |
| yards to metres | 0.9144 | metres to yards | 1.09361 |
| furlongs to kilometres | 0.201168 | kilometres to furlongs | 4.97097 |
| miles to kilometres | 1.609344 | kilometres to miles | 0.621371 |
| **Area** | | | |
| square inches to square centimetres | 6.4516 | square centimetres to square inches | 0.1550 |
| square feet to square metres | 0.092903 | square metres to square feet | 10.7639 |
| square yards to square metres | 0.836127 | square metres to square yards | 1.19599 |
| square miles to square kilometres | 2.589988 | square kilometres to square miles | 0.386102 |
| acres to square metres | 4,046.856422 | square metres to acres | 0.000247 |
| acres to hectares | 0.404685 | hectares to acres | 2.471054 |
| **Volume/capacity** | | | |
| cubic inches to cubic centimetres | 16.387064 | cubic centimetres to cubic inches | 0.061024 |
| cubic feet to cubic metres | 0.028317 | cubic metres to cubic feet | 35.3147 |
| cubic yards to cubic metres | 0.764555 | cubic metres to cubic yards | 1.30795 |
| cubic miles to cubic kilometres | 4.1682 | cubic kilometres to cubic miles | 0.239912 |

## IMPERIAL AND METRIC CONVERSION FACTORS (CONTINUED)

| Imperial to metric | | Metric to imperial | |
|---|---|---|---|
| To convert from | Multiply by | To convert from | Multiply by |
| **Volume/capacity (continued)** | | | |
| fluid ounces (imperial) to millilitres | 28.413063 | millilitres to fluid ounces (imperial) | 0.035195 |
| fluid ounces (US) to millilitres | 29.5735 | millilitres to fluid ounces (US) | 0.033814 |
| pints (imperial) to litres | 0.568261 | litres to pints (imperial) | 1.759754 |
| pints (US) to litres | 0.473176 | litres to pints (US) | 2.113377 |
| quarts (imperial) to litres | 1.136523 | litres to quarts (imperial) | 0.879877 |
| quarts (US) to litres | 0.946353 | litres to quarts (US) | 1.056688 |
| gallons (imperial) to litres | 4.54609 | litres to gallons (imperial) | 0.219969 |
| gallons (US) to litres | 3.785412 | litres to gallons (US) | 0.364172 |
| **Mass/weight** | | | |
| ounces to grams | 28.349523 | grams to ounces | 0.035274 |
| pounds to kilograms | 0.453592 | kilograms to pounds | 2.20462 |
| stones (14 lb) to kilograms | 6.350293 | kilograms to stones (14 lb) | 0.157473 |
| tons (imperial) to kilograms | 1,016.046909 | kilograms to tons (imperial) | 0.000984 |
| tons (US) to kilograms | 907.18474 | kilograms to tons (US) | 0.001102 |
| tons (imperial) to metric tonnes | 1.016047 | metric tonnes to tons (imperial) | 0.984207 |
| tons (US) to metric tonnes | 0.907185 | metric tonnes to tons (US) | 1.10231 |
| **Speed** | | | |
| miles per hour to kilometres per hour | 1.609344 | kilometres per hour to miles per hour | 0.621371 |
| feet per second to metres per second | 0.3048 | metres per second to feet per second | 3.28084 |
| **Force** | | | |
| pounds-force to newtons | 4.44822 | newtons to pounds-force | 0.224809 |
| kilograms-force to newtons | 9.80665 | newtons to kilograms-force | 0.101972 |

## IMPERIAL AND METRIC CONVERSION FACTORS (CONTINUED)

| Imperial to metric | | Metric to imperial | |
| --- | --- | --- | --- |
| To convert from | Multiply by | To convert from | Multiply by |
| **Pressure** | | | |
| pounds-force per square inch to kilopascals | 6.89476 | kilopascals to pounds-force per square inch | 0.145038 |
| tons-force per square inch (imperial) to megapascals | 15.4443 | megapascals to tons-force per square inch (imperial) | 0.064779 |
| atmospheres to newtons per square centimetre | 10.1325 | newtons per square centimetre to atmospheres | 0.098692 |
| atmospheres to pounds-force per square inch | 14.695942 | pounds-force per square inch to atmospheres | 0.068948 |
| **Energy** | | | |
| calories to joules | 4.1868 | joules to calories | 0.238846 |
| watt hours to joules | 3,600 | joules to watt hours | 0.000278 |
| **Power** | | | |
| horsepower to kilowatts | 0.7457 | kilowatts to horsepower | 1.34102 |
| **Fuel consumption** | | | |
| miles per gallon (imperial) to kilometres per litre | 0.3540 | kilometres per litre to miles per gallon (imperial) | 2.824859 |
| miles per gallon (US) to kilometres per litre | 0.4251 | kilometres per litre to miles per gallon (US) | 2.3521 |
| gallons per mile (imperial) to litres per kilometre | 2.824859 | litres per kilometre to gallons per mile (imperial) | 0.3540 |
| gallons per mile (US) to litres per kilometre | 2.3521 | litres per kilometre to gallons per mile (US) | 0.4251 |

## LARGEST COUNTRIES BY POPULATION SIZE

Countries with a population of over 100 million, 1999 and 2050.

| Rank | Country | Population (millions) | % of world population 1999 |
|------|---------|----------------------|----------------------------|
| 1 | China | 1,274 | 21.31 |
| 2 | India | 998 | 16.69 |
| 3 | United States | 276 | 4.62 |
| 4 | Indonesia | 209 | 3.10 |
| 5 | Brazil | 168 | 2.81 |
| 6 | Pakistan | 152 | 2.54 |
| 7 | Russian Federation | 147 | 2.45 |
| 8 | Bangladesh | 127 | 2.12 |
| 9 | Japan | 127 | 2.12 |
| 10 | Nigeria | 109 | 1.82 |
| **World total** | | **5,978** | |

| Rank | Country | Population (millions) | 2050 (projected) |
|------|---------|----------------------|------------------|
| 1 | India | 1,529 | 17.16 |
| 2 | China | 1,478 | 16.58 |
| 3 | United States | 349 | 3.91 |
| 4 | Pakistan | 346 | 3.88 |
| 5 | Indonesia | 312 | 3.50 |
| 6 | Nigeria | 244 | 2.73 |
| 7 | Brazil | 244 | 2.73 |
| 8 | Bangladesh | 213 | 2.39 |
| 9 | Ethiopia | 170 | 1.90 |
| 10 | Congo, Democratic Republic of | 160 | 1.79 |
| 11 | Mexico | 147 | 1.65 |
| 12 | Philippines | 131 | 1.47 |
| 13 | Vietnam | 127 | 1.42 |
| 14 | Russian Federation | 122 | 1.42 |
| 15 | Iran | 115 | 1.29 |
| 16 | Egypt | 115 | 1.29 |
| 17 | Japan | 105 | 1.17 |
| 18 | Turkey | 101 | 1.13 |
| **World total** | | **8,909** | |

Source: United Nations Population Division, Department of Economic and Social Affairs

## SOVEREIGNS OF ENGLAND AND THE UK FROM 899

| Reign | Name | Relationship |
|---|---|---|
| **West Saxon Kings** | | |
| 899–924 | Edward the Elder | son of Alfred the Great |
| 924–39 | Athelstan | son of Edward the Elder |
| 939–46 | Edmund | half-brother of Athelstan |
| 946–55 | Edred | brother of Edmund |
| 955–59 | Edwy | son of Edmund |
| 959–75 | Edgar | brother of Edwy |
| 975–78 | Edward the Martyr | son of Edgar |
| 978–1016 | Ethelred (II) the Unready | son of Edgar |
| 1016 | Edmund Ironside | son of Ethelred (II) the Unready |
| **Danish Kings** | | |
| 1016–35 | Canute | son of Sweyn I of Denmark who conquered England in 1013 |
| 1035–40 | Harold I | son of Canute |
| 1040–42 | Hardicanute | son of Canute |
| **West Saxon Kings (restored)** | | |
| 1042–66 | Edward the Confessor | son of Ethelred (II) the Unready |
| 1066 | Harold II | son of Godwin |
| **Norman Kings** | | |
| 1066–87 | William I | illegitimate son of Duke Robert the Devil |
| 1087–1100 | William II | son of William I |
| 1100–35 | Henry I | son of William I |
| 1135–54 | Stephen | grandson of William II |
| **House of Plantagenet** | | |
| 1154–89 | Henry II | son of Matilda (daughter of Henry I) |
| 1189–99 | Richard I | son of Henry II |
| 1199–1216 | John | son of Henry II |
| 1216–72 | Henry III | son of John |
| 1272–1307 | Edward I | son of Henry III |
| 1307–27 | Edward II | son of Edward I |
| 1327–77 | Edward III | son of Edward II |
| 1377–99 | Richard II | son of the Black Prince |

## SOVEREIGNS OF ENGLAND AND THE UK FROM 899 (CONTINUED)

| Reign | Name | Relationship |
|---|---|---|
| **House of Lancaster** | | |
| 1399–1413 | Henry IV | son of John of Gaunt |
| 1413–22 | Henry V | son of Henry IV |
| 1422–61, 1470–71 | Henry VI | son of Henry V |
| **House of York** | | |
| 1461–70, 1471–83 | Edward IV | son of Richard, Duke of York |
| 1483 | Edward V | son of Edward IV |
| 1483–85 | Richard III | brother of Edward IV |
| **House of Tudor** | | |
| 1485–1509 | Henry VII | son of Edmund Tudor, Earl of Richmond |
| 1509–47 | Henry VIII | son of Henry VII |
| 1547–53 | Edward VI | son of Henry VIII |
| 1553–58 | Mary I | daughter of Henry VIII |
| 1558–1603 | Elizabeth I | daughter of Henry VIII |
| **House of Stuart** | | |
| 1603–25 | James I | great-grandson of Margaret (daughter of Henry VII) |
| 1625–49 | Charles I | son of James I |
| 1649–60 | the Commonwealth | |
| **House of Stuart (restored)** | | |
| 1660–85 | Charles II | son of Charles I |
| 1685–88 | James II | son of Charles I |
| 1689–1702 | William III and Mary | son of Mary (daughter of Charles I); daughter of James II |
| 1702–14 | Anne | daughter of James II |

## SOVEREIGNS OF ENGLAND AND THE UK FROM 899 (CONTINUED)

| Reign | Name | Relationship |
|-------|------|--------------|
| **House of Hanover** | | |
| 1714–27 | George I | son of Sophia (granddaughter of James I) |
| 1727–60 | George II | son of George I |
| 1760–1820 | George III | son of Frederick (son of George II) |
| 1820–30 | George IV (regent 1811–20) | son of George III |
| 1830–37 | William IV | son of George III |
| 1837–1901 | Victoria | daughter of Edward (son of George III) |
| **House of Saxe-Coburg** | | |
| 1901–10 | Edward VII | son of Victoria |
| **House of Windsor** | | |
| 1910–36 | George V | son of Edward VII |
| 1936 | Edward VIII | son of George V |
| 1936–52 | George VI | son of George V |
| 1952– | Elizabeth II | daughter of George VI |

## PRIME MINISTERS OF GREAT BRITAIN AND THE UK

| Term | Name | Party |
|------|------|-------|
| 1721–42 | Robert Walpole[1] | Whig |
| 1742–43 | Spencer Compton, Earl of Wilmington | Whig |
| 1743–54 | Henry Pelham | Whig |
| 1754–56 | Thomas Pelham-Holles, 1st Duke of Newcastle | Whig |
| 1756–57 | William Cavendish, 4th Duke of Devonshire | Whig |
| 1757–62 | Thomas Pelham-Holles, 1st Duke of Newcastle | Whig |
| 1762–63 | John Stuart, 3rd Earl of Bute | Tory |
| 1763–65 | George Grenville | Whig |
| 1765–66 | Charles Watson Wentworth, 2nd Marquess of Rockingham | Whig |
| 1766–68 | William Pitt, 1st Earl of Chatham | Tory |
| 1768–70 | Augustus Henry Fitzroy, 3rd Duke of Grafton | Whig |
| 1770–82 | Frederick, Lord North[2] | Tory |
| 1782 | Charles Watson Wentworth, 2nd Marquess of Rockingham | Whig |
| 1782–83 | William Petty-Fitzmaurice, 2nd Earl of Shelburne[3] | Whig |
| 1783 | William Henry Cavendish-Bentinck, 3rd Duke of Portland | Whig |
| 1783–1801 | William Pitt, The Younger | Tory |
| 1801–04 | Henry Addington | Tory |
| 1804–06 | William Pitt, The Younger | Tory |
| 1806–07 | William Wyndham Grenville, 1st Baron Grenville | Whig |
| 1807–09 | William Henry Cavendish-Bentinck, 3rd Duke of Portland | Whig |
| 1809–12 | Spencer Perceval | Tory |
| 1812–27 | Robert Banks Jenkinson, 2nd Earl of Liverpool | Tory |
| 1827 | George Canning | Tory |
| 1827–28 | Frederick John Robinson, 1st Viscount Goderich | Tory |
| 1828–30 | Arthur Wellesley, 1st Duke of Wellington | Tory |
| 1830–34 | Charles Grey, 2nd Earl Grey | Whig |
| 1834 | William Lamb, 2nd Viscount Melbourne | Whig |
| 1834 | Arthur Wellesley, 1st Duke of Wellington | Tory |
| 1834–35 | Sir Robert Peel, 2nd Baronet | Tory |
| 1835–41 | William Lamb, 2nd Viscount Melbourne | Whig |
| 1841–46 | Sir Robert Peel, 2nd Baronet | Conservative |
| 1846–52 | John Russell, Lord Russell | Whig-Liberal |
| 1852 | Edward Geoffrey Stanley, 14th Earl of Derby | Conservative |
| 1852–55 | George Hamilton-Gordon, 4th Earl of Aberdeen | Peelite |
| 1855–58 | Henry John Temple, 3rd Viscount Palmerston | Liberal |
| 1858–59 | Edward Geoffrey Stanley, 14th Earl of Derby | Conservative |
| 1859–65 | Henry John Temple, 3rd Viscount Palmerston | Liberal |

## PRIME MINISTERS OF GREAT BRITAIN AND THE UK (CONTINUED)

| Term | Name | Party |
|------|------|-------|
| 1865–66 | John Russell, 1st Earl Russell | Liberal |
| 1866–68 | Edward Geoffrey Stanley, 14th Earl of Derby | Conservative |
| 1868 | Benjamin Disraeli | Conservative |
| 1868–74 | William Ewart Gladstone | Liberal |
| 1874–80 | Benjamin Disraeli[4] | Conservative |
| 1880–85 | William Ewart Gladstone | Liberal |
| 1885–86 | Robert Cecil, 3rd Marquess of Salisbury | Conservative |
| 1886 | William Ewart Gladstone | Liberal |
| 1886–92 | Robert Cecil, 3rd Marquess of Salisbury | Conservative |
| 1892–94 | William Ewart Gladstone | Liberal |
| 1894–95 | Archibald Philip Primrose, 5th Earl of Rosebery | Liberal |
| 1895–1902 | Robert Cecil, 3rd Marquess of Salisbury | Conservative |
| 1902–05 | Arthur James Balfour | Conservative |
| 1905–08 | Sir Henry Campbell-Bannerman | Liberal |
| 1908–16 | Herbert Henry Asquith | Liberal |
| 1916–22 | David Lloyd George | Liberal |
| 1922–23 | Bonar Law | Conservative |
| 1923–24 | Stanley Baldwin | Conservative |
| 1924 | Ramsay Macdonald | Labour |
| 1924–29 | Stanley Baldwin | Conservative |
| 1929–35 | Ramsay Macdonald | Labour |
| 1935–37 | Stanley Baldwin | Conservative |
| 1937–40 | Neville Chamberlain | Conservative |
| 1940–45 | Winston Churchill | Conservative |
| 1945–51 | Clement Attlee | Labour |
| 1951–55 | Winston Churchill[5] | Conservative |
| 1955–57 | Sir Anthony Eden | Conservative |
| 1957–63 | Harold Macmillan | Conservative |
| 1963–64 | Sir Alec Douglas-Home | Conservative |
| 1964–70 | Harold Wilson | Labour |
| 1970–74 | Edward Heath | Conservative |
| 1974–76 | Harold Wilson | Labour |
| 1976–79 | James Callaghan | Labour |
| 1979–90 | Margaret Thatcher | Conservative |
| 1990–97 | John Major | Conservative |
| 1997– | Tony Blair | Labour |

[1] From 1725, Sir Robert Walpole.  [3] From 1784, 1st Marquess of Lansdowne.  [5] From 1953, Sir Winston Churchill.
[2] From 1790, 2nd Earl of Guilford.  [4] From 1876, Earl of Beaconsfield.

## US PRESIDENTS

| Year elected/ took office | President | Party | Losing candidate(s) | Party |
|---|---|---|---|---|
| 1789 | 1 George Washington | Federalist | no opponent | |
| 1792 | re-elected | | no opponent | |
| 1796 | 2 John Adams | Federalist | Thomas Jefferson | Democrat–Republican |
| 1800 | 3 Thomas Jefferson | Democrat–Republican | Aaron Burr | Democrat–Republican |
| 1804 | re-elected | | Charles Pinckney | Federalist |
| 1808 | 4 James Madison | Democrat–Republican | Charles Pinckney | Federalist |
| 1812 | re-elected | | DeWitt Clinton | Federalist |
| 1816 | 5 James Monroe | Democrat–Republican | Rufus King | Federalist |
| 1820 | re-elected | | John Quincy Adams | Democrat–Republican |
| 1824 | 6 John Quincy Adams | Democrat–Republican | Andrew Jackson | Democrat–Republican |
| | | | Henry Clay | Democrat–Republican |
| | | | William H Crawford | Democrat–Republican |
| 1828 | 7 Andrew Jackson | Democrat | John Quincy Adams | National Republican |
| 1832 | re-elected | | Henry Clay | National Republican |
| 1836 | 8 Martin Van Buren | Democrat | William Henry Harrison | Whig |
| 1840 | 9 William Henry Harrison | Whig | Martin Van Buren | Democrat |
| 1841 | 10 John Tyler[1] | Whig | | |
| 1844 | 11 James K Polk | Democrat | Henry Clay | Whig |
| 1848 | 12 Zachary Taylor | Whig | Lewis Cass | Democrat |
| 1850 | 13 Millard Fillmore[2] | Whig | | |
| 1852 | 14 Franklin Pierce | Democrat | Winfield Scott | Whig |
| 1856 | 15 James Buchanan | Democrat | John C Fremont | Republican |
| 1860 | 16 Abraham Lincoln | Republican | Stephen Douglas | Democrat |
| | | | John Breckinridge | Democrat |
| | | | John Bell | Constitutional Union |

## US PRESIDENTS (CONTINUED)

| Year elected/ took office | President | Party | Losing candidate(s) | Party |
|---|---|---|---|---|
| 1864 | re-elected | | George McClellan | Democrat |
| 1865 | 17 Andrew Johnson[3] | Democrat | | |
| 1868 | 18 Ulysses S Grant | Republican | Horatio Seymour | Democrat |
| 1872 | re-elected | | Horace Greeley | Democrat–Liberal Republican |
| 1876 | 19 Rutherford B Hayes | Republican | Samuel Tilden | Democrat |
| 1880 | 20 James A Garfield | Republican | Winfield Hancock | Democrat |
| 1881 | 21 Chester A Arthur[4] | Republican | | |
| 1884 | 22 Grover Cleveland | Democrat | James Blaine | Republican |
| 1888 | 23 Benjamin Harrison | Republican | Grover Cleveland | Democrat |
| 1892 | 24 Grover Cleveland | Democrat | Benjamin Harrison | Republican |
| | | | James Weaver | People's |
| 1896 | 25 William McKinley | Republican | William J Bryan | Democrat–People's |
| 1900 | re-elected | | William J Bryan | Democrat |
| 1901 | 26 Theodore Roosevelt[5] | Republican | | |
| 1904 | re-elected | | Alton B Parker | Democrat |
| 1908 | 27 William Howard Taft | Republican | William J Bryan | Democrat |
| 1912 | 28 Woodrow Wilson | Democrat | Theodore Roosevelt | Progressive |
| | | | William Howard Taft | Republican |
| 1916 | re-elected | | Charles E Hughes | Republican |
| 1920 | 29 Warren G Harding | Republican | James M Cox | Democrat |
| 1923 | 30 Calvin Coolidge[6] | Republican | | |
| 1924 | re-elected | | John W Davis | Democrat |
| | | | Robert M LaFollette | Progressive |

## US PRESIDENTS (CONTINUED)

| Year elected/ took office | President | Party | Losing candidate(s) | Party |
|---|---|---|---|---|
| 1928 | 31 Herbert Hoover | Republican | Alfred E Smith | Democrat |
| 1932 | 32 Franklin D Roosevelt | Democrat | Herbert C Hoover | Republican |
| | | | Norman Thomas | Socialist |
| 1936 | re-elected | | Alfred Landon | Republican |
| 1940 | re-elected | | Wendell Willkie | Republican |
| 1944 | re-elected | | Thomas E Dewey | Republican |
| 1945 | 33 Harry S Truman[7] | Democrat | | |
| 1948 | re-elected | | Thomas E Dewey | Republican |
| | | | J Strom Thurmond | States' Rights |
| | | | Henry A Wallace | Progressive |
| 1952 | 34 Dwight D Eisenhower | Republican | Adlai E Stevenson | Democrat |
| 1956 | re-elected | | Adlai E Stevenson | Democrat |
| 1960 | 35 John F Kennedy | Democrat | Richard M Nixon | Republican |
| 1963 | 36 Lyndon B Johnson[8] | Democrat | | |
| 1964 | re-elected | | Barry M Goldwater | Republican |
| 1968 | 37 Richard M Nixon | Republican | Hubert H Humphrey | Democrat |
| | | | George C Wallace | American Independent |
| 1972 | re-elected | | George S McGovern | Democrat |
| 1974 | 38 Gerald R Ford[9] | Republican | | |
| 1976 | 39 James Earl Carter | Democrat | Gerald R Ford | Republican |

## US PRESIDENTS (CONTINUED)

| Year elected/ took office | President | Party | Losing candidate(s) | Party |
|---|---|---|---|---|
| 1980 | 40 Ronald Reagan | Republican | James Earl Carter | Democrat |
| | | | John B Anderson | Independent |
| 1984 | re-elected | | Walter Mondale | Democrat |
| 1988 | 41 George Bush | Republican | Michael Dukakis | Democrat |
| | | | Ross Perot | Independent |
| 1992 | 42 Bill Clinton | Democrat | George Bush | Republican |
| | | | Bob Dole | Republican |
| 1996 | re-elected | | Ross Perot | Reform |

[1] Became president on death of Harrison.
[2] Became president on death of Taylor.
[3] Became president on assassination of Lincoln.
[4] Became president on assassination of Garfield.
[5] Became president on assassination of McKinley.
[6] Became president on death of Harding.
[7] Became president on death of F D Roosevelt.
[8] Became president on assassination of Kennedy.
[9] Became president on resignation of Nixon.

## RELATIVE TIMES IN CITIES THROUGHOUT THE WORLD

The time indicated in the table below is fixed by law and is called standard time.
At 12:00 noon, GMT, the standard time elsewhere around the world is as follows:

| City | Time |
| --- | --- |
| Abu Dhabi, United Arab Emirates | 16:00 |
| Accra, Ghana | 12:00 |
| Addis Ababa, Ethiopia | 15:00 |
| Adelaide, Australia | 21:30 |
| Alexandria, Egypt | 14:00 |
| Algiers, Algeria | 13:00 |
| Al Manamah (also called Bahrain), Bahrain | 15:00 |
| Amman, Jordan | 14:00 |
| Amsterdam, Netherlands | 13:00 |
| Anchorage (AK), USA | 03:00 |
| Ankara, Turkey | 14:00 |
| Athens, Greece | 14:00 |
| Auckland, New Zealand | 24:00 |
| Baghdad, Iraq | 15:00 |
| Bahrain (also called Al Manamah), Bahrain | 15:00 |
| Bangkok, Thailand | 19:00 |
| Barcelona, Spain | 13:00 |
| Beijing, China | 20:00 |
| Beirut, Lebanon | 14:00 |
| Belgrade, Yugoslavia | 13:00 |
| Berlin, Germany | 13:00 |
| Bern, Switzerland | 13:00 |
| Bogotá, Colombia | 07:00 |
| Bonn, Germany | 13:00 |
| Brazzaville, Republic of the Congo | 13:00 |
| Brisbane, Australia | 22:00 |
| Brussels, Belgium | 13:00 |
| Bucharest, Romania | 14:00 |
| Budapest, Hungary | 13:00 |
| Buenos Aires, Argentina | 09:00 |
| Cairo, Egypt | 14:00 |
| Calcutta, India | 17:30 |
| Canberra, Australia | 22:00 |
| Cape Town, South Africa | 14:00 |

## RELATIVE TIMES IN CITIES THROUGHOUT THE WORLD (CONTINUED)

| City | Time |
| --- | --- |
| Caracas, Venezuela | 08:00 |
| Casablanca, Morocco | 12:00 |
| Chennai (formerly Madras), India | 17:30 |
| Chicago (IL), USA | 06:00 |
| Cologne, Germany | 13:00 |
| Colombo, Sri Lanka | 18:00 |
| Copenhagen, Denmark | 13:00 |
| Damascus, Syria | 14:00 |
| Dar es Salaam, Tanzania | 15:00 |
| Darwin, Australia | 21:30 |
| Delhi, India | 17:30 |
| Denver (CO), USA | 05:00 |
| Dhaka, Bangladesh | 18:00 |
| Dubai, United Arab Emirates | 16:00 |
| Dublin, Republic of Ireland | 12:00 |
| Florence, Italy | 13:00 |
| Frankfurt am Main, Germany | 13:00 |
| Gdańsk, Poland | 13:00 |
| Geneva, Switzerland | 13:00 |
| Gibraltar | 13:00 |
| Hague, The, Netherlands | 13:00 |
| Harare, Zimbabwe | 14:00 |
| Havana, Cuba | 07:00 |
| Helsinki, Finland | 14:00 |
| Hobart, Australia | 22:00 |
| Ho Chi Minh City, Vietnam | 19:00 |
| Hong Kong, China | 20:00 |
| Istanbul, Turkey | 14:00 |
| Jakarta, Indonesia | 19:00 |
| Jerusalem, Israel | 14:00 |
| Johannesburg, South Africa | 14:00 |
| Karachi, Pakistan | 17:00 |
| Kiev, Ukraine | 14:00 |
| Kuala Lumpur, Malaysia | 20:00 |
| Kuwait City, Kuwait | 15:00 |
| Kyoto, Japan | 21:00 |
| Lagos, Nigeria | 13:00 |

## RELATIVE TIMES IN CITIES THROUGHOUT THE WORLD (CONTINUED)

| City | Time |
|------|------|
| Le Havre, France | 13:00 |
| Lima, Peru | 07:00 |
| Lisbon, Portugal | 12:00 |
| London, England | 12:00 |
| Luanda, Angola | 13:00 |
| Luxembourg, Luxembourg | 13:00 |
| Lyon, France | 13:00 |
| Madrid, Spain | 13:00 |
| Manila, Philippines | 20:00 |
| Marseille, France | 13:00 |
| Mecca, Saudi Arabia | 15:00 |
| Melbourne, Australia | 22:00 |
| Mexico City, Mexico | 06:00 |
| Milan, Italy | 13:00 |
| Minsk, Belarus | 14:00 |
| Monrovia, Liberia | 12:00 |
| Montevideo, Uruguay | 09:00 |
| Montreal, Canada | 07:00 |
| Moscow, Russian Federation | 15:00 |
| Mumbai (formerly Bombay), India | 17:30 |
| Munich, Germany | 13:00 |
| Nairobi, Kenya | 15:00 |
| New Orleans (LA), USA | 06:00 |
| New York (NY), USA | 07:00 |
| Nicosia, Cyprus | 14:00 |
| Oslo, Norway | 13:00 |
| Ottawa, Canada | 07:00 |
| Panamá, Panama | 07:00 |
| Paris, France | 13:00 |
| Perth, Australia | 20:00 |
| Port Said, Egypt | 14:00 |
| Prague, Czech Republic | 13:00 |
| Rawalpindi, Pakistan | 17:00 |
| Reykjavik, Iceland | 12:00 |
| Rio de Janeiro, Brazil | 09:00 |
| Riyadh, Saudi Arabia | 15:00 |
| Rome, Italy | 13:00 |

## RELATIVE TIMES IN CITIES THROUGHOUT THE WORLD (CONTINUED)

| City | Time |
| --- | --- |
| San Francisco (CA), USA | 04:00 |
| Santiago, Chile | 08:00 |
| Seoul, South Korea | 21:00 |
| Shanghai, China | 20:00 |
| Singapore City, Singapore | 20:00 |
| Sofia, Bulgaria | 14:00 |
| St Petersburg, Russian Federation | 15:00 |
| Stockholm, Sweden | 13:00 |
| Sydney, Australia | 22:00 |
| Taipei, Taiwan | 20:00 |
| Tashkent, Uzbekistan | 17:00 |
| Tehran, Iran | 15:30 |
| Tel Aviv-Yafo, Israel | 14:00 |
| Tenerife, Canary Islands | 12:00 |
| Tokyo, Japan | 21:00 |
| Toronto, Canada | 07:00 |
| Tripoli, Libya | 13:00 |
| Tunis, Tunisia | 13:00 |
| Valparaiso, Chile | 08:00 |
| Vancouver, Canada | 04:00 |
| Vatican City | 13:00 |
| Venice, Italy | 13:00 |
| Vienna, Austria | 13:00 |
| Vladivostok, Russian Federation | 22:00 |
| Volgograd, Russian Federation | 16:00 |
| Warsaw, Poland | 13:00 |
| Wellington, New Zealand | 24:00 |
| Yangon (formerly Rangoon), Myanmar | 18:30 |
| Yokohama, Japan | 21:00 |
| Zagreb, Croatia | 13:00 |
| Zürich, Switzerland | 13:00 |